POLICY AND CHANGE

EDITED BY RANDALL SMITH
AND JANE RAISTRICK

First published in Great Britain in 1994 by

SAUS Publications
School for Advanced Urban Studies
University of Bristol
Rodney Lodge
Grange Road
Bristol BS8 4EA

Telephone (0272) 741117
Fax (0272) 737308

Selection and editorial matter © SAUS 1994
See Acknowledgements for other contributions

British Library Cataloguing in Publication Data
A catalogue record for this book is available from the British Library

ISBN   1 873575 68 8
ISSN   0268-3725

The School for Advanced Urban Studies is a centre for research, post-graduate and continuing education, and consultancy at the University of Bristol. The School's focus is the analysis, development and implementation of policy in the fields of employment, health and social care, housing, social management, and urban change and government. Its aim is to bridge the gaps between theory and practice, between different policy areas, and between academic disciplines. SAUS is committed to the wide dissemination of its findings and in addition to courses and seminars the School has established several publications series: **SAUS Studies, Occasional Papers, Working Papers, Studies in Decentralisation and Quasi-Markets, DRIC Reports and SAUS Guides and Reports**.

SAUS is working to counter discrimination on grounds of gender, race, disability, age and sexuality in all its activities.

Printed in Great Britain by BPC Wheatons Ltd, Exeter.

In memory of the late Tony Eddison, Director of SAUS 1975-1982, without whose initiative, inspiration and leadership SAUS would not be celebrating its 21st birthday.

CONTENTS

Acknowledgements
ix

Foreword
xi

Preface
xiii

Introduction
Randall Smith
1

PART 1: THE PRESSURES FOR CHANGE

CHAPTER 1
A new management in the public sector?
Paul Hoggett
15

CHAPTER 2
Quality and decentralisation:
are they connected?
Lucy Gaster
39

CHAPTER 3
The changing role of the non-profit sector in
Britain: moving toward the market
Marilyn Taylor
57

CHAPTER 4
Information technology and organisational
culture: implementing change
Susan Barrett
79

CHAPTER 5
Institutional change and rebuilding for a fast
changing economy: confronting chaos
Tom Davies
93

PART 2: THE IMPACT OF CHANGE

A: URBAN POLICY

CHAPTER 6
Inner cities: a multi-agency planning
and implementation process
Murray Stewart and Jacky Underwood
105

CHAPTER 7
The significance of urban economic
development programmes
Ken Young and Charlie Mason
122

CHAPTER 8
Future directions for urban government
in Britain and America
Robin Hambleton
131

CHAPTER 9
Urban Development Corporations: post-Fordism
in action or Fordism in retrenchment?
Paul Burton and Mo O'Toole
155

B: HEALTH AND SOCIAL POLICY

CHAPTER 10
Quasi-markets and social policy
Julian Le Grand
175

CHAPTER 11
Privatisation and quasi-markets in public
sector service delivery in the UK
Will Bartlett
189

CHAPTER 12
Need, equity and the NHS: the distribution
of health care expenditure 1974-87
Carol Propper and Richard Upward
205

CHAPTER 13
User empowerment, older people and the
UK reform of community care
Robin Means and Rachel Lart
228

C: HOUSING POLICY

CHAPTER 14
Social differentiation in urban areas:
housing or occupational class at work
Alan Murie
241

CHAPTER 15
Spatial mobility, tenure mobility, and emerging
social divisions in the UK housing market
Ray Forrest
262

CHAPTER 16
The impact of land use planning and tax
subsidies on the supply and price of housing in Britain
Glen Bramley
288

CHAPTER 17
Towards a sustainable housing renewal policy
Philip Leather and Sheila Mackintosh
325

D: LABOUR MARKET POLICY

CHAPTER 18
A perfunctory sort of post-Fordism: economic restructuring
and labour market segmentation in Britain in the 1980s
John Lovering
345

CHAPTER 19
Evaluating local labour market policy:
the case of TECs
Martin Boddy
365

CHAPTER 20
The Social Charter and the Europeanisation
of employment and social policy
Kevin Doogan
382

CHAPTER 21
Information technology skills and access to
training opportunities: Germany and the UK
Teresa Rees
399

Index
425

ACKNOWLEDGEMENTS

We would like to acknowledge with gratitude the authors and copyright holders of the chapters in this collection for their kind permission to reprint them here.

Chapter 1, 'A new management in the public sector?' by Paul Hoggett first appeared in *Policy and Politics*, 1991, vol 19, no 4, pp 243-56, published by the School for Advanced Urban Studies, University of Bristol, UK.

Chapter 2, 'Quality and decentralisation: are they different?' by Lucy Gaster first appeared in *Policy and Politics*, 1991, vol 19, no 4, pp 257-67, published by the School for Advanced Urban Studies, University of Bristol, UK.

Chapter 3, 'The changing role of the non-profit sector in Britain: moving towards the market' by Marilyn Taylor was first published in B. Gidron, R.M. Kramer and L.M. Salamon (eds) (1992) *Government and the third sector: emerging relationships in welfare states*, San Francisco, USA: Jossey-Bass Inc.

Chapter 4, 'Information technology and organisational culture: implementing change' by Susan Barrett first appeared in the *International Review of Administrative Sciences*, 1992, vol 58, no 3, pp 363-74, published by the International Institute of Administrative Sciences, Brussels, Belgium.

Chapter 5, 'Institutional change and rebuilding for a fast changing economy: confronting chaos' by Tom Davies was first published in M. Belka and J. Lipinski (eds) (1991) *Studia I Materialy*, pp 253-64, Warsaw, Poland: Instytut Nauk Ekonomicznych.

Chapter 6, 'Inner cities: a multiagency planning and implementation process' by Murray Stewart and Jacky Underwood was first published in P. Healey, G. McDougall and M.J. Thomas (eds) (1982) *Planning theory: prospects for the 1980s*, Oxford, UK: Pergamon Press.

Chapter 7, 'The significance of urban economic development programmes' by Ken Young and Charlie Mason was first published in K. Young and C. Mason (eds) (1983) *Urban economic development: new roles and relationships*, London, UK: Macmillan.

Chapter 8, 'Future directions for urban government in Britain and America' by Robin Hambleton first appeared in the *Journal of Urban Affairs*, 1990, vol 12, no 1, published by JAI Press, Greenwich, Ct, USA.

Chapter 9, 'Urban Development Corporations: post-Fordism in action or Fordism in retrenchment?' by Paul Burton and Mo O'Toole was first published in R. Imrie and H. Thomas (eds) (1993) *British urban policy and the Urban Development Corporations*, London, UK: Paul Chapman.

Chapter 10, 'Quasi-markets and social policy' by Julian Le Grand first appeared in the *Economic Journal*, 1991, vol 101, pp 1256-67, published by Blackwells, Oxford, UK on behalf of the Economic Society.

Chapter 11, 'Privatisation and quasi-markets in public sector service delivery in the UK' by Will Bartlett was first published in F. Targetti (ed) (1992) *Privatisation in Europe: West and East experiences*, Aldershot, UK: Dartmouth Publishing Company.

Chapter 12, 'Need, equity and the NHS: the distribution of health care expenditure 1974-87' by Carol Propper and Richard Upward first appeared in

x Acknowledgements

Fiscal Studies, 1992, vol 13, no 2, published by The Institute for Fiscal Studies, London, UK.

Chapter 13, 'User empowerment, older people and the reform of community care' by Robin Means and Rachel Lart was first published in D. Challis and B. Davies (eds) (1994) *Health and community care: UK and international perspectives*, Aldershot, UK: Gower.

Chapter 14, 'Social differentiation in housing provision: housing or occupational class at work' by Alan Murie first appeared in *Tijdschrift Voor Economie en Social Geografie*, 1986, vol 77, pp 345-57, published by the Royal Dutch Geographical Society, Utrecht, The Netherlands.

Chapter 15, 'Spatial mobility, tenure mobility and emerging social divisions in the UK housing market' by Ray Forrest first appeared in *Environment and Planning A*, 1987, vol 19, pp 1611-30, published by Pion Ltd, London, UK.

Chapter 16, 'The impact of land use planning and tax subsidies on the supply and price of housing in Britain' by Glen Bramley first appeared in *Urban Studies*, 1993, vol 30, no 1, pp 5-30, published by Carfax Publishing Company, Abingdon, UK.

Chapter 17, 'Towards a sustainable housing renewal policy' by Philip Leather and Sheila Mackintosh also appears in P. Williams (ed) (1993) *Sustainable housing policies*, Housing Studies Association conference proceedings, Autumn 1993, published by the Centre for Housing Management and Development, University of Wales College of Cardiff.

Chapter 18, 'A perfunctory sort of post-Fordism: economic restructuring and labour market segmentation in the 1980s' by John Lovering first appeared in *Work, Employment and Society*, 1990, vol 4, published by the British Sociological Association, Durham, UK.

Chapter 19, 'Evaluating local labour market initiatives: the case of Training and Enterprise Councils' by Martin Boddy first appeared in the *British Journal of Education and Work*, 1992, vol 5, no 3, published by Trentham Books Ltd, Stoke-on-Trent, UK.

Chapter 20, 'The Social Charter and the Europeanisation of employment and social policy' by Kevin Doogan first appeared in *Policy and Politics*, 1991, vol 20, no 2, published by the School for Advanced Urban Studies, University of Bristol, UK.

Chapter 21, 'Information technology skills and access to training opportunities: Germany and the UK' by Teresa Rees was first published in K. Dukatel (ed) *Employment and technical change in Europe: work organization, skills and training*, 1994, Cheltenham, UK: Edward Elgar.

We are also grateful to the University of Bristol for its financial support of this publication.

FOREWORD

As Director of SAUS, I was delighted to be able to persuade Randall Smith, Senior Lecturer at the School, to join with Jane Raistrick from SAUS' publications team, in producing an anniversary volume to celebrate 21 years of research, policy and practice at SAUS. The early years of the School concentrated on professional development training programmes mainly for public sector officials involved in the planning, management or delivery of urban services. Published material tended to be placed in professional journals, with just a few articles in refereed journals. From the early 1980s, more and more articles were accepted by refereed journals, so that the editors of this book were faced in 1993 with choosing from over 150 such articles, as well as over 150 chapters of books. It has not been an easy task, as they explain in their Preface, but I am sure that readers will find that the choices they have made for this book do illuminate very clearly the theme of *Policy and change*. The compilation also provides an important contribution to the further development of SAUS' research strategy in the mid 1990s.

Martin Boddy
Director, School for Advanced Urban Studies
February 1994

PREFACE

21 YEARS OF SAUS

RANDALL SMITH AND JANE RAISTRICK

The School for Advanced Urban Studies at the University of Bristol came officially into existence at the beginning of 1973, under the directorship of Sir Colin Buchanan. This was the same day on which the United Kingdom formally joined the European Community. It was also the year of the first major oil crisis, one of the factors leading to a worldwide recession in the mid 1970s. In a very real sense, the policy world of the UK began to be disturbed by these critical external factors, just as the work of SAUS was getting underway. At a more parochial level, local government and health service reorganisations in Britain were implemented in 1974 and much of the School's early work reflected the changes in administrative culture at the subnational level.

The late Tony Eddison, who became Director of SAUS in 1975, had published his book on *Local government: management and corporate planning* in 1973. With pressures on public spending becoming more intense in the mid 1970s, the emphasis of SAUS work shifted from corporate planning to a broader concern for the formulation, implementation and review of the policy process. One product of this endeavour was the publication in 1978 of Robin Hambleton's book *Policy planning and local government* followed up by his 1986 book *Rethinking policy planning*.

Another product was a book edited by Susan Barrett and Colin Fudge, *Policy and action* published in 1981. All the chapters of this book were prepared by staff at SAUS based on research and scholarship undertaken in the late 1970s. The subtitle was 'Essays on the implementation of public policy' and the volume included case studies on land policy, local employment policies, development control, services for mentally ill people, housing policy and building societies, public expenditure cuts and briefing for building design. The focus of the book as a whole provided a challenge to top-down theories of the implementation process and stressed the complex interaction between the making and implementation of policies. Further development of work on implementation theory was undertaken under the umbrella of a Social Science Research Council initiative on central-local relations, and was brought together in an article by Susan

Barrett and Michael Hill published in July 1984. Its title was 'Policy, bargaining and structure in implementation theory: towards an integrated perspective' and was placed in the journal *Policy and Politics*, which SAUS took over from Sage Publications in 1979. This stream of implementation research was also included in a textbook written by Christopher Ham and Michael Hill (1984), *The policy process in the modern capitalist state*. Since leaving SAUS Ham has sustained his interest in reflecting the policy process in the rapidly changing world of health planning and service delivery (see Ham, Robinson and Benzeval, 1990; Ham, 1991). Hill too has continued his commitment to this work and has recently edited two volumes *New agendas in the study of the policy process* and *The policy process: a reader*, both published in 1993.

The arrival in 1979 of a Conservative government with radical ideas about governance, with a commitment to a business culture through privatisation and the introduction of competition to eliminate public sector monopolies, with a determination to challenge the role of trades unions and with an unremitting hostility to local government, increased the turbulence of the environment for public service practitioners. Ideas from the private sector were to be applied to the public sector, local authorities were to lose a number of their delivery services whilst retaining responsibility for service standards, the role of the voluntary sector was to be transformed, and the health service was to be radically reorganised as was local government and the civil service. Meanwhile, policy towards the European Community seemed quite ambiguous as hostility to the idea of 'an ever closer union' was accompanied by the signing of treaties, one of which was called The Treaty on European Union. The overall drive for economy, efficiency and effectiveness was not deeply concerned with issues of equity, nor the less tangible aspects of quality. For focused commentaries by SAUS staff on these developments in respect of both housing policy and urban policy see the 1988 book by Ray Forrest and Alan Murie, *Selling the welfare state: the privatisation of public housing* and the review of the Economic and Social Research Council Inner Cities research programme by Murray Stewart in the April 1988 issue of *Policy and Politics*. The emphasis on the consumer with resources, faced with a choice of goods or services in the market-place, was extended to the (potential) user in the fields of social welfare, where the notion of choice was, at least, more problematic for frail older people, those with mental health problems or the materially poor, and where a competitive market may not, in any case, be very robust.

One response by SAUS staff in the late 1980s was to examine the reforms in the broad field of social welfare, and to introduce the notion of quasi-markets. Initial ideas, supported by the Functioning of Markets Initiative of the Economic and Social Research Council, were pulled together in a book published in 1993 edited by Julian Le Grand and Will

Bartlett, *Quasi-Markets and social policy*. All the contributions were from SAUS staff and covered the policy fields of health, community care, education and housing.

Since SAUS came into being, practitioners in public service have experienced more and more turbulence in their organisational settings and in the broader environment in which they work. At the beginning of this Preface we referred to the accession of the UK to the European Community, the reorganisation of local government and the National Health Service, and the ever increasing pressures to limit public spending in response to a deteriorating economic situation triggered by worldwide recession. Another main element in the work of SAUS in the 1980s and 1990s has been to analyse and comment on the changing environment of organisations, to chart how policy priorities shifted and to comment on how managers and workers in a variety of institutional settings were responding to the transformation of their working worlds. In particular, staff have addressed issues of decentralisation (Hambleton and Hoggett, 1987; Burns, Hambleton and Hoggett, 1994); quality of service (Gaster, 1994); the role of women managers (Clarke and Coleman, 1990; Martin, 1994); flexible personnel policies (Fudge, 1990); and consumer orientation (Hoggett, 1992). It is this broad theme of the pressures for change in the policy world which informs the choice of writings included in this anniversary volume.

Building on a strong track record, SAUS' research strength continues to grow. As a multidisciplinary department within a Faculty of Social Sciences it has done extremely well to achieve a ranking of 4 in the last two research assessment exercises undertaken by the Higher Education Funding Council for England (and its predecessor bodies). Early in 1994, SAUS academic staff were engaged in a total of 25 research projects: 3 funded by the Economic and Social Research Council; 7 by charitable foundations; 7 by central government; 6 by local and health authorities and TECs; and 2 by the European Commission or other Community institutions.

The themes of urban regeneration, local government, health and social care, housing, labour market policy and organisational change will continue to be addressed in the mid 1990s. The longstanding interest of SAUS staff in (i) the interrelationships between policy areas (such as housing and labour mobility); (ii) the linkages both between professional groups and between providers and users of services (as in community care); as well as (iii) the changing institutional environment in which the policy process is embedded, will continue to feature in our future research programme. Indeed SAUS staff themselves have the opportunity to reflect on their own links with other academics in the University of Bristol as plans are taken forward to include SAUS in a new School for Policy Studies which is developing in the context of a further strengthening of research and graduate studies across the Faculty of Social Sciences as a whole. Change and development have been constant features of SAUS' 21 years, and the

School expects to play a central role in future developments at Bristol. At the same time, it will fully sustain its commitment to (i) academic excellence and intellectual rigour; (ii) quality and value for money; (iii) linking research, policy and practice; and (iv) equal opportunities, empowerment and democracy.

From the large body of published output by SAUS staff over the past 21 years, it has been a difficult task to select those works most representative of SAUS' research excellence and most illustrative of our theme of policy and change. In 1992-93 alone SAUS staff produced (according to the annual report of the Council to the Court of the University of Bristol) 25 articles in refereed journals, 32 chapters of books, 9 books, 12 articles in professional journals, 10 monographs or working papers, 5 edited books, 30 papers in conference proceedings as well as 25 unpublished reports, mainly for central government departments. The academic editor created a rod for his own back in developing a stringent set of criteria to assess eligibility for inclusion in the book. Only articles from refereed journals and chapters from books edited (with one exception) by non-SAUS academics were eligible. A past or present member of SAUS staff could feature only once. Nothing published by SAUS itself could be included, apart from refereed articles in *Policy and Politics*, where the practice for submissions by SAUS staff is to have the proposed (anonymised) article refereed by non-SAUS members of the Editorial Board. Finally, it was felt that an equal number of papers should be included under each policy heading in the second part of the book.

Funding for this work (for SAUS is a self-funded unit within the Faculty of Social Sciences of the University of Bristol) has come from a wide range of sources, including the Economic and Social Research Council, many of the larger charitable foundations in the UK, several government departments, a range of local and health authorities, and a number of the institutions of the European Union, including the Commission itself, the European Foundation for the Improvement of Living and Working Conditions in Dublin and CEDEFOP in Berlin.

We hope that the contributions included in this anniversary volume, as well as the many other publications, both advance understanding of the implications of rapid policy change in the UK and also assist in improving the quality of the policy making process.

References

Barrett, S. and Fudge, C. (eds) (1981) *Policy and action: essays on the implementation of public policy*, London: Methuen.

Barrett, S. and Hill, M. (1984) 'Policy, bargaining and structure in implementation theory: towards an integrated perspective' *Policy and Politics*, vol 12, no 3.

Burns, D., Hambleton, R. and Hoggett, P. (1994) *The politics of decentralisation*, Basingstoke: Macmillan.

Clarke, D. and Coleman, G. (1990) *Management effectiveness for women*, Cambridge: National Extension College.

Eddison, T. (1973) *Local government: management and corporate planning*, Leighton Buzzard: Leonard Hill Books.

Forrest, R. and Murie, A. (1988) *Selling the welfare state: the privatisation of public housing*, London: Routledge.

Gaster, L. (1994) *Quality and public services: managers' choices*, Milton Keynes: Open University Press.

Ham, C. (1991) *The new NHS: organisation and management*, Oxford: Radcliffe Medical Press.

Ham , C. and Hill, M. (1984) *The policy process in the modern capitalist state*, Brighton: Harvester.

Ham, C., Robinson R. and Benzeval, M. (1990) *Health check: health care reforms in an international context*, London: King's Fund Institute.

Hambleton, R (1978) *Policy planning and local government*, London: Hutchinson.

Hambleton, R. (1986) *Rethinking policy planning: a study of planning systems linking central and local government*, Bristol: SAUS Publications, School for Advanced Urban Studies, University of Bristol.

Hambleton, R. and Hoggett, P. (1987) (eds) *Decentralisation and democracy: localising public services*, Occasional Paper no 28, Bristol: SAUS Publications, School for Advanced Urban Studies, University of Bristol.

Hill, M. (ed) (1993a) *New agendas in the study of the policy process*, Hemel Hempstead: Harvester Wheatsheaf.

Hill, M. (ed) (1993b) *The policy process: a reader*, Hemel Hempstead: Harvester Wheatsheaf.

Hoggett, P. (1992) *Consumer oriented reform in the UK public service*, Dublin: European Foundation for the Improvement of Living and Working Conditions.

Hoggett, P. (1992) *Consumer oriented reform in the UK public service*, Dublin: European Foundation for the Improvement of Living and Working Conditions.

Le Grand, J. and Bartlett, W. (eds) (1993) *Quasi-markets and social policy*, Basingstoke: Macmillan.

Martin, L. (1994) 'Power, continuity and change: women managers' experience in local government', in M. Tanton, *Women managers' learning*, London: Routledge.

INTRODUCTION

POLICY AND CHANGE

RANDALL SMITH

Over the past decade the policy environment in the United Kingdom has undergone considerable turbulence and change. A major transformation in political culture as well as shifts in organisational structures and economic conditions have all had a marked impact on most policy areas. This collection aims to draw together recent research which illustrates different aspects of this changing policy world. The first part of the book addresses the pressures for change and the second focuses on the impact of change in major policy areas in recent years in urban policy, health and social care, housing and labour markets.

The pressures for change

The first part of the book contains five chapters which chart a range of influences on organisations in both the public and independent sectors. Paul Hoggett reflects on developments in what he calls post-bureaucractic management in the public sector and identifies much more internally devolved forms of organisation in a variety of domestic settings, including local authorities under different political control. One of his themes is that of operational decentralisation. Lucy Gaster takes this theme forward by considering the links between decentralisation and quality of service delivery and, following a discussion on the definition of quality in practice, she concludes that practical guidance can be given to public sector bodies in the UK on whether and how to decentralise to improve service quality from the perspective of the consumer. Many voluntary organisations in Britain have put the requirements of the service user at the forefront of their concerns. In recent years, welfare policies in the UK and elsewhere have been moving away from government provision to a system based on market principles in which services are delivered by a variety of bodies. What are the implications for the voluntary sector? Marilyn Taylor outlines the impact of this major shift for voluntary bodies as deliverers of services and concludes that a transfer of service delivery responsibilities does not of itself transform the quality of service provision or bring it closer to the consumer. She argues for a continued role for government in a developing pluralist system so that core resources and a strategic planning function combine to avoid drastic underfunding and fragmentation of responsibility.

These three authors have addressed a variety of influences, including ideas from the business sector, on public service in the UK in the 1980s and the early 1990s. Susan Barrett has focused her attention on the opportunities presented by developments in information technology in post-industrial societies to change traditional practice and to underpin 'results oriented' organisations characterised by productivity, performance and responsiveness to customers. She eschews a top-down approach, pointing out that this is the management style of a traditional organisation and, consonant with her views on implementation theory (Barrett and Fudge, 1981, Barrett and Hill, 1984) argues that effective changes in organisational culture can best be brought about by dialogue, negotiation and learning rather than by command and control. This echoes Hoggett's comment that the new basic principle of post-bureaucratic management is to give staff "freedom within boundaries". In the context of the application of new information technologies in organisations through a process of learning, Barrett advocates the use of pilot schemes, the widespread availability of personal computers and basic software, the formation of user groups and the selection of user-friendly systems. Thus, the process of introducing new technologies can be a vehicle for bringing about change in organisational culture.

The last paper in the first part of the book offers an example of SAUS work in a non-UK setting where the turbulence of the environment has been such that the institutions of both the state and the economy are being radically restructured. Tom Davies outlines the dilemma faced by Poland and argues that the hard moral as well as economic and political choices being faced by the peoples of Central and Eastern European countries are also the hard choices that should be faced in what he characterises as hitherto static Western economies and societies. He suggests that major convulsions are affecting all societies and 'chaotic' self-sustaining ways of surviving, learning from both successes and failures, have to be adopted in all their variety and complexity, as could be beginning to happen in Poland.

The impact of change - urban policy

The second part of the book contains sixteen chapters, four each on urban policy, health and social care, housing and labour markets. The urban policy section opens with a chapter from a book on *Planning theory* by Patsy Healey *et al* (1982). Despite being published over ten years ago, the analysis by Murray Stewart and Jacky Underwood of inner cities policy retains its relevance as it illuminates the wide range of agencies involved and the process of intervention proposed to deal with the problems of inner areas. The notion of a 'partnership' approach in inner city planning remains a central theme yet it also remains as problematic to achieve as it was in the early 1980s, not least because of the shifts in the complex, institutional arrangements that have occurred over the lifetime of inner area policy. Indeed, the paper refers to inner cities policy as an "administratively constrained power struggle" (p 117) in which members of different sets of interests either collaborate or conflict.

The second chapter in the urban policy section of the book also remains very relevant despite being over ten years old and addresses the broader issue of local responses to major changes in the economic environment that have become known as the 'deindustrialisation' of major urban areas. Ken Young and Charlie Mason edited a book on urban economic development with a special focus on new roles and relationships. The concluding chapter of their book, published in 1983, addressed the significance of urban economic development programmes, the responses of city governments to the consequences of deindustrialisation, such as high levels of unemployment in the manufacturing sector, physical dereliction and a declining fiscal base. In particular, they note the tension between local concerns at the level of unemployment and national emphasis on the control of inflation rather than the fall in employment and ask whether local government can in principle manage the mixed economy of the city.

Young and Mason comment that the process of deindustrialisation has been on a much greater scale in the United States. These economic pressures, together with changing organisational arrangements and shifting political forces, are presenting urban governments in both the UK and the US with new challenges. Robin Hambleton's chapter first identifies, like Young and Mason, the global restructuring of capital and its implications for urban government, alongside the revolutionary advances in information technology which lead to a 'delocalisation' of the processes of production and consumption. Second, he notes the shift towards more decentralised forms of organisation and management, as articulated by Paul Hoggett (see Chapter 1), and third, he outlines local political movements to counter globalisation and 'delocalisation', which take the form of seeking more local autonomy and urban self-management. He argues that urban government in Britain in the 1980s moved away from bureaucratic paternalism towards two alternative models of, on the one hand, market-driven privatisation and on the other of responsive democratic forms of public service provision. On this basis, Hambleton identifies moves towards privatisation, consumerism and neighbourhood decentralisation in British urban government in the 1980s as the key elements of institutional change.

He characterises the changes in urban governance in the 1980s as reflecting post-Fordism in action. The fourth urban policy chapter in this book examines the impact of an organisational initiative in the 1980s, urban development corporations, on UK urban policy. Were they post-Fordist in

4 *Policy and change*

action or Fordism in retrenchment? Burton and O'Toole outline the key components of urban strategies since the 'rediscovery of poverty' in the 1960s and describe urban development corporations as the flagship of Conservative urban policy in the 1980s. They argue that the corporations have not been very successful in countering the impacts of macroeconomic cycles, that their managerial policy style has had to be tempered to the demands of the current planning framework, that whilst they have been able to encourage public-private sector partnerships, they have failed to produce long-term regeneration in respect of jobs and infrastructure. Burton and O'Toole end by suggesting that local government, in its new enabling and regulating form, should coordinate the very varied range of players in the inner urban policy area, which include training and enterprise councils, contracted out services and locally managed schools, as well as urban development corporations.

The impact of change - health and social policy

As already noted, there has also been considerable turbulence in the policy areas for health and social care. As well as reorganisation of both the health service and local government, the functions of health and social care agencies have been radically changed with the introduction of the purchaser-provider split notion and the expectation that local government would continue to reduce its direct service delivery functions whilst enhancing its regulatory and quality control roles. In his chapter on quasi-markets and social policy Julian Le Grand argues that "a major offensive against the bureaucratic structure for welfare provision was launched in 1988 and 1989, years that in retrospect will be seen as critical in the history of British social policy" (p 175-76). The reforms, which covered education and housing, as well as health and social care, had a fundamental similarity - the introduction of 'quasi-markets' into the delivery of welfare services. The state was to become primarily a funder or purchaser of services from a wide range of private, voluntary and public sector providers, operating in a market in competition with each other. Le Grand points out that the move away from large-scale centrally planned organisations is affecting Western countries as well as those in Eastern Europe (see Chapter 5 by Tom Davies) and that one of the reasons for this broad trend in many societies and in both the public and private sectors is the arrival of new technologies permitting decentralised budgeting and other forms of information processing (see Chapter 4 by Susan Barrett).

The second health and social care chapter by Will Bartlett builds on the ideas outlined by Le Grand. In a book on privatisation in both Eastern and Western Europe (Targetti, 1992), Bartlett outlines the UK privatisation process in health, education, community care and housing. For health, he concludes that:

> the new system of health service provision is likely to have two offsetting effects in efficiency and performance. On the one hand, the increased incentives provided to suppliers of services by the operation of market-type price signals and by the possibility ... to appropriate financial surpluses, will tend to increase efficiency and reduce costs. On the other hand, there are a variety of factors which may work in the opposite direction. (p 194)

These factors include manipulation of incomplete block contracts, increased administrative costs and increased labour costs, all of which could reduce efficiency and raise costs of providing health services.

For community care, Bartlett links the reforms to the financial crisis in local government. He points out that while it is not a central purpose of the reforms to transfer provider institutions in the public sector, like residential homes, to the private or voluntary sectors, in fact many local authorities were attempting to hand their residential homes over to housing associations or voluntary sector organisations.

Both Bartlett and Le Grand comment on the lack of impact on the UK welfare system until the third Conservative administration in the late 1980s. Indeed, Goodin and Le Grand (1987) argued that welfare resources, facilities and services inclined to benefit the educated and articulate middle classes and were not responsive to the needs of the poor and disadvantaged. A decade earlier, Le Grand (1978) had concluded that the top two socio-economic groups received 40% more health care per person reporting sick than the bottom two socio-economic groups. The third health and social care chapter examines the distribution of health care expenditure between 1974 and 1987 to assess whether the allocation of health services was according to need and whether the ability to pay was unimportant. Carol Propper and Richard Upward undertook an examination of horizontal equity in the delivery of health care, using General Household Survey data for different years (compared with single year data in earlier studies). They broadly concluded that the distribution of NHS expenditure across income groups, controlling for need, was either uniform or slightly in favour of lower income groups. "The results indicate that departures from horizontal equity are rather small" (p 219) and this in general applied to the analysis by socio-economic group as well as by income, though the distribution of expenditure across socio-economic group did appear more 'pro-rich' than that across income.

The fourth health and social care paper returns to the theme of the reforms of the community care services, in particular the stimulation of choice for service users and the empowerment of users. Robin Means and

6   *Policy and change*

Rachel Lart drew upon a study in four areas of the impact of the reforms on users, particularly older people. How far are service users or user groups involved in the process of community care planning or service delivery in the form of packages of care? Their starting points are (i) that giving more power to users over decisions entails taking power away from service providers; and (ii) that market approaches to consumer empowerment are exit-driven (find an alternative service elsewhere) and democratic approaches are voice-driven (change the service from within). They concluded that effective involvement of service users or user groups in the community care planning process required a great deal of time, and background material needed to be both clear and yet in sufficient detail. All this indicated a review of the role of the professionals in the planning process.

The impact of change - housing policy

One of the policy areas most affected by the actions of the Conservative government in the 1980s was that of housing. The consequences of the large scale sale of council houses and the residualisation of council housing have been examined in detail by both Alan Murie and Ray Forrest, both of whom have taken housing as a core element in the debate about the changing structure of British society. In his chapter, Murie has examined the relative importance of occupational class and the housing dimension of consumption sector cleavages in explaining social differentiation in urban areas. Is housing tenure position as important as occupational class in determining life chances? Should housing be placed at the centre of the debate about the sources and maintenance of social divisions and inequalities? Murie's response is one of caution. He notes differentiation within as well as between housing tenures, regional differences in preferences for home ownership based on economic buoyancy, other influences than housing on the opportunities for autonomy and self-expression, and in any case lack of ownership does not necessarily prevent autonomous self-expression.

For these and a wide range of other reasons focused on housing-based wealth, Murie suggests some caution in accepting the view that new consumption cleavages are more important than traditional class differences, and agrees with Heath et al (1985) that "housing does not form the basis for a new cleavage in British politics, but rather acts as a separate source for the maintenance of the class cleavage". However, he does accept that housing processes do introduce real inequalities. His overall view is that over time home ownership may become a much more mixed experience. Perhaps the argument that consumption cleavages in housing cross cut occupational class has been over-influenced by looking at a system in transition, and at the end of the transition "there is likely to be a better fit between occupational class and housing situation" (p 259).

Ray Forrest also focuses on social divisions in the British housing market. He, like Murie, notes the consequences of the expansion of home ownership drawing in lower income households and involving transactions between existing owners. "Problems supposedly confined to the rental tenures are now spilling over into home ownership, and there is marked social and spatial unevenness in mobility, asset appreciation and capital gains" (p 262). For example, it was becoming clear that owner occupation rather than council housing was the major housing barrier to labour mobility. Forrest argues that problems of enhanced or inhibited mobility relate to a highly differentiated structure of housing assistance which in turn relates to position in the labour market.

The general impression is of a housing market in which mobility and choice are subject to increasing social and spatial unevenness fuelled by a chaotic and inequitable system of state support and occupational subsidies, such as relocation expenses or bridging finance. All these influence the shape of housing histories, with housing assistance being available to those on the economic margins (through housing benefits) and to those in high status employment and in higher priced dwellings (through mortgage interest tax relief and occupational assistance). The large group of owner occupiers on modest incomes in cheaper housing gain a little from mortgage interest tax relief and in part discounts on council house sales. Forrest concludes that "housing histories, housing opportunities and patterns of residential movement will become increasingly socially and spatially differentiated" (p 283).

Glen Bramley's chapter, which won the Donald Robertson Memorial Prize in 1992, analyses the impact of two types of policy intervention, tax subsidies (mortgage interest tax relief) and land use planning, on the housing market in Britain. Like Forrest and Murie, Bramley's argument is based on data from the 1980s, "one of the relative boom conditions in the housing market" (p 296) and he notes that the results of his work may not be quite such a good guide to the impact of the subsequent recession and low demand on the system. His empirical work aims to quantify the impact of the land use planning system on housing output and house prices across different types of area and the effect of taxes and subsidies on housing on those areas. Do subsidies lead to the production of more housing or simply raise its price? He concludes that the effect of abolition of mortgage tax subsidy over a three year period would be likely to lead to a fall in house prices, which however would not be sustained after the end of the three years but would be eroded quite significantly. After a lag, there would also be a fall in new completions, and it was this fall that would put upward pressure on prices. A simulation of the impact of a large-scale increase in the planned release of land was also carried out. A 75% increase in the planning policy targets for housing resulted in a modest 16% increase in the flow of planning permissions which fell to 7%-8% after three years. "From a housing policy point of view, the results suggest that general exhortations or requirements to release more land through the statutory planning system do not provide a very fruitful route to the desirable goal of widening accessibility to owner-occupation" (p 319).

The final chapter in the housing policy section of the book is an analysis of the crisis in renewal policies for the private sector of the housing stock. Philip Leather and Sheila Mackintosh outline the turbulence of this policy arena by examining the background to the crisis, the operation of the current grant system and the kinds of problems which it has thrown up. They describe the short and medium-term options available to government 'to get renewal policy back on its feet again'. However, they argue for a more fundamental review of the direction of housing renewal policy. Effective strategies in the 1990s need to acknowledge that there is a an ageing housing stock and an ageing population. Housing decay is an ongoing process, not a short-term problem. With the current constraints on public expenditure likely to continue in the mid 1990s, public resources need to be used more effectively and mechanisms need to be developed to encourage higher levels of private investment by home owners in the maintenance and improvement of their dwellings.

The impact of change - labour market policy

Some of the chapters concerned with housing, health and social care and urban policy issues have also touched on issues of employment and labour markets. This is the theme of the fourth and last section of the second part of this book. John Lovering's chapter on the restructuring of the labour market in the 1980s in Britain is based on a range of primary and secondary material, especially research undertaken as part of the Economic and Social Research Council initiative, Social Change and Economic Life. He argues that the restructuring of the British economy in the 1980s, including the period of deindustrialisation in the early part of the decade, the increase in foreign investment particularly by Japan, the deregulation of the stock market and its implications for Britain's international financial role, and the impact of the spending boom and subsequent recession in the late 1980s and beyond, did not halt the relative decline of the British economy.

In labour market terms the modest recovery following the severe recession of the early 1980s led to increased employment, almost entirely accounted for by women who formed the bulk of the workforce in the growing industries but were not present in large numbers in contracting industries. Meanwhile, men dominated the major increase in self-employment in the 1980s. Lovering suggests that traditional internal labour markets, like the public sector and large manufacturing companies, are being replaced by more segmented and truncated internal labour markets. He argues that, as many of the growing industries use women workers and as working women tend to be less geographically mobile than men, especially those in part-time jobs, promotion is in effect truncated by being confined to the particular establishment in which they are working.

In contrast, external labour markets have increased in importance, both through elite professionals in high demand moving between organisations (or being self-employed) and through the development of secondary labour markets by which employers use local labour in a way that does not increase their marketable skills, give them opportunities for promotion, or indeed secure jobs.

The restructuring of the labour market has not led to the kind of flexible specialisation exemplified in Japan, and in so far as it does indicate a move away from a Fordist mode of operation, it is a deeply conservative kind of post-Fordism. Key features of the so-called restructured labour market are inherited from the past. They are the long established status inequalities associated with gender, race, age and social status which continue to form the major axes of labour market segmentation.

Against this backcloth of transformation of labour market structure underpinned by long-term discriminatory continuities, one of the specific institutional initiatives in recent years has been the establishment of Training and Enterprise Councils (TECs) in the late 1980s, which Martin Boddy describes as "the most radical reform of the country's training and enterprise infrastructure since the establishment of the Manpower Services Commission in the 1970s" (p 365). TECs were established as locally-based independent companies with a board of directors dominated by employer interests, and they were charged with developing an approach based on private sector management styles and organisational culture. Part of their remit was to evaluate the extent to which they have been able to achieve their own local priorities and objectives.

Boddy reports on the issues and problems which arose in practice in the development and implementation of individual evaluation strategies at the local level. The 'localisation' of this function meant that (i) opportunities to learn from elsewhere were limited and (ii) it was difficult to compare the performances of individual TECs as methodologies and measures differed between them. Boddy's unsurprising conclusion was that there was little incentive, on both technical and structural grounds, to develop elaborate evaluation strategies focused on the broader aims of the overall TEC initiative.

The policy areas of health and social care and housing, even urban issues until very recently, have been seen in the main as domestic concerns and not within the competence of the European Union. In this respect, labour market policies are distinct as they are seen as central to the social as well as the economic dimension of European integration. Kevin Doogan's chapter examines the extent to which labour market policy has remained national in character and how far it has been informed by practice in other member states of the European Union. He uses the discussions about the Social Charter and the subsequent Social Action Programme to illuminate the point that both sceptics of and enthusiasts for European integration paint a picture of increasing influence on the domestic policy debate about employment and labour market issues. He notes that there is less comment that the laws and procedures of the European Union may well have emerged in part through the active participation of British institutions. He argues that the policy debate is "an endogenous process in which different EC policy concerns are internalised and brought on to the domestic agenda" (p 382).

Overall, Doogan identifies tensions at the heart of the single market policy. First, market integration for goods and services is driven by a process of deregulation, whereas labour market integration involves a programme of regulation. "In a concrete sense, the integration process is moving in opposite directions in different markets" (p 391). Second, in individual member states, the institutional arrangements associated with employment policy are very varied, are deeply entrenched within the culture and traditions of different member states and are resistant to major reorganisation.

Doogan (writing before the Maastricht summit) concluded that the impact of the Social Charter as a guarantor of worker's rights was likely to be only limited, not least in the UK, whose government did not sign up to the solemn declaration. However, he does argue that expectations have been raised. Both employer and union interests in the UK are more likely to draw on practices of other member states, and the outcomes of negotiations will depend on the bargaining capabilities of the two sides of industry and the predisposition of government policy. "The institutional framework within which employment and social policy will develop will remain essentially national in character in terms of its procedures but will be far better informed of policy in other member states" (p 397). In this way domestic policy is likely to be become Europeanised.

The final chapter on labour market issues is also European in focus and reflects some of the concerns outlined by Susan Barrett in her chapter on the impact of new information technologies (NITs). Teresa Rees points up the challenges facing the European Union in the next decade including the ageing of the workforce, competition from Japan and the UK and a growing shortage of high level skills in NITs. She argues that this requires major investment in training and human resource management, particularly in relation to the under-utilisation of women in the workforce. In John Lovering's terms, this would imply a move of women workers from the secondary external labour market through development of effective and lifelong training strategies into an elite external labour market, though he could also argue that they might instead 'benefit' from a truncated internal labour market in so far as the jobs were located in large organisations.

The chapter explores access to training for NITs (particularly access for women) in the European Union by examining the potential for better participation by women in EU funded training measures, and by two 'training' case studies in Germany and the UK. The former describes opportunities for advancement through mainstream in-house continuing training for NITs, whereas the UK case study focuses on women-only workshops outside mainstream training and targets women returning to the labour market after time at home looking after children. Rees concludes that:

> patterns of gender segregation, the masculinisation of technology and the male-centredness of mainstream training provision are so entrenched that even the combined weight of the economic imperative and social justice demands are unlikely to lead to better access to training in the NITs for women as for other disadvantaged groups. Strategic policy development is needed at all levels: the European Community, the member state, the region, the firm and the training provider. (p 421)

Concluding comment

Much of the work undertaken by SAUS in the 1980s and the 1990s has analysed the impact of a changing and turbulent environment on a range of policy areas. The social science disciplines have been applied to issues of inter-institutional relationships, organisational change, economic restructuring, allocation of scarce resources and new information technologies in the policy areas of housing, health and social care, labour markets and urban regeneration. It is hoped that the chapters contained in this volume contribute to an understanding of the changing policy world and will be of value to all those interested or involved in the policy making process.

References

Barrett, S. and Fudge, C. (eds) (1981) *Policy and action: essays on the implementation of public policy*, London: Methuen.

Barrett, S. and Hill, M. (1984) 'Policy, bargaining and structure in implementation theory: towards an integrated perspective' *Policy and Politics*, vol 12, no 3.

Goodin, R. and Le Grand, J. (1987) *Not only the poor: the middle classes and the welfare state*, London: Allen and Unwin.

Healey, P., McDougall, G. and Thomas, M.J. (ed) (1982) *Planning theory: prospects for the 1980s*, Oxford: Pergamon.

Heath, A., Jowell, R. and Curtice, J. (1985) *How Britain votes*, Oxford: Pergamon.

Le Grand, J. (1978) 'The distribution of public expenditure: the case of health care' *Economica*, vol 45.

Targetti, F. (ed) (1992) *Privatisation in Europe: West and East experiences*, Aldershot: Dartmouth.

Young, K. and Mason, C. (eds) (1983) *Urban economic development: new roles and relationships*, Basingstoke: Macmillan.

PART 1:

THE PRESSURES FOR CHANGE

CHAPTER 1

A NEW MANAGEMENT IN THE PUBLIC SECTOR?

PAUL HOGGETT

Introduction

Over the last six or seven years a remarkable volume of research and argument has been generated by what is sometimes referred to as the 'restructuring debate'. This debate, conducted by a mixture of economists, geographers and sociologists, has focused upon the question of whether Western capitalist economies are beginning to generate entirely new forms of the organisation of production. The debate has by no means been simply a parochial or academic one. Many of its terms, such as post-Fordism or flexible specialisation, have been embraced by fashionable politicians, journalists, and the like. However, with a few exceptions (Cousins, 1988; Hoggett, 1987, 1990; Winckler, 1990), there has been little attempt to consider the relevance that this debate might have for understanding contemporary developments within the organisation and management of the public sector. This is the purpose of this paper.

A restructured private sector, a restructured public sector?

Here is not the place to dwell at length upon the current state of argument surrounding the nature of restructuring in the private sector. I have attempted to sketch some of the main differences of analysis in a previous paper (Hoggett, 1990). Perhaps one of the few advantages of the term 'post-Fordism' is its agnosticism about the future; it suggests that we are clearer about where we are coming from than where we are going to. Some of the most interesting analyses presently emerging from the debate are those which suggest that different nations, regions and sectors shape the new forms of organisation of production in different ways. Thus what emerges is not a single, new restructured model but a range of basic types - Californian, neo-Fordist, Saturnian, Japanese - each of which is shaped from the same basic template (Leborgne and Lipietz, 1987; Lane, 1988).

So what might this new basic template or paradigm consist of? There appear to be two essential dimensions to it. First of all it gives emphasis to flexibility - more flexible production strategies and manpower strategies. Secondly it replaces the notion of 'vertically-integrated' production (ie integrated around the centralised hierarchies of the classical industrial bureaucracy) with much more decentralised (organisationally and spatially) methods of organising production. In this paper I wish to focus primarily upon the latter of these dimensions, that is, the decentralisation of production and particularly the forms of managerial devolution that correspond to this. But before considering in more detail the nature of this development I wish to consider the notion of 'restructuring' and its possible application to the public sector.

The term 'restructuring' suggests a particular form of change, something which is discontinuous, major and qualitatively different to that which has gone before. It therefore amounts to something more than the kind of change that might be produced by switches in corporate or governmental policy. In particular it suggests some kind of basic paradigmatic change in how we think about the organisation and management of production - a qualitative shift in the techniques of organisational control. Moreover it is a shift which has been brought about by radical changes in both technological and market conditions.

Given that a consensus appears to be emerging that some such process is at work within the private sector (even though disagreement abounds concerning the particular nature of this process), is the state sector also undergoing some kind of restructuring? There would seem to be two ways of answering this question. Firstly, is the role and function of the state itself changing radically to suit the requirements of this 'post-Fordist' world (Clarke and Mayer, 1986)? Secondly, is the organisational form of the state changing in a way which corresponds to the new forms of organisational control we now see being adopted within large private companies?

I wish to concentrate on the latter of these two questions in this paper. My thesis is that during the last decade a distinctively new set of organisational forms and approaches to management have begun to emerge within the public sector, both within central and local government, education and the health service. I wish to concentrate on one facet of this development - the creation of more internally decentralised forms. Arguably in Britain forms of external decentralisation - contracting out and the creation of quasi-markets within the public sector - have been equally important, especially since the return of the third Conservative government in 1987 (Le Grand, 1990). However, I wish to concentrate on forms of internal decentralisation, partly because I am more familiar with these developments, and partly because they appear to be less specific to the distinctively New Right political project of Britain and the USA.

I would like to take as a starting point the concept of 'the new public management' to which a special issue of the journal *Governance* was recently devoted (Aucoin, 1990). Focusing primarily upon the reorganisation of the civil service, this discussion examined recent developments across a range of Western-type societies, particularly Britain, Canada, New Zealand and Australia. It might seem strange to talk about the emergence of a 'new' public management when the idea of 'management' (as opposed to administration) is a comparatively recent addition to our way of thinking about the running of the state. In a bold but, I feel, illuminating argument Aucoin (1990) suggests that we think of the discourse of public administration as one which was congruent to our thinking about the organisation of the state in an era in which the model of bureaucratic control dominated organisational practice in private and public sectors. The logic of this argument leads us to the supposition that the new forms of management are based upon essentially post-bureaucratic methods of organisational control. The purpose of this paper is not so much to test this hypothesis (an ambitious if not impossible task given that many of the changes referred to are of an extremely recent origin) as to examine it in more detail, particularly in the light of changes which occurred in the British public sector in the 1980s.

Strategies of organisational control

Within the organisational literature a tradition has emerged which focuses upon the way in which work is controlled within public and private organisations. This tradition (Edwards, 1979; Clegg, 1981; Burris, 1989) has sought to demonstrate how a variety of different strategies for control have emerged and developed over time. A full list of these control strategies would include craft, simple control, technical control, bureaucratic control and professional control. Table 1 outlines each of these control strategies, their origins and distinctive characteristics.

Within most complex organisations, where manual workers, professionals and managers coexist, more than one control strategy will be adopted. The key issue is which control strategy dominates. I would argue that for much of the 20th century there has been a relative congruence between technical and bureaucratic control strategies. It is this congruence which has provided the basis for the development of the giant industrial and public bureaucracies of the post-war period. However, bureaucratic control strategies rested very uneasily with professional control strategies. Since the Second World War, particularly within the state sector where professions have a stronger base (Johnson, 1972), professional and bureaucratic control strategies increasingly collided. In the UK, particularly since the 1970s, there has been an increasing attempt to subdue professionalism by bureaucratic control strategies. We might think of the rise of corporate management in local government in the 1970s and the

Table 1: Organisational control strategies

Strategy	Periodisation	Characteristics
Craft	- pre-capitalist - though subject to de-skilling process throughout 20th century (Braverman, 1974) some evidence exists (the 'flexible specialisation' literature) that the emerging wave of capitalist development may rehabilitate some forms of skilled/craft production	- apprenticeships - decentralised - traditionally based upon male 'labour aristocracy' - integration of 'expertise' and labour
Simple control	- 18th century to present - conditions of full employment tend to undermine the basis for its coercive approach, as does strong unionisation	- coercive authority ('macho management') - direct, personal supervision of work - 'hiring and firing' - conflictual labour relations
Technical control	- really came into its own at beginning of 20th century through the work of Frederick Taylor and Henry Ford	- control embedded in machine systems - machines dictate pace of work - worker isolation - de-skilling
Bureaucratic control	- early 20th century - Henri Fayol's *General and industrial management* (1916) was the classic exposition - an application of the ideas of 'sound administration' originally developed within the civil service of the most advanced European states	- centralisation - formalisation - specialisation - hierarchies of legitimated authority
Professional control	- some 'professions' (academia, medicine, law) essentially pre-capitalist - remarkable 'explosion' of professionalism since Second World War as educated labour becomes increasingly integral to production in private and public sectors	- self-regulation - collegiality - credentialism - semi-autonomy
Post-bureaucratic control	- first 'emerges' in mid 1970s - first detailed analysis in Mintzberg's discussion of 'adhocracy' (1979) - rides forth upon the rhetoric of 'management excellence' in the 1980s	- devolved or remote control - decentralised centralisation - formalised informalism - regulated autonomy

Source: Derived from Burris, 1989, p 4

emergence of general management within the National Health Service in the 1980s in this light. Similar trends within the American welfare sector have been charted by Alford (1975) who speaks of managers and professionals as competing structural interest groups (the professionals being dominant but managerialism being emergent). A similar line of analysis can also be found in Heydebrand's (1977) analysis of the bureaucratisation of the American legal profession.

Bureaucratic control

As I have already suggested, the apogee of bureaucratic control corresponded to the post-war period of growth and development in the Western capitalist countries. It would be foolish to separate out this particular ideology (of the organisation of production) from wider ideologies and 'ways of seeing things' which were common to the period of post-war development which is sometimes regarded as a period of 'modernism' par excellence. The mechanistic and rationalistic principles of bureaucratic organisational control appear to have corresponded to much wider, and deeply rooted, ways of visualising the world and using language.

It is difficult, if not impossible, to pin down and succinctly capture the nature of the bureaucratic organisation. Whilst Weber's 'ideal type' of model remains a valid exposition of the basic dimensions of bureaucracy, somehow or another it lacks sufficient vividness to capture the main dynamics of bureaucratic control. Countless subsequent attempts have been made to capture 'the essence' of bureaucracy (Albrow, 1970). Some have pointed to the strongly mechanistic nature of bureaucratic strategies (Morgan, 1986); others (such as Aucoin, 1990) have noted the "highly standardised systems of coordination and control, and excessive attention to formalised procedures" (p 198). Others have noted the primacy of impersonal forms of regulation, of objectivity, of detailed prescription and differentiation. Indeed, it may come as a reassurance to many public sector workers that such forms of organisational life appear to have been as prevalent within the postwar private sector as within government, health and other social services agencies.

However, to fully appreciate the nature of organisational bureaucracy, it is necessary to get away from those mechanistic ways of thinking which were so much a part of the bureaucratic world, ways which felt uncomfortable with handling paradox, contradiction, and conflict. In Table 2 I attempt to outline some of the essential characteristics of bureaucracy, but in a way which demonstrates the essential contrariness of bureaucracy (a contrariness which bureaucratic ways of thinking could never fully apprehend).

Table 2: Essential characteristics of bureaucratic organisation

Dominant principle	Inevitable consequence
Centralisation	Segmentalism
Formalisation	Informal strategies for 'making out'; Discretion

Anyone familiar with large private sector companies in Britain (such as British Aerospace), or with the National Health Service and local government in Britain in the 1970s, would be familiar with the many highly autonomous departments, enclaves and territories which characterise these large bureaucratic formations. Nevertheless, there is still some truth in suggesting that the dominant characteristic of such bureaucratic forms was centralisation, the problem being that such processes of centralisation in themselves constituted their own antithesis, an antithesis perhaps summarised most succinctly by Kanter (1984) through her analysis of organisational segmentalism. The problem of segmentalism (or 'departmentalism', 'divisionalism') became recognised as a basic dysfunction of the bureaucratic form which emerged in terms of the tension between the principle of ordered and centralised command on the one hand and the necessary forms of functional specialisation within complex bureaucracies on the other. Where this tendency towards functional specialisation overlapped with forms of professional interest group structure then the resulting compartments tended to be driven far more by the needs of occupational interest groups than the requirements of the firm (and in the context of the state this presumably provides some explanation for the behaviour of bureaucrats as 'budget maximisers'). Paradoxically, then, far from resembling monolithic structures, large bureaucratic organisations were much more akin to 'pluraliths'.

The formalisation of organisational life, which perhaps was the other essential characteristic of bureaucratic control strategies, also produced its own antithesis. Within organisational sociology the 'symbolic interactionist' literature was concerned primarily to study the informal strategies adopted by people within bureaucratic organisations to subvert the formalised and regulatory regimes in which they found themselves immersed. Within the social policy literature the same phenomenon becomes explored through the concept of 'discretion': "a ubiquitous phenomenon linked to the inherent and logical limits to control" (Ham and Hill, 1984).

An analogy may be useful here in enabling us to think through the character of the organisational regimes during the bureaucratic era. Leaving aside the issue of coercion, a very close comparison can be made between the experience of working within bureaucratic regimes and the social experience of citizenship in post-totalitarian regimes within Eastern Europe (Havel, 1987). Within both regimes we find an ascendant principle of regulatory control through attempts to define, specify and regiment all aspects of social life. We might think of such systems as bureaucratic command structures - an attempt to reach out and control all parts of society/organisation. The point is that where no formalised freedoms exist then the result is widespread, informal subversion. And this is as true within British local government or British Aerospace in the 1970s as it was within Eastern European societies under Brezhnev or Husak. The problem for bureaucratic regulationists was their failure to understand that people are always both objects and agents of social and organisational processes. So, rather than seeing informal subversion and discretion as 'dysfunctions' of bureaucracy, we need to adopt a position from which we can see how such phenomena are actually constituted by bureaucracy, and essential to its very nature.

Incapable of containing mentally the notion of such paradox, bureaucratic agents persisted in seeing segmentalism and discretion as aspects of bureaucratic dysfunction which could be controlled and remedied. The problem, however, was that the remedy was essentially 'more of the same'. Bureaucracies attempted to cope with discretion via more regulation, renewed efforts to assert hierarchical control, more information gathering and monitoring, and so on; in other words, by more bureaucracy. So the spiral continued. Similarly, as I have noted elsewhere (Hoggett, 1990), faced with the disintegrative processes of segmentalism, bureaucracies tended to fall back upon traditional methods of asserting control and in doing so merely exacerbated existing tensions. Thus, the centre of the organisation reacted to the emergence of divisionally-based, or departmentally-based, power centres by seeking to impose greater degrees of corporate regulation and control.

> Centralised units devoted to development of corporate strategy grew like Topsy, budgetmaking processes became geared to undermining the dysfunctional autonomy of the corporate sub-units, the culture of mistrust necessitated the enforcement of the principle of 'delegation upwards', and so on. (Hoggett, 1990, p 10)

Increasingly, then, the centre of bureaucracy was forced to adopt a policing role which led it towards progressive encroachment on routine and administrative operations and details themselves. Hence the constant experience of policy makers within state bureaucracies in the later 1970s and 1980s of being bogged down in detail, of never having time to focus upon real strategic issues.

The demise of bureaucratic control

Such 'dysfunctions' could be contended with so long as the bureaucratic form was congruent with prevailing market and technological conditions. In terms of their liking for centralisation, massification and 'the vertical integration of production' bureaucracies seemed geared to the mass production of goods and services. Moreover, the giant, slow moving organisations which emerged during this period could not respond swiftly to changes in the market environment. By the mid 1970s both of these conditions had altered. Turbulence within the market environment (particularly after the Opec oil price rise in 1973) had become the norm and if organisations lacked the internal capacity to adapt to changed market conditions, they would quickly go to the wall. Morris Suzuki (1984, 1986) termed this new phase of capitalist development 'the permanent innovation economy' (PIE). The need for a much greater degree of innovation (or at least an ability to imitate the innovations of competitors) has meant that organisations have had to harness the potential of their own 'expert labour' far more shrewdly than was possible under bureaucratic regimes. The problem for bureaucracies was that it was difficult for talent to flourish within regimes characterised by regulation, formality, and delegation upwards.

To summarise, the demise of bureaucratic control strategies was made possible by alterations in technique which revolutionised the handling of information concerned with the planning, design, coordination and supervision of production. But this demise was made imperative by the development of PIE, turbulent market conditions and (particularly for state democracies) the fiscal crisis of the state itself.

By the 1970s, mechanistic and rationalistic approaches to management, for example management by objectives, had more or less had their day (except in the British public sector where they were undergoing something of a renaissance). Signs of new thinking were clearly beginning to emerge through the work of the Palo Alto school of 'communications theory' (Watzlawick, Beavin and Jackson, 1968) and the important work of Gregory Bateson (1973). Bateson studied complex forms of animal learning and applied this to theories of learning within family and social systems. This in turn became the basis for thinking through issues of imitation and innovation within management learning. What some have referred to as the 'new wave' of management writing (Wood, 1989) really began to take off in the early 1980s with the work of Tom Peters and others (Peters and Waterman, 1982; Peters, 1988; Kanter, 1984). The book by Peters and Waterman (1982) announced itself as a full-blown critique of the basic managerial assumptions of the bureaucratic era. This single text has had a most remarkable impact upon the rhetoric, if not the practice, of managers in the British public sector producing a plethora of 'excellence' seminars, conferences and even annual awards (for example the winner of the annual *Local Government Chronicle* leadership award earns the chance to go on a two week Tom Peters 'skunk camp').

At a broader level the crisis of bureaucratic regulation within the British public sector was signalled clearly by the arrival of the first Thatcher government in 1979. Interestingly enough, the first attempts to begin to develop more de-bureaucratised approaches to management within the public sector came from the 'municipal left' in the early 1980s. A large number of largely Labour controlled local authorities embarked upon the administrative and political decentralisation of their services in an attempt to enhance the popularity of such services in the face of the threat of privatisation (Labour Coordinating Committee, 1984). Throughout the 1980s I developed first hand knowledge of such developments through consultancy and research work for local authorities (Hambleton and Hoggett, 1984; Hoggett and Hambleton, 1987). What eventually became clear, however, was that many of these initiatives were going to amount to little more than an attempt to disperse services spatially into districts and neighbourhoods. Management control often remained quite hierarchical and comparatively little progress was made in devolving managerial decision making. Nevertheless by as early as 1984 the Audit Commission was taking note of the fact that decentralised arrangements appeared to have an impact upon organisational efficiency (see Audit Commission, 1984).

It was not until the mid 1980s that real progress in creating more devolved managerial forms began to occur. In the National Health Service 'cost centre budgeting' was introduced through the Griffiths reforms in 1984 (Petchey, 1986). Within social services a number of shire county social services departments began to experiment with more devolved approaches to management - the Eastbourne Area Social Services Team in East Sussex was probably the first to acquire fully devolved financial and personnel powers in 1987. Such developments were followed closely by the Social Services Inspectorate of the then Department of Health and Social Security. This led to the publication of a major package of training materials, *The decentralisation of social services departments* (1988) which encouraged further developments.

The Department of Education and Science had been similarly interested in developments in Cambridgeshire's education department, where attempts were being made in the mid 1980s to devolve financial management down to the heads of schools (Burgess, 1986). The Cambridgeshire model became very much the prototype for the government's Educational Reform Act in the third term of the Conservative administration. Within the local authority housing service progress was much more uneven, most of the innovation occurring at the very localised level of the individual housing estate. Here the government's own Priority Estate Programme initiative was instrumental in disseminating ideas concerning the creation of estate-based budgets but a number of local authority housing departments, particularly Glasgow and Rochdale, had also pioneered such highly localised forms of resource devolution.

What one detects in all of these developments across a range of service areas is a process of management learning which moves backwards and forwards between local and central levels of government. That central government was quite capable of picking up on innovations from a disparate range of institutions was demonstrated most clearly through its own proposals for the reform of the civil service, proposals which drew quite heavily upon the Swedish model of state administration (Fudge and Gustafsson, 1989). As a result, the Ibbs Report *Improving management in government: the next steps* (1988) recommended reconstituting much of central government along the lines of a devolved or 'executive agency' approach.

By the late 1980s devolved approaches to management were being heralded by the Audit Commission very much as if they constituted the new orthodoxy for the public sector to follow (Audit Commission, 1988, 1989). Clearly we should remain sceptical of the extent to which such ideas have taken hold of the practice of public sector managers as opposed to the rhetoric. There has been considerable resistance to such change from trade unions, managers and politicians alike. Inadequate, and often manually-based, financial information systems presented a major block to many such developments as did the attitudes and practices of the many powerful senior officers within centralised financial, personnel and legal sections. However, it would seem that the further extension of competitive tendering through the Local Government and Housing Act of 1989 has finally provided the catalyst for a major shake up of central services. Three basic models for the reorganisation of central services appear to be emerging. The first opts for a radical devolution of financial and personnel functions to the main service departments. The second, for the creation of an internal market for support services through the construction of service level agreements (CIPFA, 1988). The third reconstitutes support services along the lines of 'quasi trading units', the difference being that in this case service departments can 'shop outside' for support services if internal suppliers are felt to be inappropriate or inadequate (LGTB, 1990).

The kinds of developments I have outlined all share the same essential characteristic: the devolution of previously centralised managerial powers to the operational level. It is important to understand that such forms of structural change do not necessarily imply an equivalent change in the culture of public sector management. Much of the new managerialism also gives emphasis to changes in style and approach - to 'learning from the customer', 'valuing one's staff', being clear about one's 'core values', and so forth. Whether such principles are taking hold as the new values-in-use or whether they remain simply 'espoused values' (Argyris and Schon, 1978) remains a moot point. As I have suggested elsewhere, more devolved patterns of management within the public sector are compatible with a range of political and institutional objectives - they can lead towards more genuinely emancipatory forms of public service management, but they can also be the means of achieving a much greater degree of financial control and service rationalisation (Hoggett and Bramley, 1989). To understand this fully we must examine in much more detail the nature of decentralisation as a dimension of the restructuring process in the private and public sectors.

Towards post-bureaucratic control?

> The centre may not be 'doing' the work in a decentralised organisation, but it makes sure that it knows how the work is going. The new technology, of course, makes it even easier for that information to flow more copiously and more immediately than ever, making it even easier to contemplate still further decentralisation, in theory at least. (Handy, 1989, p 94)

It is the revolutionary advances in the automation of information handling which have provided the conditions necessary for entirely new approaches to organisational control. The concept of decentralisation is crucial to an understanding of the emerging post-bureaucratic forms of organisation both within private and public sectors. However we tend to have a number of preconceptions concerning the term 'decentralisation' which should be suspended if we are to grasp the full meaning which I wish the term to convey.

The first thing to appreciate is that under conditions of post-bureaucratic control an essential bifurcation develops between strategic and operational levels of organisational work. The new paradigm comprises a paradoxical development through which radical forms of operational decentralisation become combined with the further centralisation of strategic command. In the case of international companies operations may be devolved and distributed across several continents but overall strategic control remains tightly centralised, albeit within vastly reduced company headquarters. Fergus Murray coined the phrase "the decentralisation of production and the centralisation of command" to describe these processes at work in Italian companies such as Olivetti (Murray, 1983). In the case of state institutions operational devolution to schools, hospitals, executive agencies, occurs in the same movement as the centralisation of strategic command via enhanced control over expenditure, the nationalisation of the curriculum, and so forth (Walker, 1988).

The key point is that such processes of decentralised centralisation occur at all institutional levels. They are as pertinent to our understanding of the relationship between the centre of a social services department and its devolved area teams as they are to an understanding of emerging patterns of central-local government relations. The point is that this new form of organisational control provides the basis for the articulation of the full range of traditional political projects but in a contemporary organisational form. Institutions committed to the pursuit of egalitarian values could benefit from the centralisation of strategic command as much as those committed to the strategy of cost-control.

The second issue to appreciate is that decentralisation may assume two basic forms - internal or external. Under internal decentralisation operational management is devolved to internal units within the organisation. In the context of the public sector I have suggested that we use the term 'devolved service unit' (DSU) to describe the new generation of schools, libraries, leisure centres, area housing and social services teams, etc operating within decentralised health and local government authorities. Under external decentralisation, operations are devolved to units and agencies outside the organisation altogether, ie contracting out. The point is that under conditions of maximum internal or external decentralisation the nature of control is actually the same - control by contract - it is just that in the first situation operations are 'contracted in' rather than out.

This brings us to a third essential characteristic of decentralisation. It is equivalent to a fundamental shift in the focus of organisational control from a concern for internal methods and procedures to a concern for results. As I have previously noted, commentators such as Aucoin (1990) have suggested that we think of the era of bureaucratic control as one corresponding to that within which the discourse of public administration dominated our thinking about the organisation of the state. Central to this was "the adherence to formalised processes and procedures" (p 118) as opposed to concern for results, performance, outcomes and effectiveness (p 197). Charles Handy (1989) makes a similar point regarding the shift in thinking within private sector management in the 1980s. He speaks of the increased pressure for results and the need for organisations to deliver. He adds, "organisational fashion used to imply that the work of most of the organisation could be precisely described and defined, and therefore carefully monitored and controlled" (p 103) whereas now organisations have to be managed by specifying "the essential core" and "by being clear about boundaries and areas of discretion by specifying the kinds of results which are required" (pp 103-4).

This new concern for results rather than methods and procedures corresponds to the abandonment of control by hierarchy and its replacement with control by contract. The development of commercial contracts between purchasers and suppliers is just one manifestation of a much broader movement towards contractual relationships within the contemporary management process, the point being that fully decentralised organisational arrangements are incompatible with traditional forms of hierarchical control, irrespective of whether these arrangements are internal to the organisation itself or an expression of external decentralisation (ie contracting out). As I have said before, my main interest in this paper is to look at internal forms of decentralisation. I have argued elsewhere (Hoggett, 1990, p 21) that in Britain the impetus towards forms of external decentralisation (ie contracting out) has come essentially from the Conservative government. The objective underlying this strategy is clearly cost control and hence, contrary to Aucoin's suggestion, it has focused more upon the specification of inputs in contractual relationships than upon outputs and results.

Cost control can clearly also be the main strategic objective underlying forms of internal decentralisation. Arguably this is the primary impulse behind the creation of 'executive agencies' within the British civil service (Winckler, 1990, pp 149-50). Full devolution of operational control to service managers can only occur within a set of clear boundaries which include 'the kind of results' the organisation is looking for. What emerges then is a form of non-legal contract between the centre and the DSUs in which the centre prescribes the framework (including values, objectives, targets, etc) within which the DSU can operate and the DSU describes clearly the forms of support it requires to convert its enhanced organisational freedom into results. Whether such 'contracts' give most emphasis to the specification of inputs, outputs or outcomes will vary according to the strategic objectives underlying the devolution. Whereas cost-led strategies will prioritise inputs, quality-led strategies will give emphasis to outcomes and outputs. In most public sector organisations in Britain the actual nature of the strategic objectives underlying devolution are by no means unproblematic. They cannot be simply read off from the formal statement of an organisation's values. Because pressures to control costs are so great there is a tendency for organisations to espouse service quality whilst privileging cost control.

Another way of thinking about this notion of control by contract is to return to the problem of discretion within bureaucratic organisational regimes. The post-bureaucratic organisation seeks to overcome 'the problem' of informal discretion by replacing it with 'formalised freedom'. It is important to note that the emphasis of much of the 'new wave management' (Wood, 1989) on 'intrapreneurialism', 'looseness', chaos, etc is not so much a sign of a shift towards a greater degree of informality within organisations as it is of a licensing (and hence control) of the informal that forms an inevitable part of all working environments. Cooper and Burrell (1988) note how the bureaucratic mentality could never get to grips with the paradox of formality within organisations. They suggest that 'post-modernist' approaches to the analysis of organisational life celebrate such contradictions rather than seeing them as irresolvable conceptual problems. They note, " 'the formal' and 'informal' reflect each other like the obverse and reverse sides of a coin; to the extent that they can never be separated, they are not just mutually defining but can be said to be self-referential" (p 109).

This development of formalised informality within organisations is equivalent to the abandonment of regimented and regulated orders by more liberal regimes of organisational authority. We might add that such liberalisation can itself assume a number of quite different forms, from being just another variant of what Marcuse once described as 'repressive tolerance' to more genuinely emancipatory forms of institutional relationships. Such liberalisation processes seek to harness human agency rather than regulate it, the latter being an impossible task as we have already seen. In this sense the new organisational regimes are far more subtle in their use of power - they insinuate themselves upon our better nature, as a quick scan of the work of Tom Peters (1988) quickly reveals.

In summary, then, I would suggest that post-bureaucratic organisational regimes recognise the inevitability of human agency within organisational life and therefore seek to formalise freedoms for it. Managerial devolution is therefore equivalent to 'freedom within boundaries', a form of regulated autonomy. It is to an investigation of this notion of 'freedom within boundaries' that I now turn.

Freedom within boundaries

If control is to be devolved rather than abrogated then devolution must take place within a given framework or set of boundaries. Within organisations these boundaries consist essentially of sets of rules and expectations, for example rules relating to financial control or expectations relating to standards of performance. Without such boundaries there could be no accountability. The point about such boundaries is that they both open-up and close-off; they define what can be done and what cannot be done; they constitute a space for legitimate action whilst precluding certain other actions as illegitimate. This holds for any kind of rule irrespective of whether it consists of a 30 mph speed limit, a rule relating to financial underspending or to the invoicing of sub-contractors. In other words a boundary constitutes both a constraint and a freedom.

Typically people operating within bureaucratic environments found that they could never do anything (other than a strictly limited number of actions prescribed by their job specification) without first going 'back up the line'. This was how 'control by hierarchy' was experienced at the individual level. Because the boundaries were so tightly drawn they invited rule-bending as a modus operandi. In a sense the development of post-bureaucratic organisational forms is equivalent to the creation of more liberal-democratic organisational regimes. Within such democracies individuals exercise freedoms within agreed frameworks of conduct. Laws only tend to be invoked when such boundaries fail to contain behaviour and transgression occurs. In this sense laws (a particular kind of rule) act as a sign or marker - we tend to behave within accepted frameworks not because 'there is a law about it' but because of the internalisation of certain standards for which laws act primarily as signifiers. So liberal-democratic regimes rely heavily upon the power of socialisation processes to regulate behaviour, and the same is true for the new forms of organisation. Hence the paramount importance given to the concept of 'organisational culture' and 'cultural change' within the management literature of the 1980s (Schein, 1985).

The concept of 'freedom within boundaries' is therefore central to the post-bureaucratic organisation. But the creation of radically devolved forms of operational management corresponds to a transformation in all aspects of management, particularly in the role of the centre. In Table 3 I attempt to sketch these changes.

The role of the centre is crucial in all this. There are many who have argued that organisational decentralisation sounds fine in theory but in practice it would crucially weaken the ability of the centre (and hence of the elected local or national politicians) to direct and influence policy. But as Handy (1989, pp 95-96) notes, in the end organisations "have to stop trying to run everything from the centre, they have to begin to let go". The paradox of contemporary developments is that it is precisely by letting go of operational matters that strategic command can be concentrated more effectively at the centre. The Thatcher government appeared to clearly appreciate this paradox. Its 'Next Steps' strategy was designed to increase efficiency in resource management within the British civil service by reorganising it on a devolved 'executive agency' basis whilst simultaneously enhancing the executive authority of ministers over their departments (Kemp, 1990). At the local governmental level it also tends to have been Conservative councils who have been quickest to appreciate the nature of this paradox. Many Labour controlled local authorities have strongly resisted devolution, particularly of financial and personnel powers, because of a feeling that it would undermine the ability of elected politicians to direct local affairs. In reality I would argue that it is only by embracing the new developments that Labour politicians have any real chance to shape and direct events at a local level; even the cut-back local councils of today are far too complex an organisational system to be controlled from the centre.

Table 3: Devolved management

Function	Contribution to devolved management
Centre: Strategic leadership	Responsible for making sure the boundaries are set - eg the core values, strategic priorities, minimum performance standards non-negotiable personnel and financial rules
Regulation/control (eg performance review)	Monitoring/policing of boundaries
Support services (eg accountancy training)	Supports managers/staff in using new freedoms
Operational management	Adapts strategic priorities and objectives to local needs, may create local policy, manages available resources to produce the most effective 'input mix' to achieve efficient and responsive service

What then is the role of the centre *vis-à-vis* the devolved units in the post-bureaucratic organisation? Firstly, to establish and maintain the corporate culture, or, in today's jargon, to create the vision or mission around which the new, liberal-consensual organisational regime can be constructed. Secondly, to be absolutely clear about the kinds of results it is looking for from operational managers through the provision of practical objectives and performance targets. Thirdly, to develop frameworks for monitoring, evaluation and inspection both to encourage, reward and develop performance and to police the boundaries for possible transgression. The key point is that it no longer has line-management (ie control through hierarchy) responsibilities and therefore no longer needs those layers of senior managers (assistant directors and principal officers) whose role, under the old regimes, always contained an ambiguous mixture of policy and administration. In the private sector, the term 'down-sizing' is given to the process of peeling off layers of redundant staff at the centre.

Delegated powers

What then are the managerial freedoms which become delegated under the new organisational arrangements? We can approach this issue by asking four questions:

i. Has the devolved unit its own budget?

ii. Has the unit any control or influence over the size of this budget?

iii. What control does the unit have over how this budget can be used?

iv. Has the unit any control over what services it provides, how they are provided, and to whom?

Taking each of these in turn we have suggested elsewhere (Hoggett and Bramley, 1989) that there are of course choices to be made in terms of how far an organisation wishes to go. Regarding the budget itself a prerequisite is that control over the revenue budget should be delegated to operational management as well as a budget for all non-major capital items. Typically the centre will maintain tight control over the allocation of such budgets but devolved units may be granted (or may claim) influence through lobbying and bidding processes. Even if the devolved unit has no control over the central allocation it may have power to raise extra revenue. Schools (through the work of parent-teacher associations) have traditionally had such powers, but housing teams may also be given the power to develop agreements with tenants tying rents to services (this has been tried in Glasgow and elsewhere) or decentralised neighbourhoods may be granted the power to generate and keep their own capital receipts (as occurs in the London Borough of Tower Hamlets).

Control over how the budget can be used (ie expenditure control rules) constitutes an essential facet of the boundaries within which the new freedoms may be exercised. A consensus seems to be emerging, encouraged in part by the Audit Commission document *Towards better financial management* (1989), which challenges overly restrictive approaches to expenditure control. Considerable scope for virement of sums between different budget heads can be provided so long as certain rules, such as preventing virement from capital into revenue budgets, are observed. Previously restrictive rules concerning underspend have also been challenged providing managers with a much greater degree of flexibility in terms of how they use their resources. Many local authorities are now delegating 'client side' functions to the level of the DSU so that schools, estate teams, leisure centres and so forth, acquire direct control over tendering processes.

Finally, there is the crucial question of the DSU's ability to influence policy. The new arrangements, as we have noted, provide the conditions for a much greater degree of centralised control over strategic issues. The point is, however, that whilst the centre is responsible for the organisation's strategic direction it does not have to perform this strategic role itself; it merely has to ensure that it gets done. Centralised responsibility for strategy is one thing, the centralised creation of strategy and policy is something entirely different. It is of course quite possible to envisage an organisation in which operational units have radically devolved financial and personnel powers and yet have no control over what services are produced, how they are delivered or to whom. It is equally possible to envisage an organisation, say for instance a social services department, within which area teams are accountable to subcommittees of locally-based councillors and user groups and where the freedom exists not just to develop local services which can respond to local needs but also to shape and influence the overall strategic direction of the department. This brings us back to the question of the values of the organisation and how the newly emerging post-bureaucratic forms have the capacity to realise a range of different service objectives.

If an organisation simply devolves financial control whilst retaining tight centralised control over policy making then it may certainly achieve greater control over costs and encourage innovation in the use of resources at operational levels but it may have done nothing to improve the degree of responsiveness or local accountability of services. Devolution will only permit greater responsiveness if DSUs either have the ability to create locally specific policies or to interpret and adapt corporate policies to local requirements. For example, this would imply that devolved units had the power to target services towards the needs of particular groups (eg elderly people, children with special learning difficulties, etc) or to introduce entirely new kinds of services to a particular area (eg a community education initiative attached to a local library or a support unit for survivors of psychiatric services) or to deliver existing services in radically new ways.

We have engaged in an extensive examination of decentralisation initiatives in the London boroughs of Islington and Tower Hamlets (Hambleton, Hoggett and Franklin, 1991). The research throws much light on many of the political and managerial choices which can shape such approaches to public service reform. Decentralisation in Tower Hamlets has been led by the local Liberal Party which took control of this area of London's East End in 1986 (the local activists eschew the new title 'Liberal Democrats' adopted by the national party to which they belong). The Liberals totally reorganised the vast majority of services that the borough traditionally provided by placing them under the de facto control of seven neighbourhoods. Political control of each neighbourhood corresponds to the strength of the political parties in that area. A deliberate and systematic attempt has been made to restrict the power of the corporate centre so that the autonomy of neighbourhoods could be maximised.

Such a radical approach to political and managerial devolution has provided the conditions necessary for the creation of locally specific policies. Thus, for example, the Stepney Neighbourhood, which was controlled by Labour between 1986 and 1990 quickly developed a reputation for allocating resources to its local community and voluntary sector primarily as a means of diverting resources to the neglected local Bangladeshi community. Globe Town, which has been controlled by the Liberals since 1986, has experimented with the further devolution of powers to much smaller areas and with the encouragement of tenant management cooperatives. Two other Liberal controlled neighbourhoods - Bethnal Green and Bow - gave priority to massive estate modernisation programmes. Of course once operational units have been given power to make local policy then traditions of uniformity in service provision may be replaced by rampant diversity as our own research in Tower Hamlets is currently revealing. Deakin and Wright raise this issue regarding decentralisation when they allude to the problem of "equity and maintaining common standards - how much diversity is tolerable if these other standards are to be met?" (1990, p 205).

In contrast, the London Borough of Islington has been far more cautious in granting autonomy to its 24 neighbourhoods. This is partly a reflection of the tradition of tight centralised political control which has been a feature of Labour's leadership in this borough. It is also a reflection of the genuine commitment of both officers and politicians in Islington to equal opportunity policies and a concern that radical devolution could undermine this commitment. However, neighbourhoods have had sufficient autonomy to interpret central policies in a way which was responsive to local requirements. In Islington, unlike Tower Hamlets, no single minority ethnic group dominates; instead a large range of smaller communities can be found dispersed in different parts of the borough. However, decentralisation has enabled neighbourhoods to respond more flexibly to the needs of the particular groups in their area - the Irish in the north of the borough, Turkish Cypriots in the east, and so on.

As by now should be clear, my view is that devolution, even in its radical forms, is not incompatible with a commitment to egalitarian values. In Tower Hamlets a strategic decision was made by the Liberals to restrict the role of the centre as much as was practically possible. But even here we have found that the power of the centre has tended to reassert itself. By devolving control over operational matters the strategic centre is freed up from absorption in day-to-day administrative detail. This facilitates a much greater degree of centralised command over those policies which provided the boundaries within which managerial freedom can be exercised. Decentralisation is an innovation in the organisational means through which policies and services are delivered; as such it is compatible with the full range of possible political and administrative values including egalitarian ones. Indeed Islington has embarked upon a programme of financial devolution to its neighbourhoods in the belief that central controls over equality policies have been securely established.

A final question to examine is the relationship between post-bureaucratic forms of public institution and democratic accountability. This is a complex issue and one should be wary of providing premature answers. Certain questions can be raised however. The radical left and the radical right may differ in terms of their preference for internal or external decentralisation (the right preferring to contract out, the left preferring to maintain a public monopoly of service provision), but whatever the preference a much greater degree of administrative and spatial separation of strategic and operational matters is likely in the future. A slimmed down centre would appear to be incompatible with a large and unwieldy political executive. On the other hand, the creation of a whole new layer of devolved service units would appear to open up the space for new political roles at the grass roots level and for much greater user involvement at the point of service delivery. Without managerial devolution there really was very little point in users becoming involved in service delivery matters except as complainants and antagonists, but once real power over decisions and resources has been located at the point of delivery user-based forms of local democracy become a more tangible possibility. The fascinating question is whether such involvement will lead to an increased bottom-up demand for public resources or whether it will absorb and side-track such demand. This would appear to be a useful topic for anyone researching the new school governing bodies to look at (Jones and Stewart, 1990).

Bureaucracy, professionalism and beyond

In this final section I would like to return to some of the issues raised at the very beginning of this paper concerning the different models of organisational control to have emerged, particularly during this century. We noted the tension between bureaucratic and professional models of control and the development of the attempt to 'subdue' professionalism through bureaucratic management. In Britain in the 1980s this struggle was most obvious in the tension between the medical profession and the new generation of 'general managers' introduced into the NHS after the Griffiths Report in 1984.

The Griffiths reforms within the NHS very much stand at the watershed between the old and the new paradigms. They contained elements of the old (rational planning, corporate management, etc) (Day and Klein, 1983) but also some elements of the new thinking. The introduction of 'cost centres' within the NHS was very much part of the latter, and we can see how further government proposals (self-managing units, general practitioner budgets) built upon this approach (Hoggett, 1990, p 23). The essential difference between the old and the new thinking seems to be this: rather than attempt to strengthen 'management' in order to control 'professionals' the strategy shifts towards creating managers out of professionals. Suddenly doctors, headteachers, or senior social workers, find themselves managing a budget (often measured in £ millions), invoicing contractors, switching money out of one budget heading into another, developing strategies for dealing with vacancy levels, etc. A new generation of unit managers begins to emerge who combine technical expertise with managerial competence. As Burris (1989, p 12) notes, professional/ bureaucratic conflicts are not so much being extended as transcended as the new form of control strategy (one she calls 'technocratic' rather than the term 'post-bureaucratic' that I have used) develops. Moreover some aspects of the rhetoric of the new management - those which emphasise team working, encourage initiative, speak about harnessing human resources - are in many ways congruent with more traditional 'collegiate' forms of professional organisation. Hence the two are more easily fused, the kickback however being that the promise of greater autonomy through financial devolution disguises the simultaneous centralisation of strategic command. Control becomes not just devolved but almost 'remote'.

Conclusion

In this paper I have tried to develop a hypothesis which could provide a framework for understanding contemporary developments in public sector management in Britain. My impression is that these kinds of development are also occurring within the public sectors of many other Western capitalist countries. I have linked these developments to broader processes of economic restructuring, processes which have been underway within the private sector since the early 1970s. I have suggested that this restructuring corresponds, among other things, to a qualitative change in techniques of organisational control which are post-bureaucratic in character. I am aware of the popularity of this particular prefix (ie 'post') at the present moment and am wary of adding to a list which already includes post-Fordism, post-modernism, etc. However, as I mentioned much earlier, the advantage of such terms is that they signify some degree of certainty about what has passed whilst being agnostic about what exactly will take its place.

It could be objected that so long as the public sector is about the rationing of scarce resources within a framework of democratic accountability then some degree of bureaucracy will always be necessary. I would not dispute this point. The key issue, however, is not whether some degree of bureaucracy is necessary but whether bureaucratic principles constitute the essential mode of organisational control within a given sector. My hypothesis is that even within the public sector an essentially new managerial paradigm is now emerging.

References

Albrow, M. (1970) *Bureaucracy*, London: Macmillan.

Alford, R. (1975) *Health care politics: ideological and interest group barriers to reform*, Chicago: University of Chicago Press.

Argyris, C. and Schon, D. (1978) *Organisation learning: a theory of action perspective*, Reading, Mass: Addison-Wesley.

Aucoin, P. (1990) 'Administrative reform in public management: paradigms, principles, paradoxes and pendulums', *Governance*, vol 3, no 2, pp 115-37.

Audit Commission (1984) *Bringing council tenants' arrears under control*, London: HMSO.

Audit Commission (1988) *The competitive council*, Management Papers no 1, London: HMSO.

Audit Commission (1989) *Towards better financial management*, London: HMSO.

Bateson, G. (1973) *Steps to an ecology of mind*, London: Paladin.

Braverman, H. (1974) *Labor and monopoly capital*, Monthly Review Press.

Burgess, T. (1986) 'Cambridgeshire's financial management initiative for schools', *Public Money*, vol 7, pp 21-24.

Burris, B. (1989) 'Technocratic organization and control', *Organization Studies*, vol 10, no 1, pp 1-22.

CIPFA (1988) *Accounting for support services*, London: Chartered Institute of Public Finance and Accountancy.

Clarke, S. and Mayer, M. (1986) 'Responding to grassroots discontent: Germany and the US', *International Journal of Urban and Regional Research*, vol 10, pp 401-17.

Clegg, S. (1981) 'Organisation and control', *Administrative Science Quarterly*, vol 26, pp 545-62.

Cooper, R. and Burrell, G. (1988) 'Modernism, post-modernism and organizational analysis', *Organization Studies*, vol 9, no 1, pp 91-112.

Cousins, C. (1988) 'The restructuring of welfare work: the introduction of general management and the contracting out of ancillary services in the NHS', *Work, Employment and Society*, vol 2, pp 210-28.

Day, P. and Klein, R. (1983) 'The mobilisation of consent versus the management of conflict: decoding the Griffiths Report', *British Medical Journal*, vol 287.

Deakin, N. and Wright, A. (eds) (1990) *Consuming public services*, London: Routledge.

DHSS Social Services Inspectorate (1988) *The decentralisation of social services departments*, nos 1-5.

Edwards, R. (1979) *Contested terrain*, New York: Basic Books.

Efficiency Unit (1983) *Improving management in government: the next steps*, London: HMSO.

Fayol, H. (1916) Administration Industrielle et Generale, Bulletin de la Societé de l'Industrie Minerale, English translation (1971), *General and Industrial Management*, London: Pitman.

Fudge, C. and Gustafsson, L. (1989) 'Administrative reform and public management in Sweden and the UK', *Public Money and Management*, vol 9, no 2, pp 29-34.

Ham, C. and Hill, M. (1984) *The policy process in the modern capitalist state*, Brighton: Wheatsheaf.

Hambleton, R. and Hoggett, P. (eds) (1984) *The politics of decentralisation: theory and practice of a radical local government initiative*, Working Paper no 46, Bristol: SAUS Publications, School for Advanced Urban Studies, University of Bristol.

Hambleton, R., Hoggett, P. and Franklin, A. (1991) *The decentralisation of public services: a research evaluation*, London: ESRC.

Handy, C. (1989) *The age of unreason*, London: Business Books Limited.

Havel, V. (1987) *Living in truth*, London: Faber.

Heydebrand, W. (1977) 'Organizational contradictions in public bureaucracies', *Sociological Quarterly*, vol 18, pp 83-107.

Hoggett, P. (1987) 'A farewell to mass production? Decentralisation as an emergent private and public sector paradigm', in P. Hoggett and R. Hambleton (eds), *Decentralisation and democracy: localising public services*, Occasional Paper no 26, Bristol: SAUS Publications, School for Advanced Urban Studies, University of Bristol, pp 215-33.

Hoggett, P. (1990) *Modernisation, political strategy and the welfare state: an organisational perspective*, Studies in Decentralisation and Quasi-Markets no 2, Bristol: SAUS Publications, School for Advanced Urban Studies, University of Bristol.

Hoggett, P. and Bramley, G. (1989) 'Devolution of local budgets', *Public Money and Management*, vol 9, no 4, pp 9-14.

Hoggett, P. and Hambleton, R. (eds) (1987) *Decentralisation and democracy: localising public services*, Occasional Paper no 26, Bristol: SAUS Publications, School for Advanced Urban Studies, University of Bristol.

Johnson, T. (1972) *Professions and power*, London: Macmillan.

Jones, G. and Stewart, J. (1990) 'Forces set in motion for more education spending', *Local Government Chronicle*, 10 August.

Kanter, R.M. (1984) *The change masters: corporate entrepreneurs at work*, London: Unwin.

Kemp, P. (1990) 'Next steps for the British civil service', *Governance*, vol 3, no 2, pp 186-96.

Labour Coordinating Committee (1984) *Go local to survive: decentralisation in local government*, London: Labour Coordinating Committee.

Lane, C. (1988) 'Industrial change in Europe: the pursuit of flexible specialisation in Britain and West Germany', *Work, Employment and Society*, vol 2, no 2.

Le Grand, J. (1990) *Quasi-markets and social policy*, Studies in Decentralisation and Quasi-Markets no 1, Bristol: SAUS Publications, School for Advanced Urban Studies, University of Bristol.

Leborgne, D. and Lipietz, A. (1987) 'New technologies, new modes of regulation: some spatial implications', Paper presented to the International Conference on Technology, Restructuring and Urban Regional Development, Dubrovnik.

LGTB (1990) *The future for central services?*, Luton: Local Government Training Board.

Mintzberg, H. (1979) *The structuring of organizations*, Englewood Cliffs: Prentice Hall.

Morgan, G. (1986) *Images of organization*, London: Sage.

Morris Suzuki, T. (1984) 'Robots and capitalism', *New Left Review*, no 147, pp 109-21.

Morris Suzuki, T. (1986) 'Capitalism in the computer age', *New Left Review*, no 160, pp 81-91.

Murray, F. (1983) 'The decentralisation of production: the decline of the mass collective worker', *Capital and Class*, vol 19.

Petchey, R. (1986) 'The Griffiths reorganization of the NHS: Fowlerism by stealth?', *Critical Social Policy*, vol 17, pp 87-101.

Peters, T. and Waterman, R. (1982) *In search of excellence*, New York: Harper and Row.

Peters, T. (1988) *Thriving on chaos*, London: Macmillan.

Schein, E. (1985) *Organizational culture and leadership*, San Francisco: Jossey-Bass.

Walker, A. (1988) 'Tendering care', *New Society*, no 83, p 1308.

Watzlawick, P., Beavin, J. and Jackson, D. (1968) *Pragmatics of human communication*, London: Faber.

Winckler, V. (1990) 'Restructuring the civil service: reorganization and relocation 1962-85', *International Journal of Urban and Regional Research*, vol 14, no 1, pp 135-57.

Wood, S. (1989) 'New wave management', *Work, Employment and Society*, vol 3, no 3, pp 379-403.

CHAPTER 2

QUALITY AND DECENTRALISATION: ARE THEY CONNECTED?

Lucy Gaster

Introduction

Two important trends can be discerned in local government in Great Britain. First, there has been a trend towards more local, neighbourhood-based service delivery. Second, in line with moves elsewhere in the public sector, attention has turned increasingly to the idea of 'quality'. Both trends have highlighted the need to look closely at relationships at the point of service delivery. By implication, at least, the role of front-line staff and their impact on and response to service users and residents, individually and collectively, must now receive more attention than in the past.

This paper looks at the connections between these two trends at that point of interaction - the front line - and offers the hypothesis that quality needs decentralisation, but decentralisation does not in itself lead to quality.

This proposition will be examined here in relation to local government. However, similar trends are present in other parts of the UK public sector (see for example Dalley, 1990a; Day, 1990; and Pollitt, 1990) and, allowing for the difference that only local government is subject to the electoral process, many of the elements in the debate will also apply elsewhere.

In order to examine whether the hypothesis suggested above holds good, some definitions and explanation are needed. The first part of the paper tries to do this. We then look at the processes needed to establish quality; the advantages and disadvantages of different approaches are examined in relation to the needs of local government workers and of consumers and citizens. Finally, an attempt will be made to clarify the connections between decentralisation and quality and to identify what can and cannot be achieved using each approach.

Decentralisation

Decentralisation takes as its starting point the centralist, bureaucratic and remote style of traditional local government, where power and decision making are concentrated in the town hall and the electoral process is the only source of democratic accountability.

Since the early 1980s, pressures for change in the operation of local government have been rapidly mounting. Some have been externally generated, such as the effects of an anti-public sector, tax-cutting government agenda (Deakin, 1987); legislation enforcing client-contractor splits and tenant choice; and the Audit Commission's inspectoral role emphasising the notions of economy, efficiency and effectiveness (Day and Klein, 1990; Henkel, 1991). Others, such as squeezed finances (Alexander, 1990) and low staff morale could be classified as internal pressures.

Most councils have concluded, in the face of these pressures, that they must not only make a fundamental re-examination of the services they have traditionally offered, but that they should make those services more attractive to local residents. Many have also seen increased sensitivity to needs and day-to-day democratic accountability as the route to change and increased public support (Hodge, 1987).

Although by no means universal, one option chosen by many departments and some councils as a whole has been to make their services more physically and geographically accessible (Stoker, Wedgwood Oppenheim and Davies, 1988).

Although this trend has generally been encapsulated as 'decentralisation', in practice it has been interpreted in a variety of ways (Stoker, 1987; Beuret and Stoker, 1986). Often, objectives have been unclear or contradictory (Gaster, 1991a). At a minimum, it has meant the establishment of local outlets for one or more of a council's services but with little other change; management hierarchies are still in place and local offices can still be, and often are, dominated by an anti-public, siege mentality.

In some councils - Basildon and Tower Hamlets, for example - the locational changes have been accompanied by devolved management and budgets (Gaster, 1991b). In some - Basildon again, and Birmingham and Islington - there have been conscious attempts to break down departmental or job boundaries through integrated or generic working. In others again, an emphasis has been on adding 'participative democracy' to the well-established 'representative democracy' symbolised by the elected councillors, through area committees, user groups and neighbourhood forums (Hoggett and Hambleton, 1987).

It has been argued (Hambleton, 1989) that full decentralisation comprises all these elements: localisation, devolution (to staff and to local residents) and integration. This requires major shifts in structures, attitudes and power relationships; few, if any, councils have yet achieved this level of decentralisation.

Quality

The private sector now claims to see quality as more important than profit, cost or schedules (Confederation of British Industry, 1988). The focus is increasingly on small scale production units producing customised, high quality goods. There is much emphasis on 'zero defects', 'fitness for purpose', conformance with requirements and being 'right first time'. While these are laudable aims, derived largely from the manufacturing sector and British Standard 5750, they are difficult to apply to service organisations, particularly those in the public sector.

As Robin Hambleton and Paul Hoggett have noted (1990), the individualistic 'consumerism' emphasised in this approach is not suitable for the public services because it fails to address some important issues. First, individual consumers, whether receiving universal services such as rubbish collection or street lighting, or being compelled by statute or tenure to receive particular services, do not have the option of going elsewhere. This weakens their power over the monopolistic service providers. Second, a solely consumerist approach omits the major requirement of public sector services, namely, collective and public accountability. In the private sector no mechanisms exist whereby consumers can positively influence decision making and policy. Annual shareholders' meetings are an extremely crude mechanism, favouring the powerful, while individual consumers can normally only influence decisions through negative action (withdrawal of custom) where there is no private monopoly.

While, therefore, ideas from the private sector are helpful, we need to look elsewhere for a definition of quality that is applicable to the public sector. Such a definition needs to be meaningful at several levels: it must be useful to service providers in all parts of the organisation, as a practical basis for evolving service standards; it must be wanted and be influenced by consumers and citizens; and it must be capable of being measured and made accountable to senior management, elected representatives and, indeed, central government.

Probably the most detailed work on definitions of quality in the service sector is that by Avedis Donabedian who produced a series of reports during the 1980s on quality in the health service in the United States (1980, 1982, 1985). While not altogether applicable to the full range of public sector services in the UK, his ideas provide a useful and easily assimilable starting point. (See also Stewart and Walsh, 1990.)

He suggests that quality has three dimensions: a technical dimension which can be equated with the concept of 'fitness for purpose' - what is the service intended to do, what are its constituent elements; a non-technical dimension, which covers the social-psychological interaction between service provider and receiver; and, third, the environment, context or ambience in which the service operates. Donabedian argues that an understanding of all three dimensions, and a recognition of their interdependence, is essential to the analysis of quality as it relates to a particular service.

While these ideas need refining and developing to take account both of the different roles that a whole range of actors play in service delivery (see below) and of the notion of public accountability referred to above, they do provide a useful jumping off point. For example, this framework both underlies the need to pay attention to how providers and consumers interact - the focus of 'customer care' programmes - and demonstrates that to pay attention only to this aspect of a service is not enough. For the overall quality of a service to be defined, and for that definition to provide a basis for the service standards increasingly highlighted as the foundation for quality in public services (Labour Party, 1991), all three dimensions of quality, especially the technical aspects, need full consideration.

A third advantage of using the Donabedian framework is that in organisations responsible for a range of services, such as local government, the possibility is created for the council-wide development of common standards cutting across all services, particularly for the non-technical and environmental dimensions; at the same time, there is room for the separate development of technical standards relating to specific services. Similarly, the power balance dilemmas of the professionalmanagerial relationships identified by Ellis (1988) and Pollitt (1990) could, at least partially, also be resolved by analysing which aspects of service are whose responsibility, and at the same time increasing awareness of the links between the different aspects.

However, it would be dangerous to be too dependent on Donabedian's definitions of quality, for three reasons. Focusing on the needs of individual clients, he takes little account of collective consumer needs, and none at all of the role of society in shaping and enforcing accountability of services. Then, partly and perhaps rightly because of the difficulties of identifying the exact contribution by the service provided to the eventual outcome, the analysis concentrates heavily on 'process'. The aims of the service are, therefore, hardly questioned. It hardly needs pointing out - although it is all too common in practice - that a well-delivered service which is not focused on society's or consumers' needs would be unlikely to deserve a quality label, at least when measured against consumer expectations and satisfaction ratings.

Finally, in order to keep the definition of quality within bounds, Donabedian excludes some criteria which, it can be argued, form an inevitable part of many local government services. These are 'accessibility', 'continuity' and 'coordination', all of which are surely important factors in improved services responsive to the pressures outlined earlier but which he sees as 'contributing factors' rather than as integral elements in quality.

Research in Birmingham neighbourhood offices (Gaster, 1991a) showed all three of these factors as inherent in 'quality' as perceived by workers there.

The utility of Donabedian's model is nevertheless very high: it identifies three important, interdependent dimensions of quality; it highlights the role of the front-line workers and of the immediate client; and it provides a foundation for a variety of approaches to suit the needs of different organisations trying to implement a programme for quality.

Refining the model for use at the front line

Who is the service provider?

Front-line staff, service providers, street-level bureaucrats: these are all terms used to describe staff in direct contact with the people using their service (Czepiel *et al*, 1985; Walsh, 1989; Lipsky, 1980). These people are in direct contact with the public, processing information and representing the organisation at its boundary with the external environment. They are the people who will create 'first impressions' among the public and who therefore have considerable power to create and mould expectations about and satisfaction with the whole organisation.

While many (most?) such staff are committed to their work and, possibly to a lesser extent, to their organisation (Day and Klein, 1987; Gaster, 1991a; Stoker and Lowndes, 1991), they are also under great stress from the conflicting demands of consumers, community, management and politicians.

> People often enter public employment, particularly street level bureaucracies, with at least some commitment to the service. ... Yet the very nature of the work prevents them from coming even close to the ideal conception of their jobs. (Lipsky, 1980, p xii)

If, as is stressed by many writers about quality (Confederation of British Industry, 1988; Stewart and Walsh, 1990; Mortiboys, 1986; Wennlund, 1990; Cassam, 1990), effective quality policies depend for their implementation on commitment from leadership and the board/politicians, the commitment from front-line staff is therefore just as important. If the commitment is not there, the level of day-to-day discretion available to front-line workers (Lipsky, 1980) leads both common sense and policy implementation theories (Ham and Hill, 1984) to tell us that the policy is likely to be implemented half-heartedly or not at all.

Two aspects need consideration: the front-line staff's ability to do their job; and the extent to which front-line staff are supported by the 'back line' - the rest of the organisation.

Apart from the necessary technical or professional training, the first question is whether staff working at the front line have the interactive skills they need to be able to use that training most effectively (Borzeix, 1990). Have they, for example, received training in non-verbal communication - as important, says Tansik (1985), as verbal communication. Do users have good information about how best to use the service (Carr-Hill *et al*, 1991)? Do the people seeking their service have accurate expectations of what is on offer, or will there be a stream of disappointed or angry consumers leaving the office (Nyquist *et al*, 1985; Birmingham CCSAP, 1989)? Do staff feel confident enough to deal with verbal or physical violence, or the threat of it? Is the environment in which they work demoralising for them and/or confusing or antagonising for their users (Maister, 1985; Wener, 1985)?

Second, how do front-line staff connect with the rest of the organisation? What is the culture of the organisation as a whole? Are structures and procedures constructive and consistent for the whole organisation (Shostack, 1985)? Are front-line staff isolated, or do they feel supported? Are frontline staff valued (James, 1989)? Is the relationship between the front line and the back line one of trust or cynicism? Do front-line staff know what is going on: what are the lines of internal communication, up, down and sideways (Gaster, 1991a)? And what is rewarded: speed of performance and throughput (eg levels of arrears, speed of repairs) or accuracy and quality (eg benefits advice, well-finished repairs that last)?

It will not be argued here that conditions at the front line must be problem-free before a policy for quality can be implemented. But, in thinking about 'what is quality?', it is argued that, for the process to be effective, the perspective of front-line staff must be included in identifying quality and formulating standards. Such a perspective - and the will to make it happen - is more likely to be meaningful if staff feel committed, involved and supported.

Who is the service user?

Talking about 'consumers', Christopher Pollitt distinguished several categories, each of which has a distinct but possibly different interest in the service (1988). These are: current users; eligible applicants for service not yet receiving it (eg waiting lists); eligible non-recipients - people who think they are ineligible or who know (or think they know) enough about the service not to want it; and future users. A further group, now receiving increasing attention, consists of the people who look after those receiving services - the carers. Finally, there are those who control the gateway to some services through their power of referral.

As well as consumers, who can relate to the service as individuals or through user or 'self-advocacy' groups (Croft and Beresford, 1990), there are those who are involved through the fact that local government services are, like other public sector services, accountable to the public at large: 'citizens', in the various senses in which that word can now be used (Deakin, 1990).

The difficulties and problems that limit real consumer and citizen impact on service delivery, priorities and policies have been well rehearsed, as have the realities of public accountability (Croft and Beresford, 1990; Day and Klein, 1987). Equally, however, the advantages of public involvement in services for a receptive organisation seem clear: there is a better chance that services will meet actual need; consumers (in the broadest sense) will know more about the services; and there will be a closer, more trusting relationship with the service providers.

Despite the difficulties, therefore, a further dimension to the question 'what is quality?' must be the democratic element, both through representative democracy (elected councillors) and through participative democracy (user groups, neighbourhood forums and other mechanisms involving local people other than at election time). A quality service is surely one that as far as possible meets the needs of users and consumers and the general public. The reality exists of constrained resources, of statutory requirements, of political values and, at the local level, of conflicts of interests and divided communities. Nevertheless, the ability of an organisation to listen, understand and respond is a prerequisite to successful community and consumer involvement in defining quality.

The organisation

The two previous sections have briefly examined the importance of involving front-line staff and the public in defining the quality of services offered by a local council. It is essential, however, not to overlook the role of the policy makers and of senior and central management. For in the end, the level, quantity and availability of the services on offer will be determined by the values and objectives of the whole organisation. And it is in this area more than any other that the importance of clear leadership and top-level commitment is paramount.

This point is repeatedly emphasised in quality assurance and quality control literature (Association of Metropolitan Authorities, 1991; Caplen, 1982), and can lead to the conclusion that quality policies are likely to be 'top-down', based on the ideas of management and senior politicians of what the service should be: 'we know best'. This is a real danger and the small amount of evidence about quality in practice bears it out (Gaster, 1991a; Dalley, 1990b). It is because of this that such emphasis has been placed in this paper on the role of the other groups described in the last two sections.

The key to an effective quality policy, it is suggested here, is that it should be formulated (ie defined) and eventually implemented both with involvement and active participation at all levels within the organisation and with practical recognition of external accountability in its widest sense.

Quality in practice: setting standards and monitoring them

If it is accepted that service quality can be defined by looking at the technical content and at how and in what circumstances the service is delivered, and if it is accepted that these definitions require the participation of the range of actors described above, what conditions are needed for a quality policy to be put into practice?

First, it seems clear that quality must be defined in a way that enables it to be assessed and reviewed. It is no good having such broad statements of quality that no-one can tell either how or whether it is put into effect. Where national quality standards exist - for trading standards, for example - then these may provide a starting point for an organisation. Does it wish to implement the national standard and be subject to nationally-based inspection and monitoring, or does it wish to go further? Or is there a case for saying that the national standard is inappropriate for local needs?

For most services, however, no national standard, even of the technical content, will exist for some time to come: here, local councils will need to define their own quality standards and to decide how these will be measured.

None of this is easy, as the rapidly increasing literature on performance measurement demonstrates (Allen, Harley and Makinson, 1987; Carter, 1989 and 1991; Flynn, 1986). Indeed, many of the issues relating to organisational management and culture, to be taken up in the next section, apply to the development of performance measures too.

Meaningful performance measures ought to be of value to those whose work is under scrutiny and to those who use the service. Otherwise, as has been demonstrated time and again, staff avoid risks and/or become cynical (Gaster, 1991a); professionals use methods such as peer review private to themselves (Pollitt, 1990); and the public is completely excluded. One difficulty is that performance indicators are easiest to develop for inputs or throughputs, much more difficult for outputs or outcomes (impact). Similarly, it is easier to measure quantitative aspects of service, not quality; indicators have therefore been most heavily concentrated on the aspects of service summed up as 'economy' and 'efficiency', while far less attention has so far been paid to 'effectiveness' or quality. Indeed, it would not be an exaggeration to suggest that, far from performance indicators measuring a service developed to meet specific objectives, it is all too often the case that the indicators apparently dictate the service, especially where ministries require returns - in health or housing for example - unrelated to local circumstances or need.

Some attempts are now being made in the social services to develop indicators of quality (Social Services Inspectorate, 1990, 1991; Hoyes, 1990). The general emphasis is on the use of an audit approach enabling, for example, particular homes to be assessed on a standard scheme. While this can take local circumstances into account and involve local residents and staff, there are two disadvantages: first, that the audit schemes were drawn up by professionals, not users and local staff; and second, they do not appear to be related to specific council policies on quality - an inherent difficulty, as already implied, in any national scheme for establishing quality and standards and partly explained by the fact that such policies and standards did not exist. Also, they are expensive in terms of the time needed to carry them out.

So a further range of qualitative and quantitative methods of data collection needs to be developed. Consumer surveys are one source of information about levels of satisfaction and attitudes towards services (Gosschalk, 1989), though the level of detail they can reasonably collect is limited and it is difficult to derive precise action plans from them.

Similarly, another frequently suggested method of ascertaining views about the quality of services is to examine complaints received. However, Seneviratne and Cracknell (1988) demonstrated clearly that there are often severe problems - no proper complaints system, ignorance or cynicism of potential complainants, and possibly fear of retribution (rubbish on the front path). Such complaints as are received, presuming they are found to be justified, should provide a basis for remedial action, but it would be dangerous to rely too heavily on them. Another suggestion, the use of 'satisfaction cards', is also liable to erratic use and misinterpretation. Research in Birmingham neighbourhood offices (Gaster, 1991a) found that, whereas one office had taken the lack of returns as a trigger for investigation and had found a host of reasons why the cards were not being filled in, another had interpreted a similar response as a sign that tenants were satisfied with the repairs service. All other evidence showed that this was unlikely to be the case.

What emerges from this are the following points: first, that while the objectives and standards needed for the development of high quality service should ideally be measurable, there are real difficulties in achieving that measurement. To balance this, a range of methods for measuring quality, largely but not exclusively depending on qualitative methods of evaluation, is being developed, although it would be unwise to rely on one method alone. Finally, there is a danger that the performance indicators are used without reference to local policies or to the needs of local staff or users/residents; they will therefore be meaningless and merely a game to be played to keep management happy.

This is a practical point. Relevant information, including quantitative data, can help current and potential consumers to know more about the service, and to decide whether they want it or want to change it. Similarly, returning to the issue of front-line commitment, staff need feedback on what they are doing, not in the competitive, league table form of much current data, but as a trigger for action and learning (Carter, 1989). This in itself should, if the organisational climate is right, encourage those who wish to consolidate and improve the quality of their services.

The organisational climate - or culture - is a key issue: indeed, it is one of the main elements that the processes to establish decentralisation and quality have in common. Before considering this connection, it is worth considering what has happened in councils trying to decentralise.

Organisational culture: lessons from decentralisation

Although it is relatively easy to set up local offices (area offices of one kind or another have existed for a long time now), it has proved far less easy to implement the other aspects of decentralisation listed at the beginning of this paper.

Take the aspect of 'integration'. The aim of integration would be, in the eyes of decentralising councils, to avoid duplication, to end 'passing the buck' and to enable staff and teams to take ownership of consumers' problems. This may be achieved through teamworking, across and within departmental boundaries, and in some councils (St Helens, Islington, Rochdale, for example) new departments have been created specifically to cut across such traditional boundaries as housing and social services. Broad job descriptions may be introduced to encourage more flexible working. Encouragement may be given to those who see themselves as 'professionals' to develop the positive side - the maintenance of high and consistent standards - and to minimise the more negative, 'boundary control' elements.

Ideally, the aim would be to develop a system where individuals can both use and share their skills and develop new ones, to the benefit of themselves, their organisation and, most of all, to the users of the service and to the community. Unfortunately, while in any organisation there will be people who are positively - sometimes desperately - wishing to expand their horizons, it is only too common to find a strongly negative, defensive attitude to change, often vociferously represented through trades unions. While lip-service may be paid to the need to change, actual behaviour may be contradictory, leaving local managers trying to implement the new policies isolated and undermined. A few decentralising authorities, for example Islington District Health Authority (Dalley, 1900a), re-examined their overall management style to reflect the changes, to become more participative and more supportive of local staff. Few local councils appear to have done so. The result has been that local managers have frequently not had the support they needed to change staff attitudes and create a team approach.

Similar processes have affected a second dimension of decentralisation: the devolution of power, both managerially within the organisation and democratically, to local people. The difficulties and disappointments that often arise from well-intentioned attempts to make services more accountable through consultation and participation have been touched upon earlier. Nevertheless, advances have been made within the context of decentralisation, as experience in Islington has shown (Barnard, 1991). The devolution of budgets to neighbourhood offices, where local forums and working parties can develop well-informed recommendations for projects, based on their own and office staff's knowledge of local needs, is an encouraging precedent for the wider development of community decision making (Gaster, 1991b).

However, it is also the case that traditionally minded councillors have perceived such initiatives as a loss of, rather than an adjunct to, their legitimate power. The result has been that, rather than negotiating what their role should and could be in new democratic structures, they resist the changes, perhaps because it was often the more radical councillors who promoted the moves, under the banner of 'empowerment' (Beuret and Stoker, 1986).

Similar processes appear to operate in relation to the devolution of power to staff. Senior officers may feel reluctant to relinquish control, or fearful of being unable to exercise their duty to ensure the implementation of council-wide policies and values. This is a natural and legitimate concern, but seems to stem from two major weaknesses in many local councils used to working in a traditional, hierarchical way: communication tends to be in one direction only - from top to bottom - and levels of trust and mutual confidence very low indeed. The ability to rethink the role of the centre and make the best use of its resources to support, develop and monitor local action are likely in these circumstances to be rather limited.

The result of such failures is that the organisation as a whole is unable to benefit from the new, localised structures. There is a danger that it fails to capitalise on the experience and knowledge of staff in local offices. Meanwhile, these staff, by force of circumstance, develop new relationships with local people and gain a much better knowledge of local needs and the relevance of the services on offer. They are unable to take advantage of this knowledge, except (and this is an important exception) to improve relationships with users. They may thus temporarily increase the credibility of the organisation with the local community, but if decision-making power has not been devolved, and all decisions have to continue to be referred upwards through the organisation, that credibility is unlikely to last.

Quality and decentralisation - related or not?

It would be disheartening if the conclusion to be drawn from the previous sections was that the consumer-oriented trends of bringing services closer to local people on the one hand, and improving service quality on the other, were doomed to failure. Both trends can be seen as the outcome of a range of pressures affecting the public sector as a whole since 1979 and, for even longer, local government in particular. Both trends can be interpreted as defensive on the one hand and altruistic and potentially empowering on the other.

Certainly, while decentralisation appears at first sight to be more of a structural change, it depends for its success, as has been shown above, on a changed organisational culture, and this is not easy to achieve. The opposite may be said about the introduction of effective quality policies: the need for cultural change, focusing on the role of management and levels of communication and trust, appear at first to be paramount. But once issues of responsiveness and accountability are included, as surely they must be, then structural questions may also need to be investigated. Certainly, both trends require changed attitudes both towards the public and towards front-line staff, at all levels within the organisation: at a minimum, to listen, value and be honest with people (Gaster, 1991a).

One very important dimension of quality is to provide an answer to the question 'what is the service intended to do?' (the technical dimension). However, as Kieron Walsh has pointed out (1989), most of what local government does is to produce services, not goods. This requires an interaction between service provider and service user (in the broadest sense); it means that the other two dimensions of quality defined by Donabedian - the interface and the ambience - are both crucial to the technical quality.

If a quality service is one that meets as nearly as possible the needs of consumers and the wider community, it follows that the definition of that quality needs to emerge from a dialogue with that community. Experience of consultation and participation shows that they will only be meaningful if there are reasonable levels of trust between the participants. That trust is based on previous and current experiences. Are promises carried out? Are those with responsibility for action accessible and responsive? Do staff feel confident that the rest of the organisation will support them in carrying out the recommendations or decisions of that dialogue? Conversely, do people in the community know enough about the realities of what services can be offered, the constraints and pressures affecting staff and councillors, to make realistic demands and to be able to assess the results fairly?

The theoretical intentions of decentralisation would appear to supply the right conditions for the development of quality services, especially those that depend most heavily on face-to-face contact. Decentralisation in practice has not fully matched the theory, to the disappointment of its advocates, but less surprising to those who recognise decentralisation as an example of organisational change. It is for this reason that it is not possible to claim that decentralisation will necessarily improve the quality of services. However, the multi-dimensional, consumer and front-line staff oriented definition of quality that is being proposed here would, with the right organisational culture and necessary training, find a favourable context for its development in a decentralised structure. To that extent, it seems possible to affirm that, while decentralisation will not by itself lead to quality, quality needs decentralisation.

A way forward

Even without fully devolved management, and possibly without integrated working, decentralisation in the sense of localisation has much to offer quality developments. Local offices can, with the right attention to the detail of staff training and support (management and technical), and with such factors as user-friendly signposting, queuing and waiting systems and a welcoming office environment, give an important message to staff, consumers and community alike. This is that there is a new culture: public service orientation (Clarke and Stewart, 1987).

Unless this is to be an example of the charm school approach, however, the new culture of openness, honesty and responsiveness implied above needs to reach up through the whole organisation. It is not enough to leave the interaction with the public to the local office while the rest of the organisation remains exactly as it was.

If this can be done, two of the important dimensions of quality - the interface and the environment - on which the effective technical quality of personally delivered services heavily depends could be much enhanced.

Further, where the 'technical' nature of the service in itself consists of a high level of personal interaction (giving advice or personal support or enforcing controls, for example), there may be even stronger arguments for basing it locally, especially if the service also depends on ease of access between provider and receiver. Where two or more such services are being delivered and - as is almost inevitable in local government - the same consumer needs more than one service, there is a strong argument for local integration through collaboration and flexible working by working in teams and, in some circumstances, by developing more generic job descriptions.

In contrast, for much of the technical side of service delivery, and for those services where the level of personal interaction is low, there are arguments for saying that a local presence is not so necessary. If that is the case, then the emphasis in terms of quality would be on accessibility, continuity and a public service orientation by other means: neighbourhood links; attendance at local offices for appointments and surgeries; good telephone systems and manner; and reliable and appropriate information technology accessible from the neighbourhoods. If these are in place, greater efficiency and economy as well as higher technical quality of direct services could be achieved through a centralised system.

Other activities related to service delivery would, in the interests of equity and consistency, be likely to remain central, informed and guided by consultation and participation from the key actors highlighted in this article: the front-line staff, consumers and the community. So the centre would be responsible for developing overall policy frameworks and corporate strategies and objectives; setting the implementation frameworks for such policies as equal opportunities and contracts; basic resource allocation; monitoring and evaluation; provision of all or part of such support services as finance, legal, personnel and new technology; and, not least, providing leadership and commitment to quality itself.

So a local authority considering whether to embark on a decentralised approach to service delivery and aiming to improve the quality of its services, might find that the answers to the following questions provide a useful framework for decision making.

i. Is the service used by many people without access to telephones or transport?

ii. Does the service expect a high number of personal callers?

iii. Does the service consist of high levels of complex, face-to-face contact?

iv. Is it important for the service provider to be able to reach the consumer quickly and easily?

v. Does the service also depend for its success on high levels of day-to-day - and preferably face-to-face - contact with other council provided services?

vi. Does the service depend for its success on high levels of staff knowledge of the local environment and community?

If the answer is 'yes' to most of these questions, then it seems likely that the quality of the service in question is likely to be enhanced if it is delivered from local offices. The desirability of an integrated approach and devolved decision making will vary from service to service. They are unlikely to be irrelevant to any of them.

If the answer is 'no', then other methods of service delivery can - and probably should - be considered.

If this framework is applied not only to distinct services, as traditionally provided by local government, but also to the different stages of services, the possibility arises of deliberately and explicitly decentralising parts of a service without feeling compelled to decentralise the rest. Examples that come to mind are: initial enquiries, where the nature of the problem and the range of possible responses can be fully explored and analysed; and complaints about the service, where locally accessible staff with clear authority to take the matter forward could encourage the constructive use of a well-publicised complaints system. If, however, these or other elements of a total service are localised in this way, the linkages between the different stages - the service design - will have to be meticulously planned and reliably implemented so as not to leave any part of the service isolated and without support. Similar tests can be applied to issues of accountability, whether at an individual or collective level, or to residents in their role as citizens.

i. Is personal accountability through visibility necessary?

ii. Are there alternative ways of ensuring the personal accountability of staff?

iii. Would collective accountability be enhanced by local staff presence, with day-to-day contact with local groups?

Again, if the answer is 'yes', a case emerges for locally-based staff responsible not only for direct service delivery, but also for ensuring that quality is enhanced through the contribution of local people at every stage of the development and implementation of quality policies.

Conclusion

The introduction of both 'quality' and 'decentralisation' (as defined in this article) depend for their success on a new organisational culture, characterised by mutual trust, two-way communication, and positive relationships with consumers and the community. In addition, it is suggested here that decentralisation can bring about improved quality, not just locally, but throughout the organisation.

This in itself requires a new approach to decentralisation: not the dogmatic 'if it can go local, it should go local' attitude of the decentralisation missionaries, but 'which services - or parts of services - would be improved by going local?'.

Using the three-dimensional, consumer and front-line definition of quality proposed here, all the services offered by local government can be tested to see if they would be qualitatively improved by being decentralised. And that is where quality and decentralisation connect.

References

Alexander, A. (1990) 'Lessons for the locals', *Marxism Today*, April, pp 16-17.

Allen, D., Harley, M. and Makinson, G.T. (1987) 'Performance indicators in the NHS', *Social Policy and Administration*, vol 21, no 1, pp 70-84.

Association of Metropolitan Authorities (1991) *Quality services: an introduction to quality assurance for local authorities*, London: AMA.

Audit Commission (1988) *Performance review in local government: a hand-book for auditors and local authorities*, Action Guide, London: HMSO.

Barnard, H. (1991) 'Neighbourhood environmental action', *Local Government Policy Making*, vol X, pp 8-14.

Beuret, K. and Stoker, G. (1986) 'The Labour Party and neighbourhood decentralisation: flirtation or commitment?', *Critical Social Policy*, vol 17, pp 4-22.

Birmingham Community Care Action Project (1989) (1) Information Pack (2) Consultation with carers report *Giving carers a voice*.

Borzeix, A. (1990) 'Mais qu'est-ce que la qualité d'un service publique?', Unpublished paper, CRNS-GIP 'Mutations lndustrielles', Paris.

Caplen, R.H. (1982) *A practical approach to quality control*, 4th edition, London: Business Books Ltd.

Carr-Hill, R., Hennessy, S., Higgins, M. and Potts, L. (1991) *Patient information survey*, Quality Management Initiatives, Centre for Health Economics, University of York.

Carter, N. (1989) 'Performance indicators: 'backseat driving' or 'hands-off' control?', *Policy and Politics*, vol 17, no 2, pp 131-38.

Carter, N. (1991) 'Learning to measure performance: the use of indicators in organisations', *Public Administration*, vol 69, Spring, pp 85-101.

Cassam, E. (1990) 'Everything to gain', *Social Work Today*, 19 July, pp 26-27.

Clarke, M. and Stewart, J. (1987) 'The public service orientation and the citizen', *Local Government Policy Making*, vol 14, no 1, pp 34-40.

Confederation of British Industries (1988) *Zero defects: a new British Standard?*, Booster Books Ltd.

Croft, S. and Beresford, P. (1990) *From paternalism to participation: involving people in social services*, Open Services Project and Joseph Rowntree Foundation.

Czepiel, J.A., Solomon, M.R. and Surprenant, C.F. (1985) *The service encounter: managing employee-customer interaction in service businesses*, Lexington Books.

Dalley, G. (1990a) *Decentralising community health care in Islington*, Kings Fund Centre for Health Service Development, Working Paper for Managers No 6.

Dalley, G. (1990b) *Quality management in action: the survey report*, Centre for Health Economics, University of York (unpublished).

Day, P. and Klein, R. (1987) *Accountabilities: five public services*, Tavistock Publications.

Day, P. and Klein, R. (1990) *Inspecting the inspectors*, Joseph Rowntree Memorial Trust.

Day, T. (1990) *Getting closer to the consumer? Locality planning in Exeter Health District*, Working Paper no 84, Bristol: SAUS Publications, School for Advanced Urban Studies, University of Bristol.

Deakin, N. (1987) *The politics of welfare*, Methuen.

Deakin, N. (1990) 'Some limits to active citizenship', in *New perspectives on citizenship*, Social Policy Series no 3, New Waverley Papers, University of Edinburgh.

Donabedian, A. (1980) *Explorations in quality assessment and monitoring, vol 1: 'The definition of quality and approaches to its assessment'*, Ann Arbor, Michigan: Health Administration Press.

Donabedian, A. (1982) *Explorations in quality assessment and monitoring, vol 2: 'The criteria and standards of quality'*, Ann Arbor, Michigan: Health Administration Press.

Donabedian, A. (1985) *Explorations in quality assessment and monitoring, vol 3: 'The methods and findings of quality assessment and monitoring'*, Ann Arbor, Michigan: Health Administration Press.

Ellis, R. (ed) (1988) *Professional competence and quality assurance in the caring professions*, Chapman and Hall.

Flynn, N. (1986) 'Performance measurement in public sector services', *Policy and Politics*, vol 14, no 3, pp 389-404.

Gaster, L. (1990) 'Defining and measuring quality', *Local Government Policy Making*, vol 17, no 2, pp 15-23.

Gaster, L. (1991a) *Quality at the front line*, Bristol: SAUS Publications, School for Advanced Urban Studies, University of Bristol.

Gaster, L. (ed) (1991b) *Local budgeting in practice*, Bristol: SAUS Publications, School for Advanced Urban Studies, University of Bristol.

Gosschalk, B. (1989) 'In the eyes of the users', *Municipal Review and AMA News*, August-September, pp 120-21.

Ham, C. and Hill, M. (1984) *The policy process in the modern capitalist state*, Brighton: Wheatsheaf Books.

Hambleton, R. (1989) *Consumerism, decentralisation and local democracy*, Working Paper no 78, Bristol: SAUS Publications, School for Advanced Urban Studies, University of Bristol.

Hambleton, R. and Hoggett, P. (1990) *Beyond excellence: quality local government in the 1990s*, Working Paper no 85, Bristol: SAUS Publications, School for Advanced Urban Studies, University of Bristol.

Henkel, M. (1991) 'The new evaluative state', *Public Administration*, vol 69, Spring, pp 121-36.

Hodge, M. (1987) 'Central/local conflicts: the view from Islington', in P. Hoggett and R. Hambleton (eds) *Decentralisation and democracy*, Occasional Paper no 28, Bristol: SAUS Publications, School for Advanced Urban Studies, University of Bristol.

Hoggett, P. and Hambleton, R. (eds) (1987) *Decentralisation and democracy*, Occasional Paper no 28, Bristol: SAUS Publications, School for Advanced Urban Studies, University of Bristol.

Hoyes, L. (1990) *Promoting an ordinary life: a checklist for assessing residential care for people with learning difficulties*, Bristol: SAUS Publications, School for Advanced Urban Studies, University of Bristol.

James, K. (1989) 'Encounter analysis: front-line conversations and their role in improving customer service', *Local Government Studies*, May/June, vol 15, no 3, pp 11-24.

Labour Party Policy Directorate (1991) *The quality commission: a consultation paper*.

Lipsky, M. (1980) *Street-level bureaucracy: dilemmas of the individual in public service*, New York: Russell Sage Foundation.

Maister, D.H. (1985) 'The psychology of waiting lines', in J.A. Czepiel *et al* (eds) *The service encounter: managing employee-customer interaction in service businesses*, Lexington Books.

Moores, B. (ed) (1986) *Are they being served? Quality consciousness in service industries*, Oxford: Philip Allan.

Mortiboys, R. (1986) 'Quality in the boardroom', in B. Moores, *Are they being served? Quality consciousness in service industries*, Oxford: Philip Allan.

Nyquist, J.D., Bitner, M.J. and Booms, B.H. (1985) 'Identifying communication difficulties in the service encounter a critical incident approach', in J.A. Czepiel *et al* (eds) *The service encounter: managing employee-customer interaction in service businesses*, Lexington Books.

Pollitt, C. (1988) 'Bringing consumers into performance measurement: concepts, consequences and constraints', *Policy and Politics*, vol 16, no 2, pp 77-88.

Pollitt, C. (1990) 'Doing business in the temple? Managers and quality assurance in the public services', *Public Administration*, vol 68, no 4, pp 435-52.

Seneviratne, M. and Cracknell, S. (1988) 'Consumer complaints in the public sector', *Public Administration*, Summer, vol 66, no 2, pp 181-93.

Shostack, G.L. (1985) 'Planning the service encounter', in J.A. Czepiel *et al* (eds) *The service encounter: managing employee-customer interaction in service businesses*, Lexington Books.

Social Services Inspectorate (1990) *Homes are for living in*, Department of Health, London: HMSO.

Social Services Inspectorate (1991) *Inspecting for quality: guidance on practice for inspection units in social services departments and other agencies*, Department of Health, London: HMSO.

Stewart, J. and Walsh, K. (1990) *The search for quality*, Luton: Local Government Training Board.

Stoker, G. and Lowndes, V. (1991) *Tower Hamlets and decentralisation: the experience of Globe Town Neighbourhood*, Luton: Local Government Training Board.

Stoker, G. (1987) 'Decentralisation and the restructuring of local government in Britain', *Local Government Policy Making*, September, vol 14, no 2, pp 3-11.

Stoker, G., Wedgwood Oppenheim, F. and Davies, M. (1988) *The challenge of change in local government: a survey of organisational and management innovation in the 1980s*, Birmingham: Institute of Local Government Studies, University of Birmingham.

Tansik, D.A. (1985) 'Non-verbal communication and high-contact employees', in J.A. Czepiel *et al* (eds) *The service encounter: managing employee-customer interaction in service businesses*, Lexington Books.

Walsh, K. (1989) *Contracts and quality*, unpublished paper, Birmingham: Institute of Local Government Studies, University of Birmingham.

Wener, R.E. (1985) 'The environmental psychology of service encounters', in J.A. Czepiel *et al* (eds) *The service encounter: managing employee-customer interaction in service businesses*, Lexington Books.

Wennlund, I.L. (1990) *Management and quality*, unpublished paper from the Quality Programme of the Swedish National Institute for Civil Service Training and Development (SIPU).

CHAPTER 3

THE CHANGING ROLE OF THE NON-PROFIT SECTOR IN BRITAIN: MOVING TOWARD THE MARKET

MARILYN TAYLOR

Introduction

Governments across the globe are looking for new ways of meeting human need. Demographic trends, technological advance, economic restructuring, environmental stress, and organisational change are all making new demands on finite resources. Many governments wish to put limits on their responsibility for welfare and encourage a more pluralistic system with a greater input from the non-statutory (that is, non-governmental) sectors, whether in the desire to release more resources or the belief that such a system is both more efficient and more responsive to individual need.

In principle, this policy trend presents considerable advantages to the voluntary or non-profit sectors, with new opportunities for service provision and the prospect of new resources. But experience suggests that there are risks as well as opportunities. To assess the likely implications of such a change of direction, this chapter looks at the British experience (exclusive of Northern Ireland), where welfare policies have been moving, over the past ten years, from a system based on government provision and financing of welfare toward one modelled on market principles. The first section examines the changing relationship between government and the voluntary sector through the 1980s and the different ideologies of welfare that have applied to Britain. The second section assesses the impact of current policies on the voluntary sector and its activities, first in relation to service delivery, then in relation to service finance. The chapter concludes that new welfare policies pay too little attention to the role that government should continue to play in a more plural system, particularly at the local level. It argues for a partnership between government and the voluntary sector that recognises the strengths of the latter not only in service provision but also in the democratic control of welfare - an element of the voluntary sector role that is neglected by policy makers and voluntary sector theoreticians alike.

This chapter first appeared in B. Gidron, R.M. Kramer and L.M. Salamon (eds) *Government and the third sector: emerging relationships in welfare states*, 1992, San Francisco: Jossey-Bass Inc.

Changing welfare strategies

Developments to 1979

The voluntary sector has long had a role in British welfare. Charity law was introduced in 1601 to encourage private citizens to share the burdens of welfare in a period of economic upheaval (Ware, 1989, p 16). The 19th century saw a renewed emphasis on philanthropy, with the birth of some of today's best-known charities. Other elements of the voluntary sector tradition also grew in importance during the Victorian era: mutual aid, especially among working-class communities; and public education or campaigning, for example, on poverty, prisons, and public health.

During the first half of this century, government came to recognise the inequities and patchiness of a system of provision that depended so much on voluntary philanthropy. During the 1940s legislation on income support, health, and education was the climax to the development of a comprehensive welfare state, with the public sector taking primary responsibility for the delivery, financing, and regulation of welfare. Under this system, the voluntary sector was for many years seen as marginal, although it is important to recognise that there was never a complete state monopoly. Aspects of welfare remained with voluntary organisations, including residential care, provision for special needs, the lifeboat service, and independent counselling and advice.

By the 1970s there was growing dissatisfaction with state welfare. To some extent the system bred the seeds of its own destruction. The improved standards of living to which it contributed, coupled with rising incomes, meant that initial satisfaction gradually gave way to rising expectations and frustration with the lack of choice offered. But there was more to the criticism than that. Provision of services was felt to be standardised and insensitive. Critics argued that public welfare was overloaded with bureaucracy and had been taken over by the professionals and the public service unions. "Public services continued often to treat people as a potentially recalcitrant mass, while the private supplier of goods and services wooed them as individuals of taste, discrimination and independence" (Corrigan et al, 1988, p 3).

Whether these shortcomings were an inevitable consequence of public sector provision of services is open to debate. Efforts were made during this period to introduce more participation into the decision-making process, particularly in housing, planning, and community development (Loney, 1983). By the end of the 1970s alternative models of welfare involving a reduced role for the state were being canvassed. Prominent among these was the concept of 'welfare pluralism' (Wolfenden Committee, 1978; Gladstone, 1979) which allowed voluntary organisations a much greater role. Gladstone argued for a 'preference-guided society' where government, in the interests of equity and social justice, would retain a major responsibility for financing welfare but the voluntary sector would take over much of the delivery. This bears considerable similarities to the pragmatic partnership model of Kramer (1981) or the third-party government model of welfare suggested by Salamon (1981, 1987a). Welfare pluralists also introduced the concept of political pluralism, where voluntary organisations are viewed as a medium not only for delivering services but also for giving different interests a voice in the political process (Hatch and Mocroft, 1983).

Critics from the right of the political spectrum saw no major role for government in welfare. Public sector provision was accused of "stifling innovation, denying choice, and voraciously and insatiably consuming people's money" (Anderson, Lair, and Marsland, 1981, p 14). Known as the New Right, this school of thought advocated using the market as the principal mechanism for welfare, claiming that its neutrality made it the only mechanism that could both respect individual liberty and, through competition, guarantee the efficient use of resources. Thinkers on the political right also preached the values of self-reliance and individual enterprise. They believed that state welfare had encouraged a "culture of dependency" (Lawson, 1987). Too much emphasis on entitlements and rights to benefits, in their eyes, undermined people's ability and will to help themselves, weakened the traditional role of the family, and 'privatised' compassion, leaving nothing to the individual but the pursuit of self-interest. Where the market failed to meet need, by implication, philanthropy and the family should provide a safety net. These different approaches are summarised in Table 1.

Table 1: Alternative approaches to welfare

Approach	Function		
	Provision	Finance	Regulation
Welfare state	Government	Government	Government
Welfare pluralism	Voluntary sector	Government	Government and voluntary sector 'mediating structures'
New Right	For-profit sector (with a voluntary sector safety net)	Private sources	The market (through individual purchase)

By 1979 public sector services were facing growing pressure from their consumers. During the 1970s a new wave of voluntary activity had arisen in direct response to the weakness of state welfare. Criticism of the growing power of professionals in public services led to the formation of self-help groups. Concern about red tape, bureaucracy, and inefficiency was reflected in the growth of advice, information, and advocacy services. Disabled people developed their own advocacy services to counteract the loss of dignity involved in state services; black and ethnic minority groups joined forces to bring into their communities the jobs, training, and services that neither the state nor the private sector was delivering. These new organisations took issue not only with the insensitivity of state bureaucracies, but also with the more traditional voluntary sector service providers, who were seen as paternalistic and disabling. These too were under pressure to develop more community-based appproaches to their work.

Significant new advocacy bodies came into existence during this time, for example Shelter (an organisation concerned with homelessness) and the Child Poverty Action Group started in the mid 1960s. Old and new, voluntary organisations drew on their experience as providers and as consumers to provide feedback to policy makers and draw public attention to new or neglected needs. For example, MIND (a national mental health agency) played a major part in drawing up the legislation enshrined in the Mental Health Act of 1983, and a coalition of voluntary organisations worked on drafting the Disabled Persons Act of 1986.

The Thatcher era

Economic recession, rising unemployment, and a series of crippling public sector strikes combined in 1979 with more general criticisms of state welfare to pave the way for the election of a Conservative government committed to rolling back the frontiers of the welfare state. During its first three terms in office, this government introduced a range of policies reflecting the influence of the New Right approach: priority for economic regeneration, in the belief that social regeneration will inevitably follow on from economic buoyancy and that the benefits accruing to the wealthy will 'trickle down' to the disadvantaged; a more open market in social welfare with the withdrawal of the public sector from service delivery; and the generation of new resources for welfare with a corresponding limitation of the state's financial responsibility.

This transition took place in two phases. The first, which spanned the first two terms of the Thatcher administration (1979-1987), featured tax cuts and the relaxation of controls over industry as well as the introduction of the more politically attractive reforms in welfare (such as the sale of public housing). This period also saw the opening moves in the dismantling of local government powers, with increasing financial controls over local government spending, the abolition of a tier of local government in the metropolitan areas, and the introduction of non-elected public bodies at the local level for specific programmes, particularly in the field of economic development (for example urban development corporations).

During this phase also, however, many local bodies, which remained in Labour Party control, sought to fashion their own response to the dissatisfactions of the 1970s by introducing decentralisation and participation policies designed to bring services closer to the consumer and the community. They drew on the experience of other countries, notably in Scandinavia, in introducing a 'public service orientation' (Clarke and Stewart, 1986). They also increased considerably their levels of funding to voluntary organisations. Local authority financial support for voluntary bodies grew by 19% in real terms between 1983/84 (when figures were first collected) and 1987/88 (Charities Aid Foundation, 1989, p 40), although it experienced a dip toward the end of this period as financial restraint began to bite. The role of voluntary organisations in extending economic development and training to disadvantaged communities and people with special needs was recognised, and joint ventures were developed. Environmental groups worked with local authorities and the private sector to reclaim wasteland or develop cooperative housing. In community care, recognition of the unique strengths of the voluntary sector led to packages in, for example, special needs housing.

The pace of this change was slow and very patchy, dictated as much by the survival instincts of a beleaguered local government as by belief in the merits of voluntary activity. And efforts at sharing power left much to be desired (Taylor, 1986). Nonetheless, the tension between the old and new orders was productive for the voluntary sector and began to foster many of the principles promoted by the welfare pluralists, including greater pluralism in provision and greater empowerment of the consumer. Voluntary organisations were not, however, looking to substitute for public sector provision but rather to supplement it. A continued major government role in finance and delivery was essential if good practice was to be guaranteed, especially to minority groups. A symbiotic relationship began to develop between the two sectors, which sought to extend the opportunities for choice within the welfare state, with government still providing the major finance but with a mixed delivery system and a voluntary sector role in regulation (broadly defined). Voluntary organisations were needed to supplement and complement public sector provision, by reaching isolated or special needs that large-scale services could not meet and by catering to the diversity of need where state services were too uniform (service pluralism), and to promote good practice in the public sector (and elsewhere) through advocacy and campaigning and through developing and demonstrating innovative alternative models for provision (democratic pluralism).

Before these local reforms could really take hold, however, the Thatcher government moved during its third term to accelerate the legislative programme and introduce more far-reaching changes in relation both to local government and to the central welfare state services of health, community care, and education. These changes included legislation that allows schools, housing, and hospitals to be taken out of local government control, as well as the introduction of compulsory competitive tendering in some public services and the encouragement of contracting out in many others.

Measures were also introduced to further restrict the autonomy and role of local government, changing its system of raising finance to one based on the community charge or poll tax, which government sees as being more accountable to ratepayers; and effectively reducing local authority influence on a range of new bodies and joint ventures through legislation that, with some exceptions, places similar restrictions on companies with a local authority interest as those placed on local authorities themselves. New legislation on community care provided the exception to the general trend, by giving primary responsibility for the planning and management of care to local authorities while encouraging them to contract out the delivery of services. However, the announcement of delays in the implementation of significant parts of this legislation until after the next election raises considerable doubts as to both the resources that will be made available to support the new arrangements and the continued political commitment to the local authority's lead role. A major review of the structure and finance of local government is currently underway (Department of the Environment, 1991). Meanwhile, the implementation of new legislation on the health service is going ahead, and could affect the balance of power between local and health authorities in this field.

The third Thatcher term also saw new efforts to contain public spending on welfare and to generate private and charitable funding. At the individual level, social security legislation reduced income support for young people on the assumption that they could still turn to their families. In 1988 entitlements to special needs grants were changed in most instances to discretionary loans through the introduction of the Social Fund. Under this system, claimants are expected to exhaust all other sources of help before coming to the state, and applicants are frequently referred to voluntary organisations in the first instance. As a result, voluntary bodies report greatly increased demand.

Beyond this, individuals are being urged to recognise their responsibilities not only toward themselves and their families but also toward others. Government is promoting the idea of 'active citizenship' where those who have gained from increased affluence are expected to recognise parallel social responsibilities.

> We are moving from the 'I care, therefore the state must provide' attitude of the 1960s to the much more practical and effective 'I produce and consume, therefore I have a moral duty to care and provide' imperative. (Patten, 1988, p 23)

Parallel to this is the promotion of corporate responsibility, harking back to the benevolent paternalism of the Victorian city fathers. Where government funding is provided, there is more of an emphasis on stewardship and value for money, with an efficiency scrutiny of government funding to the voluntary sector (Home Office, 1990) and with a growing emphasis on performance indicators and financial monitoring.

These policies may be influenced by the New Right ideology described earlier but they are not in complete harmony with it. Public spending on welfare has proved difficult to reduce, for both practical and political reasons. Opinion polls still show considerable public support for public spending (Bosanquet, 1988) and government has acknowledged a continued financial responsibility for health and education, while seeking to introduce outside funds where possible. Government agencies are being encouraged into the fund-raising business; one of the most successful appeals in the early 1990s was the Wishing Well Appeal organised by a National Health Service children's hospital in central London. Private health insurance has been given a boost through tax advantages and private insurance companies are taking an interest in the field of community care. Market principles have also been introduced wherever possible through contracting out and the introduction of internal markets.

The primary role for the voluntary sector in this scenario is that of an instrument of government (Salamon, 1989) competing with the private sector in the contractual market place. As the channel for 'active citizenship', it also has a role as a safety net for needs that cannot be met through the use of market principles. Government finance is increasingly likely to be tied to specific government policy objectives rather than providing general support (Home Office, 1990, p 9).

The impact on the voluntary sector

In assessing the impact of these changes on the voluntary sector and its activities, the second part of this chapter will address two questions. Will the new policies allow voluntary organisations to play their part in a more pluralist and diverse delivery system? Will they release new, non-governmental resources into the welfare field?

Pluralism in delivery

British welfare is moving from a position where the voluntary sector complements state delivery toward one where the voluntary and for-profit sectors are expected to substitute for state delivery. The introduction of compulsory competitive tendering in a range of service fields, the promotion of purchase-of-service contracting in others, and the introduction of 'opting out' legislation that allows agencies to become private all offer new opportunities to voluntary organisations and will bring more services into the sector. Voluntary organisations have new partners to work with, and the introduction of wide-ranging new legislation could encourage a valuable overhaul of service provision, which would recognise the different contributions that each sector can make. The emphasis on the consumer in the market could provide opportunities to consumer and community-based organisations both to provide advice and information to service users faced with a more fragmented system and to develop their own forms of provision. Many voluntary organisations also feel that contracts imply a more equal partnership than the paternalistic relationships that were so often a feature of grant aid.

Nonetheless, there are anxieties that a more open market in service delivery may discourage the innovation, diversity, flexibility, and responsiveness to consumer need that voluntary organisations are supposed to bring, and indeed that the progress made in this direction during the first two terms of the Thatcher government may be reversed. There are fears that replacing grant aid with purchase of specific services as the main form of government support may compromise organisational independence or even distort the aims of an organisation, that services will become increasingly bureaucratised, and that voluntary organisations will lose their distinctiveness in relation to the statutory services they were meant to replace. Many in the voluntary sector are concerned that the market-place will favour the larger service-providing organisations at the expense of smaller, community-based organisations. Finally, there are questions about the survival of consumer and citizen empowerment functions in a system that sees voluntary organisations as primary service providers. It is too early to say whether these fears will be realised, but evidence from other countries suggests that while anxieties over independence may be exaggerated, those who are concerned about the diversity of the sector and its empowerment functions may well have grounds for their concern.

Will a move toward purchase-of-service contracts mean that government funders will increasingly dictate the content of a voluntary agency's work? US researchers suggest that multiple funding, political influence, and government's own failure to put adequate resources into monitoring all mean that contractor organisations still have considerable room for manoeuvre. The work of Kramer and Grossman (1987) and de Hoog

(1985) suggests that voluntary organisations with an expertise that government wants are able to exert considerable influence on the shape of the final contract and that once a contract is made it is likely to be renewed.

However, commentators in Britain feel that a 'contract culture' will inevitably favour certain kinds of activities. Contracts tend to reflect the status quo and are unlikely to allow for innovation, risk taking, or uncertainty.

> The whole notion of contracted services reflects a culture that has little time for values and principles ... a culture of management in which goals are not worth setting unless they are achievable. (Dowson, 1989, p 10)

The fear is that agencies will find themselves compromised not through direct pressure from a funder, but through a gradual process of diversion into the areas that are amenable to contract funding - those that are quantifiable and easily specifiable and those that carry out government objectives. A successful bid for a contract covering part of the agency's work could absorb its energies to the extent that other work suffers. Or the agency may seek to follow the money into new areas, with the result that existing work is squeezed out. Those who voice these fears point to voluntary organisations' use of Community Programme funding (a government programme to promote job creation); they believe the opportunity to get money for providing jobs of community benefit pulled a number of agencies away from their initial aims into becoming employment and training agencies (Addy and Scott, 1988).

If government contracts do not dictate the content of voluntary agency work, will they dictate its style? There is a danger that voluntary organisations that take on mainstream services will become more and more like the statutory service providers they were meant to replace. Maria Brenton, in her study of non-profits in the United States and the Netherlands, suggests:

> The process of development of the voluntary sector to the role of monopoly or major provider with the aid of state funds seems inevitably to follow a path similar to that taken by our statutory services - the path toward professionalisation and bureaucracy. (1985, p 206)

Contracts are likely to be framed in the tried and tested operating culture of the contracting authority rather than that of the contractor, and may undervalue the different ways of working used by voluntary organisations. De Hoog's suggestion (1985) that familiar professional systems may serve as a substitute for assessing the actual outcomes of suppliers' services would reinforce this point. Kramer and Grossman (1987, pp 47-48) see the skills that are needed in order to bid for contracts as being quite "different from the traditional competencies associated with the administration of voluntary agencies dependent on community contributions". They note a tendency for successful, small agencies to become larger and more bureaucratic through engaging in the contracting process and comment that "while government agencies prefer contracting because it avoids inflexible civil service requirements, it is the voluntary agencies that inherit the rigidity of line budgeting" (p 45). It is even possible to suggest that local authorities will put out to contract the services that can be easily specified (mainstream provision) and keep the more innovative, less easy to specify work in house. This would be a complete reversal of former patterns.

The introduction of competition may, however, pull voluntary organisations into the culture of the for-profit sector rather than that of government and lead to a shift toward income-generating, as opposed to mission-based, objectives (Perlmutter and Adams, 1990). One commentator suggests:

> In a market economy non-profit organisations share the same dynamic for expansion as profit-making organisations. Indeed the dynamic may be the stronger because of limits to the ways in which non-profit-making organisations can financially reward those who direct and manage them. Expansion provides its justification for regrading senior staff and increasing their salaries. (Maxwell, 1989, p 9)

British voluntary organisations may yet find themselves in a situation similar to that faced in the United States, where for-profit organisations have challenged the tax breaks received by not-for-profits in their field.

Some of the more pessimistic commentators are suggesting that voluntary organisations will become a stepping stone on the path to true privatisation; once the for-profit sector has entered the market, they will find themselves taking a back seat. But there are other competitors too. Recent years have seen the appearance of a number of 'hybrids' in the margins between the voluntary, statutory, and for-profit sectors. Opting out policies are creating new voluntary or non-profit organisations; for example the National Health Service (NHS) trusts may well be looking to expand their field of enterprise. There are a growing number of management or employee buyouts, where local authority workers set up an independent organisation which then contracts with the authority to provide previously in-house services. In the years to come, such trends may force a complete rethink of current distinctions between the public, private, and voluntary sectors (Rein, 1989).

Critics of the market point to its tendency to concentrate production and distribution in the hands of corporate giants, who are then able to exercise considerable control over the market and over patterns of consumer choice (for example Corrigan *et al*, 1988, pp 8-9). In theory, the voluntary sector should be in a strong position to counteract this. By its nature it spawns many local, small-scale, close-to-the-consumer initiatives that offer an alternative to large institutional welfare and promote democratic pluralism by involving the consumer or community. But there is no reason to believe that, left to itself, the services market will behave any differently from the private-goods market. British researchers point out that:

> ... from the point of view of the local authority, a single large contract has the advantages that there is only one contractor to deal with and that there should be economics of scale. (Kunz, Jones, and Spencer, 1989, p 11)

Kramer and Grossman (1987, p 44) found that in the United States "larger agencies with 'track records' tended to receive contracts ... more frequently". They suggest further that the larger organisations are most likely to be able to negotiate flexibility into their contracts and thus maintain their independence, and that they are also the most able to bear the uncertainty and costs involved in preparing and negotiating contracts.

If contract funding becomes the preferred form of government support to the voluntary sector, the diversity of the sector may be threatened. Many of the smaller, community-based voluntary organisations are not in the market for large-scale service contracts and rely on more general 'arm's length' funding in support of their general objectives (National Council for Voluntary Organisations, 1984). Especially in a period of financial restraint, this kind of funding is likely to be at risk. They also depend on a well-developed network of intermediary and development agencies, which provide the information, training, and support that allows the small organisations to survive on very limited funding. This voluntary sector infrastructure is no longer likely to be at a premium in a market oriented to front-line services.

The advocates of the market see individual consumers as the regulators of provision, selecting the commodity that meets their needs most effectively. But there is no guarantee that all consumers will be able to exercise this power. Nor is it a foregone conclusion that voluntary organisations will improve on public accountability through the democratic system. "The history of voluntarism is not one simply of benevolence and altruism ... but also of self-interest, self-protectionism and class interest" (Davies, 1986, p 24). The introduction of a market style of operation may even reverse the efforts that have been made in this sector toward involving more members of the consumer community in running local projects and services:

> To the market, democratic structures of accountability and management will appear an unnecessary cost ... the model for a 'market-fit' organisation will be a non-profit making trust or company with a self-perpetuating leadership and a

management structure organised around profit centres. These will be ill-equipped to combine the provision of services with a community development role. (Maxwell, 1989, pp 8-9)

Consumers will need advice and advocacy if they are to make informed choices, especially when they are, as so often in the case of social welfare, under considerable stress. This advice will become even more critical in a fragmented market. However, the emphasis in new policies has been on voluntary organisations' role as service providers. Advocacy is supported in principle but not in the detail of new legislative requirements and, although a new funding power for advice has been put into recent local government legislation, there are no parallel resources. Indeed the pressures of poll tax are reducing the amount of money available for discretionary services, which puts existing advice services at risk and makes it difficult for new services and groups to get established.

Meanwhile, a number of major service providers in the voluntary sector are concerned that their advocacy work could suffer as they move into mainstream provision (Billis and Harris, 1986; Etherington, 1987). The larger organisations may be able to exert considerable influence as major providers and could use this influence to ensure better services and policies across the board as well as in their own service agreements. But there are questions as to how far independent advice and advocacy for service users can be provided by organisations with a central position as service providers.

The market deals with consumers as individuals. But many voluntary organisations are concerned with the impact of individual choices on the public good (they have a long tradition in combating the environmental consequences of production and promoting public health) and thus consider the individual not only as a consumer but as a citizen. Through collective action and community development, they have helped people to realise their common experience and common strengths as consumers and to tackle the wider interests of the community at large. At best, they have regard to patterns and styles of overall provision as well as individual choices, and their perspective is about changing provision by transforming its nature, not just by finding another: what Hirschman (1970) describes as the 'voice' as well as the 'exit' option. These kinds of empowerment are likely to have low priority in a welfare system designed around individual choice. While there is nothing in market theory that prevents groups of consumers from acting together in their own or the public interest, right-of-centre thinking is suspicious of allocating government or charitable money for such purposes, and it is on such income that community development and the empowerment of the disadvantaged consumer has often relied.

Pluralism in finance

The argument so far is that although government finance has been maintained in many services, as the welfare pluralists decreed, the change in its nature, with priority for purchase of service, means that it may not yield genuine pluralism in welfare. But voluntary organisations have access to alternative resources, philanthropy, and volunteering; indeed, many would see these as essential features of the sector. It could be argued that greater use of these alternative resources will overcome some of the difficulties. This brings us to the second question raised at the beginning of this section: will the new policies release new non-governmental resources into the welfare field?

Government's promotion of 'active citizenship' has led to tax concessions, firstly on payroll giving and secondly on single donations by individuals that are above £600 (Gift Aid). It has also been a factor in a new initiative to promote volunteering, launched by the Prince of Wales, and a Speaker's Commission on Citizenship, which has proposed several initiatives concerned with the promotion and recognition of volunteering. Corporate giving, too, has been encouraged and is gaining pace. Some financial institutions have introduced credit cards that generate income for charity; one of them claims to have raised £1,000,000 in 1989. The media have put their considerable resources behind major fund-raising appeals such as BandAid, Children in Need, Comic Relief, and the Telethon, and the latter three raised some £80,000,000 from corporate and individual donors in 1988. The relaxation of previous controls on charity advertising on television and radio opens up still more potential avenues.

However, these new developments are taking place against a background of a standstill in government funding. During the first two terms of the Thatcher government, total government funding for the voluntary sector rose by about 221% (in real terms 92.4%) to an estimated £4,147 million. But central government funding (direct or through central government agencies) has been standing still in real terms since 1986, while local government funding actually fell in real terms during 1985-87, although it has since recovered to its 1985 level (Charities Aid Foundation, 1988, pp 32-33).

The restriction of local government finance intensified with the introduction of poll tax, or capitation tax, and the efforts in some jurisdictions to place caps on this tax; there are growing reports of large cuts to voluntary sector budgets imposed by authorities that have in the past had a good track record in funding voluntary organisations. Initial evidence suggests that advocacy and infrastructural services are particularly hard hit. Meanwhile, major central government funding programmes in the Department of Health and the Department of Education and Science have shifted their emphasis away from long-term core funding toward short-term project funding, and although the Efficiency Scrutiny supported investing central government funding in core and infrastructural work, this was not reflected in the minister's response, which emphasised short-term funding.

Meanwhile, the shift of funding criteria from social to economic programmes, as has happened in inner-cities initiatives, and the transformation of the Community Programme into employment training geared more specifically to the needs of industry, have made it far harder for social programmes to find government funds. In the financial year ending March 1988, the Training Agency (which ran these programmes) provided some £700 million to the voluntary sector, but in 1988/89, although the change took place halfway through the financial year, the level of support was already down by 26% and several organisations, whose work was dependent on this funding source, reported serious difficulties. Cuts in the programme during 1989/90, as government sought to transfer responsibility to the private sector, caused further retrenchment and closures.

Government wishes to see other sources taking more responsibility for such programmes and welfare in general, but there are question marks over their ability to do so, their willingness to do so, and the pattern of welfare that would result. Salamon (1987a, p 39) has referred to the 'insufficiency', 'particularism' and 'paternalism' of US philanthropy. What has the British experience been so far?

Total private charitable support for the British voluntary sector was estimated to be £3,446 million as of 1987/88, mostly from individuals (Charities Aid Foundation, 1989). The sources of this support are noted in Table 2.

What is the capacity for increased giving? Donations from the private and corporate purse are on the increase. Both have more than doubled since 1979 and corporate giving is estimated to have grown by nearly 20% during 1988. However, corporate giving has not increased in line with profits and there are signs that it may be reaching a plateau, especially among the larger donors (Directory of Social Change, 1989). Recession in the economy and industrial restructuring as a consequence of the introduction of the single European market could affect these levels. Moreover, while business has shown that it is willing to engage more generously with community and voluntary organisations, there is little evidence that it is prepared to take over where it feels that government should take financial responsibility. Plans to set up 20 technical colleges in association with industry have failed to raise sufficient private sector finance, and leaders in business have criticised government for withdrawing subsidy for the arts as business sponsors are attracted. Moreover, government has an important role in promoting private investment and drawing it into new fields. Leat, Smolka and Unell (1986) found that financial support from government increases the capacity of voluntary organisations both to raise funds from elsewhere and to recruit volunteers.

Table 2: Private charitable support for UK voluntary organisations 1987/88

Source	Amount (£ million)
Households	2,260 a
Grant-making trusts	572 b
Legacies	325
Company giving (1988)	285 b
Payroll giving	4
Total	3,446

Sources: a. Based on an average between estimates by Charities Aid Foundation (1989) and Department of Employment, *Family Expenditure Survey* (1987)
b. Charities Aid Foundation, *Directory of Grant-making Trusts* (1989, p xi)

Charitable trusts are estimated to have given £572 million to the voluntary sector in 1987/88. They, too, see their role as funding innovation and experiment and do not wish to take responsibility for mainstream service provision (Burkeman, 1988). Charity Commission guidance in relation to benefit changes reinforces this stand.

> Trustees are in breach of trust if by making a grant they bring about a reduction in statutory benefit to which a person otherwise has a right. ... Funds for the relief of need, hardship or distress cannot properly be used to pay for relief or assistance which might otherwise be given by the state. (Charity Commission, 1988, p 1)

What about individual giving? Central government's hope that individuals would give more does not seem to be bearing fruit. The introduction of payroll giving has had disappointing results so far, while recent evidence indicates that slightly fewer people than in previous years are giving to charity and that the typical (median) amount given is also going down (Halfpenny, 1990, p 32). Economic recession and rising unemployment suggest that a reversal of this trend is unlikely in the immediate future.

Meanwhile, some of the major agencies concerned with volunteering are reporting a drop in numbers of new volunteers. Demographic changes may well make recruitment even more difficult at a time when the increasing numbers of frail elderly will increase demand. Rather than a surplus, which could be drawn into volunteering, there is likely to be a shortage of young people going into the labour market. Married women are therefore being encouraged back into employment, a trend that further reduces the pool from which volunteers can be recruited and puts pressure on informal care. There seems little sign as yet that early and new retirees are taking up volunteering (Rankin, 1989). However, there is a growing interest in company volunteering programmes.

The one area where there is an increase in commitment and voluntary activity is environmental concern, where membership and subscriptions are increasing by leaps and bounds (Taylor, 1990). But whether this interest will spill over into social welfare remains doubtful. And increased subscriptions are not an option for voluntary organisations whose members have low incomes, which includes many self-help and community groups.

Whatever the capacity for increasing resources, the surplus is unlikely to be sufficient to make serious inroads even into the £3.68 billion given by government to the voluntary sector in 1987/88 (Charities Aid Foundation, 1989, p 33), let alone into public expenditure on welfare as a whole. A charitable trust administrator reported in 1989 that the £42 million raised for a major children's hospital appeal over four years would "only keep the nation's health services going for one day" (Best, 1989, p 3).

Fees and charges are another potential source of income. Posnett (1988) found that such fees accounted for 61% of voluntary sector support in 1985 out of an estimated income of £12.65 billion. But in Posnett's study, 96% of this fee income was raised in the fields of housing, arts and education, and only one in three voluntary organisations received any fee income at all (Peterson, 1988, p 30). Social welfare organisations at that time raised less than 1% of total fee income. It is likely that these proportions have risen since that study, which found that newer charities were more likely to receive fee income. But raising more money from fees may well be at the risk of serving those most in need. Voluntary organisations in the fields of residential care and housing are experiencing increasing difficulties as they are forced to increase their charges, and many community-based organisations operate:

> ... in areas where paying for any other than the most essential services, such as housing, is not an option and where dealing with the results of lack of money is more urgent. (Berry, 1988, p 270)

Edwards (1988, p 136) argues:

> Charity, though the noblest of virtues, is a quixotic one, subject to the vagaries of happenstance, fads, fashions, sex appeal and media hype. ... Whatever else the market and charity may

achieve, they will not, severally or in combination, guarantee welfare provision.

There is plenty of evidence to suggest that giving is unevenly spread. It would appear that public generosity is more appropriate for relieving disaster, stimulating innovation, and filling gaps than for providing dependable basic services. It is not so readily tapped for drug addicts, ex-prisoners, or people with mental health problems. Its geographical coverage is patchy too. Leat (1985, p 30) concludes that "the voluntary sector tends to be least strong where statutory provision is least adequate, where need is greatest".

British philanthropy is most likely to go to children, animals, hospices, and medical research. Donors want to give to something they can see and are notoriously suspicious of administration. They are not likely to give to the voluntary sector infrastructure, even if it does make the difference between survival and extinction for many small and new groups. Evidence from the United States suggests that corporate foundations tend to shy away from controversy (Salamon, 1987b). Neither advocacy nor the assertive self-help and ethnic minority organisations that have given a voice to so many disadvantaged consumers are likely to be a saleable commodity compared with the image of a helpless child. But these are the very activities that are finding it more difficult to raise government funds.

Government ministers have argued that it is state welfare that creates dependency. Hence the current appeal to 'active citizenship', which is framed in terms of individual responsibilities rather than rights to state help. But charity can, to quote Salamon (1987a, p 41) "create a self-defeating sense of dependency on the part of the poor since it gives them no say over the resources that are spent on their behalf". In Britain, Hall (1989, p 26) recalls "the indignities - what I would call the offensive social contempt - which have always gone along with a system of welfare which depended only on private patronage".

The financial climate for agencies that speak out for the disadvantaged consumer has deteriorated considerably with the collapse of consensus politics. Legislation to curb the use of local authority funds for political publicity also constrains those voluntary organisations whom local authorities fund from making political statements. The White Paper on Charity Law did endorse the current guidelines on the political activities of charities so long as efforts to influence policy remained "ancillary to a charity's primary purposes, which must be clearly charitable and non-political". This judgment was reinforced by the 'efficiency scrutiny' (Home Office, 1990, p 26), but scrutiny did allow the right of departments to define the areas of activity they wished to exclude from a particular funding agreement. In addition, there have been several attacks on campaigning activity from the political right, along with media reports of government concern about left-wing influences in charities. The minister's response to scrutiny - that projects and bodies receiving government money must uphold "accepted ethical standards, for example, to support family life" (Home Office, 1990) - has caused concern among voluntary organisations working outside traditional family structures and more generally among those working with people who are not always seen as the deserving poor.

Conclusions

This chapter has described a range of policies that seek to transfer responsibility for welfare away from the state and toward other providers and funders. The voluntary sector has a crucial role in such a transfer. But it suggests that, although moves towards the market in the United Kingdom aim to promote choice and diversity and to release new resources through the increased use of voluntary organisations in welfare provision, they will not do so unless they recognise a continued government role, not only in financing welfare but also in guaranteeing that choice is available to all.

A number of writers have argued that government and the voluntary sector should not be seen as alternatives, but that systems of welfare should draw on the different strengths of both (Brenton, 1985; Kramer, 1981; Salamon, 1987a). The welfare pluralists saw a central role for government in providing the finance of welfare in the interests of equity and social justice (see, for example, Gladstone, 1979, pp 103-4). The link between government finance and social justice is reinforced by Dahrendorf (1982, pp 167-68):

> Less government is a very pertinent political demand though it must not be misunderstood as a free pass to cut services which are needed to back up the citizenship rights of all. ... Governments ... have the job of ironing out the injustices brought about by the market. ... Unless full participation in the life of society is regarded as a right for all, liberty remains an empty phrase, even a smokescreen behind which privilege thrives.

Certainly without continued government finance, choice is likely to extend only to those with money, while philanthropic provision will be weighted toward the more socially acceptable in society (the deserving poor). But earlier discussion suggests that real choices across the board depend not only on whether government finances welfare, but how it does so.

Merely to transfer service delivery from a monolithic state to large independent providers will not of itself transform the nature of service provision or bring it closer to the consumer. If real pluralism is to be encouraged, government has a role in promoting diversity within a framework of guaranteed universal provision. In such a role, government would fund specific services but would also take some financial responsibility for sustaining the health and vitality of the sector on which it depends for service delivery. This means providing development and support to allow smaller, community-based groups to get to the point where they can take on services if they so wish. It involves supporting the core costs of some organisations as a basis for innovation and project development, and investing in the voluntary sector infrastructure, which is so necessary in a time of change and new demands. It also involves recognising advice and advocacy as key services if consumers are to make their choices effective.

But government's role is not confined to finance. If the range and pattern of provision are to be appropriate to the diversity of need, and if fragmentation and confusion are to be avoided, some form of planning and oversight are necessary. This is a role that government, especially at the local level, is uniquely equipped to perform. But if government is to resume this role, then ways have to be found of resisting the centralism that overwhelmed the welfare state. To do this, government must learn to promote democratic pluralism as well as pluralism in provision. The devolution of service delivery is a first step toward this, but it is not sufficient. It requires democratic mechanisms through which people, as consumers and citizens, can influence patterns of service provision. In this respect, the erosion of local government and the poverty of current political thinking in relation to local democracy are a cause for considerable concern. But democratic mechanisms, too, are insufficient without parallel investment in the community development and public education that gives people, especially those with least power, the ability to use these mechanisms. These are not activities that find favour with the private donor, except perhaps in the environmental field.

To expect government to support this range of activities may seem utopian. But the recent Efficiency Scrutiny supported the case for core and infrastructure funding. And the growth of both the voluntary sector infrastructure and its empowerment work owes a lot to government funding during the 1970s and 1980s, especially at the local level. To suggest that government has a role in these areas is not to ask for a blank cheque. Nor does it negate the need to mobilise new resources from nongovernmental sources. Indeed, these will be all the more necessary if genuine welfare pluralism is to be supported. What is required is a recognition that government has a different role from that of the private donor. What is worrying many voluntary organisations now is the trend in government funding toward the very activities the private donor prefers to support: those which are short-term and visible, which are new, and which make for good public relations.

In such a scenario, government funding would still need to be subject to the definition of priorities and objectives and to the test of cost effectiveness. Difficult decisions would still need to be made and worthwhile work would continue to go unsupported. But a model of welfare that gives government a vital role in planning and supporting the delivery of welfare in the interests of social justice seems a more appropriate aspiration for welfare than one that leaves the fortunes of the most disadvantaged in society to the rough justice of the market.

References

Addy, T. and Scott, D. (1988) *Fatal impacts? The MSC and voluntary action*, Manchester: William Temple Foundation.

Anderson, D., Lair, J. and Marsland, D. (1981) *Breaking the spell of the welfare state*, Agenda for Debate no 1, London: The Social Affairs Unit.

Berry, L. (1988) 'The rhetoric of consumerism and the exclusion of community', *Community Development Journal*, vol 23, no 4, pp 266-72.

Best, R. (1989) 'Future directions for charitable trusts', *Search*, York: Joseph Rowntree Foundation.

Billis, D. and Harris, M. (1986) *An extended role for the voluntary sector*, Uxbridge: PORTVAC (The Brunel Programme of Research and Training into Voluntary Action).

Bosanquet, N. (1988) 'An ailing state of national health', in R. Jowell, S. Witherspoon and L. Brook (eds) *British social attitudes: the fifth report*, Social and Community Planning Research, London: Gower.

Brenton, M. (1985) *The voluntary sector in British social services*, London: Longman.

Burkeman, S. (1988) 'Plugging the gap', *Poverty*, vol 71, pp 20-21, London: Child Poverty Action Group.

Charities: a framework for the future (1989) London: HMSO.

Charities Aid Foundation (1988) *Charity trends*, (11th edition) Kent: Charities Aid Foundation.

Charities Aid Foundation (1989) *Charity trends*, (12th edition) Kent: Charities Aid Foundation.

Charities Aid Foundation (1989) *Directory of grant-making trusts*, Kent: Charities Aid Foundation.

Charity Commission (1988) *Charities for the relief of the poor: the social fund*, guidance notes, London: Charity Commission.

Clarke, M. and Stewart, J. (1986) *The public service orientation - developing the approach*, Working Paper no 3, Luton: Local Government Training Board.

Corrigan, P., Jones, T., Lloyd, J. and Young, J. (1988) *Socialism, merit and efficiency*, pamphlet no 530, London: Fabian Society.

Dahrendorf, R. (1982) *On Britain*, London: British Broadcasting Corporation.

Davies, B. (1986) 'The future for voluntary organisations in Manchester', in D. Scott and P. Wilding (eds) *Beyond welfare pluralism?*, Manchester: Manchester Council for Voluntary Service.

de Hoog, R. (1985) 'Human services contracting: environmental, behavioural and organisational conditions', *Administration and Society*, vol 16, no 4, pp 427-54.

Department of Employment (1987) *Family expenditure survey*, London: HMSO.

Department of the Environment (1991) *The structure of local government* and *New tax for local government*, London: HMSO.

Directory of Social Change (1989) *Company giving news*, London: Directory of Social Change.

Dowson, S. (1989) 'Innovation and advocacy', in *Should voluntary organisations provide more services?*, London: NCVO.

Edwards, J. (1988) 'Justice and social welfare', *Journal of Social Policy*, vol 17, no 2, pp 127-52.

Etherington, S. (1987) 'Heading for the big time', *Social Services Insight*, vol 27.

Gladstone, F. (1979) *Voluntary action in a changing world*, London: Bedford Square Press.

Halfpenny, P. (1990) 'The 1989-90 charity household survey', *Charity Trends*, (13th edition), Kent: Charities Aid Foundation.

Hall, S. (1989) *The voluntary sector under attack*, London: Islington Voluntary Action Council.

Hatch, S. and Mocroft, I. (1983) *Components of welfare*, London: Bedford Square Press.

Hirschman, A.O. (1970) *Exit, voice and loyalty: responses to decline in firms, organisations and states*, Cambridge, Mass: Harvard University Press.

Home Office (1990) 'Efficiency scrutiny of government funding of voluntary sector published' (news release), 4 April.

Kramer, R. (1981) *Voluntary agencies in the welfare state*, Berkeley: University of California Press.

Kramer, R. and Grossman, B. (1987) 'Contracting for social services: contract management and resource dependencies', *Social Services Review*, March, pp 32-55.

Kunz, C., Jones, R. and Spencer, K. (1989) *Bidding for change*, London: Community Projects Foundation and Birmingham Settlement.

Lawson, N. (1987) 'All mankind's concern ...', The Arnold Goodman Charity Lecture, *Charity*, July, pp 13-16.

Leat, D.(1985) *Privatisation and voluntarisation,* Paper presented to research seminar on 'The future of welfare', London: Economic and Social Research Council.

Leat, D., Smolka, G. and Unell, J. (1986) *A price worth paying?*, London: Policy Studies Institute.

Loney, M. (1983) *Communities against government: the British Community Development Project,* London: Heinemann Educational Books.

Maxwell, S. (1989) *Riding the tiger*, Edinburgh: Scottish Council for Voluntary Organisations.

National Council for Voluntary Organisations (1984) *Relations between the voluntary sector and government: a code for voluntary organisations,* London: National Council for Voluntary Organisations.

Patten, J. (1988) 'Launching the active citizen', *The Guardian*, 14 September.

Perlmutter, F. and Adams, C. (1990) 'The voluntary sector and for-profit ventures: the transformation of American social welfare', *Administration in Social Work*, vol 14, no 1, pp 1-13.

Peterson, J. (1988) 'Fees and charges paid to the voluntary sector', *Charity Trends 1986-7*, Kent: Charities Aid Foundation.

Posnett, J. (1988) 'Trends in the income of registered charities 1980-85', *Charity Trends 1986-7*, Kent: Charities Aid Foundation.

Rankin, M. (1989) *Active citizenship: myth or reality*, Berkhamsted: Volunteer Centre UK.

Rein, M. (1989) 'The social structure of institutions: neither public nor private', in S.B. Kamerman and A.J. Kahn, *Privatisation and the welfare state*, Princeton, NJ: Princeton University Press.

Salamon, L.M. (1981) 'Rethinking public management: third-party government and the changing forms of public action', *Public Policy*, vol 29, pp 255-75.

Salamon, L.M. (1987a) 'Of market failure, voluntary failure and third-party government: toward a theory of government-nonprofit relations in the modern welfare state', *Journal of Voluntary Action Research*, vol 16, pp 29-49.

Salamon, L.M. (1987b) 'Partners in public service: the scope and theory of government-nonprofit relations', in W.W. Howell (ed) *The nonprofit sector: a research handbook*, New Haven, CT: Yale University Press.

Salamon, L.M. (1989) *Beyond privatisation: the tools of government action*, Washington: The Urban Institute Press.

Singleton, R. (1988) Letter to *The Guardian*, October.

Taylor, M. (1990) *New times, new challenges: voluntary organisations facing 1990*, London: National Council for Voluntary Organisations.

Taylor, M. with the Newcastle and Sheffield Tenants' Associations (1986) 'For whose benefit? Decentralising housing services in two cities', *Community Development Journal*, vol 21, pp 126-32.

Ware, A. (1989) 'The changing relations between charities and the state', in A. Ware (ed) *Charities and government*, Manchester: Manchester University Press.

Wolfenden Committee (1978) *The future of voluntary organisations*, London: Croom Helm.

CHAPTER 4

INFORMATION TECHNOLOGY AND ORGANISATIONAL CULTURE: IMPLEMENTING CHANGE

SUSAN BARRETT

Introduction

Administrative modernisation is on the political agenda of most European countries, motivated both by economic pressures for increased competitiveness in a changing economic environment, and by public dissatisfaction with current performance in the delivery of services (OECD, 1990). The main thrust of current reform programmes is cost effectiveness: the transformation of public bureaucracies into 'results-oriented' organisations characterised by productivity, performance and responsiveness to clients in pursuit of policy goals (OECD, 1987). In effect this means a major cultural shift for many public organisations.

It is widely recognised that information technology (IT) will have an important role to play in supporting modernisation initiatives such as decentralised administration, performance-oriented management systems and client-oriented service delivery (Barrett, 1989b). But the relationship between IT and cultural change is less clear. Will increased reliance on electronic information handling and communication create a new 'information-oriented' culture, and will this contribute to, or be at odds with, the desired cultural change? To what extent can the process of introducing IT of itself be used as a means of bringing about cultural change? These questions form the focus of this paper.

Culture and public organisations

Organisational culture can be defined in everyday language as 'the way we do things here': the values and norms which shape the way an organisation functions. At the level of everyday experience it is possible to get the feel of an organisation's culture from such simple things as the way the reception of visitors is organised, and the manner in which transactions are conducted.

This chapter first appeared in the *International Review of Administrative Sciences*, 1992, vol 58, no 3, pp 363-74.

Public bureaucracies are traditionally characterised by hierarchical organisation and accountability structures, and concern with functional and procedural rationality, reflecting Weberian normative values of impartiality, consistency and evenhandedness in the administration of government policy. The term 'bureaucracy' has become synonymous with this way of organising and doing things, and 'bureaucratic culture' a metaphor for understanding and explaining this kind of organisational functioning. In this sense public organisations do not simply *have,* but *are* a distinct culture (Smircich, 1983).

More negatively, bureaucratic culture has become associated, in the eyes of the general public, with functional inflexibility, centralised hierarchical control and conformance with procedural rules, often as a result of experiencing apparently rule-bound behaviour and 'can't do' attitudes among front-line staff - the so-called 'street-level bureaucrats' (Lipsky, 1980). It is the *negative* cultural aspect of the functioning of public organisations which modernisation initiatives seek to address.

For the purpose of this paper, culture is conceived of as the "complex patterns of meaning in and around an organisation which together shape the attitudes and practices of those within it" (Frissen, 1989). For any particular public organisation, there will be elements of culture shared with the public sector as a whole, particularly those pertaining to functional rationality and procedural control which perhaps have the greatest influence on public perceptions. But there will also be distinctive features contingent on the particular cultural and functional environment, and subsystems reflecting different internal groupings, professional orientations and interests, including the influence of individual management styles.

The cultural impact of information technology

In European public administration, IT has been a 'normal' feature of organisational life for around 30 years. Yet the prospect of increased reliance on technology for essential information handling and communication functions of public administration is still an emotive issue for citizens and public officials alike. Debate tends to be polarised and fraught with cultural myths and stereotypes - both positive and negative. At one extreme is a negative vision of humans increasingly dependent on, and subservient to, machines, and IT as an instrument for centralised state control. There is fear that the possibilities for increased data linkage and networking of information will be used to increase state regulation of citizens' lives, with consequent loss of privacy and civil liberties. There is concern that increased mechanisation of administrative processes will result in a reduction of human interactions, and loss of responsiveness to individual needs. Increased reliance on electronic data transfer and communication may exclude an underclass of the 'information poor' from participating in processes of governance (Barrett, 1989a).

At the other extreme is a vision of technology unlocking almost unlimited possibilities for enhancing human capacity. IT is seen as a means for empowering citizens via access to more information about the functioning of government; for enhancing local democracy by facilitating decentralisation and devolution of government functions; and for increasing responsiveness by releasing human resources to concentrate on personal service. From this perspective, IT tends to be regarded as a panacea for all organisational problems or as a means, in itself, of bringing about desired changes.

The association of computers with mechanisation and centralised control reflects the history of their use in public administration. Early uses were limited by technical capacity to the mechanisation of routine tasks capable of being processed in 'batches', and the main users were central departments responsible for routine financial calculations, record handling and production of statistical management information. Procurement decisions and control of use were generally retained at corporate level, since the computing hardware and expertise required for its use was expensive and scarce. Such patterns of use and control coincided with theories of management which emphasised corporate management and economies of scale; hence the perception of computers as a tool for central management control.

As new generations of mainframe computers offered increased scope for data linkage and the handling of textual information, aspirations for potential use tended to outstrip both the technological and organisational capacity to implement, notably in the area of integrated management information systems. Disillusion and suspicion with the potential of computers arose partly from the loss of human autonomy and discretion associated with mechanisation and partly from the (often costly) failure of many grand designs and promises of information support to be realised in practice (Barrett and Leather, 1984).

The development of powerful microcomputers in the early 1980s generated a fierce debate about strategies for computerisation centred around the question of centralised or decentralised patterns of use and control. To a certain extent this debate about 'ownership' of information system development has been overtaken by the spread of distributed processing and electronic networking of information, offering the capacity for both centralised *and* decentralised information handling. Many public organisations are already combining a corporate approach to the procurement and development of hardware and software 'infrastructure' with a more user-led approach to information system development. It is now possible to regard the technology itself as 'neutral'; its impact depending on the organisational choices made about how it will be used.

IT now offers the potential for developing new *forms* of organisation and communication and new *patterns* of service delivery. Choice about the use of IT is no longer a matter of prioritising the computerisation of existing administrative processes or data-processing tasks, but involves evaluating the organisational possibilities offered by the tools in relation to change objectives. This, in turn, means explicit consideration of the *values* and *norms* embodied in these objectives, and the degree to which they will be furthered by different solutions. In other words, if it is possible to arrange service functions in a variety of ways, relatively free of former technological constraints on information handling and communication, then the important question is: what kind of *culture* is wanted? The criteria for choice will be less to do with technical feasibility and more to do with the cultural impact of different solutions. Deal and Kennedy (1982) go further to speculate that future organisation will consist of loosely coupled small units, connected through telecommunication networks. In these networks, culture will be the sole device for producing coherence and meaningful unity.

So can the introduction of IT be regarded as 'neutral' in cultural terms? Are there cultural implications associated with increased reliance on automated information-processing and communication, and will these help or hinder the realisation of modernisation objectives? In many ways it is differing assumptions about cultural impact that lie at the heart of the differing attitudes to increased use of IT.

Current developments in the use of IT in public administration represent a shift from computerisation to what has been termed 'informatisation' (Frissen, 1989). Frissen argues that IT should not be regarded as a culturally neutral set of tools because increased reliance on IT will bring with it a specific set of cultural norms and values concerning the role of information in decision making. These emphasise precision, measurement, quantitative data analysis and the codification of knowledge, rather than the qualitative or substantive 'political' rationales associated with discretionary decision making or micropolitical bargaining in implementation. Such cultural characteristics have much in common with Weberian normative values embedded in the formal structures and administrative processes of government institutions, which emphasise functional and procedural rationality and hierarchical control in decision making and execution. From this perspective it can be argued that increased reliance on IT will tend to reinforce the traditional bureaucratic culture of governmental organisations, rather than help to bring about the cultural shift needed for the achievement of modernisation objectives.

Yet the realisation of specific modernisation goals, such as structural flexibility and improved quality of service, is unlikely to be feasible *without* the increased use of IT. Governments are thus faced with an apparent paradox between the potential of IT as a force for change, and its potential to reinforce the cultural status quo.

But is it inevitable that increased use of technology will reinforce bureaucratic cultural values? Much depends on the purpose for which IT is used and the processes by which it is introduced. Until recently, most organisational change in public administrations was aimed at increasing internal productivity and efficiency. The use of IT reflected the prevailing concern with cost saving (via automation) and improved efficiency (via rationalisation of data-processing associated with internal administrative record handling). More recent IT developments offer the capacity for handling and communicating substantive and qualitative information via the integration of text, image and voice as well as data-processing. There is now the potential to offer enhancement as well as the substitution of human skills. User-oriented hardware and software offers greater self-determination for users (including citizens) in the development and control of information systems, and a shift from control to support in the role of technical experts. The potential therefore exists for a more positive vision of IT as a means for service enhancement, citizen empowerment and more participatory and responsive governance to be, at least in part, *capable* of realisation. It could be possible for IT to become a 'taken for granted' set of tools as normal as the typewriter and telephone and integrated into the cultures within which it is being used. But realisation of this potential will depend on harnessing 'subcultures' which support and benefit from such change, and on the degree to which these subcultures can influence the processes of introducing IT and managing change.

Approaches to managing change

Other recent studies of organisational aspects of IT (such as the work of Kraemer and colleagues at Irvine, California (Kraemer and King, 1986; Hirscheim, 1985; Campbell, 1990) conclude that IT does tend to reinforce the cultural status quo, but explain the observed tendency in terms of interactionist theories of power and control (eg Pfeffer, 1981), rather than as a product of the values associated with the technology itself. These studies suggest that the way IT is used in an organisation will be the result of negotiation and bargaining between different interest groups (and subcultures) represented in the organisation, and will reflect and reinforce the prevailing norms and values of those most able to influence or control the process of implementing change.

Traditionally most bureaucratic organisations have tackled the introduction of IT by means of:

i. a 'top-down' approach to policy change whereby change is initiated by politicians and/or senior management and imposed on operational and front-line staff (albeit with consultation) through the formal hierarchical management structure;

ii. the control of IT procurement and information system design placed in the hands of technical experts, either from a central IT department or brought from outside as consultants.

This top-down approach reflects the hierarchical management norms embedded in the structure and culture of public organisations; it is the 'normal' way that policy is implemented in such organisations. It also reflects the lack of IT awareness and expertise amongst managers and policy professionals within such institutions, especially policy delivery agencies. There has been a tendency for decisions about the procurement and use of IT to be left to technical specialists, and for a lack of integration between the structurally compartmentalised worlds of corporate policy makers in senior management, technology experts, service professionals and front-line staff. In this situation it is the values of senior management and technical experts which will have most influence on how IT is used; if they are convergent cultural reinforcement will take place.

But there is no automatic reinforcing convergence between those with the authority to lead change and those in a position to influence the detail of its implementation, especially where change is designed to challenge aspects of the status quo, whether in terms of culture, structure or existing power relations based on possession of information or expertise. Whilst senior managers may espouse modernisation objectives and have the authority to lead change, others, including technical experts and those lower down the management hierarchy, may not be so enthusiastic if the change appears to threaten their role in the organisation. These are the people most likely to influence the detailed implementation of change as change objectives are transmitted 'down' the formal hierarchy.

Many apparent failures to achieve change objectives can be attributed to the paradox of working within existing structures and cultures of control and expertise to bring about change in just those things. Rather than seeing an automatic tendency for IT to reinforce bureaucratic culture, perhaps the question needs to be posed a different way round, namely, how far the potential for alternative ways of perceiving and using IT can be realised in bureaucratic organisations whose dominant cultures and structures tend to reinforce the use of IT for mechanisation, codification and top-down managerial control.

Realising potential in practice

It will not be enough for senior managers to perceive IT potential and make decisions which harness it in support of modernisation objectives. The foregoing discussion suggests that appropriate tools may facilitate, but their introduction will not, of itself, *bring about* desired change. Senior managers thus also need to concern themselves with the *process* by which change is introduced, to ensure that decisions are implemented in such a way that the desired cultural change permeates the whole organisation. This may mean questioning the traditional top-down style of policy implementation in bureaucratic organisations, and developing a more flexible and negotiative approach which recognises the need to reach accommodation (if not consensus) among those responsible for implementation, on the *values* and *norms* which provide the cultural framework for, and thus influence the outcomes of, proposed change (Barrett and Fudge, 1981; Barrett and Hill, 1984).

Research evidence of historic practice does not mean that such practice is immutable. The value of such studies is to highlight a number of factors which need to be addressed explicitly in the management of change involving informatisation:

i. More attention than in the past needs to be paid to identifying, and making explicit, underlying value assumptions concerning the *expected role* of information, as a basis for identifying the nature and degree of change required in existing patterns of information handling and communication, and the likely impact of change on the status quo - cultural as well as functional. This would provide the foundations for a more coherent *information policy* embodying desired cultural norms and values, to guide the development and introduction of new information systems.

ii. Such a policy will need to be treated as an integral part of the strategy for administrative modernisation, rather than something added on or left to the technical experts by default.

iii. Such an *integrated strategy* will need to take account of, and negotiate between, differing values and interests, and the ability to pursue them amongst those upon whom implementation depends. This will require a closer integration of the worlds of policy professionals, technology experts, front-line staff and senior management; not to create 'consensus', but to develop mutual understanding and to distinguish the 'myth' of cultural stereotypes from the reality of conflicts of values and interests; to discuss and negotiate agreement on alternative possibilities for the use of IT in relation to modernisation objectives; and to renegotiate the 'social order' of organisational structures and processes which will form the basis of a strategy integrating new ways of using IT with new organisational objectives.

iv. More influence and control over the development and implementation of information systems will need to be given to those with responsibility for the functions or service to be supported (end-users), in order for IT to become a 'taken for granted' tool, rather than perceived as an alien culture imposed from outside.

However, the development of this kind of organisational capacity to cope with change is hampered by the level of *uncertainty* associated with change, and its effects on those involved, and *the communication* and *learning 'gap'* between technical experts and end-users, which prevents non-technical staff from participating on equal terms in the development of information systems, and technical staff from appreciating what is really wanted.

Change and uncertainty

Organisational change more often than not involves shifts in the balance of power - whether via change in the authority structure, or change in patterns of influence (eg via new information flows) - and uncertainty for those affected. In situations of uncertainty, people tend to seek ways of minimising their personal insecurity; either by putting pressure on senior managers to give a clear lead, or by 'digging in' and holding on to the familiar (even if it is unsatisfactory). Apparent hostility to change may thus reflect feelings of insecurity, as much as genuine conflicts of interest (Barrett and McMahon, 1990).

Even where politicians/senior managers have a clear view of the direction they wish to go in, there may be uncertainty about the best way to go about it, and a desire to discuss with operational staff the feasibility and practical implications of alternative courses of action. But, paradoxically, staff may be reluctant to engage in open discussion of alternatives because they are afraid of committing themselves whilst unclear about the implications of change. They will tend to demand clear proposals to respond to, or assurances about personal security, before being prepared to enter negotiations about how things might be done. Where IT is involved, levels of uncertainty are likely to be increased, both because of the complexity of choice related to the pace of technological change, and the lack of awareness and experience of what *is* possible amongst non-technical personnel.

Concept of strategy

All these uncertainties have implications for the *concept* of strategy. Rather than a 'master plan' what is needed is a framework for directing an ongoing process of change, which combines clarity of goals with flexibility for innovation, adaptation to changing circumstances and learning. This is more like the 'loose/tight' management approach advocated by Peters and Waterman (1982), and suggests a strategy which provides a sense of direction and purpose, which is less about control from the top or centre, but represents a framework for the steering and coordination of incremental developments and innovation often emerging from the 'bottom up', and which incorporates a strategy for organisational learning.

Sense of direction means the contextual framework of value criteria against which individual, ongoing decisions can be tested and checked for relative consistency. This might include a basic statement of organisational purpose, together with the principles which will guide organisational and service development decisions. It will also be important to know the political and senior management stance on the expected level of, and cost benefit criteria for, IT investment. Otherwise system providers and users will not have a clear 'bottom line' to inform the limits of risk and choice. In this respect, key questions to address might be:

i.   the degree of commitment to informatisation;

ii. attitude to risk investment in research and development;

iii. values informing investment in IT - what IT is *for* - eg productivity, administrative efficiency, enhancement of service to clients, greater analytical capacity, enhanced decision support, or improved management information?

The *sharing* of value principles is also an important coordinating mechanism. In practice it is often only the senior management team who are privy to bottom line values and principles. Sharing does not mean reaching consensus, but it is about openness in the interests of minimising misunderstanding and perhaps alleviating some of the insecurity created by impending change.

The *framework for steering and coordination* represents a balance between the need for central control to safeguard longer term objectives for integrated system development, and the freedom to allow users to take as much responsibility as possible for their own information handling. On this basis, such a framework will include *ground rules* for areas requiring central coordination, such as the development and maintenance of basic IT infrastructure; protocols and standards for data-handling; and guidance on hardware and software compatible with basic infrastructure. It should also include *mechanisms* and *procedural guidelines* to facilitate the necessarily ongoing dialogue and negotiation between users, technical support and senior management.

Organisational learning denotes the process of developing human resources so as to maximise the potential contribution of knowledge, experience, expertise and creativity to the process of organisational development and change. Formal education and training will play a part, but the process also crucially includes maximising opportunities for learning from experience, and for identifying and sharing the learning that takes place. A strategy for organisational learning will need to include:

i. mechanisms for identifying the human resources available (skills and enthusiasms as well as numbers and formal qualifications);

ii. ways of developing mutual awareness between the different perspectives and interests that need to interact in the process of change;

iii. means for encouraging learning through doing and experimenting (as well as via training);

iv. mechanisms for exchanging (as well as evaluating) experience.

An explicit commitment to organisational learning is an essential part of building the organisational capacity to implement change effectively, by helping to break down misunderstandings, develop necessary skills and reduce the insecurity associated with the uncertainties of change. It may also help to create a new culture, developed out of, and associated with, the *actual process* of change. The final section of this paper looks at some ways of incorporating organisational learning into the process of informatisation.

Strategies for organisational learning

Risk and uncertainty in the process of informatisation may be alleviated, and the degree of effective implementation may be greater, in organisational settings where:

i. there is a high degree of consensus and commitment to the objectives of informatisation;

ii. the scope of system development is commensurate with the resources available;

iii. there is motivation and commitment amongst those upon whom the organisation will depend for the implementation of system developments - in particular the end-users.

The problem is that such conditions rarely exist, especially in advance of system implementation. Resources are rarely committed in advance of proven benefits. People implementing the system or affected by associated changes in administrative practice may be wary and insecure about its potential impact on their roles within the organisation without either experience of the system in practice, or a demonstrable commitment from the organisation to meeting their needs for learning and voice in the process of change.

In practice, an *incremental* and *user-led* approach to informatisation may not only minimise risk, but also offer opportunities for learning in conjunction with system development, which will ultimately pay off in terms of organisational performance. The process of informatisation will be more likely to meet organisational objectives effectively if staff are participating from a basis of personal learning and experience, rather than having systems and training imposed from above. But equally the effectiveness of systems will depend on their being easy to use.

Based on the experience of working with public organisations in the UK (including my own), the following are suggestions for ways of incorporating learning into the process of system development and implementation.

i. *The use of pilot schemes or small scale subsystems as a starting point.* Such schemes can produce relatively quick results for evaluation by users, and give some immediate learning and satisfaction to the staff involved. They can act as a demonstration project/catalyst for raising awareness and enthusiasm amongst others. Pilot experiments may also be possible to develop using existing proven software (eg commercial packages).

ii. *The provision of as many staff as possible with access to personal computers and basic software* such as word processing or spreadsheets. This may mean accepting the proliferation of 'personal' systems initially, and possibly discarding the hardware after a year or two. But it will encourage people to learn at their own pace (eg by taking machines home to 'play with' in their own time), and encourage innovation and experimentation without the risk of ridicule or costly mistakes. Above all such investment demonstrates an organisational commitment to the availability and use of IT.

iii. *Encourage the formation of informal 'user groups'.* Such groups can provide important opportunities for sharing experience and solving problems. Non-technical staff find them a means of building up confidence to generate questions and to enter into dialogue with technical staff. They may also provide a mechanism for representation in corporate decisions about the use of IT.

iv. *Invest resources at the design stage to ensure that systems are genuinely 'user-friendly' and virtually self-training.* Self-training means that users need no special training, but are guided and learn as they use the system (see Baddeley and Dawes, 1987). This approach removes the barrier of technological jargon and builds user confidence. It also ensures that learning takes place as and when needed (rather than in isolation from everyday use). It can also represent a long-term saving in the cost of training, and increase the range of staff able to benefit from system use.

Learning and training

Even with such strategies to maximise informal learning, formal training will still play an essential part in fostering organisational learning, to be budgeted for as an integral part of the cost of change. But it is important to distinguish specific *skills training* from broader programmes of *education and staff development* necessary to the development of the organisational capacity to make effective use of IT.

Most organisations budget for training in the skills necessary to use particular types of software or system configuration, or to take on new tasks and responsibilities resulting from enhanced information support or changed administrative structures. However, too little attention is still paid to *retraining*, which itself can go a long way to alleviate insecurity by demonstrating that the organisation is aware, and cares about, the wider implications of change to job content and job boundaries arising from informatisation. Even fewer organisations have established strategies which incorporate broader programmes of education and staff development aimed at preparing staff (especially middle management) for engaging in both the development of IT-based systems and the administrative restructuring with which they are associated (Barrett, 1989b).

Concluding note

The opportunities offered by current trends in technology in many ways represent a challenge to traditional institutional structures, organisational roles and management practices. Associated organisational cultures cannot be maintained or changed by force, hence the emphasis in this paper on dialogue, negotiation and learning as a means of reaching accommodation rather than trying to impose change by command and control. There is a balance to be struck between developing corporate norms and values which help to integrate and provide the 'bottom line' for the process of change, and maintaining respect for differing values and interests associated with different functional perspectives.

Perhaps the main message of this paper is that the degree to which IT becomes culturally accepted as a 'taken for granted' resource to support the effective operation of the organisation or agency, will depend on developing the capacity to recognise, evaluate and use the opportunities offered, at all levels of the organisation. This will require much greater attention and investment than hitherto given to:

i. the organisational values and principles underlying the objectives for informatisation;

ii. negotiative rather than dirigiste approaches to the process of implementing change;

iii. the creation and fostering of a climate in which learning and innovation are encouraged and valued, and which seeks to make the optimum use of the human skills and enthusiasms which will ultimately determine the quality of organisational performance.

References

Baddeley, S. and Dawes, N. (1987) 'Information technology support for devolution: vision and reality in Walsall Housing Department', *Local Government Studies*, July/August.

Barrett, S. (1989a) 'Improving the quality of service to clients with information technology', Paper presented to OECD meeting on Using Information Technology to Support Administrative Modernisation, Paris, May.

Barrett, S. (1989b) 'Implementing technologies in public organisations: developing management awareness', Proceedings of the Fiera di Padova 7th Congress: *Informatica come pubblico servizio: Il cittadino Utente*, Padova.

Barrett, S. and Fudge, C. (eds) (1981) *Policy and action*, London: Methuen.

Barrett, S. and Hill, M. (1984) 'Policy, bargaining and structure in implementation theory', *Policy, and Politics*, vol 12, no 3.

Barrett, S. and Leather, P. (1984) 'Information technology in planning practice', Environment and Planning Committee Paper no 4, London: ESRC.

Barrett, S. and McMahon, L. (1990) 'Public management in uncertainty: a micropolitical perspective of the health service in the UK', *Policy and Politics*, vol 18, no 4, pp 257-68.

Campbell, H. (1990) 'Use of geographic information in local authority planning departments', unpublished PhD dissertation, University of Sheffield.

Deal, T.E. and Kennedy, A.A. (1982) *Corporate cultures: the rites and rituals of corporate life*, Reading, MA: Addison-Wesley.

Frissen, P. (1989) 'The cultural impact of informatisation in public administration', *International Review of Administrative Sciences*, vol 55, pp 569-86.

Hirscheim, R.A. (1985) *Office automation: a social and organisational perspective*, Chichester: Wiley.

Kraemer, K.L. and King, J.L. (1986) 'Computing and public organisations', *Public Administration Review*, vol 46, pp 488-96.

Lipsky, M. (1980) *Street-level bureaucracy*, Newbury Park: Russell Sage.

OECD (1987) *Administration as service: the public as client*, Paris: OECD.

OECD (1990) *Public management survey*, Paris: OECD.

Peters, T. and Waterman, R. (1982) *In search of excellence,* New York: Harper and Row.

Pfeffer. G. (1981) *Power in organisations,* London: Pitman.

Smircich, L. (1983) 'Concepts of culture and organisational analysis', *Administrative Science Quarterly,* vol 28, pp 339-58.

CHAPTER 5

INSTITUTIONAL CHANGE AND REBUILDING FOR A FAST CHANGING ECONOMY: CONFRONTING CHAOS

TOM DAVIES

Poland finds itself, as do many countries in Central and Eastern Europe, existing and re-emergent in a historical dilemma which many Western European countries would in some ways dearly love to share - a legitimate opportunity, indeed a popular demand, to reconstruct the state's and the economy's institutions from the beginning again so that the national economy and the society itself can prosper and be morally sound.

It is quite clear that restructuring is the name of the imperative. It is also quite clear that Mrs Thatcher is seen as the heroine of the historical moment not least because she made politics out of the concept even before Mr Mitterand produced his 'rigeur', or Mr Gorbachev his 'perestroika'.

Previously I have proposed a thesis of convergence between East and West and demonstrated, using evidence from Hungarian cities that the elements of the policy set used commonly in the West (privatisation, decentralisation, local democratisation, centralisation, control of local authority budgets, international competitivity, restructuring and rationalisation of industry, the linking of the education sector to the needs of the labour market, entrepreneurship, the discrediting of planning) were already detectable in the Hungary of the years 1984 to 1988 (Davies, 1991). I also demonstrated that most people in Hungary did not believe that these changes were occurring deep down in the structures of their society. They certainly did not agree with the idea that this subtle undermining of the structures which they knew would lead, together with massive popular action in some countries, to the sudden collapse of all that they thought immutable.

In a paper on 'Futures' presented to the Technical University in Helsinki in 1990, I discussed the pace of change in Central and Eastern Europe, and predicted that we were merely at the beginning of the changes to come. I was as surprised as most when the pace became an avalanche that

---

This chapter first appeared in M. Belka and J. Lipinski (eds) *Studia I Materialy*, 1991, Warsaw: Instytut Nauk Ekonomicznych.

Christmas and the societies of Central and Eastern Europe were pushed abruptly into the world's mainstream of change.

Nevertheless, during that talk I said two things which I think still hold true and which I want to concentrate on here:

i. that we were only at the beginning of massive and very turbulent changes, even after the extraordinary happenings of the year, and even if one discounts the possible outcome of the Gulf War;

ii. that the changes in Central and Eastern Europe, far from being a 'catching up' with the West, would demonstrate for the West the institutional and economic transformations which are increasingly necessary if the world economic and environmental system is to survive.

In other words, I suggested convergence between the lagging East and the leading West; now I am suggesting the opposite.

There are two reasons why I should say this, and the second follows from the first. The first is the extent of the impact of the changes in the world economy and environment upon economies and societies which have tried to maintain stasis in a fast changing world. All states try to do this. Lenin, I believe, wrote something about that. Mrs Thatcher was firmly of the opinion that the UK state was also trying to do that.

The second is the nature of the prescriptions which are pouring forth from the gurus of Western managerial thought about the need for change - not in the seekers after stable states but in the managers of the global and multinational companies which are assumed to be the leaders of the world changes, to which the puny nation state is trying desperately to respond.

The modern writers, the best sellers in particular (for example Drucker, 1989; Mintzberg, 1989; Peters, 1988; Kanter, 1989), are all proposing that 'chaos' is here to stay, that it is the main characteristic of the business environment, and that *Thriving on chaos*, as Tom Peters titled his best selling management book, is what successful modern business and other organisations are learning to do. They do this by building diverse and multiple shifting structures, by experimentation and the reward of innovation, by complex and conflicting strategies.

> I have just proposed radically changing the organisation's structure annually or even more frequently - it's a must. Changing all the procedures and then changing them again - another must. Smashing the market into bits, and then smashing it into even finer bits - a must as well. Restlessly altering the structures and markets and procedures depends upon keeping the vision and value system constant, more constant and more prominent than ever before - replacing control by procedure with control by vision and trust. ... The

> goals must be bold, even to stand still. ... Moreover, the most efficient and effective route to bold change is the participation of everyone, every day, in incremental change. ... The dramatic success symbol is usually just that, a symbol. The road to it is paved with a million experiments, a million false steps and the wholehearted participation of everyone. (Peters, 1988)

There is some evidence which suggests that successful societies have also exhibited that pattern over history. A multiplicity of changing structures seems to be associated with survival, at least over time (Hannan, 1988).

The key figure in this new process is the manager who can make sense of, indeed enjoys, the complexity of the environment in which she or he finds her or himself. In the new production technologies lauded by the best-selling commentators, the manager no longer sits in an office with the door open, she or he has a desk down on the shop floor and spends time, along with all other 'experts' progressing the chaotic process of services or products. Schonberger illustrates this in his book on world class manufacturing, based on the 'success stories' of US and Japanese companies. This book is strangely subtitled 'The lessons of simplicity applied'. It does not list 'simplicity' in the index and is in fact about 'just in time' production processes which are very complex dynamic iterative learning processes.

> Having salaried people (engineers, schedulers, buyers, plant managers, everybody) on call is common in Japan and also seems to be ingrained in Japanese subsidiary plants outside Japan. ... A problem has to be fixed quickly and everyone must help - as people do when their community suffers a flood, tornado, serious earthquake, or other disaster [interesting use of language]. ... Hewlett-Packard has a tradition of having salaried support people's desks on the factory floor. (Schonberger, 1986)

In fact, he suggests that everyone should be involved in management. Of the 17 points of his 'action agenda for manufacturing excellence' the following relate to that statement:

xi. cross-train for mastery of more than one job;

xiii. assure that line people get first crack at problem-solving - before staff experts;

xvi. seek to have plural instead of singular work stations, machines, cells and lines for each product.

One of many sets of technical suggestions for continual change in manufacturing which he proposes interacts between every employee and every aspect of the market constantly, iteratively, and increasingly.

Poland as yet does not have its global companies in the sense that it does not yet participate in the global ownership stakes, and does not yet contribute significant numbers of nationals to global management. Nation states can, by definition, not have an 'ownership' of a global company - the multinational yes, the global no. However, we shall see a fast and startling development of international trading by state and para-state, Polish private and internationally owned Polish located companies in the near future (Kaynak, 1989).

We shall also see a state policy structure which is trying to put in place the extraordinarily varied and immediately required social policies which service and deal with the consequences of the restructuring which the economy demands.

A key point which I would like to make is that the appropriate organisational and policy forms for both the economic and the social policy sectors are likely to be similar.

It is highly unlikely that the Polish state will put in place anything remotely resembling the past 'welfare states' of Nordic countries, nor even those of France or Britain. The ways in which flows from taxation, the impact of privatisation and decentralisation, and the huge scale of the convulsions of the labour market actually make themselves felt will force the Polish state, like the other Central and Eastern European states into the adoption of 'chaotic' ways of surviving - and hopefully of prospering, thriving and establishing legitimate and morally sound governance.

We should be in no doubt that the risks of failure are very high indeed. The forces which push all our societies towards 'thriving on chaos' could also push them into the decay of racism, the creation of large scale 'underclasses', nationalistic-based wars and even more widespread impoverishment than has been experienced in Europe this century.

However, those who are arguing forcibly for the development of community-based economic initiatives, those who are arguing for the release of the energies of the 'female', the 'grey', the 'informal' economies, those who argue for creative self-help and the humane governance of societies relate rather closely to the concepts of 'institutional dissolving', 'diversity' and 'dispersal' being argued in the US and Japanese management schools.

These concepts are related to the idea of 'self-reliant' development put forward by those concerned with rural areas, areas of traditional industries in decline and the 'third world', a concept itself now much in dispute. Some years ago Mattelart suggested:

> By setting out its requirements at all levels, individual and collective, local, regional and national, self-reliance refuses to take the state and its administrative apparatus as the only social subject. It is the multiplicity of organised interlocutors that characterises a self-reliance situation. A wealth of documentation from popular organisations and movements, consumers' organisations, women's organisations, environmental movements, human rights organisations, Christian groups, and also the trades union movement and working class political parties, shows the extent to which we are witnessing more and more a pressure towards a decentralised development model. As much in the central countries as in the periphery, the emergence of these new historical actors coincides with the profound crisis experienced by historical political movements and parties, which demands a change in the traditional way of conceiving of and making politics. (Mattelart, 1983)

These in turn relate very closely to the changing concepts of physical and social sciences - the so-called 'post-modern' which is really just the newest phase of the 'modern' - and the chaos theorists themselves, who have discovered that order in the world, and indeed in the universe, is not simple (Gleick, 1987). It is still possible to maintain that order as a concept has some meaning, but that it is chaotic. In other words, it is highly complex, multifaceted, turbulent and difficult to conceptualise. Not only that, but we are severely limited by the very meanings systems which we try to use to understand that order. We must constantly question and, dare I say it, 'deconstruct' our meanings system in order to proceed towards understanding the reality with which we are faced, which is itself constantly retreating in front of us at an accelerating pace.

Mrs Thatcher may or may not have appreciated the implications of this new thesis: she seemed to suggest that we must all restructure in order to arrive at a stable state. She did not suggest the nature of that state, except that some people would be very rich, and that the rest would owe their existence to the way in which the rich were prepared to reward them for hard work or for being deserving poor.

The future reality may be very different from that - it certainly will not be stable. Indeed the disputed outcome of the Thatcher experiment indicates that Britain at least has not arrived at stability. The whole concept of stability is in the process of being staggeringly redefined; the much used term 'self-sustaining', whether applied to nation or world, is not simple but conflictual and multicultural in the widest sense of that word.

It therefore follows, unless you wish to write off in a very explicit way countless numbers of the populations of every society and whole populations of many societies, that it is important to recognise that no-one is to blame for what we are about to experience, and that no one group of people ('experts' or not) is going to have the right formula; that we are all dependent upon the creativity of each other at the global scale; and that failure to recognise this will lead directly to the collapse of societies and to global war.

Peters also points out that 'failure' of a more positive kind must become a more common element of our strategies, and that we shall have to become used to failing a great deal more than in the past. Failure will be welcomed as evidence of experiment. It follows that we cannot just have one strategy which fails: the multiple strategy organisation and indeed the multiple strategy society becomes the instrument for future progress.

This has been observed in successful private sector organisations and in a way has already been acknowledged and created in the welfare programmes and social policies of Western Europe and elsewhere. Policy experimentation, the funding of pump-priming experiments - the establishment of countless new non-statutory and community-based organisations which are in many cases set up to fail - is seen everywhere in the policy set.

One of the greatest challenges presented to us by this array of multiplex policies and institutions is that there is a need for morality in the process and outcome of these organisations. They will have to experiment and to fail in order to succeed. However, they must not carelessly create in that process human casualties. We have to remember that the revolutionary change in Central and Eastern Europe was morally as well as economically based (Lukes, 1990). The solutions, although they will be 'chaotic', must also be moral, and that suggests a new 'chaotic' morality will emerge in countries such as Poland and spread westwards.

There are at least two moral dangers here. The first is that 'chaos' actually crushes the diversity which we value and which we require for a moral society. Mattelart put this danger succinctly:

> Transnational capital also needs a society splintered into a thousand movements and groups. However, it is only the atomized form of this splintering which is useful to it. In other words, not a chain of movements expressing the solidarity of groups and individuals but a series of monads isolated from one another by competition and individual consumption. The decentralisation by the market underlying the transnational project is the bearer of the dismantling of the structures of solidarity. (Mattelard, 1983)

That last sentence is redolent of meaning in the Polish setting.

On the other hand, there is of course always a temptation to move towards a single morality to replace a collapsed single system. This appears to be very dangerous for economic and for social survival.

Perhaps a clear illustration of that is the work of Professor Brian Griffiths, who has recently republished his evangelical popular moral book on *Christian alternatives to capitalism and socialism*, originally conceived at the same time as Matterlards's (Griffiths, 1989). Whilst commending to us the multiplexity of " 'the little platoons' ... the family, the school, the workplace, the professional association, the church ...", his morality is based upon a particular form of Christianity. He does not approve of course of Christian socialism, nor presumably of any other religious-based economics. His evangelical stance was adopted for the whole world and, as he was one of Mrs Thatcher's closest advisers, we must take that stance seriously. In the 1989 preface to the reissued book, he states:

> In so much modern writing, clear biblical words such as 'love', 'the poor' and 'sharing' are removed from their immediate context to become slogans for wealth distribution. ... Whilst our responsibility to others is at the heart of Jesus' teaching, it is quite wrong to make it synonymous with equality.

> By contrast, the theology of social ethics which underlies [this book] is one based on creation ethics - the search for those universal moral principles and structures which are part of the creation order and which are expanded on in Old Testament law. Despite the exegetical problems in relating the Old Testament to the modern world, there is a wealth of material which relates social structures (marriage, ownership, family, law etc) to the moral law (the Ten Commandments etc). (Griffiths, 1989)

Other more acceptable and diverse models are however being offered to us, at the global scale and nationally. Globally we are requested to discover a fourth force to underpin the new 'ethical economics'; fourth after Adam Smith's 'invisible hand', Alfred Marshall's marginal analysis, mathematics and scientific analysis, and Keynes' government role. That force, says Hamrin, is:

> ... the dominant values of the citizenry, firmly rooted in long-standing and rich philosophic-religious traditions. With such values as a guiding force, the resulting economy will indeed become a servant to, not a master of, the people. (Hamrin, 1989)

At the national level we are offered the following prescription for Japan, where the conflict between different cultural traditions is seen as the reason for a successful humanistic enterprise.

> In Japan there seems to have been an invisible principle of 'coexistence of opposites'. Historically, Japan has allowed the coexistence of various religions such as Shintoism but also

> Buddhism, Confucianism, Taoism and Christianity. ... Japan has incorporated Western science and technology on to the Eastern European culture. ... Today Japan is trying to synthesize capitalism and socialism into a new economic system. (Nakano, 1989)

Laszlo, suggests that we must be able to embrace many visions, not just the single vision which Tom Peters and others suggest.

> Our world is interdependent and, as yet, reasonably diversified. But instead of recognising interdependence and safeguarding diversity, liberals and Marxists alike dream of extending national hegemony into international uniformity. The more hawkish among them contemplate waging wars and inciting revolts to accelerate the conversion of their own wealth and power.
>
> The tables have been turned on such aggressive strategies. The classical conceptions have failed to foresee today's high degrees of interdependence and have vastly underestimated the values of diversity. Today we must 'let a hundred visions bloom'. (Laszlo, 1989)

We must ask ourselves what are the models of state apparatus for welfare - of state policies for welfare - which are being suggested to the Polish state? How robust are they for the new world situation? Are they based in fact upon failed models, the results of earlier experiments, and indeed upon old historical cultural religious battle lines, or do they look forward to their own multiple failures and multiple successes?

References

Davies, T. (1991) 'Economic restructuring and social policy: lessons from Hungary', in F. Millard (ed) *Social welfare and the market*, Occasional Paper no 15, London: Suntory-Toyota International Centre for Economics and Related Disciplines, London School of Economics, pp 50-80.

Drucker, P.F. (1989) *The new realities*, London: Heinemann.

Gleick, J. (1987) *Chaos: making a new science*, London: Heinemann.

Griffiths, B. (1989) *Morality and the market-place: Christian alternatives to capitalism and socialism*, Sevenoaks: Hodder and Stoughton.

Hamrin, R.D. (1989) 'Ethical economics: a new paradigm for global justice and stewardship', *Futures*, December, pp 608-18.

Hannan. M.T. (1988) 'Organisation, population dynamics and social change', *European Sociological Review*, vol 4, no 2, pp 95-109.

Kanter, R.M. (1989) *When giants learn to dance: mastering the challenge of strategy, management and careers in the 1990s*, New York: Simon and Schuster.

Kaynak, E. (1989) 'Managing firms across borders: operating organisations, behaviour and strategy formulation in public enterprises', *International Journal of Public Sector Management*, vol 2, no 2, pp 28-42.

Laszlo, E. (1989) *The inner limits of mankind: heretical reflections on today's values, culture and politics*, One World Books for Thoughtful People.

Lukes, S. (1990) 'Marxism and morality: reflections on the revolutions of 1989', *Ethics and International Affairs*, vol 4, pp 19-31.

Mattelart, A. (1983) *Transnationals and the third world: the struggle for culture*, South Hadley, Mass: Bergir and Garvey.

Mintzberg, H. (1989) *Mintzberg on management. Inside our strange world of organisations*, New York: Free Press.

Nakano, C. (1989) 'Principles of humanistic enterprise in Japan: a new economic system of the future', *Futures*, December 1989, pp 640-46.

Peters, T. (1988) *Thriving on chaos: handbook for a management revolution*, London: Macmillan.

Schonberger, R.J. (1986) *World class manufacturing: the lessons of simplicity applied*, London: Collier Macmillan.

PART 2:

THE IMPACT OF CHANGE

A: URBAN POLICY

CHAPTER 6

INNER CITIES: A MULTI-AGENCY PLANNING AND IMPLEMENTATION PROCESS

MURRAY STEWART AND JACKY UNDERWOOD

Introduction

This paper uses inner cities policy to address questions of 'planning' theory. There are a number of reasons why this is appropriate. First, work on inner cities represents a significant contemporary area of planning practice within which the tasks of description, explanation and prescription have become particularly confused. Second, the boundaries of the policy sector are unclear with the result that there are significant arguments about the professional, technical, organisational and political legitimacy of the different interests clustered around the inner cities policy initiative. This heightens the debate about the role of planners and planning. Third, the policy sector quite clearly suggests a range of theoretical questions both about the substance of the 'problem' (the analysis and explanation of economic and social change in inner cities) and about the process of intervention proposed to deal with the 'problem' (a central/local government, public/private sector, multi-organisational initiative introduced on a selective geographical basis and assuming a consensus on the objectives of policy).

Even these preliminary observations indicate the complexities involved in analysing inner cities policy. In terms of defining 'planning', for example, planning for inner cities is not at first sight an activity of a particular type, undertaken by a particular type of institution, does not involve the guidance/regulation of particular classes of events, and is not undertaken by particular people who consider what they do to be planning. One might indeed argue that inner cities policy is so multi-faceted yet so opaque that it defies analysis. It is, however, precisely because it is like this - and so resembles so much of the wide-ranging but ill defined planning initiatives of recent years - that it deserves attention.

In this paper we adopt an implementation perspective, for three main reasons. First, this requires arguments to be grounded in action and

---

This chapter first appeared in P. Healey, G. McDougall and M.J. Thomas (eds) *Planning theory: prospects for the 1980s*, 1982, Oxford: Pergamon.

practice, a condition we regard as important. Second, we identify the greatest tension in the initiative as that between the aspiration to consensus, coordination, coherence and (planned) order which a 'partnership' approach implies, and the reality which we have observed which is of sectional interest, conflict and pluralism (anathema to traditional concepts of planning). It is at the level of implementation of policy in a multi-agency process that this tension is most apparent and amenable to empirical observation on which analysis and explanation can be based. Third, we chose an implementation oriented approach because we believe that, far from obscuring broader questions of ideology and value in governmental action, an action/practice perspective in fact can highlight and demonstrate these broader issues.

This final point raises what we see as our most significant point. This is that whilst we accept that the concern for implementation has to an extent developed out of procedural planning theory and is in some quarters being seized upon as a rationale for a new managerial style, we do not regard it as necessary that a 'policy and implementation' perspective should ignore questions of value, social relations, historical context and so on. Our aim, therefore, is to suggest that a research task which centres on policy implementation in multi-organisational contexts need not become blinkered by micro-organisational concerns, even if the focus of study is on the relationship between organisational arrangements and policy.

In this paper, therefore, we first state what 'implementation' means to us as a conceptual tool for theorising about practice and we then describe briefly the framework used in our research. After some background information on the nature of the inner cities policy initiative, we then illustrate the application of our theoretical approach to inner cities policy.

Implementation

It would be possible to define implementation in three ways (Healey *et al*, 1981):

i. as the relapse to pragmatism, an anti-theoretical position justified by the need to 'get something done';

ii. as an analytic category within a procedural approach, where there is a rational sequential, hierarchical model of the planning process within which implementation comes at the end/bottom. The apparently diminishing efficacy of public policy suggests that something is wrong with the procedural chain of events leading from policy to action and that clear communication, more specific guidance, tighter controls from the beginning/top will suffice;

iii. as the expression of micro-organisational behaviour, explaining the way policies are defined and used, how resources are allocated and the outcome of these activities. Central themes are rules and discretion, organisational and professional culture, bargaining and negotiation.

Pragmatism is seen by Healey *et al* (1981) as oppositional to procedural theory whilst 'policy and implementation' - summarised in the terms of (iii) above - is developmental of procedural theory with studies of implementation being labelled and categorised into the procedural mode. We do not follow this over-simplified line of argument. Whilst it is true that an implementation perspective does identify and use the concepts outlined in (iii) above, and thus does begin to develop the simplistic policy-implementation model of procedural theory, we would argue that a more appropriate perspective is one which goes further in viewing implementation as a process of generating policy change. An implementation perspective, therefore, not merely focuses on *action, reaction or response*, where the nature of organisations and their behaviour influences the differential scope for action and the use made of this scope within a given policy; it also focuses on the *politics of policy* and views implementation as the continuous negotiation and renegotiation of position between a range of interests. Thus, ideology and values, and power and resources, are recognised as key determinants of the form and outcome of the 'negotiation' (or exchange or bargain or whatever form the relationship between two or more interests may take).

We are aware that the concepts embodied in the term 'politics of policy' have pluralist connotations. Certainly, this has limitations in that much of the work that has been done on implementation as a negotiation/bargaining process has focused on what *is* negotiable and consequently almost inevitably has adopted a pluralist stance. Many of the associated concepts were also developed in intra-organisational studies and, again almost inevitably, were 'contextless'. However, subsequent work has moved on from this position, in part as a result of examining relationships *between* organisations, and has recognised that it is also important to account for what is *not* negotiable and how this affects the nature of the policy implementation process (Barrett and Fudge, 1981).

Our own approach to policy and implementation seeks to accommodate this direction of thinking by recognising the structural constraints to policy development and to 'planning' action. These constraints may be observed in a variety of forms: as the emergence of a symbolic rather than substantive policy (Edelman, 1977); as the non-taking of decisions on key issues in the policy debate (Bachrach and Baratz, 1970); or as the influence of deeper value structures upon the exercise of power (Lukes, 1974). Thus, whilst starting our work from observation of practice in inner city areas, we are concerned about how the structure of interests embedded in the policy sector and represented in the organisational arrangements for inner cities set limits to the policy and implementation processes.

Within this general stance, and given the multi-organisational nature of the inner cities initiative and the variety of interests represented, we have found a useful heuristic framework to be a development of that put forward by Benson (1980).

Central to this is the concept of the 'policy sector' which Benson defines as an arena in which public policies are decided and implemented, characterised by complexes of inter-organisational resource dependencies. Two aspects of the policy sector are significant to us. First, the question of the definition of the sector and in particular its boundaries - how are these established, by whom can they be changed, in what circumstances? In practice a major source of organisational power is the ability to amend or alter the boundaries of the policy sector. Second, we are interested in the competition for space within the sector as organisations seek to give themselves elbow room for more autonomous (or collaborative) action.

Within a policy sector (again drawing on Benson) we can distinguish a number of levels of analysis each of which is constrained by the existence and operation of the 'higher' levels.

i. *The organisational structure* including:
   - the formal administrative linkages and control relationships between the organisations in the policy sector (including relationships between levels of government);
   - the patterns of resource dependencies between organisations which are functionally related to the policy substance and administrative structures and which can be considered as the 'order' which is 'negotiated' as a result of informal behavioural factors as well as more structured features;
   - the substantive content or policy orientation which is to be inferred from actual practices rather than declarations of intent.

ii. *The interest structure* - consisting of the interests embedded in the administrative arrangements and policy commitments of the sector. This we suggest may be explored through an examination of the process of negotiation which takes place over time, concerning both organisational arrangements and policy substance. It is here that we can begin to identify the power structures which are important to an understanding of the third level of analysis.

iii. *The rules of structure formation* - operating in and on the policy sector and setting limits to the operation of the other levels in terms of the relative power accorded to institutions in the sector. These 'rules' are generated by the requirements of the larger social formation.

Much of our research activity concentrates on the first two levels of analysis. Nevertheless, in adopting a framework which explicitly forces links to be made between different levels of analysis we would argue that our perspective on implementation is more than a mere development of procedural approaches to planning and policy making. This does not mean that we ignore the exercise of discretion within work situations defined by rules, organisation cultures, professional cultures and the interplay of interests. We regard as central "the significance of bargaining over resources, the negotiability of rules, directives, and policy guidance, and the conflicting demands placed on individuals and groups" (Healey *et al*, 1981).

We believe, however, that theoretical understanding - relating for example to patterns of organisational differentiation and control, resource allocation, local political systems - needs to be set within an understanding of a specific socio-historical situation and needs to articulate the relationship between economic activities, social organisation processes of social change and the nature and role of government. We would argue that a sufficiently open approach to the nature of policy and implementation, viewing implementation as one element in the politics of change and recognising policy as being subject to a range of environmental determinants, implies an approach which, as Healey *et al* (1981) suggest as desirable, "is able to relate broad economic and political forces to the detailed operation of government policy in the urban field ... a complete reversal of the contextless character of procedural planning theory".

Inner cities policy

Inner cities policy in general and the partnership/programme arrangements in particular have to be viewed within the historical context of a series of area-based policies since the late 1960s aimed at tackling problems of 'deprivation'. These are well documented elsewhere (Hambleton, 1981; Batley and Edwards, 1978), with emphasis given to two particular failings. First, there was a fragmentation of effort with departments at both local and central governmental level often pursuing their own particular initiatives at best in isolation from one another but on occasions in competition. Second, the early initiatives were focused either solely on the physical problems of particular areas or upon the characteristics (often seen as failings) of the particular populations living in the areas.

In the 1970s some lessons were learned, notably from the reports of the Community Development Projects, but also from the desk and action research of the Birmingham, Lambeth and Liverpool Inner Area Studies. These studies emphasised the need not only to see 'inner area' change as part of a broader process of economic and social change in society as a whole but also to understand the problems of 'inner areas' in structural as opposed to 'pathological' or individual-based terms. These structural arguments were understood, interpreted, and acted upon in different ways by different bodies. At central government level, the response was the announcement of a further initiative comprising the 'enhancement' of the Urban Programme with wider aims and a transfer of responsibility from the Home Office to the Department of the Environment and Welsh Office. This was accompanied in June 1977 by the White Paper *Policy for the inner city*. This partially recognised the structural questions by laying emphasis on *economic* problems and policies - the enhanced urban programme would be used to support economic and environmental projects as well as social ones, legislation would be passed to assist authorities to counter disinvestment and employment run down in inner areas, and the private sector would 'play its part'. On the *administrative* side the government announced its intention of entering into special arrangements, known as partnerships, with the county and district authorities and the health authorities of the most deprived cities with the object, first, of bringing together within one set of administrative arrangements the range of agencies responsible for action in the inner areas of those cities, and second, of redirecting main policies and programmes in favour of inner city areas.

The development of the policy has been documented elsewhere (Hambleton, 1981; Hambleton, Stewart and Underwood, 1980). Within the first two years the emphasis was on the establishment of the 'partnership' arrangements and the preparation of Inner Area Programmes in 7 partnerships and 15 other 'programme' areas. At the outset, the hallmark of the policy was its selectivity - discrimination in favour of particular groups of people and areas - and its variety and sensitivity to local circumstances as established through the work of the local partnership and programme administrative structures. At the same time central government regarded it as necessary, on grounds of rational planning, value for money, and accountability, to have some basis for making their allocations (£106 million of the £165 million urban programme allocations in 1979/80 went to partnership and programme authorities), and so safeguarding the use of public money. Thus the mechanism of the programme - the strategic statement together with a bid for resources - was borrowed from neighbouring policy areas such as Transport Policies and Programmes (TPPs) and Housing Strategies and Investment Programmes (HIPs) and seemed at the outset to encourage many authorities to carry out work on the assessment of needs and priorities, work which they themselves recognised was overdue.

Variety was, then, built into the application of the policy both explicitly and purposively, and also implicitly and more surreptitiously as the parties to the 'partnership' concept brought their own histories, perspectives and objectives to bear on the development of policy. This makes generalisation about organisational arrangements and the processes of planning difficult and it became clear that the situation in each area was different (Hambleton, Stewart and Underwood, 1980).

The basic distinction between partnership and programme areas was that the former possessed an additional formal layer in their structure - the Partnership Committee - which brought central government ministers directly into contact with the development of the policy at the local level. With the passage of time there was some disappointment at the degree of actual involvement which had occurred and the apparent confirmation of this by a 'streamlining' or reduction of the scale and frequency of meetings. A similar trend towards less involvement of central government officials, apart from Department of the Environment officials, was also apparent in the officer steering groups. Below these higher level groups there tended to be a variety of standing working groups which initially were concerned not only with developing and assessing specific projects for inclusion in the programme of urban programme funded schemes, but also with the redefinition and exploration of 'inner city problems' and a review of existing policies. These groups were usually topic-based and included representatives from other relevant agencies, with in some cases the involvement of the voluntary and private sectors.

The key distinguishing features of the programme areas were the lack of central government involvement in the formulation of the policy programme and the smaller urban programme allocation available. As a consequence, whilst most of the programme authorities took the development of initiatives seriously, they did not with a few exceptions see fit to develop a sophisticated bureaucratic machinery to deal with the policy programme. Instead, existing working arrangements were used or adapted, and there was less proliferation of special working groups.

In both partnership and programme areas, it was clear that the scale of the policy review task required, and the speed with which it had to be accomplished in the first year, had consequences for the philosophy of the policy and a lasting impact on the form and content of the planning system. A tendency to focus on a programme of individual projects and schemes rather than on a broader review of policy and attempts to 'bend' main programmes was confirmed by the change of direction following the 1979 central government election. On the substantive policy side this heralded a greater emphasis on economic and environmental initiatives at the expense of those addressing social deprivation; and on the administrative side it heralded a greater degree of intervention by central government to ensure financial accountability to overall policy goals by checking the appropriateness and acceptability of individual schemes. Hence, whilst local variation continued to exist, the balance of power between local interests was altered by the changes of direction at central level.

Application of the theoretical perspective to inner cities policy

The policy sector

Benson(1980) defines the policy sector as "an arena in which public policies are decided and implemented ... conventionally conceived with labels that are part of the public debate". The identification of what is 'conventionally conceived' as a policy and the policy label idea reflect the fact that the nature of policy is often highly ambiguous (Hill *et al*, 1979) and that the policy 'message' can be blurred and confused (Hambleton, 1981).

With these questions in mind the 'policy sector' can be looked at in three ways. What explains the emergence of the policy? What are the attributes or characteristics of the policy? What are the implications of the birth and nature of the policy for implementation given that we define implementation as a process of generating policy change?

i. *The emergence of policy*

There are two levels at which this can be discussed. First, the question (which we briefly return to later) of why there is an inner cities policy at all - or why there is planning/public intervention at all - and what is its function? Second, why did the particular initiative emerge in 1977 in the form it did? There is a growing literature on the policy agenda (Solesbury, 1976) and it is possible to suggest the reasons why inner cities got on to, or moved up, the agenda in the 1970s. Momentum was given by the series of initiatives since the late 1960s. The impetus given by the Conservatives (who initiated the Inner Areas Studies) was transmitted to and carried forward by the Labour government who were thus in a general position of having to sustain a sympathy on inner cities/deprivation as well as in a particular position of having to respond to the Inner Area Studies of Birmingham, Lambeth and Liverpool. There was therefore the need to do something, symbolic or otherwise, as well as the recognition - if not a radical interpretation - of the arguments about the structural as opposed to the pathological nature of inner city 'problems'. In addition, with the tardy arrival of the 1971 Census data, there was a greater awareness of the population and employment shifts taking place and of the resource problems of the inner districts of the metropolitan counties. More broadly there was the traditional Labour anti-New Town feeling shifting attention back to existing urban areas together with the ill-articulated feeling that since comprehensive redevelopment had failed the older areas perhaps they deserved another chance. Above all there were recurrent fears about social order as the racial tensions which had stimulated the 1960s interest in cities re-emerged as National Front activity and achieved a scale and visibility not seen for some years. It is not difficult to argue that a policy was required in the light of symptoms such as these. The question is rather how far were the pressures for a policy correctly understood or interpreted and consequently how appropriate were the policies and programmes conceived?

ii. *The attributes of policy*

The options for policy were constrained so that the emergence of inner cities policy in 1977 reflected a variety of the pressures operating on government. The aims of the policy as expressed in the White Paper (1977) together with the government's proposals for action reflected the view that the initiative needed to address economic issues and to offer new administrative arrangements, but underlying the specific proposals it is possible to identify broader constraints on policy. First, it is clear that the policy would not be able to claim many resources. Whilst the Urban Programme was enhanced the level of funds remained in absolute terms small, and the emphasis was placed on resource allocation via the bending of main programmes - the attempted pre-emption of existing programme resources. Second, it is clear that in the face of a known difficult and intransigent problem - inner area decline - the policy sought shared responsibility. If there was anything in the coordinated, unified approach then results would be achieved but if the policy were to be a failure the blame would be shared. Hence partnership, which involved all and absolved any one participant from total responsibility, but also reflected a set of consensual values about the nature of the problem and the appropriate responses. The co-option of varied interests, and the belief that there is or was a common concern, to which all these interests could subscribe, about what was to be done, how it was to be done and who was to do it, raised important theoretical questions about pluralism, corporatism, and the role of the state which we discuss later. More specifically we can see that a required attribute of the policy was its visibility given the need to be seen to be doing something. With limited financial and administrative resources, government could only become involved with some authorities, and so the special arrangements for a few areas and the selective partnership approach were developed. Finally, there was the necessity for administrative convenience and, despite the spirit of partnership, the distancing of central from local government. This necessity produced the 'programme' procedures, akin to the HIPs and TPP procedures previously developed by government, and reinforced the bidding-allocation relationship of central to local government. There is a good deal of evidence (Hambleton, 1981; Hambleton, Stewart and Underwood, 1980) that the existence of a programme mode of implementation has determined the approach to policy development and imposed a more explicitly administrative and bureaucratic style upon the policy than need have been the case.

iii. *The implications for the 'policy sector'*

From this discussion four points emerge which clarify the nature of the inner cities policy sector. First, the boundaries of the policy are drawn wide both in terms of substantive areas and organisational involvement. Inner cities policy is a meta-policy: a policy about other main programme policies as they affect inner areas, and an aspiration to influence and shift a whole range of activities. All contributors are welcome - central and local government, other public bodies, the non-statutory sector, the private sector; no-one is excluded but in consequence no-one is clearly responsible. The policy is the property of no-one and as we argued above this has benefits as well as costs. Related to this there is an ambiguity of goals. Inevitably a policy as all-embracing as inner cities will have vague broad goals (making inner cities better places to live and work) and multiple and often conflicting specific goals. It is not clear how far the policy is about economic change or about social development; whether resources are to be concentrated or dispersed (geographically or to recipients); whether the intended beneficiaries are the residents of inner areas or prospective newcomers; or whether the object is short-term remedial mopping-up or long-term change. Ambiguities of this type, inevitable as they are, desirable even in order to allow locally appropriate strategies to develop, encourage an atmosphere of uncertainty within the policy and clearly heighten the potential for the processes of redefinition and interpretation which have been evident both overall and at a local level. The third point is that whilst the breadth and openness of the policy and the ambiguity of its goals mean that there is little or no conflict over who can be involved with the policy (everybody can, whilst nobody has to be) this leaves a good deal of space *within* the boundaries of the policy for different organisations to compete for the resources such as they are and the power and influence, if any, endowed. Thus there are initial expressions of commitment to the policy followed by the stages of adoption, adaptation and exploitation to meet sectional interests. Fourth, the policy is widely perceived as being vulnerable, uncertain and largely symbolic, and there is widespread cynicism about its utility (although the money is still sought after). Although in practice the policy proved fairly robust in its early years this was precisely because of its opaque nature and because the consensus-based values of the partnership concept were widely acceptable.

It is indeed because the policy sector is so diffuse, so all embracing, and so opaque that it is the implementation process which sheds light on the politics of the policy and on the values and purposes which underlie the policy. We turn, therefore, to the three levels of analysis which are suggested in the Benson framework.

Administration and practice

i. *Administrative arrangements*

As defined by Benson these are the "patterns of differentiation and control over activities in a policy sector ... a set of rules according to which activities are divided ... the extent of control and the bases of control exercised". The arrangements established for implementing inner cities policy (described briefly earlier and more fully in Hambleton, Stewart and Underwood, 1980) can be analysed in terms of the differentiation between stages of the annual process (preparation of programme, submission, approval, implementation, review) and which organisations exercise control at different stages, or between different functions (eg the policy making, planning and intelligence, resource provision, mediating and coordination, service provision, evaluation of Hjern and Porter (1981)). The breadth of the initiative leads to a rather disorderly division of labour between the various activities within the policy sector and the researchers intended to clarify first the 'pool of organisations' involved before grouping them according to division of labour and location of control. This task was seen to be relatively simple for the clearly defined programme tasks, less easy for the vaguer initiatives with the private sector. The intention was then to follow through a variety of networks in the system (Healey and Underwood, 1978) noting the significant functions of networks for information flow, resource exchange and bargaining, and the transmission of norms and expectations. By recognising the significance of inter-personal and inter-organisational networks for the operation of these interest-based functions the authors planned to link the practice of inner cities planning and implementation to broader levels of analysis.

ii. *Inter-organisational resource dependencies*

Benson lays emphasis on the interdependence of organisations (the intersection of their policy domains) as a cause of inter-organisational collaboration or exchange of resources although he also recognises the significance of power differentials in maintaining or breaking down resource dependencies. In his analysis of planning systems and implementation Hambleton (1981), drawing on Van Meter and Van Horn (1975), argues that resource availability may promote implementation activity towards central aims, distort it towards the ends of implementers, or merely ensure that the administration of resources becomes an end in itself. The nature of the administrative arrangements - that is, for example, the existence or otherwise of block grants, specific project controls, guidelines for action, discretionary powers, accounting mechanisms etc - determines the nature of the dependency arising from resource availability. Inner cities policy offers numerous examples of the way in which promotion, distortion, and administration have occurred: the guidelines set out for voluntary projects in some local areas, the informal advice on programmes from regional offices, the excision of particular projects by individual ministers, the diversion of inner city funds to traditional lines of activity. Dependency, however, is not solely embedded in formal resource arrangements and control and discretion are not simple administrative functions. The researchers intended to make use, therefore, of the concept of 'negotiated order' (Strauss, 1978; Barrett and Fudge, 1981), to understand the (temporary) states of interdependence between organisations that are arrived at by negotiation, bargaining and compromise. There is of course a danger in focusing on negotiations in isolation from their context. Barrett and Fudge remind us that the policy environment plays an important part in the dynamics of power relations in setting the rules of the game or determining how and when the rules get changed whilst Strauss himself, has added concepts of 'structured context' and 'structural properties' which go wider than the negotiating context.

In terms of inner cities policy, the game was a fairly new one, the rules experimental (and largely unwritten), the referee a player as well as arbiter, the number of players unspecified, the length of the game variable, and the method of scoring not agreed. There was, therefore, considerable scope for moving behind the formal administrative arrangements to investigate:

- what inner cities policy in three case study authorities comprised;

- who this policy/these policies belonged to and who had a stake in them;

- how far inner city policies were related to what was going on previous to the inner city initiative;

- what were the traditions of negotiations (and the prior networks of negotiators) which may have influenced attitudes to the negotiation process *and* the policy;

- what was the complexity of negotiations - how many people were involved, from how many agencies (power/resource basis);

- what was the overt/covert nature of negotiations, eg where were the real bargains struck, as opposed to any wider process of consultation;

- whether resource dependency patterns were being constructed, maintained or changed.

iii. *The policy orientation*

Benson argues here that the policy sector has, or takes on, an orientation which is "evident in practices. ... Declarations of policy intent are quite imperfect guides ... useful as indications of assumptions and values widely shared in the sector". This mirrors his definition of the 'official' policy sector as that which is conventionally labelled arena, and our own position that practice offers the most useful insights into the meaning and purpose of policy. In research terms this means distinguishing between the various levels of rhetoric about the policy, the various accounts of justifications for practices, and the reality of those practices. Inference from practice is not inference from accounts of practice, though each have their own usefulness. It is quite clear to us that what is said about inner cities *policy* in many cases bears little relation to what is proposed in the way of programmes and projects, and for a variety of reasons, what actually happens in programmes and projects itself bears little relation to what was proposed. Thus monitoring and evaluation have become highly problematic tasks.

The interest structure

In arguing for a very grounded knowledge of administration and practice we acknowledged that organisational interaction, resource bargaining and the like were subject to both formal and informal arrangements and that both kinds of arrangement embodied power and interest in some way. Thus the interest structure consists of those interests embedded in the policy sector. Benson has conceived of various groups - demand groups, support groups, administrative groups, provider groups, and coordinating groups - in a categorisation of interests which is probably more helpful for some policy sectors (eg health) than for others, particularly inner cities.

We conceive of several ways of classifying the interests represented in the partnership and programme initiative. One is by institutional differentiation. Elsewhere (Hambleton, Stewart and Underwood, 1980) we have identified the interests of central government (ministers and officials), local government (councillors and officers), other agencies, the voluntary sector, the private sector and so forth. Alternatively one might develop a classification similar to Benson's which identified consumers (residents, workers, etc), producers (service departments or executive agencies), policy makers, lobbies, resource controllers. The difficulty, as with all pluralist models, is that the groups are not exclusive and it is clear, for example, that some local government officers fall within most categories. Given our emphasis on inner cities policy as an administratively constrained power struggle it is probably easier to recognise the existence of different sets of interests and to attempt to identify the collaboration and/or conflict between the members of these sets. One set, for example, would be the institutional set identified above (the formal organisations involved with the policy). Another would be the set of professional interests (valuation, planning, education, social work, etc to which might be added the inner city 'professional' working for an inner city unit). A further set would contain interests clustered around particular areas of action - the local economy, the environment, law and order, housing, etc. Again there are interests clustered around particular forms of provision of services - such as those who favour private provision, traditional local authority provision, innovatory local authority provision, self help, or voluntary organisation provision. All these types of interest are well represented within the inner cities initiative and different local areas see different combinations of interest (eg the voluntary movement is involved to very different degrees in different areas). The channels for exercising power also vary from the formal to the informal and we can see both the politics of action and the politics of non-action. Some interests are challenged, some reinforced. What is important to note, however, is that the nature of the inner cities policy sector makes the understanding of the interest structure more complex. This is because the boundaries of the policy are so wide and the interests so many that no one interest is likely to be either totally excluded from the policy sector or totally contained within it. Thus the inner cities sector will never be the sole arena within which an interest is being expressed. Three simple examples illustrate this. The central/local relationship cannot be analysed in terms of inner cities alone, since so much of inner city debate reflects the general relationship as it is affected by other factors (eg grant arrangements, or public expenditure control). A particular voluntary organisation will view the inner cities initiative as a possible source of funds, but its expression of interest in those funds and thus its commitment, willingness to collaborate, vulnerability or whatever will be dependent on whether it is also likely to get funds from say the EEC and how it expresses its interests to Brussels. Finally, and crucially, local authorities and central departments have their own policies and programmes and have extensive political, financial, professional and administrative resources tied up in those 'main' programmes. Their interest may in part be exercised within the inner cities policy sector but will in part be exercised elsewhere.

Rules of structure formation

Our discussion of interest structures and the administration and practice whereby they are expressed implies an open local political system, which allows competition and conflict between a variety of interests. We have recognised at various points that this pluralist view is a limited one and that there are constraints to the capacity of the political process, formal and informal, to admit and respond to the pressure of particular interests. In

Benson's terms this is a recognition of the existence of 'rules of structure formation', rules which set limits on the extent to which there is scope for change within or between particular policy sectors. He sees these limits as resulting in part from the tension between policy sectors, an example in our context being the tension between inner cities policy (aiming to channel resources to particular areas of cities) and industrial policies (seeking to encourage investment and growth wherever they are possible).

The structural rules preclude the concentration of regional aid or industrial assistance to inner areas. Structure formation rules also operate, however, upon all sectors and are generated by the requirements of the social formation, determining the particular role which will be played by government (or governments at different levels) and by the state. Different theories of the state offer different interpretations of the level and nature of the autonomy open to the 'local interests' apparently represented in the inner cities initiative. We consider it important to relate particular insights about the organisational arrangements for inner cities policy to these different interpretations and to assess the consistency between various theories of the state (which give indications about what sets the rules of structure formation) and the theoretical perspectives that can be applied at various levels.

At present three interpretations suggest themselves. First, and consistent with the general themes of competition, interest, and bargaining pervading this paper, one can consider how far the inner cities policy offers a vehicle for local pluralism, a system of interest representation in which the participants are allowed fair and open access to the political system under the auspices of a neutral and independent state. Whilst we have identified the inner cities policy space as having very wide boundaries and as offering extensive scope for individual and group pressure within it, we believe, as others such as Newton (1976) have suggested, that the rules of structure formation are likely to reflect only a limited and partial pluralism. More attractive seems a second perspective which sees inner cities policy as a form of local corporatism. Thus the policy is less an arena for the competition of contending interests and much more a specific vehicle for incorporating and legitimating (licensing) the interests of a few. The state establishes the structure within which the 'partners' come together to determine the future course of action, and indeed the state chooses which interests are to be involved with the policy. The emphasis in most corporatist writing on order, certainty, unity and coordination, the rejection of ideology in favour of neutrality, the recognition of "the pragmatic, opportunistic, informal and non-bureaucratic nature of corporatism" (Reade, 1980) all seem to fit inner cities policy reasonably well. Equally the emphasis in the policy on economic questions (investment in the inner city, improved infrastructure, training facilities) matches the direction of most corporatist activity which is regarded as being directed towards ensuring the continued viability of the economy. Enterprise zones, local enterprise trusts and advice services for small firms all reinforce the view of the inner cities initiative as local corporatism.

A third perspective on the role of the state in inner cities policy would allow the coexistence of corporatism and pluralism. The rules of structure formation would tightly constrain the functions of the policy in relation to production, that is constrain the autonomy of local interests in respect of social investment (O'Connor, 1973) whilst allowing a more competitive, pluralist approach to allocative decisions and consumption (Saunders, 1978). The inner cities arrangements deal with both production and consumption related programmes and projects and in some cases the organisational structure is differentiated to distinguish between the two whilst in other areas it is not. Again the involvement of central and local government and their relative concern for particular production or consumption aspects of the programme varies from region to region and from one partnership area to another. We would argue that it is only by fairly detailed research on the particular form and content of inner cities policy as it is reflected in practice that it is possible to develop a view about the appropriateness of this particular interpretation of the state as a coexistence of corporatist and pluralist systems.

Indeed the last thought represents our main conclusion on the contribution of theory to understanding the nature of inner cities policy. We consider that different theoretical perspectives can be used to explain the same phenomena at different levels of generality and abstraction. What is important, therefore, is less the choice of theory or theories (this will always be the consequence of personal preference) and more the attention paid to consistency in the use of theories at different levels of explanation.

Acknowledgements

This paper was drafted early on in an SSRC Central/Local Relations Panel sponsored project on inner cities policy. The paper drew on previous work on inner cities at SAUS, as well as on collaborative work carried out on other projects with colleagues at Bristol. The authors would like to acknowledge in particular the help of Sue Barrett, Robin Hambleton and especially Gill Whitting.

References

Bachrach, P. and Baratz, M.S. (1970) *Power and poverty, theory and practice*, Oxford: Oxford University Press.

Barrett, S. and Fudge, C. (eds) (1981) *Policy and action*, London: Methuen.

Batley, R. and Edwards, J. (1978) *The politics of positive discrimination*, Tavistock.

Benson, J.K. (1975) 'The inter-organisational network on political economy', *Administrative Science Quarterly*, vol 20, pp 229-49.

Edelman, M. (1977) *Political language: words that succeed and policies that fail*, New York: Academic Press.

Hambleton, R. (1981) 'Policy planning systems and implementation: some implications for planning theory', Paper to Planning theory in the 1980s conference, Oxford.

Hambleton, R., Stewart, M. and Underwood, J. (1980) *Inner cities: management and resources*, Working Paper 13, Bristol: SAUS Publications, School for Advanced Urban Studies, University of Bristol.

Healey, P. and Underwood, J. (1979) *Professional ideals and planning practice*, Oxford: Pergamon.

Healey, P., McDougall, G. and Thomas, M.J. (eds) (1982) *Planning theory: prospects for the 1980s*, Oxford: Pergamon.

Healey, P., McDougall, G. and Thomas, M.J. (1981) 'Theoretical debates in planning: towards a coherent dialogue', Paper presented to Planning theory in the 1980s conference, Oxford.

Hill, M.J. et al (1979) 'Implementation and the central-local relationship', in *Central-local government relationships*, SSRC.

Hjern, B. and Porter, D.O. (1981) 'Implementation structure: a new unit of administrative analysis', *Organisation Studies*, no 1.

Lukes, S. (1974) *Power: a radical view*, London: Macmillan.

Newton, K. (1976) *Second city politics: democratic process and decision making in Birmingham*, London: Oxford University Press.

O'Connor, J. (1973) *The fiscal crisis of the state*, New York: St James Press.

Reade, E.J. (1980) 'Town planning and the 'corporation thesis', S.I.P. Paper 10.

Saunders, P. (1979) 'Community power, urban managerialism and the 'local state", Paper presented to Urban Change and Conflict conference, Nottingham.

Solesbury, W. (1976) 'The environmental agenda', *Public Administration*, vol 54, pp 379-97.

Strauss, A. (1978) *Negotiation, values, contexts, processes and social order*, San Francisco: Jossey-Bass.

Van Meter D.S. and Van Horn, C.E. (1975) 'The policy implementation process: a conceptual framework', *Administration and Society*, vol 6, no 4, pp 445-88.

CHAPTER 7

THE SIGNIFICANCE OF URBAN ECONOMIC DEVELOPMENT PROGRAMMES

KEN YOUNG AND CHARLIE MASON

Introduction

The restructuring of advanced industrial societies is producing dramatic spatial consequences in the de-industrialisation of cities and the industrialisation of fringe and rural areas. Britain, of all the European nations, has experienced this process the most acutely, although not on a scale comparable with the United States (Hall and Hay, 1981). Our foremost concern in this chapter is not, however, with the de-industrialisation process itself, nor with the ways in which it makes itself felt at the urban level. Rather, our focus is on the responses of city governments to its least tolerable consequences. Among these are a declining fiscal base, rising welfare costs, physical obsolescence and dereliction, and the loss of industrial activity leading to high levels of unemployment in the manufacturing sector.

Of all the aspects of change, falling manufacturing employment provides the greatest single stimulus to intervention in the urban economy. As unemployment has slipped from its pre-eminent place on the national policy agenda in favour of the control of inflation it has, paradoxically, become one of the foremost concerns of local government. This 'mismatch' of concern generates a conflict of interest between central and local government (see Young and Mills, 1982).

The formulation by local authorities of programmes for economic development is in itself no novelty. Many of the activities in which they engage are long established, despite the rhetoric of innovation in which they are often cloaked. We have tried to address the issue of how far these programmes for urban economic development have brought about or arisen from changing relationships between and within governmental agencies, and between the public and the private sectors. Our overall concern has been with these changes and their consequences; in short, with the operations and role of local government in its attempts to manage the mixed economy of the city.

This chapter first appeared in K. Young and C. Mason (eds) *Urban economic development: new roles and relationships*, 1983, Basingstoke: Macmillan.

This chapter aims to focus attention on three questions. First, are economic development programmes intended to serve welfare or the market? Second, are the economic development activities of local government really substantive or merely symbolic? Third, are not all interventions in the urban economy swimming against the inexorable tide of metropolitan decline?

Welfare versus the market?

The concern of national governments with economic issues has increasingly centred on questions of efficiency and competitiveness, to the extent that the welfare concerns of the 1944 White Paper on employment seem a dim memory. In their exhortations to local planning authorities successive governments have stressed the need to take local decisions in the light of national needs. The theme was notably expounded in the late 1970s in the Circular on local government and the industrial strategy and in the White Paper on the inner cities (see Chapter 6). Circular 22/80 was more explicit, reflecting the climate of the early 1980s; it proclaims that "the planning system should play a helpful part in rebuilding the economy" and should not obstruct "the economic regeneration of the country" (Department of the Environment, 1980).

Circular 22/80 was an explicit token of the national preoccupation with efficiency and competitiveness. Since the 1960s the restructuring of key industries was actively promoted by government regardless of its spatial consequences. In the early 1980s, it was becoming clear that the older cities had borne the brunt of restructuring and had to meet - in both financial and human terms - the welfare costs of market goals (Massey and Meegan, 1978; Lawless, 1981). Here surely is an ineradicable conflict of interest. Few would dispute the propriety of a national-level concern with macro-level competitiveness. Its corollary is, however, that the local interest in welfare should aim to maintain employment and income and legitimately seek to retard the process of change, if only in the hope of buying time in which to ease the transition. Even this modest local aim begs the question of transition to what? The rhetoric of post-industrialism paints a picture of an urban future in the tertiary, quaternary and quinary sectors, reflecting the macro-level shifts in the sectoral structure of the economy (see Kumar, 1978; Hall, 1981). It should be clear that for most of the older industrial cities the prospect of so neat a substitution remains exceedingly dim. It is a dangerous temptation to confuse macro processes with micro, and local problems with national needs.

Local authorities understandably decline to define their local problems in terms of national economic imperatives. They are naturally more sensitive to the pressures which they experience directly: to serve the welfare of their local people by stemming employment decline; to secure the fiscal base and maximise their resources; and to reduce the physical and psychological blight of industrial dereliction. The almost universal justification of such measures as are taken - whether to build small factory estates or to promote the investment image of a locality - is the relief, directly or indirectly, of unemployment. Welfare is apparently the foremost concern.

It is not surprising that the welfare consequences of urban economic decline should loom so large. Disadvantaged groups - the school leaver, the unskilled, the long-term unemployed, the redundant worker - are unable to compete in the labour market. Minority ethnic groups and women, who themselves may belong to one or more of these categories, may suffer additional discrimination against their employment. At the same time, the quality of employment, the conditions of employment and the returns to employment have continued to deteriorate.

Local authorities as 'need-meeting' agencies might be expected to give priority to tackling these consequences of restructuring and recession. Yet at the same time, due to the parallel process of decline in the urban fiscal base and new and more stringent controls on local expenditure, their ability to tackle welfare problems of this magnitude is severely eroded (Rose and Page, 1982). Nor is this all. Local authorities claim to provide no more than a welfare net of the coarsest kind.

The ultimate responsibility for the maintenance of family income lies not with them but with the national system of social security. Moreover (and for our purposes more important) a closer look at local authority programmes for employment reveals that they are *not* characteristically targeted on the needs of the most vulnerable groups. Rather, it seems, a concern for employment justifies interventions that serve welfare less directly than the needs of the market itself. Welfare concerns are on this view a symbolic rather than a substantive aspect of local economic development programmes.

Symbol or substance?

The intelligent citizen has long been aware that a large part of governmental activity is symbolic rather than substantive. The basic distinction is familiar to those who have never encountered Walter Bagehot, Georges Sorel, Graham Wallas or Murray Edelman. It would, however, be a gross mistake to assume that because local economic development programmes are dignified by appeals to welfare symbolism, they necessarily conceal the workings of an 'efficient' concern with market effectiveness. Rather, the very actions themselves may be symbolic, and express no more than a felt need to act and to be seen to be acting.

Faced with their immediate economic crises, local policy makers respond to the imperative to act. The most potent argument in a novel setting is 'well, we must do something' (Young and Mills, 1983). Policy statements, new machinery and the allocation of fresh resources are almost self-justifying when they are decided upon in a climate of acute and rising public concern. There is little room for the iconoclast who asks for a firmer rationale than the comfort of 'doing something'. There are two evident problems in self-justified action. The first is that action tends to run far ahead of analysis. The second is that the political costs of monitoring and evaluating the effects of action may be seen as unacceptably high.

There is no shortage of action in this field and in some areas there is considerable expenditure on economic development programmes. Both have evidently increased over time, if from a rather higher initial base than is commonly supposed. There is far less evidence of this activity being directed towards clearly established problems in the local economy. Research and intelligence tends to follow action rather than to lead it. As such, it tends to be used descriptively, to quantify the problem to which policy is already addressed (and so to legitimate the policy) rather than analytically, to identify the problems to which policy might be addressed.

Local economic policies are not peculiar in this regard. Most attempts to define 'the natural history of social problems' emphasise the political and non-rational elements in the problem definition/intelligence/action relationships (see Young and Mills, 1983; Spector and Kitsuse, 1977). Particularly in areas where urgent solutions to perceived problems are sought, action comes first and research is used to underscore it. This is not a role that research and intelligence units welcome. On the other hand, their own involvement in economic affairs will sometimes prove an embarrassment as they seek to redefine the issues and pose new policy goals. Yet research and intelligence is often tangential to the main streams of policy determination, and some of the most professional and prolific research teams coexist with executive units whose policies and practices are impervious to the counterarguments of research. This disjuncture is perhaps especially evident where strong, freewheeling industrial development teams operate, perhaps recruited in part from the private sector.

Where there is a clear policy line it is likely to be maintained regardless of intelligence. Where there is not, research and intelligence personnel may have more opportunity to redefine the economic problem and contribute to a research-based strategy. It is, however, in just such circumstances that the gap between policy and action may be at its widest. Here we find policy waived and issues 'decided on their merits' - that is, in accordance with political and organisational power.

The second aspect of symbolic action is the deep-seated reluctance to monitor and assess the impact of economic policies. Monitoring is often dismissed as a costly and academic irrelevance. The stridency of the dismissal suggests a tacit recognition that many economic initiatives could not survive a rigorous monitoring exercise. It is still possible to encounter industrial development units who accept firms' projections of future employment growth, render financial assistance accordingly, and then provide an arithmetical justification of their activities in terms of impressively low estimates of the per capita costs of employment creation. The imperative not to monitor seems as powerful as the imperative to act, and in this respect local economic programmes share a sense of vulnerability with the far more stringently applied Department of Industry schemes (Comptroller and Auditor-General, 1981).

The precedence of symbol over substance also encourages policy makers to turn a blind eye to the increasingly apparent overlap and competition of agencies and programmes. Any evaluation of the substantive impact of local schemes of assistance would have to take a wider view than the bilateral authority-firm relationship. It would have to take into account the whole pattern of financial assistance and the true opportunity costs to the authority of any one decision to assist a firm. Such an assessment would be admittedly difficult. A major metropolitan area will possess a complex 'policy map' with possible variations in assisted area status being overlaid by variations in status under the Inner Urban Areas Act and subsequent legislation. There will be a scattering of industrial improvement areas, of estates constructed by the county, the districts or English Industrial Estates, with perhaps an enterprise zone to further complicate the pattern of available assistance and place-specific costs.

That firms may be able to play this network to maximum financial advantage is covertly recognised. The extent to which it occurs is impossible to assess, for the necessary confidentiality with which industrial assistance is handled provides a convenient barrier to cross-agency evaluation. It may not be too cynical to suggest that the widespread confusion and ignorance of industrialists is a stronger constraint on multiple funding than such arrangements for inter-agency coordination as presently exist.

Any serious attempt to articulate an economic strategy to support either welfare *or* the market and so transcend symbolic action would need to work through the multi-agency network. In so doing, it would doubtless tend towards closer scrutiny and tougher decisions on support for firms. Tougher decisions, however, imply a lower level or a slower rate of expenditure. One evident problem here is the felt need to avoid underspend and so protect (for example) the industrial promotion budget. This is just one of the ways in which economic development programmes can become institutionalised to the extent that the symbolism of executive action takes precedence over substantive results.

Swimming against the tide?

Even where research units chart the contours of local economic problems and industrial development officers have the expertise to assess firms' needs and growth potential, a lingering doubt remains as to the ultimate purpose of urban economic development initiatives. Most of the activities which we have scrutinised are conceived in terms of, at best, regenerating and, at worst, maintaining the urban economy. What are their chances of success? There are probably few local economic policy makers who are deaf to this question, but there are equally few who can face its implications. Most planning researchers and industrial development officers acknowledge the adverse trends in economic activity locally, nationally and even internationally. Yet their operating assumption is often a one-dimensional one, of a falling level of some desired quality investment, employment or real income. The image is of a gradually lowering level in a static pool, the prime task being to contain the rate of leakage to an acceptable level.

The image of a receding tide better fits the contemporary experience of urban change. In broad terms, investment is relocating to urban fringe or non-urban locations in a dynamic and cumulative tide of urban de-industrialisation (see Hall and Hay, 1981; Fothergill and Gudgin, 1982). It is on some accounts a tide of change as powerful as that which produced the modern industrial city. It is against such a tide that urban economic programmes must swim. The overall assessment of the activities we have investigated is ultimately to be made against this backcloth of change, from which several factors in particular may be picked out.

One assumption of local policies for economic development is that they are applied to an industrial decision process which is itself locally-based. This is less often true than is commonly supposed. The remarkable concentration of British industry, which accelerated during the late 1960s, bestows upon some large industrial cities the virtual status of a 'branch plant economy' (George, 1975; Dicken, 1976). The multi-plant national corporation and the multi-national have a significant (though not wholly determining) impact on urban economies. Historically, acquisitions and mergers have been followed by rationalisation and the contraction or closure of the less efficient plant, which, characteristically, is located in traditional urban areas (Daniel, 1972; Community Development Project, 1977; Massey and Meegan, 1978).

Insofar as multi-plant corporations behave in this fashion they demonstrate their greater mobility and superior assessment of the relative costs of location. But all manufacturing firms face a similar pattern of locational advantages arrayed upon the spatial surface of economic organisation. The unfavourable shift in the costs and benefits of an urban location is almost universal (Warnes, 1977; Hayden, 1978; Hamilton, 1978). Changes in transport technology make fringe locations more attractive. Modern production processes require spacious single-storey buildings. Labour costs, goods handling and site access problems accumulate in traditional urban locations. Latterly, Labour-controlled city councils have responded to the severity of the fiscal squeeze by increasing their rate levies, to the further deterioration of their locational attractiveness (Rose and Page, 1982).

Above all, it is the growing firms which have the strongest incentives to relocate, as they are the first to encounter the ceilings to growth that urban - and particularly inner urban - locations impose. In so doing, they effectively export growth potential and the prospects of rising incomes from the city to the fringe, or even to the shire county (Keeble, 1969; Fothergill and Gudgin, 1982; see also the argument as to product cycles put forward in Norton and Rees, 1979).

Cities have experienced this cycle of firm creation, growth, move and further growth since the beginning of the industrial revolution. But two factors have in the past been seen to contain its adverse effects. The first is the persistence of inter-firm linkages, which have been thought to provide a continuing centripetal attraction, ensuring that outward moves do not continue to the point of disengagement. These linkage effects may themselves have been overestimated (Keeble, 1969; Beesley, 1955; Wood, 1969; Taylor and Wood, 1973). Moreover, increasing concentration of ownership enables large firms to enjoy an internalisation of linkages and so liberate themselves from any specific location. Second, cities have been regarded as industrial incubators, capable of replacing lost industry with new firms, some of which will have the necessary potential to generate compensatory growth. While local authority policies are increasingly targeted on this sector of the urban economy, there is a growing recognition that the industrial birth rate has fallen faster within cities than outside them, and that for many types of activity the best environment for both birth and growth is no longer to be found in the city (Cameron, 1973; Firn and Swales, 1978; Nicholson et al, 1981; Fagg, 1980).

To a greater or lesser extent the arguments about industrial concentration, locational tendencies, linkages and birth rates apply to all of the older industrial cities. Yet there are also apparent differences *between* cities which remain even when we set London aside as a special case. Perhaps the most tantalising are those differences in the overall economic environment that produce startling differences in the entrepreneurial capacity of, say, Manchester as compared with Liverpool, or Leicester as compared with Derby (Lloyd and Dicken, 1980; Fothergill and Gudgin, 1982).

Current attempts to explain such differences centre on a complex of economic and non-economic factors which are best captured in that rather inexplicit term *milieu*. The very range of the concept draws attention to the cultural and political factors which interact with economic considerations to produce locally specific economic change. How important are the cumulative activities of local authorities in shaping these *milieux* for good or ill? While it is far too soon, given the fragmentary state of our knowledge, to answer this question, there may yet be value in posing it.

The full impact of local authority action on the urban *milieu* extends beyond the limits of the formally adopted, economic development role. The urban space economy at any one point in time is a shifting (but not unstable) equilibrium of centrifugal and centripetal forces. If the weight of economic argument has shifted in favour of the former, then intangible factors - beliefs, loyalties, sentiments, preferences - may still have a powerful centripetal, pro-urban effect. Fostering those intangibles might yet prove to be a more effective means of anchoring firms against the tide of urban economic decline, and it is to that end that new roles and relationships might best be geared.

References

Beesley, M. (1955) 'The birth and death of industrial establishments: experience in the West Midlands conurbation', *Industrial Economics*, vol 4, pp 45-61.

Cameron, G.C. (1973) 'Intra urban location and new plant', *Papers and Proceedings of the Regional Science Association*, vol 31, pp 125-43.

Community Development Project (1977) *The costs of industrial change*, CDP Inter-Project Team.

Comptroller and Auditor-General (1981) *Appropriation accounts*, vol 2, classes iv-ix, 1979-80, London: HMSO.

Daniel, W.W. (1972) 'Whatever happened to the workers in Woolwich?', *Political and Economic Planning*.

Department of the Environment (1980) *Development control: policy and practice*, DOE Circular 22/80.

Dicken, P. (1976) 'The multi-plant business enterprise and geographical space: some issues in the study of external control and regional development', *Regional Studies*, vol 10, pp 401-12.

Fagg, J.J. (1980) 'A re-examination of the incubator hypothesis: a case study of Greater Leicester', *Urban Studies*, vol 17, pp 35-44.

Firn, J.P. and Swales, J.K (1978) 'The formation of new manufacturing establishments in Central Clydeside and the West Midlands conurbations 1963-1972: a comparative analysis', *Regional Studies*, vol 12, no 2, pp 199-213.

Fothergill, S. and Gudgin, G. (1982) *Unequal growth*, London: Heinemann.

George, K.D. (1975) 'A note on changes in industrial concentration in the UK', *Economic Journal*, March, pp 124-27.

Hall, P. (ed) (1981) *The inner city in context*, London: Heinemann for SSRC, pp 120-23.

Hall, P. and Hay, D. (1981) *Growth centres in the European urban system*, London: Heinemann.

Hamilton, F.E.I. (1978) 'Aspects of industrial mobility in the British economy', *Regional Studies*, vol 12, pp 153-66.

Hayden, F.W. (1978) *Factors influencing the location of industry*, Research Memorandum RM528, Greater London Council.

Keeble, D.E. (1969) 'Local industrial linkage and manufacturing growth in outer London', *Town Planning Review*, vol 40, pp 163-88.

Kumar, K. (1978) *Prophecy and progress*, Harmondsworth: Penguin.

Lawless, P. (1981) 'The role of some central government agencies in urban economic regeneration', *Regional Studies*, vol 15, no 1, pp 1-14.

Lloyd, P. and Dicken, P. (1980) *New firms, small firms and job generation: the experience of Manchester and Merseyside*, North West Industry Research Unit Working Paper no 9, Manchester: School of Geography, Manchester University.

Massey, D. and Meegan, R. (1978) 'Industrial restructuring vs the cities', *Urban Studies*, vol 15, no 3, pp 273-88.

Nicholson, B.M., Brinkley, J. and Evans, A.W. (1981) 'The role of the inner city in the development of manufacturing industry', *Urban Studies*, vol 18, no 1, pp 57-72.

Norton, R.D. and Rees, J. (1979) 'The product cycle and the spatial decentralisation of American manufacturing', *Regional Studies*, vol 13, no 2, pp 141-51.

Rose, R. and Page, E. (eds) (1982) *Fiscal stress in the cities*, Cambridge: Cambridge University Press.

Spector, M. and Kitsuse, J.I. (1977) *Constructing social problems*, Menlo Park, CA: Cummings.

Taylor, M.J. and Wood, P.J. (1973) 'Industrial linkage and local agglomeration in the West Midlands metal industries', *Transactions of the Institute of British Geographers*, vol 59, pp 172-54.

Warnes, A.M. (1977) *The decentralisation of employment from the larger English cities*, Geography Department Occasional Paper no 5, London: King's College.

Wood, P.J. (1969) 'Industrial location and linkage', *Area*, vol 2, pp 32-9.

Young, K. and Mills, L. (1982) 'The decline of urban economies', in R. Rose and E. Page (eds) *Fiscal stress in the cities*, Cambridge: Cambridge University Press.

Young, K. and Mills, L. (1983) *Managing the post-industrial city*, London: Heinemann.

CHAPTER 8

FUTURE DIRECTIONS FOR URBAN GOVERNMENT IN BRITAIN AND AMERICA

ROBIN HAMBLETON

Introduction

The 1980s were a period of crisis and change for British local government. To a lesser degree the last decade was also a turbulent period for American local authorities. Drawing on a comparative review of urban government under Thatcher and Reagan (Hambleton, 1989a) we can identify a number of similarities and contrasts.

On the one hand, it is clear that there are strong parallels between the UK and the USA. The socio-economic trends impacting on urban areas are similar: both the Thatcher and the Reagan administrations reduced financial support to city governments in the name of national economic policy; and urban areas are increasingly divided, with extraordinary concentrations of deprivation and poverty in some neighbourhoods. On the other hand, alongside these similarities there are remarkable divergencies: the Thatcher government's commitment to political centralisation would be unthinkable in the United States; party politics in Britain has become highly politicised in a way which is (on the whole) foreign to American city councils; and, linked with this, attempts by local authorities to pursue radical reform programmes appear to be more widespread in Britain than in the United States.

This chapter offers a simple conceptual framework for thinking about current and future developments in urban government in Britain and America. In particular it tries to make sense of the various moves towards privatisation, consumerism and neighbourhood decentralisation. It will be suggested that the changing pressures on local government in both countries will continue, even intensify, in the 1990s.

Changing pressures on urban government

Comparative government is a fascinating but treacherous field. Major political, cultural, social, economic, racial, legal, historical and geographical

---

This chapter first appeared in the *Journal of Urban Affairs*, 1990, vol 12, no 1, pp 75-94.

differences need to be recognised. Furthermore, when the focus is local government it is important to recognise the constitutional differences. Local government in America is a creature of each of the fifty states. There is huge variation in the form and financing of American local authorities. This contrasts sharply with the high degree of institutional and fiscal uniformity found in British local government.[1]

Clearly we should beware of drawing cross-national parallels which disregard these differences. However, having made this caveat, we can point to several trends which have little regard for national boundaries.

Firstly, it can be argued that we are witnessing a global restructuring of capital that has implications for all the major cities in the USA and the UK (as well as elsewhere). Capital flight, foreign investment, multinational corporate competition, and international interdependence of production activities are all part of the "globalisation of economic relations" (Smith, 1987). From this perspective a key current issue for city government is managing the tensions between the imperatives of transnational capital accumulation and local political forces demanding a stable economic base.

The globalisation of economic relations has been accelerated by the revolutions in communication systems and micro-electronics. Advances in information technology are diminishing the significance of place and leading to a 'delocalisation' of the processes of production and consumption. We are witnessing:

> the decomposition of the processes of work and management so that different tasks can be performed in different places and assembled through signals (in the case of information) or through advanced transportation technology (standardised assembly pieces shipped away from very remote points of production). (Castells, 1983, p 6)

A second key trend, which is inextricably linked to the global restructuring of capital and the delocalisation of the processes of production and consumption, is organisational. Hoggett (1987) has argued that current shifts towards decentralised forms of organisation and management in both the private and the public sectors can be viewed as part of a new techno-managerial paradigm. On this analysis the post-war boom was based upon a 'technological style' which combined Fordist techniques of mechanised mass production with Taylorist models of management and organisation. Mass production, economies of scale, fragmentation and specialisation of work, the de-skilling of manual labour through the removal of discretion were key features of what might be called the 'Fordist' era.

Hoggett argues that the revolution in micro-electronics, robotics and information technology is leading towards the flexible, automated production of a diversified range of more custom-designed quality products. In organisational terms "the emergent techno-managerial paradigm replaces bureaucratic supervision by delegation, participation and team work organised within a subtle framework of increasingly computerised control systems" (Hoggett, 1987, p 222). Fordism stressed organisational structure and strong, centralised power control. In 'post-Fordist' organisations power is more dispersed - structures are cellular rather than pyramid-like and the units tend to regulate themselves, rather than being governed by rules and commands that flow downwards (Mulgen, 1988; Peters, 1988).

A third key trend is political. The pressures towards globalisation and delocalisation referred to earlier are being opposed by political movements seeking more local autonomy and urban self-management. In some cases, political parties feature boldly in these campaigns - this is certainly the case in the UK (Blunkett and Jackson, 1987). In many cases, however, these 'urban social movements' lie outside formal party structures (Lowe, 1986). These pressures for local autonomy are, to varying degrees, confronted by centralising trends within nation states. In the UK, for example, the central state has worked relentlessly to undermine local government in recent years (Hambleton, 1989a).

In summary, it can be suggested that these three sets of forces - the economic, the organisational and the political - dominate the development of urban government in the 1990s in both the USA and the UK. What, in practice, might this mean for urban government?

Emerging tensions : economic, organisational and political

Firstly, economic forces are likely to shrink the differences between urban government in the USA and the UK. For example, commercial property investment now operates in a very competitive global market; city authorities in both countries can be expected to extend their knowledge of and involvement with different private sector interests in order to attract inward investment. In support of this we can note that survey evidence suggests that American city councils have become very heavily involved in urban economic development since the mid 1960s (Robinson, 1988; Bowman, 1988). The strategies most American cities adopt are very business oriented, even though the social costs of this approach can be considerable (Cummings, 1988; Hambleton, 1988a; 1989b).

In Britain, too, there has been a rapid growth in the number of local authorities pursuing local economic development strategies (Young and Mason, 1983; Lovering, 1988). Many of these strategies have had a much more explicit social purpose than their American counterparts. Not surprisingly, there is ongoing conflict between central and local government about the nature and purpose of local economic development - is it about wealth creation or is it about helping local residents? (Blunkett and Jackson, 1987 pp 108-42). The general point, however, is that, whilst different political parties will emphasise different objectives, we can anticipate continued growth in public/private sector collaboration as city councils wrestle with economic restructuring.

The issue of organisational change is discussed in detail later. In general terms, we can, following Schon (1971), suggest that the institutions of urban government, like most social systems, are resistant to change to the point of exhibiting 'dynamic conservatism' - that is they fight to stay the same (Schon, 1971, p 32). This is not necessarily bad - we don't want institutions that fly apart at the seams. Our organisations of urban government "need to maintain their identity, and their ability to support the self-identity of those who belong to them, but they must at the same time be capable of frequently transforming themselves" (Schon, 1971, p 60). Schon rightly stresses that external pressures require constant innovation.

Again, at a general level it can be suggested that the organisations of urban government have not paid sufficient attention to the needs of the consumer. The burgeoning, largely American, literature on consumer oriented management suggests that superior (private or public sector) performance requires organisations to take exceptional care of their customers (Peters and Waterman, 1982; Peters and Austin, 1986). According to this line of argument, the institutions of urban government need to launch a customer revolution; they need to become obsessed with listening to their consumers and to achieve extraordinary levels of responsiveness (Peters, 1988).

The consequences of the third key trend - political change - are more difficult to predict because developments within both the UK and the USA seem to point in two directions: some would seem to be widening the differences between urban government in Britain and America whilst others could narrow the gap. On the first point the intensification of ideological conflict in British party politics might be expected to widen the gap. A variety of political movements (emanating from the political right, left and centre) are articulating and implementing radical reform programmes which seek to transform established approaches to providing and financing urban services.

These various initiatives are discussed further below - examples are: radical right privatisation and cost cutting strategies as in the London Borough of Wandsworth (Beresford, 1987); radical left neighbourhood decentralisation strategies as in the London Borough of Islington (Hodge, 1987; du Parcq, 1987); and centre party innovation with area-based management as in the London Borough of Tower Hamlets (Morphet, 1987). Whilst it is possible to imagine similar programmes being developed by American city councils, we would not expect to find such a strong party political emphasis in local government strategies for organisational change, notwithstanding developments in some progressive cities (Clavel, 1986).

This divergence in party politics is, however, only part of the picture. It is also possible to suggest that city politics in Britain is moving towards an American form in the sense that local politics is becoming more pluralistic. The electorate is certainly more heterogeneous than it was ten years ago; class is no longer the only important political cleavage. Citizens have become more assertive and more diversified and organisations based around neighbourhood, ethnicity and specific issues (such as homelessness or transport policy) are having an increasingly significant impact on local government. Urban social movements have certainly grown in Britain in the 1980s. Various writers have shown that local politics has become much more sectional and that local interest groups have become more influential (Gyford, 1986; Stoker, 1988 pp 106-128). If the upsurge in interest group politics continues it can be suggested that British urban politics will, over a period of time, become more like American city politics which has a strong pluralist tradition (Waste, 1987).

It would be wrong to imply that these three driving forces for change - the economic, the organisational and the political - are independent of one another. On the contrary, it is clear that there are strong overlaps. In particular, it is clear that major business interests are capable of dominating local interest group politics by virtue of their economic power.

In summary it can be argued that it is helpful to engage in an Anglo-American comparative study of trends affecting urban government not least because it provides insights on prospects for the coming years.[2] As explained further below, some key trends point towards an Americanisation of British urban government. If these trends continue in the 1990s we can anticipate an increase in urban conflicts as party political organisations wrestle with the pressures from new social groups and take on the challenge of developing a creative relationship with powerful (often international) business interests.

The next section outlines a conceptual framework for understanding the way British urban government has evolved since the late 1960s. The subsequent sections then expand on the key themes identified in the framework. Whilst the focus is on Britain, the discussion attempts to highlight lessons for American cities.

Understanding developments in Britain: a conceptual framework

The framework outlined in Figure 1 was originally developed by a group of staff at the School for Advanced Urban Studies (SAUS) to help us understand the strong British movement towards various forms of neighbourhood decentralisation (Hambleton and Hoggett, 1987; Hambleton, Hoggett and Tolan, 1989).[3] The framework can, however, be used to serve the broader purpose of introducing an international audience to some of the key currents of change running through British local government as a whole. Figure 1 represents a drastic simplification of a far more complex reality. Whilst it has proved useful in a number of seminars and workshops run by SAUS for local government managers and politicians, no claim is made that it provides a comprehensive map.

Figure 1: Evolving patterns of relationship between local authorities and their communities: a conceptual map

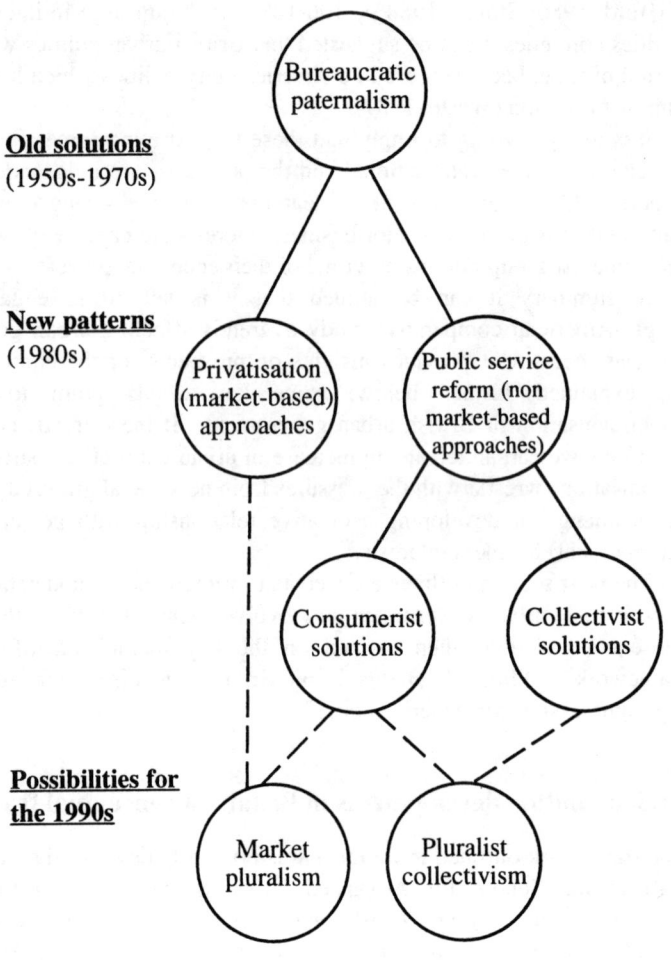

The framework contrasts 'old solutions' (broadly pre-1980) with the 'new patterns' of the 1980s and speculates about the 'possibilities' for the 1990s. The phrase 'bureaucratic paternalism' succinctly describes the old solutions that have become today's problems in local government. Too many local authority departments are large, hierarchical organisations structured to mass produce services in line with the 'Fordist' model outlined earlier. The 1980s have not only seen a crisis in these old solutions, but the emergence of two 'post-Fordist' alternatives. The first alternative, usually associated with the radical right, seeks to challenge the very notion of collective and non-market provision for public need. Centring upon the strategy of privatisation it seeks to replace public provision with private provision. The second alternative aims to preserve the notion of public provision, but seeks a radical reform of the manner in which this provision is undertaken. Thus it seeks to replace the old bureaucratic paternalist model with a much more responsive and democratic model.

This latter approach to reform appears to have two central variants, the one being essentially consumerist, the other being essentially collectivist. Consumerist approaches to reform give primary emphasis to enhancing the responsiveness of local government services to individual consumers. However many services cannot be individualised - they relate to groups of consumers or to society at large. Collective interests can only be protected through appropriate forms of political accountability. Hence, collectivist approaches place their primary emphasis on the democratisation of local government service provision. Clearly there are very close links between responsiveness and democracy. Nevertheless we have found it helpful to distinguish between the two approaches. The consumerist approach is essentially concerned with the reform of local government considered as an administrative system, whereas the collectivist approach seeks to reform local government considered as a political system.

It is important to stress the speed at which developments have been occurring. With the election of the Conservatives for a third term in June 1987 new scenarios for the public sector in the 1990s and beyond have emerged. New legislation on the contracting out of public services (referred to as compulsory competitive tendering or CCT), on the break-up of public sector housing, on changes to education (including provisions for schools to opt out of the state system), on alterations to the National Health Service, all point to the creation of more pluralist patterns of public service provision in the future. The key point is, what kind of pluralism will emerge?

A market-based pluralism which gives emphasis to deregulated, private institutional forms to run schools, housing estates, hospitals, elderly persons' homes and so on, is clearly the objective of the radical Thatcherites. An alternative pattern of pluralist collectivism is also possible. Within this scenario, provision remains 'public' but not necessarily 'state'. New forms of social provision (social trusts, management cooperatives, tenant management corporations etc) emerge accountable by contract, regulation and inspection to local authorities. The market-based pluralism scenario envisages a proliferation of profit seeking organisations providing for individualised consumers. Pluralist collectivism implies a growing diversity of non-profit organisations and trusts offering a variety of ways of meeting public needs. Needless to say American cities are replete with many examples of both kinds of organisation, and this is one of the main reasons for suggesting that an Americanisation of British local government may be in train. Having provided an overall framework we can now sketch in a few details.

There are two developing critiques of the old solutions. First, there is the political critique of massive alienating public bureaucracies. This analysis suggests that the Thatcher government cashed in on the paternalism and inadequacies of the welfare state and that the response must be radical. One influential political leader on the Left put it this way:

> We must start debating as a movement our values and the ways in which we will extend democracy, participative democracy, as well as defending what we've got; because it is partly the inadequacy of, and the alienation from, the way in which the system is worked that has enabled Thatcher to take the steps she has with such success. (Blunkett, 1985)

Second, there is the management critique of inward looking organisational cultures. There has been a widespread failure in the private as well as the public sector to put the 'customer' first. The critique has been developed in popular form by American management consultants in the best-seller *In search of excellence* (Peters and Waterman, 1982).

The key point to stress is that both the political and the managerial critiques suggest that radical rather than marginal change is needed. The next three sections of the paper highlight the key features of the three main sets of responses that emerged in Britain in the 1980s.

The radical right: expenditure cuts and privatisation

Both the Thatcher and the Reagan administrations cut central government financial support to local government. In Britain between 1979/80 and 1986/87 the government slashed the rate support grant (which resembles general revenue sharing) by £17 billion (roughly $25 billion). Similarly, the so-called 'policy earthquake' of the Reagan Omnibus Budget Reconciliation Act (OBRA) of 1981 produced sharp declines of federal aid in the 1981/82 period. One independent study revealed that federal funding for specifically urban programmes fell by $5.8 billion in fiscal 1982 from what it would have been had fiscal 1980 policy continued in effect

(Peterson, 1986). In both countries then, central government has put fiscal pressure on city councils.

In Britain this has been a running saga throughout the 1980s. There has been a torrent of legislation on local government finance including the Local Government Planning and Land Act of 1980 (to punish 'overspending'), measures to introduce 'rate capping' (in 1984), measures to replace rates with a poll tax and measures to reform housing finance and local authority capital spending (the 1989 Local Government and Housing Act). These various measures, which are discussed more fully elsewhere (Hambleton, 1989a), are all designed to restrain council spending.

But the radical right has a philosophy which goes well beyond holding down public spending. A further key feature has been the strategy of privatising local government (Ascher, 1987; Stoker, 1988, pp 173-91). In a pamphlet Nicholas Ridley, former Secretary of State for the Environment, has attempted to articulate the philosophy underlying the Conservative government's policies. This restates the view that it is essential "to constrain the growth of local authority expenditure in order to stop it taking an ever-larger proportion of the total national product at the expense of other areas of the economy" (Ridley, 1988, p 7). This view is, of course, contested - one critique offers twelve reasons why the argument is flawed (Newton and Karran, 1985, pp 20-35). For example, local government is one of the private sector's best customers and local government provides and maintains industrial infrastructure and services which are crucial to the success of the national economy. In other words local government is contributing to, not taking from, 'other areas of the economy'.

To secure better local government in the future, Ridley suggests that two of the keys to success lie in strengthening accountability and extending competition:

> To strengthen accountability we need a more direct relationship between payment for local services through local taxation and the service being provided. ...
>
> Competition is a spur to efficiency and value for money wherever it operates. Too much of the public sector has been insulated from it. The spread of competition in education, housing and other local services should do an enormous amount to improve standards of efficiency. (Ridley, 1988, p 8)

On the first point the claim of the radical right is that the poll tax (or 'community charge' as it was called officially) should strengthen accountability. All adult citizens were to be liable and, so the argument runs, would therefore have a stronger interest in holding their local councils to account through the ballot box. Opponents of the poll tax raised a string of objections. First, it was unfair in that it required everyone over 18 to pay the same, regardless of means. This would lead to a substantial redistribution of income from the less well-off to the better-off. Second, the costs of collecting the tax from a far larger number of people would be substantial; some estimates suggested that the tax would cost almost three times as much as rates to collect. Third, the compilation of the register would involve intrusion into the private lives of individuals. Fourth, even with energetic enforcement there would be substantial tax evasion, in particular it would deter young people from registering to vote. These objections did not stop the government from pressing ahead with the scheme - the tax was introduced in Scotland in April 1989 and in England and Wales in April 1990.

The second theme of competition is hinted at in the subtitle to the Ridley pamphlet: 'enabling not providing'. Thus the argument runs that the role of the local authority should no longer be that of universal provider. Rather it should be to encourage diversity and alternatives, with elements of competition between the different providers. This emphasis on competition is directly in line with New Right belief in the virtues of the market:

> As far as possible competition should prevail, or at least, every supplier should be open to competition. Neither private nor government contrivances should be allowed to obliterate or blur the crucial signalling role of the free market. (Green, 1987, pp 211-12)

More than that, the Ridley pamphlet argued that ownership should shift into private hands:

> This government goes in for private ownership, because assets in *private* hands are cared for and used efficiently, while assets in public hands have too often been allowed to decay and stagnate and become a burden on the community. (Ridley, 1988, p 23 - author's emphasis)

'Privatisation' is a term which is used rather loosely to describe a variety of policies which aim to limit the role of the public sector and increase the role of the private sector. In terms of the government's policies for local government we can identify three main aspects. First, the sale of local authority assets has been a key feature. For example, the 1980 Housing Act gave public sector housing tenants the right to buy their houses with discounts of up to 50% on the market value. Over one million council houses were sold in the period 1980-86 (Malpass and Murie, 1987, p 102). More recent legislation (the Housing and Planning Act, 1986) provided for the disposal of whole housing estates to private developers and the taking-over of housing management by non-local authority agencies.

Second is the expansion of the private sector role in service provision and investment. Thus, the private sector has moved into social service provision through a rapid growth in private homes for the elderly. Financial institutions have begun to invest more heavily in urban redevelopment, encouraged by a range of financial inducements not dissimilar to the American Urban Development Action Grant approach (Boyle, 1985).

Third and arguably of most long-term significance, is the introduction of 'market discipline' into local authority service delivery through the introduction of compulsory competitive tendering (CCT). The tendering exercise involves contracting out services previously provided in-house by the local authority. The in-house workforce is required to compete against interested private bidders. If the local authority department submits the most competitive tender the contract price becomes its budget and it operates as if it were an arms-length organisation servicing the local authority. If the private sector company wins it gets the contract and the local authority department (usually known as the direct labour organisation) is disbanded.

The underlying driving force behind the various privatisation initiatives is an ideological belief that 'private equals good' while 'public equals bad' (Dunleavy and Rhodes, 1986, p 141). These authors suggest that the Conservative electoral strategy was designed to intensify public/private conflicts. This approach, when coupled with a continuing series of measures to 'roll back the state', was seen as the main plank in a strategy to build up long-term Conservative electoral support. The importance of 'gut politics' in explaining Conservative enthusiasm for privatisation should not be underestimated but other factors are relevant (Stoker, 1988, pp 173-176). First, the strategy has developed at a time of financial austerity - selling off assets reduces pressure for public sector borrowing. Second, privatisation creates new markets and greater opportunities for the private sector - it attempts to strengthen the operation of market forces and reduce public expectations about what the state should do and what it should be responsible for.

Opponents of privatisation argue that there is no evidence to support the view that assets 'in private hands' are better cared for and used more effectively than those 'in public hands'. Rather they argue that the Conservative drive towards contracting out is part of a campaign against public sector trade unionism (Ascher, 1987, pp 46-53). Employees in the private sector are less likely to be strongly unionised. If private contractors are able to offer a cheaper service, and this is contested, it is, so the argument runs, because they are exploiting their workers.

Much of the argument over privatisation is strongly coloured by ideological prejudice. It is noteworthy, therefore, that Sir John Banham, former head of the Audit Commission, made the following remarks at a national conference:

> The best local government is superb and private enterprise could never improve on it ... with Sheffield as a shining example.

A well-managed direct labour organisation is going to be fully competitive with the best of the private sector. Sheffield collects refuse rather more economically than Southend which is privatised - a fact which went down like a lead balloon in Marsham Street, the Department of the Environment headquarters. There is no excuse for lousy management and privatisation is the last resort of a management that has given up. (Quoted in Blunkett and Jackson, 1987, p 122)

Public service reform: consumerism

The major alternative to privatisation is, as indicated in Figure 1, public service reform. This approach recognises that a successful defence of the welfare state requires a response which goes well beyond defending existing forms of service provision to develop new ways forward which will win popular support. As explained earlier, the framework distinguishes two kinds of public service reform. In this section we are concerned with the consumerist approach.

The idea of 'getting closer to the consumer' enjoyed a resurgence within the private sector during the 1980s. There are many strands to this but one study of successful American companies, *In search of excellence*, has, as mentioned earlier, been particularly influential. The authors of this book argue that despite all the lip service given to market orientation, in many firms the customer is being either ignored or regarded as a nuisance. Their findings were summarised as follows: "The excellent companies really are close to their customers. That's it. Other companies talk about it; the excellent companies do it" (Peters and Waterman, 1982, p 156).

It was not long before these private sector management ideas began to permeate through to the public sector. American local government was 'ahead' of British local government. In 1984 a Californian handbook on excellence in local government management appeared which attempted to adapt the Peters and Waterman criteria of success for use in local government - the authors were enthusiastic about the possibilities (Barbour *et al*, 1984). British local government has now also started to address the issues which arise when a local authority wants to get closer to its consumers. The Local Government Training Board produced an impressive 96-page booklet, *Getting closer to the public*, which sets out the basic ideas and approaches, provides a framework for reviewing current practice and considers some of the staff development activities needed to bring about change (Local Government Training Board, 1987). This was followed up with a further publication on *Learning from the public* (Local Government Training Board, 1988).

It would be misleading to imply that these consumerist ideas are simply the latest import from the private sector into current public sector management thinking. On the contrary, the cause of consumerism has advanced steadily over some 30 years. In saying this it is important to distinguish two definitions of consumerism - the narrow and fairly familiar meaning used to describe problems associated with the consumption of 'high street' goods and services; and the broader usage applied to problems associated with the use of public sector services. As Smith (1986) argues, this wider definition has been with us at least since the founding of the British National Consumer Council in 1975 and is implicit in a number of popular radio and television programmes which carry the 'consumer' label.

What is new is the political context within which these consumerist ideas are being debated. As outlined earlier, central government is putting enormous pressure on public sector organisations via its cost cutting/privatisation strategy and this is forcing rethinking. In addition to these pressures from above the population at large has become increasingly able to voice its views regarding public service inadequacies. These different pressures have given weight to those professionals and politicians within local authorities who are alert to the inadequacies of existing service provision and wish to develop a more consumer-oriented service.

Within the fashion for consumerism, as Pollitt (1988) observes, rival conceptions are at work "ranging all the way from cosmetic, 'charm school' approaches through improved provision of information to direct consumer participation and power-sharing". He suggests that the brands of consumerism actually being implemented tend to be at the cosmetic end of the spectrum. The established power relationship between those providing and those receiving services is not usually challenged.

An influential variant on the consumerist idea is the public service orientation (Stewart and Clarke, 1987). Such an orientation sets service for the public as the key organisational value, providing motivation and purpose both for the local authority and its staff. These authors argue that service for the public can provide a shared vision for those involved with local government at a time when local authorities are under attack. Their ideas draw on the private sector thinking outlined earlier but extend beyond the mechanistic transfer of consumerist ideas from the market place to the public sector. They claim that concern for the citizen as well as the customer distinguishes the public service orientation from the concern for the customer that should mark any service organisation. The emphasis is both on the customer for whom the service is provided and on the citizen to whom the local authority is accountable.

The sorts of measures advocated in documents like *Getting closer to the public* (Local Government Training Board, 1987) could, if implemented with enthusiasm, lead to significant improvements in local government service delivery. There are, however, two main sets of reasons why it is necessary to go beyond the consumerist/public service approach (Hambleton and Hoggett, 1987, pp 23-5). The first stems from the fact that many of these ideas have been imported from the private sector where, within limits, the consumer enjoys a degree of power by virtue of personal choice. If a retailer in the 'market place' is too expensive or sells a shoddy product it is possible (for most of us) to shop elsewhere. There are, of course, constraints on this consumer power. For example, poor, infirm consumers may be insufficiently mobile to take their business elsewhere. Also it has been clear for at least 30 years that the market is able to create desires and shape consumer wants in subtle but extremely effective ways (Packard, 1957). However, allowing for these constraints, the private sector consumer has the power of choice.

Advocates of the market approach have encountered serious problems when trying to extend consumer choice within the public sector. Even when services are privatised, individual consumer choice is not enhanced - thus individuals cannot switch their refuse collector, their fire service, their water company, their electricity board, etc. In the public sector we have built up political structures to provide a mechanism for holding service providers (whether public servants or private contractors) accountable to the citizen. For these services, which are effectively monopolies, the consumer derives power from political control, not from the ability to exercise choice within the market place. The consumerist/public service approach fails to address the issues raised by this distinction, in particular the imbalance of power in the server-served relationship which arises when the consumer has little or no choice.

The second major limitation of the consumerist/public service approach is that it has difficulty coping with the needs of groups of consumers. Many public services provide a collective rather than an individual benefit. Clean air, roads, street lighting, environmental quality, environmental health, police protection and schooling are just some of the services provided and consumed on a collective basis. In a democracy, collective needs of this kind need to be addressed collectively; conflicts of view need to be expressed and choices which take account of other people's preferences have to be made. In short, a large range of decisions which affect people's lives cannot sensibly be made by individuals operating in isolation; they must be conceived politically. This is not to imply that existing arrangements for democratic control of public service organisations are adequate. On the contrary, we need improved mechanisms for enabling different groups of consumers and citizens to influence political decision making about the collective provision of services. This leads us into a discussion of public service reform strategies which centre on empowering the consumer and the citizen.

Empowering the consumer and the citizen

The consumerist proposals discussed so far have concentrated on managerial rather than political change. While the public service orientation attempts to go beyond the supermarket model of consumerism by introducing the notion of 'concern for the citizen', it centres on improving service delivery and, as a result, does little to enhance citizenship. This is the essence of the critique offered by Rhodes who argues that local government is about more than providing services. He suggests it is a means for emancipating the individual and creating a free society through citizen participation:

> If it seems grandiloquent to load local government with idealistic goals such as emancipation, it can be countered that a sense of mission does not lie in the sale of hamburgers - with due deference to *In search of excellence* - but in the 'nobility' of the aspiration. (Rhodes, 1987, p 67)

Rhodes goes on to argue that the public service orientation should be modified to embrace a broad conception of citizenship because local government is the pre-eminent location for the integrative political experience outside Parliament.

The decentralisation of services to neighbourhood level is attracting considerable attention within local government in Britain. Making local authority services more accessible to the public, breaking down departmental barriers at local level, creating completely new avenues for staff development - these are the sorts of aspirations which explain the surge in support for decentralisation in recent years. A growing number of local authorities have now decentralised many of their services to local level and many others are either in the process of decentralising or are contemplating decentralising (Hoggett and Hambleton, 1987; Hambleton, 1988b). In one sense this is not a new development. In the 1970s there was an earlier shift towards neighbourhood management in both Britain and the United States (Yates, 1973; Hambleton, 1978). Whilst these developments often improved the responsiveness of public service bureaucracies at the margin they rarely challenged entrenched departmentalism effectively and had only modest success in raising citizen involvement (Hambleton, 1978; Ross and Stedman, 1985, pp 96-123).

There are two main reasons why the British developments of the 1980s seem to differ from the initiatives of the 1970s: one is managerial, the other is political. First, aided by new information technology, decentralised forms of organisation are rapidly developing within private sector companies across the world. These managerial innovations, which represent a shift towards the 'post-Fordist' forms of organisation referred to earlier, are now being imported into the public sector (Hoggett, 1987). Second, different forms of decentralisation are proving attractive, in varying degrees, to all the major political parties in Britain. In many cases the town hall leaders who now advocate decentralisation were active in community groups in the 1970s attacking remote, centralised decision making. Their commitment to decentralisation is often deeply held. The unifying theme of both the managerial and the political critiques of bureaucratic paternalism is the recognition of the need to disaggregate and break up organisations which have become too big and complex to manage effectively.

It would be misleading, however, to suggest that the many neighbourhood decentralisation initiatives being taken forward in Britain have been successful in empowering the consumer and the citizen. On the contrary, the need for political change is often not seen as a primary focus of interest - decentralisation is being pursued for a variety of objectives. Elsewhere I have suggested that this policy confusion can be penetrated by distinguishing five overlapping yet distinct objectives (Hambleton, 1988b). These possible objectives for decentralisation are summarised in Figure 2.

There is no need to discuss each of these objectives in detail here. We can note, however, that the potential objectives of decentralisation are wide-ranging. Some of the objectives present a fundamental challenge to familiar and well established ways of running services while others involve comparatively minor change. While some of the five objectives are reinforcing, some are in tension, if not conflict. For example, the fourth objective of increasing public support for local government links easily with the first objective of improving public services. This is difficult to achieve if the fifth objective of staff development is ignored. On the other hand, an example of possible conflict would be between the second and third objectives - a radical approach to strengthening the accountability of services to the local neighbourhood could be incompatible with the pursuit of authority-wide policies concerned to even up opportunities for neglected groups.

Despite the difficulties a number of local authorities are experimenting with new forms of local accountability and some examples are given below. These councils are not only striving for improved service responsiveness. They are concerned to encourage local political activity as a means of sustaining democracy as a whole - the advancement of 'citizenship', to use Rhode's term (1987). Whilst there is not space to explore the literature on democracy here we can, following the Widdicombe Report, note that the three main arguments for local government stem largely from democratic theory (1986, pp 45-52).

Figure 2: Possible objectives of neighbourhood decentralisation

i. Improving services
   - service delivery (convenient, one-stop, local coordination, local decisions)
   - cost effectiveness (local financial management)
   - service planning and policy (locality planning)
   - the relationship between public servants and the public

ii. Local accountability
   - varying degrees - authority or influence?
   - to whom? (local councillors? consumers? local people? a combination?)
   - community development

iii. Distribution
   - priority areas?
   - different resources for different areas/groups
   - equal opportunities policy

iv. Public support
   - win public support for local government
   - win support for a political party

v. Staff development
   - job satisfaction
   - multi-disciplinary teams
   - friendly environment
   - neighbourhood loyalty
   - central support

The first argument derives from a concern with political liberty - local government supports political pluralism and is able to moderate a tendency or temptation towards autocracy which is itself destructive of good government. Second, local government contributes to political education - it is a school in which democratic habits are acquired and practised and the infrastructure of democracy laid down. The third set of arguments revolves around responsiveness - the necessity for local needs to be locally defined in order that appropriate services can be provided, the need for constant innovation and the need to maximise public choice. These three arguments have been elaborated elsewhere (Hill, 1974; Stewart, 1983; Jones and Stewart, 1983; Gyford, 1984). Young (1986, p 18) stresses that any valid theory of local government must be a political theory: "The current fashionable concern to regard local government as simply nothing more than a convenient mechanism for the delivery of public services is, in the long run, the most dangerous to its continued survival and vitality".

These three arguments in favour of local government can, with appropriate modifications, be used to support the development of various forms of neighbourhood government, ie governmental structures below the level of the local authority. This is not to suggest that decentralisation is the only way to extend local democracy. There are many ways of strengthening local political accountability and Figure 3, in outlining four broad approaches, does not exhaust the possibilities.[4]

Figure 3: Ways of strengthening local democracy

---

i. *Improving representative democracy*
eg voter registration drives, open government, citizens' rights at meetings, better support to councillors

ii. *Extending representative democracy*
eg area committees based on wards or groups of wards, urban parish councils

iii. *Extending direct democracy*
eg funding of non-statutory groups, community development, user group participation

iv. *Infuse representative with direct democracy*
eg co-option on to committees, neighbourhood committees of councillors and representatives from community and disadvantaged groups

---

First, there is a range of steps which can be taken to improve the existing mechanisms of local representative democracy. For example, in recent years many British local authorities have developed much better support services for politicians ranging from good secretarial help through to research support and policy advice (Thomas, 1987).[5] A second approach is to extend representative democracy by creating new, more local settings within which representatives can decide on local issues. An increasing number of local authorities now have area or neighbourhood committees which have decision-making powers relating to areas of the local authority. Examples are Stockport Metropolitan Borough Council, Birmingham City Council and Walsall Borough Council. The London Borough of Tower Hamlets, which is Liberal controlled, has probably gone furthest with this model. In 1984 the council scrapped most of its central committees and handed power over to new neighbourhood committees (Morphet, 1987).

A third approach is to extend direct democracy. The central idea is to break with the notion that local government should always be the vehicle through which local needs are met and to invest in the 'voluntary' sector. This approach involves decentralising influence and power to groups rather than areas. This is important because the neighbourhood does not necessarily command its inhabitants' primary loyalties. Arrangements have developed for consultation with and provision of direct funding to a range of interest groups - for example, community relations councils, minority ethnic groups, and women's groups. In addition many councils are supporting the involvement of 'user groups' in the running of council services. Tenants' associations provide a long-standing example of a local government user group. In recent years new user groups have appeared, seeking some say over how council services are planned and delivered. This has happened particularly in the sphere of leisure and recreation where user groups are involved in running major facilities. Other groups are also emerging - for the parents of children in day nurseries, transport users' groups, parks users' groups and so on.

A fourth way of strengthening local democracy is to infuse representative democracy with direct democracy. This approach recognises the limitations to both representative democracy and direct democracy. Representative democracy has led to a professionalisation of party politics with the result that white, middle class, middle-aged men tend to dominate. Second, the form of involvement offered by representative democracy is passive and minimalist - a vote every three or four years. This form fits well with the paternalistic 'leave it to us' approach. Third, and despite the startling amount of energy and commitment many councillors invest in local politics, elected members can only effect a fragile form of accountability from service professionals to the electorate. On the other hand, direct forms of democracy can be attacked on the grounds that they are often unrepresentative and parochial in their concerns. For example, tenants' associations are sometimes criticised for being white-dominated or are accused of focusing only on the interests of tenants and disregarding the needs of those without tenancies, such as the homeless.

One interesting example of an attempt to infuse representative democracy with direct democracy is provided by the neighbourhood forums in the London Borough of Islington. Each forum covers a neighbourhood office catchment area, the aim being to enable administrative change and political reform to reinforce one another. No attempt is made to impose a blueprint upon all neighbourhoods; councillors are involved, but it is equally important that the public and organised community groups be represented. The forums try to compensate for the lack of representation of disadvantaged groups by positively discriminating in their favour (places for these groups are guaranteed). And each forum has a budget to spend of around £60,000 per annum (roughly $90,000). It is too early to assess how the Islington neighbourhood forums are working but they are a significant innovation of interest to other urban local authorities.

Conclusion

This chapter has suggested that urban government in Britain and America is confronted with a range of new pressures - economic, organisational and political. There are, of course, major constitutional differences between the governmental structures of the two countries and there are also interesting policy divergencies (Hambleton, 1989a). However, the thrust of this chapter has been to focus on forces which appear to be international in scope. If this analysis is broadly correct, there may be some convergence in British and American approaches to urban government in the 1990s.

Figure 1 provides a framework for understanding some of the key currents of change running through British local government. It is hoped that the framework can also serve as a useful prompt for reflecting on current trends within the United States. The framework is used to identify three main sets of responses to the perceived problems of local government.

i. The radical right strategy of cutting public spending and promoting privatisation.

ii. The reform of public service conceived as a management strategy for improving the responsiveness of services to the needs of consumers.

iii. The reform of public service conceived as a political strategy for empowering the consumer and the citizen in order to strengthen local democracy.

There are ways in which developments in Britain contrast sharply with American experience. For example, the Thatcher government's policy of political centralisation would be regarded as unacceptable in the United States (whether nationally or within one state). Yet, in other ways, we may be witnessing the Americanisation of British urban government. The way city councils are responding to economic restructuring often follows American models. Urban politics in Britain is becoming more pluralistic - class is no longer the only important political cleavage. The contracting out of public services to private companies, which is now receiving such attention in Britain, has been long established practice in many American cities. The push towards a consumer-oriented strategy for public sector organisations owes much to American private sector management rhetoric about 'getting closer to the consumer'. The break up of the public sector and the development of more plural forms of service provision is a further shift towards American models.

Set against the market, which attempts to individualise needs, is the notion of citizenship:

> The notion of the citizen implies a notion of the city - of the polis, of the public realm, of public purposes, publicly debated and determined. ... To narrow the scope of public power, to take activities out of the public domain and put them into the private, is, by definition, to narrow the sphere of citizenship. (Marquand, 1989).

A large number of local authorities in Britain are attempting, through a range of measures, to strengthen citizenship through political participation. These strategies seek to empower the consumer and the citizen. The argument here is that none of us are merely consumers - our relationship with society is far more complex. The citizen has a stake in all services, even in those services which he or she does not consume directly. One of the most striking urban trends of the 1980s in both Britain and the United States is the growth of social divisions. Cities became more unequal in the last decade and serious tensions have built up. The central task for urban government in the 1990s is to respond to economic, organisational and political pressures in a way which recovers a shared sense of values and renews the tradition of social idealism which city government has often stood for in the past.

Notes

1. General comparisons of local government in Britain and America are provided by Sharpe (1973), Hambleton (1978, pp 89-113), Lee (1985) and Magnusson (1986).
2. Some of the wider arguments for engaging in cross-national comparative study in the field of public administration are explored in Bull and Hambleton (1989).
3. In particular I would like to acknowledge my substantial debt to Paul Hoggett who has been heavily involved in the development of these ideas.
4. For a full discussion of these four broad approaches see Hambleton (1988b).
5. Many councils now provide good services. Examples of high quality provision are Bristol City Council, the London Borough of Hammersmith and Fulham, Manchester City Council, Wakefield Borough Council, and Strathclyde Regional Council.

References

Ascher, K. (1987) *The politics of privatisation*, London: Macmillan.

Beresford, P. (1987) *The good council guide*, Policy Study 84, London: Centre for Policy Studies.

Barbour, G.P., Fletcher, T.W. and Sipel, G.A. (1984) *Excellence in local government management*, Handbook produced by the Centre for Excellence in Local Government, Palo Alto, California.

Blunkett, D. (1985) 'Ratecap resistance', *Marxism Today*, March.

Blunkett, D. and Jackson, K. (1987) *Democracy in crisis: the town halls respond*, London: Hogarth Press.

Bowman, A.O'M. (1988) 'City government promotion of economic development', Paper presented at the annual meeting of the Urban Affairs Association, St Louis, 9-12 March.

Boyle, R. (ed) (1985) 'Symposium: leveraging urban development: a comparison of urban policy directions in the United States and Britain', *Policy and Politics*, vol 13, no 2, pp 175-210.

Bull, D. and Hambleton, R. (1989) 'The comparative study of public administration: an innovative approach', Paper presented at the 12th National Conference on Teaching Public Administration, Charlottesville, Virginia, 14-16 March.

Castells, M. (1983) 'Crisis, planning and the quality of life: managing the new historical relationships between space and society', *Environment and Planning D: Society and Space*, vol 1, pp 3-21.

Clavel, P. (1986) *The progressive city: planning and participation 1969-84*, New Jersey: Rutgers University Press.

Cummings, S. (ed) (1988) *Business elites and urban development*, Albany: State University of New York Press.

Dunleavy, P. and Rhodes, R. (1986) 'Government beyond Whitehall', in H. Drucker et al (eds) *Developments in British politics*, London: Macmillan.

du Parcq, L. (1987) 'Neighbourhood services: the Islington experience', pp 25-29 in P. Willmott (ed) *Local government decentralisation and community*, Discussion Paper 18, London: Policy Studies Institute.

Green, D. (1987) *The New Right*, London: Wheatsheaf.

Gyford, J. (1984) *Local politics in Britain*, 2nd edition, Beckenham: Croom Helm.

Gyford, J. (1986) 'Diversity, sectionalism and local democracy' in Widdicombe Report, *The conduct of local authority business*, Research, vol 4, Cmnd 9801, London: HMSO.

Hambleton, R. (1978) *Policy planning and local government*, London: Hutchinson.

Hambleton, R. (1988a) 'The new St Louis blues', *The Guardian*, 11 May.

Hambleton, R. (1988b) 'Consumerism, decentralisation and local democracy', *Public Administration*, vol 66, pp 125-47.

Hambleton, R. (1989a) 'Urban government under Thatcher and Reagan', *Urban Affairs Quarterly*, vol 24, no 3, pp 359-88.

Hambleton, R. (1989b) 'Boomtown Houston?', *Local Economy*, vol 3, no 4, pp 273-78.

Hambleton, R. and Hoggett, P. (1987) 'Beyond bureaucratic paternalism', in P. Hoggett and R. Hambleton (eds) *Decentralisation and democracy: localising public services*, Bristol: SAUS Publications, School for Advanced Urban Studies, University of Bristol.

Hambleton, R., Hoggett, P. and Tolan, F. (1989) 'The decentralisation of public services: a research agenda', *Local Government Studies*, January/February, pp 39-56.

Hill, D.M. (1974) *Democratic theory and local government*, London: George Allen and Unwin.

Hodge, M. (1987) 'Central/local conflicts: the view from Islington', in P. Hoggett and R. Hambleton (eds) *Decentralisation and democracy: localising public services*, Bristol: SAUS Publications, School for Advanced Urban Studies, University of Bristol.

Hoggett, P. (1987) 'A farewell to mass production? Decentralisation as an emergent private and public sector paradigm', in P. Hoggett and R. Hambleton (eds) *Decentralisation and democracy: localising public services*, Bristol: SAUS Publications, School for Advanced Urban Studies, University of Bristol.

Hoggett, P. and Hambleton, R. (eds) (1987) *Decentralisation and democracy: localising public services*, Bristol: SAUS Publications, School for Advanced Urban Studies, University of Bristol.

Jones, G. and Stewart, J.D. (1983) *The case for local government*, London: George Allen and Unwin.

Lee, E.C. (1985) 'Reflections on local government and politics in England and the United States', *Local Government Studies*, September/October, pp 49-67.

Local Government Training Board (1987) *Getting closer to the public*, Luton: LGTB.

Local Government Training Board (1988) *Learning from the public*, Luton: LGTB.

Lovering, J. (1988) 'The local economy and local economic strategies', *Policy and Politics*, vol 16, no 3, pp 145-57.

Lowe, S. (1986) *Urban social movements: the city after Castells*, London: Macmillan.

Magnusson, W. (1986) 'Bourgeois theories of local government', *Political Studies*, vol 34, pp 1-18.

Malpass, P. and Murie, A. (1987) *Housing policy and practice*, 2nd edition, London: Macmillan.

Marquand, D. (1989) *The unprincipled society*, London: Fontana.

Morphet, J. (1987) 'Local authority decentralisation - Tower Hamlets goes all the way', *Policy and Politics*, vol 15, no 2, pp 119-26.

Mulgen, G. (1988) 'The power of the weak', *Marxism Today*, December, pp 24-31.

Newton, K. and Karran, T.J. (1985) *The politics of local expenditure*, London: Macmillan.

Packard, V. (1957) *The hidden persuaders*, Harlow: Longman.

Peters, T. (1988) *Thriving on chaos: handbook for a management revolution*, London: Macmillan.

Peters, T. and Austin, N. (1986) *A passion for excellence*, London: Fontana.

Peters, T.J. and Waterman, R.H. (1982) *In search of excellence: lessons from America's best run companies*, New York: Harper and Row.

Peterson, G.E. (1986) 'Urban policy and the cyclical behavior of cities', pp 11-35 in G.E. Peterson and C.W. Lewis (eds) *Reagan and the cities*, Washington, DC: Urban Institute.

Pollitt, C. (1988) 'Bringing consumers into performance measurement: concepts, consequences and constraints', *Policy and Politics*, vol 16, no 2, pp 77-87.

Rhodes, R.A.W. (1987) 'Developing the public service orientation', *Local Government Studies*, May/June, pp 63-73.

Ridley, N. (1988) *The local right: enabling not providing*, Policy Study no 92, London: Centre for Policy Studies.

Robinson, C.J. (1988) Economic development planning and policy: results of a national survey of large cities, *Planning Advisory Service (PAS) Memo*, Chicago: American Planning Association.

Ross, B.H. and Stedman, M.S. (1985) *Urban politics*, 3rd edition, Illinois: Peacock.

Schon, D. A. (1971) *Beyond the stable state*, London: Temple Smith.

Sharpe, L.J. (1973) 'American democracy reconsidered', Parts 1 and 2, *British Journal of Political Science*, vol 3, pp 1-28 and 129-67.

Smith, M. (1986) *The consumer case for socialism*, Fabian Tract 513, London: Fabian Society.

Smith, M. P. (1987) 'Global capital restructuring and local political crises in the US cities', in J. Henderson and M. Castells (eds) *Global restructuring and territorial development*, London: Sage.

Stewart, J. (1983) *Local government - the conditions of local choice*, London: George Allen and Unwin.

Stewart, J. and Clarke, M. (1987) The public service orientation - issues and dilemmas, *Public Administration*, vol 65 pp 161-77.

Stoker, G. (1988) *The politics of local government*, London: Macmillan.

Thomas, Sir R. (1987) *Support services for councillors*, Report by the Association of Councillors, 2nd Edition, Croydon: Charles Knight.

Waste, R.J. (1987) *Power and pluralism in American cities*, New York: Greenwood Press.

Widdicombe Report (1986) *The conduct of local authority business*, Report of Committee of Inquiry into the conduct of local authority business, Cmnd 9797, London: HMSO.

Yates, D. (1973) *Neighborhood democracy: the politics and impacts of decentralisation*, Lexington, Mass: D.C. Heath.

Young, K. and Mason, C. (eds) (1983) *Urban economic development: new roles and relationships*, London: Macmillan.

Young, K. (1986) 'The justification of local government', in M. Goldsmith (ed) *Essays on the future of local government*, West Yorkshire Metropolitan County Council.

CHAPTER 9

URBAN DEVELOPMENT CORPORATIONS: POST-FORDISM IN ACTION OR FORDISM IN RETRENCHMENT?

PAUL BURTON AND MO O'TOOLE

Introduction

This chapter attempts to offer an account of the future directions that urban policy might take as we move towards the millennium. It begins with a brief consideration of the main factors that have driven urban policy over the last fifteen years and the particular role played by urban development corporations (UDCs) as the policy flagship of the era. We then examine the effect that the UDCs have had on urban policy development during the 1980s and the 1990s, what trends they have initiated or intensified and what pressures they have responded to. In the third section we are concerned with different perspectives on the UDCs, the way in which the UDC story is now being told. Finally we will examine the continuity and discontinuities that prevail in current urban policy. It appears that UDCs have been relegated from the position of flagship to frigate in the hierarchy of urban initiatives. We question how the role of UDCs has changed, particularly in the light of City Challenge as (ostensibly) a successor flagship. The chapter finishes by analysing the extent to which City Challenge and the Urban Regeneration Agency in particular as well as other policy vehicles have been capable of meeting the enduring problems of urban policy. The question implicit in our analysis is how better equipped are we in the 1990s to tackle these problems and what if anything have we learned from the recent experimentation in the processes of city-making.

What has driven urban policy over the last fifteen years?

Taking an overview from the mid 1960s onwards, we can see a significant shift in the analysis of urban problems. In the 1960s the so-called 'rediscovery of poverty' led to the identification of pathologically inadequate local communities, caught up in self-sustaining cycles of deprivation. These communities were nevertheless seen to be susceptible to

---

This chapter first appeared in R. Imrie and H. Thomas (eds) *British urban policy and the urban development corporations*, 1993, London: Paul Chapman.

state intervention. Policy responses took the form mainly of positive discrimination measures which targeted small areas with additional resources, using such vehicles as the Urban Programme (administered then by the Home Office), Education Priority Areas and General Improvement Areas. The consensus surrounding this approach began to break down through the work of the Community Development Projects, established in 1969, which developed a powerful critique of the scope of small scale experiments in social engineering. The Inner Areas Studies carried out in Liverpool, Birmingham and London during the early 1970s continued to shift the focus of attention onto the structural problems facing cities as they struggled to cope with rapid economic, social and demographic change, and fed directly into the White Paper *Policy for the inner city* published in 1977.

The Inner Urban Areas Act of 1978 embodied this new analysis of urban problems and adopted a much broader approach by way of response. The traditional Urban Programme was recast under the control of the Department of the Environment and the resources at its disposal increased significantly from £35 million in 1978 to £165 million in 1980. The existence of multiple deprivation within many cities and conurbations was to be tackled by partnerships of central and local government in which main spending programmes would be 'bent' in the direction of the most deprived inner city areas. Alongside environmental and social improvements, the local economic base of each of the target areas would be strengthened through direct support to local firms as well as the provision of land and premises for new business development.

While this potted history emphasises the development of analysis, understanding and awareness in policy change we should not forget the underlying political struggle. This struggle was (and continues to be) between the dispossessed minorities trapped within the 'inner city' and the representatives of the relatively privileged majority. In a sense it was an expression of the historic tension between the threats and promises of cities. The social, economic and political opportunities offered by urban life have long been contrasted with the threat of violence and social unrest associated with urban concentration (Keith and Rogers, 1991). In the second half of the 20th century this contrast has been most apparent in the distinction between a suburban ideal and an inner city problem.

Nor should we forget the racial dimension of this struggle (Indian Workers' Association, 1987). Enoch Powell's 'rivers of blood' speech in 1969 was, however, as much of a precursor of the Urban Programme as academic analyses of poverty and we should remember David Donnison's remark that "a riot makes a much bigger impact on government thinking than any amount of earnest and accurate research". From across the Atlantic the American experience of serious civil disorder between 1964 and 1968 fuelled fears that British cities might suffer a similar fate (Sills, Taylor and Golding, 1988; MacGregor and Pimlott, 1990).

The conventional wisdom, expressed in the 1977 White Paper, characterised the inner city problem in the following terms. Economic restructuring in general and deindustrialisation in particular led to a major reduction in manufacturing jobs, with little in the way of service sector replacement. Alongside this a serious skills gap opened up so that many inner city residents were unable to compete for any other job opportunities. Large areas of dereliction were created as investors sought out more attractive and profitable greenfield sites outside the conurbations, and this in turn made the inner areas even less attractive to prospective developers. In this deteriorating environment many people who were able to chose to leave, again for more attractive settings (including the new towns), leaving behind the poor, the old and relatively recent migrants from former colonies. Local authorities were then faced with a population requiring comparatively high levels of support but a dwindling local tax base.

What has driven UDCs as the flagship of urban policy?

It is important to remember that special agencies in the form of development corporations have been an important feature of British urban policy delivery for most of the post-war years. The new town programme relied on corporations not just to assemble the necessary talent and expertise to put the programme into effect, but to ensure the implementation of a national policy interest in the face of anticipated local opposition (Thomas and Cresswell, 1973).

By the early 1970s the accelerated closure of the Port of London's upstream operations, in what became known as Docklands, created enormous problems of deindustrialisation but also the opportunity for the wholesale redevelopment of an area close to the heart of the capital. While there was intense debate over the type of redevelopment needed (public or private sector housing, manufacturing or new service sector employment and so on) attention also focused on the most appropriate organisation needed to take these plans forward in the most effective manner.

The debate soon polarised into two main camps. On the one hand, were the proponents of a special development agency constituted along the same lines as a new town development corporation, and on the other hand, were the advocates of a partnership of existing local authorities. The development corporation lobby stressed the need for additional powers of land acquisition and a degree of insulation from local electoral politics. They pointed to the inevitable rivalries and disputes that would arise in any grouping of existing local authorities (five boroughs and the GLC) and argued strongly for a body that could transcend these local pressures and act in the national interest. The riparian boroughs and the GLC took a more localist line and pressed for a statutory joint committee which would reflect the interests and aspirations of East Enders in particular and Londoners in general. Local needs and local accountability therefore underpinned this approach.

The establishment of the Docklands Joint Committee in 1974 represented an acceptance of the localist case, although it must be said that the pragmatism of Geoffrey Rippon (Secretary of State for the Environment at the time) was probably more significant than the balance of the political argument. When the Conservative government took office in 1979, the new Secretary of State for the Environment, Michael Heseltine, launched a review of the policy measures inherited from his predecessors. While accepting that the partnerships established under the new Urban Programme had a continuing role to play in the regeneration of most inner city areas, he took a different view in relation to London and Merseyside, highlighting the practical capacities of special agencies, their single-mindedness and market orientation, *vis-à-vis* groupings of local authorities. It is an argument that was deployed during the lengthy inquiry into the establishment of the London Docklands Development Corporation (LDDC) carried out by a select committee of the House of Lords and subsequently during debates over the extension of UDCs to other parts of the country.

But there are at least two other arguments that can be used to explain the emergence of UDCs and their position as flagships of Conservative urban policy. The first is party political and the second may be termed structural. Party political arguments begin with the fact of an unbroken period of Conservative governments since 1979 and their mission, *inter alia*, to eradicate socialism at national and local levels. Although, as we noted above, Michael Heseltine was prepared to accept many elements of urban policy which flowed from Labour's 1977 White Paper, he was also keen to bypass Labour-controlled authorities in London and Liverpool. Indeed he went so far as to say in the course of a Commons debate on UDCs that "It was not red tape and inaction, but pure prejudiced socialism that was broken through by the LDDC" (House of Commons, 1982).

Any careful analysis of the actual plans and operations of the Docklands Joint Committee reveals the fallacy of Heseltine's accusation, but this is not to disregard entirely the significance of an anti-Labour strand to Conservative urban policy development. When we take into account the concerted attack on the powers and autonomy of local authorities, especially those controlled by Labour administrations, then we can see a party political agenda. Solesbury (1987), however, notes that the breakdown in consensus over the nature of urban problems in the late 1980s was driven as much by an assortment of clerics, academics, business groupings and local authority associations as it was by the main political parties, who remained strangely silent.

UDCs: the results

There is little doubt that the UDCs have made a significant impact on the implementation of urban regeneration policy in the 1980s. It is more problematic to disentangle their precise influence in the 'patchwork quilt' of agencies which now delivers this policy. We look at five themes in an attempt to do so; the interaction between the UDC and macroeconomic processes; policy styles and the UDCs; the UDC and place marketing; alliances to promote cities; and finally the development process. There are two points to bear in mind when attempting to evaluate the UDCs long-term contribution to urban policy making. The first is that the overview comprises evidence gathered from a range of reports that reflect diverse opinions; no comprehensive survey of UDCs had been published at the time of writing. The second lies in the specificity of the examples; it is difficult to draw a general lesson from the UDCs, either as a success or as a failure.

Macroeconomic cycles and the UDCs

It is not within the scope of this chapter to probe the debate on the nature of macroeconomic cycles, but one cannot enter into a discussion of the latter years of UDC policy without recognising the influence of such cycles on Western economies, though there is discussion as to their length and their precise impact (Elliot, 1992). However they are defined, it would seem that a combination of the cycles inherent in the development process, together with the longer and deeper movements in the global economy, are profoundly threatening to the transient, property and consumption-led development corporations. A short life span, and a property-dependent programme, have conspired to increase the vulnerability of the UDCs to the negative effects of such fluctuations (Healey et al, 1992). The late 1980s/early 1990s cycle, resulting in a vicious recession, has had a manifold impact on the plans of UDCs, but two outcomes are striking. In the short term, development and land sales have massively declined. Even where significant development has taken place, such as Trafford Park in Manchester, or in the Newcastle Business Park of Tyne and Wear's Urban Development Corporation, UDCs have failed to buck the overall downward trend in the development market. Law (1989) has described how the oversupply in office space in Trafford is aggravated by cycles. These have ultimately restructured plans which the Trafford Park Development Corporation had prepared for their flagship development.

As the pace of development slowed, and capital projects encountered difficulty, so the corporations moved in new directions. There was an increasing emphasis upon training and community development activity. The Black Country Development Corporation invested heavily in under-fives provision and creche development (BCDC, 1990). Brownill (1993) has described the increasing community and training activity which LDDC undertook as the 1980s moved to a close. Simultaneously, UDCs became more reliant on public sector finance as a primary source of funding, leverage ratios declined, and grant-in-aid peaked way above original estimates. For instance, since 1987, UDCs have received £2 billion of grant-in-aid, with the largest proportion pouring into the LDDC (*The Independent*, 25 June 1992).

It would appear that the supply side approach of the new regeneration strategies are significantly more speculative than the Keynesian strategies which predated them. But are the corporations any better equipped to deal with the vicissitudes of the macroeconomic environment than local government planning or economic development departments? In the context of interurban competition, the UDCs have influenced the capacity of the locality to engage in capital capturing activities. Returning to Trafford, the UDC has been pivotal in working to attract the Olympic Games (interview Trafford Park, 1989). Similarly the repackaging of cities in which UDCs have engaged with vigour has prompted a wider acceptance of an entrepreneurial approach to economic development (Bianchini et al, 1988).

But UDCs have been unable to assist cities to engage in strategic responses to downturns in the market. Interurban competition relies on winners and losers; as the stakes have been raised in global competition so the strategies have become even more high risk and the losses more significant. UDCs have gamely put in place strategies to win, but have been less than successful in dealing with the increasing pace of competition and the unsuccessful spatial and social projects that are bound up with this competition.

Policy styles and the UDCs

Perhaps most conspicuously the UDCs have been successful in popularising a way of doing things. The process of regeneration, indeed of city governance, now corresponds to a model promoted by the UDC. Partnerships, fast tracking and streamlining are all part of the public sector entrepreneurial kit-bag, although they do coexist with more traditional professionalised approaches to urban regeneration. The many unprompted reorganisations that have taken place alongside more radical legislative change in local government departments are a testament to the hegemonic hold that the managerial culture of the UDC has over the public sector (Stoker, 1990).

Yet the model does not really correspond to the reality. Kirklees is one of many authorities to have undertaken a reorganisation which introduces similar executive decision-making structures to those of the UDC. UDCs, however, remain predominantly reliant on the existing organisational networks of their cities. Meegan (1993) has emphasised Merseyside Development Corporation's adherence to the structure and local plans of Greater Merseyside. Tyne and Wear Development Corporation (TWDC) has been very aware of the effect that local political networks have had on their plans and have sought to accommodate the wishes of the established regional political hierarchy within the proposals for their flagship developments.

A quick response to developer interest was an essential part of the rationale for establishing UDCs and it would indeed appear that they have more room for manoeuvre in development decisions than local authority planning departments. But, as UDCs work within the present planning framework, they have inevitably been tied up with public inquiries and lengthy consultation processes such as in the Bristol spine road or the Tyne and Wear East Quayside projects. Both inquiries spread over a two year period, pushing up costs and prompting serious development problems because of changes in the market.

Perhaps the most notable feature of the UDCs' decision-making process is the extent to which they started to mimick old style local authority procedures in the field of inner city policy. This was particularly true of their community development work. Corporations found it necessary, and many found it desirable, to develop sophisticated consultation networks to appease local hostility or accommodate local desires. Residents' monitoring panels at Tyne and Wear were one such example of this process of consultation (TWDC, 1990). There have therefore been some unexpected outcomes of this process. It breathed new life into the debate on the nature of democracy within planning. The level of dissatisfaction with local authority procedures in some areas appeared no greater than discontent around UDC procedures. To some extent the presence of the UDC has allowed us to define what the planning processes should be about, particularly in the case of Docklands. The more established bureaucratic and community networks and their agendas have remained, altered but not eradicated. In most cities, a mutual accommodation has been negotiated, in many as a result of a recognition that both styles of regeneration have merit. This recognition was explicit in City Challenge where submissions that did not have evidence of a true partnership were discarded by the Department of the Environment (1991).

Place marketing

Place marketing is firmly embedded in the vocabulary of urban regeneration (for a fuller account see Wilkinson, 1992). It is used as a technique by economic development and inward investment strategists to create or illustrate the niche in the world of interurban competition which their city occupies. The marketing of cities in the context of global capital movements has become an essential prerequisite to the economic resurgence of the locality. But how does place marketing relate to the UDC? UDCs have popularised the repackaging of declining industrial cities, peripheral regions and specific sites within cities. At one end of the spectrum Canary Wharf signifies the new uses for London's East End; other examples litter the Urban Development Areas (UDAs) such as the business sites on redundant arms factories and shipbuilding yards in Tyne and Wear, the wharfside developments at Trafford Park and elsewhere, and the museums and galleries of Merseyside. But physical developments in themselves do not amount to a marketing strategy. What UDCs have done is to consolidate and, in some places, create an ethos of marketing place.

The UDC's approach has converged with that of the locality in the quest for new jobs and new populations. This has meant establishing a common sales pitch for local elites, it has required that urban infrastructure fit the new needs of the area and it has meant that training strategies should be similarly matched. Above all, it has required good publicity, whether this be in the form of glossy brochures or in undertaking damage limitation exercises when bad publicity visits the area in the form of a riot or a disturbance. New campaigns have emerged from the pens of specialised consultants and new alliances or partnerships head the promotions. Without the UDC, UDC-type processes such as place marketing would have taken much longer to ingrain themselves on the consciousness of the city. While UDCs have, therefore, been unable to live up to the expectation of catalysing wholesale regeneration, they have provided a demonstration of the implements needed to sell cities. It is their separation from the local democratic process which has allowed them to do this. But, as we shall argue in our conclusion, it is that same separation which may be the undoing of their strategies.

Public/private sector partnerships

A plethora of new alliances have been forged during the period of the UDCs. In most cities the UDC represents one part of a matrix of overlapping elites and organisational, commercial and professional interests. Frequently, the board members rotate around new institutions having sprung from established ones. UDCs have also become synonymous with the new type of partnership that now presides over what was previously public policy making in a new configuration of roles and responsibilities.

But is the UDC integral to the formation of the new alliances that are being struck up in the interest of reclaiming cities and city regions? A number of examples suggest not. For instance, the Sheffield Economic Regeneration Committee was originally established to pre-empt a development corporation. In other areas, such as Manchester and

Liverpool, the UDC forum was but one element of the decision-making jigsaw. In Birmingham most notoriously, but countless other examples exist, partnerships thrive without UDC intervention in any form, though it must be acknowledged in this latter example that resistance to the imposition of a UDC acted as a catalyst for the creation of the Heartlands project.

Despite this almost intangible relationship between UDCs and new alliances it does appear that the UDC has popularised the notion of blurring the divisions between public and private sectors that can result in the success of regeneration strategies. The UDC represents only one form of partnership, but it has assumed a flagship role in promoting the concept. What is common to both partnerships and to UDCs is an apparent credibility, premised on three things: a privatised decision-making environment, the involvement of the private sector in policy formulation rather than simply being the instruments of implementation, and the relegation of the respective local authorities in the development arena.

The development process

The term regeneration has produced much argument, and, for many, it suggests a brief beyond physical redevelopment (Centre for Local Economic Strategies, 1990; Lawless, 1991). Within this broader meaning, UDCs have failed to produce long-term regeneration in terms of jobs and infrastructure. But physical development has taken place, and in many environments where it previously would have been unthinkable. The problem about these developments is that they are not necessarily matched to the requirements of the immediate locality, even if they are suitable for the long-term redevelopment of the area.

The dispute between TWDC and Shepards, a local scrapdealer in the east end of Newcastle, serves to illustrate this point. TWDC had been diligent in their sensitivity to housing needs for social purposes. But in siting an executive housing development at St Peter's Basin, a site overlooked by a Shephards scrap metal mountain, we see the mismatch of needs that can occur in UDAs between developers and promoters of new uses for derelict areas, and local employers and employees who engage in traditional uses on the sites. There are, of course, more significant examples all of which illustrate the chasm between necessity and aesthetics, between profit and social justice which urban policy seems to underscore. More importantly, especially in relation to infrastructure, they show how the fragmentation of the institutions involved in regeneration has resulted in less than satisfactory responses to city wide or regional planning strategies.

Securing leverage was seen originally as a means to capture private investment at the same time as limiting public expenditure. Alas, as reports have shown (*The Independent*, 21 June 1992) leverage ratios are strikingly uneven and universally disappointing. The built environments of UDAs remain persistently dependent on public finance. The UDCs have been, in effect, a tacit agreement to redirect and repackage development expenditure between central government and the development industry.

Perspectives: what really happened?

So far, we have looked at how we arrived at the UDCs and the key issues to have emerged from them as we have progressed through the quagmire of Thatcherite urban policy. But it is equally important to look at the range of views that have interpreted the UDCs and how they might usefully serve us in sorting out where we go next in inner city policy. There are perhaps as many perspectives on what UDCs are about as perceptions on what they have achieved. Although we have categorised them within five frameworks which encompass the thrust of UDC experiment, we recognise that they are not discrete agendas, that there is in fact considerable overlap. Nevertheless it is valuable to distinguish between the key perspectives as they begin to draw a distinctively post-Fordist view of the process of urban governance and regeneration.

The new right has spawned two elements within the UDC agenda, the limitation of public sector bureaucracies alongside an unfettered property market. Although the left, and certainly the left in local government, has perceived the UDC firmly within the boundaries of this philosophy there has always been an ambiguity within central government circles. The criticisms emerging from the Adam Smith Institute, among others, have had a significant impact on the post-Thatcher impasse in UDC policy. The free market approach to urban regeneration, pragmatically espoused by Margaret Thatcher and Nicholas Ridley, considered the UDC to be an instrument that would disentangle bureaucracy from the urban landmarket. The critique which subsequently developed and which has, in part, been directed at that other proponent of UDC policy, Michael Heseltine, suggests that the UDCs have gone 'native', that they now represent the worst element of interference in the market place and that they have become a captive of the public sector.

This is extremely pertinent to studies of locality. There is a good deal of evidence to suggest that UDCs have gone 'native' in many of the cities in which they have been located. They meet regularly in joint public sector forums and their decisions have been in line with other public sector organisations in many localities. The extent of their conversion to local values varies; Bristol, for instance, representing a striking example of the failure to establish a trusting relationship and joint working practices. But, in other subregions, like Tyne and Wear, or in cities like Sheffield, board member networks, built up through sectoral and historical relationships, ensure a greater coherence with the whole. In other areas traditions of working amongst UDC personnel have the same effect. But ultimately the corporations are bound by their remit to regenerate an area, and in turn very much subject to the views of the Secretary of State and their board on what the appropriate method of regeneration might be. This has often resulted in conflict between the corporation and established interests already involved in the UDAs over the preferred uses for development sites.

In sketching some suggestions as to why the new right should engage in this critique we are also challenging the critics of the left who see the process of the imposition of UDCs as a one-dimensional inorganic process. The UDCs have ensured that we can no longer underestimate the power of locality as a structured force of resistance to a nationally imposed policy.

The second critique of some importance is that of the democratic pluralist. At one level, this view is most clearly espoused by the Audit Commission or the House of Commons Select Committee on Employment (National Audit Office, 1989). But there are equally cogent arguments ranged against the UDCs by both academics and local government representatives (Centre for Local Economic Strategies, 1990, 1992; Imrie and Thomas, 1992). The democratic pluralist critique hinges on the definition of regeneration, and upon arguments about accountability in the planning process. It argues, on the one hand, that efficiency, effectiveness and economy, or value for money, should be indicative of policy success, and, on the other hand, that a commitment to quality and accountability can facilitate such success. Equally, it sees local government as being equal to the task of regeneration if given similar resources with which to work. Whereas the new right theorist views the UDC as an instrument of the market, the democratic pluralist sees it as a mechanism to deal with market failure.

The democratic pluralist interpretation is also significant in our third strand, the local government view. This has its roots in the tension between central and local government. During the 1980s the increasingly hostile and polarised stance of these protagonists spawned a number of competing, and sometimes overlapping, views within a central-local state framework. There has been a stream of criticism emanating from local government associations, local councillors and opposition members in Parliament since the introduction of the UDCs, asserting the potential damage to local-central relations. But the local government agenda, which was profoundly party political, also had an important intellectual backdrop. These include the views of social theorists, such as Saunders and others, who developed the dual state thesis, distinguishing theoretically between the central and local elements in state intervention processes and identifying UDCs as examples of local corporatism. Cawson (1985), Saunders (1981) and Batley (1989) argued that they were examples of central corporatism operating locally.

There is considerable continuity between the views of the democratic pluralist, and those of the defenders of local government in the planning process. But the local government perspective is clearly committed to the appropriateness of an evolving local and accountable structure, a structure not unlike that which coexists with the development corporation but is, they would argue, decidedly more neutral.

The community and labourist perspective achieved its nadir during the mid 1980s. It is a view that is rooted in communities who continue to struggle against the demise of the manufacturing economy and the Keynesian management systems associated with that economic paradigm. The production processes which mark the era of Fordism were accompanied, it has been argued, by associated modes of social and cultural development. While the front line of resistance to the dramatic restructuring has taken place within those industries, there has been corresponding resistance within communities. These communities and their cultures have remained somewhat stubborn in the face of post-Fordist and post-modern renewal and within the context of a democratic planning process they have utilised both institutional and non-institutionalised forms of protest. The culture is influenced by a public sector that is local and accountable or at least if not accountable, intelligible to local constituents. The criticisms by the Centre for Local Economic Strategies (1990) and Byrne (1993) reflect this. They are not alone, as one northern MP recently commented:

> Effectively we are paying through the nose for a policy that has done nothing to regenerate Britain's manufacturing base. ... The overall effect is to concentrate resources on a few flagship projects ... while the manufacturing regions go to the wall.
> (*The Independent*, 16 July 1992)

UDCs were not established to regenerate the manufacturing base, nor would they in themselves be capable of this or a suitable vehicle for it. What is interesting about this view and the communities who hold it is the extent to which they have been able to secure progressive gains from the development corporations.

Finally there is a more all encompassing critique that places the UDC firmly within the debate on Fordism and post-Fordism, and correspondingly modernism and post-modernism. Within this field there is argument about how completely one should embrace the notion of post-Fordism (Amin and Robins, 1991) and there are nuances amongst those who broadly agree, but we would argue strongly that the views of three authors, Meyer (1991), Harvey (1989b) and Stoker (1991), have captured the mechanisms of transformation in Western cities and in doing so have revealed and contextualised the work of UDCs more instructively than anybody else. Our synthesis of their work is perhaps a little vulgar but they broadly conceive of UDC mechanisms as being part of a complex power struggle for control of the new urban governance; they are about an agenda for change, about managerialism versus entrepreneurialism and they are about a transformation in rules and values on which a new stage in capitalist development is predicated (Harvey, 1989a).

Whilst Harvey's emphasis has always been the spatial dimension of urban policy development, Meyer (1991) and Stoker (1991) add to his analysis by concentrating on other imperatives. Meyer's conception of the dual city explains the interrelationship between the idealised city of the UDCs' publicity brochures and that of the urban underclass eschewed by the mainstream, as both a precondition of a post-Fordist agenda and a potential for progressive struggles within the arena of the state (Meyer, 1991). Stoker, like Meyer, has utilised the regulation approach (Aglietta, 1982) to analyse the transformation in urban governance which the UDCs represent. He is equivocal about how far we have progressed into a post-Fordist regime but he does view the state as providing the necessary institutional backdrop, a regime of regulation for the transition to a more successful mode of accumulation. He sees the vehicle of urban governance as developing three characteristics to deal with the transformation: firstly, it internalises the methods of production, operating service delivery and policy development in accordance with the dominant mode of production; secondly, both left and right have evolved strategies for dealing with the transition and this makes the decision arena a live and active one where disputation, shifting ground and constant repositioning take place; finally, he argues that the inner city package did not have any coherence until the post-election period of 1987 and then the coherence was in the form of marketing and rhetoric rather than in substantive policymaking (Stoker, 1989).

When used to analyse the changing nature of UDCs, and the mounting problems they now face, this analytical stance is fruitful. UDCs have been forced to compromise on their initial position. They have begun to realise that social, as well as physical, infrastructure is needed for effective regeneration; they have found that public involvement (if not outright accountability) tends to facilitate better quality proposals as well as defusing local political unrest; and they have found that local needs cannot be ignored or left to the alleged trickle down of benefits from an unfettered market. As the property market moved from boom to bust in the 1990s the tensions which prompted this drift became even more exposed, to the point that UDCs seemed likely to be squeezed between the return to partnership embodied in City Challenge and the single-minded approach of the proposed Urban Regeneration Agency (URA).

Whither urban policy?

The future of the UDCs is a matter of interesting and somewhat tentative speculation. Overall, we have suggested that they have had a more significant ideological, and organisational, impact than in the matters of physical regeneration and inner city redevelopment. There was much speculation in the late 1980s about their potential as a post-modernist spearhead in a post-Fordist society, yet post-modernism has taken a severe critical denting in the 1990s while the UDCs have been challenged by subsequent policy initiatives, particularly City Challenge and the URA. In this section we will look at what may happen and why initiatives such as City Challenge and the URA have emerged before finally going on to say what we believe needs to happen in urban policy in Britain in the 1990s.

The urban policy debate of the 1980s consisted of five main questions: whether to concentrate on stimulating growth or access to and the distribution of the benefits of growth; whether to focus on problems or on opportunities; whether to invest in people or in places; whether to rely on market or bureaucratic/political means to effect change; and whether to use agents or develop partnerships for the delivery of policy (Solesbury, 1987). To a great extent, the UDC approach involved a clear answer to each of these questions - investment in places by centrally-appointed agents would stimulate markets and lead to self-sustaining growth, the benefits of which would eventually trickle down to everyone. City Challenge marked a break with this tradition in many if not all respects. All the areas invited to submit bids were deemed to be experiencing a wide range of serious problems, but their proposals had to show how they planned to grasp local opportunities for regeneration. Indigenous economic growth remained an important goal but great weight was also given to the development of mechanisms which linked these opportunities to local people.

Investment in human resources - not just in skills training for employment, but in the more nebulous notion of 'capacity building' - has been well established, alongside investment in physical infrastructure. The development of effective partnership arrangements has been given more attention than previously, with proposals scrutinised rigorously for signs of genuine rather than superficial partnerships. Finally, market mechanisms have been given most prominence in the competitive element of the whole challenge process. Areas have been forced to compete openly for scarce resources and there is some evidence that this sharpened up the preparation of regeneration strategies following a period in which the urban programme management initiative had succeeded in stifling much local initiative. City Challenge, therefore, reflected a shift in symbolic acronym - from the three Es (efficiency, economy and effectiveness) of the 1980s to the three Cs of the 1990s (cooperation, concentration and competition) (Department of the Environment, 1992).

Solesbury (1987) identified two additional issues in the urban policy debate of the late 1980s. The first was whether urban problems would continue to be addressed directly or tangentially through other policy measures, and the second concerned the criteria that would be used in making the inevitable choices between the competing claims of different urban areas. The second of these can be seen to have been 'resolved' through the competitive process of City Challenge. Areas or authorities have been forced to play a game in which there are a limited number of winners. The option of deciding not to play existed in principle but in practice no one took that step. In fact, during the first round of bidding, a handful of authorities threw their stake money onto the table without receiving an invitation!

The issue of whether urban problems will continue to be tackled through explicit, dedicated, urban policy measures remains somewhat clouded. The launch of Action for Cities in 1987 was widely interpreted as little more than an exercise in repackaging, pulling together a battery of existing policies and programmes into a glossy document with a preface by the Prime Minister. Academic commentators revelled in the opportunity to apply the critique of 'symbolic policy' to this, adding a twist to Mrs Thatcher's oft-quoted remark, "We must do something about those inner cities", so that it became, "We must appear to be doing something but it doesn't really matter what". Moreover, since the early 1980s a plethora of developments had been taking place on the broader policy stage which impinged, positively and negatively, on the quality of life and opportunities in the inner cities. The establishment of Training and Enterprise Councils (TECs) as relatively autonomous agents of labour market planning, the introduction of local management in schools, compulsory competitive tendering in the provision of local services and the sale of council houses illustrate the diversity of influential non-inner city policies.

At the time of writing (summer 1992) the future of an explicit, dedicated policy for the inner cities is very uncertain. A report from the Policy Studies Institute (Willmott and Hutchinson, 1992) demonstrated the failure of 15 years of intervention in closing the gap between inner city areas and the rest of the country; civil disorder has erupted in many towns and cities, often in areas that have been targeted with special measures; the outer estates are now seen as suffering similar problems to inner areas; and the notion of an 'underclass' is used extensively to describe the source and cause of the most pressing social problems of the day.

Ministers appear to be casting around for something new with which to tackle the inner city problem and have come up with plans for a new Urban Regeneration Agency (relabelled in 1993 English Partnerships). This seems little more than a peripatetic development corporation designed to avoid the problem of getting bogged down, expensively, in certain locations. It represents a return to the single-mindedness thought so important when

UDCs were first launched, the (re)creation of a specialist property development machine following the diversification of activities seen in the second and third generation UDCs.

What does all this tell us about the tractability of urban or inner city problems and the capacity of the state to intervene effectively? Drawing again on the lessons of the new towns we can say that large-scale redevelopment schemes require a lot of time, money, expertise, careful planning, political will and luck if they are to succeed. More ambitious aspirations to achieve comprehensive social and economic regeneration require the same mix but on a greater scale. Perhaps it is a deep seated recognition of our relative ignorance of the underlying dynamics of urban change and development which makes us all susceptible to the attraction of quick fixes. The more we criticise existing measures the more we increase the pressure to produce dramatically better alternatives. And these must be seen to work not over a period of decades but within the lifetime of parliaments.

We must begin to recognise the scope for effective urban policy measures in the context of broader social and economic change. This means making realistic assessments of the likely impact of spending programmes measured in tens of millions of pounds and doing this in comparison with the total budgets of local authorities and other agencies. It means examining the potential of local job creation programmes in comparison with the scale of job growth (or loss) in the economy at large. It means assessing the scope for countering discrimination in inner city labour markets against a wider backdrop of racism, sexism and other forms of discrimination. The UDCs have only served to emphasise these needs, but they have also illustrated the necessity of other policy mechanisms; for instance, the importance of an integrated strategic plan for the urban region, linking social and economic considerations as well as the polarised populations who now inhabit the same territory.

Flexibility in programme development based upon clearly developed and understood entrance and exit strategies should also be built into all urban initiatives. This would serve to improve continuity for local populations and assist in their capacity building process. Above all, local government should be able to capitalise on this enforced reorganisation to perform a new and crucial role in inner city policy, one which can accommodate UDCs and City Challenges. This would be to coordinate the now disparate functionaries of the urban infrastructure, TECs, locally managed schools, contracted out services and Housing Action Trusts, within a framework that is strategically linked and operationally consistent.

References

Aglietta, M. (1982) 'World capitalism in the eighties', *New Left Review*, vol 137, pp 5-42.

Amin, A. and Robins, K. (1991) 'The re-emergence of regional economies? The mythical geography of flexible accumulation', *Environment and Planning D: Society and Space*, vol 8, no 1, pp 7-34.

Batley, R. (1989) 'London Docklands: an analysis of power relations between UDCs and local government', *Public Administration*, vol 67, no 2, pp 167-87.

Bianchini, F., Dawson, J. and Evans, R. (1988) 'Re-imagining the city', unpublished paper.

Black Country Development Corporation (1990) *Corporate plan 1990*, Birmingham: BCDC.

Brownill, S. (1993) 'The Docklands experience: locality and community in London', in R. Imrie and H. Thomas (eds) *British urban policy and the urban development corporations*, London: Paul Chapman.

Byrne, D. (1993) 'Property development and petty markets versus maritime industrialism: past, present and future', in R. Imrie and H. Thomas (eds) *British urban policy and the urban development corporations*, London: Paul Chapman.

Cawson, A. (1985) 'Corporatism and local politics', in W. Grant (ed) *The political economy of corporatism*, London: Macmillan.

Centre for Local Economic Strategies (1990) *First year report of the CLES monitoring project on UDCs*, Manchester: CLES.

Centre for Local Economic Strategies (1992) *Social regenerataion - directions for urban policy in the 1990s*, Manchester: CLES.

Department of the Environment (1991) *City challenge: draft guidance*, London: DOE.

Department of the Environment (1992) *The urban regeneration agency: a consultation paper*, London: DOE.

Elliot, L. (1992) *The Guardian*, 24 August.

Harvey, D. (1989a) *The condition of post-modernity*, Oxford: Blackwell.

Harvey, D. (1989b) 'Transformation in urban governance in late capitalism', *Geografiska Annaler*, vol 71B, pp 3-17.

Healey, P., Davoudi, S., O'Toole, M., Tavsanoglu, S. and Usher, D. (1992) *Rebuilding the city: property-led urban regeneration*, London: E & FN Spon.

House of Commons (1982) *Official Record*, col 265, 21 April, London: HMSO.

Imrie, R. and Thomas, H. (1992) 'The wrong side of the tracks: a case study of local economic regeneration in Britain', *Policy and Politics*, vol 20, no 3, pp 213-26.

Indian Workers' Association (1987) *The regeneration of racism: the hypocrisy of inner city policies*, Middlesex: IWA.

Keith, M. and Rogers, A. (eds) (1991) *Hollow promises? Rhetoric and reality in the inner city*, London: Mansell.

Law, C.M. (1989) 'Inner city policy on the ground: the Manchester experience', *Cities*, vol 4, pp 336-46.

Lawless, P. (1991) 'Urban policy in the Thatcher decade: English inner-city policy 1979-90', *Environment and Planning C: Government and Policy*, vol 9, pp 15-30.

MacGregor, S. and Pimlott, B. (1990) 'Action and inaction in the cities', in S. Macgregor and B. Pimlott (eds) *Tackling the inner cities: 1980s reviewed: prospects for the 1990s*, Oxford: Clarendon Press.

Meegan, R. (1993) 'Urban development corporations, urban entrepreneurialism and locality', in R. Imrie and H. Thomas (eds) *British urban policy and the urban development corporations*, London: Paul Chapman.

Meyer, M. (1991) 'Politics in the post-Fordist city', *Socialist Review*, vol 91, no 1, pp 105-23.

National Audit Office (1989) *Regenerating the inner cities*, London: HMSO.

Saunders, P. (1981) *Social theory and the urban question*, London: Hutchinson.

Sills, A., Taylor, G. and Golding, P. (1988) *The politics of the urban crisis*, London: Hutchinson.

Solesbury, W. (1987) 'Urban policy in the 1980s: the issues and arguments', *The Planner*, June, pp 18-22.

Stoker, G. (1989) 'Urban development corporations: a review', *Regional Studies*, vol 23, no 2, pp 159-73.

Stoker, G. (1990) 'Regulation theory, local government and the transition to Fordism', in D. King and J. Pierre (eds) *Challenges to local government*, London: Sage.

Stoker, G. (1991) *The politics of local government*, London: Macmillan.

Thomas, R. and Cresswell, P. (1973) *The new town idea*, Milton Keynes: Open University Press.

Tyne and Wear Development Corporation (1990) *A vision of the future*, Newcastle: TWDC.

Willmott, P. and Hutchinson, R. (1992) *Urban trends 1: a report on Britain's deprived areas*, London: Policy Studies Institute.

Wilkinson, S. (1992) 'Towards a new city? A case study of image improvement initiatives in Newcastle upon Tyne', in P. Healey, S. Davoudi, M. O'Toole, S. Tavsanoglu and D. Usher (1992) *Rebuilding the city: property-led urban regeneration*, London: E & FN Spon.

B: HEALTH AND SOCIAL POLICY

CHAPTER 10

QUASI-MARKETS AND SOCIAL POLICY

JULIAN LE GRAND

Introduction

When the Thatcher government came into power in 1979, the welfare state was the biggest area of non-market activity in the British economy. The vast bulk of social security, education and health care, and a large proportion of housing and social care, were produced, allocated and distributed by bureaucratic mechanisms. Many of these activities dwarfed market activities. The National Health Service, for example, was the largest employer in Western Europe; and the welfare state as a whole consumed almost a quarter of the Gross Domestic Product.

In these areas, how much was produced and who got the fruits of production were not the unintended consequences of self-interested decisions made by individual producers and consumers operating in a competitive market. Rather they were the outcome of conscious decisions of politicians, bureaucrats and professionals operating in a bureaucratic environment and, ostensibly at least, intending to further the public interest.

Given the market ideology of the 1979 government and the rhetoric that accompanied its arrival, it might have been expected that the welfare state would be an immediate casualty of the war against the Keynesian mixed economy consensus that the new government was supposed to launch. However, to the surprise of many commentators, on the whole the first two Thatcher administrations avoided direct confrontations with the welfare system. With the major exception of council house sales, the basic structure of the welfare state in 1987 was much the same as in 1979. The vast majority of the population was still served by state-funded and state-provided systems of education, health care, social services and social security. Even the proportion of national resources going into public welfare did not change significantly; in 1987/88 it was exactly the same percentage of the GDP (23%) as it had been in 1978/79 (Le Grand, 1990b).

Quite why there was this fundamental stability is an interesting question but one that I shall not address here (it has been extensively discussed elsewhere; see, for example, Le Grand and Winter, 1987, and Le Grand, 1990b). Whatever the reason, the peace was not to last. A major offensive against the basic structures of welfare provision was launched in 1988 and

---

This chapter first appeared in the *Economic Journal*, 1991, vol 101, pp 1256-67.

1989: years that in retrospect will be seen as critical in the history of British social policy. For it was then that the Conservative government began to apply a programme of market oriented change to the welfare state.

In 1988 the Education Reform Act was passed: perhaps the most significant Education Act since the Second World War. The Department of Education began to introduce a different funding system for universities and polytechnics; it also proposed the introduction of student loans (Department of Education and Science, 1988). That year also saw the setting up of a comprehensive review into the National Health Service, a review that finally reported in January 1989 with radical proposals for the reorganisation of the NHS (Department of Health, 1989b). In the same year, the Griffiths Report on personal social services (Griffiths, 1988) was published; its recommendations were finally accepted by the government in a White Paper in December 1989 (Department of Health, 1989a). Two major acts concerning public housing were also passed in those years, the Housing Act of 1988 and the Housing and Local Government Act of 1989.

All these reforms had a fundamental similarity: the introduction of what might be termed 'quasi-markets' into the delivery of welfare services. In each case, the intention is for the state to stop being both the funder and the provider of services. Instead it is to become primarily a funder, with services being provided by a variety of private, voluntary and public suppliers, all operating in competition with one another. The method of funding is also to change. Resources are no longer to be allocated directly to providers through a bureaucratic machinery. In some cases the state continues to act as the principal purchaser, but resources are allocated through a bidding process. In other cases, an earmarked budget or 'voucher' is given directly to potential users, or to agents acting on their behalf, who can then allocate the budget as they choose between the competing providers.

If these reforms are carried through to their conclusion, the welfare state in the 1990s will be a very different animal from the welfare state of the previous 45 years. Under the 'old' system of welfare local governments owned, operated and directly financed nursery, primary and secondary schools; they funded and operated local colleges and polytechnics; they owned and managed large stocks of public housing, letting them out to tenants at subsidised rents; they owned and operated residential homes and other facilities for children, for elderly people and for people with physical or mental handicaps. Similarly, the central government owned and operated hospitals and other medical facilities; it funded and provided a general practitioner service and it financed and allocated student numbers to universities.

In the 1990s central government or local authorities will still be financing most of these activities. But, if the reform process proceeds as intended, they will not be providing the services concerned (or, if they do, their role will be increasingly that of a residual provider). Instead, welfare services will be supplied primarily by a variety of independent agencies. Opted-out and other schools will be competing for state-financed pupils; independent colleges, polytechnics and universities will be competing for students, more and more of whom will be privately financed. Independent hospitals of various kinds will be competing with directly managed hospitals for patients; private and voluntary homes will be catering for the clients of local authority social services; housing associations, or even private landlords, will be managing erstwhile council estates.

These changes thus represent a major break with the past. They also present a challenge for the analysis of social policy. What are the likely consequences of these reforms? Will they bring about greater responsiveness to the needs and wants of users of welfare services, coupled with reduced costs of service delivery, as their proponents argue? Or will they create other sources of inefficiency while simultaneously causing greater inequity, as their critics allege? We cannot properly answer these questions until the changes have fully worked their way through the system: and this is likely to be several years away. However, it is possible to make some theoretical speculations as to some of the likely consequences of the reforms, both desirable and undesirable, and this forms the basis for most of the rest of this paper. But first, a little more discussion of the quasi-market phenomenon itself is required.

The quasi-market phenomenon

So far as the welfare state is concerned the introduction of quasi-markets began in a small way in the early years of the Conservative government, with the contracting out of catering and cleaning services for the National Health Service, the assisted places scheme in education, and with the inclusion of a residential allowance in the system of social security for elderly people. The contracting out of catering and cleaning was an early instance of the state ceasing to be a provider and becoming primarily a purchaser. The assisted places scheme and the residential allowance for elderly people also involved the state as purchaser, but with the added dimension that the funding took the form of what is effectively a voucher, with the resources 'following' the choices made by the users of the services concerned.

But the 'big bang' occurred with the reforms of 1988 and 1989. The 1988 Education Reform Act incorporated two quasi-market elements: open enrolment and the ability of schools to 'opt out' from local authority control. Under the open enrolment proposals, parents are permitted to enrol their child at any school of their choice; under formula funding, schools will then receive a funding allocation based on the numbers of pupils enrolled, an allocation which, under the local management provisions, they can spend as they wish. The opting-out provisions permit schools to opt out of direct local authority finance and control and instead to receive a grant directly from central government. All these changes together can be viewed as the introduction of a form of education voucher funded by central government, with the setting up of essentially 'independent' schools and with the allocation of state funds to schools being determined by the pattern of parental choices instead of through a bureaucratic planning process.[1]

In higher education there are a variety of changes under way. Universities and polytechnics now have to bid for funds for student teaching purposes from their respective funding councils.[2] At the same time the fees for students are being raised; student grants are being frozen and top-up loans being introduced. Again these changes reflect a shift from the state as purchaser and provider to the state as purchaser only. Further, the student grant/loan system constitutes the basic elements of a voucher scheme (although this time part of the voucher would be repayable) with the students exercising their choices between independent institutions and with the pattern of resource allocation between these institutions being partly determined by the pattern of student choice.

The National Health Service reforms also include the introduction of quasi-markets. As of 1 April 1991, hospitals and other service units have been allowed to opt out from health authority control; 57 have done so already and a large number of others have expressed an interest in being in the second wave. These and other independent hospitals and health clinics will be able to tender for contracts with health authorities and general practitioners. Also GPs with practices over a certain size may have budgets for each of their patients that they will be able to spend on hospital and other treatments of their choice. The proposed budgets for health authorities and GPs to be spent on patient treatment provided by competing independent institutions is again a proposal for a form of voucher, with the difference that the choice is exercised not by the actual consumers, patients, but by the GP or the health authority acting as their agent.

Under the White Paper on social care, a 'case manager' would be appointed for each client to construct a package of care for the client concerned, based on a predetermined budget. In making up the package of care, the case manager would consider bids from competing provider organisations, including public, voluntary and private sector agencies. The proposed system can be viewed as essentially a voucher system with case managers allocating vouchers on behalf of their clients between competing institutions. Again the allocation of resources is determined by client choice (as delegated to case managers), instead of by central allocation procedures.

Under the 1988 Housing Act, the state continues to subsidise local authority tenants (primarily through housing benefit); but they are now able to choose their landlords from between competing suppliers. The mechanism of choice is slightly different (a majority of tenants are required either to vote in favour of a particular proposal or abstain), but the principle is the same: instead of the bureaucrat, the choices of consumers, or an agent acting on their behalf (in this case a collectivity of the tenants themselves), determine the allocation of state funds to providers.

All these developments thus involve the introduction of quasi-markets into the welfare state. They are 'markets' because they replace monolithic state providers with competitive independent ones. They are 'quasi' because they differ from conventional markets in a number of key ways. The differences are on both the supply and the demand sides. On the supply side, as with conventional markets, there is competition between productive enterprises or service suppliers. Thus, in all the schemes described there are independent institutions (schools, universities, hospitals, residential homes, housing associations, private landlords) competing for customers. However, in contrast to conventional markets, these organisations are not necessarily out to maximise their profits; nor are they necessarily privately owned. Precisely what such enterprises maximise, or could be expected to maximise, is unclear, as is their ownership structure.

On the demand side, consumer purchasing power is not expressed in money terms. Instead it takes the form of an earmarked budget or 'voucher' confined to the purchase of a specific service. Also on the demand side, in some of the areas concerned such as health and social services, the immediate consumer is not the one who exercises the choices concerning purchasing decisions; instead those choices are delegated to a third party (a case manager, a GP, or a health authority).

These welfare quasi-markets thus differ from conventional markets in one or more of three ways: not-for-profit organisations competing for public contracts, sometimes in competition with for-profit organisations; consumer purchasing power in the form of vouchers rather than cash; and, in some cases, the consumers represented in the market by agents instead of operating by themselves.

All of these changes are of course the product of the Conservative government; many of them emanate from the right wing think tanks such as the Institute for Economic Affairs and the Adam Smith Institute. However, an important aspect of the quasi-market phenomenon is that proposals of this kind are not confined to the Conservative end of the political spectrum. In the centre-left publication *Samizdat*, Michael Young has proposed a voucher system for GPs, to replace the present payment structure based on capitation fees (Young, 1989). As at present, doctors would receive a payment for each patient they had on their list. Unlike the present system, however, every year patients would have to choose their doctor, or confirm the choice they had already made. In Young's view,

... this would bring it home to patients that it is they, as taxpayers, who are paying the doctors; and likewise to the doctors who would be less likely, when faced by patients who have their doctors' salaries in their pockets, to consider they are being paid by 'the state'.

Accountability as well as choice would be enhanced.

In the same issue of *Samizdat*, Patricia Hewitt, an erstwhile aide to Neil Kinnock employed at the 'left' think tank, the Institute of Public Policy Research, has suggested applying the voucher idea to child care for the under-fives (Hewitt, 1989). The voucher would be given to each parent at the end of the period of parental leave. Parents could then 'spend' the voucher on a range of approved child care provision. The value of the voucher could be higher for single parents and for children with special needs. The voucher could only be spent on approved facilities.

The voucher idea has also been extended to the other end of the education ladder (Le Grand, 1987; Barr and Barnes, 1988). The suggestion is that all institutions of higher education should charge full-cost fees, and that all students should receive a non-means-tested grant (or voucher) that would cover those fees plus a generous allowance for maintenance. There is an equity issue here, in that many students (indeed most) come from well-off backgrounds; moreover, many will go on to well-paid jobs as a consequence of the education they have received at the public expense. But this could be overcome by the introduction of a graduate tax, originally suggested by Glennerster (Glennerster, Merrett and Wilson, 1968) and currently being implemented in Australia. This would be a tax set as a proportion of income levied on higher education graduates and collected through the income tax, or, as recommended by Barr, through the national insurance system (Barr, 1989). The advantages of the graduate tax would be that, unlike the repayment of conventional loans, people on low incomes would pay less than those on high incomes: hence any deterrent effect on graduates of taking up low-paid activities would be reduced.

A quasi-market idea that was actually put into practice well before the Conservative government in the 1980s is the replacement of concessionary fare schemes by transport vouchers. The problems with the former are numerous. They are usually confined to one form of transport (such as buses or trains) thus disadvantaging those who, for one reason or another, cannot use that particular form (such as those in wheel-chairs, for instance). They are also usually specific to one area, so that they provide no help for cross-boundary travel or for travel outside the area. Also for the authority operating them they represent an open-ended commitment, with little idea of exactly how much they will be called upon to contribute.

It is not widely known, but there is a system of transport vouchers already in operation. In the 1970s a consortium of public transport organisations set up a non-profit-making company, National Transport

Tokens Limited. This provides transport vouchers to local authorities or any other authority operating a concessionary fares scheme. The issuing authority buys a quantity of vouchers (in the form of coin-shaped tokens) from the company and then issues the tokens to eligible concessionary travel users. They use the tokens as full payment for their travel to any participating operator (buses, trains or taxis). Finally, the operator returns the tokens to the company, who redeems them at their face value, plus a handling charge. Any surplus from the scheme is shared with the operating authorities. The scheme has obvious advantages. To the users the scheme offers far greater flexibility than concessionary fare schemes, for the tokens can be used for any form of public transport, so long as the relevant operator accepts them. And to the issuing authority it offers budgetary certainty: they know exactly when, where and how much they are paying for the service.

From this list of 'alternative' quasi-market proposals, it is apparent that the quasi-market phenomenon is not confined to the public sector policies of the government. Indeed, as Hoggett (1990) has pointed out, changes of this type are not even confined to the public sector. So-called 'post-Fordist' changes of a similar kind are occurring in the private sector, with some companies that were hitherto vertically integrated and tightly controlled from the centre now increasingly contracting out their operations and engaging in other forms of decentralisation. More widely, there is a general move away from large-scale centrally planned organisations: most obviously in Eastern Europe, but in most Western countries as well.

The reasons for this trend are not entirely clear. The advent of new technology permitting decentralised budgeting and other forms of information processing is undoubtedly a factor, as is a worldwide disenchantment with the perceived inefficiency and dehumanising character of large organisations, public or private. Industrial relations may also play a role; it may be easier to reduce the power of trade unions if suppliers are fragmented. Whatever the reason, the very universality of the phenomenon suggests that there are perhaps fundamental forces at work which it may be difficult, if not impossible, to override, even if it were thought desirable to do so.

Quasi-markets and welfare

But would it be desirable to do so? Part of the pressure for the quasi-market reforms in the welfare area arose because there were perceived to be real problems with the previous system. These perceptions were held by critics from all parts of the political spectrum. From the Right came the accusation that the welfare bureaucracies were wasting resources on excessive administration; and they tended to protect their employees' interests at the expense of those of their users. Perhaps more importantly, they offered little choice to the client or 'consumer' of welfare services; in consequence, they were often either unable or unwilling to respond adequately to clients' specific needs and wants. In economists' terms, they were both x-inefficient and allocatively inefficient.

One aspect of this last point was echoed by other critics more sympathetic to the concerns of equity as well as efficiency. They argued that the welfare system was particularly unresponsive to the needs and wants of the very people it was set up primarily to help: the poor and disadvantaged. Resources and facilities were often diverted to those best able to manipulate the system: the educated and articulate middle classes (Le Grand, 1982; Goodin and Le Grand, 1987; Bramley, Le Grand and Low, 1989). The consequent pattern of distribution was, therefore, likely to be inequitable as well as inefficient.

The introduction of quasi-markets may help resolve some of these problems - at least in theory. The introduction of competition is supposed to encourage a more economical use of resources, thus improving x-efficiency. More importantly, the introduction of competing suppliers should improve allocative efficiency. Welfare users, or their agents, should now have alternative sources of supply. Confronted with the uncooperative teacher, with the insensitive consultant, or with the recalcitrant housing clerk, they can take their business elsewhere. This not only extends the choice of users, it gives them real power; in the battle for resources, the uncooperative, the insensitive and the recalcitrant will lose out, while the helpful, the considerate and the flexible will flourish. It may even help the poor, for under many of the quasi-market proposals they will have a measure of real economic power; if suppliers do not respond to their wishes, they can take their business elsewhere. Hence the outcome may be both more efficient and more equitable.

Thus quasi-markets are argued to have advantages in terms of both efficiency and equity over their predecessors. However, these arguments gloss over a number of serious problems, which need more detailed attention.

X-efficiency

As we have seen, a major justification for the introduction of quasi-markets is that they would promote X-efficiency. But this is open to question. The indeterminacy of enterprises' objectives (profits, turnover, social welfare?) makes it difficult to predict how they will respond to market incentives. Even if enterprises were unambiguously profit-maximising, there are well-known reasons why, for welfare services, conventional markets may be X-efficient. These include imperfect information on the part of users, the existence of professional monopolies, and increasing returns to scale. Would quasi-markets be significantly different in this respect?

A particular worry concerns the effect on costs. The switch from public monopoly provider to competitive private providers is often advocated on the grounds that it will reduce the costs of service delivery. It is argued that public providers are inherently wasteful and inefficient, partly because they are publicly owned and hence not driven by the profit motive and partly because they face no competition. The switch to competitive provision will, on this argument, reduce costs and thus release resources for more services (or reduce the burden on the taxpayer).

The fact that under the new quasi-market arrangements many providers will still not necessarily be profit-maximisers casts some doubt on this argument. But even if they were, the privatisation of provision may create an upward pressure on costs, for a wide variety of reasons.

First, there are costs involved in setting up the infrastructure for markets to operate efficiently. For instance, marketed activities must be accurately costed and their purchasers billed. If the market relationship is a contractual one, then contracts must be devised, their implementation monitored and, if necessary, enforced. All these procedures use resources and are therefore costly.

This is not to imply that resources used in this way are necessarily wasted. Properly costing activities can improve efficiency through improving decisions about resource allocation. With or without the quasi-market reforms it is likely that some form of improved costing procedures would have been introduced throughout the welfare area; indeed, this was already happening in the National Health Service. But it is important to note that measures to improve resource allocation can themselves be costly - and that perhaps on occasion they will cost more than the savings they create.

Second, competing institutions will use resources for advertising and other ways of trying to increase their market share. Again, these resources may not be wasted: spending on advertising may make for better informed consumers, and thus ultimately for more efficient decisions. But again the costs of the resources involved has to be set against any eventual gain in efficiency.

Third, the switch from monopolistic providers to competitive ones may bring about a rise in labour and in other input costs. Staff in many areas of welfare provision are organised in trade unions or in powerful professional associations which in key respects operate very much like trade unions. Economic theory suggests the power of a labour supply monopoly can be offset by a monopoly purchaser of labour. However, if there is competition for labour, then the competitors, bidding against one another, will drive up wages. This in turn will put considerable pressure on budgets, leading either to strong political representations for an increase in the budget limit or to reduction in service quality or output - which can then be used as ammunition for a further attempt to raise the budget.

The proposed changes for the National Health Service can be used to illustrate the point (Mayston, 1990). One of the major factors contributing to the relatively low costs of the NHS is its ability to hold down the wages and salaries of medical and other personnel. It is virtually a monopoly employer and is therefore able to bargain more effectively with the relevant professional associations and trade unions. However, under the quasi-market proposals, the NHS as a monopoly employer is about to be broken up. Independent hospital trusts are to be set up, which will be able to determine pay and conditions for staff. If enough hospitals become independent, the consequence will be the conversion of the NHS from being a (virtual) monopoly purchaser of labour to a (virtual) monopoly purchaser of services. It will now buy services from competitive hospitals, themselves competing for doctors, nurses and ancillary staff. Economic theory would predict that this change will bring about a widening in the dispersion of wages and salaries and probably a rise in their mean levels as well. This prediction has been borne out in the United States, where hospital wage rates have been found to be higher in competitive than in concentrated labour markets (Sloan and Elnicki, 1978; Feldman and Scheffler, 1982; Robinson, 1988).

Again, this is not to imply that if wages do rise it is automatically undesirable (Kings Fund Institute, 1989). Monopolies of any kind can be exploitative. Wage rises may have a positive impact on morale and productivity. Also there are differences between the relevant labour markets in Britain and the United States that suggest the desirability of caution in making comparisons (for example, the fact that consultants in Britain can already make large sums from private practice). Yet there remains a real concern that one of the major virtues of a 'monolithic' public sector, its ability to control the power of the professions and hence an important part of its overall labour costs, will be lost.

Fourth, the difficulty in assessing quality of outcome in many areas of welfare services in market situations often leads to a focus on the quality or quantity of inputs. Thus hospitals may compete on the basis of their level of capital equipment or the 'star' status of their consultants; schools on their laboratory facilities or their playing fields. Inevitably this will impact on input costs. If there is a direct relationship between the quality and quantity of inputs and the quantity and quality of outcomes this may not matter, since the latter will improve with the former; but if there is not (and in many welfare areas the link between inputs and outcomes has yet to be established empirically) then we are likely to see an upward pressure on costs, with no corresponding improvement in service.

Finally, costs may rise in the short term due to political pressures. In many cases the providers of welfare services are hostile to the proposed changes, partly from conservatism, partly because the changes threaten their job security, and partly because they have a genuine fear that the changes will harm the people they serve. Faced with such hostility, the government may try to defuse it by increasing salaries and other resources.

Allocative efficiency

Advocates of quasi-markets often argue that, even if there are no cost savings, there will at least be an expansion of consumer choice - desirable in itself in that it will create greater allocative efficiency. But will there necessarily be more choice in quasi-markets than under bureaucratic systems? How much choice do parents have if there is only one school in an area? How much choice will patients have if there is only one local GP, or if changing GPs is difficult? How much choice is there for either patients or GPs if there is only one local hospital? Will enough potential landlords offer themselves to the tenants of problem estates to allow a real choice? Under the Griffiths proposals, how much choice will the clients of case managers actually have? Will they, for instance, be able to choose their case manager?

Indeed in the case of residential care in particular, the quasi-market proposals could actually be viewed as having restricted choice in comparison with the previous situation. The elderly in need of residential care already had a kind of voucher: a social security payment for that care, for which entitlement was simply a test of means. Under the Griffiths proposals, the money will be channelled through local authorities and entitlement will now only be established by professional assessment.

A partial solution to the problems created by the absence of local competition might be transport vouchers of the kind discussed above. These could be given, for instance, to parents to accompany education vouchers so to widen their choice of schools, at least geographically. Or they could be given to prospective patients who have to travel to a distant hospital - and to their families for visiting them. However, transport vouchers can only reduce the direct financial costs of transport. There will still be, perhaps considerable, costs in terms of travel time and inconvenience, barriers that may still effectively restrict choice, particularly for the poor (Goodin, Le Grand and Gibson, 1985).

A possible solution to the problems that may arise due to agents, rather than the consumers themselves, making the relevant decisions, is to ensure that potential users can choose the agent who is to work on their behalf. The Young proposals for GPs mentioned above are an example of this. The idea could be extended to social care. People in need of such care could be allocated a voucher and allowed to choose their case managers who would help them decide how the voucher would be spent. Their need or entitlement could be established by a relatively simple procedure based on age, degree of disability, or, in the case of those with learning difficulties, on a test of mental aptitude. Whatever the system, it would seem important that assessment for entitlement for any earmarked budget or voucher should be separated from the decision as to how the voucher should be spent.

Equity

A common criticism of conventional markets (and a common justification for their replacement by bureaucracies) is that they foster and maintain inequalities and therefore social injustice. Quasi-markets may well have similar effects. In particular they may create problems of selectivity.

In education, selective schools may arise that cream off the most able pupils, leaving 'sink' schools for the remainder. Health care providers, such as GPs with practice budgets, or self-governing hospitals, will compete for the custom of the young and comparatively healthy, while ignoring the elderly or chronically sick. In social care, residential homes will compete for healthy elderly people, while ignoring those who are senile and incontinent. Since there is likely to be a greater concentration of the 'bad risks' among the poor and deprived, the latter may end up receiving fewer services relative to those received by the better-off, thus widening inequality.

A possible solution to this is the Positively Discriminatory Voucher or PDV (Le Grand, 1989). Here poorer individuals and/or those with greater needs are given larger vouchers or budget allocations. This gives providers of services a greater incentive to take on such people; indeed if the discrimination is large enough they may specialise in the provision of services to them. PDVs in education could be used to give schools an incentive to take on children from poorer backgrounds; similar schemes in health and social care would encourage suppliers of such care to look after those who need it most.

A difficulty with PDVs is that if income were used as the basis for discrimination, so that in general poorer families received larger vouchers, there might have to be some elaborate means test, with the attendant problems of stigma, administrative complexity and low takeup. An attractive alternative here is to use place of residence as the basis for discrimination, with larger vouchers being given to families who live in poorer areas. The wealth of an area could be assessed by a sample survey of the gross capital value of houses in the area. This would have the advantage of impeding the relatively wealthy from moving into the area to benefit from the larger voucher; for if they did so, house prices would rise and the value of the voucher would fall.

Quasi-markets: the way forward?

The list of potential problems with quasi-markets is impressive. But the old style welfare state was itself far from perfect. There is much yet to be discovered about quasi-markets. Some of the consequences of introducing them may be beneficial, others less so. What is important is not to take an *a priori* stand either for or against all the ideas. In some ways the present government has made a gift to economists analysing social policy. Many of the ideas are directly amenable to economic analysis, both standard microeconomic theory and more recent developments such as transactions costs analysis (Williamson, 1975, 1985). It has also provided a set of quasi-market 'experiments' against which to test those theories. Properly monitored, these should be able to provide us with evidence as to whether, suitably adapted and extended, quasi-markets constitute the way forward for social policy - or whether they are a retrograde development that will need reversing as soon as is politically or practically feasible.

Notes

1. Vouchers in education have been extensively discussed (see Blaug, 1984, and the references therein) but rarely implemented. The experience of what was perhaps the only voucher experiment prior to open enrolment is discussed in Maynard (1975).
2. The bidding process was suspended in 1990/91 for universities, but, at the time of writing, is still intended to form the basis of future university funding.

References

Barr, N. (1989) *Student loans: the next steps*, David Hume Paper no 15, Aberdeen: Aberdeen University Press.

Barr, N. and Barnes, A. (1988) *Strategies for higher education*, Aberdeen: Aberdeen University Press.

Blaug, M. (1984) 'Education vouchers - it all depends on what you mean', in J. Le Grand and R. Robinson (eds) *Privatisation and the welfare state*, London: Unwin Hyman.

Bramley, G., Le Grand, J. and Low, W. (1989) 'How far is the poll tax a "community charge?" The implications of service usage evidence', *Policy and Politics*, vol 17, pp 187-205.

Department of Education and Science (1988) *Top-up loans for students*, Cm 520, London: HMSO.

Department of Health (1989a) *Caring for people: community care in the next decade and beyond*, Cm 849, London: HMSO.

Department of Health (1989b) *Working for patients*, Cm 555, London: HMSO.

Feldman, R. and Scheffler, R. (1982) 'The union impact on hospital wages and fringe benefits', *Industrial and Labor Relations Review*, vol 35, pp 196-206.

Glennerster, H., Merrett, S. and Wilson, G. (1968) 'A graduate tax', *Higher Education Review*, vol 1, pp 26-38.

Goodin, R. and Le Grand, J. (1987) *Not only the poor: the middle classes and the welfare state*, London: Allen and Unwin.

Goodin, R., Le Grand, J. and Gibson, D. (1985) ' 'Come and get it'; distributional biases in social service delivery systems', *Policy and Politics*, vol 13, no 2, pp 109-25.

Griffiths, R. (1988) *Community care: agenda for action*, London: HMSO.

Hewitt, P. (1989) 'A way to cope with the world as it is', *Samizdat*, no 6, pp 3-4.

Hoggett, P. (1990) *Modernisation, political strategy and the welfare state: an organisational perspective*, Bristol: SAUS Publications, School for Advanced Urban Studies, University of Bristol.

Kings Fund Institute (1989) *Managed competition: a new approach to health care in Britain*, Briefing Paper no 9, London: Kings Fund Institute.

Le Grand, J. (1982) *The strategy of equality*, London: Allen and Unwin.

Le Grand, J. (1987) 'The middle class use of the British social services' in R. Goodin and J. Le Grand, *Not only the poor: the middle classes and the welfare state*, London: Allen and Unwin.

Le Grand, J. (1989) 'Markets, welfare and equality' in J. Le Grand and S. Estrin, (eds) *Market socialism*, Oxford: Oxford University Press.

Le Grand, J. (1990a) *Quasi-markets and social policy*, Studies in Decentralisation and Quasi-Markets no 1, Bristol: SAUS Publications, School for Advanced Urban Studies, University of Bristol.

Le Grand, J. (1990b) 'The state of welfare' in J. Hills, (ed) *The State of welfare: the welfare state in Britain from 1974*, Oxford: Oxford University Press.

Le Grand, J. and Winter, D. (1987) 'The middle classes and the welfare state under Conservative and Labour governments', *Journal of Public Policy*, vol 6, pp 399-430.

Maynard, A. (1975) *Experiment with choice in education*, London: Institute of Economic Affairs.

Mayston, D. (1990) 'NHS resourcing: a financial and economic analysis', in A. Culyer, A. Maynard and J. Posnett (eds) *Competition in health care*, London: Macmillan.

Robinson, J. (1988) 'Market structure, employment and skill mix in the hospital industry', *Southern Economic Journal*, vol 55, pp 315-25.

Sloan, F. and Elnicki, R. (1978) 'Professional nurse wage setting in hospitals' in F. Sloan (ed) *Equalizing access to nursing services*, Washington, DC: US Department of Health and Social Services.

Williamson, O. (1975) *Markets and hierarchies*, New York: The Free Press.

Williamson, O. (1985) *The economic institutions of capitalism*, New York: The Free Press.

Young, M. (1989) 'A place for vouchers in the NHS' *Samizdat*, no 6, pp 4-5.

CHAPTER 11

PRIVATISATION AND QUASI-MARKETS IN PUBLIC SECTOR SERVICE DELIVERY IN THE UNITED KINGDOM

WILL BARTLETT

Introduction

The privatisation revolution began in earnest under Mrs Thatcher's government in the United Kingdom between 1979 and 1990. Yet, looking back over this period it is remarkable that one of the largest systems of public sector service delivery in the Western world went largely unaffected by this revolution until very late on. Indeed, public spending on the welfare state (including health, education, housing, social security and the personal social services) actually rose slightly from 22.9% of GDP in 1979/80 to 23.2% of GDP by 1987/8, under a system of state ownership and allocation. However, in 1988 and the two subsequent years, a set of legislative Acts was passed which promised to extend the privatisation process throughout the whole area of public sector service delivery in the UK.

This paper describes this revolution in the making, a product of 'late Thatcherism', and considers some of its likely consequences. Following a general introductory discussion of the introduction of the quasi-market reforms in the public services sector, the paper presents a detailed discussion of the privatisation in public sector service delivery and the way in which quasi-markets operate in the areas of health, education, social services and housing in the UK. The concluding section provides an assessment of the likely effects on the efficiency of service delivery in the new system.

Quasi-markets in public services

In general terms, the quasi-markets revolution involves a process of separation of state finance from state provision of welfare services, alongside the introduction of competition in the provision of services between independent agencies. These agencies may be under private or public ownership, and may have profit or not-for-profit objectives, but are

---

This chapter first appeared in F. Targetti (ed) *Privatisation in Europe: West and East experiences*, 1992, Aldershot: Dartmouth.

no longer to be under exclusive public control. The agencies involved are to operate systems of service delivery that involve the extension of consumer choice and competition between private, voluntary or public suppliers within a framework of rules and funding set out by the state. Examples include provisions for 'opting out' of state control and/or ownership; the use of vouchers, or voucher-like arrangements; the development of internal markets in place of bureaucratic allocation; and competitive tendering within various sectors. In contrast to the privatisation programme in the public sector, it is not envisaged that publicly owned institutions will be sold to private owners through a share issue. Instead, where a transfer of ownership to the private sector takes place, it is to be effected through a process of conversion of ownership to a new set of non-profit institutions.

The sectors involved include education, health, the personal social services and a wide variety of other government services. In the provision of health services, for example, 'self-managing' hospitals are now allowed to opt out of local health authority control and establish themselves as independent 'hospital trusts'. The first 57 such NHS trusts were established in April 1991. Most of the trusts comprise hospitals or groups of hospitals, although some trusts provide other health services such as ambulance services, or community health services. They earn their revenues through commercial operations on a quasi-market by competitive contracting for patients with health authorities and some general practitioners, who are the budget holders financed by the state. In personal social services, social service professionals have become 'care managers' and are budget holders taking bids from competitive provider organisations (eg old people's homes) so that resources are no longer to be allocated by a central bureaucratic process. In education, schools may opt out of local authority control and, through the open enrolment system, compete for pupils with other independent schools in both the public and private sectors. Schools' revenues are to be determined on a competitive capitation basis so that total revenue reflects competitive success. And in housing, not-for-profit housing associations are taking a larger role in the provision of housing to rent, and tenants of council estates have the power to opt out of local authority control.

Health

By far the greatest part of health care in the UK is provided through the National Health Service (NHS). The NHS is one of the largest organisations in the world, employing over a million people throughout the UK. Throughout the 1980s, the NHS increased its share of public spending, and the Department of Health was and remains the second largest spending department, with an expenditure of £21.57 billion on the NHS in England alone in 1990/91. Moreover, by some measures the efficiency of service delivery improved throughout the 1980s: the number of patients per bed increased from 16 in 1980 to over 23 in 1988/89; average bed occupancy stood at 80%, compared to 55-65% in the residual private health care sector.

Yet some problems remain. There is a large and growing waiting list, which passed the one million mark in 1990. Inefficiencies and inequities can arise in the way in which priorities are set to manage this large queue. More significantly perhaps, it is claimed by some critics of the system that there are high levels of microeconomic inefficiency in the allocation of resources, both spatially on account of the historically-determined geographical allocation of resources, and across different types of health care, due to the implicit nature of decision criteria (Barr, 1987).

The NHS and Community Care Act was introduced by the Thatcher government in 1990, partly in response to these criticisms, and partly in reflection of the general policy trend towards the extension of the domain of operation of market forces into an area seen by Mrs Thatcher as one of the remaining bastions of 'crypto-communism': the post-war welfare state. More recently, the post-Thatcher conservatives have been at pains to stress the merits of the National Health Service, and have cast the reforms as an attempt to improve its efficiency, rather than as an attempt to replace it with something entirely new and different.

The Act, as with other elements of the quasi-market reforms, introduced both a decentralisation of control to independent provider units, and elements of a transfer of state ownership to organisations with a non-profit status. The decentralisation of control is effected through a splitting of the NHS into two sets of 'purchaser' and 'provider' units. Firstly, in the new system the district health authorities (DHAs) and budget holding general practices (GPs) (still a minority of GPs) become the purchasers, along with private individuals, insurance companies and employers. Secondly, services are supplied by providers which include the hospitals which remain under DHA control (directly managed units), GPs, and other newly independent 'provider units': the NHS hospital trusts.

Thus, to take one example, from April 1991 the Bristol and Weston DHA purchased services from two newly independent hospital trusts (each comprising a group of several hospitals), as well as a directly managed supply unit. Two large GP practices began to manage their own budgets, although others remained within the ambit of the local family health service authority.

It is intended that the new system should address some of the critics' concerns about the micro-efficiency of the system. For example, both DHAs and GP budget holders receive their revenue on a capitation basis: DHAs on the basis of their resident population, in line with previous trends towards a more consistent spatial allocation of resources; GPs on the basis of their patient list size, with the intention of offering a more effective system of incentives to stimulate GP effort.

The most significant new departure from previous arrangements, however, is to be found in the creation of a system of independent non-profit hospital trusts. The first wave of conversions of NHS hospitals into independent trusts took place in April 1991, when some 57 hospital trusts were established. This first wave of conversions covers only 2% of the 2,800 hospitals in the UK, but they are on average rather large and important ones. They account for 6% of the NHS budget; 13% of hospital beds; and £3.8 billion of assets. They were followed by a second wave of conversions in April 1992, when decisions were made concerning a further 111 applications for trust status.

A hospital trust is run by a board of directors, which consists of a chairperson, five non-executive directors, and five executive directors. The non-executive members of the board consist of two 'community directors' appointed by the regional health authority, and up to three others appointed by the Department of Health, and are likely to include people with top-level management experience in finance, information technology, legal services and personnel management. The executive directors, drawn from the upper echelons of the medical and administrative staff represent the employee and professional interest, and give substance to the Act's description of the trusts as 'self-managing' units.

The board is able to run the trust as an independent business, so that trusts can establish their own input mix (type and mix of staff, materials etc), and to agree output levels with the various purchaser units with which they draw up contracts. They are able to set levels of remuneration, bonus payments, and working conditions for their own workforce. They are able to retain financial services, and re-invest such surpluses in the trust. Income is generated on the basis of contracts drawn up with a variety of purchasers, including DHAs (not necessarily entirely with the parent DHA), GP budget holders, insurance companies, employers, individuals and other hospital trusts and directly managed units.

The assets of the hospitals and other service units which comprise a new NHS trust are transferred to its ownership when it is established. The trust becomes the new owner, free to dispose of any of the assets as the directors see fit, and to purchase and develop new sets of assets. Sales of assets are subject to the veto of the Secretary of State for asset disposals valued at over £1 million, whilst development schemes with a value of over £10 million require approval from the NHS Management Executive.

At the same time the trust is debited with a debt equivalent to the current market value of the transferred assets. This debt is held in two forms. The first part is a fixed interest rate loan in the form of interest-bearing debt (IBD). The second part, however, is a public equity stake in the form of 'public dividend capital' (PDC). The exact proportions in which these two types of debt are to be held by each individual trust is declared by the Secretary of State at the time the trust is established. Proportions tend to vary between a two-thirds/one-third split between PDC and IBD, to a fifty/fifty split between them. The important point, however, is that the dividend on the PDC is a form of (non-voting) equity dividend, payable only when the trust is in financial surplus. In this way, part of the debt service payment is made contingent upon the state of the world prevailing at any particular time, and this has the effect of shifting a proportion of the risk involved in managing an NHS trust onto the state.

Central to the operation and performance of the new arrangements for health care provision is the system of contracts which links the purchasers and providers on the new quasi-market, and on which the new system of resource allocation rests (Bartlett, 1991). Contracts are of two types. The first type is a cost-per-case contract. This, as one can imagine, sets a cost, or price, for each type of treatment. Contract prices can be set on an average cost basis, or on a marginal cost basis where there is excess capacity. Prices are regulated so that trusts make a 6% return on their assets, when entering into contracts with NHS purchasers, although they are allowed to exceed this target when entering into a contract with the private sector. The cost-per-case contract cannot be a complete contract, in the sense of specifying a separate price contingent on every set of circumstances. Nevertheless, any such contract is likely to require a far greater degree of price information than is currently available, since in most cases, individual treatment costs are just not known. In addition, such contracts tend to be costly to write, implement and enforce, the more so the more complete the nature of the contract. It is not surprising, therefore, that a survey of the intentions of those units which applied for trust status in the first round found that only 14% of such applicants intended to operate mainly on the basis of cost-per-case contracts (Newchurch, 1990).

The second type of contract in common use is the block contract. This is an incomplete contract under which the purchaser agrees to pay the trust an annual fee in return for access to a broadly defined range of services. Broad performance targets, such as an increase in the proportion of day cases, maximum target waiting lists, reduced lengths of stay, etc, are also laid down in the contract. The contract also specifies the mechanisms by which quality is to be monitored, and the remedies available if a trust fails to meet the terms of the contract. However, such contracts are inevitably incomplete, in the technical sense that they cannot specify a fee structure which is contingent upon every possible state of nature (ie every contingency). Moreover, an asymmetry of information exists between purchaser and provider concerning the level to which the contract is fulfilled, despite the implementation of medical audit procedures designed to monitor service quality. Since block contracts are incomplete, and since information is asymmetric, they are open to the problem of what

Williamson (1975) calls "opportunism". This problem occurs once an incomplete contract is agreed, and purchaser and supplier are locked in to the contract. The provider unit is then in a position to vary its performance strategy, and choose an imperfectly observed set of actions, in pursuit of its own private interests, resulting in a level and mix of service quality which may not optimise the purchaser's interest. In the present context, this could just as easily be a level of service quality that is too high in some prestigious areas (relative to the efficient level), as a level that is too low due to an excessively lax set of working practices. This 'opportunism' effect (a form of moral hazard) may work to increase the costs of service delivery over and above that which would obtain under an integrated purchaser/provider system (such as existed before the reforms were introduced).

In addition, the existence of uncertainty about the exact costs involved in meeting an incompletely specified set of obligations can impose a high degree of risk upon the provider, given that under a block contract the contract fee is fixed, even though the delivery costs are variable, and only partially controllable by the provider unit itself. In the case where trusts are risk-averse, such uncertainty over cost outcomes may increase the desired fee for any specified quantity and quality of service delivery, since the contract fee will have to include an element to cover their risk premium. This may be an additional factor tending to increase the cost of operating a contract-based system of health service delivery, the more so the greater the extent to which risk is shifted onto the provider. In practice, an element of risk-sharing is built into the system through the use of public dividend capital to fund the trust's debt.

Thus, the new system of health service provision is likely to have two offsetting effects on efficiency and performance. On the one hand, the increased incentives provided to suppliers of service by the operation of market-type price signals, and by the possibility which the new arrangements give to the independent provider units to appropriate financial surpluses tend to increase efficiency and reduce costs. On the other hand, there are a variety of factors which may work in the opposite direction. The likelihood that providers may adopt opportunistic strategies in the face of incomplete 'block' contracts; the increased risk premia required by risk-averse providers; the increased administrative costs of fully specified cost-per-case contracts; and the increased labour costs which may follow the break up of the NHS monopsony on the labour market, all tend to reduce efficiency and to raise the costs of supplying health services. The outcome of these opposing factors is as yet indeterminate, and careful theoretical and empirical research is required to estimate and determine their relative impact.

Education

Education services in the UK have hitherto been provided and financed by 104 Local Education Authorities (LEAs). There is also a small private sector (accounting for more than 6% of school children and 10% of expenditure) and some schools are run by voluntary bodies, all of which are established as charities. Education is both free and compulsory from the age of 5 to 16, and organised into a primary sector (age 5 to 11), and a secondary sector (age 11 to 19) which is largely comprehensive (ie nonselective) in nature. Within the state sector, teachers are employed by the local LEA, and salaries are paid according to an agreed national scale (the Burnham Scale). LEAs manage administrative and advisory services for the schools in their area, and, before the 1988 Education Reform Act, have had the power to allocate resources and manpower between their schools. They have also had the power to allocate children to schools in a school's catchment area, subject to an appeals procedure. Thus, although nominally under the direction of the Secretary of State for Education, in practice the locus of power over the allocation of resources in the educational sector has lain within the LEAs.

There has been much debate over the quality of education provided by the education system. Criticism has come largely from the right wing, which argues that resources are wasted through the system of administrative planning of education carried out at the local level by the LEAs. The criticism was especially vindictive in the case of the Inner London Education Authority (ILEA) which was actually abolished by the 1988 Act, and its powers transferred to the London borough authorities. Few studies of the efficiency properties of the education system have been undertaken, partly due no doubt to the difficulty of measuring the quality of education services. However, a cross section study by Lord (1984) failed to find any correlation between expenditure patterns and performance.

Various reform proposals have been debated, although few have argued in favour of a completely private system of education because of the absence of the standard conditions for the efficiency of a competitive market (such as perfect information and perfect capital markets). More widespread has been the advocacy of a voucher system. Under such a scheme, the voucher would cover the average cost of a place at a state school, and under some schemes its value could be topped up out of a parent's disposable income. Consumer choice would be enhanced through the ability of parents to send their children to the school of their choice, and schools would be free to select pupils and to organise waiting lists. Others, concerned with the adverse distributional effect of such schemes, argue that topping up should not be allowed and have suggested a modified scheme involving the use of discriminatory vouchers, whose value would be linked inversely to income levels, or to local property values (Le Grand, 1990).

The privatisation of the education sector has been a long-standing aim of the Thatcherite wing of the Conservative Party, and the first steps in this direction were introduced through the 1988 Education Reform Act. There are four main elements in the Act. Firstly it introduces a national curriculum, which takes the power to set the 'output mix' out of the hands of the LEA. Secondly it devolves the financial management of the school budget to the individual school's governing body. This arrangement, known as local management of schools (or LMS), reduces the ability of the LEA to interfere in the day-to-day management of the school. Thirdly, it introduces a competitive system of capitation funding based on open enrolment at the level of the individual school. This funding system reduces the ability of the LEA to control the allocation of resources between schools, and introduces instead a form of voucher system. And fourthly, it makes provision for individual schools to opt out of LEA control altogether, and establish themselves as independent grant maintained (GM) schools funded directly by the Department of Education and Science.

Even within the state system, the new arrangements introduce elements of decentralisation and quasi-market competition between schools. Budgetary devolution through LMS enables head teachers to control the day-to-day management of the school and allows school governors to make key strategic decisions concerning the management of the school such as the appropriate level and mix of inputs (staffing, materials, heating, maintenance etc), admissions policy, and educational priorities within the constraints set by the national curriculum. Quasi-market competition, associated with open enrolment and capitation funding, means that the more successful schools are in attracting pupils, the greater is their capitation-based budget.

In addition the LEA is no longer able directly to control the distribution of pupils among schools by administrative means. Under the new arrangements, schools compete for pupils under a system of open enrolment which presents parents with the ability to choose to which school to send their child. Schools, however, retain some control over admissions policy, especially where demand for places is high, and the school roll is full. The normal capacity of a school in terms of the number of pupils which may be admitted (known as the 'standard number') is set by the Secretary of State (rather than, as previously, the LEA). In most cases it is set at the number which were admitted either in 1979 or in 1988, whichever is the greater. Whilst this normal capacity may be exceeded by agreement between the LEA and the governing body in any year (or by appeal to the Secretary of State if no agreement can be reached between them), there is no obligation to exceed the standard number, on account of an excess demand for places. Thus popular schools may be in a position to discriminate in their admissions policy in order to influence the quality of the new pupil intake. However, since school rolls have been falling since 1979, there is a surplus of available school places, and it is likely that most schools will have to compete strongly to fill their available capacity. It is intended that such competition should make consumer choice more effective, and should bring about a distribution of resources that rewards the more popular schools and penalises the less popular.

The dynamic properties of this system are worth considering. Since performance depends much on the initial quality of the pupil intake, successful schools want to screen out less able pupils, and so enhance the likelihood of achieving high performance results, greater popularity, higher student numbers, and hence higher budget allocations, than less successful schools. Less successful schools are likely to be located in poorer areas, and so the selection mechanism reinforces class-based differences in educational provision. Over time these differences will increase as capitation funding allows successful schools to prosper and to become ever more appealing to prospective pupils. One way round such a process would be to allow genuinely free access to schools by removing the existing upper limits ('standard numbers') to open enrolment altogether. More popular and successful schools would find their teacher-pupil ratios falling, and, without the power to restrict entry of new pupils, this would place a limit on their ability to increase quality by selectively admitting only the brighter and/or more socially advantaged pupils.

The most radical part of the new measures, however, are associated with the provisions which allow individual schools to opt out of LEA control altogether. Under these measures, schools which opt out, known as grant maintained schools, need not relate to the LEA in any way once they have become independent. Any secondary school, and any primary school with more than 300 pupils can opt out of the state system following a secret vote of all the parents who send children to the school. Schools which an LEA proposes to close may also opt out, provided the closure has not been approved by the Secretary of State by the time the decision to ballot has been taken by the governors (or by a group of parents, the number of which must exceed 20% of the number of children at the school).

The governing body of a grant maintained school is composed of five elected parent-governors and either one or two elected teacher-governors. These governors serve a four-year term of office. In addition, the head teacher is an ex-officio governor. This group then appoints nine 'foundation' governors from among the local community, including representatives from local business, to serve for a term which lasts between five and seven years. Thus, there is some element of employee participation in decision making in the new system, although the majority on the governing body is held by lay parent and community representatives. Following the conversion, the governing body gains corporate status; it can enter into contracts and be sued; and individual governors become personally liable.

Privatisation of the school is effected when, upon conversion, the ownership of the assets of the school is transferred to the governing body. This includes all the land, buildings and all property used for the purpose of the school, with the sole exception of any property vested in the LEA or former governing body as trustees (in which case only the trustee rights are transferred). The governing body then has complete rights over this property to use and to sell it. The governing body may also buy new property, and has the power to invest available liquid funds. In contrast to the case of the NHS hospital trust, however, there is no equivalent creation of an initial debt; in fact, any existing debts are retained by the LEA, who must continue to pay interest on any outstanding loans. GM schools have an added advantage over state schools in that they can apply for 100% capital grants from the Department of Education and Science to support capital development programmes.

The grant maintained school is financed directly from the Department of Education and Science, on a capitation basis, which initially mimics that which it would have received had it remained within the control of the LEA, plus its share of expenditure on central services. This amount is recovered by the Department from the LEA revenues. The grant maintained school thus differs from a private school in that it does not receive its revenue from charging fees to parents, but by direct capitation payment from the state.

The governing body has complete discretion over admissions policy, up to a maximum limit of admissions specified in the articles of government. The admissions policy must, however, be consistent with the 'character' of the school as it was under LEA control (as, for example, a comprehensive school, or in its particular religious orientation). This character can be changed, but only with the agreement of the Secretary of State. Thus, grant maintained schools can adopt explicitly selective policies of admissions, and so the dynamic consequences for the evolution of the quality of provision are likely to be even more pronounced with the grant maintained schools 'skimming the cream' of the talented pupils away from the state sector.

In sum, the introduction of quasi-market reforms in the education sector has been based upon the separation of purchaser and provider functions primarily through the delegation of financial and managerial control to the individual schools' governing bodies (LMS). Schools' revenues are based on a system of capitation funding and open enrolment which introduces a voucher-type system designed to increase consumer choice and encourage competition for pupils between schools. This has been backed up by provisions for schools to opt out of LEA ownership and control and convert themselves into independent grant maintained non-profit units. Privatisation breaks the residual links between individual schools and the LEA which under LMS continues to supply central services to individual schools and so retains a measure of influence over their performance. Consequently, grant maintained schools are likely to have greater flexibility than LMS schools over choice of levels of inputs and the input mix which they adopt. In each case the funding arrangements take the form of contracts which are linear in service output - in some respects similar to the health sector cost-per-case contracts discussed above. Under a system of this type the provider unit bears all the risk of financial losses, and reaps the benefit of financial success. In contrast to the arrangements for NHS trusts, there are no provisions for sharing the increased burden of risk, which is shifted onto the provider unit in its entirety. On the other hand, the introduction of quasi-markets in education is likely to result in a closer and more direct relationship between consumers' choices and the flow of funds to provider units than is the case in the health sector. Parents can learn about the quality of the education services provided by an individual school over time through repeated sampling of quality performance. By contrast, in the health sector, often only a single sample of quality of service delivery can be taken by direct consumers, who rely instead upon GPs and DHAs to act as their agents. These institutional purchasers have considerable power to influence allocative outcomes and to create a system of "managed competition" (Appleby *et al*, 1990). Thus competitive forces are likely to have a greater influence on the provision of education services than on the provision of health services. Whether or not this leads to improvements in the efficiency of services depends largely upon the way in which the dynamics of the competitive process operates.

Social services (community care)

Changes to the system of provision of community care services (for elderly people, people with learning difficulties, physical disabilities and mental health problems) were first introduced through the NHS and Community Care Act of 1990. The main elements of privatisation in this field relate to the encouragement of a separation of the purchaser and provider roles at the level of the local authority social services department. It was intended that local authorities should no longer be responsible for the direct supply of all community care services but should take on more of an 'enabling' role through the allocation of funds. They are expected to appoint 'care managers', at a local level, who may be autonomous budget holders, purchasing the best package of care for individual clients from a wide variety of competing agencies, only one of which need be the local authority.

A typical example of this process is in the provision of residential homes for older people. Care managers are expected to cast a wide net among competing local authority, private and voluntary sector providers. All providers have to meet stringent quality control standards enforced through an independent inspectorate. The standards required in many cases exceed the existing practice in many local authorities. In addition, whilst the costs of care for clients in a private residential home are met through the national social security budget, the costs of care in a local authority home have to be met directly by the local authority itself. The policy envisages the encouragement of a high degree of private sector entry into a area which up till now has been largely dominated by public sector providers. Due partly to the financial implications for local authority budgets during a period of reorganisation and crisis in the system of local authority finance, however, the implementation of the reforms in this sector was delayed until April 1993. Despite this delay, and as a by-product of the financial crisis, privatisation in this area of community care provision is proceeding rapidly in many areas. Even though it was not a major intention of the reform of the community care services that existing provider institutions under public ownership would transfer their assets to the private or to the voluntary sector, in practice many local authorities are handing over their residential homes to housing associations and voluntary sector organisations. This process is occurring essentially because in many cases local authorities can no longer afford to administer their residential homes under the combined effect of the new financial regime and the new quality control constraints.

Housing

Since the end of the Second World War a large publicly owned rented housing sector had been built up in the UK, owned and managed by the local authorities ('council housing'). Such housing has normally been let at subsidised rents which did not reflect the current market value of the housing assets. Designed to provide for the basic housing needs of the poorer groups in society, security of tenure soon led to a situation in which there was little correlation between council house tenancy and the income level of a tenant household. As the average income levels of council house tenants rose, privatisation on the basis of the direct sale of property to sitting tenants became a feasible policy. Legislation introduced in 1980 gave council tenants a statutory right to buy their rented accommodation. The policy was popular, and discounts were set at high enough levels to make purchase of a council house attractive to large numbers of households. In addition public sector tenants were given a right to receive a mortgage loan from their local authority. As the privatisation programme proceeded the size of the discounts on offer increased, so that by 1986 they had reached a level of 60% of assessed house value after 30 years tenancy (70% for a flat). By 1988 the proceeds from privatisation of council housing had reached £14 billion. This figure should be compared to the £18 billion raised from all industrial privatisations undertaken up till that time, including British Gas, British Telecom and Cable and Wireless (Forrest, 1991).

Eventually, however, it became more difficult to increase the rate of privatisation. The higher income tenants had bought their council houses, leaving predominantly low income or older households behind as a residual lump of public sector tenants. By 1988, some 57% of council house tenants were in the bottom three deciles of the income distribution (Forrest and Murie, 1988), and over half the heads of household in the public sector were aged over 60. In this situation a modified policy of privatisation was introduced in the housing sector, reflecting the general trends of the quasi-markets programme.

The 1988 Housing Act offered council tenants the possibility to convert their entire estate, en bloc, into the ownership of voluntary housing associations. 'Tenants' choice' was to be effected by the tenants' democratic ballot to strip the local council of the ownership of their estates, and to opt out of the public sector. The new landlord could be a housing association, a housing cooperative or even a private landlord. This legislation is designed to increase the variety of service providers in a locality and thus stimulate competition between them. Rents were to be set at levels the market could bear, and housing subsidies channelled through means-tested personal housing allowances (Housing Benefit) to low income families, rather than through the directly subsidised rents of the earlier system. Transactions within the quasi-market in rental housing were to be actual market transactions, rather than contract-based, or voucher-based. Thus the new market which is created in rental housing is much more like a real market than are the quasi-markets which are being set up in the other public sector services.

Assessment

The essential ingredient of the quasi-market reforms which have taken place in the period of 'late Thatcherism' in the UK has been the transformation of a system of administrative state provision of welfare services into a market-type system based on the creation of new sets of institutions on both the demand side of the quasi-market (purchasers) and on the supply side of the quasi-market (providers). This separation of the functions of purchaser and provider supports the creation of a market in public services in which transactions are to be based variously on contracts (health), voucher-like arrangements (education), devolved budgets (community care) and market prices (housing). In several cases, but not in all, this has involved a process of privatisation of the provider organisations. Often the mere separation of functions, and the devolution of budgets (as in the case of care managers, local management of schools, directly managed units in the NHS) has been thought sufficient to give providers a sufficiently increased incentive to improve the quality of service delivery.

Often, however, this separation of the two sides of the market has been supported by a process of privatisation, where ownership has been transferred to provider units such as hospital trusts, grant maintained schools, or housing association landlords. Privatisation may support the incentive effects of quasi-market competition where the transfer of ownership results in an institutional arrangement where the provider organisations gain the right to claim the residual surplus (or loss) which results from their activities (eg from an improvement in productivity).

The separation of purchaser and provider functions gives rise to an increased asymmetry of information concerning the actions and performance of the provider units. Principle agent theory suggests that in such circumstances an optimal fee structure (contract) will be linear in output, with fixed fee contracts as a limiting case (Ross, 1973). Further, where providers are more risk averse than purchasers, an optimal contract involves some degree of risk sharing between the purchaser and the provider. This is because a provider's risk aversion increases the required costs of service delivery by an amount related to the provider's 'risk premium', and which is greater, the greater the share of risk the provider is asked to bear. This introduces a potential inefficiency into the system wherever contracts are not designed to achieve the most efficient means of sharing risk between the purchaser and provider, and may offset the advantages obtained from the heightened incentives due to quasi-market competition. In addition, the possibility that provider units may engage in opportunistic behaviour creates a potential further inefficiency within the new system, tending to increase the cost of service delivery. However, there is a trade-off between these two sources of inefficiency in terms of the variable degree to which risk is shared between purchaser and provider. Contracts which shift risk entirely onto the provider, such as a fixed fee (block) contract, minimise the incentives to providers to indulge in opportunistic behaviour, since they themselves bear the full amount of any resulting cost increases. They therefore minimise the costs associated with opportunism. On the other hand, such contracts, precisely by virtue of the fact that they shift the burden of risk entirely on to the provider, maximise the risk premium required to support the contract, and so maximise the costs associated with risk-shifting. This trade-off could be taken into account in the design of 'incentive contracts', so as to reduce the combined effect of the two sources of contract cost as far as possible. Such contracts would involve some optimal degree of risk-sharing, so that the costs of financial loss and the benefits of financial success would be shared in the most efficient way between purchaser and provider. Such optimal incentive contracts balance the costs which arise from increased opportunism against the savings from reduced risk premia (Laffont and Tirole, 1986; McAfee and McMillan, 1988).

This discussion suggests that the existing contractual arrangements which have been established in the UK quasi-market reforms have not always been designed to efficiently minimise the costs arising from these effects. For example, in the health sector, the cost sharing arrangements associated with the system of public dividend capital introduce a non-linear element into the reward structure of the provider units. When in financial surplus they must pay a dividend on such capital; yet when they make a loss they must bear the full burden themselves. The discussion of optimal incentive contracts suggests that efficient risk sharing would require the purchaser also to bear some part of any losses made by provider units, and so share the risk of uncertain and unexpected cost increases. To take another example, in education, the capitation funding system is equivalent to a contract linear in output, but it makes no provision for cost sharing between purchaser and provider. An optimal incentive contract would, in contrast, involve some element of risk sharing. This could be instituted by creating an equivalent public interest in the independent provider units' financial structure by the creation of a public dividend capital debt, perhaps held by the local authority. This would be similar to that created for the hospital trusts, which would earn dividends from financial surpluses earned by schools, but on account of which the local authority would also partially cover any losses which such schools realised in a particular year. In this way schools would share the benefit of success with the local education authority, but would also be to some extent (but not entirely) insured against the consequences of financial failure, which may be due in part to circumstances beyond their control.

Sometimes, however, the costs and inefficiencies involved in operating a quasi-market can be expected to be so great that they outweigh the improved incentives which might be stimulated by financial and managerial decentralisation, even where such positive incentives are reinforced by privatisation of 'opted out' provider units. For example, the transactions costs involved in operating a quasi-market in health services may be excessive due to the administrative costs of developing a satisfactory system of pricing, and the uncertainty surrounding the outcomes of particular treatments. Labour costs may be increased by a market system which replaces the monopsonistic position in the labour market previously held by the administrative agencies of the state, such as the NHS health authorities. Moreover, even if optimal contracts were to be designed, providers' opportunistic strategies could raise the costs of service provision. Similarly, in the provision of education services, even with effective competition between providers, market dynamics may permit inefficient outcomes when better endowed, and hence more popular schools screen new pupil entrants to influence the quality of their intake. So, inequalities in service provision may be inefficiently widened by the introduction of the quasi-market. There are, therefore, a set of circumstances under which it may be relatively more efficient to forego privatisation and the quasi-market, and to operate services within an integrated system under public ownership and management. However, the way in which the balance of positive and negative incentives and effects works out in practice is essentially an empirical issue. Careful research of an empirical nature is required to investigate the comparative performance of the new varieties of privatisations which are emerging in the welfare sector in the UK in the 1990s.

References

Appleby, J. et al (1990) 'The use of markets in the health service: the NHS reforms and managed competition', *Public Money and Management*, (winter), pp 27-33.

Barr, N. (1987) *The economics of the welfare state*, London: Weidenfeld and Nicolson.

Bartlett, W. (1991) *Quasi-markets and contracts: a market and hierarchies perspective on the NHS reforms*, Studies in Decentralisation and Quasi-Markets no 3, Bristol: SAUS Publications, School for Advanced Urban Studies, University of Bristol.

Forrest, R. (1991) 'Privatisation and housing under Thatcherism', *Journal of Urban Affairs*, vol 13, pp 201-19.

Forrest, R. and Murie, A. (1988) *Selling the welfare state*, London: Routledge.

Laffont, J.J. and Tirole, J. (1986) 'Using cost observations to regulate firms', *Journal of Political Economy*, vol 94, no 3, pp 614-41.

Le Grand, J. (1990) *Quasi-markets and social policy*, Studies in Decentralisation and Quasi-Markets no 1, Bristol: SAUS Publications, School for Advanced Urban Studies, University of Bristol.

Leonard, M. (1988) *The 1988 Education Act: a tactical guide for schools*, Oxford: Blackwell.

Lord, R. (1984) *Value for money in education*, London: Chartered Institute of Public Finance and Accountancy.

McAfee, R.P. and McMillan, J. (1988) *Incentives in government contracting*, Toronto: University of Toronto Press.

Newchurch (1990) *The Newchurch guide to NHS trust applications*, London: Newchurch and Co.

Ross, S.A. (1973) 'The economic theory of agency: the principal's problem', *American Economic Review*, vol 63, no 2, pp 134-39.

Williamson, E.O. (1975) *Markets and hierarchies: analysis and anti-trust implications*, New York: The Free Press.

CHAPTER 12

NEED, EQUITY AND THE NHS: THE DISTRIBUTION OF HEALTH CARE EXPENDITURE 1974-87

CAROL PROPPER AND RICHARD UPWARD

Introduction

It is a widely accepted proposition that one of the aims of the UK National Health Service is to allocate health care on the basis of need. However, while there may be considerable consensus over the legitimacy of this goal, there is also considerable debate as to whether the goal has been met. If care is allocated according to need, then the corollary is, after controlling for differences in need, there should be no systematic differences in the amount of care received by persons of different ability to pay. Allocation according to need means that ability to pay should be unimportant. Thus an empirical test of whether the NHS allocates according to need is to examine horizontal equity in the delivery of health care, controlling for differences in need.

In an early study of this distribution, Forster (1976) took class as a measure of ability to pay. His results showed the utilisation of publicly funded health care was positively associated with class for men, but independent of class for women. Le Grand (1978), using the same methodological approach, and data for 1972, reached the conclusion that the top two socio-economic groups received 40% more health care per person reporting sick than the bottom two socio-economic groups. Hurst (1985) used data for 1976 and reached a similar conclusion. These findings have formed part of a body of evidence which has been used to support the hypothesis of middle class capture of the welfare state (Goodin and Le Grand, 1987). However, later research on the distribution of public-sector-provided health care reached different conclusions. Collins and Klein (1980), Puffer (1986), O'Donnell and Propper (1991) and Evandrou et al (1991) all found considerably smaller and less systematic departures from horizontal equity.

One conclusion might be that there has been a genuine decrease in horizontal inequity in the delivery of health care in the UK. The studies cited above all use data from the same national cross-sectional household

---

This chapter first appeared in *Fiscal Studies*, 1992, vol 13, no 2, pp 1-21.

survey, but the data are drawn from various points within a 15-year time span. During this period there were considerable changes in the NHS. Some of these were explicitly directed at removing inequalities in the distribution of health care, for example, RAWP (Resource Allocation Working Party, Department of Health and Social Security, 1976). Although RAWP was aimed at the reduction of geographical inequality, it may have had a second-order effect on the distribution of health care across individuals. However, before this conclusion can be drawn, a number of methodological issues need to be considered. The definitions of ability to pay, utilisation of medical care and need for medical care are not consistent across all the studies cited here. The manner in which health care is adjusted for need varies across the studies. Some studies use a regression approach; others compare standardised ratios of health care received to need. While some of the later studies use a similar methodological approach and the same data set (for example, Puffer and Evandrou *et al* use regression analysis; O'Donnell and Propper replicate the methodologies used by Le Grand and Collins and Klein), in each study only one year of data is examined. These data are taken from surveys carried out in different years. Thus it is not possible from this body of evidence to distinguish between change over time, sampling variability and differences in methodology.

In the present research we seek to shed some light on these issues by undertaking a replication of a subset of these studies. We do not propose a new definition of horizontal equity in the distribution of publicly funded health care expenditure. Instead, we adopt three methodologies that have been used in previous research. These methodologies are used to analyse four sets of data, covering the period 1974 to 1987, taken from the same cross-sectional national survey. Common definitions of all variables in the analyses were employed. Only by adopting this approach can change over time be disentangled from differences in methodology and sampling variability.

The paper is organised in six sections dealing with the following: (i) the methodological approaches that are adopted in this replication study; (ii) the data used; (iii) the distributions of need; (iv) tests of departures from horizontal equity of health care expenditure; (v) a discussion of results; and (vi) some concluding comments.

Methodological approaches

Horizontal equity in the allocation of public resources requires that individuals defined as equal should be treated equally. The characteristics of any individual can be divided into two sets. In the first set are those characteristics which are established by policy as the basis for resource allocation. In the second set are those which are deemed to be irrelevant for the purposes of resource allocation. The horizontal equity principle requires that allocation should be based only on characteristics falling in the first set. More precisely, individuals who are identical in terms of first-set characteristics, but differ in terms of second-set characteristics, should receive the same allocation. In the case of the allocation of publicly funded health care, Wagstaff and van Doorslaer (1992) have argued that a departure from allocation according to need is a departure from horizontal equity. Once the characteristic need is taken into account, the NHS goal should imply that there are no systematic differences in allocation of health care across individuals. Systematic differences across income, socio-economic group or any other measure of ability to pay thus represent departures from horizontal equity.

Since allocation should differ across individuals in different need, in order to examine departures from horizontal equity, it is necessary to define an allocation standardised for need. Different researchers have adopted different definitions and measures of this key variable. In this replication, we wished to make use of micro data. Given our aim of disentangling change over time from differences in methodology and sampling variability, we could replicate only those methodological approaches suited to analysis of the type of data derived from large-scale, representative data sets. We also wished to be able to compare our findings with those from earlier research, in particular the influential work of Le Grand (1978). We therefore employed three different methodological definitions of the allocation of publicly funded health care, standardised for need. These measures are not those that would be adopted in an explanation of the determinants of health care expenditure. They are not intended for this purpose. Instead, they are summary measures of the variable of interest, the distribution of health care standardised for need. These measures can be used to examine departures from horizontal equity.

Le Grand (1978), following Forster, defined the summary measure as the ratio of health service utilisation in an ability-to-pay group to the need of that ability-to-pay group. Collins and Klein (1980) proposed examination of the variation in utilisation of services by individuals of a given need across ability-to-pay groups. The two studies reached different conclusions, Le Grand finding evidence of substantial inequality, Collins and Klein concluding there was little evidence of departures from equality. The differences may be due to differences in the health services examined. Le Grand examined the distribution of all NHS care while Collins and Klein looked only at primary care. However, the differences in conclusions may also be due to differences in methodology.

O'Donnell and Propper (1991) have argued that if need for medical care is not distributed equally across ability-to-pay groups, the ratio of use to need approach adopted by Le Grand will produce systematically different results from an examination of the amount of use within need groups. Let there be only two need groups, the ill and the not-ill. Let x_i and x'_i be the amount of services used by the ill and the not-ill respectively in group i. i indexes ability to pay. The Collins and Klein approach involves examination of two ratios:

$$x_i / n_i \text{ and } x'_i / n'_i \text{ for each } i \qquad (1)$$

where n_i = the numbers of ill in group i;
n'_i = the numbers of not-ill in group i.

If these ratios are the same across all i then equal treatment for equal need is achieved. Using the same notation, the Le Grand measure of standardised expenditure is:

$$(x_i + x'_i) / n_i \text{ for each } i. \qquad (2)$$

Equal treatment for equal need requires that this ratio does not vary systematically across i.

If the distribution of the not-ill varies systematically across income groups, and this variation is such that the rich are more likely to be not-ill (as is the case in the UK) then the two measures will produce different results. Equation (2) will indicate that expenditure is more pro-rich than equation (1). More formally, let a_i and a'_i be the average utilisation of health care within the ill and not-ill groups respectively:

$$a_i = x_i / n_i$$
$$a'_i = x'_i / n'_i$$

Substituting these definitions into (2), the Le Grand use-need ratio is:

$$a_i + (a'_i n'_i) / n_i \qquad (3)$$

In the case of equal treatment for equal need, $a_i = a$ for all i, and (3) becomes:

$$a + (a'n'_i) / n_i \qquad (4)$$

Equation (4) makes it clear that equal treatment for equal need is not sufficient for the Le Grand use-need ratio to be equal across income groups. A further condition is that n'_i/n_i is constant across i.

The Le Grand measure, equation (2), requires the auxiliary assumption that those who are recorded as not-ill are not in need. By contrast, equation (1) allows that they may be in need, but makes no *a priori* assumption about the level of need for this group relative to that of those recorded as ill. Given that in any empirical analysis, observed measures of need will be used, the question of which measure is more appropriate is to a large extent an empirical issue and concerns the relationship between observed measures of need and the 'true' latent variable need.

The literature on the relationship between recorded need and true medical need indicates that individuals can have illnesses (and so a need for medical treatment) of which they are not aware (Blaxter, 1990). In addition, the empirical observations of need used in all the studies discussed here are self-assessed measures of need. They are also relatively few in number and apply to a period which does not always correspond to the period for which utilisation of health care is recorded. In some cases, the need measure applies to a shorter time span than the period over which utilisation is recorded. Thus an individual may have been in need, received health care and as a result subsequently, at the time of the survey, recorded themselves as no longer ill. However, this does not imply that this individual was not in need at the time health care was received. For these reasons, it would appear to be more useful to examine explicitly the distribution of NHS resources across individuals in different need categories, rather than make the Le Grand assumption that those who do not report illness have zero need. However, in this particular paper, in order to allow comparison with earlier research, both methodologies (1) and (2) are used.

While equation (1) makes no *a priori* assumption about the weighting of various measures of need, it does not provide a single summary measure of the distribution of health care expenditure. A separate ratio is calculated for each measure of medical need. An extension which provides a single summary measure has been proposed by Wagstaff and van Doorslaer (1992). This measure is:

$$\sum_m (x_{mi} / n_{mi}) n_m / N \tag{5}$$

where n_m = the number in the population in need group m,
x_{mi} / n_{mi} = average utilisation of health care by those in need group m and ability-to-pay group i;
N = total sample size.

Equation (5) is a weighted sum of the average use of individuals in need group m, where the weights are the population proportion reporting that measure of need. Equation (5) is referred to as the Comac methodology. As with all measures discussed here, this statistic embodies a value judgement, in this case that the weights for each measure of need reflect the incidence of each measure of need in the population. Other types of weight may be preferred (for example, to give greater weight to those who are in greater need).[1]

To compare the distributions of health care utilisation standardised for need requires some summary statistic. The statistic used was the concentration index. Let x represent ability to pay and y health care standardised for need. If horizontal equity is violated, then $y = g(x)$. The concentration curve for health care y is the share of total y received by observations with ability to pay of x or less, plotted against the population share of those with an income no greater than x. The concentration index is 1 minus twice the area under the concentration curve (Jenkins, 1988). The concentration index (CI) is of the same form as the Gini coefficient. The larger the absolute value of the index, the greater the extent of inequality. A variable which is distributed proportionately more to those observations with high values for x will have a positive index. An example would be the CI for income (the Gini coefficient). A variable which is distributed proportionately more to those observations with low values of x will have a negative index. The index ranges from +1 to -1; so for example if the whole distribution is concentrated in the observation with the lowest x, the CI will be -1. The CIs were calculated from micro data using a method suggested by Jenkins (1988).[2]

Data

To carry out this research, data on the utilisation of NHS services, ability to pay, socio-demographic characteristics and measures of medical need are required. The data used in this research are from the General Household Survey (GHS). This is a national cross-sectional micro data set of over 10,000 households and 25,000 individuals. It includes measures of individuals' health care utilisation, need and ability to pay. In this replication, data from four years of the survey were used, the years chosen to span as long a time period as possible, subject to the constraint that the same data were available in all the samples. The selected years were 1974, 1982, 1985 and 1987. Data for 1976-81 on key variables were not comparable with those of later or earlier years. Data for 1982 are incomplete, as the utilisation of health services for children is not recorded. For the full four years analysis was possible for an adult-only sample. Analysis was undertaken using data on all individuals for the other three years. Any differences in the pattern of results using the two samples are reported.

The GHS imposes certain constraints on the empirical measures of health care utilisation. It provides information on the utilisation of primary care (general practitioner visits), out-patient, accident and emergency and in-patient care, but for three of the four years provides no information on individuals' length of stay as in-patients. It was therefore assumed that average length of stay was constant across individuals.[3] No measure of quality of service was provided, so it was assumed quality does not vary systematically across individuals. The GHS does not survey the institutionalised population. Thus a major omission from our analysis (and of earlier analyses) is the distribution of institutional care. Individuals resident in NHS institutions are likely to be amongst the poorest members of society and most intensive users of health care. Their omission will reduce the relative use of health care recorded for the poor. But the health status of the institutionalised population is generally very low and so it is not possible to predict what the impact of their omission on the distribution of health care relative to need will be. In all, it is estimated that the data in the GHS account for approximately 60% of total NHS expenditure. To identify aggregate NHS utilisation it is necessary to weight the various types of health care. Service usage was therefore multiplied by unit costs to produce total NHS expenditure on each group.[4]

Various measures of self-reported morbidity were used as proxies for the latent variable need. The questions asked in the GHS are designed to distinguish between health state and health status. As a measure of health state, individuals are asked whether they have experienced an illness or injury which has restricted their usual activity in the preceding two-week period. Health status is measured by asking individuals whether they have any long-standing illness, disability or infirmity. Those responding positively are asked whether they experienced limited functioning due to this illness. These questions were asked both of adults and to adults about their children. In addition, adults are asked to rate their general health as 'good', 'fairly good' or 'not good'. It has previously been established that these measures reflect different facets of need (Blaxter, 1990). We therefore undertake analyses using either all these measures or a subset of them where dictated by the needs of replication.

As a measure of ability to pay, previous research has used both (current) income and socio-economic group. We have argued elsewhere (O'Donnell and Propper, 1991) that socio-economic group (essentially occupation) is often used as a proxy for other variables, such as income, education and social attitude. Rather than use a composite measure which may be weakly associated with any one of the variables which it proxies, we argue that it is more sensible to use current income appropriately equivalised for family type. However, earlier analyses have used socio-economic group (SEG), so for purposes of comparability, replications of the Le Grand methodology were undertaken using both income and SEG.

The income variable is gross family income, adjusted for the size and structure of the family (ie equivalent family income). Family rather than individual or household income is used, since this makes the most plausible assumption about the degree of income pooling which generally occurs within households.[5]

Factors other than need may affect the utilisation of publicly provided health care services. If these factors are correlated with ability to pay and account is not taken of this, there is a possibility that the association between these factors and utilisation will be mistaken for an association between ability to pay and utilisation. In a dynamic model, and with appropriate panel data, such associations could be fully modelled. In cross-sectional data this is not possible. All the studies replicated here fitted linear terms in age and sex to control for differences in the distribution of age and sex across income groups. While it is accepted that this does not address the issue of causality, and would be inappropriate if the aim of the research were to develop an explanatory model of the utilisation of health care standardisation, adopting this procedure allows replication of, and so comparison with, earlier research. Thus the distributions of health care presented in this paper are after standardisation for age and sex.[6]

Distributions of need

Prior to an analysis of the distribution of utilisation adjusted for need, we analyse the distribution of need, ie of self-assessed morbidity. It has been established that the extent of self-assessed morbidity has been rising since the 1970s (Hills, 1990). However, change in the distribution, as distinct from the level, has been less noted. Table 1 shows the number of individuals in each income group reporting different types of morbidity, as a percentage of all individuals reporting that type of morbidity. The distributions show that need, as proxied by three of the four measures, is negatively associated with income. The measure of non-limiting chronic illness is an exception.

The extent of inequity varies across the different morbidity measures. The CIs indicate that the distribution of the general health status (labelled 'general health rated as not good' in Table 1) is more unequal than the measure of limiting chronic illness, which in turn is more unequal than the distribution of acute illness. Non-limiting chronic illness has the smallest degree of inequity, with the rich reporting slightly more, as noted above. This pattern is stable across all years, indicating that it is not due to sample variation.

These results confirm previous findings for individual years (Hurst, 1985; O'Donnell and Propper, 1991). Those in lower income groups, on the basis of three of the four measures of morbidity, are sicker. With the exception of non-limiting chronic illness (the most difficult measure to interpret in terms of severity) the patterns of inequity are similar across all measures of need. Inequity increases from 1974 to 1985 and then falls in

1987, though comparing 1974 with 1987 there appears to be little worsening of inequity.

Table 1: Percentage of total morbidity of various types reported by each income quintile (adults only, standardised by age and sex)

Income quintile	1974	1982	1985	1987
(i) Acute illness				
Bottom	21.9	21.8	26.4	22.0
2nd	21.7	22.6	21.4	22.1
3rd	19.2	19.7	18.5	19.6
4th	18.6	16.9	15.1	18.0
Top	18.6	19.0	18.6	18.3
Concentration index	-0.039	-0.045	-0.088	-0.047
(ii) Non-limiting chronic illness				
Bottom	19.9	19.6	17.9	18.9
2nd	21.6	20.1	19.4	18.4
3rd	19.4	19.9	21.2	20.2
4th	18.6	21.2	19.3	21.9
Top	20.6	19.2	22.2	20.6
Concentration index	-0.007	-0.001	0.044	0.028
(iii) Limiting chronic illness				
Bottom	25.7	25.3	29.1	26.3
2nd	23.5	25.1	24.1	23.0
3rd	18.7	19.0	17.7	18.8
4th	16.8	15.7	15.2	16.8
Top	15.3	14.9	13.8	15.1
Concentration index	-0.113	-0.123	-0.157	-0.122
(iv) General health rated as 'not good'				
Bottom	-	29.3	33.6	29.2
2nd	-	26.2	26.4	25.3
3rd	-	17.4	17.0	19.7
4th	-	15.2	13.1	15.2
Top	-	11.9	9.8	10.5
Concentration index	-	-0.192	-0.257	-0.147

Earlier research has indicated that the measure of general health is very subjective. For the same medical conditions, individuals of different ages and gender report different levels of general health (Wright, 1986). Thus given this measure, variation across individuals is non-random across age, sex and probably also income. Thus this measure (labelled 'general health rated as not good' in Table 1) was not used in the analyses of the distribution of utilisation adjusted for need.

In Table 2 we present a measure of the absolute level of self-reported morbidity. The table shows the percentage in each quintile who report acute and/or limiting chronic illness (the measure of need used by Le Grand, 1978). For all five income quintiles the proportion reporting morbidity has increased by about one-third. There is a slightly greater increase for the poorer groups: the poorest quintile report 33% more morbidity, while the richest increased by 28%. Overall, however, whilst reporting of morbidity has increased, increases are of a similar magnitude across all income groups. (The distribution by SEG follows similar patterns.)

Table 2: Percentage of each gross equivalent income quintile reporting acute and/or limiting chronic illness (adults only, standardised by age and sex)

Income quintile	1974	1982	1985	1987
Bottom	29.0	33.4	37.2	38.6
2nd	27.5	33.1	31.1	35.8
3rd	23.1	27.1	25.2	29.7
4th	21.6	23.0	21.7	27.7
Top	20.7	23.3	22.7	26.4

The reasons for this increase in reporting of morbidity are not clear. It seems unlikely that this large rise is due mainly to the population actually becoming sicker: over the period 1975 to 1987 mortality, as measured by the crude death rate, fell by about 4% (Office of Health Economics, 1990). It seems more likely that greater awareness and intolerance of ill health and greater reporting are the cause. A similar pattern has been observed in North America, particularly in the reporting of long-term disability (similar to the limiting chronic measure used here). Various hypotheses have been advanced for this increase. These include the ageing of the population, increases in unemployment for which individuals avoid social stigma by reporting themselves disabled and the introduction of social welfare programmes which treat the disabled unemployed more favourably than others out of work (Wolfe and Haveman, 1990). In empirical analyses all of these factors appear to be important. Disney and Webb (1991) found that the most important determinant of the increase in invalidity benefit claims in the UK was aggregate unemployment. If self-reported morbidity is correlated with claiming invalidity benefit, then some of the increase in self-reported morbidity may be caused by an increase in aggregate unemployment. The differential impact of unemployment on lower income groups may be an explanation for the increase in inequality in 1985.

Horizontal equity of NHS expenditure

To undertake replication, we used the three methodologies outlined earlier. For each methodology, the percentage share of per person standardised expenditure received by each ability-to-pay group is reported. Ability to pay is defined as equivalised income, except in the case of a replication of the Le Grand results using SEG. Horizontal equity requires that each group receives the same share of standardised expenditure.[7] A positive value for the CI statistic indicates a pro-rich distribution, a negative value a pro-poor distribution.

Table 3 shows the amount of expenditure on each morbidity group using the Collins and Klein measure. The CIs for the distribution of expenditure standardised for acute illness, non-limiting and limiting chronic illness separately are all negative, indicating that departures from equity favour the poor. The absolute values are small, in all but two cases below 0.1. There is no very clear pattern in the absolute values of the CIs across the years. The CIs are smallest in 1982 for all three measures, but the largest absolute value for acute is in 1987, for non-limiting chronic is in 1985 and for limiting chronic is in 1974.[8]

Table 4 presents the results of analysis using the Comac methodology. The CIs in the table show a standardised distribution of NHS expenditure which favours the lower income groups in all four years. The extent of this 'pro-poorness' does not alter greatly between 1974 and 1987. The distribution does, however, become slightly more favourable to those in higher income quintiles in 1985 and 1987, as indicated by the slight decrease in the size of the concentration indices.

The estimated expenditures in Table 4 are calculated as the product of the estimated probability of the observation incurring any expenditure and the estimated mean amount of expenditure for that observation conditional on expenditure being positive. That is:

$$E(exp) = Pr(exp>0) \times E(exp/exp>0)$$

where E denotes the expectation, Pr the probability and exp the standardised utilisation.

Table 3: Collins and Klein methodology: percentage shares of standardised NHS expenditure (adults only, standardised by age and sex)

Income quintile	1974	1982	1985	1987
(i) Acute				
Bottom	23.8	20.6	21.8	23.7
2nd	22.2	20.2	23.5	20.8
3rd	19.5	20.1	20.3	19.0
4th	19.3	23.2	18.3	22.0
Top	15.3	15.9	16.0	14.5
Concentration index	-0.085	-0.047	-0.068	-0.099
(ii) Non-limiting chronic				
Bottom	27.7	23.5	26.9	22.1
2nd	14.3	20.9	19.8	24.1
3rd	18.6	16.8	21.2	18.1
4th	20.8	21.5	18.2	19.7
Top	18.6	17.3	14.0	16.0
Concentration index	-0.047	-0.045	-0.126	-0.067
(iii) Limiting chronic				
Bottom	25.1	21.0	22.7	23.0
2nd	22.3	19.9	24.6	22.7
3rd	21.2	22.5	19.1	20.3
4th	18.1	22.4	17.9	19.2
Top	13.4	14.2	15.7	14.8
Concentration index	-0.117	-0.026	-0.084	-0.085

The distribution across income group of the probability of utilisation and the conditional level of utilisation may differ. The higher expenditure on the poor may be the result of a greater probability of access to health services and/or the receipt of a higher level of expenditure once access has occurred. In the UK health care system, a plausible hypothesis is that (after standardisation for need) initial contact is more unevenly distributed than the amount of expenditure received conditional on care being initiated. The direct financial costs of care in the UK system are zero, but access costs, such as lack of information, travel costs etc, have been argued to be greater barriers to initiation of treatment for low income groups (Barr, 1987).

Table 4: Comac methodology: percentage shares of standardised NHS expenditure (adults only, standardised by age, sex, acute, limiting and non-limiting chronic illness)

Income quintile	1974	1982	1985	1987
Bottom	24.6	22.5	22.7	22.7
2nd	21.6	20.3	22.7	21.2
3rd	19.3	21.1	19.7	19.9
4th	17.9	21.7	18.9	19.8
Top	16.6	14.5	16.1	16.3
Concentration index	-0.083	-0.092	-0.070	-0.062

However, once care has been initiated, the lack of co-payment may mean that the level of care is exogenous to the demander, and is determined by the provider. Given the zero co-payment, providers may not take into account the income of their patients. Indeed, their stated goal is allocation according to need. If this is the case, the level of care given to those who have had initial contact should not vary systematically with ability to pay.

Concentration indices calculated for the distributions of the two components of expenditure suggest that those in the lower income quintiles have a very slightly higher probability of access, but also get a greater share of expenditure once treatment is initiated. The difference in CIs for probability of access and conditional expenditure are small. Thus the data do not support the differential access/treatment hypothesis.

The results using the Le Grand use-need ratio as the method of standardisation are presented in Table 5.[9] For purposes of comparability with Le Grand (1978), need was defined as positive if an individual reported limiting chronic and/or acute illness, and as zero otherwise. These distributions, though still just favouring the lower income groups, are somewhat flatter than those in Table 4, as indicated by the smaller concentration indices. As explained earlier, because the numbers 'not-ill' are greater in the richer income groups, then the Le Grand ratios will have a 'pro-rich' bias. Tables 4 and 5 cannot be directly compared, because need in the former is measured by three indicators, and in the latter by two. However, the additional measure used in Table 4 is non-limiting chronic illness, and the effect of omitting this measure is small as it is distributed fairly evenly across income groups (Table 1). Thus it is probably reasonable to conclude that the smaller absolute values for the CIs in Table 5 are the consequence of the pro-rich bias in the Le Grand methodology.

Table 5: Le Grand methodology: percentage share of standardised NHS expenditure (adults only, standardised by age, sex, limiting chronic and acute illness)

Income quintile	1974	1982	1985	1987
Bottom	21.6	19.6	19.1	20.6
2nd	20.1	18.0	21.1	19.9
3rd	20.0	20.6	20.7	20.4
4th	19.7	23.9	21.1	21.4
Top	18.7	17.9	18.0	17.7
Concentration index	-0.029	0.010	-0.009	-0.017

Note: Figure for each quintile = $[(x'_j + x_j) / n_j] / \sum_j [(x'_j + x_j) / n_j]$

Table 6: Le Grand methodology by SEG: percentage share of standardised NHS expenditure (adults only, standardised by age, sex, acute and limiting chronic illness)

SEG		1974	1982	1985	1987
1+2	Professional, employers and managers	24.7	-	26.4	25.9
3	Intermediate and junior non-manual	23.9	-	23.6	23.9
4	Skilled manual	26.0	-	26.4	25.2
5+6	Semi-skilled and unskilled manual	25.4	-	23.6	25.0

Note: SEG defined as own, father's (if not in work) or husband's

In the actual analyses undertaken by Le Grand (1978), SEG rather than income was used to define ability to pay. This analysis was replicated here and the results are presented in Table 6. Using 1972 data Le Grand concluded that the top two groups received 40% more health care than the bottom two groups. No such relationship is evident from the data in Table 6. The distributions do not favour the lowest class. Expenditure is always greater in the skilled manual than in the unskilled class, and in two years (1985 and 1987) the professional/ managerial class has the highest share.

Discussion of results

The results presented here suggest that the distribution of NHS expenditure across income groups, controlling for need, is either uniform or slightly in favour of lower income groups. This distribution appears to have been fairly stable over the four years used in the analysis, though there is the expected evidence of sampling variability. No one year appears to be a particular outlier. The flat or weakly 'pro-poor' distribution is also found in the distribution of the components of expenditure, ie in the probability of contact and the amount of expenditure received conditional on contact with the health service. Far from suggesting that the NHS is 'pro-rich', the results indicate that departures from horizontal equity are rather small.[10]

In earlier research (O'Donnell and Propper, 1991), which compared the Le Grand results for 1972 with those for 1985, it appeared that there had been a shift from a pro-rich to a uniform distribution. In that paper it was suggested that changes in the distribution of self-reported morbidity may have accounted for the change in the distribution of resources standardised for need. On the basis of the additional information presented here, this conclusion would appear to be incorrect. First, all the distributions using the Le Grand methodology are fairly flat. Second, the change between 1974 and 1985 is from a more pro-poor to a less pro-poor distribution, not, as suggested by point comparisons between 1972 and 1985 data, from a pro-rich to a less pro-rich distribution. Third, Table 2 indicates that increases in reporting of morbidity are spread fairly evenly across income groups. If anything, the increase in reporting of morbidity has been greater in low than in high income groups. Thus the difference between the 1972 data and that presented here (and in O'Donnell and Propper, 1991) cannot be due to changes in the reporting of morbidity. These findings suggest that the year used in the Le Grand analysis may have been an 'outlier'.

Whether the slight pro-poorness of most of the distributions in the present paper represents 'unequal treatment for equal need' depends on whether the morbidity proxies for need measure the same levels of need across income groups. O'Donnell and Propper (1991), using not the GHS but the Health and Lifestyle Survey (HLS), found that within morbidity groups defined similarly to those in the GHS, income was negatively correlated with poor health. In other words, the poor within each morbidity group were sicker. In all the methodologies used in this paper, it is assumed, within each type of morbidity group, all respondents are in equal need. If it was the case that of those reporting illness, the poor were more sick than the rich, any given distribution of standardised health care would be more 'pro-rich' than indicated by the summary statistics given in Tables 3 to 6.

O'Donnell and Propper (1991) used data from the HLS to examine this issue because no data on the extent of sickness within morbidity groups are routinely provided in the GHS. However, such information was collected in the 1974 GHS. If respondents to the 1974 GHS replied in the affirmative to the questions about incidence of chronic and acute illness, they were asked to state the number of conditions of that type they suffered from. Table 7 shows the distribution of the number of chronic and acute conditions among those with a positive number of conditions. For both limiting and non-limiting chronic conditions, it is clear that the poor have more conditions than the rich. This is not the case for the incidence of acute illness. Thus, for two of the morbidity categories used in the analyses of this paper, the poor in 1974 had greater need than the rich. If this is the case for all years, then the weakly 'pro-poor' distributions obtained in this paper may in fact be neutral or even 'pro-rich'.

Table 7: Numbers of illnesses suffered by those who are sick, by income quintile, 1974 data (adults only, standardised by age and sex)

Income quintile	Average number of non-limiting chronic illnesses	Average number of limiting chronic illnesses	Average number of acute illnesses
Bottom	1.14	1.28	1.04
2nd	1.10	1.26	1.02
3rd	1.08	1.19	1.03
4th	1.09	1.23	1.03
Top	1.09	1.15	1.04

Our findings indicate that the distribution of expenditure across SEG is not dissimilar to that across income. Our broad conclusion that there is little systematic evidence of horizontal inequity applies for SEG as for income. However, the measure of ability to pay does appear to matter to some extent: the distribution across SEG does appear more 'pro-rich' than that across income. One possible explanation is that the middle classes make most use of the welfare state, the rich being able and willing to buy private services. The top SEG contains not only the rich, but also the less well-off middle classes. A pro-middle-class bias will not show up in an income distribution, as by definition the top quintile are the richest, but will show up in an SEG distribution.

The data used here give some support to this hypothesis. First, as expected, given the correlation between income and SEG is less than 1, the distribution of income by SEG is more even than the distribution of income *per se* (see Appendix 2). Second, the distribution of private health insurance is pro-rich, with a concentration index of over 0.6 (O'Donnell,

Propper and Upward, 1992). Analysis for 1985 indicates that the distribution of all health care expenditure is more pro-rich than for NHS expenditure. These data suggest that the rich are more likely to use private health care. Thus we would expect that the distribution of NHS care across income groups is less extreme than the distribution across class groups, which is the result found here.

This finding raises the question of which measure of ability to pay is appropriate. We would suggest that the answer depends on the hypothesis under consideration. If the hypothesis is one of purchasing power, then income seems most appropriate and indeed is the measure most often used in public finance analysis of ability to pay. Given that payment for the NHS is on the basis of current income, a legitimate question to ask is how benefits from the NHS are distributed across income groups. If the hypothesis is rather more sociological and concerns the ability of certain social groups to use services and influence service providers to their advantage, then the appropriate measure might be SEG. Whichever measure is judged more appropriate, our results suggest that SEG produces a more pro-rich distribution than income, and that the Le Grand methodology produces a slightly more pro-rich result than either the Comac or the Collins and Klein methodologies. This perhaps explains why Le Grand's 1972 results indicate considerably more expenditure on the middle classes.

Finally, it was noted earlier that age-sex standardisation may mask relationships of interest. In the current case, it may hide a systematic relationship across income between gender and expenditure. The Comac methodology was used to examine departures from horizontal equity within gender groups. The findings, which are for 1987 data, are given in Table 8.

Table 8: Percentage shares of standardised NHS expenditure, men and women separated, 1987 (adults only, standardised by age, acute, limiting and non-limiting chronic illness)

Income quintile	Women	Men
Bottom	23.8	20.7
2nd	21.2	21.3
3rd	19.6	20.4
4th	20.4	18.5
Top	14.9	19.1
Concentration index	-0.087	-0.070

The results indicate that while the distribution across income groups for men is basically fairly flat, the comparable distribution for women indicates that women in poorer families receive more expenditure for a given need. Evandrou *et al* (1991) found evidence that social class was an important determinant of GP contact for females aged under 40, and for men over 60. The latter group is small numerically, so that when analysis is undertaken across all age groups the distribution across men may be unaffected by this class effect for older men. Women under 40, on the other hand, account for a significant proportion of the female population. Thus our analysis, although by income rather than class, may therefore be indicative of a similar process for total expenditure.

Conclusions

In this study we have attempted to resolve the issue of whether there are significant departures from horizontal equity in NHS expenditure. Previous studies have reached different conclusions. However, the studies are not directly comparable. Researchers used data from different years, different definitions of ability to pay, utilisation and need, and different methodologies. In contrast, the present research has taken three different methodologies, and applied these to data with common definitions of the key variables and for four years between 1974 and 1987.

The conclusions, from this analysis are as follows. First, irrespective of the definition of need or of ability to pay, the distribution of NHS resources, standardised for need, does not appear to be pro-rich. The summary statistics calculated here indicate that NHS expenditure, as recorded in the General Household Survey, is weakly pro-poor. Second, there do not appear to have been large changes in this distribution over the period 1974 to 1987, though there is some evidence of a shift in later years in favour of higher income groups. Third, the different measures of utilisation standardised for need will give different results if need is unequally distributed across ability to pay. However, in empirical terms, these differences do not appear to be large. All three methodologies tested in this paper produce an almost flat or slightly pro-poor distribution of expenditure. Fourth, the definition of ability to pay does appear to affect the results, as does the choice of proxy measures for need. The distribution by SEG appears to favour the highest SEG more than the distribution by income groups favours the richest income quintile. The addition of more, and more finely categorised, measures of need reduces the extent of pro-poorness in the observed distribution of NHS resources. In conclusion, our results provide some explanation for the different results of earlier research into horizontal equity in the allocation of resources in the NHS. Nevertheless, once methodological differences are distinguished from change over time, this study indicates that departures from horizontal equity do not appear to be large and there does not appear to have been large change in the distribution of NHS resources in the period 1974 to 1987.

Appendix 1: Standardisation of need and expenditure

1. Morbidity was standardised as:

$$\Sigma_j \Sigma_k (m_{ijk} / n_{ijk}) ((n_i n_{jk}) / n) \qquad (A1)$$

where m_{ijk} = the number of individuals reporting morbidity in the ith income group, jth age-group and kth sex group;
 n_{ijk} = the number of individuals in the ijkth income-age-sex group;
 n_i = the number of individuals in the ith income group;
 n_{jk} = the number of individuals in the jkth age-sex group;
 n = the number of individuals in the whole sample;
 n_{mjk} = the number of individuals in the mjkth morbidity-age-sex group.

Distributions for all three of the methodologies outlined earlier in this paper were standardised by age and sex.

2. The Collins and Klein use-need ratios, x_{mi}/n_{mi}, are standardised as:

$$\Sigma_j \Sigma_k (x_{mijk}/n_{mijk}) (n_{mjk}/n_m) \qquad (A2)$$

where x_{mi} = the amount of expenditure on the ith income group and the mth morbidity group;
 n_{mi} = the number of individuals in the ith income group and the mth morbidity group.
 Other definitions as above.

3. Standardised Comac methodology (Wagstaff and van Doorslaer, 1992).

$$E(\exp) = \Pr(\exp>0) E(\exp/\exp>0)$$

where $\Pr(\exp>0) = \Sigma_m \Sigma_j \Sigma_k (p_{mijk}) (n_{mjk}/n) \qquad (A3)$

and $E(\exp/\exp>0) = \Sigma_m \Sigma_j \Sigma_k (S_{mijk}) (n_{mjk}/n) \qquad (A4)$

where p_{mijk} = the mean probability of expenditure in the $mijk$th morbidity-income-age-sex group
 = $\bar{n}_{mijk}/n_{mijk}$;

S_{mijk} = average amount of expenditure for those with positive expenditure in *mijk*th group

= $x_{mijk}/\bar{n}_{mijk}$;

n_{mijk} = number of persons with positive expenditure in *mijk*th group;

$\bar{n}_{mijk}$ = number of persons in *mijk*th group.

Other definitions as above.

4. The standardised Le Grand use-need ratio

$$= [\Sigma_j \Sigma_k (x_{ijk}) (n_{jk}/n)] / [\Sigma_j \Sigma_k (m_{ijk}/n_{ijk}) ((n_i n_{jk})/n)]$$

Table A1: Distribution of income across quintiles and SEG 1987

	Mean yearly equivalised income	Standard deviation
Income quintile		
Bottom	£3,771	£885
2nd	£5,980	£716
3rd	£8,521	£748
4th	£11,444	£1,009
Top	£19,258	£9,893
SEG		
Professional	£15,437	£10,203
Employers and managers	£13,044	£9,317
Intermediate	£10,486	£7,209
Skilled manual	£8,715	£4,475
Semi-skilled	£7,333	£4,408
Unskilled manual	£6,429	£3,416

Table A1 shows the mean and standard deviation of gross equivalised family income across income quintiles and collapsed SEG groups (a similar result was found for 1974 data).

Notes

1. We are grateful to Julian Le Grand for bringing this to our attention.
2. Jenkins (1988) exploits the result that the concentration index can be rewritten in the form of a linear transformation of the covariance between an observation's rank in the x distribution and the value of $y = g(x)$, to show how

the CI can be calculated using micro data. In the present case x = ability to pay and y = standardised health care expenditure.

3. An exception is the data for 1974. Use of length-of-stay data is considered in the discussion of results.

4. The cost of an average in-patient stay and out-patient visits were from Department of Health (1990) and Department of Health and Social Security (1986), for 'mainly acute' non-teaching hospitals, as defined in *Health Service Costing Returns* (Department of Health and Social Security and Welsh Office, 1987). The cost per GP consultation was estimated by dividing the total number of GP consultations into the total general medical FPS expenditure for each year. Cost per prescription was calculated as total expenditure on prescriptions divided by the total number of consultations where a prescription was issued. Data were from Office of Health Economics (1990). The table below summarises the costs used.

	In-patient stay	Out-patient visit	GP without prescription	GP with prescription
1974	£247.61	£6.52	(£1.31+£1.73=£3.04)	
1982	£697.66	£21.44	£4.17	£12.61
1985	£726.99	£24.47	£5.65	£17.09
1987	£763.79	£26.05	£5.80	£17.92

The resulting estimate of NHS expenditure was compared with actual expenditure in the relevant years. Excluding expenditure not covered by the GHS (such as maternity and capital expenditure) the estimate produced by grossing up the costs above accounted for between 60% and 70% of actual expenditure. Some of the difference is due to the omission from the GHS of persons in institutions.

5. The equivalence scale is McClements (1978).

6. The general effect of standardisation was to slightly reduce the inequality of the distributions, but the absolute value of the impact of standardisation was generally small. The method of standardisation is given in Appendix 1. It is equivalent to standardisation through regression with dummy variables (van Vliet and van de Ven, 1985).

7. For all methodologies, the distribution of utilisation standardised for need is unaffected by size of ability-to-pay group.

8. The CI for general health status reported as 'not good' is positive for 1982 and 1985 and negative for 1987, but in all three cases is small in absolute value.

9. Le Grand (1978) presents these ratios in terms of absolute amounts, not shares.

10. The distributions for all persons (adults plus children) for 1974, 1985 and 1987 are similar.

References

Barr, N. (1987) *The economics of the welfare state*, London: Weidenfeld and Nicolson.

Blaxter, M. (1990) 'A comparison of measures of inequality in morbidity' in J. Fox (ed) *Health inequalities in European countries*, London: Gower.

Collins, E. and Klein, R. (1980) 'Equity and the NHS: self reported morbidity, access and primary care', *British Medical Journal*, vol 281, pp 1111-15.

Department of Health (1990) *Health and personal social services statistics for England 1990*, London: HMSO.

Department of Health and Social Security (1986) *Health and personal social services statistics for England 1986*, London: HMSO.

Department of Health and Social Security and Welsh Office (1987) *Health service costing returns 1985/86*, London: HMSO.

Disney, R. and Webb, S. (1991) 'Why are there so many long-term sick in Britain?', *Economic Journal*, vol 101, no 405, pp 252-62 (Conference Supplement).

Evandrou, M., Falkingham, J., Le Grand, J. and Winter, D. (1991) 'Equity in health and social care', LSE STICERD Welfare State Programme Discussion Paper, WSP/52.

Forster, D.P. (1976) 'Social class differences in sickness and general practitioner consultations', *Health Trends*, vol 8, pp 29-32.

General Household Survey (1974, 1982, 1985, 1987) London: HMSO.

Goodin, R. E., and Le Grand, J. (1987) *Not only the poor: the middle classes and the welfare state*, London: Allen and Unwin.

Health and Lifestyle Survey (1987) London: Health Promotion Research Trust.

Hills, J. (ed) (1990) *The state of welfare: the welfare state in Britain from 1974*, Oxford: Oxford University Press.

Hurst, J.W. (1985) *Financing health services in the United States, Canada and Britain*, London: Kings Fund.

Jenkins, S. (1988) 'Calculating income distributions from micro-data', *National Tax Journal*, vol 41, pp 139-42.

Le Grand, J. (1978) 'The distribution of public expenditure: the case of health care', *Economica*, vol 45, pp 125-142.

McClements, L.D. (1978) *The economics of social security*, London: Heinemann.

O'Donnell, O. and Propper, C. (1991) 'Equity and the distribution of National Health Service resources', *Journal of Health Economics*, vol 10, pp 1-21.

O'Donnell, O., Propper, C. and Upward, R. (1992) 'Equity in the finance and delivery of health care in Britain' in E. van Doorslaer, A. Wagstaff and F. Rutten (eds), *Equity in the finance and delivery of health care: an international perspective*, Oxford: Oxford University Press.

Office of Health Economics (1990), *Compendium of health statistics 1989*, London: OHE.

Puffer, F. (1986) 'Access to primary care: a comparison of the US and the UK', *Journal of Social Policy*, vol 15, pp 293-313.

van Vliet, R. and van de Ven, W. (1985) 'Differences in medical consumption between publicly and privately insured in the Netherlands: standardisation by means of multiple regression', Paper presented at International Meeting on Health Econometrics.

Wagstaff, A. and van Doorslaer, E. (1992) 'Methodology of the COMAC-HSR project' in E. van Doorslaer, A. Wagstaff and F. Rutten (eds), *Equity in the finance and delivery of health care: an international perspective*, Oxford: Oxford University Press.

Wolfe, B. and Haveman, R. (1990) 'Trends in the prevalence of work disability from 1962 to 1984, and their correlates', *The Milbank Quarterly*, vol 68, no 1, pp 53-80.

Wright, S.J. (1986) 'Age, sex and health: a summary of findings from the York Health Evaluation Survey', Discussion Paper 15, York: Centre for Health Economics, University of York.

CHAPTER 13

USER EMPOWERMENT, OLDER PEOPLE AND THE UK REFORM OF COMMUNITY CARE

ROBIN MEANS AND RACHEL LART

Introduction

This paper draws upon a two-year research project, funded by the Joseph Rowntree Foundation, which looked at the impact of the UK reform of community care on users in four contrasting local authorities. It explores three key questions, namely:

i. What assumptions about how best to achieve user empowerment lie behind different broad approaches to the provision of community care services?

ii. How are users and user groups being consulted or becoming involved in the community care planning procedures of the four case study authorities?

iii. How do issues of empowerment vary between the different care groups, and, in particular, what, if any, issues are specific to older people?

The background of this paper is the UK reform of community care. *Caring for people*, the White Paper on community care (Department of Health, 1989) and the subsequent National Health Service and Community Care Act 1990 gave the lead agency role to local authority social services departments for all the main care groups, including older people. However, this lead agency role was to take the form of stimulating service provision by the independent sector rather than through the monopoly provision of state services. At a strategic level, local authorities would be expected to publish community care plans on an annual basis after wide consultation with other key agencies and with user and carer groups. At an operational level, care managers would be expected to assess need and put together flexible packages of care. A key justification for these changes given in the White Paper was the need to stimulate choice for service users, while

---

This chapter first appeared in D. Challis and B. Davies (eds) *Health and community care: UK and international perspectives*, 1994, Aldershot: Gower, pp 33-43.

subsequent guidance has gone further in arguing that "the rationale for this reorganisation is the empowerment of users and carers" (Department of Health/Social Services Inspectorate, 1991). But what is user empowerment and how can it be achieved?

Theories of empowerment

This section draws heavily from a recent working paper on *User empowerment in community care: unravelling the issues* (Taylor et al, 1992). There is no simple answer as to what does and what does not represent user empowerment since it is a contested concept. However, a good starting point is to underline that it involves giving more power to users over decisions, and hence it probably necessitates taking power away from service providers. It is also clear that empowerment can involve different degrees of authority. Figure 1 shows a ladder of empowerment with degrees of power that can be conferred on, or taken by, varying users.

Figure 1:   Ladder of empowerment

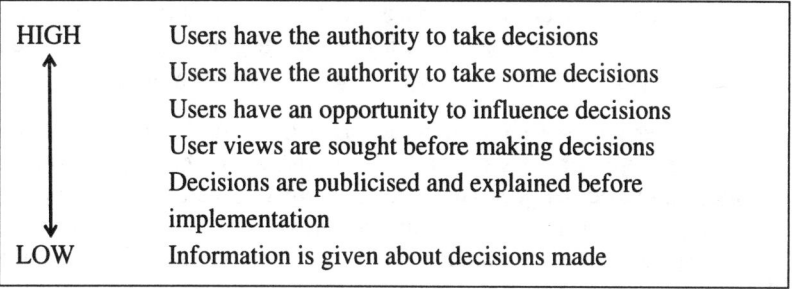

There are very different views about how to achieve progress up this ladder and not all would agree about the importance of all the steps. For example, the inclination of Ramon (1991) is to reserve the term empowerment for situations where real power and control is taken by users. She complains of "the use of the concept of empowerment by politicians, who are constantly cutting back on services and benefits available to people with disabilities" since they confuse "buying power with empowerment" (p 17). This requires us to look at different theories of empowerment and the assumptions that they make.

One of the difficulties in addressing theories of empowerment is that there are a number of intertwined yet separate debates which might be drawn upon to illuminate the issue. These include debates about the strengths and weaknesses of:

i.   markets versus democracy;
ii. markets versus hierarchies;
iii. exit versus voice;
iv. consumer versus citizen.

The emphasis of this chaper will be on 'exit' (and its relationship to markets) and 'voice' (and its relationship to democratic accountability). Market and democratic approaches to consumer empowerment differ in the following ways.

i.   The market approach seeks to empower consumers by giving them choice between alternatives and the option of exit from a service and/or provider if dissatisfied. Here the total pattern of provision is dictated by the sum of consumer choices - those services which are not chosen will go to the wall. In other words, if you don't like your day centre, you move to another one. Day centres which are unpopular will cease to trade.

ii. The democratic approach would keep more services in the public sector but seeks to empower users by giving them a voice in services and thereby the chance to change (ie transform) their existing service or service organisation. In other words, if you don't like your day centre, you join the user committee and change it to your liking.

Three further points need to be made. Exit is not fully synonymous with the market approach. Users can be given the choice between a range of publicly provided services and hence the right of exit. And competing providers from the public, voluntary and private sectors can each place a high emphasis on representation and voice for their service consumers. Nevertheless, it is possible to argue that market approaches are exit driven and democratic approaches are voice driven in ideology if not always in practice.

Second, some older people are in a position to self-provide or to buy their own services directly (Oldman, 1991) but most are not, and this situation is unlikely to change dramatically in the 1990s (Bosanquet and Propper, 1991). The reforms of central government are essentially about creating quasi rather than pure markets (Bartlett and Le Grand, 1993). The intention is for competition to be created in service provision, and an agent (ie care manager) working on behalf of the client can then use this market to buy in appropriate care packages (Hoyes and Means, 1991).

Third, all individual local authorities include a complex mixture of community care activities which are underpinned by a mixture of exit and voice assumptions and strategies. An authority which contracted out all its services would still have a legal obligation to pursue the voice strategy of producing a community care plan after consultation with others including user and carer groups. However, local authorities are tackling the community care reforms from very different starting points in terms of previous patterns of provision and in terms of their interpretation of how best to move forward. This can be illustrated by our four case study authorities. These are: Devon; Oxfordshire; Hammersmith and Fulham; and St Helens.

The senior managers of all four authorities express enthusiasm for developing a mixed economy of social care. But the majority Labour group of councillors in the latter two authorities are hostile to the further development of a service delivery role by the private sector. St Helens has a far smaller voluntary sector with paid workers than Hammersmith and Fulham. Devon was an early enthusiast for an internal split between purchaser and provider functions within social services at the field level, but Oxfordshire was initially far more sceptical.

Overall, the most important question is not which 'exit' or 'voice' is the best way to empower users. Rather, researchers need to clarify what combination of exit and voice driven strategies are most effective in empowering users, and whether this combination should be the same for all the main care groups.

Involving users in community care planning

This section looks at how user and carer groups have been involved in the community care planning procedures of our four case study authorities. It should be noted that the community care reforms are usually seen as market or exit driven yet consultation over community care plans is a voice mechanism. This section draws extensively from a recent article by Hoyes and Lart (1992). The strategies of the four authorities varied from using an enhanced version of existing networks and relationships, to an attempt to create a whole new framework for communication and planning. Each approach had implications for the authority in terms of time, identifying who to involve and how, arranging that involvement, giving people sufficient time to reflect and contribute, and effectively using that contribution.

Hammersmith and Fulham started their planning process a year ahead, using the network of relationships within the existing joint planning structure which was 'tidied up' and strengthened. Joint planning teams, with increased voluntary sector representation, produced analyses of need of different client groups; social services highlighted those elements which they considered their responsibility. A small group of senior officers, including the director, took charge of overall coordination of the plan. A series of open days for users and carers was held prior to producing the

1991/92 plan. The 1992/93 community care plan was circulated for comments early in 1992, and a series of open meetings was held.

In St Helens, the community care plan was drafted by a team of four officers from the personal services department. This group drew upon a number of initiatives, including a care management pilot, a multi-agency quality assurance group and a voluntary sector committee on community care. Perhaps the key initiative was a collaborative group of managers from health and social services which was seen as having a very positive impact on working relationships. The chosen process involved only limited direct input from users and carers, although the voluntary sector committee did carry out a small survey of user and carer views and its membership did include the parent of a physically disabled child. The draft community care plan was circulated widely for comment in early 1992.

In Oxfordshire, each of the six social services divisions took responsibility for producing its own plan, but with an obligation to involve users and carers. This involvement varied from large, well-attended public meetings, spawning further, more focused participation, to voluntary organisations and individuals attending planning team meetings. Over 1,000 users and carers were consulted at this stage in an untidy but comprehensive process. A single county-wide community care plan was drawn together, written up by a professional journalist and circulated widely, but with only six weeks for consultation. The divisional plans were published in the following autumn and provide a basis for ongoing participation at a local level.

Devon social services department required each of its 32 districts to establish forums for consultation including users, carers and local voluntary organisations, as well as health and housing agencies. This structure was not yet well enough established to be used for the community care plan consultation process. The plan was written by a small group of senior officers and a draft distributed very widely for comment between October 1991 and January 1992. Ten thousand copies were distributed, 6,000 in a magazine for people with disabilities produced by the authority. Devon's community care plan was probably seen by more individual users and carers than those of other authorities. However, people were being asked to comment on a statement of policy aims and strategic objectives rather than a detailed description of planned services. A more detailed reference file was made available at district offices.

Social services departments were experiencing contradictory pressures in relation to planning. On the one hand, they were being urged to pursue consultation and participation; on the other hand, they were operating in a context which made it difficult to be explicit about their plans. For example, Devon's community care plan was criticised for lacking financial details. Yet uncertainty about the amount of Department of Social Security funds to be transferred to individual social services departments, together with the annual basis of local government funding, make it difficult to publish detailed proposals and give time for meaningful consultation.

Developing effective means of including users and carers takes time and commitment. From experiences in the four social services departments, the research team came to the following conclusions.

i. Building on existing networks, largely through the voluntary sector, raises questions of representativeness.

ii. Creating new networks at a very local level takes time and a pro-active approach, but can reap rewards.

iii. Consulting large numbers of people at open meetings requires clarity and mechanisms for taking on board the messages that come out of discussion.

iv. Distributing documents widely for comment requires that documents are readable (or available in non-written forms) and yet detailed enough that people are clear about what they are being asked to comment on.

v. Plenty of time is needed for groups to consult their own members/constituencies.

In terms of how user groups representing different care groups either engaged with community care planning or linked more generally with the statutory agencies, we were struck by how few user groups drew their strength from older users of community care services. On the carer side, all four case studies had active branches of the Alzheimer's Disease Society while each had active Age Concern branches which were often involved in service delivery developments. However, older people themselves seemed to have very little opportunity to comment on strategic directions compared to the other care groups.

Is this inevitable, given that older service users are likely to be either very frail or experiencing severe mental health problems? Can carers, more active older people or other disabled people act as proxies on their behalf? These are complicated questions made all the more urgent by the Allen *et al* study (1992) which found that at the level of individual assessment and care packaging, elderly people were given little say or influence over services received. This is moving us towards the issue of whether all care groups have common needs and common interests.

Common needs? Common interests?

The final section considers whether all users have common needs and common interests. Service recipients are frequently allocated by bureaucracies to one of a limited number of large care groups, the most commonly used being: older people; people with physical or sensory impairments; people with learning disabilities; and people with mental health problems.

An important issue is to what extent an emphasis upon such categories helps or hinders the process of user empowerment. Many champions of the social model of disability argue that considering different care groups separately is supportive of the medical model and obscures how the disabling character of society and of nearly all social policy applies to all disability groups. Their alternative way forward is to support the further growth of a self-help disability movement which can join other oppressed and marginalised groups in challenging the existing political system (Oliver, 1990; Morris, 1991).

However, not all agree with this view. For example, some 'survivors' may feel discussions in the disability movement continue to place too much emphasis upon physical access, unless, of course, they have a physical impairment themselves. This debate has similarities to the racial dualism discourse in which some argue that a simple black-white dichotomy has served to marginalise the Asian experience of Britain (Modood, 1991). Equally, some survivors have spent so long trying to escape the stigmatising effect of the disability label that they do not define themselves as disabled - people with aural and visual impairments have expressed a similar opinion on occasions.

However, there is a danger of caricaturing the common interests perspective. A political position which emphasises the commonality of oppression does not preclude the recognition that different groups have specific needs, both in terms of services required and in terms of the processes which may be required to empower them at an individual and strategic level. But to what extent does such variation reflect the different disabilities of the conventional community care groupings?

The answer to this is only to a limited extent. Certainly, empowerment requires a challenging of professional stereotypes about old age, mental health, learning disabilities and physical disability, and this needs to be replaced by a much deeper understanding of the problems faced by older people and people with disabilities. Whittaker (1990) provides a clear account of what this means for professionals wishing to involve people with learning disabilities in meetings, by drawing on her experience as an adviser to the self-advocacy organisation, People First. For example she points out:

> It is useful to remember that what happens ordinarily at meetings; there are people who talk too much while others

may say virtually nothing; some people stick to the topic while others are inclined to wander off.

Professionals need to ensure that people with learning disabilities are not expected to be super participants who never stray off the subject, nor should they be given special treatment.

It is also clear that the stage of development of user groups is not evenly spread. People with physical impairments seem to have the strongest profile. Mental health self-advocacy groups have grown since the formation of Survivors Speak Out in January 1986, although Campbell (1990) estimated there to be only 35 groups in early 1990. Numerous self-help groups campaign on behalf of people with learning difficulties, but many are essentially composed of parents/carers rather than the users themselves. Research in the early 1990s revealed that social services managers complained about 'decibel planning' by which such groups, composed of articulate middle class parents, were attracting resources to the detriment of others, such as those with mental health problems, who were seen as poorly organised and transient to the locality (Hoyes, Means and Le Grand, 1992). Older people seem to be another badly organised group; voluntary organisations such as Age Concern claim to speak on their behalf but genuine user groups are far less common and tend to focus on broad preventive health issues (Meade and Carter, 1990). However, there are numerous carers' groups who focus on the needs of those providing informal care for older people with mental health problems (eg Alzheimer's Disease Society).

Some groups seem to find it harder than others to express dissatisfaction with the quality and appropriateness of services provided. Older people are especially reluctant to be critical. Consumer surveys generate very positive responses about services being received, but a much less clear-cut picture emerges when the interviewer explores levels of satisfaction through a more in-depth discussion with the user (Harrison and Means, 1990). But is this also true of younger adults with physical disabilities or are they much more likely to complain direct to the service provider? In a recent study, a Crossroads scheme organiser claimed her organisation had been asked to work with this group because home help organisers from the local authority were too used to working with passive older people (Hoyes and Means, 1991). But it is hard to be sure whether such views are well grounded or reflections of societal stereotypes (ie passive older women and aggressive young males in wheelchairs).

Overall, these broad care groups contain too wide a spectrum of situations to allow any simple generalisations to be made. The capacity of an 85 year old with a broken hip to express an opinion about required services is very different to that of an 85 year old in advanced stages of senile dementia. To participate in a meeting, someone in a wheelchair needs physical access to the building while someone with an induction impairment may need an induction loop. Many individuals have a complex combination of impairments and illness. For example, people with learning disabilities grow older and this may see them having to cope with the illnesses and physical disabilities most commonly associated with later life. Perhaps most striking is the importance of the level of impairment or the stage of impairment. Severe learning disability or the advanced stages of senile dementia can limit communication between user and professional, especially over planning rather than individual care management issues. People close to death or in great pain who are struggling for survival on a day-to-day basis are unlikely to get involved in abstract decision-making processes, although some will have a deep desire to try and improve service delivery for future users in a similar position to themselves.

The biggest weakness of a narrow focus upon the nature of the impairment is that it encourages a denial of other sources of disadvantage and discrimination, and the implications of this for user empowerment. For example, people continue to be male and female after reaching retirement age. Some frail older people can afford to pay a cleaner to look after their house and garden, but the majority cannot. An increasing percentage of Britain's older population comes from minority ethnic groups (Phillipson, Fennell and Evers, 1988). There is now a growing literature on how issues of race and gender intertwine with being a user or potential user of community care. For example, a feminist perspective has increasingly been brought to bear on British ageing studies as several authors have stressed that most older people are women, and that this has important consequences for likely income levels, and for how they are treated by health and social care professionals (Peace, 1985; Arber and Ginn, 1991).

There is a more limited literature for race and ethnicity than for gender. However, studies are beginning to emerge such as the work of Baxter *et al* (1990) on issues and services for people with learning disabilities from black and ethnic minority communities. Their starting point is to argue that:

> only now are the white cultural assumptions underpinning current community care policies being recognised, their limitations understood and their relevance to services for people with learning difficulties from black and ethnic communities challenged. (p 2)

Certainly for all groups, the colour-blind nature of much previous provision means that many potential recipients of services may have failed to come forward to express their needs. This, in turn, may have helped to perpetuate complacency about previous services and to encourage sweeping assumptions about the capacity and desire of 'black' families to care for all members without support from publicly funded services (Bowling, 1990).

Such a situation may mean present service recipients are skewed to certain types of user, and a real danger exists that a simplistic approach to user empowerment may fail to recognise the unmet needs of many potential users. The avoidance of this requires key agencies to involve black and ethnic minority communities in service planning (Baxter *et al*, 1990, pp 199-201; Atkin, 1991).

Conclusion

It is important that researchers make a contribution to drawing out not only common principles which need to be applied if empowerment is to be fostered, but also to think through the detailed implications of this for both users and carers, for the different care groups, and for different kinds of user within each of the main carer groups.

Our brief look at community care planning underlined how far our four local authorities have to travel in terms of developing general principles of empowerment, and then applying them appropriately to a wide range of users and carers. In fairness to senior managers, most are very aware of how much is left to be achieved. Overall, if we are to "give individuals a central place in the delivery of services" as claimed by the Citizen's Charter, then local authorities must persevere in their efforts to develop a sensitivity to the views of service users and local communities, based on a mixture of voice and exit mechanisms.

References

Allen, I., Hogg, O. and Peace, S. (1992) *Elderly people: choice, participation and satisfaction*, London: Policy Studies Institute.

Arber, S. and Ginn, J. (1991) 'The invisibility of age: gender and class in later life', *Sociological Review*, vol 29, no 2, pp 260-91.

Atkin, K. (1991) 'Community care in a multi-racial society: incorporating the user view', *Policy and Politics*, vol 19, no 3, pp 159-66.

Bartlett, W. and Le Grand, J. (1993) (eds) *Quasi-markets and social policy*, London: Macmillan.

Baxter, C., Poonia, K., Ward, L. and Nadirshaw, Z. (1990) *Double discrimination: issues and services for people with learning difficulties from black and ethnic minority communities*, London: King's Fund Centre/Commission for Racial Equality.

Bosanquet, N. and Propper, C. (1991) 'Charting the grey economy in the 1990's', *Policy and Politics*, vol 19, no 4, pp 269-81.

Bowling, B. (1990) *Elderly people from ethnic minorities: a report on four projects*, London: Age Concern Institute of Gerontology.

Campbell, P. (1990) 'Mental health self-advocacy' in L. Winn (ed) *Power to the people: the key to responsive services in health and social care*, London: King's Fund Centre.

Department of Health (1989) *Caring for people: community care in the next decade and beyond*, London: HMSO.

Department of Health/Social Services Inspectorate (1991) *Care management and assessment: summary of practice guidance*, London: HMSO.

Harrison, L. and Means, R. (1990) *Housing: the essential element in community care*, London: Anchor Housing Trust/SHAC.

Hoyes, L. and Lart, R. (1992) 'Taking care', *Community Care*, 20 August, pp 14-15.

Hoyes, L. and Means, R. (1991) *Implementing the White Paper on community care*, Studies in Decentralisation and Quasi-Markets no 4, Bristol: SAUS Publications, School for Advanced Urban Studies, University of Bristol.

Hoyes, L., Means, R. and Le Grand, J. (1992) *Made to measure? Performance indicators, performance measurement and the reform of community care*, Bristol: SAUS Publications, School for Advanced Urban Studies, University of Bristol.

Meade, K. and Carter, T. (1990) 'Empowering older users: some starting points' in L. Winn (ed) *Power to the people: the key to responsive services in health and social care*, London: King's Fund Centre.

Modood, T. (1991) 'The Indian economic success: a challenge to some race relations assumptions', *Policy and Politics*, vol 19, no 3, pp 171-90.

Morris, J. (1991) *Pride against prejudice: transforming attitudes to disability*, London: The Women's Press.

Oldman, C. (1991) *Paying for Care*, York: Joseph Rowntree Foundation.

Oliver, M. (1990) *The politics of disablement*, London: Macmillan.

Peace, S. (1985) 'The forgotten female: social policy and older women' in C. Phillipson and A. Walker (eds) *Ageing and social policy*, Aldershot: Gower.

Phillipson, C., Fennell, G. and Evers, H. (1988) *The sociology of old age*, Milton Keynes: Open University Press.

Ramon, S. (1991) 'Principles and conceptual knowledge' in S. Ramon (ed) *Beyond community care: normalisation and integration work*, London: Macmillan.

Taylor, M. (1991) *Consulting disabled people in Avon*, available from the Equal Opportunities Unit, Avon County Council.

Taylor, M., Hoyes, L., Lart, R. and Means, R. (1992) *User empowerment and community care: unravelling the issues*, Studies in Decentralisation and Quasi-Markets no 11, Bristol: SAUS Publications, School for Advanced Urban Studies, University of Bristol.

Whittaker, A. (1990) 'Involving people with learning difficulties in meetings' in L. Winn (ed) *Power to the people: the key to responsive services in health and social care*, London: King's Fund Centre.

C: HOUSING POLICY

CHAPTER 14

SOCIAL DIFFERENTIATION IN URBAN AREAS: HOUSING OR OCCUPATIONAL CLASS AT WORK?

ALAN MURIE

Introduction

This paper is concerned with the debate about the importance of housing to social differences in urban areas. This debate relates to whether occupational class is of primary importance in structuring access to consumption and the pattern of benefits gained or whether consumption sectors share certain fundamental and common interests which do not really coincide with differences in occupational class. This is an important debate offering a challenge to both conventional class-based analyses and to those which assert the importance of factors other than occupational class. It forms part of an alternative to, and more tangible formulation of, the changing importance of class than the embourgeoisement thesis. It has been drawn on to explain the outcome of British general elections in 1979 and 1983 and the evidence on voting behaviour (eg Dunleavy, 1979) has in turn been drawn on to substantiate the view that consumption sector cleavages are of key importance. Housing is not the only dimension of consumption cleavages referred to in this debate but is the most prominent and the one for which 'different fundamental interests' can most easily be argued. This paper refers purely to the housing dimension of the debate. It is principally concerned to contribute to the discussion of whether consumption sectors in housing share certain common fundamental interests; whether class and inequality are no longer phenomena of the organisation of production alone; whether housing tenure position may be as important as (occupational) class location in determining life chances; and whether class is of declining importance in understanding developing patterns of power, privilege and inequality. These propositions are a long way away from ones which regard housing differences as mere reflections of other processes or details of interest only to environmental health and other professionals. They place housing at the centre of debate about the sources and maintenance of social divisions and inequalities. Indeed it is

---

This chapter first appeared in *Tijdschrift Voor Economie en Social Geografie*, 1986, vol 77, pp 345-57.

salutory to compare Vere Hole's (1972) view of only 15 years ago, that housing was a subject of interest to only a minority of sociologists and was regarded either as part of the physical environment with little importance for sociological study or the province of social administrators and those concerned with the amelioration of social problems, with Peter Saunders' more challenging view of today:

> Social and economic divisions arising out of ownership of key means of consumption such as housing are now coming to represent a new major fault line in British society (and perhaps in others too), ... privatisation of welfare provision is intensifying this cleavage to the point where sectoral alignments in regard to consumption may come to outweigh class alignments in respect to production, and ... housing tenure remains the most important single aspect of such alignments because of the accumulative potential of house ownership and the significance of private housing as an expression of personal identity and as a source of ontological security. (Saunders, 1984, p 203)

Saunders (1986) has identified the emergence of consumption cleavages as a challenge to 19th century conceptions of class and inequality as phenomena of the organisation of production alone. This is not because of some blindness of 19th century writers but because the phenomena did not exist in the 19th century. Current levels of accumulation and inheritance associated with housing were inconceivable even 70 years ago. And consumption sectors "have only arisen in the period of advanced capitalism in which the state has intervened directly both in the organisation of production and consumption. They are products ... of the use of state power in civil society and as such they have only appeared in the period since Marx and Weber were writing". Divisions between public and private sector consumers or workers "cannot be assimilated directly into either Marx's or Weber's theoretical schema" and "cannot be treated merely as forms or expressions of deeper class divisions" or "as examples of Weberian status groups or parties". The significance of the enhanced state role for the class structure and system of social inequality is not easily expressed using theories of stratification which were developed when "the basic factor deterring most aspects of people's lives in capitalist societies was their class location and the exercise of class power".

The same theme is referred to by other writers. For example, Pahl (1984, p 314) has stated:

> The assumption that the occupation of the male chief earner is the most important determinant of the social and political consciousness of the household is open to serious doubt. The division between the more affluent home-owning households

of ordinary working people and the less advantaged under class households is coming to be more significant than conventional divisions based on the manual/non-manual distinction. (Pahl, 1984, p 314)

Assertions about the impact of home ownership go further:

Among the characteristics ... which are bringing working class consciousness to an end are the enormous increase in home ownership which has marked the last 30 years. (Vaizey in Zweig, 1976, p 7)

And Farmer and Barrell (1981) have argued that house price inflation and the opportunities for accumulation through home ownership have meant that "entrepreneurial ability has been sucked into the home owning sector".

In the housing context this draws attention to the ways in which the housing market has changed this century - to the changing tenure structure, the changing meanings of tenures and the role of the state in the development of tenures. The identification of the consumption of housing as a key element in social inequality is associated with this change. The particular 'fit' between housing position and occupational class position will be affected by this process of change. A bad 'fit' may be associated with a temporary, transitional phase. An acknowledgement that housing processes arc important sources of social difference should not lead us to overstate this importance, to deny links between housing situation and employment or to ignore the context of a changing housing market and current trends to commodification and privatisation or to ignore other emerging differences.

The emergence of housing class: council housing

In Britain in 1919 some 90% of dwellings were rented from private landlords. State housing was negligible and state financial support to housing in whatever tenure was minimal. In the period since then private renting has declined to a relatively small role. Both home ownership and council housing have passed private renting in importance. Both tenures have grown under state sponsorship. A similar pattern can be observed in most of industrialised Europe although Britain presents a more extreme picture in the extent of growth of home ownership, the depth of decline of private landlordism and the scale of direct provision through state landlordism. The two emerging tenures have had particular attributes which have been reflected in the analysis of residential patterns. The private rented sector was an open access sector differentiated in price, quality and location. High rents relative to income, eviction and distraint as well as flitting ensured that unemployment or loss of income resulted in moving down market. And the condition of properties encouraged regular moves in any event (Englander, 1983). The consequence was a pattern of residence where income and wealth directly determined and reflected place and type of residence. The two emerging tenures, however, have involved a different organisation of the market which resulted in a less simple fit between housing and income and wealth.

Access to council housing in Britain has been determined by family status and housing need variables which have enabled people to obtain high quality housing which they often could not have obtained or afforded in the private rented sector. While different phases in the development of council housing resulted in differing levels of rent, patterns of access and quality of housing (Murie, 1983) the overall effect of the development of council housing has been to break the association between housing and income and wealth. Because of the various forms of subsidy and of tenancy rights in council housing improved income status did not (as in the USA) result in loss of occupancy rights. Tenants' circumstances changed over time and rather than trading up or down many tenants remained in high quality dwellings throughout. The sector was not homogeneous, was stratified internally but as a tenure was marked by social mix. The resulting pattern is a long way from that suggested by a simple economic determinism. Timms (1971, p 80) has argued that in a society in which there are a variety of interventions designed to regulate the market, the classical ecological model which suggests that residential differentiation will faithfully mirror the income and wealth characteristics of the population is less clearly relevant and residential differentiation occurs in terms of many other population characteristics than wealth.

Robson (1969, p 154), in his analysis of Sunderland, demonstrated that council housing introduced new elements and new combinations of traits into the structure of towns. In council house areas low class is no longer associated with poor housing (even though the association with high density per room persists), and in terms of age and household composition, the population differs radically from areas within the private housing sector regardless of whether such areas are of high or low social class.

Rex and Moore (1967), in their study of Birmingham, identified the competition for housing in a zone of transition and emphasised the important role played by local authorities in the allocation of housing. To be allocated a dwelling in the public housing sector was seen as "a considerable prize in a society where housing is a scarce resource". It can bring into being (and help to sustain) an especially privileged group. They suggested that "there is a class struggle over the use of houses ... [which] is the central process of the city as a social unit". In saying this, they followed Max Weber, who saw that:

> class struggle was apt to emerge wherever people in a market situation enjoyed differential access to property and that such class struggles might therefore arise not merely around the use

of the means of industrial production, but around the control of domestic property.

Persons in the same labour situation:

> may come to have differential degrees of access to housing and it is this which immediately determines the class conflicts of the city as distinct from those of the workplace. (pp 273-74)

In developing a concept of housing class, Rex and Moore were not denying the importance of capitalist economics or the system of production but were simply extending understanding of the nature of social relationships and conflicts. Rex has stressed that conflict of housing resources is only one of a number of factors helping to determine the character of encounters in the city. He has also acknowledged that more complex models of conflict could and should be built, to make explicit the importance of the variety of value systems which exist and affect urban situations (Rex, 1971). A range of criticisms has been levelled at Rex and Moore's specific presentation of housing class. The most significant critique is associated with Haddon (1970), who argued that Rex and Moore had identified 'status groups' and not classes. The distinction is particularly important for a debate which is about key social cleavages and differences in behaviour and interest associated with notions of class.

Whatever view is taken of these issues, at this stage the debate is a long way from asserting the primacy of housing. Rex and Moore's housing classes are, however, based on an assertion of differing interest related to housing situations which do not simply reflect position in the system of production. Subsequently research on 'urban managers' and on race and gender has consistently restated this position. The way council housing works means that housing situation can not be read off from economic position.

The establishment of housing class? - home ownership

The second key feature of the emerging dominant tenures relates to accumulation. The early literature on housing classes refers to differences in access to owner occupation. Analyses of access and eligibility to home ownership stressed that income and wealth alone were not sufficient explanations of who was where in home ownership. For example, mortgage arrangements made manual and non-manual workers competitors for the same dwellings in spite of differences in income. In proportion to their income, non-manual workers may purchase more expensive houses because the ease of entry into the housing market through mortgage funds was related to occupation and not to income (Barbolet, 1969).

Following Rex and Moore, Pahl (1975) suggested that if the means of access, rather than current housing situation, are regarded as central, then the important differentiating factor between households was capital. But the real shift in focus in the debate is associated with discussions of consumption cleavages and consumption sectors. Saunders (1977) adopted the concept of 'domestic property class'. He indicated a real division between home owners and tenants and emphasised differences in potential exchange value, rights of use, control and disposal. The emphasis on wealth accumulation rather than access to housing is of key importance.

Saunders' position stresses the exchange value of housing and wealth accumulation as opposed to access to housing. This distinguishes Saunders' division between owners and tenants into 'domestic property classes' from Rex and Moore's 'housing classes'. The use of the term 'class' remained problematic and Saunders himself expressed various doubts about it. His reformulation involved a framework of consumption sectors rather than a reformulation of class. Dunleavy had outlined this approach:

> The concept of sector is a means of characterising and grouping together non-class or 'immediate' social interests distributed in systematic ways by economic, political and ideological structures. Basically, sectors are lines of vertical division in a society, such that certain common interests are shared between social classes in the same sector, while within a social class, sectoral differences reflect a measure of conflict of interests. (Dunleavy, 1979, p 419)

This approach remains the basis for the most plausible current contributions. It does not seek to rewrite class as such but identifies an additional source of alignments and interests.

It could be that such alignments and interests could be read off from class, would be directly determined by class, and so would deepen and strengthen class differences rather than cut across or confuse them. The proponents of consumption sector cleavages however have asserted their independent and cross-cutting effect.

The primacy of occupational class?

The challenge to the consumption cleavage position has been strongly expressed by Preteceille (1986). This does not attempt to argue that occupational class directly determines consumption differences. Instead, it asserts the primacy of class. Preteceille argues that the separation between work processes and consumption is a material, economic and ideological reality of capitalist societies but is not necessarily an absolute separation and varies from one city and country to another. Collective consumption is not a separate activity and has more than vague and general connections with the rest of people's lives and particularly their lives at work. State intervention in the provision of consumption goods and services can and does generate new inequalities and divisions over and above those generated through the class system. But class position structures access to consumption (eg size and security of income) and different consumers may derive different benefits and costs from state provision according to their class. Class determination does not mean that consumption practices should be the same for, or specific to, particular occupational class groups. Rather the position of each individual in the actual work process has major consequences for life outside work. The critique of the mechanistic and functionalist view of the reproduction of the labour force does not have to lead to the loosening of the links between collective consumption and economic processes. Preteceille argues that it is not only present relations of production that tend to organise life, but also the past ones of individuals and of their parents and relatives. Furthermore, determinations between work and consumption processes work both ways. To consider consumption differences as mere reflections or direct consequences of class situation is a gross oversimplification. There are important differences in consumption conditions of the members of each class, but some consumption processes are particularly active components of the (re)production of class differences. None of the wide range of differences in consumption are independent from class relations but rather are produced by a specific set of social processes which are structured by, and express in different ways, capitalist relations of production. And the basic source of diversity in needs lies in the situation of those groups in the production process, the division of labour and related power structures.

Thus, to return to 'housing classes', they may be regarded as a source of social difference but they relate to position in the work process and are most clearly understood in relation to it. A specific analysis of the processes converging to produce consumption difference indicates the primacy of class relations.

Saunders (1986) has responded to this position. He states that notwithstanding their internal fragmentation it may still be the case that consumption sectors share certain *fundamental* interests in common. Other differences between owner occupiers cannot undermine their common and fundamental interest in maintaining domestic property values, reducing mortgage interest rates, increasing state subsidies through tax relief or grants and so on. Saunders argues that recognition of the significance of class in affecting access to consumption does not necessarily indicate the primacy of class location. Class is often a poor guide to a household's consumption location, for certain forms of private consumption (most crucially private housing) are commonly purchased in many capitalist societies by large sections of the population, including many working-class families. The key factors structuring access to forms of consumption may have less to do with class *per se* as with whether or not people are engaged in formal employment of any kind and whether households can draw upon more than one income. Seen in this way, class divisions may turn out to have less significance than divisions between employed and unemployed, or between single and multiple earner households. Saunders argues that more significant than this, is the fact that consumption location may generate effects which far outweigh those associated with class location. Ownership of housing is the key factor here. With 60% of households in the owner-occupied sector in Britain (and an even higher proportion in some other countries), a majority of the population are in a position to accumulate such capital gains as may accrue through the housing market. Inheritance associated with housing, loans secured through housing collateral, access to favourable locations with positive externalities, and release of current income from the need to secure capital sums in old age, all suggest that consumption location may be every bit as important as class location in determining life chances.

Saunders' argument moves on from accumulation to assert the importance of ownership of housing in opening up the possibility for some degree of autonomous self-expression through a world of objects created or modified through our own labour. He asserts that people do seem to achieve a real and deep satisfaction from the ability to express their own identities through reproducing their own immediate surroundings in which they enjoy an exclusive right of ownership. While Saunders acknowledges constraints and qualifications which need to be taken into account. he asserts that "it is this sense of meaningful experience which people may derive from different modes of consumption which has been lacking hitherto in the debate over consumption sectors" and "it remains crucial to an analysis of consumption sector cleavages that we understand the association which undoubtedly exists for many people between individualised consumption and personal autonomy".

In this way the debate in Britain has moved from housing class to consumption sectors and from examination of the role of council housing to home ownership. Home ownership is the only growing tenure in Britain and the inflation of house prices involves real gains associated with housing. In the early and mid 1980s house price increases in London and the south east delivered larger gains than were available through wages and salaries obtained through work. Housing and housing tenure position are the key example of sectoral differences within social classes - differences which it is suggested involve a measure of conflict of interest. It is suggested that home owners have common interests irrespective of class and separate from non-owners in the same class. These interests relate to two elements: accumulation of wealth and the real and deep satisfaction and ability to express identity through exclusive rights of ownership.

Grounds for caution

The focus for different contributions on housing class and consumption cleavages is housing tenure. The growth of home ownership and council housing has resulted in a polarised, dual tenure system. Home ownership provides a capacity to accumulate wealth and has resulted in a real redistribution of wealth, real differences in opportunity, life-styles and access to credit, real influences on decisions to move, trade up and speculate in housing. Tax expenditures and other encouragements to home ownership do not distinguish between housing as an investment and housing for use and encourage over-consumption and trading up. Home owners then have different interests and opportunities which correlate with voting and political behaviour and divide those who are otherwise in the same class situation. To the extent that there is an emerging consensus it is based on a plausible model and is more tangible and visible than the embourgeoisement thesis. The fact that tenure status is easily identified and that the growth of a nation of home owners can be documented is however not sufficient demonstration of new social alignment and interests.

The general thesis around housing consumption sectors can be addressed in various ways. In this paper three elements in the debate are referred to and it is suggested that a closer examination of these gives ground for caution in relation to the thesis.

Tenure in general

The thesis implies a general consensus over what tenure is and what it delivers. However there is growing evidence and analysis of differentiation within tenures, and of differences in meanings attached to tenures over time and spatially. None of the major categories are homogeneous. Not all council housing comprises stigmatised estates and run-down or badly designed flats and maisonettes. Similarly, not all owner-occupied properties are well maintained, detached villas in leafy desirable suburbs. The meaning, attitudes, and material interests associated with home ownership have changed over time and vary between different types of owner occupation (Forrest, 1983). Spatial differences between tenures became more marked in Britain in the 1980s. In some areas it was owner occupation which formed the less desirable residual stock of dwellings taken up by those who were marginalised economically and politically. In other areas it was parts of the council stock which fulfilled this role (Forrest and Murie, 1986). The slower rate of house price inflation in the northern regions of England and in Scotland compared with Greater London and the south east of England related to affluence and economic buoyancy. It resulted in a situation where the package of benefits associated with owner occupation and the perceptions of that tenure were very different. It seems likely that this partly explains regional differences in preferences for home ownership.

Furthermore, the images of attitude to dwelling associated with ownership are not generally sustained. Saunders' arguments about the extension of personal autonomy and the possibility for some degree of autonomous self-expression are linked to ownership rather than to the house or home in all tenures. Three considerations can be offered in response to this. Firstly, that not all owners are likely to identify the same advantages of ownership. Secondly, that the opportunities for autonomy and self-expression are likely to reflect the wider life experience and to be a product of work and family and community situation as well as housing. Thirdly, it is evident that just as some owners do not respond to ownership in the way implied, so many tenants do invest time and effort in rented accommodation and do not find lack of ownership prevents autonomous self-expression. There may be differences in the degree of alienation and powerlessness associated with different tenures and households may express themselves in different ways in different tenures. In council housing it may be internal decoration rather than external display (see, for example, Holme, 1985). What is difficult to sustain is a view that such attributes are exclusive to tenures or derive from ownership rather than life experience and attitudes which may often coincide with tenure status. In this context we also have to recognise that in Britain dwelling types and rights in use differ between tenures. These differences affect what can be done in the dwelling including the nature of any 'production' work being carried out within the home.

Accumulation

The significance of housing as a source and store of wealth has become more marked in Britain in the 1980s. Statistics on the distribution of wealth provide ample evidence of the importance of the growth of individual ownership and the capital appreciation of owner-occupied dwellings. The evidence provided by the Royal Commission on the Distribution of Income and Wealth in 1977 provides the fullest evidence on housing and wealth and has been discussed elsewhere (Murie and Forrest, 1980; Murie, 1983). The importance of housing in wealth does not just reflect a growth of owner occupation (or a decline in private renting) but also depends on the movement of house prices relative to retail prices and to the value of other assets. Bearing in mind the reservations with this data it does seem possible that, as a result of the impact of house price movements and of the economic recession on the value of other assets, the importance of housing assets in wealth has probably increased since 1978 and in 1986.

Because relatively few large wealth holders continue to hold a large proportion of their assets in the form of dwellings, the increase in the value of houses compared with other assets has meant that the gap in wealth between house owners with few other assets and those with substantial other assets has narrowed. However, at the same time, the gap between house owners and households with few assets of any kind, and not including a house, has widened. Thus, under the influence of inflation, house owners have largely moved out of the categories of households with least net wealth, and dwellings represent an increasing proportion of wealth in the middle and higher ranges of wealth holding. The Royal Commission evidence showed that persons in the bottom range of wealth owners had below average holdings of dwellings and land. For those in the middle range, dwellings accounted for more than 50% of assets. In view of the dominance of house property in the assets of these households it is evident that few households who do not own dwellings can accumulate wealth on a scale comparable with the house owner.

Descriptive data on the distribution of wealth are easily marshalled to support a view that accumulation through housing processes is substantial and has been increasing. It contributes both to arguments that changes in the ownership of dwellings has had a considerable impact on social inequality and has either reduced class inequalities or introduced interests and conflicts of interest which complicate class relations. It can be mobilised to indicate a reduction in inequality or the importance of class in society or a redrawing of social divisions along housing tenure lines. Home owners in contrast to tenants are able to make real capital gains from their own house. As a result owners have a source of income in addition to the job market and have real interests around this.

The analysis of housing in statistics on wealth initially demonstrates the importance of housing in wealth. However, such an analysis as it stands begs a considerable number of questions. Initially, and most obviously, the definition of wealth must be one which relates to real accumulation which extends and enhances life chances or is a source of social and economic power and which consequently places the home owner in a different social situation with different interests than say the tenant or the owner of other highly priced commodities.

If entitlement to flows of income through subsidy for council housing (or owner occupation) is represented as wealth then housing processes become more significant determinants of the value of gross personal wealth. Complications arise especially concerning measuring the value of entitlements. Rent pooling, historic cost accounting and subsidy withdrawal are all features of council housing which complicate any measurement of the capital value of entitlements. However, these are technical objections and the more fundamental concern relates back to adopting a definition which will indicate differences in immediate command over resources which could be constituted in a variety of forms and switched between them rather than a flow of income over time. Except insofar as, say, council tenants could 'sell' their tenancy entitlements for cash there is no sense in which the capital value of the use of a council house can be realised or the tenant can shift the form in which entitlement is held. While access to non-marketed assets (ie the council dwelling) constitutes a real capital value it does not constitute accumulation which can be legally realised, or transferred into other forms of wealth, or which can be borrowed against. The process which enables individuals to accumulate wealth (through housing) which can be realised and transferred is almost exclusively the prerogative of owners of dwellings including both landlords and owner occupiers. But do all home owners own a realisable and transferable asset? A home owner with a new 100% mortgage does not; an owner whose property is depreciating in value or has a market value of less than the outstanding debt may not. Furthermore, it is strongly and reasonably argued that sale or transfer for many home owners is conditional upon the purchase of another dwelling. These home owners could not realise the value of their asset and reinvest it in some other form of capital holding.

These are all issues which must be addressed if the nature and extent to which housing processes facilitate accumulation is to be placed in a realistic perspective.

Starting from a view that what it is necessary to identify is the extent to which housing processes provide opportunities to make money gains which can be realised and transferred three propositions can be put forward as the basis for modification of the picture presented:

i. that money gains are not made by all owners but are realisable where owners trade down or are in a position to trade down in the housing market;

ii. that where owners do move but do not trade down in some cases there is substantial 'leakage';

iii. that where owners do not move in some cases the appreciation of the value of the asset is such that they move into a position where they *could* trade down (especially to a smaller house) or do realise some of the capital value through borrowing on the security of the dwelling.

These kinds of considerations would suggest that the realisable wealth associated with home ownership is overstated by conventional statistics of wealth which refer to total asset value. However, realisable wealth is more significant than is indicated by leakage associated with moving house or increasing borrowing. It may be argued that in many cases this realisable wealth is not realised during the lifetime of the home owner but this is to impose an alternative concept of wealth which becomes a denial of the notion of wealth itself. Nonetheless, it is in this context that the inheritance of wealth through house property becomes important.

There is a growing body of evidence on marginal and failed owners. In some parts of the owner-occupied market processes of obsolescence and house price changes leave owners with a diminishing asset value net of the debt involved. In some cases the mortgage debt exceeds market value. In these cases there is no realisable money gain. In some cases the realisation of money gain is problematic because there is nowhere to 'trade down' to. Supply and access restrictions may prevent a move to rented property being a mechanism for realising money gains. Evidence of mortgage failure and repossession, negative real rates of accumulation and wide regional and local disparities in rates of house price increase are the most immediate challenge to any view that all owners are in the same position in relation to accumulation (see, for example, Moreton and Tate, 1986; Munro and Maclennan, 1987; Doling et al, 1986; Karn et al, 1985).

In contrast to this evidence there is growing evidence on issues of credit and leakage associated with home ownership. Remortgaging of houses in order to finance the purchase of consumer durables has been associated with the 1972/73 house price boom in Britain. The 1980s boom involves the same process (Johnson, 1984; Turnbull, 1984). The boom of mortgage credit has been a pivotal factor behind the buoyancy of expenditure. Since 1980 the growth in mortgage lending has far outstripped the personal sector's housing investment and has not, therefore, been directed solely towards the acquisition of additional and better housing. Mortgage funds have therefore circulated within the personal sector, thereby becoming available for consumption purposes via a process known as 'equity withdrawal'.

The conventional view (expressed by Turnbull) is that this more rapid growth in mortgage lending is not accounted for by direct lending for consumer expenditure. Rather, it is associated with decisions not to reinvest the full proceeds from the sale of a previous dwelling. Equity withdrawal rose appreciably after 1980 and was associated with the increasing percentage of purchase price funded by a mortgage. According to Ball (1986) in 1980 only 46% of purchase price on average was funded by a mortgage and this had risen to 59% in 1984. First time buyers were also borrowing a larger proportion of purchase price. These figures related both to what was realisable wealth and to actual realisation through equity withdrawal. While actual realisation did grow, the extent to which home ownership represented debt rather than ownership also grew for those with mortgages.

Increasing indebtedness is associated with increased levels of home ownership, increased borrowing by individuals to facilitate home purchase, or improvement and increased use of the home as a source of credit which is spent in areas other than housing. To the extent that the last of these aspects is involved home owners are realising the wealth accumulated through housing during their lifetime and converting it into disposable income. They may be doing this in order to cope with other problems or in pursuit of various other strategies.

The problems of estimating the extent of capital leakage are considerable. A cautious consideration by Kemeny and Thomas (1984) suggests that between 0.6 and 1.0% of the total value of personal sector dwellings is realised each year. This includes (but is likely to underestimate) the leakage of capital released to last-time sellers. Nevertheless, these estimates:

> mean that capital leakage represented 20-35% of net total advances on house purchase in 1980. Consequently, it must be concluded that as a result of capital leakage there is a demand for extra housing finance which goes beyond that necessary to sustain an expanding owner-occupied sector.

The Bank of England estimated (1985) that 'net cash withdrawal' from the private housing market totalled £7.2 billion in 1984 and was equivalent to 3% of total consumer spending. Not all of this was spent on consumption but went into savings. The discussion of capital leakage is normally linked with questions of distortion of the savings market (and impact on finance to productive industry) and distortions of the housing market (and the need to reform housing finance to reduce subsidies to consumption and discourage capital leakage). The extent of leakage is a consequence of the fiscal arrangements associated with owner occupation and would be modified by changes in these arrangements. However, in terms of the discussion in this paper, capital leakage associated with remortgaging is a manifest realisation of housing wealth. Leaving aside issues of inheritance and realisation affecting beneficiaries, the *potential* extent of realisation of wealth held in housing is considerably greater. In terms of a distinction between measures of asset holding and measures of realisable wealth this is significant.

The analysis of leakage includes that associated with last-time sellers. While this may include persons moving out of home ownership for various reasons, it will include sales following transfers of ownership through inheritance. The issue of inheritance is an important one in the discussion of accumulation as it offers the most tangible realisation and transfer of an asset. The more direct housing consequences of inheritance have been speculated upon elsewhere (Murie and Forrest, 1980).

The preceding discussion of housing as wealth has raised issues of definition and measurement which are important in identifying the extent and nature of accumulation through housing. But there is another dimension to the concept of wealth which the discussion has neglected. In much of the analysis of wealth and inequalities in wealth the important dimension is not the money value of assets at a particular time but the power and control that is associated with the ownership of assets. Hird and Irvine (1979) state:

> It is almost a precondition for producing wealth in our society that one own and control capital. This is also perhaps the main factor determining the distribution of wealth: workers can generally fight for higher wages only while owners and managers make the investment decisions which determine what will be produced, how and where. Capital is thus different from other forms of wealth: shares in an industrial company, for example, will typically grow in value over time, produce a regular dividend, confer legal ownership over part of the company's material assets, and are, moreover, easily marketable when necessary. Other forms of wealth are quite different: consumer goods generally depreciate and have a low second-hand value; the value of houses may in the main appreciate, but they are often difficult to sell, and the owner generally needs to buy another as replacement; pensions provide an entitlement to a future income only for as long as the pensioner lives, are not transferable, and often depreciate in value; and cash, although it confers immediate economic power through its purchasing power, generally depreciates. It is changes in the ownership and control of the means of production that need to be treated as the central criterion in assessing the distribution of wealth for changes in other forms of wealth are intimately related to these.

In these terms it is not sufficient to distinguish between whether and to what extent housing assets are marketable or realisable. Rather it is important to distinguish between housing as a category of asset which has a market value and other assets which have a market value but also involve ownership and control of the process of wealth creation. Hird and Irvine refer to this latter category as capital (company securities, listed ordinary shares, land). They go on to argue that the effective control of other wealth lies with a smaller group of managers rather than with the owners of assets. The direction of such an argument is that wider ownership of wealth or of realisable wealth through housing is a trend which does not involve wider ownership of capital or equality in economic power. In that sense it does not imply increasing equality or classlessness and raises doubts about the strength of the common interest involved in home ownership.

These kinds of considerations relate back to the debate around housing classes and the extent to which the accumulative capacity of owner occupation provides a significant cleavage in the interests of persons in the same position in relation to the means of production but in different housing tenures. The considerations outlined in this section suggest that the analysis of accumulation is misleading if reference is made to the money value of owner-occupied dwellings. Reference should be to realisable wealth. As a result it is apparent that not all house owners accumulate through housing and that the extent of accumulation is considerably less than is implied if asset values are referred to. The discussion of leakage and inheritance demonstrates that actual housing wealth is realised and transferred both within lifetimes and between generations. The potential for such realisation through remortgaging and trading down is considerably greater. Nevertheless the capacity for accumulation is not in itself a source of economic power. The extent to which it affects the interests and orientations of home owners is very much less than would be the case otherwise. Owners of houses do have material interests relating to the ways their dwellings are financed and exchanged but the extent to which these distort or override other interests, say in the sphere of production, are likely to be very much less significant than would be the case if total asset values were realisable or if wealth held in the form of housing provided economic power.

Accumulation through home ownership is not the necessary experience of all home owners and the rate of accumulation varies considerably over time, between different locations and in different parts of the housing market.

Housing and employment careers

The terminology of housing ladders and escalators is associated with owner occupation in academic as well as other literature. In spite of doubts cast on the nature and extent of filtering there is an implication that because substantial capital gains can be made from housing and because these can be substantial compared to the income derived from the work process housing careerists, spiralists or entrepreneurs are at work. These individuals demonstrate a difference of interest and behaviour associated with housing. They have so far identified a separate world of consumption as the route to accumulation that their energies and their political priorities are focused on housing consumption rather than on the workplace. Farmer and Barrell's (1981) representation of this group suggests that it is an exotic group with secure jobs rather than a large sector of home owners. Attempts to identify the group in practice suggest they are a minor protected species. Even among those who have moved up and through the owner-occupied market there is little to suggest that manipulation of the housing world has been a central feature of this movement. Rather, those who have reached the top rungs of the ladder have often progressed through a series of job-related moves often assisted by the employer and often designed to enable future job-related mobility rather than to maximise accumulation through housing (Forrest and Murie, 1987). There may be others (and civil servants have been suggested) where high paid secure jobs do not involve regular relocation and where entrepreneurial energies are left to be exercised in the housing market. But the case is not proven. Indeed it seems likely that family and educational considerations will be more significant triggers to movement and determinants of where to move than speculation.

Evidence on why people move or do not, what determines where they move and on preferences and choices does not support any general assumption of speculative activity. There is little evidence that people pursue housing careers in the sense of planned trajectories related to maximising financial gains. Rather the evidence does support a primacy of work process. The immobile home owner is clearly not speculating; few of those who do move move from the bottom to the top of the market and reasons for moving are likely to relate to housing and family; those who do move often and who accumulate through housing moves are often doing so because their job dictates. In the discussion of different interests associated with housing, evidence about speculative movers does not offer a great source of support.

Implications

What are the implications of the considerations outlined above for the debate about the primacy of class in consumption? It has been argued that the nature of the work process, and the extent to which mobility is a necessary aspect of job career, structures the way that benefits are taken from housing consumption. It has also been argued that the accumulative dimension of home ownership tends to be overstated, is uneven and is by no means general. These considerations and differentiation within tenures lead to some caution about the over-enthusiastic assertion that new consumption cleavages are more important than traditional class differences. As against this it is evident that housing processes do introduce real inequalities. Where people own houses, when they own them and for how long affects accumulation. The size of inter-generational transfers also relates to this. There is no doubt that Saunders is correct in asserting that inequalities generated through consumption are of key importance. Insofar as these can be explained by employment and work the connection is often indirect and can not be read off from general descriptions of occupational class. The assertion of the primacy of class becomes a problem only if it is seen to deny that the differences which develop from position in relation to consumption can outweigh the differences associated with the sphere of production, or if it is 'ontological security' which is stressed. Employees in similar occupational categories earning similar amounts and moving house as a result of the requirements of employment will move more or less often, at different times and to different locations. Their housing situation and rate of accumulation is undoubtedly structured by the work process. Their rate of accumulation and their position in relation to consumption although structured by the same process will be very different. Rates of gain and the importance of consumption sector gains relative to those directly associated with employment may diverge considerably. What this does not establish is that the political and social attitudes of those who own or those who benefit most from owning are changed by this. The evidence on voting behaviour in Britain is far from conclusive and the view that the growth of working-class owner occupation represents a 'new working class' more inclined to vote Conservative has been challenged. For example, Heath, Jowell and Curtice (1985) state that:

> changes in the distribution of housing tell us little that the changes in class structure had not told us already.

They continue:

> While we agree with Dunleavy (1979) that 'consumption patterns ... in housing ... raise important questions for political analysis', we disagree that housing has 'political effects cross cutting those of occupational class'. Housing does not form the basis for a new cleavage in British politics, but rather acts as a separate source for the maintenance of the class cleavage. (Heath, Jowell and Curtice, 1985)

Further considerations

Much of what has been stated above casts doubts on the thesis of the 'primacy of ownership'. The differences which emerge from housing processes can cross cut occupational class differences. However, these housing consumption differences cannot be read off from housing tenure. It is only in parts of home ownership that significant gains arise. Regional and local differences in the status and meaning of different tenures and in rates of accumulation or loss are of major importance and it is not clear that autonomy, self-expression, identity and ontological security are attributes restricted to home ownership.

The primacy of ownership is also open to question in three other respects. Firstly, the demand to own and the returns made from ownership are strongly influenced by policy. The growing demand for home ownership in Britain has been strongly influenced by significant and increasing financial and ideological support. The discussion about the interests generated by ownership refer to a set of historically specific circumstances rather than necessary attributes of the tenure. These are, in particular, that house prices have risen faster than the rate of inflation and housing investment has provided greater returns than other forms of investment; that mortgage interest rates have been lower than inflation rates; and that tax relief and fiscal arrangements have privileged the housing sector relative to other forms of investment. Changes in policy, in rates of inflation, in interest rates and in other factors influence the nature and extent of gains to be made from different parts of the home ownership world. Changes in policy towards other tenures and the desirability of those tenures is also relevant.

Secondly, as home ownership grows, it is less determined by new building, is more dependent on second-hand sales and chains of sales, becomes more unstable and liable to rapid fluctuations in price and market collapse (see, for example, Ball, 1986). So the variation in the owner-occupied market will become more marked and the primacy of ownership become more doubtful.

Thirdly, the underlying trends in the British market - commodification, privatisation and marginalisation within each tenure - involve a reassertion of the connection between housing and income and wealth. As home ownership approaches a 70% share of the market, the problems of disrepair, repossession, eviction, flitting and homelessness are more apparent. The growth phase of home ownership in the period of transition in which the form of private housing provision has changed from rentier landlordism to individual owner occupier is likely to have had different characteristics than a later phase. In the growth phase home ownership has been associated with the younger employed, in a growing full employment economy with an expanding welfare service net. In a later phase recession and unemployment and declining welfare provision mean that home ownership and home owners have a much more mixed experience. The sector is increasingly dependent on grants and state subsidy. The most vulnerable owners are less likely to be able to sustain ownership status. As home ownership includes more of those who are marginal in the production process and is more affected by recession so there will be more who move from owning to renting or move down market in owner occupation because they cannot maintain the costs involved. The quality of housing which people are in and the rate of accumulation involved will increasingly reflect income and wealth and status in work. Both housing and economic trends suggest that inequalities deriving from consumption in housing will become more closely associated with occupational class. The excitement over the extent to which consumption cleavages in housing cross cut occupational class should be tempered by a recognition that we have been looking at a system in transition and that at the end of transition there is likely to be a better fit between occupational class and housing situation. In this situation it may be that we should be looking for new key social divisions within housing tenures in relation to the impact of recession, to marginalisation and the position of those who are not in employment or in the growth sectors of the economy and to differences in relation to region, gender and race as well as class rather than to housing classes or consumption sectors conceived in terms of housing tenures.

References

Ball, M. (1986) *Home ownership: a suitable case for reform,* London: Shelter.
Bank of England (1985) *Quarterly Bulletin,* March.
Barbolet, R.H. (1969) *Housing classes and the socio-ecological system,* University Working Paper no 4, London: Centre for Environmental Studies.
Doling, J. et al (1986) 'The impact of unemployment on owner occupation', *Housing Studies,* vol 1, pp 49-60.
Dunleavy, P. (1979) 'The urban basis of political alignment: social class, domestic property ownership and state intervention in consumption processes', *British Journal of Political Science,* vol 9, pp 409-43.
Englander, D. (1983) *Landlord and tenant in urban Britain 1838-1918,* Oxford: Clarendon Press.
Farmer, M.K. and Barrell, R. (1981) 'Entrepreneurship and government policy: the case of the housing market', *Journal of Public Policy,* vol 1, pp 307-32.
Forrest, R. (1983) 'The meaning of home ownership', *Environment and Planning D: Society and Space,* vol 1, pp 205-16.
Forrest, R. and Murie, A. (1986) 'Marginalization and subsidized individualism', *International Journal of Urban and Regional Research,* vol 10, pp 46-65.
Forrest, R. and Murie, A. (1987) 'The affluent homeowner', *Sociological Review,* vol 35, no 2, pp 370-403.
Haddon, R. (1970) 'A minority in a welfare state society', *New Atlantis,* vol 2, pp 80-133.
Heath, A., Jowell, R. and Curtice, J. (1985) *How Britain votes,* Oxford: Pergamon.
Hird, C. and Irvine, J. (1979) 'The poverty of wealth statistics', in J. Irvine, I. Miles and J. Evans (eds) *Demystifying social statistics,* pp 190-211, London: Pluto Press.
Hole, V. (1972) 'Housing in social research', in E. Gittus (ed) *Key variables in social research, volume 1: religion, housing, locality,* London: Heinemann.
Holme, A. (1985) *Housing and young families in East London,* London: Routledge and Kegan Paul.
Johnson, C. (1984) 'Borrowing without tears', *Lloyds Bank Economic Bulletin No 62.*
Karn, V., Kemeny, J. and Williams, P. (1985) *Salvation or despair? Home ownership in the inner city,* Aldershot: Gower.
Kemeny, J. and Thomas, A. (1984) 'Capital leakage from owner-occupied housing', *Policy and Politics,* vol 12, pp 13-30.
Moreton, N. and Tate, J. (1986) 'House prices in the older housing stock of Birmingham', *Housing Review,* vol 35, May/June, pp 85-87.
Munro, M. and Maclennan D. (1987) Intra urban changes in housing prices: Glasgow 1972-83, *Housing Studies,* vol 2, no 2, pp 65-81.
Murie, A. (1983) *Housing inequality and deprivation,* London: Heinemann.
Murie, A. and Forrest, R. (1980) 'Wealth inheritance and housing policy', *Policy and Politics,* vol 8, pp 1-19.

Pahl, R.E. (1975) *Whose city?*, Harmondsworth: Penguin.

Pahl, R.E. (1984) *Divisions of labour,* Oxford: Basil Blackwell.

Preteceille, E. (1986) 'Collective consumption, urban segregation, and social classes', *Environment and Planning D: Society and Space,* vol 4, pp 145-54.

Rex, J. (1971) 'The concept of housing class and the sociology of race relations', *Race,* vol 12, January, pp 293-301.

Rex, J. and Moore, R. (1967), *Race, community and conflict,* London: Oxford University Press.

Robson, B.T. (1969) *Urban analysis,* Cambridge: Cambridge University Press.

Royal Commission on the Distribution of Income and Wealth (1977) *Third report on the standing reference,* Cmnd 6999, London: HMSO.

Saunders, P. (1977) *Housing tenure and class interests,* Brighton: University of Sussex.

Saunders, P. (1984) 'Beyond housing classes: the sociological significance of private property rights in means of consumption', *International Journal of Urban and Regional Research,* vol 8, pp 202-27.

Saunders, P. (1986) 'Comment on Dunleavy and Preteceille', *Environment and Planning D: Society and Space,* vol 4, pp 155-63.

Timms, D.W. (1971) *The urban mosaic,* Cambridge: Cambridge University Press.

Turnbull, P. (1984) 'Mortgage lending and consumers' expenditure', *The Investment Analyst,* vol 72, April, pp 3-6.

Zweig, F. (1976) *The new acquisitive society,* London: Barry Rose.

CHAPTER 15

SPATIAL MOBILITY, TENURE MOBILITY, AND EMERGING SOCIAL DIVISIONS IN THE UK HOUSING MARKET

RAY FORREST

Introduction

In the housing debate there is growing recognition that the reduced and changed role for public sector housing in Britain is paralleled by transformations in the nature of owner occupation. As home ownership expands and draws in lower income households, as the owner-occupied market becomes progressively more dominated by transactions involving existing owners, new problems are arising in the production, distribution, and exchange of owned and mortgaged dwellings. Problems supposedly confined to the rental tenures are now spilling over into home ownership and there is marked social and spatial unevenness in mobility, asset appreciation, and capital gains. As the debate progresses, it is clear that we need a more sensitive understanding of the divisions within the British housing market if we are to move beyond an analysis which simply polarises tenures, groups, or areas. In this paper I review the current policy and theoretical debates, indicate a renewal of interest in processes of migration, mobility, and household behaviour, and relate divisions in the housing market to transformations in the labour market. In the final section a typology of housing histories is offered in an attempt to link broader changes in the social structure to the shaping of individual housing experiences.

New issues, new debates

As housing re-emerges as a prominent issue in Britain, there is political, theoretical, and policy confusion. The Labour Party offers qualified support to the sale of council houses and has turned its attention to the reform of home ownership. It would seem that the seeds of future modes of socialist housing provision are contained within the contradictions of home ownership rather than within the contracting rump of council housing (for

---

This chapter first appeared in *Environment and Planning A*, 1987, vol 19, pp 1611-30.

example, see Ball, 1986). And for those who have single-mindedly promoted the growth of home ownership there is a recognition that *rental* housing is also needed and that problems of decay, maintenance, poverty, and inequality are by no means confined to the rental tenures. Critical reports highlighting lack of investment in the physical fabric of dwellings, the problems of marginal home owners, and the chaotic and inequitable system of housing finance have emanated from the Church of England (1985) and the Inquiry into British Housing chaired by the Duke of Edinburgh (NFHA, 1985). A report published by the Department of the Environment estimated that £19 billion was required to refurbish the existing housing stock (Department of the Environment, 1985).

Council housing in its traditional form may now have few friends or supporters, but enthusiasm for the further promotion of home ownership is by no means unqualified. It has become evident that for an increasing number of households home ownership is a tenure of constraint rather than choice. Faced with declining rental opportunities, many lower income households have little choice but to enter the owner-occupied sector, only to find themselves financially overcommitted, occupying a property in need of substantial investment, and perhaps at an inappropriate stage in the family life-cycle. Describing some of the areas of inner-city home ownership in Liverpool and Birmingham, Karn *et al* (1985, p 128) suggest that Britain:

> could even experience the same wholesale abandonment or dereliction of owner-occupied housing as found in inner areas of US cities, especially if prices begin to fall in absolute as well as relative terms in response to increasing fabric deterioration and the inability to raise a mortgage or find a buyer.

Although Britain appears to be far from this situation at present, the reputation and image of home ownership is being damaged by the increase in mortgage arrears and repossession cases. The number of homeless households accepted by English local authorities for rehousing in 1979 was 50,000 (*Hansard*, 1986d). This had risen to almost 100,000 by the mid 1980s. And within those figures an increasing proportion of households became homeless through mortgage default (from 4% in 1979 to 10% in 1985). In 1985 some 59,000 court actions were begun for repossession (*Hansard*, 1986d). Although it would be misguided to overestimate the scale of the problem, representing as it does a small proportion of all owner occupiers, it is nevertheless an issue of increasing prominence with damaging political and fiscal implications. A shrinking public sector is facing increasing demands from displaced home owners. And the cost of mortgage interest payments to people who had been unemployed for up to six months was around £61 million in 1983 (*Hansard*, 1986e). Both government and the major housing institutions such as the building societies began to acknowledge the need for more rental housing and greater flexibility and choice in the housing market.

In early 1987, however, it was the issue of differential house prices which gained media attention and became preeminent in housing debates. This was significant because of its perceived impact on labour mobility (of central concern to government social and economic policy) and because it related to the basic structure and dynamics of the owner-occupied housing market. These problems are therefore not located on the margins of home ownership or related to residual processes in the rental sectors. Moreover, they are not confined to the working classes. As a range of institutions channel ever-increasing amounts of money into owner occupation, the 'hard sell' of a highly competitive mortgage finance market combines with the uneven impact of recession to produce overheating in some sectors of the housing market. With the parallel reduction in rental opportunities it became almost impossible for many households to contemplate moving from the north to the south of England. Ironically, and contrary to the beliefs and claims of the past, it was owner occupation rather than council housing which emerged as the major *housing* barrier to labour mobility.

The extent and nature of this barrier to labour mobility depends upon who is being impeded from moving. This needs careful scrutiny. Council housing contains an increasingly economically inactive population. In 1979, 41% of council tenants were in this category. By 1984 this had risen to 53% (OPCS, 1986, p 54). For this group at least, issues of *labour* as opposed to *residential* mobility are not relevant. And for the unemployed, regardless of housing tenure, the prospects on offer elsewhere are likely to be in the low paid, personal service sector, part-time employment for females, or in highly paid professional, managerial, or skilled work, typically for white males and typically for graduates (Massey, 1984). The jobs are likely to be unsuitable or to offer little financial gain, particularly given higher housing costs and the dominance of owner occupation in more affluent areas. The ways in which council housing has inhibited long-distance labour mobility may also have been somewhat overstated. Although the residential qualifications which have to be satisfied by new tenants moving to another authority have been a factor in limiting movement, most residential movement by tenants is over short distances "well within the constraints arising from local authority procedures" (for example, see Pickup, 1984, p 23). And sociological and anthropological evidence on social and kinship networks indicates that this pattern of movement is also a product of attachment to home and locale within working-class culture rather than merely a reflection of bureaucratic constraints. Moreover, it is a prominent feature of working-class home ownership. It is erroneous, therefore, to interpret immobility or limited mobility as necessarily a product of *constraint* rather than *choice* (for a general discussion see Franklin, 1986).

The significant point is that concern with the impact of house price differentials on spatial mobility relates to those in *employment* and in owner occupation. More specifically it is likely to relate to the traditionally mobile sections of the middle classes - those identified as 'spiralists' and 'cosmopolitans' in sociological literature of the 1960s (for example, see Watson, 1964; Merton, 1968). The costs and problems of relocating such employees became a prominent concern of the Confederation of British Industry which set up an Employee Relocation Council. Reports by specialist relocation consultants in the mid 1980s highlighted housing costs as an increasingly important factor inhibiting employee mobility (for example, see Black Horse Relocation, 1986; Merrill Lynch, 1986). And in a study of recruitment difficulties among firms in mid Berkshire it was concluded that "the main difficulties are related to the recruitment from lower cost housing areas of professional and managerial staff who are already owner occupiers" (Parsons, 1987, p 34).

How far the mobility of this group is impeded by house price differentials will depend on specific personnel policies and will vary between firms and between sectors. But the evident concern with house price movements and crude north/south divisions is less about the impact on unemployment levels than about the financial burden borne by firms and individuals in higher status jobs requiring high mobility. This is evident in a speech by Lord Young, the Secretary of State for Employment when he claimed that:

> At the moment ... there are probably few vacancies in any part of the country which cannot be filled from within the local area, possibly with some training. Thus it would be wrong to suppose that a higher level of mobility would lead to a major reduction in unemployment though it might have some effect at the margin. (NEDC, 1986, p 2)

Regional imbalances in housing costs and house price rises are significant not because they damage the mobility prospects of tenants or those on the margins of home ownership but because they are potentially dysfunctional to the growth sectors of the economy and represent an increasing expense for private capital when relocating key personnel.

Housing, social consumption and urban change

There is also a resurgence of interest in academic debates in residential movement and mobility. In some ways this can be seen as a return to some of the concerns of the 1960s and 1970s when a considerable amount of housing research was devoted to studies of mobility and residential choice (for a useful review see Murie, 1974). The questions are, however, being posed in a substantially changed political, theoretical, and economic context. Most obviously, in previous research a particular and pervasive pattern of state intervention in the housing market was assumed. Council housing was expanding, the economy was relatively buoyant, and, although there was considerable emphasis on life-cycle factors and institutional barriers, the general tone of the discussion was of choice rather than constraint, mobility rather than entrapment. Moreover, discussion of subsectors in the housing market was largely divorced from issues of class, labour market segmentation, and spatial differentiation. The transformation of the tenure structure, the reorientation of state intervention, and the uneven impact of recession and economic restructuring have produced a quite different research and policy agenda. Consideration of housing market processes and patterns of residential differentiation is now (and should be) more thoroughly enmeshed in broader sociological and economic debate. Within the narrower confines of housing research, discussion has focused on tenurial polarisation (Hamnett, 1984; Bentham, 1986), the residualisation and marginalisation of council tenants (Forrest and Murie, 1983; 1987a), and differentiation and stratification within the owner-occupied sector (Thorns, 1981; Karn et al, 1985; Doling et al, 1986). These essentially housing-led debates connect directly to more broadly based discussion and research on social polarisation (Pahl, 1986), economic crisis and social stratification (Rose et al, 1984), the spatial division of labour and local social and economic structures (Massey, 1984; Robson, 1986). Indeed, housing processes occupy a prominent position in these broader debates. Pahl (1986, p 8) comments:

> The rupture of a continuum of housing conditions by the sharp distinction between owner and non-ownership may be a more divisive element in the working-class than skill, ethnic origin or gender.

Similarly Marshall et al (1985, p 274) suggest that:

> One particularly important feature of changes in consumption patterns which is of crucial importance in the formation of social identities is home ownership.

And a particularly important and evolving debate has concentrated on sectoral divisions within the sphere of consumption (see in particular Dunleavy, 1986; Preteceille, 1986; Saunders, 1986a). In this context the divisions between owners and renters and the accumulative potential of owner occupation are argued to be among the most powerful factors contributing to an increasingly bifurcated society.

Such claims (which are essentially aspatial), however, need to be set within a more sensitive appreciation of the geography of recession and economic restructuring and the operation of housing markets and submarkets in different localities. Tenure cannot be assumed to convey similar benefits or disbenefits, images and meanings in all localities. As Hamnett and Randolph (1988) correctly argue in relation to tenurial polarisation:

> to the extent that socio-tenurial polarisation has occurred, then its expression varies considerably both between and within different regions depending on the local structure of both housing and labour markets and the nature of local political intervention in housing provision.

In a similar vein, Forrest and Murie (1986) have shown that the associations between the marginalised sections of the urban population and council housing will vary between areas and that apparently similar outcomes can be the product of different relationships and processes. In some cases, marginality will be highly tenure specific; in others, minority ethnic groups, the unemployed, the insecurely employed, and the working-class elderly may be heavily represented in all tenures.

This emphasis on space and locality goes beyond simple north/south distinctions (although the emerging geography of corporate dominance, higher status employment, tenure change, urban decay, and gentrification indicates that this is an increasingly significant distinction), and indicates the need for more detailed analyses of marginalisation and fragmentation within, as well as between, localities. The unemployed council tenant occupying a high-rise flat in inner London is likely to experience more chronic and multiple disadvantage than the unemployed tenant of a three-bedroomed house in the north of England where affluence and poverty may not so obviously coexist. Equally, however, those in the most privileged housing circumstance are likely to be multiple earning households living in the least affluent areas. Living in localities where the cost of housing services and other commodities is generally low, they will enjoy highly privileged life-styles. Pahl (1986, p 8) suggests it is the couple who are both earners which is the optimum survival unit in the late 20th century, and that a fragmented group of single people at all stages in the family life-cycle are relatively and increasingly disadvantaged. Equally, however, he emphasises that the life-styles and living conditions of core and marginal groups will vary according to whether they are living in depressed or affluent areas and between the north and south of the country. Indeed, for all households, mobility between localities experiencing different economic conditions may be problematic, albeit for different reasons.

What is emerging from this literature on housing and social and economic change is a complex mosaic of social differentiation according to ethnicity, class, gender, and locality. Although stark contrasts between chronic deprivation and decay and rampant gentrification can be found in the inner areas of, for example, London or Bristol, these are exotic and concentrated representations of a pervasive polarisation of life-styles and living standards.

This concern with contemporary developments in the British housing market, with enhanced or inhibited spatial mobility, sits then within a developing interest in the sociology of consumption. This interest is both the product of, and a reaction to, much of the structural Marxism of the 1960s and 1970s when concern with aspects of social consumption was implicitly if not explicitly seen as bourgeois liberalism. Deep structures are no longer viewed as the exclusive preserve of social relations in the sphere of production. And concern with 'structure' is no longer limited to political economic and macrosociological issues. As Giddens (1986, p 291) remarks, "activity in micro-contexts has strongly defined structural properties". And in this developing fusion of time geography and structuration theory the dwelling as physical artefact and the home as a social construction are deeply implicated. Dwelling design, dwelling location, residential movement, and social relations within the home are not the fragmentary concerns of architects, housing researchers, or anthropologists, but are emerging as central to our understanding of human interaction, relation of class and patriarchy, and the meaningfulness of human activity (Hayden, 1984; Giddens, 1986). Research on housing histories and the notion of housing 'careers' - the idea that different groups pursue distinct culturally embedded housing 'practices' (Franklin, 1986) - connects with the reemergence of interest in the individual as a biographical project:

> A person may live in the house of his or her parents, for example, until establishing a new residence or marriage. This may be associated with a change of job, such that home and workplace as 'stations' along the daily trajectory become altered. Mobility within the housing market, marital separation or career progression, amid a host of other possible factors, may influence typical life-paths. (Giddens, 1986, p 268)

From a different perspective, and deriving in part from his work on consumption cleavages referred to earlier, Saunders (1986b) has recently called for the development of a "sociology of consumption with its own distinctive theories and concerns". This is not to suggest that the sphere of production is unconnected or irrelevant to this development but to acknowledge that we are using rather blunt theoretical tools in attempting to understand the significant but often subtle divisions within consumption. Issues of class, culture, the life-cycle, status, need to be combined with a more detailed analysis of state intervention and the historical development of the welfare state. This latter point has been taken up in a recent paper by Harrison (1986). Drawing on previous writings by Titmuss and others (see in particular Titmuss, 1958), he argues that urban theorists have tended to work with stereotypical images of the welfare state, with crude public and private distinctions and have neglected a social division of welfare which is more complex and relates to the social division of labour (see also Forrest and Murie, 1987c). This perspective is particularly relevant to the latter sections of this paper where it is suggested that patterns of enhanced or inhibited mobility relate to a highly differentiated structure of housing assistance which in turn relates to position in the labour market. Moreover, if we are to escape from overemphasising housing tenure divisions and avoid generating a set of apparently disconnected concerns with, for example, house price barriers, down-graded council tenants, or marginal home owners, we need to develop a more unified and processual framework in which to situate debates about social divisions in housing.

Spatial mobility and tenure

A consultant's report in the mid 1980s had a section headed "Two nations - house prices divide the country" (Reward Regional Surveys, 1986). It suggested that the "soaring cost of house prices [sic] in the south east is driving a wedge between this region and the rest of the country" (p i). It contrasted the price of a four-bedroomed detached house in the Greater London area at £79,325 with an equivalent dwelling in Yorkshire priced at £46,125. Over the previous year prices in the first area had risen by 19% compared with 5% in the second: "The message for companies is clear - relocating employees to the south east, and particularly to London, is a very expensive business" (p i). The 1987 report on house prices from the Nationwide Building Society showed a further widening of the 'north/south divide'. House prices in London on average were 23% higher than a year previously compared with 21% higher in the year to September. This was over ten times the increase in Northern Ireland and nearly eight times the increase in the northern Region and Scotland (Nationwide Building Society, 1987).

Drawing on reports such as the above, and using more anecdotal evidence, national daily newspapers (and television) published regular accounts of this widening gap in property values and house price inflation (for example, see *The Observer*, 1986b; *Financial Times*, 1986a; 1986b; *The Daily Telegraph*, 1987). But it is not the problems of access to home ownership for those on low incomes, rising homelessness, or the mobility problems of the unemployed which have produced such widespread concern, but the difficulties experienced by the mobile sections of the middle classes.

Patterns of residential mobility have always been highly differentiated by class and occupational status (for example, see Murie, 1974; Donnison, 1961). Those in higher status jobs tend to move more frequently and over longer distances. Working-class mobility tends to be more local and less frequent. And perhaps contrary to popular belief, the expansion of home ownership over this century appears to have been paralleled by a reduction in mobility - particularly in the post-war period. Franklin (1986) claims that it was the period 1860-1940 which contained the highest levels of regional and national migration. Citing a procession of studies of kinship and social networks he suggests that "since the war we have been seeing greater degrees of sedimentation to locality" (p 27). One explanation offered by Franklin is that the spread of home ownership, rather than facilitating greater mobility, may have enhanced the possibilities of maintaining social and kinship networks. This would be particularly true in areas where house prices have been relatively low and access has not been restricted to higher earning households. Analyses of the 1981 census also produced evidence of decreasing mobility (Brant, 1984). Those who moved tended to move within one district of a town (57%). Long distance moves were very much the exception. And throughout the 1970s the number of house moves fell by approximately one-fifth (Davis, 1986).

Within this general picture of reduced migration and declining residential mobility, there are a number of interrelated processes which affect different groups in different ways. There is certainly no simple association between mobility or immobility and choice or constraint. For example, to attribute a reduction in residential mobility to the impact of economic recession would be to ignore the points raised by Franklin (1986) and others (for example, see NEDC, 1986, annex 1). And research on highly mobile affluent home owners has suggested that, even among this group, residential movement is a reflection of job constraints, of 'career path migration' (Salt, 1984) rather than residential choice (Forrest and Murie, 1987c). Implicit in much of the literature is a view that people have a strong and unrelenting desire to move. Evident patterns are, it seems, too often interpreted as revealed preferences.

The general point is that explanations for differing migration and mobility patterns, and for emerging social divisions in the housing market, are not to be found primarily in the distinctions between tenures but in processes of labour-market segmentation, the operation of internal labour markets, and expansion of those groups on the social and economic margins. Whereas the most evident division is between the employed majority and the expanding unemployed and underemployed minority (Hudson and Williams, 1986), sharp divisions are also emerging between those with highly localised housing and job histories and a group of increasingly mobile core workers who move from positions of job strength within internal labour markets (Craig *et al*, 1985; Salt, 1985). To some extent, therefore, there is a housing market division which corresponds to the familiar distinction between primary and secondary labour markets. Although such a bifurcation of the labour market is generally recognised as requiring considerable refinement and qualification (for a useful review and discussion see Gleave and Sellens, 1984), such a conception usefully "captures the essence of the structure" (Weeks, 1980, p 557). Past research established strong interconnections between employment in the secondary labour market, low geographic mobility, and the public housing sector (Gleave and Palmer, 1980). Recession, economic restructuring, and tenure restructuring (principally through council house sales, minimal public sector building, and the progressive penetration of home ownership down the income structure) indicate the need for a reappraisal of these relationships. In general terms, the rental tenures increasingly accommodate the economically inactive and redundant, and labour market divisions may now be of more relevance in explaining contrasting trajectories and mobility patterns *within* home ownership.

Those in the core positions, typically households with white male professionals in the growth sectors of the economy, move in national, indeed, international housing markets (White, 1986, quoted by Findlay, 1986). An early nomadic existence around branch plants and subsidiaries culminates in the career objective of a senior post in a headquarters located typically in London or the south east. They occupy subsectors of housing markets, often up-market new housing developments offering easy access and disposal, which are connected to similar subsectors in other towns rather than to the local housing market. To facilitate and encourage residential and job mobility, and to compensate for the social and financial disruptions associated with such moves, companies are forced increasingly to provide generous subsidies. Although these subsidies are associated particularly with movement from low to higher priced areas for housing, they cover removal expenses, legal fees, bridging finance, grants for new fixtures and fittings, and free rented accommodation during search times for the next dwellings, and extend to allowances and low interest loans for school fees (for example, see Merrill Lynch, 1986).

Generous assistance with increased mortgage costs may also be a significant element and it is this extensive pattern of benefits which distinguishes this group from employees in the banking and financial sector, who have access to low interest loans (Green *et al*, 1984). In some cases, increased mortgage allowances are limited to moves to the London area but this is not always so. Take these two accounts of such company policies:

> Each area was indexed and if you moved into the home counties I think the index was something like 1.5 - so if you were moving from the north where the index was 1, to an area where the index was 1.5 then if you had your house valued at £50,000 you multiplied it by the index and you had a maximum IMA [increased mortgage allowance] of £25,000. ...

> We take note of Nationwide Building Society's index. What it does is it takes the reference of your current location and say

you're moving to this location which has a multiplier of 1.1, or 1.6 say, if it's London. This is the maximum the company would expect you to have to pay. Assuming you maintain equity the company will finance the delta in the interest costs. It does it for the first three years. (author's transcripts)

The volume and extent of such subsidies and allowances have not been thoroughly investigated (but see Johnson et al, 1974; Salt, 1985), but it is evident that many households simply could not contemplate moving to the south east without generous financial assistance. Refusal or reluctance to move could seriously jeopardise career prospects and an unassisted move would necessitate a significant drop in living standards ("Try selling in Bristol at the sort of price we're going to get and move back to Surrey - what would we get - a tent?"). And the prospect of a final move to the London area necessitates maintaining maximum investment in housing if eventual promotion to a senior post is not to be accompanied by a reduction in housing space and quality.

Not all moves are, of course, in this direction. Prohibitive commercial and residential costs have been a major factor in encouraging decentralisation from the core of London to the outer periphery and Britain's 'sunbelt' - a temperate zone of relative affluence and economic growth stretching along the M4 motorway from London to Bristol. Employees choosing to relocate with a company in this situation benefit doubly from employer-related housing assistance and lower house prices. An example is provided by London Life Association, a major financial institution, which moved its head office activities from in and around London to Bristol. To facilitate the move the company allowed 10 days' paid holiday for house hunting, paid all legal and removal costs, offered more generous car purchase loans, and even bought ten furnished flats in one of the more attractive parts of Bristol which were rented to staff as a temporary staging post. Before moving to Bristol 79% of households were owner occupiers. This proportion rose to 98% after (or soon after) relocation. Moreover, more than a third of the relocated households were able to maintain or enhance their housing standards whilst extracting significant amounts of equity from the proceeds of the sale of their previous dwellings (average £5,400) (City of Bristol Planning Department, 1985). There was also some evidence of a shortage of suitable, high value, high status accommodation. These sorts of moves may be contributing towards increasing polarisation of housing markets and residential areas in places like Bristol. Whereas house prices in one area may be determined by essentially local factors, in others the relocation of employees from higher priced areas (combined with retirement migration) may fuel excessive house price inflation in certain subsectors and create widening price divisions between those areas where demand is essentially local and those sought by affluent in-migrants. The expectation would be that, in the future, retirement migration among owner occupiers in London and the south east could be a significant aspect of housing demand in rural and urban areas offering attractive environments. It may also lead to a gradual shift in supply and demand, reducing house price differentials. Overall economic trends still indicate, however, a shift in economic activity towards the south and east. There are also suggestions that "should the Channel Tunnel be completed the pull to the south will probably strengthen" (Morrell, 1986, p 45).

If these economic patterns continue, we shall experience increasing contrasts between housing circumstances in areas of growth and decline, between rich and poor in all localities, and between the factors inhibiting and enhancing the mobility of different groups in the population. These contrasts are most apparent when the housing circumstances of middle-class professionals in the growth sectors are compared with marginalised groups in the rental sectors and the low value, low quality subsectors of owner occupation. The entrapment, decay, and deprivation on the inner-city, high-rise council estates and the dump estates on urban peripheries provide an extreme contrast. There are, however, strata of middle-class and working-class owner occupiers whose subsidies are limited to mortgage interest tax relief and whose ability to move and enhance their housing conditions is determined largely by the vicissitudes of the housing market. Within this group, housing histories are increasingly differentiated by their spatial histories. Take the position of the average earner who bought a modest dwelling in London in the mid 1960s. Whether or not they have moved house they will be sitting on a valuable asset. The value of the dwelling may be some ten times annual salary. On retirement they could move and maintain their housing standards whilst realising a substantial capital gain. The majority of owners elsewhere are likely to have more modest prospects. A 1987 report by Nationwide Building Society indicated that on average home owners in Greater London enjoyed an annual rate of return on their dwelling of 18% between 1975 and 1985. This compared with 11% in the West Midlands or 12% in Yorkshire and Humberside (Nationwide Building Society, 1987). And this imbalance in housing costs and rates of accumulation is reflected in the spatial distribution of the revenue costs of tax relief on mortgage interest. Whereas the south east of England contains 41% of all mortgagors, it accounts for 47% of the revenue costs of tax relief (*Hansard*, 1986b).

Even for those in relatively well-paid professional employment (such as university lecturers?) the prospects of a better job in the south east would have to be balanced against a significant and inevitable fall in living standards. The optimum housing position is to be in a multiple-earning household with one or more members in professional or managerial employment with a long housing history in London or the south east and in an occupation offering generous relocation allowances. This is evident from a 1986 report on new house sales in Surrey, in the Greater London area. Trend data indicate that in-migration from outside the Greater London area had declined. Almost half of all movers had principal earners in professional or managerial employment and a similar proportion had more than one earner. Only 6% of moves originated from outside the county and these were predominantly work-related moves by people in high status, well paid employment (Surrey County Council Planning Department, 1986). In other words, those who moved into new owner-occupied housing in Surrey either from within the county or from outside tended to have optimum household structures and to be in occupations which were likely to offer the sorts of mobility privileges referred to earlier. The effect of what might be regarded as modest assistance with housing moves is illustrated by calculations carried out by the Nationwide Building Society (1986, p 3):

> The effect of transaction costs associated with moving is clearly brought out. For instance the average borrower who purchased a house 15 years ago and has stayed put will have enjoyed a net rate of return of 17%. A person who first bought at the same time but who moved to a larger house every five years will under our assumptions have paid out an additional £4,677 in transaction costs and reduced the net return to 15%.

It would appear that the owner-occupied market in the south east (and subsectors within housing markets in other localities) is becoming a closed shop, an exclusive club with escalating membership costs. Whether or not this is a temporary state of affairs or whether it indicates a developing structural fission in the owner-occupied market in the United Kingdom remains to be seen.

Less debatable, and of more pressing concern, is the widening rift between the housing circumstances of the mass of home owners and those on the social and economic margins. Although marginal groups such as the long-term unemployed, ethnic minorities, working-class youth, and single-parent families, are not concentrated exclusively in the state housing sector, the largest spatial concentrations are to be found in the council estates of the inner city or urban periphery. Harrison (1983) has provided a vivid description of the living conditions in Hackney, in inner London. What he refers to as 'the inner city within the inner city':

> Within the council sector, the allocation game creates pockets of even greater deprivation: the dump estates. If the inner city is like a chemistry laboratory full of dangerous social reagents, the dump estate is the test-tube where they are most corrosively combined. These are the least attractive, worst sited, worst provided with amenities. Usually they are unmodernised estates of pre-war flats, but sometimes more modern estates,

more deeply flawed than usual with architectural blunders.
(p 225)

Just as there is no neat coincidence of marginality with tenure (Forrest and Murie, 1986), neither are deprivation and disadvantage confined to inner-city areas. Most evidently, the mass high-rise housing estates on the urban peripheries present one of the most visible features of social differentiation in European housing systems (Burton *et al*, 1986). Their size, the concentration of disadvantage, and their monotenurial nature set them apart from the older, inner-city neighbourhoods which tend to be smaller scale, more diverse, and more socially integrated into the broader urban social fabric. A study of four such estates in the United Kingdom concluded with a disturbing description of peripheral isolation, entrapment, immobility, and decline:

> The most striking common factor in all four case studies is the very high level of social and economic deprivation, all of them having roughly three times the national rate of unemployment in 1981. Even though the average proportional increase in unemployment during the 1970s was no higher than the national increase, it has been suggested that because unemployment was already high the income of the outer estates has decreased even further relative to the national average, and that in some sense, all four estates may now have to be regarded as 'subsistence' communities, with very low disposable incomes. The estates have all 'converged' to almost the same very high levels of unemployment and have possibly reached a basic level of dependency, where unemployment and/or receiving state benefits is a majority condition and where further increases in unemployment may make less and less difference to the local income. (CES Ltd, 1984, p 30)

This is not the place to discuss the evidence demonstrating an increasingly residual status for council housing (see Forrest and Murie, 1983; Hamnett and Randolph, 1987; Murphy and Sullivan, 1986). The most relevant general point is that the housing histories of a new underclass are diverging sharply from what might be regarded as a social norm of housing consumption. Public sector housebuilding is at its lowest level since the 1920s. This fact, combined with the disposal of council housing through council house sales is limiting access to, and movement within, the public sector. Moreover, sales tend to be concentrated in those areas where the level of owner occupation is already above average and where unemployment is relatively low (Dunn *et al*, 1987). This has a number of implications for spatial mobility. The employment opportunities available to marginal groups are likely to be in localities where the opportunities to rent publicly or privately are most restricted and where access to home ownership is most expensive. Stated bluntly, for those seeking work the choice may be between staying put and remaining jobless or moving and becoming homeless. A house price boom combined with shrinking rental opportunities presents the worst of all possible worlds for those in search of employment. And, for those who move in search of work, employment prospects are limited and housing prospects bleak. A report from Shelter's Housing Aid Centre (Conway and Ramsay, 1986) has highlighted the housing difficulties faced by job seekers moving to London. From their analysis of a self-selected sample of households who had approached SHAC for housing aid and advice the authors of the report conclude:

> The various mobility schemes, set up to make moving for work easier, are in fact totally inadequate to meet the enormous demands placed on them. For example, under the main scheme, the National Mobility Scheme, local authorities are meant to be able to provide rented housing for movers; but because of other severe pressures on their stock, particularly from households already resident in their areas, they cannot offer much help to people from elsewhere. For owner occupiers, there are also major barriers to moving house, and this is particularly the case for those moving to areas of high housing prices, such as the south east. Not only are there very limited housing opportunities for job movers, but recent government regulations for those living in board and lodgings are specifically designed to discourage young unemployed people from staying in any one place for more than a few weeks: this makes it extremely hard to get a job anywhere.
> (p 7)

The report also found that employer assistance with housing mobility costs was restricted generally to higher status workers. Neither the state nor private capital is prepared to subsidise moving costs for the less skilled. And there is little economic logic in encouraging increased mobility of the working-class unemployed or underemployed. Whilst the structure of the housing market and housing policy conspires to inhibit the spatial mobility of low paid and marginalised groups, any dislocation between employment and housing policy relates to the mobility of the core workers in employment. For these lucky few, the costs are more appropriately borne by individual firms rather than by the state.

For the state, the more immediate and pressing political problem is those groups on the periphery of both the housing and labour market; the homeless migrants sleeping rough in the inner cities (official figures indicate that since 1970 the number of homeless households accepted by London boroughs has increased by 700%), those trapped at the bottom end of the owner-occupied market, and marginal groups in both the rental tenures. This divergence of life-styles and life chances between those in employment, many of whom have experienced real increases in living standards, and the expanding underclass is multidimensional. For example, two-thirds of council tenants are reliant on public transport (itself subject to fiscal and privatising pressures) and 40% of council tenants lack telephones (OPCS, 1986, p 50). But it is the young working-class unemployed, and especially those from minority ethnic groups who face the greatest degree of exclusion. Although a procession of social surveys indicates increasing expectation of access to home ownership (for example, see Boleat, 1986), for the young unemployed this is likely to prove impossible. Their early housing histories are more likely to be characterised by delayed household formation, longer periods of sharing with parents, with limited aspirations of access to a dwindling local authority stock.

Tenure mobility

The most obvious result of tenure change in Britain in the 1980s is the continuing expansion of home ownership paralleled by an absolute and relative decline in council housing. The growth of home ownership has not been the result of a smooth and progressive penetration of the income structure, but has been socially and spatially uneven with different groups entering under different conditions at different times. The latest layer has been largely the result of the structural privatisation of council housing. Around one million council tenants have entered home ownership without changing dwelling and at significantly less than the market price. The social and spatial pattern of this process is well documented (see Forrest and Murie, 1987b). What is less clear is the way in which council house purchase will affect the housing market trajectories of former tenants. A significant number will have bought an accumulating asset enabling them to realise or reinvest a capital gain on resale. The equity stored and ultimately realised will depend upon a number of factors: principally the size of the original discount, the specific nature and location of the dwelling, and house price movements in the locality. In some cases, particularly in London, substantial gains can be realised. For example, a tenant qualifying for a 60% discount on a dwelling valued at £40,000 (which is not unusual for council houses in London) would pay £16,000. Given house price trends in London in the 1980s of 20% per annum it could be worth almost £100,000 after five years. This would offer on resale the possibility of trading up, substantial equity withdrawal, and/or an attractively located dwelling on retirement. Even if the house price increases of former council dwellings remain significantly less than similar dwellings on the private market, a valuable asset will have been acquired. It should also be noted that not all council dwellings were purpose built. Many were acquired by local authorities for renovation and are indistinguishable from other privately owned properties. Moreover, they are not located on large council estates.

By contrast, the housing future is rather less optimistic for a tenant purchasing a less popular house or flat on a large estate in an area of low housing demand. The resale value could be extremely low. Indeed, the combined effect of rising rents, rising discounts, and falling interest rates could produce a situation where for some tenants day-to-day housing costs could be reduced by house purchase.

Predictably, rental costs and purchase costs are least divergent in areas of economic decline. But purchasing (say) a high-rise flat on a peripheral estate in Liverpool under these conditions may have little to do with tenure preference and offer minimal prospects of social or spatial mobility. For public sector tenants who do not qualify for full housing benefit, whose rents are moving nearer market rents, the move into owner occupation may be a reflection of constraint rather than choice - a coping strategy to reduce housing costs. In such circumstances the move from tenant to owner occupier status could more thoroughly entrap the household. In a recent newspaper feature on 'Winners and losers in the great council house sales bonanza' (*The Observer*, 1986a) two purchasers were contrasted, one in London, the other in Birmingham. The tenant in London who had purchased his dwelling for £30,000 had it valued four months later for £67,000. The tenant in Birmingham paid £4,000 for a house with structural defects which had proved unsaleable for £15,000 six years later (see also *New Society*, 1986, pp 10-11).

Failed tenure mobility as indicated by the rising numbers of repossession cases was referred to earlier in the paper. Mortgage default and mounting arrears are evident in all areas and are by no means restricted to those who purchase under the Right to Buy (Housing Act, 1980). Indeed, given the generous discounts on offer, the expectation might be that council house purchasers are less vulnerable to arrears and repossession than those low income purchasers paying the market price for an older, cheaper property requiring substantial repair and maintenance. By March 1985, however, almost 12% of Right to Buy loans were at least one month in arrears. Although the proportion in serious arrears was less than 3%, this indicates nevertheless a worrying trend among relatively recent borrowers. And there was a striking geography to this development. In areas where the housing market was relatively buoyant such as inner and outer London the proportion of borrowers at least one month in arrears was around 8%. In South and West Yorkshire, however, the figures were 18 and 20%, respectively (AMA, 1986). It may be that higher house prices in London restricted council house purchase to those on higher incomes and in more secure employment. Alternatively, the ability to sell up or borrow on the property might have been easier in areas of high demand. But a 1986 study contains the comment that:

the problem may be less easily solved especially in areas where property prices are stagnant and on estates or in blocks of flats where sales have failed to 'take off'.

The report continues:

Local authorities may have to adopt new strategies for dealing with mortgage arrears in such circumstances if they want to avoid the danger of having a high level of abandonments and repossessions. (AMA, 1986, p 24).

The privatisation of council housing has generated a significant increase in the level of home ownership, but movement between the two main tenures is not all one way. Failed owners are increasingly accommodated by local authorities. Not only has the local authority stock borne the burden of the further extension of home ownership, its dwindling resources have to accommodate the victims of the recession and the casualties of owner occupation. As the most valuable physical assets of the public sector are absorbed by the private market, the redundant and surplus human assets remain in or return to a social housing sector with increasingly residual status. In a useful paper Murphy and Sullivan (1986) have examined the developing relationships between unemployment and tenure among young adults. Their calculations from the Labour Force Survey showed that:

movers into local authority housing from all tenures are about six times more likely to be unemployed at the time of the survey than are movers over the same period into an owner-occupied home. (p 217)

Further measures were being introduced to encourage tenure and residential mobility. Legislative proposals in the second half of the 1980s were intended to facilitate the disposal of public dwellings en masse to the private sector. Tenants could find their status changing from public to private if management functions were transferred to private and quasi-public trusts and companies. There was some experimentation with transferable discounts which would provide council tenants with the money equivalent of their discount entitlement to purchase a dwelling on the private market. This sort of policy is better news for the building industry and potentially creates vacancies for those in greater housing need. It does, however, create a further layer of inequalities between those who qualify and those who have to enter home ownership through the 'normal' channels. On any scale, it would also be inflationary and enormously expensive. A similar scheme introduced for tenants of English housing associations and taken up on only a modest basis by about 4% of those eligible was calculated to cost some £100 million (*Hansard*, 1986c). Apparent profligacy in the context of declared austerity was not, however, directed exclusively at owner occupation. Some of those most highly mobile and most highly subsidised households were those temporarily in bed and breakfast accommodation. By December 1985, the number had grown to over 4,000, heavily concentrated in inner London, and costing considerably more in social security payments than the provision of a council house.

Housing histories, housing assistance, and spatial mobility

This paper has ranged widely across issues of economic restructuring, residential movement, tenure change, and the changing nature of the housing market and housing debates in the United Kingdom. The general impression is of a housing market in which mobility and choice are subject to increasing social and spatial unevenness fuelled by a chaotic and inequitable system of state and occupational subsidies. In drawing to a conclusion, I suggest some general connections between shifts in the occupational and class structure, the pattern of housing assistance, and the shaping of housing histories.

Some terminological clarification is appropriate at this stage. Common reference is made to housing 'careers' (Forrest and Kemeny, 1982; Kendig, 1984). The notion of housing career, however, conveys intendedness, suggests a series of moves towards a particular goal, an upward trajectory through the housing market, and a certain autonomy of housing processes. Although some housing histories may contain a strong 'career' element (for example, see Farmer and Barrell, 1981) in the sense of being planned and chosen, others are chaotic and characterised by constraints and coping strategies. Alternatively, one could refer to housing *pathways* (for example, see Payne and Payne, 1977). Again, however, such terminology indicates a series of moves through space and would be inappropriate when applied to immobile or relatively immobile households. Without labouring the point, the more neutral term, housing *history* retains the processual element and allows for more detailed examination of the *specific* processes shaping housing histories according to class, age, gender, race, and locality.

In an interesting paper on social polarisation and the economic crisis in Britain, Pahl (1986, p 9) has suggested that "the social structure is turning from a pyramid into an onion-shaped structure in terms of household income". Whilst those at the top end of the household income structure have fared exceptionally well in recent years, those at the bottom have done exceptionally badly. The bulging middle strata of predominantly home owners with one or more members in employment have, however, also enjoyed a relative increase in their living standards. Pahl speculates from this that "those in category 3 [see below] unless they are exceptionally concentrated geographically are in danger of being electorally dispensable" (p 10).

Such a threefold distinction can be developed further in relation to the different ways in which housing histories are shaped and structured. From what has been said earlier, it is clear that the housing market and its relationship to the social structure is considerably more complicated than a division between owners and renters. Those in strong bargaining positions, those with marketable and non-substitutable skills and expertise, move in a privileged housing circuit with enhanced possibilities of capital gains and various forms of mobility assistance (category 1). Conversely, those on the economic margins (category 3), the casualties of the recession, experience exclusion which is multidimensional. Their powerlessness, their exclusion from trades unions, their economic irrelevance, form part of the explanation for the increasing minimal and stigmatised services on offer to them (Forrest and Murie, 1983). Between these groups sits a bulging middle mass which is typically, but variously, accommodated by local labour and housing markets (category 2).

The popular image of the structure of housing assistance is of a pyramid shape with state subsidy concentrated at the lower end of the income structure. This is closest to the official representation (particularly if subsidies are narrowly defined) and limited to an assessment of state-provided assistance. Although there is increasing recognition and acceptance that mortgage interest tax relief must be included in the equation, of equal importance is the recognition of the marked inequalities in the distribution of state assistance within home ownership. Greater fiscal benefits accrue to higher earning households paying above the standard rate of tax and occupying higher priced dwellings. For a mortgagor with a total annual income of over £30,000, the annual value in 1987 of tax relief would be around £1,500. In contrast, a mortgagor earning less than £4,000 would receive around £100 per annum in mortgage interest tax relief (*Hansard*, 1986a; see also Kelly, 1986). And when we take account of occupational and sectoral forms of housing assistance another layer of advantage accrues to those in the higher earning core category. In fact, rather than the level and range of assistance progressively reducing as we move up the income range, it tapers towards the middle and expands as we move into category 1. Housing assistance is concentrated at either end of the social-income structure. Those in category 3 qualify for housing benefits through the social security system and this covers the repairs and maintenance costs of their dwellings. Another group straddling categories 2 and 3 benefit from discounts on council house sales and mortgage interest tax relief. Those at the narrowest point are the owner occupiers on modest income occupying relatively inexpensive dwellings gaining only modest benefits from mortgage interest tax relief. Repairs and maintenance may be a significant cost and rates of house price inflation low to moderate. The level of subsidy expands as we move towards those with higher priced dwellings paying above the standard rate of tax and gaining greater benefit from mortgage interest tax relief. This is a group in higher status employment, but who are part of an essentially local housing and labour market. The core households in category 1, however, benefit doubly from their higher tax status and from occupational assistance.

This representation could be subject to considerable elaboration and qualification. The main point is that different forms of housing assistance operate at different points of the social structure, and the pattern, level, and nature of assistance relates to bargaining power in the labour market, the social and spatial division of labour, and the necessary costs of maintaining the surplus and marginalised population.

This pattern of assistance can in turn be associated with housing histories shaped in qualitatively different ways. The matrix below (Table 1) is intended as an explanatory summary device and it is neither exhaustive in terms of the associations illustrated nor does it imply that groups or individuals can be neatly allocated to particular categories. Moreover, the three typologies illustrated do not correspond to housing tenures. Type A housing history is characterised by frequent long distance moves in pursuit of a successful occupational career for the principal earner (who is usually male). It may be an exclusively owner-occupied housing history with occasional periods in luxury rented accommodation in shorter term managerial or professional positions. Even late entrants to home ownership, however, will have experienced a steep and rapid trajectory through the owner-occupied market. Not only will their housing market accumulation be significant, but their investment will be relatively well protected by their employers (for example, low cost or no cost bridging finance, guaranteed selling prices, increased mortgage allowance). In that sense, they are at least risk from the vagaries of the owner-occupied market, but are likely to gain most in terms of lifetime asset appreciation and ultimate wealth transference. For this category, the key gatekeeper in terms of access to housing resources is the company personnel manager rather than the housing exchange or mortgage professionals.

Those in type B, typically the bulging middle stratum of home owners, are exposed to the greatest risks in the housing market. This is where the home ownership lottery is at work with the prizes on offer dependent on what you live in and where you live. For the majority of households in this category, the owner-occupied dwelling will be their major asset - an asset which may accumulate rapidly, but more typically, offer only modest gains. Their housing subsidy will be almost exclusively in the form of mortgage interest tax relief. Assistance from employers will be limited or non-existent. Residential mobility patterns will generally be confined to a localised labour market and housing moves will be associated with stages in the family life-cycle rather than job-led. In contrast to type A, housing histories may have a strong matrilocal dimension.

Those in type C may be low income and/or elderly outright owners or tenants in the public or private sectors. For this category the key gatekeepers to housing resources are not the allocators of mortgage finance but the state bureaucrats administering benefits, access to, and exchanges within council housing, bed and breakfast accommodation, and hostels. Public subsidy is substantial, stigmatised, and under pressure. There is no employer assistance. Mobility is inhibited and bureaucratically determined. There is no opportunity to accumulate through the owner-occupied housing market. Owners in this category are liable to be in dwellings requiring substantial investment with limited resale value. Council tenants are likely to be in unpopular estates with minimal prospects of entry to home ownership.

Table 1:   A typification of contrasting housing histories

Typo-logy	Key gate-keepers	Public subsidy	Occupational subsidy	Nature of mobility	Housing market accumulation
A	Personnel managers	High	High	Contractual; national, international	High
B	Housing credit managers	Low to moderate	Low	Localised or familial	Low to moderate
C	State bureaucrats	High	Nil	Inhibited or bureaucratic	Nil or minimal

Concluding comments

The indications are that housing histories, housing opportunities, and patterns of residential movement will become increasingly socially and spatially differentiated. Housing consumption costs will be progressively subject to the vagaries of the market and differentials will reflect more directly the broader pattern of economic growth and decline. Within the housing market, the divisions between the marginalised excluded underclass and the employed majority will be more evident. And within the owner-occupied market there is likely to be more marked variation in terms of housing quality, mobility patterns, rates of accumulation, and subsidy both between and within localities. There is no common housing ladder with shared lower rungs but different rates of progress. Rather it is highly fragmented; some housing experience does not involve more than one rung and some involves leaping to a higher rung without using those below. Some households, those with highly marketable skills, move in an exclusive national and international housing market generously assisted by their employers. Others whose labour is easily substitutable or who experience deskilling are excluded from such occupational benefits and will have highly localised, immobile, and stigmatised housing histories. Although it is the imperatives of employment which shape the housing histories of core workers, for a mass of locally employed, middle earning, middle strata the pattern of residential movement is more likely to be associated with life-cycle stages and family growth and decline. For those on the social and economic margins their housing histories will be shaped by bureaucratic rules and procedures in conditions of greater scarcity and control. There are also indications that these rules and procedures will be increasingly applied and managed by organisations other than local authorities. But while the state continues to bear the financial burden of maintaining and containing an expanding surplus population, it is likely that pressure on mortgage interest tax relief will mean that individuals and households in the middle strata will have to bear a higher proportion of their housing costs. Outside this, however, will be an increasingly privileged circuit of core workers in strong bargaining positions whose household mobility, housing standards, and general life-styles will be protected and enhanced through employer-related subsidies and assistance.

References

AMA (1986) *Mortgage arrears: owner occupiers at risk*, London: Association of Metropolitan Authorities.

Ball, M. (1986) *Home ownership - a suitable case for reform*, London: Shelter.

Bentham, G. (1986) 'Socio-tenurial polarization in the United Kingdom 1953-83', *Urban Studies*, vol 2, pp 157-62.

Black Horse Relocation (1986) *Point to point*, autumn issue, Windsor: Black Horse Relocation.

Boleat, M. (1986) *Housing in Britain*, London: Building Societies Association.

Brant, J. (1984) 'Patterns of migration from the 1981 census', *Population Trends*, no 35, pp 23-33, Office of Population Censuses and Surveys, London: HMSO.

Burton, P., Forrest, R. and Stewart, M. (1986) *Living conditions in urban areas*, Dublin: European Foundation for the Improvement of Living and Working Conditions.

CES Ltd (1984) *Outer estates in Britain*, Interim report, London: CES Ltd.

Church of England (1985) *Faith in our city*, London: Church of England.

City of Bristol Planning Department (1985) *Moving to Bristol*, Bristol: City of Bristol.

Conway, J. and Ramsay, E. (1986) 'A job to move', RR-8, London: SHAC.

Craig, C., Rubery, J., Tarling, R. and Wilkinson, F. (1985) 'Economic, social and political factors in the operation of the labour market', in B. Roberts, R. Finnegan and D. Gallie (eds) *New approaches to economic life*, Manchester: Manchester University Press, pp 105-123.

Daily Telegraph (1987) 'Differentials: wider still and wider', 10 January.

Davis, N. (1986) 'Training for change', in P.E. Hart (ed) *Unemployment and labour market policies*, Aldershot: Gower, pp 82-97.

Department of the Environment (1985) *An inquiry into the condition of the local authority stock in England*, London: Department of the Environment.

Doling, J., Karn, V. and Stafford, B. (1986) 'The impact of unemployment on home ownership', *Housing Studies*, vol 1, pp 49-59.

Donnison, D.V. (1961) 'The movement of households in England', *Journal of the Royal Statistical Society*, Series A, Part I, pp 60-80.

Dunleavy, P. (1986) 'The growth of sectoral cleavages and the stabilization of state expenditures', *Environment and Planning D: Society and Space*, vol 4, pp 129-44.

Dunn, R., Forrest, R. and Murie, A. (1987) 'The geography of council house sales in England 1979-85', *Urban Studies*, vol 24, pp 47-59.

Farmer, M. and Barrell, R. (1981) 'Entrepreneurship and government policy: the case of the housing market', *Journal of Public Policy*, vol 1, pp 307-32.

Financial Times (1986a) 'How house prices fuel wage rises', 23 October.

Financial Times (1986b) 'The great housing barrier', 27 November.

Findlay, A.M. (1986) 'The impact of international migration on British localities', Paper presented to the ESRC conference on Localities in an International Economy, Cardiff, 11-12 September.

Forrest, R. and Kemeny, J. (1982) 'Middle class housing careers: the relationship between furnished renting and owner occupation', *Sociological Review*, vol 30, pp 208-22.

Forrest, R. and Murie, A. (1983) 'Residualisation and council housing: aspects of the changing social relations of housing tenure', *Journal of Social Policy*, vol 12, pp 453-68.

Forrest, R. and Murie, A. (1986) 'Marginalisation and subsidized individualism', *International Journal of Urban and Regional Research*, vol 10, pp 46-66.

Forrest, R. and Murie, A. (1987a) 'Fiscal reorientation, centralisation and the privatisation of council housing', in W. Van Vliet (ed) *Housing markets and policies in conditions of fiscal austerity*, Westport, CT: Greenwood Press.

Forrest, R. and Murie, A. (1987b) *Selling the welfare state*, Beckenham: Croom Helm.

Forrest, R. and Murie, A. (1987c) 'The affluent homeowner: labour market position and the shaping of housing histories', in N.J. Thrift and P. Williams (eds) *Class and space*, Andover: Routledge and Kegan Paul.

Franklin, A. (1986) *Owner occupation, privatism and ontological security: a critical reformulation*, Working Paper no 62, Bristol: SAUS Publications, School for Advanced Urban Studies, University of Bristol.

Gleave, D. and Palmer, D. (1980) 'The relationship between geographic and occupational mobility in the context of regional economic growth', in J. Hobcraft and P. Rees (eds) *Regional demographic development*, Beckenham: Croom Helm, pp 188-210.

Gleave, D. and Sellens, R. (1984) *An investigation into British labour market processes*, Redhill: Government Publishing Company.

Giddens, A. (1986) 'Time, space and regionalisation', in D. Gregory and J. Urry (eds) *Social relations and spatial structures*, London: Macmillan, pp 265-95.

Green, F., Hadjimatheou, G. and Smail, R. (1984) *Unequal fringes*, London: Bedford Square Press.

Hamnett, C. (1984) 'Housing the two nations: socio-tenurial polarization in England and Wales 1961-1981', *Urban Studies*, vol 43, pp 389-405.

Hamnett, C. and Randolph, W. (1988) 'Socio-tenurial polarization in London: a longitudinal analysis', *Urban Studies*, vol 44, pp 338-98.

Hansard (1986a) vol 95, cols 125-126, 9 April, London: HMSO.

Hansard (1986b) vol 97, cols 345-346, 12 May, London: HMSO.

Hansard (1986c) vol 98, cols 503-505, 5 June, London: HMSO.

Hansard (1986d) vol 99, cols 127-130, 10 June, London: HMSO.

Hansard (1986e) vol 99, cols 200-201, 12 June, London: HMSO.

Harrison, M. (1986) 'Consumption and urban theory: an alternative approach based on the social division of welfare', *International Journal of Urban and Regional Research*, vol 10, pp 232-42.

Harrison, P. (1983) *Inside the inner city*, Harmondsworth: Penguin Books.

Hayden, D. (1984) *Redesigning the American dream*, London: W.W. Norton.

Housing Act (1980) *Public general acts - Elizabeth II*, chapter 51, London: HMSO.

Hudson, R. and Williams, A. (1986) *The United Kingdom: western Europe economic and social studies*, London: Harper and Row.

Johnson, J.H., Salt, J. and Wood, P.A. (1974) *Housing and the migration of labour in England and Wales*, Aldershot: Saxon House.

Karn, V., Kemeny, J. and Williams, P. (1985) *Home ownership in the inner city - salvation or despair?*, Aldershot: Gower.

Kelly, I. (1986) *Heading for rubble: the political need for housing finance reform*, London: Catholic Housing Aid Society.

Kendig, H. (1984) 'Housing careers, life cycle and residential mobility: implications for the housing market', *Urban Studies*, vol 21, pp 271-83.

Marshall, G., Rose, D., Vogler, C. and Newby, H. (1985) 'Class, citizenship and distributional conflict in modern Britain', *British Journal of Sociology*, vol 36, pp 257-84.

Massey, D. (1984) *Spatial divisions of labour*, London: Macmillan.

Merton, R. (1968) *Social theory and social structure*, London: Collier Macmillan.

Merrill Lynch Relocation Management International Ltd (1986) *Third annual study of employee relocation policies among major UK companies*, London.

Morrell, J. (1986) *Business forecasts for the housing market to 1991*, London: James Morrell Ltd.

Murie, A. (1974) *Household movement and housing choice*, Occasional Paper no 28, Birmingham: Centre for Urban and Regional Studies, University of Birmingham.

Murphy, M. and Sullivan, 0. (1986) 'Unemployment, housing and household structure among young adults', *Journal of Social Policy*, vol 15, pp 205-22.

Nationwide Building Society (1986) *Housing as an investment*, London: Nationwide Building Society.

Nationwide Building Society (1987) *House prices in 1987*, London: Nationwide Building Society.

NEDC (1986) *Geographical mobility and housing*, Paper by the Secretary of State for Employment, London: National Economic Development Council.

New Society (1986) 'Cashing in on the property boom', 10 October.

NFHA (1985) *Inquiry into British housing: the report*, London: National Federation of Housing Associations.
Observer (1986a) 'Paying price of an ideal home of your own', 22 June.
Observer (1986b) 'The boom that divides a nation', 30 November.
OPCS (1986) *General household survey 1984*, series GHS, no 14, Office of Population Censuses and Surveys, London: HMSO.
Pahl, R.E. (1986) 'Social polarization and the economic crisis', Draft paper prepared for seminar organised by The Hungarian Academy of Sciences, Budapest, March.
Parsons, D. (1987) 'Recruitment difficulties and the housing market', *The Planner*, vol 73, no 1, pp 30-74.
Payne, J. and Payne, G. (1977) 'Housing pathways and stratification: a study of life chances in the housing market', *Journal of Social Policy*, vol 6, pp 125-56.
Pickup, L. (1984) *Residential mobility among council tenants: the role of transport and accessibility*, Crowthorne: Transport and Road Research Laboratory.
Preteceille, E. (1986) 'Collective consumption, urban segmentation, and social classes', *Environment and Planning D: Society and Space*, vol 4, pp 145-54.
Reward Regional Surveys (1986) *Cost of living report: regional comparisons*, Stone: Reward House.
Robson, B. (1986) 'Research issues in the changing urban and regional system', *Regional Studies*, vol 20, pp 203-08.
Rose, D., Vogler, C., Marshall, G. and Newby, H. (1984) 'Economic restructuring: the British experience', *Annals of the American Academy*, vol 475, September, pp 137-57.
Salt, J. (1984) 'High level manpower movements in North Western Europe and the role of careers', *International Migration Review*, vol 17, pp 633-51.
Salt, J. (1985) 'Housing and labour migration', Paper presented at conference on housing and labour market change, Parsifal College, London, 12-13 December.
Salt, J. and Flowerdew, R. (1986) 'Occupational selectivity in labour migration', Paper presented to the Conference on Comparative Population Geography of the United Kingdom and the Netherlands, St Edmund Hall, Oxford, September.
Saunders, P. (1986a) 'Comment on Dunleavy and Preteceille', *Environment and Planning D: Society and Space*, vol 4, pp 155-63.
Saunders, P. (1986b) 'Space, the city and urban sociology', in D. Gregory and J. Urry (eds) *Social relations and spatial structures*, London: Macmillan, pp 67-89.
Surrey County Council Planning Department (1986) *New house sales surveys 1979-1983*, Kingston upon Thames: Surrey County Council.
Thorns, D. (1981) 'The implications of differential rates of capital gain from owner occupation for the formation and development of housing classes', *International Journal of Urban and Regional Research*, vol 5, pp 205-17.
Titmuss, R. (1958) 'The social division of welfare', in *Essays on the welfare state*, Hemel Hempstead: Allen and Unwin, pp 34-55.
Watson, W. (1964) 'Social mobility and social class in industrial society', in M. Gluckmann and E. Devons (eds) *Closed systems and open minds*, Edinburgh: Oliver and Boyd.
Weeks, G.C. (1980) 'Labour markets, class interests and the technology of production', *Journal of Economic Issues*, vol 14, pp 553-66.

CHAPTER 16

THE IMPACT OF LAND USE PLANNING AND TAX SUBSIDIES ON THE SUPPLY AND PRICE OF HOUSING IN BRITAIN

GLEN BRAMLEY

Introduction

This paper presents some new empirical estimates of the impact of two types of policy intervention on the housing market in Britain. These are the use of mortgage interest tax relief (MITR) as a subsidy to owner occupier housing (the dominant tenure group), and the control of land supply for new housing through the land use planning system. The estimates are derived from a set of models representing the demand and supply sides of the market for new private housebuilding which include an explicit land supply element. The models are fitted to cross-sectional data at the inter-urban (local authority) level, and then employed in medium period simulations of alternative policies. Modelling at this level enables estimates to be made of the extent of variation between local markets in the elasticity of supply and also in the impacts of policy measures, including the capitalisation of tax subsidies.

The paper is part of the output of a research project[1] entitled, rather clumsily, 'The local supply response of new private sector housebuilding to financial and market conditions in the British land use planning context'. It arose out of work on housing supply undertaken in Bristol on a housing finance research programme[2] in the preceding two years (see Bramley, 1989; Bartlett, 1989; Lambert, 1990; Bramley et al, 1990). The central concern of this work was to estimate supply responsiveness (elasticity) and to understand the factors underlying it. The reason for this concern was primarily that the impact and effectiveness of housing subsidies depends crucially on supply elasticity. The follow up project was designed to exploit opportunities of new data availability and to fill a widely acknowledged gap in current models of the British housing market.

This chapter first appeared in *Urban Studies*, 1993, vol 30, no 1, pp 5-30, and was the Donald Robertson Memorial Prizewinner 1992.

Background

Theory and research

It seems fair to say that there is a relative lack of attention to the supply side in housing research in general (Ball, 1983) and in economic modelling of the housing market specifically. Bartlett (1989) shows that there is a considerable literature on the long run elasticity of supply associated with the standard urban economic model, a tradition particularly associated with Muth (1969), but this literature has several significant limitations. These include the emphasis on long run equilibrium, their partial coverage of supply, and the distinctive American context.

The other well-trodden path in economic modelling of housing is the short run time series approach applied to national (and sometimes regional) data. This has been much used in Britain, with its recent history of spectacular house price fluctuations, and has drawn attention to the key relationships between variables like credit availability, interest rates, and macroeconomic conditions for the movement in house prices. Some of the modelling has had no explicit supply side, while other models contain supply equations of a limited kind (Whitehead, 1974; Mayes, 1979; Tsoukis and Westaway, 1991). Economists have frequently suggested that much of the 'problem' with the housing market arises because supply is rigid, and that supply is rigid because of planning. Yet these remain assertions because the characteristic economic tools, the macro models, contain no explicit submodels or variables relating to planning and land supply. This study can be seen as in part an attempt to plug that gap.

Some economists recognise a considerable regional dimension to housing market behaviour, for example in relation to price trends and ripple effects (Giussani and Hadjimatheou, 1990; Coombes and Raybould, 1991), and sometimes the point that planning control may be tighter in some regions than others is made (Evans, 1988a and 1988b). Yet no systematic attempt is made to build in the fact that, because land is locationally fixed, the supply side of the housing market is likely to be quite different as between different local market areas, let alone regions. Consequently, nobody has convincingly quantified the impact of the planning system on housing output and house prices overall and across different types of area (Cheshire and Sheppard, 1989, is a partial attempt based on two towns). Similarly, suggestions that the 'capitalisation' of taxes and subsidies on housing might apply differentially to different areas or sectors of the market have remained at the level of theoretical speculation (O'Sullivan, 1983).

Policy issues

Planning is a major state intervention in the housing market. While planning is assumed by some economists to restrict supply and push up house prices, this assumption is not accepted by all of those involved in the planning process. The debate between Evans (1988b) and Grigson (1986), rehearsed in Monk et al (1991), illustrates this. Grigson expresses a typical planning perspective by arguing that prices are determined by demand, not supply, because new build supply is only a tiny part of the total supply and cannot adapt quickly to the major demand fluctuations induced by financial and other factors. Evans, by contrast, argues that restricting the total supply of land is bound in the longer term to raise prices, and also to raise densities (thereby reducing welfare). Direct and systematic evidence of the extent of the impact of planning on prices is very limited, apart from the work of Cheshire and Sheppard (1989) mentioned above.

The housebuilding industry has long argued that planning restricts output and forces up prices, reducing access to buy and, therefore, increasing the amount of unmet housing need. Following a number of land availability studies in the 1970s, the 1980s saw the institution of specific procedures to ensure an 'adequate' short term (five year) land supply, albeit with adequacy defined in relation to planning targets.

In an earlier paper (Bramley, 1989) this author argued, drawing on the work of Evans (1983), Neutze (1987) and others, that housing supply would not be completely elastic even in the absence of planning. Indeed, it is possible to envisage a scenario where planning, by reducing uncertainty, increases supply. Attention was drawn to other market uncertainties that may also inhibit response, even where land with planning permission is available. That paper also argued that planning might be in practice quite responsive to market pressures, especially in the 1980s.

The level of private housebuilding output would be taken to be of at least indirect policy concern to most governments. In the 1980s, with the boom in house prices, access and affordability came to be seen as key issues, as in Bramley (1989 and 1990). From this perspective house prices have effects which are also a concern of policy.

The immediate stimulus to this study was a concern about the impact of housing subsidies. Crudely, do particular subsidies (eg mortgage interest tax relief) cause more housing to be produced, or simply raise the price of housing? The equity, efficiency and effectiveness of subsidy policies depend on the answers to these questions. And the impact depends mainly on the elasticity of supply, for which there is a lack of British evidence (Bartlett, 1989). In addition, the Rowntree studies[3] were premised on the presumption that supply elasticities would vary a good deal between local market areas and possibly between different subsectors within these. The fiscal advantages of some, perhaps already the better off among owners, might be further reinforced by the greater capitalisation of the subsidy in the relevant submarkets. The differential accumulation and subsequent passing on of housing wealth has attracted increasing attention (Hamnett *et al*, 1991; Longley *et al*, 1991), with it being widely held that some classes of people and regions are benefiting disproportionately; if so, the supply side (including planning) might have something to do with this.

Another area of policy for which this study has relevance is macroeconomic policy. There has been increasing concern about the interaction between housing and the national economy in the late 1980s (Muellbauer, 1990). For example, it has been argued that the combination of tax subsidy, land supply constraint and financial deregulation caused both an excessive house price boom and large swings in the savings ratio (through equity withdrawal), causing consequential problems of inflation and balance of payments deficit. Closely related is the field of regional policy, since some of the macroeconomic arguments have a regional dimension associated with labour mobility and housing supply (Bover *et al*, 1989; Ermisch, 1990).

The model and its assumptions

This study adopts a distinct framework which is internally consistent and which distinguishes it from some other models of the housing market. The core assumptions are as follows.

i. The owner occupier housing market may be modelled as the flow of housing units bought and sold each year ('a house is a house is a house'); completions is the measure of new build output.

ii. The model is of medium term flow equilibrium with lags; the market can clear at the going price in one year, although new construction supply is likely to reflect prices and conditions one-two years earlier (Whitehead, 1974, Chapter 8; Mayes, 1979, pp 88-90; Lambert, 1990, pp 3-4 and 20; Monk, 1991).

iii. Output is influenced or constrained by the current and expected supply of land with planning permission for housing, as well as by prices and profitability.

iv. Local housing markets may be approximated by districts, and are sufficiently separate for differential local demand and supply conditions to affect prices and output, but also sufficiently open for national and structural factors to have a strong influence on prices.

v. Local markets are relatively integrated internally, so that second-hand and new housing are close substitutes with closely related prices.

vi. Planning policies are in part autonomous, but planning decisions are also in part responsive to market demand.

vii. The land market is endogenous, with land prices being determined by the current and expected profitability of housebuilding, that is the residual difference between house prices and construction costs.

These assumptions are quite restrictive, but may be seen as a consistent, interconnected set which renders the analysis tractable and fits in with the types of data available. Thus, at the local level at which land supply operates, we only have consistent data on flows of units and only for a small number of years at district level. However, it is also argued that these assumptions are reasonable on the basis of existing knowledge about the operation of the planning system, the private housebuilding industry and the land market (as reviewed in Bramley, 1989; Lambert, 1990; Monk et al, 1991; and Monk, 1991). The role of planning and market factors in affecting the supply of 'housing services' from given land, particularly density variations, is being explored in another part of this study.

On the basis of the work done so far on this project and a general appreciation of the nature of the industry, the model that seems to provide the best framework for the analysis is what may be termed the 'lagged response' model. This model is illustrated graphically in Figures 1-2. Output is determined by price, land supply and other supply factors in a preceding period (a one-two year lag); price is determined by current period demand conditions in conjunction with actual current output. Formally, this model comprises four equations.

Demand

The first is a demand equation with price (standardised) as the dependent variable:

$$P_j = P(Q_j, D_s(Y_j, G_j, Z_j), D_L(H_j, E_j, Q_{aj}, T_L)) \tag{1}$$

where j subscripts denote local market areas

Q = output (private completions per year);
D_s = 'structural' demand function;
D_L = 'locally variable' demand function;
H = vector or index of demographic variables;
E = vector of employment variables;
Y = average household income index;
Q_a = measure(s) of alternative social rented housing supply;
G = vector of geographical/locational attributes;
Z = vector of social characteristics;
T_L = local tax bills or fiscal measures.

Land use planning, tax subsidies and housing in Britain   293

Figure 1:   Lagged response supply model

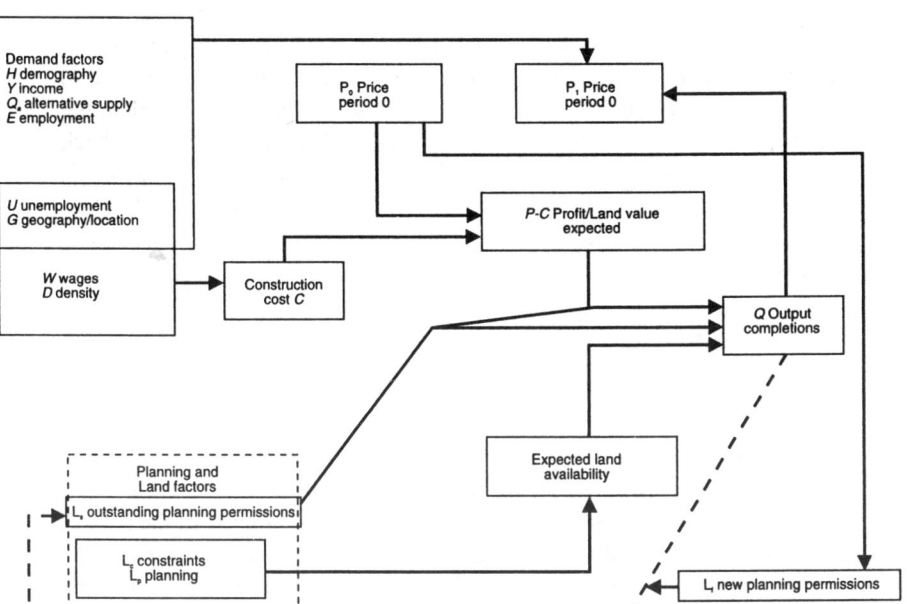

Figure 2:   Lagged response to demand shift

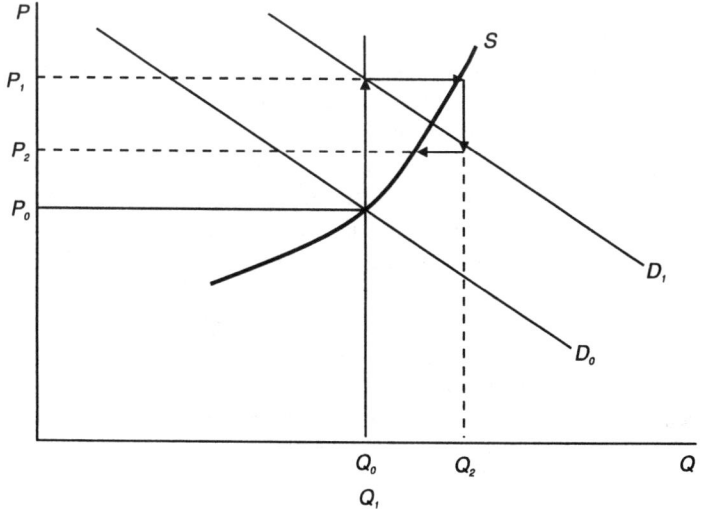

The exogenous demand side variables are grouped into two categories: 'structural' (D_S) are those that reflect relatively permanent features (eg location) determining an area's position in the national price structure; 'locally variable' (D_L) are those which can vary significantly both from one (adjacent) district to another over time. The effect of Q_j on P_j is related to the local price elasticity of demand. But it should be noted that the openness of local markets means that much of this output-price feedback may leak out into a wider market, shown by a small coefficient on Q_j (equivalent to high local elasticity). The overall system-wide effect of output on price is captured by an aggregate mechanism which in its simplest form is as follows:

$$\frac{\Delta P_N}{P} = \frac{\Sigma \Delta Q}{\varepsilon \Sigma (Q_N + Q_S)} - \frac{\Delta P_L}{P} \qquad (2)$$

This is simply a rearrangement of the identity defining the price elasticity of demand, splitting the price change into two components, a local component ΔP_L (from (1) above) and a national component ΔP_N. Supply in the market includes both new build (Q_N) and second-hand (Q_S), the latter being assumed to be invariant with price. The overall price elasticity of demand ε is not estimated but imposed on the basis of a range of other studies, which suggest a central estimate of -0.7. In simulations this national price adjustment mechanism is assumed for convenience to operate with a one-year lag.

Supply

The preferred supply function expresses output as a lagged function of profitability (price minus construction cost), land with planning permission for housing, and expected future land supply based on policies and constraints. Comparing with other supply models (Whitehead, 1974; Mayes, 1979; Tsoukis and Westaway, 1991), the use of price and cost or profit is a common feature; financial variables are not relevant in a cross-sectional model, while the inclusion of land and planning variables is the main innovation, based on ideas originally sketched out in Bramley (1989).

$$Q_j = S_{-1}((P_j - C(W_j, U_j, E_{cj}, N_j/A_j)), L_{sj}, L_{cj}, L_{Pj}) \qquad (3)$$

where S_{-1} refers to a function of suitably (one-two year) lagged values of the relevant data and C is a function for construction cost per unit, and
W = wage rates relevant to construction;
U = unemployment rate;
E_c = construction employment;

N/A = density of population;
L_s = stock of land with outstanding planning permission for housing;
L_c = constraints on future land supply;
L_P = planning policy for land release for private housing.

Output and (where appropriate) other variables (eg land available) are expressed in housing units per 1,000 owner occupier households, to standardise for the scale of the local market. Construction cost is based on published indices (RICS, 1991) available down to county level, with statistical estimation used to interpolate values for districts using four indicators (wages, unemployment, density and distance from London). A possible shortcoming of this version of the model is that these are treated as exogenous. 'Profit' ($P-C$) is also effectively equivalent to residual land value per unit. Price or profit is expected to interact with the amount of land available (L_s), because you cannot build without land with planning permission. This in turn is the principal mechanism causing the responsiveness of output to price to vary between localities.

On the basis of qualitative evidence (Lambert, 1990) and econometric tests it is believed that housebuilders have expectations about future land supply which can be represented by variables relating to potential land constraints (L_c) and planning policy (L_P) and which influence output positively. Planning may operate successfully in an indicative mode as well as through the direct use of development control. If this view is correct, these variables may be expected to enter the supply equation directly, as in equation (3). The hypothesis is as follows: if a housebuilder with a limited supply of existing land with permission expects little further land to be released, s/he will reduce output to maintain an even workload into the coming years, and exploit the probable rise in price/profit that would result from land shortage. If the land supply is expected to increase, the reverse may be expected to happen.

Planning

It seems natural to treat planning as an autonomous policy variable (assumption (vi) above). Yet it is possible that the supply of planning permissions is in part endogenous, influenced by market conditions (which are determined within the model) as well as by exogenous policy and constraint factors. This perspective is captured in equation (4), where the planning permissions flow L_f (and hence indirectly the stock L_s) is modelled as a function of: the amount of potentially available unconstrained land; local planning policy stance and targets; and the demand in the local market. Lags apply broadly as in the supply model. Demand may be expressed directly, or may operate through or be proxied by lagged price or price change.

$$L_{fj} = L_{f-1}(L_{cj}, L_{pj}, L_{sj}, P_{j-1}, \Delta P_{j-1}) \qquad (4)$$

The stocks and flows of planning permissions are linked by the identity:

$$L_{sj} = L_{sj-1} + L_{fj-1} - Q_{j-1} \qquad (5)$$

Area sample and data sources

A sample of districts

The choice of districts as the basic spatial unit, an approximation to a local housing market area, was mentioned earlier. The feasibility of collecting the wide variety of data required for this study was a major factor in this choice. While some of the data could relatively easily be obtained, from a variety of official and other sources, for all districts in England, certain crucial data on planning and land required a special enquiry through the local (county) authorities and other data would have been costly to obtain for all districts.

It was therefore decided to collect data for a large sample of 90 districts, about a quarter of the total in England The sampling strategy was not random; all districts were chosen from 13 counties, the counties themselves representing a solid wedge of territory running north and west from the boundary of London.[4] The primary reason for choosing a sample in this way was to exploit at least cost the opportunities for using the County Planning Departments as a vehicle for data collection, supplemented in some cases by regional contacts.

The area sample resulting has some disadvantages but some advantages too. It does not represent areas at two extremes of the housing market very well: London and declining/depressed/northern urban areas. One substantive advantage of sampling a solid wedge is that underlying spatial trends in the data may be identified and taken account of. The sample also represents a particular time period, also dictated in part by data availability. Most data refer to the period 1986-88. This time period represents one of the relative boom conditions in the housing market in these regions. On the whole this is useful because it enables us to identify the responsiveness of the supply side when it is under most pressure. However, our results may not be quite such a good guide to the impact of recession and low demand on the system, such as are being experienced at the time of writing.

Data

Appendix 1 provides a list of the variables used and referred to in this paper, together with summary statisitics. These data fall into a number of broad categories as follows:

i. demographic data (usually prefixed N or H) which measure the overall scale of the market, potential demand flows, and alternative supply flows (especially household dissolutions), derived from official annual estimates, the 1981 Census, and some district level household projections;

ii. economic data comprising employment (E) indicators, unemployment (U), earnings (W), indirect proxy-based indicators of household income (Y) from Bramley (1991), and some socio-economic indicators like class (Z); these economic variables play an important role in the demand equation (1) but also feature in the construction costs submodel;

iii. geographical variables (G) include attractiveness factors like distances from London, regional capitals, and north-south, and tourism measures, and measures of the land potentially available for housing or constrained (L_C), including built-up areas, green belts and areas of outstanding natural beauty; the latter variables were the most difficult to measure due to the poorly developed state of land use data in Britain;

iv. planning policies (L_P) and land supply (L_S) were obtained mainly from county planning departments but cross-checked against official returns and corrected for consistency (a labour-intensive task); some subjective dummy variables for policy stance were assigned on the basis of planning documents;

v. housing supply (Q) data were obtained mainly from official returns, with cross-checking against another source (NHBC data) for one year (1988); apart from new private completions other indicators of alternative tenures supply, vacancies, and poor quality dwellings were tested, some of uncertain accuracy or rather dated (1981);

vi. house prices were based on two separate sources: a major lender (Nationwide) covering mainly second-hand sales and the registration agency NHBC covering new sales, with approximate standardisation for age, type and size in both cases; assumption (vii) relieves us of the need for direct data on land values, which are unavailable or unreliable at local level.

For all its shortcomings this data set is unique in a British context and offers a range of possibilities for analysis of housing supply and the housing market.

Modelling private housebuilding

Demand and prices

The preferred 'lagged response' model sketched out earlier is one where current demand factors along with current output determine price (equation (1)), while output is determined by lagged values of price, land availability, construction costs and so on (equation (3)). The assumption of lags on the supply side is both plausible and convenient, since it avoids recourse to the special econometric procedures associated with simultaneous equation systems (eg instrumental variables). The simultaneous equation approach has also been explored, but demand side models for quantity work much less well than demand side models for price.

Exploratory work shows that care is needed to ensure an adequate specification of the demand model, including appropriate geographical variables, because of the strong spatial trends in the data.

Table 1 shows demand models for both second-hand and new house prices using a broad range of variables, selecting those from the various categories that seem to have a significant effect in one or other case. These models conform with the lagged response framework by containing current completions (QDN8) as an explanatory variable, for which the hypothesized effect is of course negative and related to the local price elasticity of demand.

In general, the results confirm that prices are determined by a number of locational, economic, demographic, supply and other variables in ways that are consistent with an *a priori* conception of demand within the flow of units framework. The geographical location factors, particularly distance from London and how far north, are still powerful influences even after allowing for other variables. Three employment variables have significant effects in the direction expected, as does unemployment, in the case of second-hand prices; with new prices these effects are weaker. Of the two demographic variables included, an estimate of household dissolutions (H4) has the predicted negative effect, while gross household formation has the 'wrong' effect but is not statistically significant at the 90% level. Vacancies have also been tested as an additional indicator of alternative supply from the existing stock, but with inconclusive results.

Table 1: Regression demand models for second-hand and new house prices in lagged response framework

Explanatory variables	PS8 Second-hand house prices (NABS)	PN8 New house prices (NHBC)
Constant	192.3 (8.33)	230.1 (3.75)
Supply		
QDN8 Private completions	-0.0583 (-0.94)	-0.524 (-3.1)
Geographical		
H7LN ln(distance London)	-17.6 (-7.1)	-24.1 (-3.7)
G8LN ln(dist Bristol/B'ham)	-2.20 (-2.9)	-0.43 (-0.2)
G9 distance north	-0.0648 (-8.2)	-0.107 (-5.0)
DW ward density	-0.019 (-0.3)	0.286 (1.5)
Economic		
E1 jobs/workers	11.74 (2.23)	13.2 (0.94)
E3 job growth 1984-7 %	0.509 (2.88)	0.549 (1.15)
E10 manufacturing jobs	-0.166 (-3.0)	-0.204 (-1.38)
U8 unemployment rate %	-0.729 (-2.05)	-0.68 (-0.7)
Y1 household income (£pw)	0.036 (1.12)	-0.0905 (-1.0)
z3 high social class	0.166 (1.69)	0.825 (3.1)
Demographic		
H3A gross household form'n	-0.24 (-1.36)	-0.59 (-1.24)
H4 household dissolutions	-2.74 (-1.77)	-12.23 (-2.97)
Alternative supply/quality		
QA1 social lettings	-0.0502 (-0.53)	0.259 (1.0)
N7 Private renting	0.079 (0.58)	0.726 (1.98)
LSBATH lack/share bath	-0.63 (-1.22)	-0.219 (-0.16)
Fiscal		
DOMRB7 domestic rate bill	-0.255 (-2.41)	0.0099 (0.35)
adjusted r-squared	0.908	0.763
F-ratio	50.5	17.2
no of cases	85.0	85.0

Note: Dependent variables PS8 and PN8 are second-hand and new house prices 1988 in £'000, standardised for type and age. The table shows regression coefficients with t-statistics in brackets

The impact of social rented lettings seems to be inconsistent in direction and not statistically significant, while private renting tends to have a positive effect. The quality of the older stock is reflected in the variable LSBATH which has the expected negative effect on second-hand prices although again this is barely significant. Finally, the fiscal variable DOMRB7 has the expected negative effect on second-hand (but not new) prices.

An overall impression from comparing the new and second-hand models is that there may be significant and systematic differences in the determination of prices in the two subsectors. As a generalisation, demand factors seem to have less effect on new than on second-hand prices, whereas the supply factor is more important in the case of new house prices.

The results are particularly interesting in relation to the output (completions) variable, QDN8. Higher output has only a very small effect on second-hand prices and this is not statistically very significant (the chances of the coefficient differing from zero are only 65%). By contrast, the coefficient on new prices is much larger and clearly statistically significant; this result holds across a number of variant model specifications. A slightly stronger coefficient on second-hand prices emerges when we use a more restricted approach to the specification of the rest of the model, based on prior knowledge/judgement.

There is a case for grouping demand side variables together into composite measures. Firstly, this can clarify the overall shape of the model in terms of the basic structure proposed in equation (1). Secondly, with considerable multicollinearity coefficients on individual variables may display some instability which can distract from the overall picture. Demand variables are divided into two classes: those that reflect relatively permanent features (eg location) determining an area's position in the national price structure (D_S); and those like employment that represent influences that can vary significantly from district to district and over time (D_L). Appendix 1 shows how the variables are grouped; the versions reported here (DEMANDS1 AND DEMANDL1) use equal weightings on each variable in standardised form. The demand model conforming with equation (1) can now be estimated using three explanatory variables, as follows (t statistics in brackets):

$$PS8 = 54.77 + 17.55.D_S + 8.91.D_L - 0.121.Q + u$$
$$(14.1) \quad (5.2) \quad (1.8)$$
$$\text{adj } r^2 = 0.844$$

and for new house prices:

$$PN8 = 88.45 + 29.22.D_S + 13.73.D_L - 0.81.Q + u$$
$$(9.41) \quad (3.2) \quad (-4.83)$$
$$\text{adj } r^2 = 0.657$$

These models have somewhat lower r-squared but have the advantage of parsimony and a very clear theoretical framework, with less dubious or spurious relationships included. The coefficients on the two composite demand indicators may be compared because they are in standardised units. This, together with the t-statistics, shows that the effect of the structural demand factors is about double the effect of the local factors, but both clearly operate in a significant way. Alternative formulations of the composite indicators, separating out stock supply (including vacancies) suggest that local demand factors may be weaker.

The negative coefficient on output in the second-hand price model is now significant at the 93% level, while that in the new price equation is again much larger and highly significant. But the basic conclusion remains: the local impact of supply on second-hand prices is small. This is consistent with the view that local markets are very open, which in turn is consistent with the evidence that the spatial factors are very powerful (ie prices are mainly determined by position in a national system). By contrast, the local negative impact of output levels on the prices of those new houses seems to be quite substantial. This result may be partially spurious, if there are systematic quality biases in the new price data which we are unable to standardise for. Insofar as this result is genuine, it suggests that the assumption (v) of integrated local markets with closely related new and second-hand prices may not be fully justified.

An attempt was made to incorporate measures of the 'openness' of local markets interacting with D_L and Q in these models, but so far unsuccessfully in terms of improving the specification. Further exploration of possible subregional feedback effects has also so far failed to indicate clearer supply-price feedback at either county or travel-to-work area levels.

The estimated coefficient for second-hand prices using composite demand indices shown above (-0.121) implies that ten extra completions per 1,000 existing owner occupiers (ie 1% on the stock) reduces prices by £1,210, which is about 2.3%. This very low local price response to output corresponds to a very high local price elasticity of demand of -24. This is a very high figure compared with most general estimates of this parameter, which tend to lie in the range -0.5 to -0.9. But a low response/high elasticity is expected, because we are measuring here the local effect and all local markets are open, as emphasised by the importance of our structural demand variable (D_S). Much of the price feedback effect is diffused into a wider regional and national market, and is captured in this model through equation (2).

The effect on new prices is a good deal stronger at the local level, assuming the NHBC price data are not biased. The elasticity is -5.3 (-8.3 from Table 1), which is a lot lower than the second-hand price elasticity, but still relatively high (housebuilders are still mainly price-takers). One standard deviation in output would alter new prices by £18,400 or about 25%, and the difference between maximum and minimum output levels is equivalent to £30,700 or 41%.

The evidence from these models of a rather different pattern of price determination for new houses, including a stronger supply-price feedback, suggests that more attention needs to be given to the possible segmentation of new and second-hand markets and the mechanisms of adjustment within and between them at the local level. A partial test of the hypothesis that second-hand prices adapt to output over a longer period (three years) was not supported by the data. Regressing new prices on lagged or predicted second-hand prices plus the other demand variables does not support the segmentation hypothesis, since new prices seem to be mainly determined by second-hand prices.

Supply models

The RICS (1990) Building Cost Information Service publish an annual guide to house rebuilding costs, which provides the basis for a construction cost submodel. A set of rebuilding cost figures per unit of floor area for different house types can be used to estimate baseline cost for standard house types. A regional cost index available down to county level is used as the dependent variable in a regression equation including a number of relevant indicators of location (distance from London), difficulty (simple and ward density), and labour supply and cost (unemployment and manual earnings). The regression based formula is intended to interpolate values for districts and is:

$$\text{DCOSTIND} = 1.234 + 0.00161.(N/A) \\ - 0.000043.D_w \\ - 0.0718.\text{G7LN} + 0.000747.\text{W1} \\ - 0.00923.\text{U8}$$

The adjusted r-squared was 0.76 and all variables were significant at the 90% level except D_w. This index is then multiplied by the rebuilding cost for each standard house type. Subtracting construction cost from price gives a figure for gross profit or residual land bid value per unit (PCN8 for new, PCS8 for second-hand).

Construction costs do not vary dramatically, the range being from 0.874 to 1.13 at district level. Thus the main influence on differences in profitability or land value between districts is prices. (It could be argued that construction cost should be treated as endogenous, but tests indicate that this makes little difference to the results.) The land share or gross profit percentages for 1988 (the peak of the market) varies from 12% to

73% of the price of new houses at district level, while the residual price per hectare of land ranges from £76,000 to £3,669,450.

Within the basic lagged response framework a number of variant supply models (equation (3)) were tested, involving the use of individual variables or composites and the use of interaction terms. Table 2 shows a basic linear model with nine individual variables giving a reasonable fit (adjusted r-squared of 57%) and most individual variables significant with the expected sign.[5]

The model shows clearly that land supply and planning variables make an important contribution to explaining local levels of output, as expected. The land with planning permissions variable (LSF7) is in fact the sum of outstanding permissions and new permissions in the year, since in earlier tests the separate variables had similar coefficients. The significant role of a number of variables reflecting land constraints and planning policies seems to support the view that expectations of future land supply influence current output.

Developers decisions are not solely influenced by the current stock of permissions. The only variable whose sign is not as expected is unconstrained land (LTRLN), and the negative coefficient here is not statistically significant at the 75% level.

For further work on the supply model it is convenient to adopt the same expedient as was used in the demand model, and group some of these variables together into composite factors, for the same sorts of reasons (clarity, parsimony, avoidance of spurious relationships, use of interactions). Two composites are constructed. The first (CONST1) represents the general constraints on development in an area, and comprises the sum of the three variables under the constraints heading in Table 2 (DW, G18 and LTR2LN), standardised and with equal weight (but negative, so that the index should be positively associated with output). Green belt is put in this category, rather than policy, because experience suggests that green belts are rather permanent features (Elson, 1986). The second composite (PPS1) represents planning policy stance, and comprises the equally weighted sum of the standardised values of the four variables under the policy heading in Table 2 (PPD1, PPD2, LP, PPRAT), the first two having negative weights so that the index is again positively associated with expected land supply and output.

The effect of applying the restriction on the model that these groups of variables should have equal (standardised) coefficients, which results from substituting the composites in the regression, is no loss of explanatory power; indeed, the resulting equation shows a slight improvement in the adjusted r-squared and F ratios.

Table 2: Regression models for output of completions in 1988: lagged response models (dependent variables: QDN8 completions per 1,000 owners, 1988; average of DOE and NHBC data)

Explanatory variables	(1)	(2)	(3)
Constant	12.00	12.89	12.27
Price/profit			
PCS6 second-hand price-cost 1986	0.433 (4.0)	0.381 (4.0)	
Land			
LSF7 land with planning permission for housing 1987	0.0412 (2.94)	0.0358 (3.0)	0.0414 (3.9)
PCS6*LSF7 price-land interaction			0.00571 (4.2)
Constraints			
DW ward density	−0.267 (−3.2)		
G18 Green Belt	−0.054 (−1.83)		
LTRLN Log unconstrained land	−0.393 (−0.8)		
CONST1 Composite (lack of constraints)		5.34 (4.9)	4.48 (4.4)
Planning policy			
PPD1 Very restrictive dummy	−7.38 (−3.1)		
PPD2 Restrictive dummy	−3.93 (−2.5)		
LP Structure plan provision	0.122 (1.12)		
PPRAT Permissions % of applications	0.134 (1.58)		
PPS1 Composite policy		6.36 (3.6)	5.12 (3.4)
Adjusted r-squared	0.572	0.579	0.658
F	12.5	27.5	30.6
N	77.0	77.0	77.0

Note: The following variables are expressed per 1,000 owner occupier households: LSF7, LTR(LN), LP; G18 and PPRAT are percentages. CONST1 and PPS1 are standardised sums of the relevant variables, with positive values indicating less constraints or restrictions.

One of the key underlying objectives of this research is to measure the local supply response (elasticity), which brings a presumption that the elasticity of supply varies between one locality, or type of locality, and another. Models like those in columns (1) and (2) of Table 2 assume a constant effect of price on output. It is necessary to adopt a more complex functional form to allow for varying local response, and so interactions between some or all of the explanatory variables are tested. Since developers cannot build any houses if they have no land with planning permission on which to build, we would in particular expect the market demand forces, expressed mainly through the price or profit variable (PCS6), to interact with the land supply variable (LSF7). The model in column (3) of Table 2 includes such an interaction term and is a significant improvement on the simple linear models. Thus the hypothesis of locally variable supply response seems to be supported. Price may also interact with planning and constraint variables, or have non-linear effects, although tests suggested these were not very significant. Overall, we can explain two-thirds of the variance in the rate of new build supply (per thousand stock).

Once the price-land interaction is included, the price variable on its own ceases to operate in the same way. The sign becomes negative and the statistical significance is marginal (barely significant at the 75% level). It is difficult to know how to interpret this, although one possibility might be a tendency to speculative witholding of land from development in high price areas. Because of uncertainty in the interpretation of this coefficient and its low level of statistical significance it seems preferable to exclude this in the final preferred model (column (3) of Table 2).

One of the debates in modelling the housing market is over whether the demand factors which affect output decisions are adequately captured by price (or profit in our formulation), or whether other direct quantities on the demand side directly influence output decisions as well (Tsoukis and Westaway, 1991). Without going into details, our results suggest that price adequately captures demand.

Planning permissions model

The theoretical model includes an endogenous supply of planning permissions (L_f) seen as a function of policy, constraints, and market conditions (Bramley, 1989). The general justification for this is that the determinants of L_f may be relatively systematic, and we wish to forecast output, which we now know to depend heavily on land supply with planning permission Secondly, planning is responsive; planning permissions are only granted where developers make planning applications, and we would expect developers to follow economic influences quite strongly. Thirdly, the planners may themselves be subject to market pressures, because of concern about rising prices and affordability, the labour market, or government pressure and guidance on land availability.

A simple single equation model for planning permissions flow is shown in Table 3. The choice of explanatory variables is based on equation (4) and similar to that in the supply model. Lagged stock of permissions (LS6) is included to reflect a stock adjustment perspective, and lagged output (QD6) to reflect a possible 'momentum of development' effect. The first of these does not work in the expected negative way. Demand is reflected primarily by price/profit (PCS6) and price change (PAV26), although direct demand indicators were tested.

Table 3: Regression model for the annual flow of new planning permissions (LF67, housing units per 1000 owner occupiers, 1986-7)

Explanatory variables	
Constant	-6.95 (0.97)
Demand	
PCS6 price/profit '86	0.0496 (0.19)
PAV26 price change 82-6	0.222 (1.72)
Constraints	
CONST1 composite	7.64 (2.90)
Planning policy	
PPS1 composite	3.85 (0.87)
Stock adjustment/momentum	
LS6 land with outstanding planning permission	-0.0064 (-0.17)
QD6 output	0.142 (0.68)
Interactions	
PCS6*PPS1	0.117 (0.33)
Adjusted r-squared	0.181
F	3.4
N	77.0

Note: LF67 is indirectly calculated from outstanding permissions and completions, for 1986-87

On the whole these models do suggest that market prices affect the flow of planning permissions. Direct demand indicators (DEMANDL1) do not add to the model using prices. The effect of price/profit itself is weak and inconsistent, but the lagged rate of price change (PAV26) seems to be more effective than price *per se*. Interactions of price and policy only improve the model slightly. There is no particular support for the notion of landowners withholding land when prices accelerate.

The 'constraints' on land supply seem to be important in determining planning permissions, unsurprisingly. The composite variable CONST1 has a consistent and significant impact in the expected direction. What is really surprising in these results is the weak effect of planning policy variables. When the composite PPS1 is used this has the wrong sign in some equations and tends not to be statistically significant when it is included. While the planning policy indicators available are admittedly poor in some cases, what ought to be the most important measure, structure plan provision (LP), is pretty reliable, and this does not work well on its own. Before rushing to the judgement that planning policy is ineffective in its implementation, tempting though this may be, we should bear in mind that, as shown in an earlier section, planning policy had a clear positive effect on output, presumably because of expectations effects. This relationship also shows up in reduced form equations. Thus the policy is implemented to some extent by developers in spite, as it were, of development control.

It is only fair to say that the results are not very consistent across different models or versions of the dependent variable, nor with some of our prior hypotheses, although both the poor fit and some multicollinearity contribute to this. The model shown was chosen for use in the simulations because the more important signs were in the expected direction, not because its overall fit was good.

Overall, the results of this part of the research so far are not discouraging, and do provide some interesting and suggestive material for discussion, as well as a forecasting equation for simulation work.

Simulations of policy impact

Local supply elasticities

A basic objective of this research is to estimate the magnitude and variation in local supply elasticities for private sector house building. In this section the results of the supply modelling work are put together with two other elements to give an overall assessment of supply elasticities. The two other elements are the second order 'induced supply' response via the planning system (if any) and the place of new build in the overall supply of units for sale in the market. The modelling of planning permissions (Table 3) provides a basis for the induced supply estimates, while the overall supply issue requires a discussion of demographics and turnover, which we take first.

Within the flow-of-units framework (assumption i), total housing supply on the market in a period (one year) comprises the sum of new building, conversions, transfers from other tenures or vacancies, and sales of properties released by death and household dissolution, by moves out of owner occupation, and by moves within owner occupation. However, since in this framework 'a house is a house is a house', moves within the tenure and within the market area have an equal impact on the supply and demand side, and can be netted out. This means that at local level we can subtract (ignore) all intra-local owner occupier moves; only out-migration adds to the net local supply. 'Trading up' is discounted by the assumption of homogeneity of stock in this model.

To calculate the effective elasticities in the market, that is those which will determine the interaction of supply and demand, we need to allow for these other sources of supply apart from new build, particularly those (like dissolutions) which do contribute to net supply. There is very little relevant evidence on the responsiveness of these components to market conditions, but it is clear that the fundamental causes of most of the other net supply components are essentially demographic rather than economic (death; frailty associated with ageing; divorce and relationship breakdown). Therefore, it seems justifiable as a first approximation to assume that these components are not responsive to price. The effect of this assumption is that the supply elasticity is reduced in the same proportion that new build represents in total net supply.

We can put some flesh on this outline by attempting to estimate the average magnitude of the various sources of supply of housing units for sale at the national level. Table 4 provides some estimates for 1987. These have been built up by the author from a variety of sources, influenced by two previous attempts to make such estimates at local/regional level (Merrett, 1989; Bramley *et al* 1990).

The detailed sources and assumptions used in deriving these figures are not discussed here to save space. The main conclusions are as follows. New build represents less than one-quarter of net flow supply (22.5% in a good year like 1987).

It could be argued that certain other elements of supply, particularly conversions and former private rented units, might move in step with new build in response to price changes, raising the the responsive supply to 26-30%. This means that estimates of supply elasticity from new build models should be divided by a factor of between 3 and 4 to obtain the effective elasticity of supply in the market.

These are national averages. At local level, the various components of net flow supply will in fact represent very different shares. It is possible to make an attempt to estimate values for local supply components, using relevant demographic, tenure and other variables and controlling the totals to be consistent with Table 4. As a proportion of estimated net flow supply, new build ranges from 3.9% (Oxford) to 34.9% (Basingstoke). This range helps to explain the rather extreme elasticity figures reported below. These variations indicate that the 'market' supply elasticity will not be a simple mapping of the new build elasticity.

Given a choice of output model the computation of supply elasticity is a mechanical operation. The preferred output equation is that in column (3) of Table 2. This gives a basic elasticity of new build with respect to price which varies locally according to the availability of land with planning permission and actual price and output levels. The average value is 0.99 and the range of variation is from 0.29 (Birmingham) to 2.11 (Worcester). The low values are unsurprising, but some of the high ones are affected by extreme values, for example a low existing level of completions. This model embodies a two-year lag.

Table 4: Estimates of gross and net flow of units supply of housing for owner occupation in Great Britain in 1987

	Number in thousands	Percent net supply
New build	180	23
Conversions	28	4
Void ex private rented	47	6
Dissolutions		
- death and related	180	23
- divorce	40	5
- marriage	30	4
- other	30	4
- subtotal	(280)	35
Moves into renting	65	8
Moving owners		
- inter-local migrants	200	25
- local movers	800	
- subtotal	(1000)	
Total gross supply	1600	
Total net supply	800	100

The average new build elasticity is very similar to that obtained from time series analysis for the Bristol subregion in Bramley *et al* (1990, pp 65-67). It may also be compared with results from other time series studies of 0.75-

1.62 (Whitehead, 1974) and 0.27-0.55 on profitability (Mayes, 1979, p 93). Ermisch (1984, p 56) suggests from a review of other literature a figure of 0.6 for Britain, but Bartlett's (1989) review suggests an overall long run figure of over 5.

The allowance for a secondary induced supply effect adds some complication to the computation but it remains essentially mechanical. The preferred equation for planning permissions flow is that shown in Table 3. This equation has the virtue of having plausible or 'correct' signs on the relevant variables (ie positive on PCS6, PAV26 and PCS6*PPS1) although the fit is poor and the statistical significance of the coefficients is low. It serves to illustrate the kind of order of magnitude of a possible induced supply effect, within the same two-year period, rather than an accurate final estimate.

The average supply elasticity rises from 0.99 to 1.15 after allowing for the induced land supply effect. This is not a very large increase, because the relevant coefficients in the planning permissions equation are, as we have seen, small in magnitude. The range of variation is now wider, from 0.26 (Birmingham again) to 3.94 (Oxford). The very high values look to be rather freakish, as they are areas with very tight constraints (very low existing output is the explanation in the case of Oxford).

The final stage in the calculation is to re-estimate the elasticity in terms of proportional change in net supply, using the information on the other components of net supply developed earlier in this section. The result is to divide the elasticity of supply by rather more than three, to give an average figure of 0.31. This may be closer to the correct figure to compare with estimates like Ermisch's (1984) referred to above, where the concern is with subsidy impact in the short to medium term. The range of variation now is from 0.04 (Birmingham) to 0.86 (The Wrekin, which includes Telford new town); other high values include Northavon (0.80) Worcester (0.71) and Bracknell (0.61), the common factor being high existing stocks of land with planning permission.

The finding that elasticities are low in the most urbanised areas in the sample (eg West Midlands metropolitan area) is precisely in line with our *a priori* and theoretical expectations. The identity of some of the districts with high elasticities is surprising, but may be affected by the output or net flow elements of the denominator. Overall, as Table 5 shows, elasticities are higher in the south east. This result may still be affected by the arbitrary restrictions of the functional form used.

The estimates of supply elasticity just presented provide a useful shorthand indication of the responsiveness (or lack thereof) characteristic of the private housebuilding industry operating in the British land use planning context. However, to gain a fuller picture of the impact of particular types of change, it is preferable to see how the whole system might change over several years, allowing for various feedback effects. This is the role of simulations, which use the estimated forecasting equations for prices, output and planning permissions, together with certain definitional identities and assumptions, to construct alternative scenarios for the development of the housing market in our quasi-national system of 90 districts over a number of years.

Table 5: Price elasticities of supply by county

County	ELAS11 New-build direct	ELAST11 with induced land	MELAST11 Market net flow supply
Berkshire	1.23	1.73	0.36
Hampshire	0.91	1.12	0.28
Oxfordshire	1.31	1.82	0.36
Avon	0.98	1.15	0.31
Dorset	1.19	1.41	0.35
Gloucestershire	1.08	1.19	0.35
Somerset	0.80	0.88	0.30
Wiltshire	0.98	1.12	0.36
Hereford and Worcester	1.11	1.14	0.38
Shropshire	0.89	0.86	0.31
Staffordshire	0.73	0.69	0.21
Warwickshire	0.82	0.84	0.22
West Midlands Metropolitan Area	0.77	0.72	0.15
Whole sample	0.99	1.15	0.30

How a typical set of simulations operates for one annual cycle, and how the results in that year form the inputs into the next annual cycle, may be judged from Figure 1. The sequence is roughly to forecast first the flow of new planning permissions, then update the stock of permissions, then forecast output, then estimate prices. Price levels and changes and other variables, including output, then feed into the projections for the following year. At this point the national output-price feedback mechanism (equation (2)) applies. First a baseline projection is made, and this is checked to ensure that its results look reasonable. The work done so far is for a six-year period from 1987 to 1993. The baseline assumes stable national conditions from 1988 onwards, in respect of key variables like interest rates; it also assumes zero inflation for convenience. Thus it is nothing like a forecast of the emerging reality, because it does not build in the dramatic downturn in 1989 and 1990 that was caused by the record level of interest rates, nor the subsequent general recession.

Broadly speaking we are interested in two types of simulation, one dealing with changes on the demand side and the other dealing with changes on the supply side associated with planning policy. Each of these is illustrated in turn.

Effect of mortgage tax subsidy change

The starting point for this research was a concern with how housing finance and subsidy impacts on the housing market, and in particular with the extent to which tax subsidies to owner occupiers result in higher house prices rather than a greater supply of housing. The most obvious tax subsidy to owner occupation is mortgage interest tax relief (MITR, often referred to as MIRAS). In the light of recent policy debates (Hills, 1991; Joseph Rowntree Foundation, 1991; MacLennan et al, 1991; Pearce and Wilcox, 1991) it would seem that the likely direction of subsidy change is reduction or phasing out. What would be the effect of this on the housing market? We are now in a position to use the simulation technique on our database to test out this question.

A rather crude attempt is made to model the abolition of MITR. The assumed route to abolition is a phased reduction in the maximum eligible loan, which at the time of writing stood at £30,000. This is phased out in three equal annual steps, between 1988 and 1990. This rather short sharp phasing is convenient for our computations rather than a judgement about a realistic choice of reform phasing. (It can be argued that the announcement of phasing out of MITR would be very quickly capitalised, in which case the price and other effects would happen more quickly.) The model deals in averages; we assume that, because 'a house is a house', everyone buys at the average standardised second-hand price with a 66% mortgage (this is the national average for mortgaged purchases, the vast majority). The immediate effect of the withdrawal of relief is modelled by assuming that the 'post tax relief' price paid by consumers remains the same after the change. To achieve this, the actual market price must fall by an appropriate amount; how much depends on where the operative upper MIRAS limits bite in the local housing market.

If P_1 is the market price before the change, and P_2 after, M_1^* and M_2^* are the respective MIRAS limits, then:

$$0.66(1-0.25)P_1 = 0.66(1-0.25)P_2 \quad \text{where } 0.66P_1 < M_1^* \quad (6a)$$
$$P_2 = P_1$$
$$P_2 = P_1 + 0.25(M_2^* - 0.66P_1) \quad \text{where } 0.66P_1 < M_1^* \quad (6b)$$
$$\text{and } 0.66P_1 > M_2^*$$
$$P_2 = P_1 + 0.25(M_2^* - M_1^*) \quad \text{where } 0.66P_1 >= M_1^* \quad (6c)$$
$$\text{and } 0.66P_1 >= M_2^*$$

The initial effect of the MITR withdrawal on prices is quite direct in our model, with the effect of each phase of withdrawal being as given by the above expression. In districts where the average price is above £45,000, so bringing the upper MIRAS limit into play, the reduction over the three years will be 25% of £30,000, or £7,500. In districts below this level the reduction will be 25% of 66%, ie 16.5%, of the price. The sample average value of the loss of subsidy is £6,400, or about 11.8% of baseline 1988 prices. The interesting issue is what then happens to supply, and what this means for prices in the longer term.

A fall in price causes, after a lag, a fall in new build output, for any given land supply, through the output equation. It also leads to some reduction in the flow of new planning applications, which themselves will affect output. As output falls, the national price feedback mechanism comes into play, putting some upward pressure on prices. This begins to moderate the process; the price reductions initially recorded begin to fade as supply falls off progressively.

Table 6 summarises the results of this crude simulation. Sure enough, the price of housing falls sharply and progressively as the abolition of MITR is implemented up to 1990. But it should be noted that at no stage does the price fall reach the level of 16.5% that might theoretically have happened if all mortgages attracted relief. The maximum attained is 12.5%, which is what would be expected given that in 1988 the average mortgage would have been above the limit. What is most interesting is the fact that this price fall is not sustained, but erodes quite significantly. In three more years it is down to 6.9%. The extent of this effect does depend in part on the externally imported value of the national elasticity of demand, so some sensitivity tests on this parameter would also be useful.

The effect on output builds up more gradually, but towards the end of the period it has reached significant proportions. Completions are 15% below the baseline level in year 5, but then the gap seems to narrow again. This seems, superficially at least, quite a large output effect, but it is rather what our elasticity estimates (including induced land supply) would lead us to expect. It should be remembered that the change in net flow supply resulting would be about a quarter to one third of this. In the longer term, with the price fall moderating the output gap should also gradually close. But a significant cumulative amount of investment in the stock would not have happened.

Table 6: Simulation of mortgage interest tax relief abolition phased over three years (1988-90)

'National'	1988	1989	1990	1991	1992	1993
Price (second-hand £)						
baseline	54,100	53,800	51,100	48,400	49,200	51,900
MITR abol	51,800	49,100	44,600	43,000	45,200	48,300
% difference	-3.5	-8.7	-12.5	-11.2	-8.1	-6.9
Output (comps/1,000 owners)						
baseline	17.6	19.7	22.0	21.5	19.4	17.4
MITR abol	17.6	19.1	20.7	19.0	16.5	15.2
% difference	0.0	-3.1	-5.7	-11.3	-15.2	-12.4

The results of Pearce and Wilcox (1991) may be directly compared. They use a version of the Treasury model of the British economy to simulate various MITR abolition scenarios, emphasising that the results depend crucially upon the way the authorities do or do not compensate in fiscal or monetary policy (our model implicitly assumes some form of compensation). They find that, with the most favourable option of constant money supply/lower interest rates, immediate abolition would lower prices by up to 10% in years 1-2, falling to 7% in years 3-4. For a phased withdrawal the figures are 4% and 6%. With the least favourable option of non-compensation prices would fall by 17% in years 1-2 and 26% by years 3-4. As we would expect, our results are closer to the former scenario, and indeed very similar in magnitude.

The model enables differential local and regional effects to be studied. On the basis of this first simulation, at the end of the period analysed (year 6) output would have fallen by 15-16% relative to baseline in some West Midland counties, but only by 7.5% in high demand Berkshire (see Table 7).

Table 7: Impact of mortgage interest tax relief abolition on prices and output by county (after five years)

County	Price (percentage diference)	Output (percentage difference)
Berkshire	-4.4	-7.5
Hampshire	-5.3	-10.0
Oxfordshire	-4.8	-10.0
Avon	-6.7	-13.8
Dorset	-6.8	-12.3
Gloucestershire	-6.8	-14.0
Somerset	-8.0	-12.4
Wiltshire	-6.1	-12.6
Hereford and Worcester	-8.5	-15.1
Shropshire	-9.7	-15.7
Staffordshire	-9.4	-13.0
Warwickshire	-8.5	-15.0
West Midlands Metropolitan Area	-10.7	-10.2
Whole sample	-6.9	-12.4

The price falls associated with this are similar in absolute terms (£3-4000), but much lower in percentage terms in high-priced Berkshire (-4.4%) than in the West Midlands conurbation (-10.7%). The main reason for uniform price effects is that local markets are very open with high local price elasticities of demand.[6] In percentage terms price changes range from minus 4% (Windsor, Wokingham) to -11% (Birmingham). These figures may be interpreted as the capitalised value of MITR. They show that the capitalisation of this subsidy is if anything more pronounced, in relative terms at least, in lower priced areas. But the £30,000 limit on MITR plays a major role in bringing this result about.

The effect of raising the MITR limit to £60,000 was also tested. Under the simplified assumptions of this model the effect is confined to higher priced areas, while prices fall slightly in lower priced areas due to the national supply-price feedback. Price changes range from +8% in Berkshire to -2% in much of the West Midlands. Thus, the overall impact of MITR with a higher limit would be greater in high demand/high price areas.

Further work on this aspect of the model could include simulating over a longer period, using models based on new house prices, testing different demand elasticities, testing alternative forms of change in tax subsidy, and examining the impact of changes in local taxation.

Planning policy and releasing more land

The availability of land for private housebuilding and its possible role in restricting supply and pushing up house prices have been the focus of policy debate since the early 1970s. Yet there remains no consensus either among academics or among practitioners about the true effects of planning on the housing market (Monk *et al*, 1991).

The models developed in this research are quite well adapted to the examination of this issue. A simulation of the impact of a large-scale increase in the planned release of land can be briefly described.

The primary vehicle for expressing planning policy for housing is the structure plan 'provision' level or target, which constitutes the variable L_P in this model. As an illustrative scenario we consider the implications of doubling structure plan targets, where feasible, and making consequential adjustments in other policy variables (PPD2, PPRAT, and PPS1). 'Where feasible' means where there is enough unconstrained land to last for over 100 years at the new rate of release. The result of constraints is that more than half (49) of our 90 districts have unchanged levels of provision, while a further 9 are constrained at a level below double present provision. Despite this the total level of planned provision jumps by 75%. Certain districts provide a disproportionate share of the extra potential land. Table 8 shows the results of this simulation at the 'national' level, which are in some respects remarkable.

Table 8: Simulation of major increase in land release through planning system

'National'	1987	1988	1989	1990	1991	1992
Price (second-hand £)						
baseline	47,500	54,100	53,600	50,900	48,300	49,200
extra land	47,500	53,600	48,100	45,100	42,800	46,800
% difference		-1.0	-10.3	-11.4	-11.4	-4.9
Output (comps/1000 owners)						
baseline		17.6	19.6	22.0	21.5	19.5
extra land		21.7	24.0	26.3	23.2	21.1
% difference		+23.0	+22.0	+19.5	+7.9	+8.2
Planning permissions flow						
baseline	18.4	19.8	20.5	17.5	14.1	
extra land	21.5	23.0	24.0	18.7	15.2	
% difference	+16.8	+16.2	+17.0	+6.9	+7.8	

A 75% increase in the planning policy targets for housing results in a measly 16% or so increase in the flow of planning permissions, which cannot be sustained and which falls to 7-8% after three years. There is a maximum 23% increase in output, but this too falls to about 8% at the end of the period. The consequential fall in house prices builds up to a plateau of 11-12% in years 3-4 and then falls off to only 5% at the end of the period.

These results bring home dramatically the problems that the present British land use planning system has in implementing its policies. It is one thing to change structure plan provision, but quite another to see those changes take place. This result echoes the experiences of many planning practitioners over recent years (but see also Healey et al, 1985).

From a housing policy point of view, the results suggest that general exhortations or requirements to release more land through the statutory planning system do not provide a very fruitful route to the desirable goal of widening accessibility to owner occupation. A fairly draconian increase in targets results in a price fall of 10-12%, subsequently falling off to about 5%. According to a model of affordability developed by this author in a different study (Bramley, 1991), price reductions of this order would increase the proportion of new households able to afford to buy by about 3-6 percentage points. This would be a useful achievement but would not solve housing problems in the high demand regions, where half or more of new households cannot afford to buy.

This result suggests that it would be more fruitful to re-examine more direct methods of getting land into the system of housing production and also more direct ways of making some of that housing 'affordable' to households on lower and moderate incomes.

Conclusions and implications

This paper has demonstrated the feasibility and usefulness of an approach to the analysis of housing markets based on the cross-sectional models at the interurban level. By incorporating explicit local data on land use planning policies and outcomes, the importance of this particular British form of intervention for housing market response is confirmed.

The study has shown that the elasticity of supply of new private housing in Britain is quite low, although far from negligible. The elasticity of new build with respect to price change is on average around unity after two years, or 1.15 including induced land supply. Assuming other components of stock supply are essentially demographic and unresponsive to price, the net flow supply of housing units for sale in the market has a price elasticity averaging 0.3, with local values ranging from 0.04 to 0.86. The long run elasticity of density with respect to price seems to be very low in Britain compared with comparable American evidence.[7]

Low supply elasticity has a number of policy implications. Firstly, demand subsidies such as mortgage tax relief (MITR) are partially capitalised in higher prices. Simulations suggest the present MITR system adds £3-4,000 (7% on average) to house prices in the medium term. To this extent it is failing to achieve some housing policy objectives in relation to access and, in part, output. Although there is a regressive or 'pro-rich' redistribution as a result of MITR (Hills, 1991; MacLennan *et al*, 1991) these effects, and their partial capitalisation in higher house prices in richer areas, would be worse were the £30,000 MITR limit not biting quite sharply.

The implication of this general finding is that subsidies or other policy measures to promote access to and a supply of housing for lower income groups should both be more discriminating than MITR and probably also have a supply side element.

Another major implication of low short run supply elasticity is that macroeconomic fluctuations in demand are likely to impact sharply on prices and risk destabilising the economy. Although the supply elasticity is low, it is not zero and it builds up over time. This means that large demand-induced price fluctuations are not just a monetary and price phenomenon; they have large real effects in the output and employment in the construction and allied industries. The debilitating effects of chronic instability in this industry are arguably a serious policy issue in their own right.

Variations in supply response do contribute to some variations between localities in the capitalisation of subsidies into prices, although the openness of local housing markets makes such differences less than expected. The present MITR with its £30,000 limit causes a relatively flat pattern of absolute price increases, which are proportionally more significant in the lower priced (and less wealthy) areas of the Midlands (and north).

General planning policies for land release (especially Structure Plans) have quite a substantial effect on housebuilding output, although this is far from being a one-for-one relationship. However, the effect of local land release targets and policies on local house prices in general is very weak indeed, again because of the openness of local markets in Britain.

At national and regional level one might expect that a concerted land release policy would have a greater impact. Such a policy seems likely to be difficult to bring about, politically and administratively. There is also clearly a major 'implementation gap' in planning, when even a dramatic concerted 75% increase in structure plan targets would achieve a relatively feeble 5-12% price reduction which would widen access by only 3-6% of new households.

One of the hypotheses at the outset of this research was that planning might turn out to be more responsive to market forces than it is usually portrayed. The evidence in fact gives only partial support to this proposition. Higher prices and price rises do give rise to slightly more land release, but mainly because developers apply for more permissions.

More work is to be carried out using the model to simulate the response of the housing sector to a variety of other influences including regional employment shifts, macro demand fluctuations, and local taxation changes.

Notes

1. The research on which this paper is based was funded by the Joseph Rowntree Foundation, whose support is gratefully acknowledged. A number of organisations contributed to the assembly of data required for the study, including 13 County Planning Departments, the Department of the Environment, National House Building Council, South East Regional Research Laboratory, and Nationwide Anglia Building Society, and their assistance is also acknowledged. Particular thanks are due to Gill Court who undertook the bulk of the painstaking task of assembling the dataset, to Will Bartlett and Chris Lambert for valuable ideas and input at various stages, and to Edwin Deutsch and other participants at the Vienna Housing Finance Systems workshop (Jan. 1992) for insightful comments. The author takes responsibility for any opinions or policy recommendations expressed, as well as for any errors and omissions in the analysis.

2. The Housing Finance Research Programme supported by the Joseph Rowntree Foundation over the period 1987-91 under the direction of Professor Duncan MacLennan of Glasgow University has been the largest recent programme of research on housing finance in Britain. The programme included six local case studies including one of Bristol led by the author and reported in Bramley *et al* (1990).

3. See Note 2.

4. The counties from which the districts in the sample were chosen were Avon, Berkshire, Dorset, Gloucestershire, Hampshire, Hereford and Worcester, Oxford, Shropshire, Stafford, Somerset, Warwick, West Midlands and Wiltshire.

5. The output models do not suffer from the spatial autocorrelation tendency exhibited by the price models. However, there are some signs of heteroscedasticity in the residuals. Particular versions of the model have been subject to various tests, which have given ambiguous results. It might be possible to improve the specification in some way to reduce this problem, but it does not seem to be overwhelming.

6. If we had used the new price model, more local variation in price effects would have shown up. New price data are only currently available in this dataset for 1988, so it is not possible to estimate a full lagged response set of equations using new prices.

7. The elasticity of density with respect to price is examined in another part of this research. Using data for the interurban sample the elasticity of

substitution between land and construction is very low compared with US studies.

References

Ball, M. (1983) *Housing policy and economic power: the political economy of owner occupation*, London: Methuen.

Bartlett, W. (1989) *The economics of housing supply*, York: Joseph Rowntree Memorial Trust Housing Finance Discussion Paper.

Bover, O., Muellbauer, J. and Murphy, A. (1989) 'Housing, wages and UK labour markets', in Wages and house prices symposium, *Oxford Bulletin of Economics and Statistics*, vol 51, pp 97-162.

Bramley, G. (1989) *Land supply, planning and private housebuilding*, Working Paper 81, Bristol: SAUS Publications, School for Advanced Urban Studies, University of Bristol.

Bramley, G. (1991) *Bridging the affordability gap in 1990: an update of research on housing access and affordability*, Birmingham: BEC Publications.

Bramley, G., Bartlett, W., Franklin, A. and Lambert C. (1990) *Housing finance and the housing market in Bristol*, York: Joseph Rowntree Foundation.

Cheshire, P. and Sheppard, S. (1989) 'British planning policy and access to housing: some empirical estimates', *Urban Studies*, vol 26, pp 469-85.

Coombes, M., and Raybould, S. (1991) 'Local trends in house price inflation', *Housing Research Findings*, no 30, York: Joseph Rowntree Foundation.

Elson, M. (1986) *Green belts: conflict mediation in the urban fringe*, London: Heinemann.

Ermisch, J. (1984) *Housing finance: who gains?*, London: Policy Studies Institute.

Ermisch, J. (ed) (1990) *Housing and the national economy*, Aldershot: Avebury.

Evans, A. W. (1983) 'The determination of the price of land', *Urban Studies*, vol 20, pp 119-29.

Evans, A. W. (1988a) 'South East England in the eighties: explanations for a house price explosion', in M. Breheny and P. Congdon (eds) *Growth and change in a core region: the case of South East England*, London: Pion.

Evans, A. W. (1988b) *No Room! No Room! The costs of the British town and country planning system*, IEA Occasional Paper 79, London: Institutue of Economic Affairs.

Grigson, W. S. (1986) *House prices in perspective: a review of South East evidence*, London: SERPLAN.

Giussani, B., and Hadjimatheou, G. (1990) *Econometric model of regional house prices in the UK*, The Apex Centre Economics Discussion Papers 90/2, Kingston, Surrey: Kingston Polytechnic.

Hamnett, C., Harmer, M., and Williams, P. (1991) *Safe as houses: housing inheritance in Britain*, London: Paul Chapman.

Healey, P., Doak, A., McNamara, P., and Elson, M. (1985) *The implementation of planning policies and the role of development plans*, vols I and II. Oxford: Oxford Polytechnic Dept of Town Planning.

Hills, J. (1991) *Unravelling housing finance: subsidies, benefits and taxation*, Oxford: Clarendon Press.

Joseph Rowntree Foundation (1991) *Inquiry into British housing*, Second report, June 1991, York: Joseph Rowntree Foundation.

Lambert, C. (1990) *New housebuilding and the development industry in the Bristol area*, Working Paper 86, Bristol: SAUS Publications, School for Advanced Urban Studies, University of Bristol.

Longley, P., Clarke, M., Williams, H. (1991) 'Housing careers, asset accumulation and subsidies to owner occupation - a microsimulation', *Housing Studies*, vol 8, no 1, pp 57-69.

MacLennan, D., Gibb, K., and More, A. (1991) *Fairer subsidies, faster growth*, York: Joseph Rowntree Foundation.

Mayes, D. (1979) *The property boom: the effects of Building Society behaviour on house prices*, Oxford: Martin Robertson.

Merrett, S. (1989) *The Denarius hypothesis: house price inflation in owner occupied London*, London: University College Housing Finance Project Discussion Paper.

Monk, S., Pearce, B., and Whitehead, C. (1991) *Planning, land supply and house prices: a literature review*, Department of Land Economy Monograph 21, Cambridge: Granta.

Monk, S. (1991) *The speculative housebuilder: a review of empirical research*, Department of Land Economy Discussion Paper 31, Cambridge: Granta

Muellbauer, J. (1990) 'The great British housing disaster', *Roof*, May/June.

Muth, R. (1969) *Cities and housing*, Chicago: University of Chicago Press.

Neutze, M. (1987) 'The supply of land for a particular use', *Urban Studies*, vol 24, pp 379-88.

O'Sullivan, A. (1983) 'Some misconceptions in the current housing subsidy debate', *Policy and Politics*, vol 12, no 2, pp 119-43.

Pearce, B. and Wilcox, S. (1991) *Home ownership, taxation and the economy*, York: Joseph Rowntree Foundation.

RICS (1991) *Guide to house rebuilding costs 1991*, Building Cost Information Service, London: Royal Institution of Chartered Surveyors.

Rydin, Y (1986) *Housing land policy*, Aldershot: Gower.

Tsoukis, C. and Westaway, P. (1991) *A forward-looking model of housing construction in the UK*, Paper presented at London Business School International Conference on the Economics of Housing Markets, September 1991, London: National Institute of Economic and Social Research.

Whitehead, C. (1974) *The UK housing market: an econometric model*, Farnborough, Hants: Saxon House.

Appendix: List of variables with summary statistics

Variable	Mean	Standard deviation	Minimum	Maximum	N	Label
NO1	30446.00	24985.00	7522.00	216362.00	90	NO.OWN OCC HHOLDS EST 1986
H3A	20.15	3.91	8.59	33.81	90	GROSS HHOLD FORMATION PA/1,000 HH
H4	0.95	0.30	0.00	1.67	90	HHOLD DISSOLUTIONS PA/100 HH
E1	0.36	0.10	0.19	0.73	90	TOTAL EMPLOYMENT/ POPULATION
E3	1.57	2.60	-3.10	12.87	90	CHANGE PA TOTAL EMPLOYMENT %
E10	26.80	9.70	9.95	52.95	90	MANUFACTURING EMPLOYMENT % OF TOTAL
U8	7.18	3.07	2.30	16.30	90	UNEMPLOYMENT 1987-8 % OF EA RESIDENTS
Y1	246.56	34.05	194.60	347.10	90	EST MEDIAN GROSS HH INCOME 1989 P.W.
Z3	33.35	7.80	15.10	54.80	90	HIGH SOCIAL CLASS 1981 % OF EA
G7LN	5.07	0.43	3.69	5.69	90	LOG DISTANCE FROM LONDON
G8LN	3.91	0.78	1.10	4.95	90	LOG DISTANCE BRISTOL OR BIRMINGHAM
G9	207.30	78.60	75.00	355.00	90	LATITUDE KM NORTH
DW	19.47	12.33	1.51	53.71	90	WEIGHTED WARD DENSITY PERSONS/HA
DS	10.87	12.74	0.34	46.58	90	SIMPLE DENSITY PERSONS/HA
QA1	12.31	7.39	3.06	50.90	90	TOTAL LETTINGS SOC.HO
N7	13.63	4.97	5.20	25.70	90	PRIVATE RENTING 1981 % OF HH
LSBATH	2.46	1.33	0.40	6.20	90	LACK OR SHARE BATH 1981 % OF HH
DOMRB7	409.00	62.20	278.00	545.00	90	AVE DOMESTIC RATE (TAX) BILL 1987 £
DEMANDS1	0.00	0.52	-1.28	1.14	90	STRUCTURAL DEMAND INDEX D_S
DEMANDL1	0.00	0.38	-1.44	0.88	90	LOCALLY VARIABLE DEMAND INDEX D_L
LS7	80.40	53.60	13.40	345.60	90	LAND O/S PLG PERM HSG 1987 UNITS/1,000 OWNERS
LS6	75.40	46.20	14.30	360.10	90	LAND O/S PLG PERM HSG 1986 UNITS/1,000 OWNERS
LF67	20.60	18.90	1.00	110.60	90	PLANNING PERMS FLOW PA 1986-87/1,000 OWNERS
LSF7	101.50	63.40	18.30	426.60	90	PLG PERMS STOCK + FLOW 1987/ 1,000 OWNERS
G18	28.70	34.80	0.00	100.00	90	AREA GREEN BELT % OF NON-URBAN AREA
LTR2LN	8.58	2.95	0.33	12.57	90	LOG OF UNCONSTRAINED LAND UNITS/1,000 OWNERS
CONST1	-0.06	0.63	-1.63	0.82	90	PHYSICAL NON-CONSTRAINTS INDEX
PPD1	0.14	0.35	0.00	1.00	90	V.RESTRICTIVE PLAN. POLICIES DUMMY

PPD2	0.34	0.48	0.00	1.00	90	MOD.RESTRICTIVE PLAN. POLICIES DUMMY
LP	20.60	8.86	7.45	51.10	90	STRUCTURE PLAN TARGET UNITS PA/1,000 OWNERS
PPRAT	69.20	10.14	43.82	89.50	90	AVE HOUSING PLAN.PERMS. SUCCESS RATE %
PPS1	0.00	0.52	-1.19	1.18	90	PLANNING POLICY STANCE INDEX
QD8	18.80	10.00	1.98	43.90	87	DOE 1988 COMPLETIONS /1,000 OWNERS
QN8	16.40	7.80	2.47	35.30	90	NHBC 1988 COMPLETIONS/1,000 OWNERS
QDN8	17.60	8.56	2.66	36.70	87	AVE DOE/NHBC COMPLETIONS/1,000 OWNERS
QD7	18.60	12.40	1.76	80.30	90	DOE 1988 COMPLETIONS/1,000 OWNERS
QD6	15.70	7.97	0.74	52.90	90	DOE 1987 COMPLETIONS/1,000 OWNERS
QD3YA	17.20	7.39	3.30	38.80	87	AVE 1986-8 COMPLETIONS/1,000 OWNERS
PS8	52.10	12.39	22.27	79.90	90	PRICE STANDARD MODERN HOUSE NABS 1988 £'000
PN8	74.60	21.49	41.25	151.40	90	PRICE STD NEW HOUSE NHBC 1988 £'000
PS6	41.00	9.96	26.25	63.50	80	PRICE STANDARD MODERN HOUSE NABS 1986 £'000
PCS6	5.21	8.39	-7.58	23.60	80	PRICE-COST STD MOD HOUSE 1988 £'000
PCN8	36.10	19.99	4.91	108.81	90	PRICE-COST STD NEW HOUSE 1988 £'000
PAV26	48.20	15.79	1.16	91.10	90	CHANGE AVG PRICE 1982-6 %
DCOSTIND	0.98	0.05	0.874	1.128	90	BCIS REBUILDING COST INDEX INTERPOLATED
CN8	38.40	2.12	34.33	44.32	90	BUILDING COST STD NEW HOUSE 1988 £'000
CS8	39.80	2.20	35.52	45.85	90	REBUILDING COST STD MOD HOUSE 1988 £'000
CS6	35.50	1.96	31.72	40.95	90	REBUILDING COST STD HOUSE 1986 £'000

Components of composite indicators

Four composite indicators are constructed as the unweighted standardised sum of their components, as follows:

DEMANDS1 - G7LN - G8LN - G9 + Y1 + Z3 + N7 - LSBATH
DEMANDL1 + E1 + E3 - E10 - U8 + H3A - H4 - QA1 - DOMRB7
CONST1 - DW - G18 - LTRLN
PPS1 - PPD1 - PPD2* + LP + PPRAT

CHAPTER 17

TOWARDS A SUSTAINABLE HOUSING RENEWAL POLICY

PHILIP LEATHER AND SHEILA MACKINTOSH

Introduction

Throughout the 1980s private sector housing renewal policies took a back seat to the major issues of the decade such as the privatisation of the public sector housing stock. In the renewal field, attention focused on the public sector through initiatives such as the Priority Estates Projects and Estates Action. Despite the completion of a review of renewal policy in 1985 (Cmnd 9513, 1985), it was not until 1989 that legislation to revise the improvement grant system went through Parliament. The new system involved radical changes to the previous approach, which had remained substantially unchanged since the early 1970s.

But expectations that housing renewal policy would settle into a smooth period of implementation proved wrong. After only a year of operation the legislation underwent its first official review which resulted in a number of minor changes. But a few months later, before the findings of the first review had been implemented, the government announced a second, more major review of grant policy. The new legislation had created a demand for grant aid which could not realistically be met within current and likely future public spending levels. A key aim of the review was to find ways of managing or eliminating this demand. In this chapter, we firstly examine the background to the crisis in renewal policy, the operation of the new grant system in the first three years, the nature of the problems which occurred, and the options which are available to government and to local authorities in the short and medium term to get renewal policy back on its feet again. But in our view there is a need for a more fundamental re-assessment of where renewal policy is going. The second part of the chapter will argue that what is needed are policies which recognise that Britain has an ageing housing stock and an ageing population. Effective renewal strategies for the 1990s and beyond will need to recognise that housing decay is not a short-term problem found only in the older housing

---

This paper also appears in P. Williams (ed) *Sustainable housing policies*, Housing Studies Association conference proceedings, Autumn 1993, published by the Centre for Housing Management and Development, University of Wales College of Cardiff.

stock but an ongoing process. With limitations on public spending only likely to increase, new ways need to be found to use the resources which are available more effectively while at the same time developing mechanisms to increase the level of private investment by home owners in the repair, improvement and ongoing maintenance of their housing.

The housing renewal crisis

Successive national house condition surveys have shown a continuing problem of poor physical housing conditions, although comparisons over time and between the components of the United Kingdom are difficult because of national differences and changes in definitions over time and variations in survey methodology. Table 1 shows the extent of unfitness, lacking amenities, and urgent disrepair revealed by various surveys covering the constituent parts of the UK. In total more than 1.7 million dwellings are unfit for human habitation or in Scotland below the tolerable standard. This figure would be higher if up-to-date information for Wales were available. As an alternative measure, more than 3.7 million dwellings are in a state of serious disrepair, with urgent repair costs in excess of £1000, although many of the unfit dwellings would also fall within this category. While there are problems in the local authority and housing association sectors, the majority of houses in poor condition are to be found in the owner-occupied and privately rented sectors. In 1991, some 81% of occupied dwellings in England, Scotland and Northern Ireland with urgent repair costs in excess of £1,000 were privately owned.

Housing renewal policies

We have described the historical development of housing renewal policies in more detail elsewhere (Leather and Mackintosh, 1992). After a period in the 1950s and 1960s when demolition and rebuilding were the preferred options, the emphasis of public policy in the 1970s and 1980s switched to the provision of grant aid to owner occupiers and private landlords. Enormous sums were invested by local authorities in the improvement of privately owned housing during this period. From April 1981 to March 1992 alone, some £8.3 billion was spent on grants in England (at 1990/91 prices), together with almost £1.0 billion in Wales, £1.6 billion in Scotland, and £0.8 billion in Northern Ireland (Mackintosh and Leather, 1993).

But such levels of expenditure are now a thing of the past. While the number of grants provided in England exceeded 200,000 per annum at its peak in 1982-84, the level of activity subsequently fell back to less than 100,000, and dropped even more dramatically after the introduction of the new grant system in 1990. Only 22,000 renovation grants were provided in

England and Wales in 1991, and 44,000 in 1992, compared with 114,000 improvement, intermediate or repair grants under the previous system in 1990. At this rate, it will take more than 30 years simply to deal with properties identified as unfit in 1991.

Table 1: Housing conditions in Britain 1991

	Unfit/ BTS*	Lacking amenities	Urgent repairs over £1,000	Average cost urgent repairs
Number of dwellings				
England	1,498,000	205,000	3,511,000	664
Wales (1986)	71,700	42,200	Not avail	Not avail
Northern Ireland	50,360	19,100	91,900	222
Scotland	95,000	13,000	109,500	899
Percentage of dwellings				
England	7.6	1.0	17.8	-
Wales (1986)	7.0	4.1	Not avail	-
Northern Ireland	8.8	3.3	15.9	-
Scotland	4.7	0.6	5.4	-

Sources: Department of the Environment (1993a); Welsh Office (1988); Northern Ireland Housing Executive (1993); Scottish Homes (1993); EHCS 1991 special tabulation; SHCS 1991 special tabulation

Note*: Figures for unfitness in Wales are not comparable because they relate to the pre-1989 standard. Figures for Scotland are for dwellings below the tolerable standard, which differs from the fitness standard in various ways, particularly by the exclusion of disrepair.

Despite its scale, the programme of capital grants to home owners has never been fully evaluated. The main emphasis has been on the effectiveness of area-based renewal through housing action areas (HAAs) or general improvement areas (GIAs) but these have only accounted for a small proportion of the programme. A recently completed study by the authors, funded by the Joseph Rowntree Foundation, examined the effectiveness of grant policy, and concluded that there were a number of criticisms which could be levelled.

The effectiveness of grants

Firstly, the durability of the work which was carried out with grant aid is open to question. It was intended that much of the work would last for 30 years but surveys carried out as part of our study showed that this was often not the case. One problem was the lack of supervision of the quality of work carried out. The local authorities which administered grant aid were given few powers to ensure that work was carried out properly by competent builders. In most cases, building work was only inspected on completion or when interim payments were required. Local authorities lacked powers to require work to be uncovered to check what had been done, and there is ample anecdotal evidence of poor workmanship and fraudulent practices.

Limitations on the type of work eligible for grant aid also prevented long-lasting solutions in some cases. The initial emphasis of grants was on the provision of amenities. Government awareness of the need to deal with disrepair problems did not emerge until the 1980s. Many properties which were provided with amenities during the 1970s remained in a state of considerable disrepair despite the provision of grant aid. On top of this, the limits on the costs of work eligible for grant were not regularly updated to keep pace with building costs so many authorities were forced to cut standards or to omit important items of work if jobs were to go ahead at all. There were not enough resources for the achievement of long-term solutions.

Few local authorities took any steps to encourage grant recipients to maintain their houses and there are no powers to compel owners to maintain their houses after they have had a grant. Benko (1991) has described experimental arrangements in the Netherlands to require grant recipients to enter into a maintenance agreement. With few exceptions, local authorities have taken no action at all in this area, as most regard subsequent maintenance as being the responsibility of the owner. In Birmingham, a network of area caretakers was set up and their duties included carrying out minor jobs in areas which had been subject to improvement activity. Rochdale, Leicester and a few other local authorities developed local maintenance initiatives, and other authorities prepared booklets for distribution to owners. But these activities were the exception.

Finally, it can be argued that grant policy over the 1969-90 period was in itself a deterrent to maintenance investment. The gradual increase in the scope of grant aided work from basic amenities to improvements, repairs and finally enveloping may have provided a message to owners to encourage them to neglect the condition of their properties, as in the long term grant aid from the state would probably be forthcoming. Our study showed that second or third grants had been provided for a substantial proportion of properties already improved with grant aid in the past.

The pattern of grant provision

There were also problems with the targeting of grants. From 1969 onwards, area improvement was a key component of policy, with the aim of stimulating or levering in private investment to build on that made available through grants. But more than 80% of grants went to properties located outside such areas. Only 17% of properties in the worst condition and 12% of properties in unsatisfactory condition in 1981 were included in area-based programmes between 1981 and 1986. Furthermore, the 1986 English house condition survey (Department of the Environment, 1988) showed some disappointing results relating to scattered grant investment over the 1981-86 period. Much grant aid had not been directed towards the worst properties. Some 30% of the grants provided had gone to dwellings which in 1981 were found to be in satisfactory condition. Only 14% of grants went to properties which were unfit and in serious disrepair.

It is also clear that improvement grant investment was only a minor element of total expenditure by households on repair and improvement activity, despite the scale of provision. The 1986 English house condition survey revealed that some £13.6 billion was spent by owner occupiers and private landlords on the repair and improvement of dwellings in 1986, of which only about £0.4 billion (3%) was accounted for by grants (Department of the Environment, 1988). Some 59% of this investment was on less essential work such as internal decorations, extensions, central heating, double glazing and porches. But even if this expenditure, much of which is carried out by more affluent owners who are already living in satisfactory conditions, is deducted, the proportion of investment accounted for by grant aid only increases to 7% of the remaining £5.8 billion. It is individual investment decisions made by private owners which determine the overwhelming majority of expenditure on the repair, improvement and maintenance of the older housing stock and hence its overall condition, rather than public investment policies. Changes in housing conditions result from increasing or decreasing investment levels relative to rates of decay and obsolescence. In periods of boom, such as the late 1980s, it is likely that the overall condition of the housing stock improved, as individuals borrowed more or invested their savings or income in building work, encouraged by rising incomes, low interest rates and rising house prices. During the current recession, it is more likely that the level of investment has declined, with the investment decisions of many home owners influenced by the problems some households have experienced with mortgage payments, and by the problem of negative equity under which falling house prices have led many recent purchasers to have a mortgage for more than their house is worth.

The uneven spatial pattern of improvement grant investment at local level means that there are some exceptions to this pattern. In a few cities such as Glasgow, Belfast, Birmingham, and Leicester, higher levels of public investment and successful area improvement programmes led the impact of grant activity to be much greater than in areas where investment was more scattered. But this impact was confined to a small number of cities and often to relatively small areas within those cities. The scope for intensive area renewal was also reduced because of the way in which grant resources were allocated - or rather not allocated - to individual local authorities. Although larger towns and cities have spent more on the provision of improvement than smaller districts, they have generally been unable to achieve as much in terms of relative indicators such as the provision of grants per 100 pre-1919 private sector dwellings. In part this arose as a result of policy decisions by many urban authorities to spend housing capital resources on other activities such as public sector renovation. But the main cause has been the government's capital expenditure allocation policy (including the arrangements for the use of capital receipts) which has rarely isolated an overall sum for investment in the private housing stock and allocated that sum directly to this programme on the basis of need. If this had been done, area improvement programmes in towns and cities might have been better funded and more effective.

In overall terms, it can be concluded that while a great deal of improvement has been achieved through the grant system, much effort has also been wasted through the absence of targeting on those most in need, the failure of government to concentrate resources in the worst areas, and a lack of powers for local authorities to ensure that the work funded by grants was properly carried out. Housing renewal policy in many areas of pre-1919 housing is now based on an entrenched expectation by owners and practitioners that grants will continue to be available. Yet there is little prospect that adequate levels of public resources will be forthcoming.

The new grant system

The main aim of the new grant system introduced in 1990 was to target grant expenditure more effectively on unfit properties and low income households. The mechanism for achieving this aim was a means test to determine eligibility for grant. At the same time, the government decided to make grant aid available as of right for any work required to make dwellings meet the revised standard of fitness, provided that the owner was eligible on income grounds. A fuller description can be found elsewhere (Mackintosh and Leather, 1992a). But this apparently open-ended commitment was modified by the retention of a strict system of overall control on local authority capital expenditure which by a combination of restrictions and penalties ensured that the overall level of grant activity was limited.

The crisis

As we have suggested, by mid 1993 the new system was already heading towards serious problems. There were concerns in many areas that the demand for mandatory grant aid would soon outstrip the available resources. This was officially recognised late in 1992, when the government announced the second review.

As we have indicated, the rate of progress with grant investment was far too slow to make any rapid impact on existing house condition problems, let alone those arising as a result of the ongoing deterioration of the housing stock. In addition the average amount of grant provided rose very sharply. In 1990, the average grant under the old system was approximately £3,500. By the second quarter of 1992, average mandatory renovation grants paid under the new grant system had reached £9,900 in England and £16,000 in Wales, representing increases of 283% and 478%. Although some of this increase is accounted for by the fact that 100% grants are now being paid, it is also likely that the amount of work being done per property has increased substantially and that more comprehensive solutions (renewing rather than repairing or patching) are being undertaken. It is most unlikely that this is what the government intended. What has emerged is a new system which provides a much higher level of support for greatly reduced number of households with no help at all in prospect for the remainder. Unless more resources are forthcoming, it seems unlikely that the present approach can be sustained.

The pressure on limited resources was compounded by the increasing demand for disabled facilities grants. In the second quarter of 1992 these made up 35% of the total number of grants given (excluding minor works grants) and 16% of total grant expenditure. These grants are an essential part of policies to encourage care in the community and demand is likely to gather momentum as rates of home ownership increase amongst older and disabled people and more of these groups remain living at home. The demand for mandatory grants also limited the extent to which discretionary grants such as minor works assistance could be provided. These grants allow older people on means-tested benefits to carry out small repairs and adaptations to improve the safety and comfort of their homes. Such grants are especially useful to enable someone to return home from hospital or to prevent a move into institutional care.

The options

But what are the options for the review? There is little room for manoeuvre. The first option is to provide more funding to enable local authorities to meet a higher proportion of the demand for grants. In 1991/92 local authorities in England spent only £335 million, compared with £840 million in 1985/86 (at 1991/92 prices) and £1.7 billion in 1983/84. A programme of 90,000 renovation grants a year (twice the current level but still representing only 7% of the 1.5 million unfit properties in England in 1991) at an average cost of £10,000 per grant would require public expenditure of well in excess £1 billion per annum, if other types of grant are also allowed for.

But public expenditure plans show a decrease in the government's contribution to the costs of private sector renovation rather than the threefold increase which this proposal would require, as Table 2 shows (Department of the Environment, 1993b). For 1993/94, there was a reduction in the amount of specified capital grant (SCG) available although this was portrayed as an increase in resources. This feat was achieved by lowering the rate of SCG provided by the government from 75% to 60% of local authority expenditure. To enable them to find the extra resources, local authorities were given permission to reinvest a higher proportion of capital receipts for a limited period. The table also makes it clear that further cuts in the rate at which SCG is paid will be necessary in 1994/95 simply to keep expenditure at its planned 1992/93 level.

Table 2: Public expenditure on renovation grants (£ million)

	91/92 outturn	92/93 est	93/94 plans	94/95 plans
Specified capital grant for renovation of private housing	251.7	329.6	302.7	228.4
Amount available for grants assuming subsidy rate of:				
75%	335.6	439.5	403.6	304.5
60%	NA	NA	504.5	380.6
50%	NA	NA	NA	456.8
33%	NA	NA	NA	692.1

Source: Department of the Environment, 1993b

Most authorities are already under severe pressure on both the capital and revenue sides and a major boost to grant expenditure borne to such an extent from their own resources is unlikely to materialise. At the end of the 1980s the government was providing subsidy at an effective rate of about 95% on grant spending. Nor do broader prospects look very promising. With the continuing likelihood of a large public sector borrowing requirement, demographic and economic pressures pushing up spending on social security, pensions and health provision, and no signs of a government-led investment boom to revive the economy, it would be very optimistic indeed to expect much priority to be given to the renovation grant programme despite the extent of need revealed by the national house condition surveys.

A second option is to modify or abolish the right to a grant when a property is found to be unfit. It might also be necessary to remove the parallel right to a disabled facilities grant. This would not only require new legislation but would also represent a very obvious abandonment of the government's commitment to dealing with poor housing conditions. Some practitioners have, controversially, suggested a partial relaxation of the right to a grant in areas where local authorities can demonstrate that they have a coherent strategy for dealing with older housing. But this would be very difficult to define and could provide the government with an easy way of shifting the blame for the loss of entitlement to a renovation grant on to those local authorities which declared that they had a renewal strategy. The removal of the mandatory right to a disabled facilities grant would also be in conflict with the expressed aim of increasing care in the community.

The third option is for the government to require local authorities to take a narrower view of the fitness standard. This would enable the cost of making a dwelling fit to be substantially reduced, and spread resources more thinly across a far greater number of properties. There is a limit to how far this could be taken, and it is certainly a measure which would meet with almost unanimous opposition from those involved in the provision of grants. But a reduction of average grants to 1990 levels would enable the number of grants to be trebled and thus make it unnecessary to take the politically embarrassing step of abolishing existing rights to grant aid. The disadvantage would be that the long-term impact of grant investment on the housing stock would greatly reduced. But in all probability the government no longer sees itself as being in the business of long-term investment in private housing anyway.

The next step

These debates will be resolved in the coming months and their outcomes will determine the shape of renewal policy in the mid 1990s and beyond. For many people on low incomes living in poor condition properties grant aid is realistically the only way they have of undertaking necessary repairs so a system of grant aid will continue to be required. But the review also provides an opportunity to re-examine the broader question of what housing renewal policies are trying to achieve. To do this, we need to understand how radically housing circumstances have changed since rehabilitation policies began in earnest in the late 1960s. The key factor is that the ownership and ultimate responsibility for the repair, improvement and maintenance of almost three-quarters of the housing stock now lies with individuals. This implies that there should be two elements to public policy in relation to privately owned housing in poor condition.

The first would be to ensure that the public sector resources which are available are spent in the best way, the way which draws in most private finance, and the way which achieves the greatest impact on the poorest housing conditions. This may mean challenging the view that capital grants, and the present system in particular, are a cost-effective way of using the available resources.

The second element of a new renewal policy would be to persuade private owners to invest more of their own resources in repair, improvement and maintenance, and to ensure that the money they spend is used in ways which have the maximum long-term impact on poor housing conditions. With limited public resources available, it is essential that policies to attract private investment should be more effective than the present, largely token, efforts. This may involve far more intervention than under the present system.

Stimulating private investment

There are a variety of ways in which home owners could be persuaded to increase the amount which they invest in the repair of their houses to maximise the long-term impact of this investment on poor housing conditions. In the past housing renewal policy has attempted to focus on older housing in the poorest condition, but a key objective of policy in future should be to adopt a more preventative approach by developing measures which also focus on properties in better condition. There are various measures to stimulate private investment and these are discussed further below.

Borrowing

Private owners fund the bulk of investment in repair, improvement and maintenance from their own resources. Income and savings are the main sources of funding for this work. But if owners are to be persuaded to undertake more substantial amounts of investment, or if those on low incomes, who do not have any savings, are to undertake work, it is essential to develop mechanisms which enable owners to afford to borrow, using the equity tied up in their houses as security. These could include the following.

i. The reintroduction of mortgage interest tax relief (MITR) on loans for certain types of repair, improvement and maintenance. To avoid abuse, lenders could be required to inspect completed work.

ii. The extension of proposals for a system of mortgage benefit payments to low income households to cover loans for repair, improvement and maintenance.

iii. Households could be allowed to set expenditure on repair, improvement and maintenance against tax liabilities, including inheritance tax.

But many households do not borrow to carry out repairs because they cannot afford to do so. New mechanisms are therefore needed to reduce or defer the repayment cost of loans.

i. Equity-sharing loans like those proposed by the government in its 1985 Green Paper on housing renewal policy but subsequently dropped, have great potential (Cmnd 9513, 1985). In lieu of repayments, households would assign a share of the value of their house to a lender, probably a local authority. Providing support for a scheme of this kind (and meeting the inevitable losses) could be an alternative use for some of the public sector resources currently used for grants.

ii. Rolled up interest loans, on which repayments of both capital and interest are deferred, may have some potential in paying for smaller jobs. This is mainly an option for older people as the size of the overall debt can increase rapidly after a few years.

iii. Department of Social Security help with interest payments on maturity loans for building work for older people on income support could potentially be used more extensively, provided that the practical difficulties in obtaining it, and the general reluctance of older people to borrow, could be overcome. Unfortunately the Department of Social Security has recently proposed the removal of entitlement to help with interest payments on further loans, such as those for building work, for those on income support, so this option seems unlikely to find favour.

iv. Fixed rate or subsidised interest rate loans supported either by public subsidies or from 'ethical' lending sources (where capital is provided by charities or individuals which are willing to accept a lower than market rate of return) have been used successfully in the USA (Leather and Mackintosh, 1993).

The problems associated with persuading individuals on low incomes to borrow should not be underestimated. Those houses in the poorest condition are generally those where there is the least borrowing potential. Likewise, older people, who often have the most potential to borrow because they have paid off their mortgages, may be the most resistant to doing so. Younger people, who might be willing to take on loans, may be too heavily indebted as a result of house purchase costs. In the longer term, however, it is inevitable that more people will be forced to turn to borrowing to meet the costs of building work. So long as they can afford to do so, it is better that they should use their accumulated housing wealth in this way rather than saving it to pass on to their heirs.

Insurance or savings schemes

A number of commercial mechanisms have recently been introduced to enable people to insure themselves against the need for future repair and maintenance work, or to save in order to cover these costs. This might be an alternative to borrowing. Such schemes fall into three main categories.

i. Comprehensive insurance schemes provide a package of services including an annual survey, internal and external maintenance cover, an emergency repairs service, defects insurance, and security measures for which participants pay an annual fee. Take up of such schemes so far is extremely limited. The initial costs of bringing properties into a good state of repair and the high premiums are a major disincentive.

ii. Emergency repair services provide cover for a limited range of repairs to items such as central heating, plumbing, drains, roof, locks, windows, and gas or electricity supply on an annual or monthly subscription basis. The costs are much less than those of more comprehensive schemes and take up is greater. Several schemes are operated on a national basis by companies mainly providing car breakdown services. The technology associated with such services and the experience in providing and managing a large network of garages can readily be applied to the operation of an emergency house repair service using a network of vetted builders.

iii. Mechanisms for saving to meet repair costs could also be established. In the mid 1980s a national building society examined the feasibility of an unsecured budget-type savings account (with the facility to overdraw) specifically to cover the costs of building work. Savers were also entitled to free technical advice, an emergency service, and access to a list of recommended builders. On the basis of market research the scheme was not launched, but there is potential for the introduction of such savings accounts particularly if government contributions were available as an inducement.

The take up of emergency repair services has demonstrated that there is a demand for such schemes, but there is little evidence of widespread public interest in more comprehensive maintenance schemes at the present time. In the long term, insurance-based schemes are more likely to appeal to more affluent households than to those on low incomes who could not afford to save or to pay premiums, unless help were available from the Department of Social Security. As assistance with rent through housing benefit includes provision for repair and maintenance costs, it could be argued that low income home owners should also be provided with help in meeting these costs.

Maintenance funds

A more radical approach would be the establishment of compulsory sinking funds for all privately owned houses to ensure that resources would be available for all necessary building work. A fund, managed by building societies, surveying practices, or local authorities, could be established for each privately owned property when it was next sold. The size of the fund would be set at a level necessary to cover the estimated cost of all work needed over a specified period falling into certain pre-defined categories. These would include essential repairs to ensure that the building was wind and weather-proof and structurally stable; work required to meet the fitness standard; and work needed to bring the property up to a specified energy rating. The fund could also be used for work to ensure that older and disabled people are able to remain living independently in comfort and safety in their own homes. We have proposed such a standard of fitness for community care elsewhere (Mackintosh and Leather, 1992b).

The money to establish the fund could come from the seller in the form of a deduction from the proceeds received on the sale of the house. This would act as an incentive to owners to keep their properties in good repair. At the point of each subsequent sale a new estimate would be made of the amount of resources needed to replenish the fund.

A great deal more work is required to develop an option of this kind. This approach is far more interventionist than any existing controls over the rights and duties of private owners, but in the long run it may the only way to ensure that the right type of work is carried out and that the resources are available to meet the costs. Effectively this solution would prevent equity leakage and ensure that money from the sale of properties was reinvested in the repair, improvement and maintenance of the housing stock.

Changes to the housing market, the building regulations, and lending requirements

There are also more long-term changes to the operation of the housing market, the building and planning regulations and the requirements imposed by mortgage lenders which could encourage or require owners to pay more attention to the condition of their houses:

i. making vendors responsible for latent property defects for a period of time after the sale of the dwelling;

ii. extending the coverage of the building regulations to deal with more repair work, and enforcing the regulations more strictly, for example by requiring vendors to produce certificates of compliance at the point of sale;

iii. requiring all work of specified kinds such as electrical work or gas installation to be carried out by qualified contractors; again this would need to be enforced through the production of certificates at the point of sale;

iv. persuading building societies to be more demanding about house conditions when they agree to lend;

v. encouraging the establishment and use of warranties or guarantees covering a much wider range of building work, to ensure that home owners are able to get redress for poor workmanship.

Education, information, advice, and practical help to owners

Surveys have shown that there is a substantial lack of awareness of the need for repair, improvement and maintenance investment (see for example Department of the Environment, 1988). There has been a good deal of progress in recent years in overcoming these problems. Some local authorities have distributed information booklets. In Leicester, the city council has gone further and appointed urban management officers and home maintenance advisers to carry out surveys and provide technical advice, financial advice and access to a list of competent builders. The United Kingdom also has a well-established network of home improvement agencies which provide help with the diagnosis of house condition problems, finding reliable builders, organising the finance to pay for work, and supervising the work on site.

But to raise awareness of house condition problems and to encourage more effective repair, improvement and maintenance behaviour a number of other measures are also desirable:

i. regular campaigns to educate home owners on both house condition problems and solutions;

ii. support from government and the private sector for adult education courses on repair and maintenance strategies and techniques;

iii. free or low priced surveys to advise home owners on what work is required over a specified period;

iv. extension of the existing home improvement agency network to give comprehensive national coverage.

Past experience suggests that the private sector will not contribute substantial sums to the provision of such services and it is likely that the main burden of funding will fall on central and local government.

Reform of the building industry

The sector of the building industry which deals with small scale repair and maintenance work also poses many problems for those seeking to carry out repairs or improvements. This sector generally has a poor reputation and the fear of experiencing problems can deter home owners from carrying out work. Older people are especially vulnerable to exploitation. If people are to be encouraged to undertake more work to their homes the following reforms are necessary.

i. People need to be able to find reliable builders and tradespeople and to have guarantees that the work carried out will be of a reasonable standard. This requires government involvement in the promotion and backing of guarantee schemes and proper vetting of builders who offer them.

ii. 'Cowboy' builders should not be able to undercut reputable builders in price terms. Stricter enforcement of health and safety standards and the requirement that only qualified contractors can carry out certain types of work would help to prevent this.

iii. The government should provide practical support for builders in setting up and running businesses, together with encouragement and financial support for building industry training schemes.

Strategies for public sector investment

The policies described above would aim to increase the amount of private investment in repair, improvement and maintenance. If this occurred, the role of public investment could change significantly in the future. Public expenditure could aim to lever in private investment wherever possible. Grant aid, or other new forms of direct public support, could then be targeted on those cases where there was no real potential for private investment. To take account of local variations, housing authorities could be given powers to provide assistance to home owners with repair, improvement and maintenance in the form which most suited their local needs. Government preferences and priorities could be expressed through decisions on the level of financial resources to be provided to support local initiatives.

We have already discussed several of the most promising options for making more effective use of limited public sector resources. Instead of providing capital grants for renovation, local authorities could provide grant aid towards interest payments in cases where loans had been taken out to cover work required to bring houses up to a minimum standard. The amount of assistance could be linked to an applicant's resources in a similar way to the present grant system. The disadvantage of this approach is that the owner would need to submit to a periodic test of resources. But this could also be seen as an advantage as the amount of help provided could be tailored to reflect changes in the owner's circumstances. The chief advantage, however, is that the amount of work which could be funded from public resources would be much higher than under the present system of capital grants. The precise amount would be dependent on interest rates, loan repayment rates, the average level of support required, and the amount borrowed by home owners, but even under fairly conservative assumptions it could be some two to three times as great as the annual cost to the public sector. A mixture of this approach and the current grant system could provide a limited capital grant together with assistance with loan charges to pay the remaining costs.

A further alternative would be the provision of equity-sharing loans. This would not lead to any increase in the amount of work funded in the short term. But in the longer term, when loans begin to be repaid, there is the potential for recycling receipts to increase the volume of lending. However, it is quite likely that losses would accrue on many properties in poorer condition. If commercial lenders could be persuaded to become involved in equity-sharing loans on older houses, this would also increase the resources available, but this seems unlikely.

A more radical approach would be to earmark some public resources for particular purposes, for example by limiting grant aid to designated renewal areas, or to other areas designated as priorities within a broader renewal strategy. Resources could also be concentrated on clearance and site preparation in particular areas where the condition of the stock made this the most sensible option.

Elements of a sustainable renewal policy

We have argued in this chapter that the housing renewal policies pursued over the last two decades have in many ways proved unsuccessful and short-term in impact, and that the current set of policies is unsustainable in the current economic climate because of the shortfall of resources in relation to need. We have examined a range of measures which could produce investment both to bring houses up to a reasonable standard and to enable them to remain in good condition. This includes not only repair and improvement but also regular maintenance. The key step in developing sustainable housing renewal policies is to accept that housing decay and disrepair are ongoing processes and that policies to tackle them must produce long-term and affordable solutions.

In the private sector, with which this chapter is concerned, the key problem is that many of those who own, or who are buying, houses simply cannot afford to keep them in good repair. The most significant step to improve their ability to do so would be to increase the sensitivity of house prices to repair costs. If this could be achieved, houses which were more expensive to repair or to maintain would fall in price relative to other dwellings, as people became more aware of the true costs of ownership.

Making owners more aware of the need to prepare to meet repair, improvement and maintenance costs, would change attitudes to borrowing, saving, and other forms of preparation such as insurance schemes. It would become as important to plan to meet housing repair costs in old age as to obtain an adequate pension. Houses would come to be seen as liabilities as well as assets. Owners would be persuaded to see housing equity as a resource for repair and improvement work rather than as a source of wealth to be passed on through inheritance. First time buyers would be less willing to pay high prices for houses in poor condition or less able to find lenders to assist them to do so. In inner city areas, there would be a relative decline in purchase prices, releasing money to be used for repair, improvement and maintenance. Many more people would see owning as less desirable than renting.

Many, although not all, of these proposals are a long way from implementation and some may prove to be impractical. Our aim in this chapter has been to stimulate debate rather than to provide solutions. But we are convinced that, sooner rather than later, there will be a need for a fundamental rethink of renewal policy in which these, or similar initiatives, will play a crucial part. Unless we find measures which encourage investment by the vast majority of owners who are never likely to receive grant aid, the prospects of developing a sustainable housing renewal policy are limited.

References

Benko, A. (1991) *Home maintenance insurance schemes: the Dutch experience*, Oxford: Anchor Housing Trust.
Cmnd 9513 (1985) *Home improvement - a new approach*, London: HMSO
Department of the Environment (1988) *English house condition survey 1986*, London: HMSO.
Department of the Environment (1993a) *English house condition survey 1991*, London: HMSO.
Department of the Environment (1993b) *Annual report 1993*, London: HMSO.
Leather, P. and Mackintosh, S. (1992) *Maintaining home ownership: the agency approach*, London: Longman/Institute of Housing.
Leather, P. and Mackintosh, S. (1993) 'Neighbourhood housing renewal', in R. Hambleton and M. Taylor (eds) *People in cities: a transatlantic policy exchange*, Bristol: SAUS Publications, School for Advanced Urban Studies, University of Bristol.
Mackintosh, S. and Leather, P. (1992a) *Home improvement under the new regime*, Occasional Paper no 38, Bristol: SAUS Publications, School for Advanced Urban Studies, University of Bristol.
Mackintosh, S. and Leather, P. (1992b) *Staying Put revisited*, Oxford: Anchor Housing Trust.
Mackintosh, S. and Leather, P. (1993) *Renovation file: a profile of housing conditions and housing renewal policies in the United Kingdom*, Oxford: Anchor Housing Trust.
Northern Ireland Housing Executive (1993) *Northern Ireland house condition survey 1991*, Belfast: NIHE.
Scottish Homes (1993) *Scottish house condition survey 1991: survey report*, Edinburgh: Scottish Homes.
Welsh Office (1988) *1986 Welsh house condition survey*, Cardiff: Welsh Office.

D: LABOUR MARKET POLICY

CHAPTER 18

A PERFUNCTORY SORT OF POST-FORDISM: ECONOMIC RESTRUCTURING AND LABOUR MARKET SEGMENTATION IN BRITAIN IN THE 1980s

JOHN LOVERING

A transition from Fordism to post-Fordism?

The 1980s was a decade of change but in which direction? What changed and what remained unchanged? A number of writers in a range of disciplines have claimed that contemporary economic restructuring represents a qualitative transformation from the Fordist mode of operation of the capitalist economic system, towards a post-Fordist variant (Lipietz, 1986; Sabel, 1989; Hirst and Zeitlin, 1989).[1] An alternative analysis describes this as a transformation from organised to disorganised capitalism (Lash and Urry, 1987). Some argue that post-Fordism will be characterised by flexible accumulation. Companies are deconcentrating in order to become more flexible and gain economies of scope rather than economies of scale (Cooke, 1987). This is achieved by introducing new technologies, inventory policies and work practices, and by extending the use of subcontractors. This in turn implies that new tendencies are at work in the labour market. One theory suggests that the flexible firm requires a 'core' force of 'polyvalent' task-flexible workers and a numerically-flexible 'periphery' of unskilled labour (Child, 1985). Core workers will tend to become "cocooned by an internal labour market" (Atkinson, 1984), while those on the periphery are fully exposed to the turbulence of the market.

Economic restructuring

I want to suggest that the restructuring of the British economy in the last decade has indeed modified some features and potentials of economic life significantly. But it has been less innovatory than a simple reading of the post-Fordist literature would suggest. It may represent the demise of Fordism, but it does not necessarily represent the creation of a regime of flexible specialisation as this is generally understood.

This chapter first appeared in *Work, Employment and Society*, 1990, vol 4, pp 9-28.

It is perhaps best to begin a review of economic change in the 1980s by recognising that the cycle of severe recession (1979-83), modest recovery (1983-87), over-heating (1987-89) and governmentally-induced recession (1989-), is extremely familiar. So much so, in fact, that equally familiar analyses of Britain's economic problems have been resuscitated (for example Coutts and Godley, 1989; Labour Party, 1989). However, some developments have undoubtedly had an enduring impact and have altered parameters of the economic structure and the labour market.

Firstly, there has been a sustained and major redistribution of income. The share of profits in national income rose from a low of 7.4% in 1975 to 17.6% in 1987. But this redistribution from labour to capital has not precipitated a corresponding increase in investment. The ratio of profits to gross capital formation (as proportions of GDP) nearly doubled between 1975 and 1989. The workforce, therefore, has had to produce more to bring forth a given rate of investment.

Income was also redistributed between households. The disposable income of the top quintile was nearly eight times as much as that of the lowest quintile and the differential widened in the 1980s. The poor did particularly badly, partly due to changes in the market, and partly to changes in the tax-benefit system.[2] Aggregate consumption spending rose half as fast again as output. In real terms the spending power of the top quintile increased by a quarter between 1981 and 1986, while that of the lowest quintile hardly rose at all. Spending on household durables rose twice as fast and spending on 'other services' nearly three times as fast, as total household expenditure (*Social Trends*, 1989, p 102).

The development of industry and employment of restructuring has been driven by a small set of 'motors of growth'. Following the precipitate de-industrialisation of 1979-82, manufacturing GDP began to increase, albeit more slowly than the output of services. A number of British companies established positions in international markets, notably in specialist high technology niches (Hannah, 1989), although growth here was modest compared with other countries such as the USA (Oakey and Cooper, 1989). Another part of the manufacturing revival was propelled by foreign investment. Although it accounted for under a fifth of the EEC market, Britain attracted two-fifths of Japanese investment in Europe. The UK offered multinational companies a unique mix of labour quality and low costs for mass market industries. *The Economist* recently noted that: "Taiwan once played this role" (*The Economist*, 1989, p 70).[3] An important part of service growth was driven by the reconstruction of Britain's international financial role. London became a first order international centre along with New York. The deregulation of the stock market precipitated a rapid corporate restructuring and concentration of capital, as the Bank of England had intended (Reid, 1989, p 55).[4] The 'de-nationalisation' of circuits of capital and exchange was reflected in the share of profits sent abroad in national income, an average of 17% of GDP in the 1980s, and in the growth of an international stratum in the labour market (Reid, 1989). In and out-migration between the UK, EEC and USA almost doubled between the late 1970s and mid 1980s (*Social Trends*, 1989, Table 1, p 14). A large part of employment growth derived from expanding domestic markets driven by the spending boom. Markets were created by, in effect, commodifying the future (eg insurance), the past (eg the heritage industry), place (eg distance tourism) and various aspects of lifestyles. This accelerating commodification particularly affected growth industries such as consumer services which rest on 'cultural products' (Lash and Urry, 1987; Urry, 1989).

Meanwhile, the state declined as a determinant of the level and direction of economic growth. The internationalisation of production meant that governments could play the traditional Keynesian role as a regulator/damper of market disturbances to a much diminished degree (Radice, 1984; Tomlinson, 1989a; Labour Party, 1989). The public sector also had less influence over longer-term economic development. Public fixed capital formation declined as a proportion of all investment with every cycle since 1967, reaching a record low of 19% in 1987.

On most economic indicators, all these developments did not stop Britain's slide down the international rankings. GDP grew slightly more rapidly in the 1980s than in the 1970s, but the rate was well below that of France, Italy or Denmark, only half that of the USA and a third that of Japan. The UK represented a declining share of the metropolitan market. The rate of investment was also relatively low, especially in manufacturing (Tomlinson, 1989b, p 262). Although capital formation per head increased, it nevertheless fell to half that of the USA and a fifth that of Japan.

This relative economic diminution was accompanied by further relative decline in the average standard of living. Between 1979 and 1986 British GDP per capita fell below that of Japan and continued to sink below that of West Germany and the USA. In the European Community only Spain, Portugal, Ireland and Greece were markedly poorer than Britain (Heseltine, 1987). The increase in inequality meant that the standard of living of many increased little, if at all. Measures of GDP are, of course, constructs based on commodity exchange-values and are only obliquely indicators of welfare or well-being. There can be little doubt that for many people the quality of life declined absolutely.[5]

Restructuring the labour market

When the recession associated with the first Thatcher government gave way to recovery, employment began to increase. Changes in circumstances and in demography combined to expand the supply of labour significantly. The recorded workforce expanded by 1.7 million in 4 years, equivalent to adding a second Wales and Northern Ireland (*Social Trends*, 1989, p 72).

Nine out of ten people in jobs work for others. Women accounted for the entire increase in this working class. This was less because women replaced men in existing jobs than because they formed the bulk of the workforce in growing industries and were largely excluded from contracting ones (Table 1). Meanwhile, between 1981 and 1988 twice as many jobs were created in self-employment. This new petty bourgeoisie was predominantly male (Tables 2 and 3).

Table 1: **Gender and employment increase 1981-88**

	Increase in total employment	Female % (1988) of employees
All manufacturing:	- 2.7%	30.2%
All services:	5.0%	54.8%
All industries and services:	2.4%	46.0%

Source: *Social Trends* 19, 1989, Table 4.10

Table 2: **Industrial change**

	1979		1988	
	employees	self-employed	employees	self-employed
Agriculture, forestry, fishing:	380	286	313	269
Energy, water:	722	1	459	1
Extraction:	1,147	6	771	13
Metal goods, engineering, vehicles:	3,374	42	2,219	77
Other:	2,732	93	2,108	165
Total manufacturing:	7,253	141	5,097	265
Construction:	1,239	352	1,022	576
Distribution, hotels, catering, repairs:	4,257	652	4,551	840
Transport, communications:	1,479	88	1,372	166
Banking, finance, business services:	1,647	148	2,468	324
Other:	6,197	238	6,820	544
Total services:	13,580	1,126	15,212	1,874
All	23,173	1,906	22,104	2,985

Source: *Social Trends* 19, 1989, Tables 4.10 and 4.11

Table 3: Self-employed - males as % (1988)

Sector	%
Manufacturing	79
Services	65
All	75

Source: *Social Trends* 19, 1989, Table 4.11

These outcomes reflect a range of processes. One way to approach these is to distinguish between the *structures* of the labour market and the *distributive processes* through which people are allocated to them. The restructuring of the 1980s entailed changes in both dimensions.

Restructuring the map of labour market 'places'

The occupation structure can be regarded as a set of 'places', each of which designates a set of tasks and rewards and a position in a network of social relations. Each place (job) also offers a set of longer-term opportunities, to the extent that it imparts the chance to acquire 'credentials' or 'skills'. Credentialism is traditionally regarded as the mode of advance in internal labour markets (ILMs). In external labour markets (ELMs), on the other hand, advancement is traditionally understood in terms of the acquisition of marketable 'human capital'. The labour market as a whole can be envisaged as consisting of sets of internal and external labour markets, unevenly mapped geographically, offering a specific set of ELMs and ports of entry to ILMs in each local labour market. The literature offers many ways of conceptualising this network. As a first approximation, it is useful to distinguish between 'traditional' and 'truncated' internal labour markets and 'elite' and 'secondary' external labour markets.[6] There are indications that the network of opportunities formed by these four types of labour market changed significantly in the 1980s.

Many large British companies, especially in manufacturing and the public sector, formerly provided internal labour markets in which promotion ladders were both 'broad' and 'long'. In some industries and locations these employers dominated the local labour market. One study identified over 200 'dominated local labour markets' in the 1970s. These were typically dominated by employers with Fordist ILMs (Lever, 1979). While there is room for debate over the degree to which this 'Fordist' employment pattern described the British labour market as a whole or played a hegemonic role nationally, there can be little doubt it has declined in terms of the employment provided. Deindustrialisation has hit precisely these manufacturing industries (Harrison and Bluestone, 1988, p 212). The

ILM has also been in decline in service industries. Rajan estimates that the number of employees working in ILMs fell from 68% to 52% in banks, 50% to 40% in building societies and 68% to 63% in insurance companies (Savage *et al*, 1988, p 462). The decline of internal labour markets has had a concentrated effect in many local labour markets. A particularly vivid illustration is provided by the case of Plymouth, where the run-down of the former Admiralty dockyard at Devonport has been reducing a workforce of 14,000 to one of 5,000. The dockyard was formerly part of the civil service, staff were automatically eligible for promotion up a career ladder by virtue of seniority and 'mobile grades' had the chance of promotion to other Admiralty sites in the UK or beyond. The contraction of the yard, together with privatisation, has meant that both sets of ladders have been severed. This particular labour market was, of course, effectively confined to white males and its decline was not compensated by the emergence of any new large ILM for women. Few of Plymouth's new employers offer major internal labour markets, most are small firms.

Meanwhile, there is growing evidence that employers in the 're-industrialising' industries are changing their employment practices in ways that have implications for surviving internal labour markets. The post-Fordism debate has focused on these changes and it has been suggested that employers are systematically replacing 'job ladders' with arrangements for 'contingent labor' (Harrison and Bluestone, 1988, p 44). The evidence in Britain is consistent with a rather more complex picture, in which employers are creating more segmented and truncated ILMs.

This may be illustrated by one, probably fairly typical, example. A leading manufacturer has redesigned its recruitment and promotion procedure in order: "to use people-resources like we use financial resources."[7] This requires the competitive use of labour in the short term and human resource development in the longer term. The latter involves careful targeting of training and promotion opportunities. Graduate entrants are to be more closely monitored and differentiated according to promotion potential, suitable candidates being slotted into the management development programme. The corporate view is that: "management development is a process, and it really means management elimination". Graded pay structures have been eliminated throughout professional technical occupations in favour of individual appraisal. Three lists of staff have been prepared. The first includes some 10-20 people who: "the board ought to know about now". The second lists 100 or so employees thought to be ready in five years and the third lists about a thousand who are likely to be suitable ten years ahead. The strategy is designed to ensure that the company: "identifies the superguys [sic] and develops them". One corollary is that the pay of favoured individuals has begun to rise much faster than previously.

Similar trends are evident in many manufacturing companies. Component features can also be found in the public sector, formerly one of the largest providers of traditional, large, internal labour markets. The terms of employment of public employees have been changing as the Civil Service model is abandoned. The Ministry of Defence, for example, is linking pay more closely to performance, with supplements for scarce occupations. One effect of this, described explicitly as an attempt "to get at market forces", was that, while most professionals received a 7% pay rise in 1989, a few received rises up to 20%. If the 'traditional' ILM is in decline, or is being modified by policy changes, there are signs that new types of internal labour markets are emerging elsewhere. Studies of companies in growing sectors have found that many are adopting new personnel policies in order to overcome shortages of experienced staff by 'growing their own', securing loyalty and reducing turnover. In catering and retail, where employee-customer interaction is important to competitiveness, some large companies are also constructing new career ladders and promotion incentives to attract an "improved calibre of staff" (Lovering, 1994). As capital in these sectors becomes increasingly concentrated, the proportion of companies able to provide such career ladders increases. Some have begun to advertise management careers which cut across subsidiary companies. Moreover, many of these new industries rely heavily on 'gendered jobs' and their new internal labour markets tend to be segmented accordingly. In building societies and banks new 'career clerical hierarchies' have been created, through which some women have been able to rise to assistant branch manager level, but few advance much further. In a number of studies Crompton traced the displacement of large white collar bureaucracies by segmented structures associated with multi-level recruitment and shorter hierarchies (Crompton, 1989a, 1989b). As working women tend to be more highly localised and geographically immobile than many men, promotion ladders for women are often effectively confined to the establishment. This is particularly true in part-time jobs.

So, although there are signs that new internal labour markets are emerging, the indications are that they will not be comparable in length or breadth to those which are manifestly disappearing within large manufacturing companies and the public sector. The emergent ILM is characteristically a 'truncated' one.

External labour markets appear to have increased in importance.[8] A number of case studies of employers identified the significance of external labour markets, especially in the better-paid professions. At the same time, they have shown that many employers have also relied on external labour markets for supplies of routine labour. These polar types of external labour market are differentiated by an enduring asymmetry of supply and demand. In the first 'elite' ELMs' demand consistently exceeds supply, while in the latter, 'secondary' ELMs the reverse is the case (Boddy, Lovering and

Bassett, 1986, chapter 5; Dale, 1987; Fielder, 1989). In their study of professionals in Berkshire Savage *et al* (1988) outlined some properties of the 'elite' type. Many professionals had moved between firms rather than worked their way up a corporate hierarchy. Far from being "cocooned in internal labour markets" these "core workers" were too marketable to contain in an ILM. Secondary external labour markets, on the other hand, tend to utilise labour which is more localised. Many smaller manufacturing and service establishments draw their workforce mainly from nearby housing estates. For such workers, especially women, the job does not generally impart 'skills', credentials or information which will enable them to advance to higher positions in these or other firms. Symptomatically, some employers describe their recruitment procedures for these groups in terms of the application of 'knock out factors' to reduce the number of applications to a manageable level (Boddy, Lovering and Bassett, 1986).

The growth of self-employment has created another form of external labour market. Self-employment may form part of a circuit through which elite career paths are constructed:

> the new service class is ... highly mobile between employers and into self-employment ... eg electronics engineers ...
> (Savage *et al*, 1988, p 465)

A single employer is likely to draw on several types of labour markets at once. Employers can achieve 'flexibility' by playing judiciously across these markets. They generally find professional workers through external markets. The employees most likely to be in remaining and new ILMs are those whose experience or social characteristics are important for competitiveness, although their work is essentially routine. ILMs are used to motivate such employees and reduce staff wastage by extending modest promotional opportunities. But there is little incentive to extend these concessions to the more disposable routine low skill workers (Smith, 1989). ILMs are least likely to survive or emerge in those many enterprises which have grown on the basis of low wages, or where the combination of work flow and management strategies is not conducive to guarantees of long-term full-time employment. A major part of the British workforce is employed under such 'secondary' conditions (although they are by no means secondary to the needs of employers; part-time shift workers, for example, may be the effective 'core' of an employer's workforce).

Allocation to places in the labour market: recruitment channels and selection criteria

A growing body of research has drawn attention to the social processes through which individuals find their ways to places in the labour market.

Studies of employers tend to find that employment criteria are not reducible to a rationalistic calculus of economic productivity. Recruitment practices frequently mobilise 'social criteria':

> whether actively through the positive selection of individuals with particular social characteristics or passively through a lack of concern with technical qualifications. (Rees, Williamson and Winkler, 1989, p 241)

Although this is foreign to much of the economic literature on labour markets, it should not be surprising. Recent work in institutional economics has reminded us that employers are *necessarily* concerned with the social characteristics of recruits, since they need them to cooperate in a set of social relationships.[9]

The substance of employers' selection criteria may be expected to vary across different labour markets. The various internal and external labour markets entail not only a different balance of supply and demand and thence bargaining power, but also different degrees of 'privacy' and negotiability of selection practices. To this extent, the shifting balance of internal and external labour markets implies a change in the weight of different selection criteria in the labour market as a whole. The traditional Fordist 'broad and long' internal labour market rested on a formalised selection process in which criteria were publicly laid out. In principle, promotion could be won by following the rules.[10] In many public and private bureaucracies, for example, seniority by virtue of length of service was a major credential. This does not of course mean that these labour markets were free from any taint of 'social selection'. The exclusion of women and ethnic minorities at the point of entry to internal labour markets has been well documented (for example Walby, 1986).[11] In external labour markets the criteria for selection are not conditioned by any such 'public' practices. The selection process is privatised, but this does not mean that it is less likely to be exclusionary. On the contrary, employers are free to mobilise whichever criteria they prefer. There are theoretical and empirical reasons to expect that these will tend to incorporate social criteria, especially in labour markets characterised by excess supply (Lovering, 1994; Rees, Williamson and Winkler, 1989). What is more, these criteria count at every stage of an individual's progress, rather than subsiding before formalised meritocratic criteria beyond the initial point of entry, as in ILMs. The decline of the corporatist ILM, the emergence of 'truncated' new ILMs, and the dualistic growth of ELMs, together imply that the salience of social criteria may be increasing.

'Systematic noise' in the labour market: the restructuring of institutions

The institutional context of recruitment has not received the attention it deserves. However, it seems likely that the restructuring of the recruitment industry is having important effects. Two strands of government policy have been particularly important here. Firstly, the public placement service has been marginalised. Secondly, the state has extended its influence over the supply of young workers and the unemployed. There are reasons to believe that these developments may deepen the barriers between the labour markets for advantaged and 'disadvantaged' workers.

Jobcentres deal with about a third of vacancies. The bulk of vacancies are filled through private agencies, the press, and informal networks. Private recruitment agencies have proliferated, especially in specialist technical occupations. The ability of the public service to affect recruitment processes has almost certainly declined in the 1980s. Jobcentres lack basic modern office technologies such as computerised records. Staff shortages have been worsened by relatively declining pay and conditions and increasing workloads. Jobcentres have been prevented from marketing themselves to employers. Jobcentre staff have increasingly become the 'recruiting sergeants' for government training schemes, notably Employment Training (Finn, 1988). They are under pressure to get people off the register (Taylor, 1987). Jobcentres have also become more closely associated with the coercive aspects of social security legislation. Eligibility for benefit is becoming conditional on evidence of job-search. Many jobcentres and benefit offices have been relocated into the same building.

Interviews with employers repeatedly confirm that they associate jobcentres with the lower end of the vacancy market. These institutional developments are likely to consolidate this prejudice. The more jobcentres are seen as pushing reluctant claimants to apply for vacancies, the more reluctant and selective will employers be in using them and the more their clients will be relegated to secondary ELMs.

The expansion and consolidation of training schemes has created a vast apparatus which only self-sufficient job-seekers (such as the already employed) can avoid. One effect has been to create a new network of recruitment channels, which is itself segmented. A number of studies have shown how institutional discrimination has been reproduced as a result (for example Fenton *et al*, 1984). For many employers the main value of low cost training programmes such as Youth Training Scheme and Employment Training lies in providing them with the opportunity for extended recruitment procedures (Finn, 1988; Pollert, 1988). The state subsidises and legitimates 'privatised' recruitment practices, allowing employers to use whichever criteria they choose, provided they appear to remain within the law. This type of 'flexibility' is likely to be reinforced by the move to a decentralised system of training, designed to gear provision to local needs as defined by employers (Department of Employment, 1988).

We do not have enough historical data to assess the extent to which public labour market agencies have been displaced in favour of private and informal agencies and public training provision assimilated to employers' recruitment practices. However, it seems probable that these developments have reinforced and systematised the 'noise' which characterises information flows in the labour market. Different social groups use markedly different recruitment channels and are exposed to different sets of opportunities. The importance of highly localised and socially specific recruitment networks has been recognised (Willis, 1977). At the 'elite' pole these tend to be male-dominated networks through which labour poaching is institutionalised, often explicitly. High level jobs are often filled entirely and explicitly through informal social networks. At the other pole, equally informal networks ensure that recruitment in certain jobs and industries is targeted towards minority ethnic groups and women (for example Stanley and Temple, 1989). These networks overlay to form a complex set of information channels, such that different actors inhabit different informational worlds. Private recruitment agencies and the unemployed rarely come into contact with one another.[12] The contrast between the channels used by men and women is roughly indicated in Table 4.

Table 4: Segmentation of recruitment channels: methods of seeking work

	All men	Married women	Unmarried women
Jobcentres, etc	35.0	22.0	35.4
Private agency	1.4	-	2.5
Reply to adverts	10.6	13.3	10.8
Study newspaper sits. vac	28.6	43.4	29.7
Direct application	7.5	5.4	7.2
Word of mouth, trade union, etc	11.5	8.1	8.4
Other	5.7	6.5	6.0

Source: *Employment Gazette*, April 1988, p 194

To the extent that recruitment networks become more segmented, employers are less likely to make the 'mistake' of recruiting from groups outside their targeted categories. There is less chance that deviant cases will have a corrective effect on their selection criteria and on the expectations of job-seekers. The restructuring of the recruitment network appears to be legitimating and funding the extension of employers' private, unreconstructed, recruitment practices.

Assessment: segmentation into the 1990s

In this section I want to draw out some implications of this account of restructuring. The first is that continuities with the past are very much in evidence. The most significant trends bear little resemblance to flexible specialisation versions of post-Fordism. Rather than taking us into a qualitatively new era, many of the changes have sustained or reactivated labour market practices from a more distant past.

The restructuring may have created a "more self-confident, and more efficient capitalism than we have known for many decades" (Hannah, 1988, p 48) but the relatively low level of investment has meant that this capitalism is in general premissed on a low wage and low skill labour force (Senker, 1989). Demographic and social changes have sustained the plentiful supply of 'routine labour'. Yet at the same time, the demand for labour with scarce skills and experience could not be completely suppressed or satisfied. This divergence reflects the poor level of education and of training in industry. As Hannah (1989, p 47) has put it Britain has "the worst of both worlds, individuals do not invest in their own training as readily as in other countries, and neither do firms". These circumstances would help explain why much investment appears fairly conventional in terms of the tasks it demands of labour; radical innovations are rare. Econometric studies generally suggest that new investment has not been the major factor raising productivity in manufacturing (Oulton, 1989). The more effective use of, and greater effort of, the workforce has probably been more important. This is quite understandable if investment has followed the grain of the labour market.

In the language of the Fordist debate, the resulting development is closer to an intensified neo-Fordism than to flexible accumulation. If employers have gained more flexibility in the utilisation of labour, this is mostly flexibility of a conventional kind, using greater employer control to intensify effort. In her study of Coventry for example, Purcell (1994) found most of the increase in 'flexible labour' to be "in areas where such flexibility is traditional rather than an innovation, hospitals, retailing, clerical, etc". In a low wage, segmented labour market, most employers have found enough flexibility without having to train their workers to become 'polyvalent' and entrepreneurial employees. One recent management-oriented textbook has claimed that a third of the British workforce is flexible (Leighton and Syrett, 1989). This flexibility would seem to consist largely of the ability of employers to pick and choose labour with less inhibition from formalised and public personnel practices. Talk of 'the flexible workforce', so much in vogue in management and academic business circles (for example Coyle, 1989), speaks mainly to the changed balance of power in the labour market.

This form of restructuring does little to undermine the institutional bases of segmentation. As large industries and the public sector decline in scale most local labour markets offer fewer and shorter 'ladders' for advancement within internal labour markets. And the divergence of opportunities between those on 'fast tracks' within ILMs and those excluded appears to be widening. Career and non-career paths through external labour markets may also be widening, due to the uneven acquisition of transferable knowledge and skills. Access to the elite external labour markets which are taking the place of the upper layers of ILMs depends on the possession of experience and qualifications. Most of those working in internal labour markets, and secondary external labour markets, are unlikely to acquire these. To this extent, as Savage *et al* (1988) suggest, the labour market is probably becoming more 'closed'. Moreover, it is likely to be closing along the lines of pre-existing social divisions.

These changes mean that, in general, a smaller proportion of workers are able to make careers simply by 'following the rules'. As the Fordist internal labour market disappears 'public' criteria give way to employers 'private' criteria. The main gatekeepers of the labour market are less constrained by the need for accountability. From the employee point of view the path through the labour market depends increasingly on individual characteristics and practices. But where employers invoke social criteria, those 'characteristics' are systematically associated with social categories such as gender, race and class (or, more strictly, status). Similarly, the reliance in elite external markets on qualifications and track record, elevates the significance of pre-market education and circumstances outside the labour market. To the extent that these processes are at work, the 'individualisation' of the labour market is not really individualistic at all.

Although traditional Fordist ILMs were largely the domain of men, they did in principle open opportunities for women if they possessed the correct formal qualities. In the finance sector an increasing number of women have taken advantage of this, although the goalposts have been moved against them (Crompton, 1990). In engineering the number of women professionals increased five times faster than the number of men in the 1980s. This increase was concentrated in the largest companies, which is to say those in which internal labour markets were prominent. (Of course, the *absolute* number of women involved has been small.) These may be signs that 'direct discrimination' within the more traditional internal labour markets is diminishing somewhat as women exploit equal opportunities legislation and as companies modernise their selection criteria. But these labour markets are becoming less discriminatory just as they are becoming scarce. Meanwhile, the ladders for upward mobility for women emerging in the newer industries tend to be both 'truncated' and gender segmented.

The expansion of elite external labour markets provides some new opportunities for advantaged women. But the greatest expansion would seem to be in those 'secondary' external markets in which women are targeted due to their amenability as disadvantaged workers. The contrasts between men and women, and between different women workers, underline the importance of "earnings potential and earnings needs" in differentiating the markets for female labour (Bruegel, 1989, p 58). Needs and expectations are clearly conditioned by gender for it is widely accepted that "it is the implicit assumption that most married women are not the sole earners in the household which leads to the low price of part-time labour" (Dale, 1987, p 346), but categories such as ethnicity and status are also crucial. The restructuring of the labour market has been profoundly influenced by the enhanced ability of employers to capitalise on the differentiation of labour supply associated with deep rooted ideologies of gender, race, age, etc and associated asymmetries of bargaining power.

The character of final demand also has significance here. There is a lively debate on the character of the goods and services that the better-off want to buy, captured in the notion of 'positional goods' (Lash and Urry, 1987; Urry, 1989). Economically influential spenders are buying not only a selection of products but also a range of services, notably those provided directly by the worker: entertainment, catering, etc. The demand for these consumer services is often a demand for the visible performance of an activity, unlike the demand for products, where the production process is invisible to consumers and does not impact on the use-value they derive. The demands of high-income groups are stimulating some activities where the social characteristics of the worker are germane to the use-value the buyer derives. Since the big spenders are men it is perhaps not surprising that so many of the new servants are women: barmaids, receptionists, hostesses, etc.

The peculiarities of British 'post-Fordism'

The trends of the 1980s offer little indication that a new hegemonic model of flexible specialisation is being established in Britain. The economic restructuring of the last decade would seem to be post-Fordist only in the semantic sense, it is different in some respects from the previous period which might be described as Fordist.

The social character of the restructured labour market has been conditioned by the coexistence of a stratum of society which has enjoyed expanding purchasing power and an expanding working population, large sections of which have not. The availability of cheap labour has shaped the pattern of investment. New demands have grown alongside a supply of workers to serve them. This juxtaposition has been made possible by a number of political conditions, in particular the encouragement of high incomes, the redistribution of income through taxes etc, the political construction of new markets (deregulation) and increased extra-economic coercion on labour. Growth based on a combination of domestic consumption and modest export expansion has not created systematic incentives for major increases or radical changes in investment. In comparison with other countries there has been little pressure to innovate in the labour market, beyond dismantling corporatist labour market institutions and enhancing management control.

The post-Fordist element of this restructuring would seem to consist mainly in the reduced impact of institutionalised compromises between employers and their workforces as collectivities. Labour is increasingly regulated instead through markets, in the form of a set of socially differentiated labour markets. Ideologies of gender, race and age are deeply embedded in this structure. In some markets differentiation arises 'economistically' by virtue of genuine differences of supply of labour with scarce skills. But social categories such as gender, race and class are major axes of difference here too, since they are closely associated with access to educational qualifications and enabling or constraining circumstances outside the workplace. Given that many companies have survived by acquiring rather than training labour, existing social divisions in the labour market have been exploited rather than challenged. Gender, race, age and status continue to form the major axes of segmentation. Men still monopolise the scarce and best paid occupations, women fill the jobs where employees have less bargaining power, black women fill those where they have least. This perfunctory version of post-Fordism rests on the mobilisation of existing social inequalities through the labour market.

These dynamics are closely related to government policies. While industrial and industrial relations measures have intensified the decline of extended internal labour markets, labour market policies have widened the differentiation between groups in short, or excess, supply. Social policies have influenced the disadvantages suffered by different groups of workers such as women, black people, residents of deprived areas. It is widely recognised, for example, that the high proportion of part-time work amongst women partly reflects Britain's marked lack of state child-care provision (Dex, 1985). Public policy played the major role in restructuring the recruitment and training networks which govern entry to the labour market. The resulting changes appear to be reinforcing employers' selection practices and generally heightening the barriers between different labour markets as a result. Meanwhile, many on the fringes of the labour market are discouraged or coerced into withdrawal. Of course, explicit policies may have less significance for the working of the labour market than the ideological climate induced by government, but this can only be guessed at here.

The political economy of restructuring in Britain

The direction of growth has shifted further away from 'horizontal' accumulation, based on expanding output, employment and incomes, and further towards 'vertical' accumulation based on a dualism between a high wage, high productivity sector and a large low wage sector (Hymer, 1972, pp 117-8). If this is a move towards post-Fordism it is a variant which has little in common with the model of flexible specialisation exemplified in Japan or the 'Third Italy'. It has greater affinities with the model offered by the USA. Accordingly, Mike Davis's analysis of US experience may have some relevance. He interprets the restructuring of the US economy in terms of a dynamic of *over-consumption*:

> the increasing political subsidisation of a sub-bourgeois, mass layer of managers, professionals, new entrepreneurs and rentiers who ... have been overwhelmingly successful in profiting from both inflation and expanded state expenditure. (Davis, 1986, p 211)

Britain has also experienced a redistribution towards the fortunate but this stratum seems to lack some properties of its equivalent in the USA (Heseltine, 1987). The British service class is much smaller than that in the USA (Lash and Urry, 1987) and less likely to be in industry. The number of professionals in science and engineering in Britain is stagnant, in contrast to the USA, Japan and most of Europe.

The beneficiaries in Britain are not so much rich as those better off than their neighbours. Their relative national advantages are more the result of the disintegration of a national economy in relative and, in parts, absolute decline. Propulsive sectors of the British economy have captured niches on world markets and generated some relatively high income groups. Their spending has promoted some new domestic growth markets. But these achievements have not required or generated a radical and general change in the way the labour market works. On the contrary, the enhanced power of employers has weakened the constraints on their selection and employment practices. This freedom has been used, following lines of least resistance, to differentiate workers according to traditional social divisions. If this form of restructuring represents a transition away from Fordism, the kind of post-Fordism it promises is deeply conservative.

Notes

1. For a critique of some theoretical issues, see Lovering (1990).
2. The marked decline in the inequality of the distribution of wealth also came to a halt. The share of marketable wealth plus occupational and state pension

rights owned by the richest 1% of the population stabilised at just over 25% of the total, that of the richest 10% at 36%.

3. It remains to be seen whether Britain can continue to play this role in the face of new competition from highly skilled and cheap Eastern European labour.

4. These developments revived the long-standing debate over the relationship between the City and domestic industry (see Moorhouse, 1989).

5. The rise of homelessness and crime are perhaps important indicators. Even on the minimal basis of published figures, the number of the homeless 'in priority need' rose from 80,000 to 107,000 between 1984 and 1987. Notifiable criminal offences rose by an average of 5.5% every year, while the clear-up rate fell (*Social Trends*, 1989, Table 8.6, Table 12.1).

6. A similar and compatible categorisation is offered by Crompton (1989), who differentiates between 'upper' and 'lower' internal labour markets. See also Dale (1987).

7. Quotes are from interviews with personnel directors or managers.

8. The Department of Employment London Labour Market study found the highest rate of recruitment in occupations where one would expect various types of external labour markets to be most prevalent, ie retail/catering and non-management professionals (Meadows, Cooper and Bartholomew, 1988, p 30).

9. Although the capitalist firm operates within markets it is itself: 'an important non-market institution' (Hodgson, 1989, p 295).

10. The following argument stresses the potentially meritocratic aspects of internal labour markets. This dimension has been under-emphasised in the theoretical literature, which traditionally portrayed the ILM as the arena of discriminatory social closure (Parkin, 1974). I would argue that this one-sidedness arose from two premises. Firstly, these Weberian accounts took as their starting point the apparently obvious fact that some groups try to improve their lot at the expense of others (Parkin, 1982, p 100). But they paid little attention to the ideological and political preconditions which differentiated these collective actors. As a result, there was a tendency for an ahistoric, ideal typical model, drawn from specific male-dominated industries in specific countries in a specific period, to be taken as a description of the the *necessary* characteristics of all ILMs. Secondly, they assumed that while the ILM was cocooned by organisational norms, the external (secondary) labour market was governed by pristine economic forces unmediated by cultural or political intervention. This dichotomy is overstretched. My argument is that social ideologies of difference (gender and race etc) and power relations are also implicated in the structure of external labour markets. The *entire* labour market is socially constructed. However, we do not know enough about how historical ILMs actually operated, as opposed to the way they might have worked. The whole contrast between the Fordist and post-Fordist scenario sketched here is subject to this caveat.

11. As a clerk in a nationalised industry in the 1960s it was my job to shortlist applicants for vacancies. This involved stacking their record cards in order of seniority. In many cases I was told to remove those who were black because they would be 'unsuitable' (the practice stopped, officially, with legislation

against racial discrimination). Promotion was virtually automatic for the remaining applicant, unless some misdemeanour was discovered.
12. 70% of London's unemployed never use private agencies (Meadows, Cooper and Bartholemew, 1988, para 78).

References

Atkinson, J. (1984) *Flexibility, uncertainty and manpower management*, Brighton: Institute of Manpower Studies.
Boddy, M., Lovering, J. and Bassett, K. (1986) *Sunbelt city?*, Oxford: Clarendon Press.
Bruegel, I. (1989) 'Sex and race in the labour market', *Feminist Review*, vol 32, pp 49-68.
Child, J. (1985) 'Management strategies, new technology, and the labour process', in D. Knights, H. Willmott and D. Collinson (eds) *Job redesign*, Aldershot: Gower.
Cooke, P. (1987) 'Spatial development processes: organised or disorganised?', in N. Thrift and P. Williams (eds) *Class and space: the making of urban society*, London: Routledge, pp 306-29.
Coutts, K. and Godley, W. (1989) 'The British economy under Mrs Thatcher', *Political Quarterly*, Summer, pp 137-51.
Coyle, D. (1989) 'Staff jobs are yesterday's game', *Investors Chronicle*, 25 August, pp 143-15.
Crompton, R. (1989a) *Occupational segregation*, Working Paper 2, ESRC Social Change and Economic Life Initiative.
Crompton, R. (1989b) 'Women in banking: continuity and change since the Second World War', *Work, Employment and Society*, vol 3, pp 141-56.
Crompton, R. (1990) 'Professions in the current context', *Work, Employment and Society*, vol 4, special issue.
Dale, A. (1987) 'Occupational inequality, gender and life-cycle', *Work, Employment and Society*, vol 1, no 3, pp 326-51.
Davis, M. (1986) *Prisoners of the American dream*, London: Verso.
Dex, S. (1985) *The sexual division of work*, Brighton: Wheatsheaf.
The Economist (1989) 'Europe's Taiwan', 26 August.
Department of Employment (1988) *Training for employment*, Cm316, London: HMSO.
Fenton, S., Davies, T., Means, R. and Burton, P. (1984) *Ethnic minorities and the Youth Training Scheme*, Sheffield: Manpower Services Commission.
Fielder, S. (1989) 'Recruitment, training and local labour markets: a review', ESRC research programme on Institutional Determinants of Employer's Training Strategies, Social Research Unit, University of Wales, Cardiff, and School for Advanced Urban Studies, University, of Bristol.
Finn, D. (1988) 'Training and unemployment schemes for the long-term unemployed: British government policy for the 1990s', *Work, Employment and Sociey*, vol 2, no 4, pp 521-34.

Hannah, L. (1989) 'Mrs Thatcher: capital basher?', in D. Kavanagh and A. Seldon (eds) *The Thatcher effect*, Oxford: Oxford University Press, pp 38-48.

Harrison, B. and Bluestone, B. (1988) *The great U-turn*, New York: Basic Books.

Heseltine, M. (1987) *Where there's a will*, London: Hutchinson.

Hirst, P. and Zeitlin, J. (1989) 'Flexible specialisation and the competitive failure of UK manufacturing', *Political Quarterly*, Summer, pp 164-78.

Hodgson, G. (1989) *Economics and institutions*, Cambridge: Polity Press.

Hymer, S. (1972) 'The multinational corporation and the law of uneven development' in J.N. Bhagwati (ed) *Economics and world order*, New York: Macmillan, pp 113-40.

Labour Party (1989) *Meet the challenge, make the change*, Final report of Labour's Policy Review for the 1990s, London: Labour Party.

Lash, S. and Urry, J. (1987) *The end of organised capitalism*, Cambridge: Polity Press.

Leighton, P. and Syrett, M. (1989) *New work patterns: putting policy into practice*, London: Pitman.

Lever, W.F. (1979) 'Industry and labour market in Great Britain' in F. Hamilton and G. Linge (eds) *Spatial analysis, industry and the industrial environment*, Chichester: Wiley.

Lipietz, A. (1986) *Miracles and mirages*, London: Verso.

Lovering, J. (1990) 'Fordism's unknown successor', *International Journal of Urban and Regional Research*, vol 14, no 1, pp 159-74..

Lovering, J. (1994) 'Employers, the sex-typing of jobs and economic restructuring' in A. Scott (ed) *Gender, segregation and social change*, Oxford: Blackwell, pp 329-355.

Meadows, P., Cooper, H. and Bartholomew, R. (1988) *The London labour market*, London: Department of Employment, Employment Group.

Moorhouse, H.F. (1989) 'No mean city? The financial sector and the decline of manufacturing in Britain', *Work, Employment and Society*, vol 3, no 1, pp 105-18.

Oakey, R.P. and Cooper, S.Y. (1989) 'High-technology industry, agglomeration and the potential for peripherally sited small firms', *Regional Studies*, vol 23, pp 347-60.

Oulton, N. (1989) 'Productivity growth in manufacturing 1963-85: the roles of new investment and scrapping', *National Institute Economic Review*, February, pp 64-75.

Parkin, F. (1974) *The social analysis of class structure*, London: Tavistock.

Parkin, F. (1982) *Max Weber*, London: Tavistock.

Pollert, A. (1988) 'The flexible firm: fixation or fact?', *Work, Employment and Society*, vol 2, no 3, pp 281-316.

Purcell, K. (1994) 'Industrial restructuring, gender and patterns of employment in Coventry' in A. Scott (ed) *Gender, segregation and social change*, Oxford: Blackwell.

Radice, H. (1984) 'The national economy - a Keynesian myth?,' *Capital and Class*, vol 22, pp 111-90.

Reid, M. (1989) 'Mrs Thatcher and the city' in D. Kavanagh and A. Seldon (eds) *The Thatcher effect*, Oxford: Oxford University Press, pp 49-63.

Rees, G., Williamson, H. and Winkler, W. (1989) 'The new vocationalism: further education and local labour markets', *Journal of Education Policy*, vol 4, pp 227-44.

Sabel, C. (1989) 'Flexible specialisation and the re-emergence of regional economies' in P. Hirst and J. Zeitlin (eds) *Reversing industrial decline?*, London: Berg, pp 17-71.

Senker, P. (1989) 'Ten years of Thatcherism: triumph of ideology over economics', *Political Quarterly*, Summer, pp 179-89.

Savage, M., Dickens, P. and Fielding, T. (1988) 'Some social and political implications of the contemporary fragmentation of the service class in Britain', *International Journal of Urban and Regional Research*, vol 12, pp 455-75.

Smith, C. (1989)'Flexible specialisation, automation and mass production', *Work, Employment and Society*, vol 3, no 2, pp 204-19.

Stanley, L. and Temple, B. (1989) 'Work, community, household', Paper presented at the Work, Employment and Society Conference, University of Durham, September.

Taylor, D. (1987) 'Living with unemployment', in A. Walker and C. Walker (eds) *The growing divide: a social audit 1979-1987*, London: Child Poverty Action Group.

Tomlinson, J. (1989a) 'Employment policy and economic management', in P. Alcock, A. Gamble, I. Gough, P. Lee and A. Walker (eds) *The social economy and the democratic state*, London: Lawrence and Wishart, pp 32-56.

Tomlinson, J. (1989b) 'Macroeconomic management and industrial policy' in P. Hirst and J. Zeitlin (eds) *Reversing industrial decline?*, London: Berg.

Walby, S. (1986) *Patriarchy at work*, Cambridge: Polity Press.

Willis, P. (1977) *Learning to labour*, Farnborough: Saxon House.

Urry, J. (1989) 'Work, production and societies', Paper presented at the Work, Employment and Society Conference, University of Durham, September.

CHAPTER 19

EVALUATING LOCAL LABOUR MARKET POLICY: THE CASE OF TECs

MARTIN BODDY

Introduction

In the early 1990s, 82 employer-led Training and Enterprise Councils (TECs) took over responsibility for delivering much of publicly funded training and enterprise support in England and Wales. With the status of independent private sector companies operating under contract to the Employment Department, TECs took over responsibility from the then Training Agency for delivery of Youth Training, Employment Training and other programmes. They also took over the Enterprise Allowance Scheme and other business support initiatives. Since then their remit has expanded further, giving them responsibilities in relation to the Careers Service, Compacts and Further Education. The intention was that TECs would tailor existing programmes to meet local needs. They were also, however, to pursue a broader set of national objectives to increase the commitment of employers and individuals to training, improve the quality and relevance of training, and encourage enterprise (see Figure 1).

The TEC initiative amounted to the most radical reform of the country's training and enterprise infrastructure since the establishment of the Manpower Services Commission in the 1970s. TECs themselves were constituted as new organisations, "born of the enterprise culture" (Employment Department, 1989a) with an emphasis on radical reform, performance and value for money. There were major implications as well for relations between TECs and the Employment Department. TECs represented a radically different form of delivery mechanism replacing what might be characterised as the top-down, bureaucratic, civil service model. This raised important issues of financial control and accountability. It also raised a range of wider strategic issues of policy control and evaluation.

The origin and structure of TECs and emerging issues have been discussed elsewhere (Evans, 1990, 1992; Peck, 1991a, 1991b; Peck and Emmerich, 1991; Meager, 1991; Danson *et al*, 1992). Here, the focus is on issues relating to policy evaluation and accountability which the TEC

A version of this chapter first appeared in the *British Journal of Education and Work*, vol 5, no 3, pp 43-56.

initiative and the new relationship between TECs and the Employment Department brought to the fore.

Figure 1: **Major priorities for the 1990s**

Employers must invest more effectively in the skills their businesses need;

Young people must have the motivation to achieve their full potential and to develop the skills the economy needs;

Individuals must be persuaded that training pays and that they should take more responsibility for their own development;

People who are unemployed and those at a disadvantage in the jobs market must be helped to get back to work and to develop their abilities to the full;

The providers of education and training must offer high quality and flexible provision which meets the needs of individuals and employers;

Enterprise must be encouraged throughout the economy, particularly through the continued growth of small business and self-employment.

Source: Employment Department (1990) *1990s: The skills decade*.

The paper first identifies key features of the TEC initiative which relate in particular to evaluation; it discusses the role of evaluation as this has developed in the TEC context; and it discusses problems and issues which have arisen with the development of evaluation and evaluation strategy. This latter section draws in particular on the author's experience of working closely with TECs and the Employment Department Regional Office in the South West, providing support for the development of evaluation and evaluation research over a two-year period. It also draws more widely on extensive discussion of issues relating to evaluation with TEC personnel and the Employment Department nationally over this period.[1]

TEC structure and function

Turning first to key features of the TEC initiative relevant to the issue of evaluation, five broad principles for reform were set out in the initial government 'prospectus' on how it saw the TEC framework (Figure 2). These principles shaped the TEC system, emphasising in particular the shift in organisational structure, management and culture which the government was seeking to achieve.

Figure 2: Principles for reform

---

i. *A locally based system*

In a world which demands flexibility and innovation, national training and enterprise programmes need to be tailored to the needs of local labour markets ...

ii. *An employer-led partnership*

Within a broad national framework set by government, planning and management of enterprise and training need to shift from the public to the private sector. Employers are best placed to identify key skill needs and to ensure that the level and quality of training and business services meet those needs ... While employers will play a pre-eminent role, they must do so in the context of a partnership that is forged to pursue benefits for the whole community ...

iii. *A focused approach*

The boundaries that fragment training, vocational education and enterprise development must be tackled ... the TEC will focus its investment to secure the broader aims of community revitalisation and the best possible coordination of policies and programmes.

iv. *An accent on performance*

... better value for money, greater efficiency, and a higher return on our investment. The contract with each TEC will contain an incentive to achieve progressively better performance.

v. *An enterprise organisation*

Finally, a new kind of organisation will be needed, capable of driving radical reform ... an organisation, born of the enterprise culture, with a bold vision that stretches beyond existing programmes, institutions and traditional methods of delivery ...

Source: Employment Department (1989a) *Training and Enterprise Councils: a prospectus for the 1990s.*

TECs were to be locally-based and employer led. They were constructed out of the existing Training Agency Area Office structure, largely staffed, initially, by Employment Department staff on secondment. They were, however, intended to develop as new kinds of 'enterprise organisation' built around principles of performance, value for money and return on investment. They were established as independent companies, limited by guarantee, with private sector employer-dominated boards of directors. There was also an explicit strategy to import private sector management techniques and organisational culture into TECs in contrast to what was seen as the existing centralised, bureaucratic, civil service ethos.

TECs took over responsibility for existing national training and enterprise programmes including Youth Training, Employment Training, the Enterprise Allowance scheme and other programmes. They were also, however, charged with pursuing a broader set of national priorities (Figure 2) set by the Secretary of State for Employment. These were to form priorities for action and key issues for TECs to address and were reaffirmed and spelled out in more detail when the Secretary of State set out the government's priorities for 1992/93, *A strategy for skills* (Employment Department, 1991). TECs were, at the same time, to be locally focused. They were expected to tailor existing programmes and develop new initiatives to meet local needs. The TEC would, it was anticipated, act as "a catalyst for change within its community" (Employment Department, 1989a) and as "a vehicle to bring decision makers together in the interests of broader economic development and of creating active local leadership" (Employment Department, 1988). To this end, they were explicitly required (see below) to establish their own strategic objectives relating national priorities to local circumstances.

TECs operate in effect as intermediaries, under contract to the Employment Department to provide services as specified on behalf of the Department. Contracts set out in considerable detail the way in which services are to be provided, the management and monitoring information required by the Department and financial arrangements for payment against performance indicators. Actual provision of services is, in turn, largely contracted out by the TEC to organisations providing training, enterprise support or other services. This also generates a major demand for management information and monitoring in relation to service providers.

TECs are predominantly funded from the public sector, with the majority of this funding tied to continued provision of inherited national programmes, in particular Youth Training and Employment Training. There is an element of discretionary expenditure in the form of the Local Initiative Fund and they are free to spend any operating surpluses generated. Both allow a degree of innovation. They are, however, very limited by comparison with main programme funding. In keeping with the accent on performance, TEC funds are in part specifically output related, dependent on achieving targets set by the Employment Department. Output related funding is based on "quantitative outcome measures relating to target groups to be served such as qualifications to be obtained, acceptable job placement rates, business support activities and unit cost requirements" (Employment Department, 1988, p 42). Initially limited in scope, Output Related Funding will account for an increasing proportion of the total. As

Evans (1992) has described, however, funding as a whole was significantly cut back in late 1989 and only partially restored subsequently in the face of strong protest from the TECs. This further limited the scope for innovation and development.

With the launch of TECs, expectations were raised and high profile local employers signed up via boards of directors. The TECs were encouraged to set ambitious objectives and develop innovative plans and initiatives. In practice overall budgets remained tight and as described were in fact cut in the initial period, just as TECs were getting off the ground. Private sector funding which it was intended would supplement public finance failed, moreover, to materialise to any significant degree, in part because of the recession (Peck and Emmerich, 1991; Evans, 1992). As Evans and others describe (House of Commons, 1991a, 1991b; Peck and Emmerich, 1991; Evans, 1992), TECs also operate within the constraints of very detailed financial and contractual arrangements, structured, in particular, around the continuing requirement to run inherited national programmes. TECs themselves have argued vehemently both for additional funds and, equally, for greater freedom to pursue the objectives they have been encouraged to develop, particularly through the G10 group of leading TEC chairmen with direct access to the Employment Secretary (House of Commons, 1991a, 1991b). The capacity of TECs to pursue national priorities and their own strategic objectives as opposed to delivering national programmes in a way which is somewhat more flexible and appropriate, has therefore been severely limited. So, at one level, the TEC system represents a radical restructuring of the national infrastructure for training and enterprise support. There was, however, as many commentators have observed, a gap between the rhetoric and reality (Peck, 1991a, 1991b; Peck and Emmerich, 1991; Evans, 1992).

The role of evaluation

The organisational and managerial structure of TECs coupled with new roles and relations between TECs and the Employment Department brought to the fore issues of accountability and evaluation. Training and enterprise provision had previously been delivered through a bureaucratic, top-down departmental structure. TECs, however, though linked contractually with the Department and reliant on public funding were constituted as independent, decentralised and privatised bodies, encouraged - indeed required - to develop locally focused strategies and programmes. The nature of this relationship inevitably raised issues of control and accountability at a number of levels from finance and audit through to broad policy concerns. As the House of Commons Employment Committee concluded:

> There is an inherent tension between the desire to give independence to the TECs as local, market-led, employer run voluntary organisations and the need to provide a national service to the public and to industry and commerce. As more and more tasks involving public money are laid on TECs it is essential for means to be found to reconcile national objectives with local decision making. (House of Commons, 1991, p xiv)

For the Employment Department and ultimately the Treasury, there are clearly issues of financial accountability for the use of public funds. A major concern for TECs, on the other hand, has been the extent of the detailed and complex control which they experienced on a day-to-day basis (House of Commons, 1991, p vii). At a broader policy level there is the question of how to ensure that TECs pursue policy priorities. This is made more complex by the fact that such priorities include the objective that TECs should tailor provision to local needs - the government has explicitly sought to build in to the TEC system a greater degree of flexibility and autonomy. Implicit in this is the idea that TECs should establish their own priorities and objectives at the local level and, as described below, undertake their own evaluation of the extent to which these are achieved.

Detailed operating agreements specify monitoring information and performance indicators to be provided by TECs to the Employment Department, running to several pages of requirements. Payments are then made against a set of input and output measures. As Marquand (1991) has emphasised, however, the system of payment against performance indicators does not in itself ensure that TECs pursue broader objectives as set by the Secretary of State or measure the extent to which they contribute to meeting the objectives. Nor does it ensure that TECs themselves establish and pursue objectives which specifically relate to local needs or measure, in turn, the extent to which these local priorities are achieved. What this entails is the need for an effective framework for evaluation both in accountability terms as a means of demonstrating achievements and as a management tool in order to enhance performance. Given the nature of the relationship between itself and TECs the Employment Department was keen to ensure that an effective framework for evaluation was established which met these objectives. Evaluation was also seen as central to the management structure and organisational culture which the Government was seeking to establish in TECs themselves given the priority accorded to private sector management techniques, performance measures and value for money - it was seen as an essential management tool for TECs. For both these reasons, the requirement to establish strategies for evaluation was, therefore, explicitly built in to the TEC planning framework. This was done through the contractual arrangements established between the Department and TECs and the specific management structures TECs were required to establish.

Contracts with TECs are awarded and renewed against three-year corporate plans and annual business plans, negotiated with and approved by the Department. The Department issued guidance as to what it expected in terms of plan structure and content (Employment Department, 1989b). The Corporate Plan was to set out the TEC's overall 'mission'; 'three-year strategic objectives' setting out goals to be met in order to fulfil the TEC role in its mission statement; and a 'framework for action' setting out a plan to achieve the strategic objectives (Employment Department, 1989). The business plan would then set out detailed quantified and costed plans, targets and administrative arrangements. TECs were specifically required, as an integral part of their three-year corporate plan and framework for action, to establish an evaluation strategy:

> A systematic and comprehensive approach to evaluation is needed because it will provide a much fuller picture of progress towards objectives and the relevance of those objectives, than can be obtained from performance indicators alone. Each TEC will therefore need its own evaluation strategy which it will review and update annually. (Employment Department, 1989b, p 12)

Business plans were in turn required to set out in detail work related to evaluation to be undertaken over the year. The strategy as a whole would then be revised and rolled forward annually with the TEC planning cycle. Alongside the evaluation strategy, TECs were also required to develop strategies for quality management, marketing and promotion, and equal opportunities.

The two main purposes of the evaluation strategy were, according to the Employment Department, "to assist TECs in achieving their objectives as effectively and efficiently as possible" and "to enable them to account adequately for their expenditure of public money" (Employment Department, 1989, p 12), the first relating primarily to TECs themselves, the second to their relationship with the Department:

> Evaluation is a key management tool. It provides the means of assessing whether strategic objectives are being achieved and analysing obstacles to their achievement. It will also show the extent to which achievement of these objectives has actually helped to meet the needs of customers in the local community. (Employment Department, 1989b, p 12)

This emphasis on performance, targets, objective-setting and evaluation reflects, more generally, the principles which the government sought to establish in TECs. TECs were to an extent constructed out of the old Employment Department Area Office structure and, as Evans (1992) describes, largely staffed initially at least with secondees from the

Department. There was, however, a conscious strategy to establish private sector management techniques and organisational culture in TECs. To repeat from earlier:

> ... a new kind of organisation will be needed, capable of driving radical reform ... an organisation born of the enterprise culture, with a bold vision that stretches beyond existing programmes, institutions and traditional methods of delivery. (Employment Department, 1989a)

There was to be "an accent on performance" emphasising "better value for money, greater efficiency, and a higher return on our investment" (Employment Department, 1989a). This desire for a shift in organisational culture was reflected in the establishment of TECs as private companies with employer-led boards of directors and the sort of planning and strategic framework outlined above. There was also increasing recruitment from outside of the Department, particularly at more senior levels, mainly from the private sector. This included chief executives recruited in from the business sector in part as an explicit move to import private sector values in terms of management and organisational culture. The requirement to evaluate was thus built in to the structure of TECs in formal terms. It was reinforced, however, by the more general shift in organisational and management culture.

From an Employment Department perspective, evaluation is, then, a means of ensuring accountability to its broad policy objectives. It is also a management tool providing information as to how best to meet those objectives. The Department has a continuing concern with the extent to which national programmes, as delivered and modified by TECs, meet established objectives. It also has a longer-term concern to evaluate TECs as a delivery mechanism and the success of the TEC initiative as a whole.

From a TEC perspective, evaluation in part mirrors this. It is a means of demonstrating its achievements to the Employment Department on whom it is largely dependent for funds. It is also a form of accountability at the local level, a means of demonstrating achievements to local employers and other bodies in the local area whom it is seeking to influence and collaborate with; a means of legitimating its activities and enlisting support. Again, it is also a key management tool. It should provide information to help TECs both to review current programmes and initiatives and, at a strategic level, establish the extent to which they are meeting objectives. It should also allow TECs to review the extent to which their established objectives remain relevant. In the process, evaluation should, in theory, guide TECs in terms of any necessary revision of programmes and activities.

TECs were, therefore, required to establish and implement strategies for evaluation. This was seen by the Department as a necessary component of the new organisational and management structure it sought to create in TECs. It was also seen as an important element of the Department's continuing relationship with TECs. The form it took was, however, essentially a requirement for self-evaluation. The Department established the general requirement. It was the responsibility of individual TECs to devise an appropriate evaluation strategy and to agree this with the Department as part of its overall contract. Significantly as well, the Department provided little in the way of a blueprint or 'model' form of evaluation strategy as a guide for TECs or as a basis against which they themselves could assess evaluation strategies as proposed by individual TECs.

Evaluation strategies formed part of TEC corporate and business plans put to the Department as a basis for agreeing a contract and operating agreement. There was an element of negotiation over the form and content of plans - including those elements relating to evaluation - and the Department was able, therefore, to some extent to influence plans for evaluation on paper at least. Guidance provided by the Department remained, however, at a very general level. A good practice guide issued by the Department provided a definition of evaluation as "the explicit review of operations - to help make good plans, meet objectives and demonstrate achievements" observing that "each TEC will need to evaluate how far its activities actually contribute towards its aims and objectives" (Employment Department, 1990, p 3). Key questions, according to the good practice guide, related to the economy, efficiency and effectiveness of TEC operations and those of its contractors delivering products and services on its behalf; evaluation would assess TEC activities against its aims and objectives and ask how efficiently and effectively the TEC was meeting its strategic aims and objectives (Employment Department, 1990, pp 4-5).

Support was provided to TECs by Employment Department Head Office on a regional basis during and after the planning stage and contract negotiation with the Department. This helped to spell out at a general level a model of evaluation and the sort of questions which evaluation was expected to address. As indicated by the good practice guide, the Department generally adhered to a straight-forward rational planning model of evaluation with the emphasis on the 'three Es' of economy, efficiency and effectiveness, little different from a conventional Treasury-type of approach. Evaluation would draw on monitoring information and performance measures. It would also, however, draw on a wider range of information and research activity. A comprehensive approach would address individual programmes and initiatives to establish the extent to which they meet their internal objectives. It would also address the extent to which a TEC was meeting its overall aims and objectives (Employment Department, 1990).

As indicated, the model of evaluation supported by the Employment Department was generally a traditional, top-down, judgemental approach. Evaluation was seen as an integral part of the rational planning process set out in the guide to planning (Employment Department, 1989b) and represents only one of a number of possible models. It is close to what Guba and Lincoln (1989, p 30) term "third generation" evaluation in which "evaluation was characterised by efforts to reach judgements and in which the evaluator assumed the role of judge, while retaining the earlier technical and descriptive functions as well". This they contrast with "fourth generation" evaluation in which "the claims, concerns and issues of stakeholders serve as ... the basis for determining what information is needed"; evaluation is based more on negotiation between the main stakeholders in the policy rather than through a top-down, external and judgemental process.

The distinction between 'third' and 'fourth' generation evaluation is analogous to the distinction between 'positivist' approaches based around the traditional model of scientific explanation and emphasising quantitative measures of output and 'humanist' or interpretive approaches frequently based around qualitative approaches and emphasised by Patton (1987) - what Guba and Lincoln earlier term "naturalistic" as opposed to "scientific" approaches to evaluation (Guba and Lincoln, 1981). In practice there is a range of overlapping models. Doctors and Wokutch (1980), for example, distinguish between six broad types including social process audit, experimental and quasi-experimental design, goal-free evaluation, systems evaluation, cost-benefit analysis and accountability programme evaluation. Similar distinctions are drawn by Schneider (1986) and, more recently, Shefer and Kaess (1990).

Evaluation in practice

This final section looks at issues and problems which arose in practice in the development and implementation of evaluation strategy at TEC level. Here the analysis draws more directly on the author's experience of working closely with TECs over a period of two years, mainly in the south west region, in support of their development of evaluation strategy. Individual TECs have developed different approaches influenced in part by specific consultancy inputs and differences in relationships and negotiation with the Employment Department and regional support mechanisms across the country. Discussion with Employment Department staff from head office and with other TECs from outside of the south west supports the view, however, that the experience of TECs in the south west is not in any significant sense atypical. Findings and conclusions reported here are likely, therefore, to have more general validity.

An initial observation is that evaluation strategies, as agreed in the context of contract negotiations and set out in corporate and business plans, varied widely across different TECs. There were a number of reasons for this. First, as noted earlier, there was little in the way of formal guidance as to what an evaluation strategy should look like or any requirement for them to follow a common format. There was considerable scope, therefore, for variation dependent on the ideas and experience of TEC staff and whatever consultants or advisers they drew on. Second, because the Department itself had nothing in the way of a blueprint for evaluation strategy against which to assess evaluation frameworks as proposed by individual TECs, it was not in a position to impose a common format in the course of negotiation. Third, evaluation was only one of several elements of the overall planning framework which TECs were required to develop and negotiate and to do so under tight time constraints. The priority given to evaluation in this process varied. Finally, both the support and advice available to TECs and the more formal aspects of contract negotiation were organised on a regional basis. There was, therefore, an element of variation in Departmental guidance and influence between regions as to what was required in terms of an evaluation strategy.

The lack of formal guidance and extent of variation across TECs means that, in practical terms, there was considerable duplication of effort and inefficiency in the separate development of evaluation strategy by 82 different TECs. There were some opportunities for cross-fertilisation and learning but these were relatively limited. This was a penalty of the commitment to decentralisation and 'privatisation' noted earlier which constituted the TECs as independent organisations. This was reinforced by the organisational and management culture of TECs which sought to break away from the centralised, bureaucratic structures out of which they had been created.

This fragmentation had other consequences - beyond diseconomies and the limitations on learning or development of best practice. Priorities, methodologies and measures in terms of evaluation vary across TECs, even where they have been seeking to evaluate the same programmes or essentially the same objectives. This means there is little possibility for comparison between TECs. This is significant for TECs themselves - they have little opportunity to measure how well they are doing relative to other TECs or whether their own policies or procedures are more effective. It is significant as well from the Department's perspective. In terms of accountability, given the variation in individual strategies, TECs' own self-evaluation is less valuable for establishing the effectiveness of different TECs' pursuit of national policy and priorities. Nor will the aggregate output of TECs' own evaluation do much to help the government evaluate the effectiveness of the TEC initiative as a whole or the effectiveness of TECs as a delivery mechanism.

The Department did initiate work in 1991/92 on 'local environmental indicators'. The intention was to establish a set of indicators which would measure the degree of difficulty faced by different TECs in implementing policies - TECs in localities with high levels of unemployment, adverse industrial structure and poor economic growth prospects, for example, could not be expected to achieve as much as TECs in more favourable localities. In terms of actually measuring TEC performance, however, while the Department has a considerable volume of monitoring information relating to specific programmes, it does not have any consistent set of broader evaluation indicators of the extent to which TECs are meeting broader priorities and objectives. The Department continues to evaluate national programmes and initiatives and it has instituted evaluation work in relation to the TEC framework as a whole. This remains, however, somewhat piecemeal and fragmentary

Turning to the development of evaluation strategy at the TEC level itself, as emphasised earlier, evaluation was embedded in the formal planning process and contractual arrangements. While TECs had established plans for evaluation at the contract stage and set these out in strategic and business plans, these proved in practice to be little more than paper policies. They were adequate for the purposes of obtaining plan approval but there was little clear idea as to how to implement plans in practice and only limited organisational understanding of the issues or commitment to implementing an effective evaluation strategy. These issues only started to be thought through in any detail *after* TECs became operational. As Marquand (1991, p 8) has observed, TECs "found this one of their more difficult obligations to meet".

There were significant problems, initially at least, given that staff seconded from the Employment Department primarily at Area Office, lacked the experience and expertise needed to develop and implement evaluation and evaluation research. Responsibilities for different areas of work within TECs were frequently established relatively late on, after TECs became live. Few of those responsible for evaluation, moreover, had any specific expertise or experience relating to research and evaluation. Evaluation, as the literature makes clear, is in itself complex and technically difficult especially when it is intended to address broad objectives as well as specific programmes. To develop and implement the sort of strategies required of TECs needed, as well, considerable knowledge of labour market processes, information sources and research techniques - especially given the particular complexity and difficulties posed by the task. These were areas which largely lay outside of the experience of the initial TEC staff and which required rapid learning.

The strategy was frequently to engage outside consultants. The problem here was that consultants, too, were starting well down the learning curve on these issues. They themselves often lacked the skills or the combination of skills needed to develop appropriate, empirically grounded evaluation strategies. Where management consultants were taken on they tended to lack the necessary level of specific labour market and local economic skills and knowledge required. Those with more academic, labour market expertise tended to lack skills in relation to organisational development. It was apparent, as well, that while consultants might have the skills to undertake a review or assessment of issues, there was frequently a lack of expertise specifically in relation to setting up ongoing systems for evaluation. The very range of activities over which TECs operate compounded the problem.

The complexity of the issues caused major problems in terms of information sources and research methodology, particularly in relation to broader objectives. Thus it might have been possible to say something about the outputs from a specific TEC programme or initiative. It was much harder to establish effective mechanisms to measure the overall impact of the TEC on the local labour market or economy or the extent to which broad strategic objectives have been achieved. It is difficult, for example, to measure change over time in the survival and profitability of small firms, to distinguish the specific impact of the TEC from the range of other factors operating ('additionality') and to take account of any side-effects ('displacement'). Similar problems are faced in trying to determine, for example, the extent to which a TEC has encouraged greater investment in training by employers or raised the level of skills in the local labour market. In practice, evaluation can usually give some idea as to policy effectiveness but it will usually fall well short of the ideal model.

In part, these problems reflected the nature of the strategic objectives adopted by TECs. Ideally, strategic objectives should be 'SMART': specific, measurable, agreed upon, realistic and time-constrained. Few TEC strategic objectives matched up to these criteria and few were drawn up with evaluation in mind. It was difficult, therefore to draw up and implement an effective evaluation strategy. In practice, strategic objectives needed to be unpacked or refined in order to allow evaluation. This reflected the process through which objectives were drawn up. In theory, a TEC's own strategic objectives were to reflect a combination of national priorities as set by the Secretary of State modified in the light of the TEC's own assessment of the needs of the local economy and labour market. In practice, the rational, technical process implied by this played a relatively minor part. Objectives generally emerged out of a lengthy and complex process of discussion, debate and consultation among employers, advisers, potential TEC staff and other interested parties. This formed part of the process of organisational development and establishing local commitment to the TEC particularly on the part of employers and other board members.

Reflecting this, there was a lack of clarity, initially at least, in distinguishing between strategic level evaluation, programme level evaluation, performance indicators and monitoring against targets and milestones set out in action plans. The tendency was to focus more on monitoring and on the more immediately tangible and more readily measurable indicators. There was an operational rather than strategic focus to early TEC activity. In part this related to the technical problems mentioned above of evaluation in relation to broader objectives rather than more tangible and contained programmes. It also reflected the day-to-day concern with short-term, immediate performance indicators engendered by contractual and financial arrangements with the Employment Department. This was underlined by the fact that financial payments to the TEC are tied to such indicators. There was a major requirement as part of this, to provide the Department with detailed management information. Short-term information needs tended, therefore, to take precedence in management terms over longer-term evaluation and evaluation research. TECs, moreover, had a range of simultaneous and overlapping research and information needs. These related to marketing, product development, labour market assessment, quality assurance, and performance indicators and contract management - as well as to evaluation. In this context it was difficult to distinguish and prioritise the specific needs of evaluation, particularly given that these appeared to be rather less immediate than other needs in the initial period.

Underlining this, the priority demanded by day-to-day operational issues was generally, though with some exceptions, reflected in a lack of commitment to evaluation and evaluation strategy on the part of senior management and board members. It was not clear how it fitted in to immediate concerns and given the pressures under which TECs were operating. The result was that, without senior management support or priority at board level, evaluation tended to be marginalised in operational terms. Reflecting this there was frequently a failure, early on at least, to link evaluation back to policy review and strategic planning. This compounded the marginality of evaluation activity. For this reason it tended to be accorded a relatively low priority within the overall structure of TEC activity.

Evaluation tended, therefore, to develop and to feed back into TEC policy and strategy most effectively when taken up at senior management or board level. At the same time there was a need to enlist those managers responsible for programmes and initiatives at an operational level both in order to embed programme level evaluation firmly across the TEC and in order to make the links from the operational to the strategic level. Evaluation could not remain the responsibility of an isolated staff member or unit. It needed to be linked in to the organisational development of the TEC in terms of its structure and culture and in terms of the expertise and capacity of its personnel - something closer to Guba and Lincoln's fourth generation approach (1989). The difficulty, as already noted, was that operational staff were preoccupied with maintaining and developing initiatives on a day-to-day basis while coping with the demands of a shifting organisational and management environment, new operating procedures and new forms of relationship with the Employment Department.

Having said that, it has to be acknowledged that the capacity for significant change in policy or strategic direction remained limited by the inherited structure of national programmes the TECs were required to implement and by the financial constraints under which they operate. However effective the evaluation, any change could only be slow and relatively marginal. As noted earlier, the rhetoric of radical innovation was much greater than the reality. Evaluation tended, therefore, to be seen as of limited relevance and its development was frustrated. There was little incentive in any case for TECs to evaluate national programmes as inherited; it was self-evident to TECs that the inherited programmes had not been designed to meet national priorities as set out by the Secretary of State and they were far from the programmes TECs themselves might have designed to meet their own strategic objectives. Evaluation of national programmes against the Secretary of State's priorities or local strategic objectives was seen, therefore, as of little relevance.

Conclusion

The TEC initiative resulted in a radical restructuring of training provision and enterprise support across England and Wales. The new organisational and managerial principles around which TECs were structured and the new relationship between TECs and the Employment Department brought to the fore issues of accountability and evaluation. TECs were required by the Employment Department to set out their plans for evaluation as an integral part of the initial planning process. Evaluation was to be a key management tool for TECs. It was also to be an important means of ensuring accountability in policy terms, ensuring that TEC activities were directed to achieving agreed priorities and objectives. Strategies for evaluation were, accordingly, drawn up in negotiation with the Employment Department and incorporated into TECs' corporate and business plans.

Subsequently, however, TECs experienced considerable difficulty in translating paper policies into practical strategies and action. There was also considerable variation in approaches to evaluation across different TECs. TECs clearly found this one of the more difficult of their requirements to meet. There were a number of different reasons for this. There were problems initially in terms of the skills and experience of staff charged with developing evaluation strategy, which use of outside consultants and advisers only partially solved. The technical issues involved in establishing a comprehensive strategy relating both to programmes and to broader objectives were in any case considerable, not helped by the nature of TECs' own objectives which had rarely been drawn up with evaluation in mind. Evaluation in relation to longer-term strategic objectives tended to get marginalised by very real short-term operational pressures, with little priority given to evaluation by senior management and board members or by operational staff concerned with day-to-day running of programmes.

The development of evaluation, in practice, cannot be understood simply in operational or technical terms. It reflected as well more structural factors. Autonomy and independence as opposed to bureaucratic, centralised control are inherent in the TEC framework. It was impossible, therefore, to impose in any great detail a requirement for evaluation or indeed to support its development except in a relatively low key fashion. TECs' contractual and financial constraints and the extent to which they were tied to delivering existing programmes, moreover, severely limited their capacity to pursue broader priorities and objectives. There was little incentive, therefore, to develop elaborate evaluation strategies focused on these broader strategic aims.

Note

1. The author worked as an independent regional adviser, supporting the development of evaluation strategy in TECs and TEED Regional Office in the South West Region, funded by the Employment Department: Training, Enterprise and Education Directorate. Thanks are due to the many TEC and TEED staff with whom I worked over this period. I remain, however, fully responsible for the views expressed in this chapter.

References

Danson, M.W., Lloyd, M.G. and Newlands, D. (1992) 'Privatism in business development and training: a new approach', *British Journal of Education and Work*, vol 5, no 3, pp 7-15.

Doctors, S.I. and Wokutch, R.E. (1980) 'Social program evaluation: six models', *New Directions for Program Evaluation* 7, London: Jossey-Bass.

Employment Department (1988) *Employment for the 1990s*, Cmnd 540, London: HMSO.

Employment Department (1989a) *Training and Enterprise Councils: a prospectus for the 1990s*, London: Employment Department.

Employment Department (1989b) *Training and Enterprise Councils: guide to planning*, London: Employment Department.

Employment Department (1990) *1990s: the skills decade*, London: Employment Department.

Employment Department (1991) *A strategy for skills*, London: Employment Department.

Evans, R. (1990) 'Training and Enterprise Councils - an initial assessment', *Regional Studies*, vol 25, no 2, pp 173-84.

Evans, R. (1992) 'Strategic development issues facing TECs in the north west', *British Journal of Education and Work*, vol 5, no 3, pp 17-41.

Guba, E.G. and Lincoln, Y.S. (1981) *Effective evaluation*, San Francisco: Jossey-Bass.

Guba, E.G. and Lincoln, Y.S. (1989) *Fourth generation evaluation*, London: Sage.

House of Commons (1991a) Report and Proceedings, House of Commons Employment Committee, *House of Commons Papers* 285-I, 24 July, London: HMSO.

House of Commons (1991b) Minutes of evidence, House of Commons Employment Committee, *House of Commons Papers* 285-II, 24 July, London: HMSO.

Main, D. (1990), 'Training and Enterprise Councils: an agenda for action', *Regional Studies*, vol 24, no 1, pp 69-71.

Marquand, J. (1991), 'Evaluation, decentralisation and accountability: the case of the British Training and Enteprise Councils (TECs)', conference paper, mimeo.

Meager, N. (1991), 'TECs: a revolution in training and enterprise, or old wine in new bottles', *Local Economy*, vol 6, no 1, pp 4-20.

Patton, M.Q. (1987) *How to use qualitative methods in evaluation*, London: Sage.

Peck, J. (1991a), 'The politics of training in Britain: contradictions in the TEC initiative', *Capital and Class*, vol 44, pp 23-34.

Peck, J. (1991b), 'Letting the market decide (with public money): Training and Enterprise Councils and the future of labour market programmes', *Local Economy*, vol 6, no 4, pp 4-17.

Peck, J. and Emmerich, M. (1991), *Challenging the TECs: first year interim report of the CLES TEC/LEC monitoring project*, Manchester: Centre for Local Economic Strategies.

Schneider, A.L. (1986), 'The evolution of a policy orientation for evaluation research: a guide to practice', *Public Administration Review*, July/August, pp 356-63.

Shefer, D. and Kaess, L. (1990), 'Evaluation methods in urban and regional planning', *Town Planning Review*, vol 61, no 1, pp 75-88.

CHAPTER 20

THE SOCIAL CHARTER AND THE EUROPEANISATION OF EMPLOYMENT AND SOCIAL POLICY

KEVIN DOOGAN

Introduction

In Britain much of the political debate about European integration has been couched in terms of external pressures and internal consequences. In some circles the assumption underlying the 'conveyor belt' towards federalism is that integration is an act that is being perpetrated against the British. Gravitational forces, the creation of a foreign bureaucracy, are pulling the British people and their institutions towards the centre of Europe. The public is left with the strong impression that either overtly, through the imposition of foreign standards and the exercise of supra-national authority, or covertly, 'through the back door', a foreign ideology is being visited upon the good citizens of this country. Rarely is there expressed the view that the European Community, with its laws and procedures, is something that British institutions take an active part in building.

In this respect there is a curious overlap in the perceptions of Euro sceptics and Euro enthusiasts. While sceptics rail against alien custom and practice, enthusiasts talk of importing better continental standards and conditions and anticipate the benign impact of supra-national legislation. Nowhere are these perceptions more apparent than in the social dimension debates. On one side of the discussion of the Social Charter there are impassioned pleas decrying foreign intrusion and meddling, whilst others await longingly the social advancement that will attend the arrival of continental rights and entitlements.

The purpose of this paper is to contribute to redressing the imbalances of the political debate and to discuss policy making, in large part as an endogenous process, in which different EC policy concerns are internalised and brought onto the domestic agenda. It is also hoped that an examination of the controversies surrounding the Social Charter will provide insights into the contradictory process of European integration and enhance the understanding of the 'Europeanisation' of domestic policy making. This paper looks at the scope and legal basis of the Charter and its Action

---

This chapter first appeared in *Policy and Politics*, 1992, vol 20, no 3, pp 167-76.

Programme and the institutional framework that provides the context for its implementation. It then goes on to consider the elements of an assessment of its possible impact on domestic employment and social policy.

The scope of the Social Charter

It is worth remembering that in the moves towards the completion of the Single European Market (SEM) a 'social dimension' was identified in three ways. In the first instance the project of establishing a single market within the twelve member states, constituted by the free movement of goods, services and people, demanded the integration of both capital and labour markets. Accordingly it was contended there were economic and social aspects to European integration. Secondly, it was argued that the appeal of a new European Community had to be based upon a broader sentiment than simply the economic interests of industrialists and consumers. The benefits of SEM should appear to accrue to all social groups within the Community. Finally, and more specifically, the need to provide assurances of the benefits of European integration to trades unions, many of whom were previously wedded to ideas of protectionism and attracted to import controls, added another impetus to the development of employment and social policy in the Community. For as Delors argued, during the process of economic restructuring the Charter's "sole object is to provide a formal reminder that the Community has no intention of sacrificing fundamental workers rights on the altar of economic efficiency" (Jacques Delors, Bruges, 17 October 1989). Therefore, if the advance towards SEM was to proceed with a sense of 'partnership', however defined, the employment and social rights of the Community's workforce had to be preserved and enhanced in the process.

The most visible expression of commitment to the social dimension by the architects of SEM is the Social Charter - The Community Charter of Fundamental Rights of Workers - adopted at the Strasbourg summit 9 December 1989. It constitutes a set of solemn declarations in respect of a number of 'basic social rights'. These include the following.

i. *Freedom of movement*, in which workers in the EC shall have the right of freedom of movement throughout the community.

ii. *Employment and remuneration*, in which any citizen of the Community has the right to employment and fair remuneration for their efforts with a 'decent basic wage'.

iii. *Improvement of living and working conditions*, in which the development of SEM aims to secure the harmonisation and improvement of working and living conditions of EC citizens.

iv. *Social protection*, which entitles EC citizens, regardless of status, to adequate social protection and the means of subsistence.

v. *Freedom of association and collective bargaining*, recognises the right of workers to join, or not to join, trades unions and professional associations, in defence of their economic and social interests and the right to conclude collective agreements.

vi. *Vocational training*, in which public authorities, companies and social partners are called upon to ensure the rights of workers to continue their vocational training throughout their working lives.

vii. *Equal treatment for men and women*, which calls for the intensification of efforts to ensure the equality of treatment and opportunity for men and women particularly in regard to access to employment, social protection, education, training and career development.

viii. *Worker information, consultation and participation*, in which employees are entitled to be informed 'and even consulted' on major events affecting their companies likely to have an impact on their working conditions and employment continuity. It is intended that this will have specific effects in companies operating in several member states.

ix. *Health and safety protection at the workplace*, acknowledges that every worker has the right to satisfactory health and safety conditions at his or her workplace and implies further harmonisation and improvement of conditions in each member state.

x. *Protection of children and adolescents*, aims to secure a minimum working age for young people in the Community and gives young people in employment the right to a fair wage and offers entitlement to two years training after compulsory education.

xi. *Elderly people*, upon retirement all people are to be entitled to a pension enabling the maintenance of a decent standard of living or the right to a minimum income, social protection and social and medical assistance

xii. *Disabled people*, in which people with disabilities are entitled to additional measures to improve their social integration and rehabilitation particularly in relation to their employment, housing and mobility.

From the list above it can be seen that the Charter maps out a formidable area of policy making in which to establish social and employment rights. However the range of issues covered should not obscure significant omissions. The Community's 15 million unemployed, of whom roughly half are long-term unemployed, fail to provide a focus for policy making in this arena. This is at odds with the priority status of long-term unemployment as one of the five objectives of the operation of the structural funds. It is more than a little surprising that treatment of their specific needs in re-entering the workforce should not be deemed an entitlement under the terms of the Charter. Arguably this neglect, however, is less significant than the treatment of migrants and the absence of attention to labour market discrimination on the grounds of race. In regard to the latter the introduction to the Action Programme states in somewhat muted tones that "while the Commission is not making any proposal in respect of discrimination on the grounds of race, colour and religion, it none the less stresses the need for such practices to be eradicated". In the hierarchy of policy objectives it would appear that the interrelated concerns of migrants and racial discrimination had slipped off the agenda. This is all the more surprising when considered against objective need and indeed when consideration is given to the prominence of concern for migrants and their experience in the labour market in earlier Commission publications. For instance, in the quaintly titled *The common market and the common man* (Commission of the European Communities, 1969), migration was one of the major issues in the discussion of social policy in the European Community. In the first set of proposals for immediate action arising out of the Social Action Programme of 1973 migrants were in the forefront of policy deliberations and merited a specific action programme to cater for their needs. Even as late as 1983, EC social policy significantly referred to migrants, emphasising the concern for "integrating migrant workers and their families into working and social life" (Commission of the European Communities, 1983). However, in the discussions of *1992: the social dimension* (Commission of the European Communities, 1990a) they received barely a mention and were not discussed at all in other publications such as *A human face for Europe* (Commission of the European Communities, 1990b). As regards the Charter, EC thinking on the issue was spelled out in the general introduction to the subject:

> The Commission will closely follow the development of all the problems concerning the beneficiaries of free movement and the social security of migrant workers. It intends to return to this matter at a later stage but considers that the proposals submitted to the Council satisfy the main preoccupation in this area. (Buron, 1990 p 61)

The fact that labour market discrimination on the basis of race and ethnicity, and that the rights of migrant workers fell outside of the 'main preoccupations' of employment and social discussion in EC circles represented a short-sightedness of considerable proportions. Indeed with the possibility of mass migration from Northern Africa and from Eastern and Central Europe this lack of vision may be sorely regretted in future discussion in the Council of Ministers.

The legal basis of the Charter and the Action Programme

The legal basis of the Charter and its provision is the subject of some considerable dispute. In the first instance it is difficult to locate the Charter in the armoury of legal provisions at the disposal of the Commission. It falls outside the two groups of measures, one of which is legally binding and takes the form of regulations, decisions and directives and the other set of Community instruments which are not legally binding including memoranda, communications, opinions, recommendations and resolutions. The measures of the Social Charter's Action Programme which was produced to give effect to the declarations of the Charter are more easily classified. The programme involved a package of some 47 proposals which in 1992 were at various stages in the process of formulation, consultation and negotiation. Approximately half of the Action Programme measures was to be non-legislative and half was to involve new legislative measures of differing legal status. In all they comprised 23 directives (specifying outcomes but not process) in the social field, including 11 in the field of health and safety and 5 measures described as 'Community instruments'. There were, in addition, 5 recommendations and 20 other measures. They also varied in the specificity and generality of their application. Some health and safety directives referred to minimum requirements for medical assistance on board vessels, open cast mining and asbestos, whereas of more widespread significance were the directives relating to working time, proof of employment contract and entitlements to maternity leave (COM 89; Confederation of British Industry, 1990). The basis within the Treaty of Rome, upon which each legal measure was founded has also been hotly contested. For instance, employment protection legislation requires unanimous approval in the Council of Ministers, compared to health and safety measures which require only qualified voting majorities to secure their passage. In employers' circles the view has been expressed that some initiatives requiring unanimous approval might be passed through on the back of health and safety (Article 118a), or measures necessary for the completion of the internal market (Article 100a), requiring only qualified voting majorities (Confederation of British Industry, 1989).

The development of the Social Charter and the Action Programme has aroused considerable controversy and provides the focus for a debate which continues, albeit in a more relaxed manner, with the emergence of the draft directives arising out of the Action Programme. Significantly however, at various stages in the Charter's development and implementation, different sets of concerns have been expressed and different groups have displayed their anxieties about its possible implications for employment policy in each member state. A brief review of the history of the Charter reveals the high profile and low profile of policy development and the shifting sets of expectations that have been evoked by its passage.

A brief history of the Social Charter

It is possible to break down the development of the Social Charter into distinct phases marked by particular events. The genesis of the Charter dates, in some accounts, from a Belgian initiative at the Council of Ministers for Social Affairs in May 1987 which decided to examine "the basic social rights of workers which cannot be called into question by the pressures of competition and by the search for competitiveness" (Teague, 1989). The following May, at the 1988 European Trade Union Confederation (ETUC) conference in Stockholm, Jacques Delors referred to a 'platform' which could be negotiated between the two sides of industry and then adopted by Community law. In addition he discussed the recognition of rights to vocational training by all Community wage earners and of the creation of the European company as a legal entity, the operating rules of which would ensure workers' participation in the decision-making process (Commission of the European Communities, 1988). Later in the autumn of 1988 the Commission sought the opinion of the Economic and Social Committee as to the scope and content of these rights and to suggest the appropriate method for their development and implementation.

The policy development process, from the ETUC conference in 1988 to ratification in Strasbourg in December 1989, may be characterised as a period of high expectation of the Social Charter. Some of the earlier literature produced by the Commission reflected these ambitions describing the Charter's role in ushering a new Europe as a "new social area", an "area of solidarity", a Europe committed to the promotion of equality between men and women (Venturini, 1989). The Hanover summit of June 1988 agreed that the "single market must be conceived in such a way as to benefit all people" . The subsequent Madrid summit considered that in completing the internal market, social aspects should be given the same importance as economic aspects and should accordingly be developed in a balanced fashion (NALGO, 1990). In line with the Madrid thinking the employment and social affairs commissioner Papandreou argued forcibly that social policy did not take second place to economic policy and that social objectives were not secondary to economic objectives:

> Let us be quite clear we are not advocating a social dimension so as to give us a good conscience or to demonstrate to the workers and citizens of Europe that we have a social concern -

> that of alleviating the harshness of economic and social development. Bringing about the social dimension should not be a rescue operation and we are not playing the role of 'Red Cross' on the battlefield. The social dimension is not some kind of sweet to be offered at the end of the meal; it is an integral part and parcel of the internal market and of building up the Community. (Papandreou, 1989)

Of course where expectations were high in some circles the reservations and indeed opposition grew in other parts of the Community. The stage was then set for the Strasbourg summit in December 1989 where the UK opposition to the Charter denied its unanimous adoption at the heads of state conference. Although Mrs Thatcher was alone in declining support for the Charter at the conference it is argued that reservations about its impact were by no means confined to the UK government (Rhodes, 1991). Moreover the disagreements so visibly expressed at Strasbourg may have served to obscure the drafting changes that had been made over previous months in the process of achieving pan-European consensus. Blackwell (1990) has noted:

> By contrast with an earlier draft, dated early October 1989, the provisions in the Charter adopted in December 1989 have been weakened, and more emphasis is now placed on the responsibility of the individual member states and the two sides of industry. For instance a passage which said 'a decent wage shall be established, particularly at the level of the basic wage' has been deleted; proposed improvements to maximum duration of working time and weekend working, night work, shift work and systematic overtime have been deleted. Draft rights to 'adequate levels of social security benefits proportional, where appropriate, to length and service of pay and to their financial contribution to the appropriate social protection system' have been changed to 'shall enjoy an adequate level of social security benefits'. (Blackwell, 1990, p 360)

From the European Parliament the reaction to the adoption of the final version of the Charter was deeply critical. The MEP Martine Bourne, a member of the Committee on Social Affairs and rapporteur on the Charter of Basic Social Rights complained that "the very content and text adopted by the eleven member states seems to be distinctly inadequate and of a tone which weakens its message considerably, so there is a great concern about the effectiveness of this declaration of principles". However, not only was the European Parliament disappointed in the redrafting process, their exclusion from the consultation procedures deeply offended their constitutional sensibilities and raised hostilities to the legal form and content of the Action Programme. So much so that the majority grouping in the Parliament even discussed the use of their power of censure to sack the Commission.

Following the announcement of the Action Programme the Commission released for consultation a number of draft directives covering part-time and temporary work, working time, the protection of pregnant women at work, health and safety on construction sites, the control of asbestos, and the form of proof of employment relationship. Often the release of directives confirmed earlier anxieties in government and employers' circles that employment protection legislation, requiring unanimous support from the member states, was being passed through on the back of health and safety measures that simply required qualified voting majorities. In the meantime government departments were busy assessing the costs of implementation of measures each of which was the subject of extensive consultation between the Union of Industrial and Employers Confederations of Europe (UNICE), the European Trade Union Confederation (ETUC), the Economic and Social Committee (ECOSOC) and a wide range of other interested parties.

Subsidiarity, controversy and diversity

Previously the notion of 'complementarity' had been built into the assumptions upon which EC employment and social policy making would be developed. Thus "what is best done at the local, regional or national level must not be undertaken at the Community level. The Commission must only enact those regulations that are essential" (Jacques Delors, Cologne, 23 September 1988). Such an approach to policy formulation was taken one step forward in the discussion of the implementation of the principles of the Charter. Critically this refers to the principle of subsidiarity, which not only provides for different levels of intervention from Community level to the member state, with the latter given priority, but also for legally binding and collective negotiated agreements. The Action Programme states in paragraph 3:

> In accordance with the principle of subsidiarity whereby the Community acts when the set objectives can be reached more effectively at its level than that of the member states, the Commission proposals relate to only part of the issues raised in certain articles of the draft Charter. The Commission takes the view that responsibility for the initiatives to be taken as regards the implementation of social rights lies with the member states, their constituent parts, or the two sides of industry as well as within the limits of its powers with the European Community. (COM(89)568, p 4)

In providing a set of implementation principles this formulation throws open a number of issues to do with the competence or appropriateness of the level of government intervention from supra-national to local government. The term 'subsidiarity' has been much debated. The summary report of the Select Committee on European Communities argued that "subsidiarity is a word with no meaning in English (except for those well versed in the social philosophy of the Roman Catholic Church)"(House of Commons, 1991). By its very nature it is a term that is open to many interpretations. Thus central government stresses that responsibility for policy making resides with the member state government, and only in the last instance with the Community. However in similar vein local and regional government are keen to stress that subsidiarity means that the business of government is best conducted at the lowest level, ie nearest to the electorate. It must also be stressed, amidst the debate about appropriate government, that in connection with employment and social policy, the principle of subsidiarity also confirms that there are two viable routes to take in a legislative or a collective bargaining approach towards social policy objectives.

As a mechanism of trans-European labour market integration and regulation the Charter has been reduced in significance by the adoption of subsidiarity principles. Staedelin, a rapporteur for the opinion on the Basic Social Rights asks "why use the instruments provided for by the Treaties in the fields of agriculture, finance, tax, standardization and competition and devise a special less binding fate for the social aspect?" (Staedelin, 1990). Furthermore the policy areas in which Community legislation is necessary is open to interpretation. UNICE, for instance, contend that on a quick count some eight to ten measures belong outside the Community's sphere of influence.

Rather than discussing each directive in turn this paper seeks to address the basis for controversy and tension in the development and implementation of the Social Charter. For it is not the case that the reluctance to embrace the concept of employment and social rights has a single source within the Community. Nor has there been a common set of concerns expressed in the harmonisation of the labour market in the Community. In some circles, particularly amongst trades union leaders of northern member states, there is disquiet about the prospects of 'social dumping' arising out of the downward pressure on labour costs and social protection that might evolve from labour market deregulation and the completion of SEM. In other quarters reservations are expressed about the operating restrictions and costs imposed upon employers as witnessed in the CBI comments, "The benefits of European integration could be all too easily realised elsewhere if we are more concerned with rights than with duties, preoccupied with the distribution of wealth rather than its creation" (Banham, 1989, 1991). On a more overtly political note, the opposition to the Charter of new right commentators is evident in Lingle's warnings against its implicit social democratic ideology, and the dangers it contains of bureaucratisation and social regulation (Lingle, 1991).

This paper argues that there is a tension at the heart of the SEM project. In the first instance it must be stressed that the integration of capital and product markets is of a different nature to the integration of labour markets. In short the harmonisation of the market for goods and services is driven by a process of deregulation, whereas in sharp contrast labour market integration involves a programme of regulation. In a concrete sense the integration process is moving in opposite directions in different markets. Secondly, the institutional arrangements that govern the development of employment and social policy are extremely diverse and are deeply entrenched within the traditions, culture and history of different member states and are resistant to substantial reorganisation.

Deregulation of the market for goods and services, *inter alia*, removes the state protection of industry, unfair competition arising from the use of public subsidy and seeks to expose public procurement practices to the full force of competition. By curtailing the role of government in the economy the industries of the community will be compelled to operate at greater levels of efficiency necessary to compete in the expanded market. Deregulation has consequences for all parties within industry, removing state involvement from the realm of the employer and employee.

By contrast the harmonisation of the European labour markets within member states involves the government and/or the social partners in the establishment of mutually recognisable standards and entitlements. The Commission seeks to reduce the prospect of bidding down wages and conditions through a fair wage policy and seeks guarantees of workers access to the decision-making and consultation process. In short, EC policy seeks to reconcile the protection of workers in the process of increasing industrial competition, at the same time as it seeks to remove the state protection of industries in order to permit the further expression of market forces. Rhodes describes this tension for social policy making and labour market regulation thus:

> For while the logic of monetary union and market restructuring make a 'social dimension' politically desirable, they also make it difficult to achieve. Right from the start, it was clear that, whether they derived from innovations in EC legislation or from European 'social dialogue', the new rules of the 'social dimension' would be far from constraining, due to political opposition and the incompatibility of strong social and labour market regulation with the essentially liberal market logic of the 1992 programme. (Rhodes, 1991, pp 257)

In addition to reconciling the divergence of integrative processes, the harmonisation of labour market conditions and employment practices is also made difficult by the diverse nature of industrial relations and social protection operating within the Community. The role of government in industry, the form and extent of 'social partnership' in each country, and the diversity of collective bargaining structures, organised on either a national, sectoral, regional or company basis all govern the form and extent of the implementation of the Charter's objectives.

Due, Madsen and Jensen (1991) have usefully described the existence of three traditions of labour market regulation in the EC, namely the Roman-Germanic system, the Anglo-Irish system and the Nordic system. The Roman-Germanic system, found in countries such as Belgium, France, Germany, Greece, Italy, Luxembourg and the Netherlands, operates with the state occupying a central role in industrial relations. The constitutions of each of these countries provide a core of fundamental rights and freedoms that lie at the heart of their industrial relations systems. This system is also distinguished by a comprehensive set of labour market regulations governing various areas, such as the length of the working day, rest periods, workers' representation etc. The Anglo-Irish system, by contrast, offers a very limited role to the state in industrial relations. It is a voluntarist system, in which the state only regulates in highly selective fashion the rights and obligations arising from contractual relations. The Nordic system similarly affords a limited role to the state, but rests upon an extensive set of labour market agreements negotiated between unions and employers' associations. These negotiations have laid the basis for a 'permanent', 'basic' agreement that is the heart of the institutional framework of Nordic labour markets

More specifically a number of issues reveal the heterogeneity of industrial relations and social protection systems. For instance the minimum wage policies at work across member states reveal differences in standards and in enforcement systems. A brief survey of European systems shows the range of minimum wage regimes and begins to illustrate the difficulties of establishing pan-European minimum wage policies:

> Of the twelve member states of the EC, five (France, Luxembourg, the Netherlands, Portugal and Spain) have statutory national minimum wages varying in their application by age of worker of 18 to 23; two, Belgium and Greece, have a general minimum wage set by collective agreement at national level. In the remaining five countries, minimum rates of pay are set either by collective agreement at industry level (Denmark, West Germany or Italy) or only for certain industries through special bodies. The latter is the case in Ireland and the UK, where Joint Labour Committees and Wages Councils respectively operate. (Blackwell, 1990)

In the sphere of social protection there is a similar variation in the organisation, philosophy and the extent of income maintenance systems. Historically, the organising principles on which social protection systems in Europe are founded differ significantly between member states, most notably between the Beveridge and Bismarckian principles of income maintenance (Le Grand, 1991). They also vary in the extent of employers' social insurance provision. The social security costs of employers range from 4% and 7% of total labour costs in Denmark and the UK to 22% and 31% in Belgium and Italy respectively.

Finally, the structure of the workforce describes different patterns of participation, demography and working arrangements. Thus the Commission reference to 'atypical' in its earlier directives caused not inconsiderable annoyance in member states where large numbers of workers are employed on a part-time or temporary basis. It may make some sense to talk of atypical in Italy where women part-timers represent 10% of employed women, but in Holland where nearly 60% of employed women work part-time it is illogical to describe workers in this manner. The distribution of temporary workers is similarly uneven and the range of restrictions on temporary work varies widely between member states. In Denmark, Ireland and Luxembourg there are virtually no restrictions on temporary work; in West Germany some restrictions apply whereas in Belgium temporary work is only permitted in certain circumstances (Teague and Grahl, 1991).

The diverse character of industrial relations and social protection systems determines that employment and social policy objectives are concerned with ends rather than means, with outcomes rather than process. The Social Charter does not compel a uniformity of approach nor does it seek to create a "level playing field" of the European labour market (Teague and Grahl, 1991). It deals with relative categories and not absolute categories, seeking, for instance, to maintain a fair wage in each member state rather than a trans-European minimum income. For this reason Due, Madsen and Jensen are quite perceptive when they argue:

> the proposals are not intended to create a parity of convergence between the schemes operating in various countries. Thus there will not be uniform notice of dismissal for part-time workers in Germany, France, Italy etc. The contents [of the proposals] thus involve an attempt to create harmonisation within the boundaries of the individual member state (of the conditions pertaining to part-time and full-time employees), rather than the attempt to create intra-Community convergence. (Due *et al*, 1991, p 99)

It therefore seems reasonable that the 'principle of subsidiarity', upon which the development of the Action Programme is based, does not only represent an expediency of employment and social policy. It is not simply a pragmatism which reduces the effect of contentious issues and reduces the annoyance of unsympathetic government. In view of the heterogeneous nature of systems described above it is difficult to imagine the implementation of the Action Programme on any other basis than subsidiarity principles. This is not to argue that the principles of subsidiarity remove controversy from employment and social policy discussion in Europe. The 'competence' of different levels of government and the role of the social partners in 'co-determination' have been the subject of a vigorous debate across the Community and will continue until a common position is reached on the final directive of the Action Programme.

Assessing the impact of the Social Charter

In terms of the factors identified at the beginning of this paper that have given momentum to the development of the Social Charter what can be said about its possible impact? Obviously there is enough evidence available to inform a minimalist perspective.

> What could the workers worried about the acceleration in the restructuring of the undertakings and services at European Scale, and in anguish about the threats of delocalization, 'social dumping' and dismantling the structure of labour law, expect from yet another 'solemn declaration'? (Buron, 1990, p 15)

This point of view must have some substance particularly in light of the pre-existence of the Council of Europe's Social Charter and the conventions established by the International Labour Organisation both of which have had little bearing upon employment and industrial relations practice in Europe (Blackwell, 1990). The extent, therefore, to which the Charter can act as a some kind of legal guarantor of workers rights during the anticipated programme of economic restructuring is significantly limited and particularly so in Britain. The key issue will be the domestic impact on employment and industrial relations policy. Obviously the precise implications are unpredictable in the sense that the directives arising out of the Charter await full development and adoption. It is also difficult to deduce from the text of the directive the concrete application in employment and social policy. Once common positions are secured and directives adopted in national legislation, or agreement reached in collective bargaining, evaluation will remain difficult. Enforcement procedures and mechanisms await discussion and hence final impacts and outcomes remain highly speculative. The Maastricht Summit held in December 1991 also had an important bearing on future developments as preparatory negotiations on the Social Chapter promised further controversy.

Most commentators have sought to explore the legal consequences of EC policy development in the field of employment and social policy. As stressed at the beginning of the paper, there is a preoccupation with the implications of supra-national policy making. In the British case at least this is particularly short-sighted. Two points are worth re-emphasising. In the first instance the principles of subsidiarity imply two means of implementing policy objectives, one being legislative and the other being collective agreements established between the two sides of industry. Thus in the three models of labour market regulation outlined above, with the Anglo-Irish system of labour market regulation according little importance to government intervention, the non-legislative implications of the Charter take on a special significance. The analysis must move on to the uncertain terrain of deregulated industrial relations in which bargaining power is a critical determinant of policy outcomes. It must also consider the political balance of forces and the ideological predisposition of political parties and employers and union organisations.

There have also been a number of unforeseen outcomes as a result of the Charter. No-one had predicted that the British Labour Party would abandon its traditional support for the closed shop on the pretext of some adherence to the principles of the Charter. Equally surprising, however, was the rush of enthusiasm exhibited by the Boilermakers Union which, in the month following Strasbourg, issued its 30,000 shop stewards with an action guide to force companies to implement the terms of the Social Charter (*Financial Times*, 1990). The response of employers has also sometimes been unpredictable. Reports of a U-turn in the approach of UNICE to the Social Charter described the employers considering a retreat on their traditional opposition to collective European agreement with trades unions. In preference to the Commission establishment of legally binding agreements in Community-wide undertakings, UNICE has sought to outflank the Commission and set up its own agreements with the unions. "Given a choice between being shot at dawn and life imprisonment, imprisonment begins to look like an acceptable option" (*Guardian*, 1991). Finally, the opportunism of the British government is worthy of special mention. While voicing implacable opposition to foreign intrusion in domestic employment matters, particularly in relation to the working time directive, complaining of the additional costs imposed on industry and the consequent loss of jobs, the government has shown that its opposition is not impartial. Thus the energy secretary told the House of Commons in November 1991 that he intended to repeal the 1908 Coal Mines Regulation Act, which prohibits working more than a seven and a half hour shift, to allow miners to work shift up to thirteen hours, in order "to bring legislation in line with the European directive on working hours" (*Observer*, 1991).

The assessment of the 'non-legislative impacts' of the Social Charter and the Action Programme is also presented with the difficulty of disentangling the European from the domestic shifts in policy making. When there is convergence of national and EC policy objectives, as in the realms of health and safety or in training and education, the influence of the EC on the member state is directly related to the influence of the member state on EC policy. It becomes impossible to discuss more than the mutual reinforcement of employment policy making nationally and in the community as a whole. This however is not without significance.

In recent years the march of the British Labour Party to the centre ground of British politics has been facilitated to some considerable extent by the reversal of policy position in respect of the EC. As the *Guardian* has suggested, the Labour Party has "endorsed the Social Charter as part of its march to European style social democracy" (*Guardian*, 15 August 1991). In respect of the Labour Party Bridgeford and Stirling have pointed out:

> Europe has provided a useful taking off point for many of its employment policy proposals. ... It has incorporated the principles of the draft directives giving part-timers the same rights as full-timers into its policy statements. It has now accepted a policy establishing a national minimum wage on the basis that it will bring Britain into line with the rest of the EC even though the Social Charter has been considerably weakened on this point. On equal opportunities it has used European standards as the basis for proposed measures on childcare and parental leave. There is no doubt that Europe is playing an increasing role in shaping British party political approaches to industrial relations. (Bridgeford and Stirling, 1991, p 270)

However, it is not only the Labour Party that has caught the Euro bug. The Charter has served to embed the concept of social partnership and ensure the positions of employers and trades union leaders at the top table of European policy making. British trades union leaders, for so many years excluded from the policy making arenas by the Thatcher government, find this particularly attractive and help seal their conversion to the cause of European integration. The 1991 conference of the Trades Union Conference was organised under the theme of 'social partnership'. Of special interest is the fact that it rejected a motion seeking the repeal of the Conservative government's anti-trades union legislation on the grounds that the motion ran contrary to European approaches to employment policy matters. Behind the banner of the EC British trades union leaders are following the Labour Party into the centre of British politics.

Finally, although some of the most optimistic expectations of the Social Charter did not survive the production of the Action Programme, the first five draft directives promised real impact and tangible benefits. The UK government, for instance, has assessed the financial costs of the five directives to British industry at £3 billion (Employment Department, 1990).

Of course progress is speedier where the mutual interests and benefits of both sides can be established as in the case of health and safety measures. Conversely progress is slower in contentious areas such as worker participation or fair wage policy. Nonetheless expectations have been raised. The process of drawing comparison with employment and social policy in other members states, inspired by the Social Charter, has become widespread. The domestic bargaining agenda will increasingly take on board practices in other member states. This applies both to employers and to union negotiators and the extent to which these comparisons serve to raise or lower standards and entitlement will depend upon the bargaining strengths of the social partners and the predisposition of government policy. The institutional framework within which employment and social policy will develop will remain essentially national in character in terms of its procedures but will be far better informed of policy in other member states. In this sense one might observe, over time, an osmotic process in which domestic policy development becomes Europeanised.

References

Banham, J. (1989) 'Business and the social charter', *International Freedom Review*, vol 1, no 4, Autumn.

Banham, J. (1991) 'The Social Charter: an opportunity missed', *International Journal of Manpower*, vol 12, no 2.

Blackwell, J. (1990) 'The EC Social Charter and the labour market in Ireland', in A. Foley and M. Mulreaney (eds) *The Single European Market and the Irish economy*, Dublin: The Institute of Public Administration.

Bridgeford, J. and Stirling, J. (1991*)* 'Britain in a social Europe: industrial relations and 1992', *Industrial Relations Journal*, vol 22, no 4, pp 263-73.

Buron, M. (1990) 'Community Charter of basic social rights for workers', *Social Europe*, no 1.

COM 89, *Communication from the Commission concerning its action programme relating to the implementation of the Community Charter of Basic Social Rights for Workers*, (568) final, Brussels, 29 November.

Commission of the European Communities (1969) *The common market and the common man: social policy and working and living conditions in the European Community*, Brussels: European Communities' Press and Information Office.

Commission of the European Communities (1983) *The social policy of the European Community*, Periodical 5, European Documentation, Brussels.

Commission of the European Communities (1988) 'Some ideas for a Social Europe, without which a Europe without frontiers cannot succeed', *Monthly Newsletter on the Single European Market*, June.

Commission of the European Communities (1990a) *1992: The social dimension*, Periodical 2, European Documentation, Brussels.

Commission of the European Communities (1990b) *A human face for Europe*, Periodical 4, European Documentation, Brussels.

Confederation of British Industry (1989) *Submission by the Confederation of British Industry to the House of Lords European Communities Committee, Sub-committee C (Social and Consumer Affairs) on the Community Charter of Fundamental Rights*, London: CBI.

Confederation of British Industry (1990) 'After the Social Charter: the Action Programme', *Employment Affairs Report* January/February.

Due, J., Madsen, J. and Jensen, C. (1991) 'The social dimension: convergence or diversification of IR in the Single European Market', *Industrial Relations Journal*, vol 22 no 2, pp 85-102.

Employment Department (1990) *The United Kingdom in Europe; people, jobs and progress*, London: HMSO.

Financial Times (1990) 'GMB campaigns to lobby employers over social charter', 9 January.

Guardian (1991) 'Of harm and harmony', 24 May.

House of Commons (1991) *Political union: law-making powers and procedures*, Select Committee on the European Communities, Session 1990-1991, 17th Report.

Le Grand, J. (1991) 'Some implications of 1992 and beyond: social security in Europe', Paper presented to the DSS/ESRC Consultation Seminar, Planning a Strategy for Social Security in the 1990s, 23-24 January, School for Advanced Urban Studies, University of Bristol.

Lingle, C. (1991) 'The EC Social Charter, social democracy and post 1992 Europe', *West European Politics*, January, pp 129-38.

NALGO (1990) *NALGO, the European Community and 1992*, Report of the National Executive Council's Single European Act Working Party, London.

Observer (1991) 'Tories increase miners' hours', 3 November.

Papandreou, V. (1989) 'Towards a European social policy', Paper presented to British Local Government in a Single Europe conference organised by the Association of London Authorities, the Association of Greater Manchester Authorities and the School for Advanced Urban Studies, Oldham, September.

Rhodes, M. (1991) 'The social dimension of the Single European Market: national versus transnational regulation', *European Journal of Political Research*, vol 19, pp 245-80.

Staedelin, F. (1990) 'Social Policy Social Charter, basic rights', *Social Europe*, no 1.

Teague, P. (1989) 'Constitution or regime? The social dimension to the 1992 project', *British Journal of Industrial Relations*, November, pp 310-29.

Teague, P. and Grahl, J. (1991) 'The European Community Social Charter and labour market regulation', *Journal of Public Policy*, vol 11, no 2, pp 207-32.

Venturini, P. (1989) *1992: the social dimension*, Luxembourg: Office for Official Publications of the European Community.

CHAPTER 21

INFORMATION TECHNOLOGY SKILLS AND ACCESS TO TRAINING OPPORTUNITIES: GERMANY AND THE UK

Teresa Rees

Introduction

The European Community (EC) faces a number of challenges in the next decade, such as an ageing workforce, increased competition with Japan and the USA, and a growing shortage of high level new information technology (NIT) skills. All these factors imply that more attention should be paid in future to training and human resource management, and in particular to the under-utilisation of women in the workforce. An emerging awareness of the adverse economic consequences of inequalities in education, training and employment coincides with a more pressing climate of opinion favouring social justice between people with different characteristics, for example, gender, age and ethnic origin. But how equal is access to training opportunities in the NITs in the EC? Are training systems acting as a catalyst for change, are they reinforcing the status quo, or indeed, are they aiding and abetting further polarisation between social groups in the labour market?

Technological changes are creating a need for a more skilled workforce. NITs themselves provide one imperative: their development, manufacture, service and repair, and the training and support of users in a wide variety of sectors all require growing numbers of people with technological know-how of various degrees of sophistication. Moreover, the all-pervasiveness of NITs means that few workers remain untouched. Even those in caring professions, such as nursing, or 'front-of-house' occupations, such as hotel receptionists, find that increasingly, despite the people-based orientation of their work, they need to be technologically literate.

Specific skill shortages in NITs are already being experienced in tight labour markets. The lack of people with 'hybrid skills' combining business sense and technical competences, for example, is recognised as a threat to the competitiveness of the EC. Moreover, the combination of skills required is changing: increasingly NIT skills are required alongside 'social

---

This chapter first appeared in K. Dukatel (ed) *Employment and technical change in Europe: work organisation, skills and training*, 1994, Cheltenham: Edward Elgar.

skills', known in Germany as the 'new pedagogics'. These were listed by Mercedes Benz[1] as a capacity for abstract thinking, team-working, self-reliance, enhanced communication skills, a greater degree of responsibility, and so forth. The emphasis in training for NITs at Mercedes Benz now includes training in social behaviour, group work and communication, in order to ensure that workers are able to discuss and solve problems amongst themselves (see Rees, 1990).

The use of NITs is closely related to patterns of work organisation and the need to cope with the perennial problems which face industry, such as wanting to be more efficient, improve products and levels of productivity, stream-line work processes, and increasingly, enhance standards of quality control and customer care. NITs throw question marks over the appropriateness of traditional forms of work organisation, in particular rigid structures of labour market segmentation. There are new pressures to increase the adaptability of an ageing workforce, currently socialised into thinking of training as an initial one-off experience rather than a life-long process.

The effective introduction and development of NITs implies job redesign, continuing training, and changes in patterns of work organisation. NITs can enrich jobs or deskill and enlarge them (Gallie, 1991) according to how people are trained to use them, how jobs are designed and how work is organised. Continuing training in NITs can potentially facilitate career development and progression, and the breakdown of the manual/non-manual divide.

Social characteristics, in particular gender and race, are key organising principles in the allocation of workers in a segmented labour market. To what extent could vocational training systems in the EC facilitate the movement of disadvantaged workers such as women, ethnic minorities and disabled people from low skilled jobs up into more highly regarded and highly rewarded work? A key issue here is access to training. Training systems can be an agent of change and open up opportunities to women and people from diverse backgrounds disadvantaged in the labour market by increasing their cultural capital and making them more marketable. Alternatively, they can in effect reinforce the status quo or even polarise people further by allocating opportunities for advancement to those who already have the correct combination of ascribed characteristics. Vocational and educational training systems tend to be as segregated as the labour force itself, further exacerbating patterns of segregation. The question then is to what extent will these new imperatives leading to enhanced training, open up access and create a labour force less structured by ascriptive characteristics?

This chapter explores access to training for NITs in the European Community, and in particular access for women, through a focus on three arenas. In the first section, access to EC funded training measures are examined. There is currently a deepening concern at EC level that a laissez faire approach to training for women reflects the inequalities that characterise the member states, leading to widening gaps in skill levels.

Two country case studies follow, focusing on Germany and the UK. The German case study explores change through work reorganisation and the development of continuing training for upskilling in some state of the art high-tech companies. Here the economic imperative is leading to policies which should benefit unskilled and semi-skilled workers who have previously not enjoyed opportunities for progression.

The German dual training system, which is generally well regarded, offers young people a highly prescribed programme of credentialised hands-on work-based learning experience alternated with classroom-based theoretical instruction. But access to the system is uneven, and it is facing challenges in adapting flexibly to the speed of development of NITs. Meanwhile, access to continuing training is playing an increasingly important role in determining occupational lifechances. The reorganisation of work, the need to enhance the skill level of all workers and increased expenditure on continuing training bodes well for widening access for some workers previously denied opportunities for progression, but again, access is dependent upon a range of determining factors such as sector, size of enterprise, and location.

By contrast, the UK case study focuses on women-only workshops outside mainstream training, designed to bring trainees up to the level of skills and experience necessary in order to compete for intermediate level NITs jobs, or to be accepted for further training in the mainstream. The workshops target disadvantaged women returning to the workplace after a period at home looking after children. In the UK, the training culture is not as developed as in Germany, gender segregation in the labour market is particularly marked and vocational education and training systems are as segmented as the workplace. The case study demonstrates the effectiveness of positive action training specifically designed to meet women's training needs and highlights the inappropriateness of much mainstream training for transforming women's skills and filling skill shortages in NITs.

Widening access for all is recognised as of growing significance at the European level. However, for three related reasons, reflected in the case studies in this chapter, the issue of access for women in training for NITs is of particular concern. Women are seen as playing an increasingly important role in the labour force; gender segregation is particularly marked in the NITs, and there is a problematic relationship between women and technology. Each issue is discussed in turn.

Women and the new technologies

Increasing dependence on women in the workforce

Women will represent the majority of new labour market entrants between now and the end of the century, given the decline in school-leavers. They constitute the majority of the EC's unemployed, part-time workers, unskilled and semi-skilled, and economically inactive latent workforce. As technological developments even out in different parts of the global economy, it has been argued, it is the use made of human resources and the speed of adaptation to new products and services and markets which determine competitive edge. This puts the emphasis on developing 'intangible capital', that is, the skill levels of the workforce, and enhancing its adaptability and capacity for innovation (European Round Table of Industrialists, 1989; Schmehr and Millner, 1992). Women's training is therefore a priority. There is a particular need to address the training needs of women returning to work after a period of child-rearing, whose skills may be out of date because of technological change, and whose confidence may have eroded, affecting their ability to learn. The under-utilisation of women's potential generally is increasingly being recognised as an economic as well as a social issue.

Gender segregation in employment

The EC workforce is highly segregated[2], both horizontally (whereby women and men tend to work in different industries and occupations) and vertically (whereby women are clustered at the bottom of occupational hierarchies). Segregation has been described as the single most significant determinant of the differences between women's and men's access to training, promotion, and equal pay (Walby, 1990). Over three-quarters of working women in the EC are in the service sector (compared with just over half the working men), many of them are in low paid part-time jobs in catering, cleaning and retailing. In Southern European countries, the agricultural sector remains an important, if declining source of employment for women.

The EC's 'dissimilarity index' seeks to measure segregation by comparing women's participation in each sector with the percentage of women in employment in each member state. The results show that despite an overall increase in female economic activity rates in the last five years, and despite the growth in qualification levels among women in the EC, segregation patterns remain clear cut in every member state (Commission of the European Communities, 1992b).

Training can make an impact on women's occupational lifechances, particularly in those areas of work where entry requirements are clear. Women tend to fare better in gaining entry to professions for which there are laid down entry qualifications, such as medicine, law and teaching, than those where internal labour markets operate with cloudier criteria, for example business and management (Crompton and Sanderson, 1990). Here informal criteria such as networks and 'fitting in' can effectively exclude women generally, together with male members of ethnic minorities.

The new jobs evolving as a result of the NITs are less tainted with the history of sex-stereotyping and demand less use of brawn and more of brain. Moreover, IT jobs have a clean (superclean sometimes) image compared with some of the old male-dominated industries such as steel and coal. All this might be expected to contribute to less gender segregation in the NITs. However, women tend to be concentrated in very low level work, as Connor and Pearson (1986, p 75) report in a study of the UK:

> The IT profession is characterised by a low representation of women, although large numbers of women are employed in IT at lower levels on data input and electronics assembly operations. Women typically represented only 1-2% of a company's electronic engineers, although they could be as much as 10% in the larger electronics and telecoms groups. In software jobs, the proportion of women was generally higher, averaging 15-20%.

In occupations whose main component involves the design, development, and service of use of IT, women are predominantly found in relatively low level work, and have no access to career tracks that would lead to their filling high level skill shortages (see Rees, 1992). Women predominate in the lower rungs of IT work, such as secretarial and word processing work, stock control, clerical and office VDU users, data preparation, data entry. They are also increasingly found in user support where their abilities to communicate and appease are considered significant attributes (Fielder and Rees, 1991). Men, meanwhile, are dominant in the top jobs: systems analysts, engineers, software engineers, designers, programmers, management, administration and planning operators. There are few routes of progression: distinctly different recruitment mechanisms are used for the two categories of jobs.

Finally, there are national differences in patterns of gender segregation. The numbers of women entering computing employment, for example, is increasing in some member states but decreasing in others. Computing is seen as a more woman friendly profession in France but less so in Denmark and the UK (Rubery and Fagan, 1992).

The 'masculinisation of technologies'

It has been argued that women's access to training and employment in high level NITs (where skill shortages are growing) is compounded by the growing 'masculinisation of technologies' (Cockburn, 1985; Rees, 1992; Wajcman, 1991). High level NITs have become male territory, hence women feel relatively technically incompetent and are deterred from trying to learn what they perceive to be 'male skills' (Cockburn, 1985, 1986). As a consequence women have specific barriers to face such as low levels of confidence, lack of appropriate initial qualifications to gain entry to NITs courses, and exclusionary mechanisms practised by men.

There is a powerful association between men, machinery and the concept of technical competence. Children learn early on that computing is male territory. Male computer hacks are accused of indulging male fantasies of sport, adventure and violence through the design of games of speed, war, and 'alien zapping' (Wajcman, 1991). Computers in schools throughout the EC are usually linked with mathematics departments, which are often devoid of women teachers (Pelgrum and Plomp, 1991), when they could arguably be as easily and logically located in language departments, emphasising the communication element. School-based computer clubs quickly become male dominated space. In the UK, parents are far more likely to buy computers for home use for their sons than for their daughters (Newton, 1991).

NITs are perceived as the territory of the young, white, middle class male (encapsulated in the stereotype of the computer 'hacker'), and this operates as a barrier to the training and recruitment of women and some men. The pool of people from which people can be recruited to fill skill shortages is circumscribed, and it ensures that the masculine ethos of NITs, as reflected in computer games, and the use to which they are put, are self-perpetuating.

Limitations are imposed upon technically competent women in a number of workplaces. As Cockburn (1986, p 185) says "for a woman to aspire to technical competence is, in a very real sense, to transgress the rules of gender". In her study in the UK of women and men working in three fields where new technology had been introduced (warehousing, manufacturing and hospital X-ray), and in the engineering firms which developed these technologies, Cockburn (1985) revealed that gender divisions remain clear cut. Even where women learned new technologies, men continued to be the 'technologists' and women the low paid 'operators'. She argues that:

> Whatever opportunities the new technologies appear to offer the operator, they do not in themselves enable her to cross a certain invisible barrier that exists between operating the controls that put a machine to work and taking the casing off it in order to intervene in its mechanism. This is the difference

between an operator and a technician or engineer. For an operator there is always someone who is assumed to know better than she about the technology of the machine on which she is working. That someone is almost invariably a man. (Cockburn, 1986, p 181)

Wajcman (1991, p 158) argues cogently that technology is a cultural product which is integral to the constitution of male gender identity. The female gender identity is the negation of that of the male, and so the stereotyped cultural ideal of a woman, in the ideology of sexual difference, must be technically incompetent. She underlines the significance of this technological 'ownership' as a source of power in gender relations.

In seeking access to training for NITs, then, women and men do not start from the same base position. The masculinisation of technology means that girls are far less likely to leave school with appropriate qualifications to move on to higher education and training courses which would equip them for work at technological frontiers. Women are far less likely than men to be given employer sponsored training which would enhance their promotion prospects (Deroure, 1990). A policy of equal access in training for NITs which relies on participants putting themselves forward, therefore, will inevitably generate more men than women, just as training for 'feminised' jobs such as secretarial work attracts more female trainees than male. Equality of access does not generate equality of outcome, as the next section on the European Community demonstrates.

Women and access to training for NITs in the European Community

The issue of access to training is taking on a new political significance at the EC level. The European Commission has published a proposal for a Council of Ministers' recommendation on access to continuing vocational training (Commission of the European Communities, 1992a), while the social partners of employers' and trade unions' representatives (Union of Industrial and Employers Confederation of Europe and European Trade Union Confederation) have issued a joint opinion on access to continuing training (Task Force, 1991). Access to training for NITs is increasingly recognised as vital. However, it is access for women which has attracted the most attention: indeed the social partners have now agreed a joint opinion focusing specifically on women and training, and the European Commission is seeking to ensure that its resources, both through the Social Fund and the innovative programmes developed by the Commission's Task Force Human Resources, Education, Training and Youth (the Task Force) are designed to address women's training needs more effectively.

Gender segregation in training in the EC

Women comprise less than half the EC undergraduate population overall and considerably less than half the post-graduate population in the EC. As girls are less likely than boys to leave school with appropriate qualifications to study IT related subjects, women are less likely to have had training in high level NIT skills. The training they do receive tends to lead overwhelmingly to jobs traditionally done by women.

In courses particularly associated with the NITs, women remain in a minority, ranging from just over a third of all students in the EC in natural sciences, under a third in mathematics and computing, to only 9.0% in engineering (see Table 1).

Women constitute less than a third of employer sponsored trainees on in-firm training and are less likely to be in management posts, or other senior posts where in-firm training is often concentrated.

There are variations in the different member states. In Southern European countries undergoing massive restructuring and modernisation, gender segregation in education and training at least appears to be less entrenched than in some of the more stable Northern countries.

Table 1: Students in IT related degree and postgraduate degree courses in the EC (percentage women)

	Natural sciences	Mathematics and computer science	Engineering
Belgium (combined)	(39.6)		11.9
Denmark	30.4	22.9	12.0
FRG	30.9	23.6	6.5
Greece	37.0	36.0	19.7
Spain	45.5	37.5	10.7
France	32.5	17.0	16.1
Italy	53.4	43.3	54.7
Netherlands	23.0	14.4	8.4
Portugal	63.8	54.0	22.0
UK (combined)	(32.1)		8.7
Europe 12	36.6	30.0	9.0

Source: Calculated from Tables 4 and 5, Eurostat (1988)

Notes: No figures available for Ireland and Luxembourg. These headings refer to ISCED Fields 42, 46 and 54. Figures include full and part-time students.

Women in EC funded training programmes

The Treaty of Rome in 1957 enshrined the principle of equal treatment for men and women, and in general terms it could be argued that the Commission has acted as a catalyst to the promotion of equal opportunities within the member states. In 1987 the Commission adopted a Recommendation on Vocational Training for Women which called upon member states to ensure that women have equal access to all types and levels of vocational training, particularly in professions likely to expand in the future and those in which women have been historically under represented (Commission of the European Communities, 1987).

But what effect have the various EC funded training programmes had on women? Has that effect been transformative? In other words, are women's employment prospects qualitatively improved, both in terms of being able to obtain a job in the NITs, and by securing a job with prospects of further training and promotion, as a result of their participation? Or does their access to and participation in training opportunities merely steer them into low level, low skilled, low paid 'women's' work, with poor terms and conditions of employment?

The Directorate-General for Employment, Industrial Relations and Social Affairs (DGV) of the European Commission has wrestled over the years with the issue of women's training as an identifiable heading; the Organisation for Economic Cooperation and Development has similarly oscillated from the view that earmarked sums are potentially ghettoising and patronising through to focusing on the fact that women tend to lose out in mainstream provision despite 'equality of access'. Earmarking has moved from targeting poorly qualified unemployed women and returners (from 1977-1983) to funding training and employment measures in sectors where women are under-represented (1984-89). Women received 41% of European Social Fund (ESF) resources in 1990 (Commission of the European Communities, 1991), an increase from previous years (see Table 2). In individual countries the figure ranges from a third to almost half. However, it is difficult to judge to what extent these resources are effective in transforming women's skills rather than channelling them into low level 'women's work'. The Commission is setting up a more systematic procedure for assessing women's participation in ESF activities. The Commission does support a New Opportunities for Women (NOW) programme aimed at the integration of women into the workforce through training as part of its Third Action Programme on Equality between Men and Women.

Table 2: Women's training and the European Social Fund 1987

	Number of female trainees	Females as a % total trainees
Belgium	15,637	45.3
Denmark	10,124	49.2
Germany	38,167	47.1
Greece	107,394	40.8
Spain	211,590	31.8
France	95,490	42.1
Ireland	69,874	43.3
Italy	197,872	37.3
Luxembourg	1,339	31.6
Netherlands	8,055	33.6
Portugal	112,207	39.0
UK	354,456	43.7
EC	1,222,205	39.3

Source: Extracted from Table 5.7, Commission of the European Communities (1989)

Task Force programmes are directed at a range of target groups and for the most part involve transnational partnerships and exchanges of young people, trainees, trainers, higher education students and staff, employers and employees (see Table 3).

Figures on gender distribution among participants on Task Force funded programmes have not been kept systematically by the projects: on some there is excellent information, on others it is patchy. Following a question asked by Madame Fontaine in the European Parliament on the participation of young people, ethnic minorities and women in the programmes, the issue of gender monitoring (but not ethnic monitoring) is being addressed more systematically in the new round of programmes due to be launched in the mid 1990s. Research commissioned by the Task Force revealed that women's participation rates, not unexpectedly, broadly reflect their existing pattern of representation in the various target groups (Rees, 1993). PETRA, for example, which is aimed at young people in initial vocational training, where there are likely to be broadly similar numbers of young men and women, shows a strong trend towards equality of the genders. COMETT by contrast, which is concerned with continuing training in advanced technologies, is drawing from a pool of potential participants which is overwhelmingly male: this is reflected in the figures of actual participants. Projects are, as Bucci writes (1992, p 25) "obviously affected by the balance between the sexes of those who are its potential beneficiaries". They reflect existing patterns, and hence reinforce existing gender divisions in level and type of skill.

Table 3: Task Force education and training programmes 1986-92

Short title	Full title	Duration	Current budget estimate (MECU)
COMETT	Programme on cooperation between universities and industry regarding training in the field of technology	1986-94	282.5
ERASMUS	European Community action scheme for the Mobility of University Students	1987-	300
EUROTEC-NET	Action programme to promote innovation in the field of vocational training resulting from technological change in the European Community	1990-94	7.5 (1990-92)
FORCE	Action Programme for the development of continuing vocational training in the European Community	1991-94	32 (1991-92)
LINGUA	Action Programme to promote foreign language competence in the European Community	1990-94	200
PETRA	Action Programme for the vocational training of young people and their preparation for adult and working life	1988-94	218.9
TEMPUS	Trans-European Mobility Scheme for University Studies	1990-94	318
YOUTH FOR EUROPE	Action Programme for the promotion of youth exchanges in the European Community - 'Youth for Europe' programme	1988-94	45.5
IRIS	European Network of Vocational Training Projects for Women	1988-93	0.75

In COMETT, however, one of the 125 University-Enterprise Training Partnerships (UETPs), Women in Technology (WITEC), focuses specifically on the needs of women in technology and has played an active role in alerting other UETPs to issues relating to women and technology. There are some noteworthy, innovative COMETT projects featuring women, but the figures on female participation vary by strand within COMETT and by country, in relation to the rough proportions of women in science, engineering and technology. Interestingly enough, in line with women's much greater participation in engineering in Eastern European countries, Christiansen (1992) points out that Bulgaria has imposed a 50% ceiling on women in engineering participating in TEMPUS in response to a fear that they will 'take over'.

The Task Force's new initiative, FORCE, is designed to ensure more even access to continuing training for people with different socio-economic and demographic characteristics, but it is too early to judge its effectiveness in terms of access to women. The Task Force has also funded several initiatives in women's training, in particular IRIS, the European Network of Training Schemes for Women, which facilitates women's training projects to visit each other and develop transnational training.

The Task Force is seeking to improve women's access to training, but has limited resources and, therefore, impact, compared with the structural funds of the EC. Both DGV and the Task Force are considering methods of ensuring higher female participation within existing programmes by making them more compatible with women's needs and the reality of their daily lives. A draft joint communication on women and training has been prepared for the Council of Ministers underlying the importance of women's role in the economy. If future programmes were systematically designed to ensure better participation of women, then the Commission would be in a strong position, through its management of substantial resources for training, to act as a catalyst to member states' own policies and practices in the future.

Germany: in-firm continuing training

Introduction

The dual training system of the former Federal Republic of Germany has been described as the envy of the world, certainly in terms of training for intermediate qualifications. Training regulations governing the competencies which must be achieved before an individual can become a qualified worker are strictly controlled. The two sides of industry cooperate with the state in identifying the required skills for any occupation. Some 70% of school-leavers enter the training system, a far higher figure than in other member states, and a further 20% stay on in full-time higher education. More resources are spent on training than elsewhere in the EC, some 3% of the national pay-roll (Federal Minister for Education and Science, 1992). There are attempts to ensure that as far as possible, the same standards operate across regions, firms, industries and state recognised occupations. Training is part of the work culture of those people in occupations for which a system of tiered qualifications exists, linked to occupational status and pay.

Companies in Germany have adopted NITs to a far greater extent than elsewhere. A Commission survey discovered that 90% of firms in mechanical engineering, textiles, retail trade and services used information and communication systems, 68% had centralised computer systems, and personal computers were used by 61% (Commission of the European Communities, 1988). Given the importance of training in extracting the full potential of what NITs have to offer, it is presumably no accident that Germany has some of the most successful companies in the world, not simply in using new technologies, but in their development and manufacture as well. This is a major reason for selecting Germany as a case study.

However, the very strengths of the dual training system can also be seen as weaknesses in the context of the training needs created by the emergent NITs. The system provides systematic delivery of carefully considered curricula for occupations in a range of industries, and the opportunity for both college-based teaching for theoretical aspects of the work and firm-based practical learning. The impact of NITs on patterns of work organisation is having the effect of breaking down barriers between recognised occupations: workers are now required to be more flexible. The nature of some jobs is changing dramatically: the new skills required are not simply technical, but include the new pedagogics (team working, ability to take responsibility, diagnostic and communication skills etc). These qualities are not traditionally taught in the dual training system, and trainers are not used to bringing them out in their trainees. There is increasingly a blurring of the functions of classroom-based training and in-firm learning where established staff are now expected to take on a training role.

The dual training system has also been accused of being inflexible: there is a long gestation period for introducing changes into the training regulations which govern occupations. NITs are developing with great rapidity and there is a danger that the training can lag behind by many years.

Finally, demographic changes imply that there will be a shift from initial training to continuing training, as older workers are retrained, women returners are recruited, and the unemployed and ethnic minorities are increasingly looked to as a new source of labour. Unlike initial training, the state does not regulate continuing education and training. As a consequence, access to it varies considerably, and the quality can vary too. Moreover, whereas young people are well socialised into accepting the importance of the initial training for their career prospects, there are cultural factors which restrict the enthusiasm of existing unskilled and semi-skilled employees for continuing training.

There are some tensions between what is clearly a highly developed initial training system and the demands of NITs in Germany. There are likely to be increasing disparities between experiences at the level of the firm, the region and the individual. Patterns of polarisation are already developing. In that sense, one of the strengths of the dual training system, in offering at least a limited standardisation of access, is potentially threatened. The discussion here focuses on the effect of these changes on patterns of individuals' access to training.

An individual's access to quality training will depend upon the region where they live and in which industrial sector they work. There are different standards in the dual training system between the northern and southern Länders because of differences in the quality of the training schools and in the standards of the enterprises, despite the attempts to standardise monitored by the Chambers of Industry and Commerce and the Chambers of Crafts and Trades. Larger companies in the commercial sector and the high technology industries are having few problems in arranging the training to suit their needs. However, smaller companies, in the craft sector in particular, are experiencing some difficulties although size is not the only variable (see Rees, 1990).

For major companies, spending on continuing training has increased dramatically in recent years and is projected to continue to rise substantially. Bosch, for example, spent approximately 90,000DM on continuing training in 1988. In AEG spending increased by 15% in 1988 and a similar percentage again in 1989. Siemens too are now spending nearly twice as much on continuing training as they do on initial training.

There are some jobs whose incumbents never expected to have to undergo further training, or, indeed, to have the prospects of more rewarding work and better pay opened up to them. One respondent from AEG reported:

> People who had been employed to manufacture cables had been working in one of our firms without training. The new recruits are skilled workers who know the new technologies. The unskilled workers can now have opportunities for training as we now need more skilled workers. The machines now require people who have more knowledge about them, those who work with them need more skills. We used to have six different machines involved in the process of making cables, whereas now all that work is done by just one highly complex

machine. (translated from an interview with Head of Technical and Professional Training, AEG, Berlin)

However, the response to such opportunities has been mixed. AEG reported that some unskilled Turkish women workers, for example, are not enthusiastic about any changes: cultural factors associated with the family and gendered roles within it intervene in responses to new opportunities and roles. Nevertheless, half the AEG workforce have taken a course within the last year.

Trade unions are keen supporters of continuing training as an alternative to redundancy for workers whose skills have become outmoded. 'Employment plans' were introduced in many German firms facing mass redundancies in the 1980s combining company funds with public resources for regional development to offer people who would otherwise become unemployed places in training or job creation schemes (Bosch, 1990). Collective bargaining has been used effectively during rationalisation agreements to encourage employers to invest in the training of their older workers. There are subsidies available from the Länder in the case of industries which are being completely restructured and where wholesale redundancies would otherwise have a major impact on unemployment in the region. But, more generally, firms are expected to fund their own programmes of continuing training, with perhaps some contribution from the individual employee.

Access for women

Gender segregation in the labour force in Germany is as entrenched as in many other European countries, despite a number of measures designed to dilute it. A major difficulty facing young girls wanting an apprenticeship in one of the major companies specialising in training in the new technologies, is that they are less likely than boys to have taken the appropriate qualifications at school. Fewer girls take computing and mathematics, for example, and the number of girls who do diminishes dramatically as they grow older (Schiersmann, 1988). Siemens confirmed a shortage of young women with the basic technical qualifications; despite an increase in the number of girls coming on to apprenticeships, it was felt it would be some generations before substantially more women are taken on.

Women may well benefit from the growth in continuing training, given that they are disproportionately in the unskilled and semi-skilled jobs. Some companies run women-only training to try to break down what are seen as particular barriers facing women wanting to learn new technologies. AEG, for example, run a course for women in electronics: they are not awarded the full qualification, but they can enhance their pay and get better jobs within the company. Computer courses run by women for women tend, as in the UK, to be highly successful in training women in NITs. One evaluation emphasised their 'stress free' atmosphere, and the fact that tuition is offered at times of the day suitable for the women. In the afternoons, the equipment is made freely available to the women for practice (see Sessar-Karp, 1988).

Older workers

It is often said and frequently believed that older people have more difficulty in learning NITs than younger workers, who are increasingly likely to be brought up with video recorders, microwaves and home computers. It is difficult to find empirical evidence for this, but it is likely that the belief informs certain training strategies. Moreover, older people's own attitudes towards such training opportunities may well be affected by such perceptions. Clearly, the push for more continuing training can only be to the advantage of older workers, but not all will welcome it and many will feel threatened. As older women are expected to comprise the bulk of new labour market entrants, their age disadvantage of not having grown up with new technologies, will be compounded by that of their gender.

Siemens discovered, like some other companies, that apprentices learn the new technology so quickly that they are in danger of rapidly eroding the skill differentials between them and the older workers. This can cause problems of resentment given the traditional status difference between qualified workers and apprentices, so it has been necessary to introduce special policies. Ways are found to retain the status and pay differential; for example, by rewarding their seniority. Old systems of production are retained to be used by some of the older workers alongside the new ones. Continuing training is used to up-date the skills of other older workers. In effect, social policies are needed as a complement to training policies. However, older workers are also encouraged to take early retirement, at say 56 or 57, rather than 60 or 63.

More generally, some older workers will clearly benefit from having career trajectories opened up for them as a result of NITs and new working arrangements. There are reports of skilled workers going to university. Qualified workers in the banking industry, for example, are increasingly taking a degree in accountancy as mature-age students. They then have excellent prospects for their remaining careers.

Ethnic minorities

The old FRG has a migrant population of about 4 million. The sons and daughters of migrant workers have experienced particular difficulties in securing access to the dual training system: they figure disproportionately among the small minority of school-leavers who neither stay on at school with a view to pursuing higher education, nor enter the dual training system. There are, of course, differences between the different ethnic groups. Participation in the dual training system was much higher in the mid 1980s among the Spanish and (the then) Yugoslavians, at around 22%, compared with the Portuguese and Turkish populations (nearer 11%). Turkish girls are the least likely of all to secure an apprenticeship. Those with the greatest difficulties appear to suffer language problems (particularly written skills) and/or to have arrived in the Germany relatively recently (Schweikert, 1982).

It is unlikely that the changes outlined above will have much impact on their opportunities for training, except insofar as there will be a general increase in the demand for labour. There have been a series of special projects for the children of migrant workers (Schweikert, 1982). But ethnic minorities may have lost their place in the queue for attention in training matters, given the urgency of harmonising the training of the New Länder and the need to up-date the skills of New Länder workers in line with the technical demands of Western industry.

The unemployed

Opportunities for the unemployed are simultaneously improving because of specific labour shortages, and diminishing because of the political imperative of training people from the New Länder, and the recession. There has been an increase in the number of private sector companies providing training in NITs for the unemployed, prompted by the availability of finance for such courses through the Länder and through European Social Fund (ESF) monies. The first six weeks of such courses focus on motivation: the trainees have to start at 7 am They can train in manual qualifications and can then specialise in NITs such as computer numerical control (CNC) for metal cutting, industrial mechanics or hydraulics.

The new Länder

Unification between the FRG and the DDR prompted a major task in merging the training systems. It is clear that in the New Länder, qualifications and trades are much more specialised than those even, for example, in the metal trades that have just been replaced. Much attention is being focused on rapidly training residents of the New Länder in accordance with the training standards and practices in the old FRG. A particular problem is the fact that the New Länder have a very small commercial and service sector where demand for trained people is likely to increase dramatically.

Conclusion

In the main, changes in the training system in Germany are being introduced to reflect the reality of the changes in the working world brought about through the introduction of NITs. The rigidity of the dual training system is creating difficulties, in particular in ensuring a standard currency in the value of that training in different parts of the country. Continuing training is opening up more opportunities, but some are better able to take advantage of this than others. There is a danger of the gap between the skill level of the employed, and the unemployed and non-economically active, widening even further. Members of ethnic minorities, in the context of an increasingly racist Europe, face additional problems of access, especially if they are located in those regions where small and medium-sized enterprises are having difficulty in collaborating to provide adequate initial training. Older people face erosion of the value of their skills and seniority. The merger of the two Germanies in itself poses a major challenge in harmonisation and improving training in NITs.

Overall, NITs have opened up opportunities for enhanced training in what were routine jobs, and career trajectories where none existed before. It is clear, however, that access to these opportunities will not be evenly distributed through the population. Social characteristics and spatial specificities will influence the allocation of training opportunities.

UK: women-only training workshops

Introduction

Gender segregation in the UK is particularly marked. Forty per cent of the female workforce work part-time: the fact that the level of child-care provision for the under fives is the among the lowest in Europe is undoubtedly a contributory factor. Opportunities for part-time work in professional and intermediate grades remain few and far between however, and tend to be negotiated on an individual basis. Career breaks are associated with downward occupational mobility, particularly when women return to work part-time (Lindley, 1992). It is clear that women in the UK are grossly under-used as a human resource.

The UK has been described as having a poorly educated and trained workforce compared with its competitors (Finegold and Soskice 1988). If levels of expenditure are any guide, UK employers cannot be said to set a great store by training: considerably less is spent than by their counterparts in Germany. Most employers do not have a long-term strategic commitment to training despite providing training for their employees

(Clarke, 1991). Moreover, some reports suggest that most UK companies are:

> still using IT to cut costs rather than underpin their business strategy. ... Only 39% of a sample of more than 70 companies indicated that they were fully aware of the benefits of IT. (Cane, 1990)

Only one in five companies were reported by Cane as relating their business strategy to their information systems.

Training and Enterprise Councils (TECs) were set up in England and Wales, and Local Enterprise Companies (LECs) in Scotland as part of Government policy to ensure private sector involvement in the identification of local training needs and the delivery of training (see Meager, 1991). Executive boards are made up predominantly of chief executives of major local employers, the vast majority of whom are men. TECs and LECs in effect privatise and localise training service delivery, leading to sharper spatial inequalities in the amount and quality of training provided, and as a result, greater polarisation in patterns of access. The policy of gearing training to the needs of local industry is likely to have a particular impact on women wanting to return to the labour force, whose needs are ill understood and met in a haphazard way. Early reports suggest a disappointing performance overall, and considerable variation between TECs (Equal Opportunities Commission, 1993). Resources are made available from central government for the training of the registered unemployed, but this tends to be low level and in any case many married women are ineligible to register.[3]

Women predominated in the development of programming and software in the early post-war days of computers (Wajcman, 1991), but the proportion of women in NITs in all but low level data preparation work has since diminished (Perry and Greber, 1990). Wellington (1989) noted that 95% of data preparation staff were women, but only 18% of programmers and 2% of data processing managers.

It was only in the 1970s that a well defined education and training route to high level IT jobs emerged in the UK. The decline in women's involvement in programming and software is reflected in IT training and education. In the mid 1980s, women formed a fifth of high level computing workers (Newton and Haslam, 1988). By that time the proportion of girls taking degrees in computer science and computer studies, the main access route into programming and systems analysis, had diminished to 10%. University admissions figures reveal a fall in female students in IT related subjects from 26% in 1979 to 14% in 1986 (Blaazer 1988). In 1989, women formed only 12.7% of new graduates with first degrees in computing in the UK. Lovegrove and Hall (1987) recount the specific example of Southampton University where women made up a third of computer students in 1978/79 but by 1985/86, there were no women at all enroled in this subject area.

In the mainstream of training, then, NITs have become clearly colonised as male territory except in low level skills. However, there have been some highly innovative positive action training projects in the voluntary sector, often started by groups of women themselves, which meet Cockburn's (1985) criterion of effectiveness by being women-only. The availability of funds from the ESF enabled such groups to persuade local authorities (in the main) to provide matching funds, although funding has remained piecemeal and precarious. Such training in other member states is more likely to be integrated into the mainstream. While for the most part such positive action projects have been in low level IT skills such as keyboard skills, word processing, spreadsheets and basic programming, (and have therefore been successful in attracting disadvantaged women), they have paid particular attention to career guidance and progression, confidence building and assertiveness training, and de-stereotyping the masculine ethos of NITs, thereby going beyond ITeC and further education colleges which prepare young women in 'office skills'.

Women-only training workshops in NITs

Women-only training workshops evolved in the mid 1980s as a direct outcome of the women's movement. Although set up on the whole by feminists, they were aimed at training disadvantaged women who were quite unlikely to see themselves as part of the women's movement. The motivation for setting them up came from a recognition of the importance of training to occupational lifechances, an understanding of the needs of women wanting to return to the labour force after a period at home with children, and an observation of the inadequacies of existing training provision to meet those needs. Women-only training emerged as a strategy to provide a comfortable environment for women to learn skills not usually associated with their gender. Indeed, some of the early workshops were in construction skills, but latterly NITs became the main focus. The tutors tended to be female too, again to provide a woman-friendly learning environment and to offer role models of women competent in NITs. Trainees' child-care and other domestic commitments have been included in the planning of the courses: some have on-site creches, most are organised in school term times and during school hours.

South Glamorgan women's workshop

One of best known examples and longest running examples of a women-only initiative in this field is the South Glamorgan Women's Workshop

(SGWW), a member of the IRIS network, which was set up in 1983 by a group of women in Cardiff operating as a collective cooperative. Funded by ESF and local authority monies, its aim was to train poorly qualified, disadvantaged women over 25 who wanted to return to work, in particular single parents, and black and ethnic minority women. Women from low income families and with disabilities are given priority (see Essex *et al*, 1986; MacNamara, 1990).

Training is offered in skills judged to be in demand in the local labour market, microelectronics and computing. Some 50 women have been trained each year, on a part-time basis, between the hours of 9.30 am and 3.00 pm, which both accommodates child-care commitments and allows women to travel in daylight hours. In addition to the specific skills training, there is attention paid to social skills, confidence building, de-stereotyping, work placements and counselling. Work placements with local employers improve skills and confidence and have led to trainees being offered employment, while enabling employers to recognise that such women are capable of the work. The workshop is located centrally near bus and train stations, as women on the whole have relatively poor access to private transport, even when there is a car in the household.

The vast majority of trainees go on to further training or employment. Often employment has to be part-time because of the lack of child-care facilities in the area, but the workshop has provided some places in its on-site nursery to ex-trainees who have found employment places they could not otherwise take up. One group has started a cooperative advising firms on software choices.

There are now two part-time courses, in business computing and electronics, and a series of short courses in evenings and weekends on various business computer packages: over 350 women attend courses each year. Recent activities supplementing the workshop's main training courses include a computer club for girls and an access course for Asian women, some of whom then graduate on to the main course at the workshop. Mature aged Asian women often find mixed gender courses unacceptable, particularly where women will be in a small minority.

The SGWW is now offering EC funded advanced training in computer networking and telecommunications, its reputation as woman-friendly helping to overcome the reluctance of some women to put themselves forward for such training. Skills shortages in the area ensure the women are likely to be recruited into high level NIT employment.

Conclusion

The SGWW is an example of 'best practice' positive action training which gives disadvantaged women confidence and skills, and demystifies technology. It has potentially wide application elsewhere. Like other such heavily oversubscribed workshops in Northern Ireland, Liverpool and London, further training is a major destination of trainees (Murphy and Mullan, 1989; Women's Technology Scheme, 1989). By the time they leave the women-only environment, they have developed sufficient confidence to tackle a traditional course where they are likely to be the only woman: they would not have done so before. Such workshops provide a new route back into traditional vocational education and training systems which currently divert women away from training for high level NITs.

However, the provision of opportunities for women returners wishing to train in NITs in women-only workshops are few and far between. Such workshops continue to operate on a shoe-string at the margins of mainstream training. TECs have not on the whole taken advantage of their existence to improve opportunities for women, nor have they emulated their example. The increased complexity of European Commission funding limits access to experienced European players. This combined with the withdrawal of the Urban Programme as a source of matching funding further constrains the growth potential of such initiatives, despite their success.

Conclusion

The effective utilisation of NITs is crucial to the EC's future competitiveness. Yet these core technologies are currently colonised by young, white males, so that access to jobs in and training for NITs is restricted to a small segment of the population. Broadening access to training is crucial to widen the catchment of employment in the development, manufacture, service and utilisation of NITs. It is particularly important to demythologise the association between masculinities and technology, so that women can benefit from training in NITs.

The European Commission is seeking to ensure that resources put into training benefit men and women more equitably in the future, but so far funds have merely reinforced existing divisions.

In German high-tech companies, the increasing emphasis on continuing training, work reorganisation and career progression across the old manual/non-manual divide implied by NITs may well open up opportunities to both men and women.

In the UK, changes appear to be increasing rather then diminishing gender segregation in the high level NIT skills. Successful examples of positive action training for women in NITs remain outside the mainstream, and funding is increasingly scarce. Traditional vocational and educational systems may open up a little to mature aged women in the light of demographic changes, but there is little evidence that women are taking up training in computing - quite the contrary.

Patterns of gender segregation, the masculinisation of technology and the male-centredness of mainstream training provision are so entrenched that even the combined weight of the economic imperative and social justice demands are unlikely to lead to better access to training in the NITs for women or for other disadvantaged groups. Strategic policy development is needed at all levels: the European Community, the member state, the region, the firm and the training provider.

Notes

1. This chapter draws upon documentary material and interviews conducted by the author with training and personnel directors of major companies using advanced technologies in Germany. The study was conducted with Gareth Rees and the original report of the study is Rees (1990).
2. Over half the women of working age in the EC are economically active, although the rates vary by country and by region. Some 28% work part-time, compared with 38% of men. The registered unemployment rate for women is 11.9% compared with 7.0% for men (1990 figures from Commission of the European Communities, 1990). Much of the paid work which women undertake in the EC, for example by Italian homeworkers or Greek family workers, is under-recorded. Steps are being taken by the EC to try to make women's contribution to the agricultural sector and to family businesses more visible.
3. The UK is an exception to the general pattern because of restrictions on certain women, particularly those who are married or who are only available to work part-time, qualifying to receive unemployment benefit.

References

Blaazer, C. (1988) 'The top jobs that are just waiting for the right women' *The Times*, 7 January.

Bosch, G. (1990) *Retraining - not redundancy: innovative approaches to industrial restructuring in Germany and France*, Geneva: International Institute for Labour Studies.

Bucci, M. (1992) 'Report on the access of young people to community programmes in the field of education and training', Internal Report, EC Task Force Human Resources, Education, Training and Youth.

Cane, A. (1990) 'UK lags behind the computer times', *Financial Times*, 11 July.

Christiansen, D. (1992) 'Female participation in the training programmes of the Task Force Human Resources', Unpublished paper presented to the Social Dialogue seminar on Women, Training and Equal Opportunities, held in Madrid, February.

Clarke, K. (1991) *Women and training: a review*, Manchester: Equal Opportunities Commission.

Cockburn, C. (1985) *Machinery of dominance: women, men and technical know-how*, London: Pluto Press.

Cockburn, C. (1986) 'Women and new technology: opportunity is not enough', in K. Purcell, S. Woods, A. Waton and S. Allen (eds) *The changing experience of employment: restructuring and recession*, London: Macmillan.

Commission of the European Communities (1987) 'Commission Recommendation of 24 November 1987 on vocational training for women', *Official Journal of the European Communities*, no L 342/35, 4 December.

Commission of the European Communities (1988) 'New technologies and social change', *Social Europe*, no 1.

Commission of the European Communities (1989) 'Women in graphics', *Women of Europe*, supplement no 30, Brussels: Commission of the European Communities.

Commission of the European Communities (1991) *Standing committee on employment situation of women in the Community*, Commission staff working paper.

Commission of the European Communities (1992a) *Proposal for a Council Recommendation on access to vocational training*, Brussels: Commission of the European Communities.

Commission of the European Communities (1992b) 'The position of women on the labour market: trends and developments in the twelve member states of the European Community 1983-1990', *Women of Europe*, Supplement no 36, Brussels: Commission of the European Communities.

Connor, H. and Pearson, R. (1986) *Information technology manpower into the 1990s*, Brighton: Institute of Manpower Studies.

Crompton, R. and Sanderson, K. (1990) *Gendered jobs and social change*, London: Unwin Hyman.

Deroure, F. (1990) *Accompanying measures in women's training: vocational training for women*, Brussels: DGV Commission of the European Communities.

Equal Opportunities Commission (1993) *Formal investigation into the publicly-funded vocational training system in England and Wales*, Manchester: Equal Opportunities Commission.

Essex, S., Callender, C., Rees, T. and Winckler, V. (1986) *New styles of training for women: an evaluation of South Glamorgan women's workshop*, Manchester: Equal Opportunities Commission.

European Round Table of Industrialists (1989) *Reshaping Europe*, Brussels: European Round Table of Industrialists.

Eurostat (1988) *Full-time education in the European Community in 1985/86*, Rapid Reports: Population and Social Conditions no 1, Luxembourg: Eurostat.

Federal Minister for Education and Science (1992) *Vocational training in the dual system in the Federal Republic of Germany: an investment in the future*, Bonn: Federal Minister for Education and Science.

Fielder, S. and Rees, T. (1991) *High level IT, training and women's employment*, Cardiff: Social Research Unit, School of Social and Administrative Studies, University of Wales College of Cardiff.

Finegold, D. and Soskice, D. (1988) 'The failure of training in Britain: an analysis and interpretation', *Oxford Review of Economic Policy*, vol 4, no 3, pp 46-62.

Gallie, D. (1991) 'Patterns of skill change: upskilling, deskilling or the polarisation of skills', *Work, Employment and Society*, vol 5, no 1, pp 319-51.

Lefebvre, M.C. (1992) 'Evaluation of women's involvement in ESF cofinanced measures', Report to DGV of the Commission of the European Communities.

Lindley, R. (ed) (1992) *Women's employment: Britain in the single European market*, Manchester: Equal Opportunities Commission.

Lovegrove, G. and Hall, W. (1987) 'Where have all the girls gone?', *University Computing*, no 9, pp 207-10.

MacNamara, F. (1990) *Women and training*, Unpublished dissertation, Cardiff: University of Wales College of Cardiff, MSc Econ Women's Studies.

Meager, N. (1991) 'TECs: A revolution in training and enterprise or old wine in new bottles?', *Local Economy*, vol 6, no 1, pp 4-20.

Murphy, P. and Mullan, T. (1989) 'Time for women in IT', Jordanstown: Department of Education, University of Ulster.

Newton, P. (1991) 'Computing: an ideal occupation for women?', in J. Firth-Cozens and M.A. West (eds) *Women at work*, Milton Keynes: Open University Press.

Newton, P. and Haslam, S. (1988) 'Girls and computers in secondary schools: a systems failure?', Paper presented at the British Psychological Society Annual Conference, University of Leeds.

OECD (1986) *New information technologies: a challenge for education*, Paris: OECD.

PA Consultants (1992) *An evaluation of the IRIS network*, Cambridge: PA Cambridge Economic Consultants.

Pelgrum, W.J. and Plomp, T. (1991) *The use of computers in education worldwide*, Oxford: Pergamon Press/International Association for the Evaluation of Educational Achievement.

Perry, R. and Greber, L. (1990) 'Women and computers: an introduction', *Signs*, vol 16, no 4, pp 74-101.

Rees, G. (1990) 'New information technologies and vocational training in the European communities: the challenge of the 1990s', Report for the EC's Project on Employment and Training in the New Information Technologies in the European Communities, Cardiff, University of Wales College of Cardiff.

Rees, T. (1992) *Skill shortages, women and the new information technologies*, Luxembourg: Commission of the European Communities.

Rees, T. (1993) *Women and the EC training programmes*, Report to the European Commission Task Force for Human Resources, Education, Training and Youth, Bristol: School for Advanced Urban Studies.

Rubery, J. and Fagan, C. (1992) *Occupational segregation amongst women and men in the European Community*, Brussels: Commission of the European Communities.

Schiersmann, C. (ed) (1988) *Mehr risiken als chancen? Frauen und neue technologien*, Hannover: Institut Frau und Gesellschaft.

Schmehr, H.J. and Millner, G. (1992) *Skills for a competitive Europe: a human resources outlook for the 1990s*, Brussels: Commission of the European Communities Task Force Human Resources Education, Training and Youth.

Schweikert, K. (1982) *Vocational training of young migrants in the Federal Republic of Germany*, Berlin: CEDEFOP.

Sessar-Karpp, E. (1988) 'Comuterkurse von frauen fur frauen', in C. Schiersmann (ed) *Mehr risiken als chancen? Frauen und neue technologien*, Hannover: Institut Frau und Gesellschaft.

Task Force Human Resources, Education, Training and Youth (1991) *Joint opinion on access to continuing training*, Brussels: Commission of the European Communities.

Wajcman, J. (1991) *Feminism confronts technology*, Oxford: Polity Press.
Walby, S. (1988) (ed) *Gender segregation at work*, Milton Keynes: Open University Press.
Walby, S. (1990) *Theorising patriarchy,* Oxford: Blackwell.
Wellington, J.J. (1989) *Education for employment: the place of information technology*, Windsor: National Foundation for Education Research.
Women's Technology Scheme (1989) *Annual report 1989*, Liverpool: Women's Technology Scheme.

INDEX

Page references in italic indicate figures or tables.

ability to pay, and health care, 205, 206, 207, 222
  measures, 211-12, 214, 215, *218*, 221
access
  health care, 216-17
  home ownership, 245-46, 247-48
  NITs training, 11, 400-01, 405-10, *406, 408, 409*, 413-20
accessibility, and local government quality, 42-43
accountability, public, 45, 139-40, 146
accumulation of wealth, housing as, 246, 248, 250-56, 282, 283, *283*
Action for Cities, 169
Action Programme, Social Charter, 10, 382-83, 386-87, 389
'active citizenship', 62-63, 69, 73
Adams, C., 66
'additionality', and impact of TECs, 377
Addy, T., 65
administration, 'policy sector' concept, 115-17
admissions policy, schools, 196-97, 198
advice, housing improvement, 338-39
advocacy work, voluntary bodies, 60, 68
AEG, NIT training, 412-13
age, and employment, 358, 359
Aglietta, M., 167
Albrow, M., 19
Alexander, A., 40
Alford, R., 19
Allen, D., 46
Allen, I., 233
allocative efficiency, quasi-markets, 185
AMA (Association of Metropolitan Authorities), 45, 278, 279
ambiguity of goals, inner city policy, 114
Amin, A., 166
Anderson, D., 59
Anglo-Irish labour market regulation, 392, 395
Appleby, J., 199
area committees, 148
Arber, S., 236
Argyris, C., 24
Ascher, K., 139, 141

assets
  control through ownership, 255
  sale of local authority, 140, 141
assisted places scheme, education, 177
Association of Metropolitan Authorities, (AMA), 45, 278, 279
Atkin, K., 237
Atkinson, J., 345
Aucoin, P., 16, 17, 19, 26
Audit Commission, 23, 24, 31
audit schemes, social services, 47
Austin, N., 134

Bachrach, P., 107
Baddeley, S., 90
Ball, M., 253, 259, 263, 289
Banham, J., 390
Bank of England, 254
Baratz, M.S., 107
Barbolet, R.H., 245
Barbour, G.P., 142
Barnard, H., 49
Barnes, A., 180
Barr, N., 180, 191, 216
Barrell, R., 243, 256, 280
Barrett, S., xiii, xiv, 2, 79, 81, 85, 86, 90, 107, 116
Bartholomew, R., 361, 362
Bartlett, W., xv, 193, 230, 288, 289, 290, 310
Basildon, London Borough of, 40
Bassett, K., 352
Bateson, G., 22
Batley, R., 109, 165
Baxter, C., 236, 237
BCDC (Black Country Development Corporation), 159
Beavin, J., 22
Beesley, M., 128
Benko, A., 328
Benson, J.K., 108, 112, 115, 117
Bentham, G., 266
Benzeval, M., xiv
Beresford, P., 44, 45, 134
Berry, L., 72
Best, R., 72
Beuret, K., 40, 49
Bianchini, F., 160

Billis, D., 68
Birmingham
    council housing, 244
    quality assessment, 47
Birmingham CCSAP (Community Care Action Project), 44
Blaazer, C., 417
Black Country Development Corporation (BCDC), 159
Black Horse Relocation, 265
Blackwell, J., 388, 392, 394
Blaug, M., 187
Blaxter, M., 209, 211
block contracts, health care, 193-94
Bluestone, B., 349, 350
Blunkett, D., 133, 138, 142
Boddy, M., 351, 352
Boilermakers Union, Social Charter reaction, 395
Boleat, M., 277
borrowing, for housing improvements, 334-36
Borzeix, A., 44
Bosanquet, N., 63, 230
Bosch, G., 413
Bosch, NITs training, 412
boundaries of inner city policy, 114
Bourne, Martine, 388
Bover, O., 291
Bowling, B., 236
Bowman, A.O'M., 133
Boyle, R., 141
Bramley, G., 25, 31, 182, 297, 308, 309, 318, 320
    1989, 288, 290, 292, 294, 305
Brant, J., 270
Braverman, H., *18*
Brenton, M., 65, 74
Bridgeford, J., 396
Brownill, S., 159
Bruegel, I., 358
Bucci, M., 408
budget devolution, 31-32, 190, 196, 199, 201-02
building industry reform, and housing improvements, 339
building regulations, and housing improvements, 338
Bull, D., 151
bureaucratic control, 16, 17-25, *18, 20,* 34-35
    demise of, 22-25
    and NITs, 80, 82-83, 84
    post-, *18,* 25-34, *30*
'bureaucratic paternalism', *136,* 137
Burgess, T., 23
Burkeman, S., 71

Burns, D., xv
Buron, M., 385, 394
Burrell, G., 27
Burris, B., 17, 18, 35
Burton, P., 275
Byrne, D., 166

Cambridgeshire education department, 23
Cameron, G.C., 128
Campbell, H., 83
Campbell, P., 235
Cane, A.,
capital appreciation, housing, 246, 248, 250-56, 282, 283, *283*
capital leakage, housing, 252, 253, 254
capitation funding of schools, 196, 197
Caplen, R.H., 45
care managers, 178, 190, 199-200, 228
'career clerical hierarchies', 351
'career path migration', 270
Caring for People, 228
Carr-Hill, R., 44
Carter, N., 46, 48
Carter, T., 235
case managers. *See* care managers
Cassam, E., 43
Castells, M., 132
catering services, NHS, 177
Cawson, A., 165
CBI, *See* Confederation of British Industry
CCT. *See* compulsory competitive tendering
central/local needs conflict 118, 122, 123-24, 133, 165
central services, and devolution, 24, 29-30, *30*
centralisation, 20, *20,* 21
Centre for Local Economic Strategies, 165, 163, 166
CES Ltd, 275
'chaotic' survival, Poland, 2, 93-101, 94, 96-97
charitable support, voluntary sector, 70-73, *71*
Charities Aid Foundation, 61, 69, 70, *71,* 72
Charity Commission, 71
Cheshire, P., 289, 290
Child, S., 345
childcare voucher idea, 180
Christian alternatives to capitalism and socialism, 99
Christiansen, D., 410
chronic illness, and income, 220, *220*
Church of England, 263
CIPFA (Chartered Institute of Public Finance and Accountancy), 24
Circular 22/80, 123
cities, differences between, 128-29

Index 427

citizen empowerment, 68, 144, 145-50, *147*
citizenship, 45, 62-63, 69, 73, 146, 151
City of Bristol Planning Department, 272
City Challenge, 155, 161, 167, 168-69
civil service reform, 24, 29
Clarke, D., xv
Clarke, K., 417
Clarke, M., 51, 61, 143
Clarke, S., 16
class. *See* occupational class
Clavel, P., 134
cleaning services, NHS, 177
Clegg, S., 17
Cmnd 9513, 325, 335
Cockburn, C., 404, 405, 418
'coexistence of opposites', 99-100
Coleman, G., xv
collective consumption, and class, 246-48
collectivist public sector reform, *136*, 137-38
Collins, E., 205, 206, 207, 208, 215, *216*
COM 89, 386, 389
Comac methodology, 209-10, 215, *217*, 221
COMETT programme, EC, 408, *409*, 410
Commission of the European Communities, 385, 387, 402, 405, 407, *408*, 411, 421
commodification, 347
'communications theory', 22
community-based organisations, Poland, 98
community care services, 5-6, 62, 190, 199-200, 222-38
  common needs and interests, 234-37
  empowerment theories, 229-31, *229*
  user involvement, 231-33
community charge, 139-40
Community Development Projects, 127, 156
community development work, UDCs, 161
community view of UDCs, 166
Community Programme, 65
competition, service provision, 126, 139, 140, 168, 189-90
  and efficiency, 182-83
  schools, 196-97, 199
  inner city organisations, 114
  voluntary organisations, 66
competitive tendering, 24, 62, 64, 141, 190
complaints examinations, and quality, 47
'complementarity', EC policy, 389
Comptroller and Auditor-General, 126
compulsory competitive tendering (CCT), 24, 62, 64, 141, 190
concentration, British industrial, 127-28
concentration index (CI), 210, 217
concessionary fare schemes, 180
Confederation of British Industry (CBI), 41, 43, 386, 390

Connor, H., 403
Conservative government policies, xiv, 112, 158, 179
  See also Thatcher era
constraints variables, housing models, 303, *304*, *306*, 307, 316
construction costs, housebuilding models, 302-03
consultant role, TEC evaluation, 376-77, 379
consumer empowerment, 144, 145-50, *147*
consumer surveys, and quality, 47
consumerism, xiv, xv, 41, 131, 134
  and public sector reform, *136*, 137, 142-45
  voluntary sector, 67-68
consumers of services, 44-45
consumption cleavages, 6, 241-42, 246, 249, 268
consumption sectors, 242, 246-48, 266
'contingent labor', 350
'continuity', and local government quality, 42-43
contracting out of services, 177
  See also competitive tendering
contracts, purchaser/provider, 202-03
  control by, 26-28
  NHS, 193-94
  schools, 199
  voluntary sector, 64-67
control, and ownership, 255
control strategies, organisational, 17-19, *18*
Conway, J., 276
Cooke, P., 345
Coombes, M., 289
Cooper. H., 361, 362
Cooper, R., 27,
Cooper, S.Y., 346
'coordination', and local government quality, 42-43
corporate giving, 69, 70
corporate responsibility, 63
corporatism, local, 119-20, 165
Corrigan, P., 58, 66
'cost centre budgeting', 23, 34
cost control, and decentralisation, 27
cost-per-case contracts, 193
costs, quasi-markets, 183-85, 202-03
council housing, 243-45, 248, 249, 262-63, 264
  and accumulation, 251, 252
  sale of, 6, 200-01, 275, 277-79
council tenants, marginalisation, 266, 267
Cousins, C., 15
Coutts, K., 346
Coyle, D., 357
Cracknell, S., 47

craft control strategies, 17, *18*
Craig, C., 270
credentialism, 349
credit cards, and charity income, 69
Cresswell, P., 157
criminal offences, 361
Croft, S., 44, 45
Crompton, R., 351, 357, 361, 403
cultural change. *See* organisational culture
Cummings, 133
Curtice, J., 258
Czepiel, J.A., 43

Dahrendorf, R., 74
Daily Telegraph, 269
Dale, A., 352, 358, 361
Dalley, G., 39, 45, 48
Daniel, W.W., 127
Danson, M.W., 365
Davies, B., 67
Davies, M., 40
Davies, T., 93
Davis, M., 360
Davis, N., 270
Dawes, N., 90
Day, P., 34, 40, 43, 45
Day, T., 39
Deal, T.E., 82
Deakin, N., 33, 40, 45
decentralisation, xv, 1, 16-35, 39-40, 48-49
　bureaucratic control, 19-25, *20*
　control strategies, 17-19, *18*
　delegated powers, 30-34
　freedom within boundaries, 28-30, *30*
　and NITs, 81, 132-33, 145
　neighbourhood, 131, 145-50, *147*
　post-bureaucratic control, 25-28
　and quality, 50-53
　of TECs, 365, 375
Decentralisation of social services departments, 23
deindustrialisation, urban, 3, 122, 127
delegated powers, 30-34
delivery pluralism, 64-68
'delocalisation' of production and consumption, 3, 132
Delors, Jacques, 383, 387, 389
demand equation, 'lagged response' model, 292-94, *293*
demand models, private housebuilding, 298-302, *299*
democracy, local, 148, *148*
democratic accountability, 33-34
democratic approach to empowerment, 230
democratic pluralism, 62, 75, 165
democratic public service provision, 3
　See also empowerment

demographic change, and German NITs training, 411-12
demographic variables, housing models, 297, 298, *299*, 323-24
Department of Education, 176
Department of Education and Science, 23, 176
Department of Employment, *71*, 355
Department of the Environment, 62, 123, 161, 168, 263, *327*, 329, 332, *332*, 338
Department of Health, 176, 190, 225, 229, 228
Department of Health and Social Security, 23, 206, 225
Deroure, F., 405
devolved management, 16, 23-30, *30*, 40, 49
　delegated powers, 30-34
'devolved service units' (DSUs), 26, 27
Devon, community care, 231, 232-33
Dex, S., 359
DHAs (district health authorities), 191
Dicken, P., 127, 128
direct democracy, *148*, 148-49
Directory of Social Change, 70
disabled facilities grants, 331, 333
disabled people
　commonality of needs, 234-35
　housing improvements, 331, 333, 337
　NITs employment, 400
'discretion', bureaucratic organisation, *20*, 20-1, 27
discrimination, labour market, 357, 385
　See also age; gender; race; segmentation
Disney, R., 215
'displacement', and TEC impact, 377
'dissimilarity index', EC, 402
district health authorities (DHAs), 191
diversity of European labour market policies, 10, 391-92
Docklands Joint Committee, 157-58
Doctors, S.I., 374
doctors. *See* GPs
Doling, J., 253, 266
'domestic property class', 246
'dominated local labour markets', 349
Donabedian, A., 41, 42, 43
Donnison, D.V., 156, 269
Doorslaer, E. van, 207, 209
Dowson, S., 65
Drucker, P., 94
DSUs ('devolved service units'), 26, 27
du Parcq, L., 134
dual city concept, 167
dual state thesis, 165
dual training system, Germany, 410-16
Due, J., 392, 393
dump estates, 274-75

Dunleavy, P., 141, 241, 246, 258, 266
Dunn, R., 275
'dynamic conservatism', 134

Eastbourne Area Social Services Team, 23
Eastern Europe
  regulatory control, 21
  structural change, 93-94
  See also Poland
economic development programmes. *See*
  urban economic development
  programmes
economic restructuring, 8, 132, 345-47,
  358-60
  global, 3, 132, 133
  and labour market, 347-58, *348, 349,
  355*
  Poland, 93-101
economic tensions, urban government, 133-35
economic variables, housing models, 297,
  298, 299, 323-24
economies of scale, voluntary sector, 66-67
Economist, 346
Eddison, T. xiii
Edelman, M., 107
education
  housing improvement, 338-39
  policy, 23, 62, 190, 195-99
  vouchers, 178, 180, 187
Education Reform Act 1988, 176, 177, 196
Edwards, J., 72, 109
Edwards, R., 17
efficiency of quasi-markets, 182-86, 202-03
'efficiency scrutiny', voluntary sector, 73, 75
elderly people. *See* older people
'elite' external labour markets, 349, 351,
  352, 357, 358
Elliot, L., 159
Ellis, R., 42
ELMs. *See* external labour markets
Elnicki, R., 184
Elson, M., 303
emergency repair services insurance, 336
Emmerich, M., 365, 369
employer-led partnerships, TECs as, *367*
employment careers, and housing, 256-57
Employment Department, 365, *366, 367,
  368*, 371, 372, 373, 374, 376, 396
Employment Gazette, 355
Employment Training, 354, 368
employment variable, housing models, 298
empowerment, 144, 145-50, *147, 148,*
  228-38
  community care planning, 231-33
  theories, 229-31, *229*
  users' needs, 234-37

voluntary sector, 64, 68
Englander, D., 244
English Partnerships. *See* Urban
  Regeneration Agency
enrolment, school, 177-78, 196, 197
Enterprise Allowance, 368
enterprise organisations, TECs as, *367*,
  367-68
environmental concern, voluntary activity,
  72
environmental dimension, quality, 41-42
Equal Opportunities Commission, 417
equity issues, quasi-markets, 182, 186
equity sharing loans, for housing
  improvements, 335, 340
equity withdrawal, housing, 252, 253, 254
Ermisch, J., 291, 310
Essex, S., 419
Etherington, S., 68
ethnic minorities. *See* race
ETUC (European Trade Union
  Confederation), 387, 389, 405
European Community, xiv, 9-11
  NITs training, 400, 402-10, *406, 408,
  409*
  See also Social Charter
European Round Table of Industrialists, 402
European Social Fund (ESF), 407, *408*
European Trade Union Confederation
  (ETUC), 387, 389, 405
Europeanisation of employment policy. *See*
  Social Charter
Eurostat, 406
evaluation of TECs, 365-66, 369-74
  in practice, 374-79
Evandrou, M., 205, 206, 222
Evans, A.W., 289, 290
Evans, R., 365, 369, 371
Evers, H., 236
'excellence', 22-23, 95-96, 142
exit-driven approaches to empowerment,
  230, 231
expenditure cuts, to local government,
  138-42
expenditure distribution, health service,
  205-27
  data, 210-12
  departures from horizontal equity, 215-18, *216, 217, 218*
  methodological approaches, 206-10
  need distribution, 212-15, *213, 214*
  results, 219-22, *220, 221*
  standardisation of need and expenditure,
  223-24, *224*
'expert' approach, policy change, 84
external decentralisation, 16, 26, 27
  See also quasi-markets

Index 429

external labour markets (ELMs), 9, 349, 351-52, 353, 357, 361

Fagan, C., 403
Fagg, J.J., 128
'failure' strategies, and restructuring, 98
family influences on mobility, 284
Farmer, M.K., 243, 256, 280
Fayol, H., *18*
Federal Minister for Education and Science, 411
fee income, voluntary sector, 72
Feldman, R., 184
female workers. *See* women
Fennell, G., 236
Fenton, S., 354
Fielder, S., 352, 403
finance pluralism, voluntary sector, 69-74, *71*
finance/provision separation. *See* quasi-markets
financial control, devolution of, 31-32, 190, 196, 199, 201-02
Financial Times, 269, 395
financing. *See* funding
Findlay, A.M., 271
Finegold, D., 416
Finn, D., 354
Firn, J.P., 128
fiscal variable, housing models, *299*, 300
fixed rate loans, for housing improvements, 335
flexible specialisation, 15, 345, 356-57, 358
flexibility
 labour markets, 352
 personnel and production policies, 15-16
Flynn, N., 46
FORCE, *409*, 410
Fordism, 132-33, 349
foreign investment, and restructuring, 346-47
formalisation, bureaucratic organisations, 20, *20*, 27-28
'formalised freedom', devolution, 27-30, *30*
Forrest, R., 201, 249, 280
 and Murie, A.
  1980, 250, 254
  1983, 266, 281
  1986, 249, 267, 275
  1987, 256, 266, 269, 270, 277
  1988, xiv
Forster, D.P., 205, 207
Fothergill, S., 127, 128
'fourth generation' evaluation, 374, 378
framework for steering IT change, 87
Franklin, A., 32, 264, 268, 270

'freedom within boundaries', 2, 28-30, 30
 delegated powers, 30-34
Frissen, P., 80, 82
front-line staff, 43-44, 80
Fudge, C., xiii, xv, 2, 24, 85, 107, 116
funding
 inner city policy, 113
 TECs, 368-69
 university, 176, 178
 voluntary sector, 69-70

Gallie, D., 400
Gaster, L., xv, 40, 43, 44, 45, 46, 47, 49, 50
gender
 and employment. *See* women
 health expenditure, 221-22, *221*
 and user empowerment, 236
'general health' measure, *213*, 214
General Household Survey (GHS), 210-11, 222
geographical variables, housing models, 297, 298, *299*, 323-24
George, K.D., 127
Germany, NITs training, 401, 410-16
 access for women, 413-16
Getting closer to the public, 142, 143
GHS (General Household Survey), 210-11, 220
Gibson, D., 185
Giddens, A., 268
Gift Aid, 69
Gini coefficient, 210
Ginn, J., 236
Giussani, B., 289
Gladstone, F., 58, 74
Gleave, D., 271
Gleick, J., 97
Glennerster, H., 180
global companies, 96
global restructuring, 3, 132, 133
Globe Town, 33
GM (grant maintained) schools, 196, 197-99
Godley, W., 346
Golding, P., 157
Goodin, R., 5, 182, 185, 205
Gosschalk, B., 47
governing bodies, GM schools, 197-98
government
 changing welfare strategies, 58-60, *59*
 contracts, 64-66
 inner cities, 110-11, 112
 and Social Charter, 395
 training schemes, 354
 and voluntary sector, 57, 58, 69-70, 74-76

Index 431

See also Conservative government;
    Labour government; Thatcher era
GPs
    budgets, 178, 191-92
    cost of consultation, *225*, 225
    payment structure, 179-80
    graduate tax, 180
Grahl, J., 393
grant maintained (GM) schools, 196, 197-99
grant policy, housing improvements, 325-33
    effectiveness, 327-28
    future options, 331-33, *332*
    new system, 330-31
    pattern of provision, 329-30
Greber, L., 417
Green, D., 140
Green, F., 271
Griffiths, B., 99
Griffiths, R., 34-35, 176
Grigson, W.S., 290
Grossman, B., 64, 65, 67
Guardian, 395, 396
Guba, E.G., 374, 378
Gudgin, G., 127, 128
Gustafsson, L., 24
Gyford, J., 147

Haddon, R., 245
Hadjimatheou, G., 289
Halfpenny, P., 71
Hall, P., 122, 123, 127
Hall, W., 417
Ham, C., xiv, 20, 43
Hambleton, R., xiii, 109, 110, 112, 113,
    115, 131, 133, 145, 146, 150, 151
    and Hoggett, P., xv, 23, 32, 40, 41, 135,
        139, 144, 145
    and Stewart, M. and Underwood, J.,
        110, 111, 113, 115, 117
Hamilton, F.E.I., 127
Hammersmith and Fulham, community care
    planning, 231, 231-32
Hamnett, C., 266, 267, 275, 291
Hamrin, R.D., 99
Handy, C., 25, 26, 29
Hannah, L., 346, 356
Hannan, M.T., 95
Hansard, 263, 273, 279, 281
Harley, M., 46
Harris, M., 68
Harrison, B., 349, 350
Harrison, L., 235
Harrison, P., 268, 274
Harvey, D., 166, 167
Haslam, S., 417
Hatch, S., 59
Havel, V., 21

Haveman, R., 214
Hay, D., 122, 127
Hayden, D., 268
Hayden, F.W., 127
Healey, P., 2, 106, 107, 109, 115, 159, 318
health care expenditure. *See* expenditure
    distribution, health service
Health and Lifestyle Survey (HLS), 219-20
health policy, 4-6
    See also expenditure distribution; GPs;
        National Health Service
health service quality, US, 41-42
Heath, A., 6, 258
Henkel, M., 40
Heseltine, Michael, 158, 347
Hewitt, P., 180
Heydebrand, W., 19
'hierarchy', control by, 26-27, 28-29
higher education changes, 176, 178, 180
Hill, D.M., 147
Hill, M., xiv, 2, 20, 43, 85, 112
Hills, J., 212, 312, 319
Hird, C., 255
Hirscheim, R.A., 83
Hirschman, A.O., 68
Hirst, P., 345
Hjern, B., 115
HLS (Health and Lifestyle Survey), 219-20
Hodge, M., 40, 134
Hodgson, G., 361
Hoggett, P., 2, 15, 21, 25, 27, 31, 34, 132,
    133, 151, 181
    and Hambleton, R., xv, 23, 32, 40, 41,
        135, 139, 144, 145
Hole, V., 242
Holme, A., 250
Home Office, 63, 73, 74
home ownership, 6, 7, 242, 243, 262-66,
    270, 276-77, 279
    and mobility, 270
    and occupational class, 245-46, 249-50
    primacy of, 258-60
    See also accumulation of wealth;
        council houses: sale of
homelessness, 276-77, 361
Hoog, R. de, 64, 65
horizontal equity, health care provision,
    205-07, 215-18, *216*, *217*, *218*, 219, 222
Horn, C.E. Van, 115
hospital trusts, 192-93
hospitals, 'self-managing', 178, 190
House of Commons, 158, 369-70, 390
house prices. *See* prices, house
housebuilding modelling, 298-307, *299*,
    304, *306*
Housing Act 1980, 278
Housing Act 1988, 176, 178, 201

432 Index

housing assistance, 276, 280-03, *283*
    See also subsidies, housing; tax subsidies
housing associations, 201
housing benefit, 201, 281
'housing careers', 280
'housing classes', 245, 246, 247, 249, 255
housing decay. See renewal, housing
housing histories, 280-03
Housing and Local Government Act 1989, 176
housing market changes, and housing improvements, 338
housing 'pathways', 280
housing policy, 6-8, 190
    devolved management, 23-24
    quasi-markets, 176, 178-79, 200-01
    See also mobility; occupational class; renewal; supply elasticity
housing renewal. See renewal, housing
Hoyes, L., 47, 230, 231, 235
Hudson, R., 270
Hungary, structural change, 93
Hurst, J.W., 205, 212
Hutchinson, R., 169
hybrid organisations, 66
Hymer, S., 360

Ibbs Report, 24
ILMs. See internal labour markets
implementation oriented approach, inner city planning, 105-06, 106-09
improvement grant system, 325
implementation theory, xiii-xiv, 2
Imrie, R., 165
in-patient stays, costs, 211, 225, *225*
In search of excellence, 22-23, 95-96, 138, 142
'incentive contracts', 202-03
income, as ability-to-pay measure, 211-12, 215, 222
    and self-assessed morbidity, 212-15, *213*, *214*
    and socio-economic group, 220-21
income redistribution, restructuring, 346, 360-61
incremental approach to informisation, 89
incremental change, 95
Independent, 160, 163, 166
Indian Workers' Association, 156
'induced supply' response, 307, 310
industrial incubators, cities as, 128
industrial relations, European diversity, 392, 393, 395
informal strategies, bureaucracy, 20, 20-1, 27-28

information networks, labour markets, 354-55
information policy, 85
'information poor', 81
information technology (NI or NITs), 2, 3, 10-11, 25, 79-92, 145, 181, 399-424
    cultural impact, 80-83
    culture, 79-80
    EC, 402-10, *406*, *408*, *409*
    Germany, 410-16
    and globalisation, 132
    managing change, 83-84
    organisational learning strategies, 88-90
    realising potential, 84-86
    UK, 416-20
    uncertainty and change, 86-88
'informisation', 82, 87, 88
    managing change, 83-90
infrastructure, voluntary sector, 67, 75
Inner Area Studies, 109-10, 156
inner cities, 2-3, 105-21
    home ownership, 263, 274
    implementation approach, 106-09
    policy, 109-11, 169, 170
    political struggles, 156-57
    theoretical perspectives, 112-20
    UDCs, 161
Inner Urban Areas Act 1978, 156
institutional care, health expenditure analysis, 211
institutional change, Poland, 93
insurance schemes, housing improvements, 336
integrated working, 40, 48, 52
interest bearing debt (IBD), 192
interest group politics, 135, 149
interest structure, 'policy sector' concept, 108, 117-18
inter-firm linkages, 128
internal decentralisation, 16, 26, 27
internal labour markets (ILMs), 9, 190, 345, 349-51, 352, 361
    recruitment, 353
international finance, Britain's role, 346
investment, stimulating private housing, 334-39
IRIS programme, EC, *409*, 410
Irvine, J., 255
Islington, London Borough, 32, 33, 40, 149-50
Islington District Health Authority, 48
IT. See information technology

Jackson, D., 22
Jackson, K., 133, 142
James, K., 44
Japan

Index 433

coexistence of opposites, 99-100
investment in Britain, 346
management involvement, 95
Jenkins, S., 210, 224
Jensen, C., 392, 393
jobcentres, 354
Johnson, C., 253
Johnson, J.H., 272
Johnson, T., 17
joint ventures, local authority/voluntary sector, 61
Jones, G., 34, 147
Jones, R., 67
Joseph Rowntree Foundation, 290, 312, 320
Jowell, R., 258
'just in time' production processes, 95

Kaess, L., 374
Kanter, R.M., 20, 22, 94
Karn, V., 253, 263, 266
Karran, T.J., 139
Kaynak, E., 96
Keeble, D.E., 128
Keith, M., 156
Kelly, I., 281
Kemeny, J., 254, 280
Kemp, P., 29
Kendig, H., 280
Kennedy, A.A., 82
King, J.L., 83
Kings Fund Institute, 184
Kitsuse, J.I., 125
Klein, R., 34, 40, 43, 45, 205, 206, 207, 208, 215, *216*
Kraemer, K.L., 83
Kramer, R., 59, 64, 65, 67, 74
Kumar, K., 123
Kunz, C., 67

Labour Coordinating Committee, 23
Labour government, inner city policy, 112, 157-58
labour market policy, 8-11, 262, 345-65
allocation to 'places', 352-53
EC regulation, 391
economic restructuring, 347-49, *348, 349*
and mobility, 270-01
'places', 349-54
segmentation, 356-58
'systematic noise', 354-56, *355*
See also Social Charter; training; Training and Education Councils
Labour Party, 42, 346, 347
housing policy, 262
and Social Charter, 395, 396
labourist view of UDCs, 166

Laffont, J.J., 203
'lagged response' model. *See* supply elasticity
Lair, J., 59
Lambert, C., 288, 291, 292, 295
land release policy, 316-18, *317*, 319-20
land use planning. *See* supply elasticity
land variables, housing models, 303, *304*
Länder, training in German, 415-16
Lane, C., 15
Lart, R., 231
Lash, S., 345, 347, 358, 360
Laszlo, E., 100
Law, C.M., 159
Lawless, P., 123, 163
Lawson, N., 59
LDDC (London Docklands Development Corporation), 158, 160
Le Grand, J., xiv, 5, 185, 206, 208, *218*, 219, 224, 230, 235
1978, 205, 207, 214, 217, 218, 225
1982, 182
1987, 180
1989, 186
1990, 16, 175, 195
1991, 393
leakage, house capital, 252, 253, 254
Learning from the public, 142
Leat, D., 70, 73
Leather, P., 81, 326, 330, 335, 337
Leborgne, D., 15
Lee, E.C., 151
Leighton, P., 356
lending requirements, and housing improvements, 338
length of stay as in-patients, 211, 225
Lever, W.F., 349
leverage ratios, 163-64
LGTB (Local Government Training Board), 24, 142, 143
life-cycle stages, and mobility, 284
Lincoln, Y.S., 374, 378
Lindley, R., 416
Lingle, C., 391
linkages, inter-firm, 128
Lipietz, A., 15, 345
Lipsky, M., 43, 80
Lloyd, P., 128
LMS (local management of schools), 196
loans, housing improvement, 335, 340
local authorities
decentralisation, 23, 24, 29-30
democratic theory, 146-48
economic development programmes, 122, 123-24, 129
government policy towards, 61, 62, 158
inner city interests, 118

434 Index

spending constraints, 138-39
view of UDCs, 165-66, 170
voluntary body support, 61, 69-70
See also management of the public sector; quality of service delivery; urban government
local corporatism, inner city policy as, 119-20, 165
local democracy, 148, *148*
Local Education Authorities (LEAs), 195
Local Enterprise Companies (LECs), 417
'local environmental indicators', 376
local focus of TECs, *367*, 368
  conflict with national requirements, 369-70
Local Government Training Board (LGTB), 24, 142, 143
local management of schools (LMS), 196
local market effects, housing models, 301-02
local/national needs conflict 118, 122, 123-24, 133, 165
localisation of services, 40, 49, 51, 52
locational tendencies, industrial, 128
locality studies, 164-65
London, decentralisation, 272
London Docklands Development Corporation (LDDC), 158, 160
London Life Association, 272
Loney, M., 58
Longley, P., 291
Lord, R., 195
Lovegrove, G., 417
Lovering, J., 133, 351, 353, 360
Low, W., 182
low-income households, improvement grants, 330
Lowe, S., 133
Lowndes, V., 43
Lukes, S., 98, 107

MacGregor, S., 157
Mackintosh, S., 326, 330, 335, 337
MacLennan, D., 253, 312, 319
MacNamara, F., 419
macroeconomic cycles, and UDCs, 159-60
Madsen, J., 392, 393
Magnusson, W., 151
maintenance funds, 337
maintenance insurance schemes, 336, 337
maintenance investment, post-grant, 328
Maister, D.H., 44
Makinson, G.T., 46
male workers, 348, 348, 349, 351
Malpass, P., 140
management, and institutional change, Poland, 95-96

management of the public sector, 15-38
  bureaucratic control, 19-25, *20*, 34-35
  delegated powers, 30-34
  freedom within boundaries, 28-30, *30*
  post-bureaucratic control, 25-28
  restructuring, 15-17
  strategies of organisational control, 17-19, *18*
management writings, 22-23, 94
managerial culture, UDCs, 160
manufacturing change, Poland, 96
manufacturing revival, 346
marginal groups, and home ownership, 274-76
marginalisation of council tenants, 266, 267
market approach to empowerment, 230
market pluralism, *136*, 137-38
market principles, 63, 67-68, 141, 164, 201
  and welfare, 59, 123-24, 176, 183
  See also quasi-markets
marketing of cities, 161-62
Marquand, D., 151, 370, 376
Marshall, G., 266
Marsland, D., 59
Martin, L., xv
'masculinisation of technologies', 404
Mason, C., 3, 133
Massey, D., 123, 127, 264, 266
Mattelart, A., 96-97, 98
Maxwell, S., 66, 68
Mayer, M., 16
Mayes, D., 289, 291, 294, 310
Maynard, A., 187
Mayston, D., 184
McAffee, R.P., 203
McClements, L.D., 225
McMahon, L., 86
McMillan, J., 203
Meade, K., 235
Meadows, P., 361, 362
Meager, N., 365, 417
Means, R., 230, 235
mechanistic management approaches, 19, 22
media fund-raising appeals, 69
Meegan, R., 123, 127, 161
mental health user groups, 235
Mercedes Benz, NITs training, 400
Merrett, S., 180, 308
Merrill Lynch, 265, 271
Merseyside Development Corporation, 161
Merton, R., 265
Meter, D.S. Van, 115
methodological approaches, health expenditure studies, 206, 206-10
Meyer, M., 166, 167
migrant workers, and Social Charter, 385-86

milieu, local, 128-29
Millner, G., 402
Mills, L., 122, 125
minimum wage regulations, 392
Ministry of Defence, 351
Mintzberg, H., *18*, 94
MIRAS. *See* mortgage interest tax relief
MITR. *See* mortgage interest tax relief
mobility, and housing, 7, 262-87
    and house prices, 264, 265
    and housing assistance and histories, 280-03, *283*
    social consumption and urban change, 265-69
    spatial, and tenure, 269-77
    tenure, 277-80
Mocroft, I., 59
modernisation goals, and information technology, 82-83
Modood, T., 234
monitoring
    economic policies, 125-26
    quality, 46-48
    TECs, 365-66, 369-79
Monk, S., 290, 291, 292, 316
monopolies v. competing providers, 183-84
Moore, R., 244, 245
Moorhouse, H.F., 361
moral basis for change, Poland, 2, 98-99
morbidity, as latent variable need, 211
    distribution, 212-15, *213*, *214*, 219
Moreton, N., 253
Morgan, G., 19
Morphet, J., 134, 148
Morrell, J., 273
Morris, J., 234
Morris Suzuki, T., 22
mortgage arrears, 263, 278
mortgage assistance, and mobility, 271-72, 276
mortgage benefit payments, housing improvements, 335
mortgage interest tax relief (MITR or MIRAS), 7, 281-82
    model, 291-96, *293*
    simulations of policy impact, 312-16, *314*, *315*, 319
Mortiboys, R., 43
Muellbauer, J., 291
Mulgen, G., 133
Mullan, T., 420
multi-agency approach, inner cities, 110, 114
multi-plant corporations, impact on local urban economy, 127-28
Munro, M., 253
Murie, A., xiv, 140, 201, 244, 265

and Forrest, R.,
    1980, 250, 254
    1983, 266, 281
    1986, 249, 267, 275
    1987, 256, 266, 269, 270, 277
    1988, xiv
Murphy, M., 275, 279
Murphy, P., 420
Murray, F., 25
Muth, R., 289
mutual reinforcement of policies, EC, 396-97

Nakano, C., 100
NALGO, 387
National Audit Office, 165
National Council for Voluntary Organisations, 67
National Health Service (NHS)
    devolved management, 23, 34-35
    quasi-markets, 176, 177, 178, 184, 190-04
    trusts, 190
    See also expenditure distribution
National Health Service and Community Care Act 1990, 191, 199, 228
national/local needs conflict, 118, 122, 123-24, 133, 165
National Mobility Scheme, 276
national training programmes, TECs, 354, 368, 379
National Transport Tokens Limited, 181
Nationwide Building Society, 269, 273, 274, 297
NEDC, 265, 270
need for medical care, 205, 206, 207-10, 211
    distribution, 212-15, *213*, *214*
    standardisation, 212, 215, 223-24, *224*, 225
'negotiated order', 116
neighbourhood committees, 148
neighbourhood decentralisation, 131, 135, *136*, 146, *147*
neighbourhood forums, Islington, 150
neo-Fordism, 356
Neutze, M., 290
new build model, 307, 308-10, *309*
new houses, prices, 300, 301-02
new information technologies (NITs). *See* information technology
New Opportunities for Women (NOW) programme, 407
'new public management', 16-17
New Right, 59, 59, 60, 63, 164, 165
New Society, 278
'new wave' management, 22-23, 27

Newchurch, 193
Newton, K., 119, 139
Newton, P., 404, 417
NFHA, 263
NHBC, 297
NHS. *See* National Health Service
Nicholson, B.M., 128
NITs (new information technologies). *See* information technology
'noise', labour market, 255
non-profit sector. *See* voluntary sector
non-technical dimension, quality, 41-42
Nordic labour market regulation, 392
Northern Ireland Housing Executive, *327*
Norton, R.D., 128
Nyquist, J.D., 44

Oakey, R.P., 346
objectives, TEcs, 371, 377-78
Observer, 269, 278, 395
occupational class
  and housing, 6, 241-61, 280-03
  accumulation, 250-56
  council housing, 243-45
  employment careers, 256-57
  home ownership, 245-46
  primacy of, 246-48
  residential mobility patterns, 269-70, 280
  tenure, 249-50, 258-59
  measure of ability to pay. *See* socio-economic groups
O'Connor, J., 120
O'Donnell, O., 205, 206, 207, 211, 212, 219, 220
OECD, 79
Office of Health Economics, 214, 225
older people
  empowerment, 233, 235, 236
  housing improvement assistance, 335, 337
  residential care, 177, 185, 199-200
older workers, NITs training, 414
Oldman, C., 230
Oliver, M., 234
OPCS, 264, 277
open enrolment, schools, 177-78, 196, 197
operational decentralisation, 1, 25, 29
'opportunism', 194
optimal incentive contracts, 202-03
opting out provisions, 190
  hospitals, 178
  schools, 177, 178, 196, 197
  and voluntary sector, 64
organisation, and quality, 45-46
organisational change, xv, 29, 79, 83-91,
  managing, 83-86

organisational learning, 88-90
  and uncertainty, 86-88
organisational control strategies, 17-19, *18*
organisational culture, 29, 44, 79-80
  and decentralisation, 48-49
  impact of NITs, 80-83
  See also organisational change
organisational decentralisation, 132-33
organisational learning, 2, 87-88, 88-90
organisational structure, 'policy sector' concept, 108, 115-17
organisational tensions, urban government, 133-35
O'Sullivan, A., 289
Oulton, N., 356
out-patient visits, costs, 211, 225, *225*
output related funding, 368-69
output variable, housing models, *299*, 300, 301-02, 313, *314*
over-consumption, 360
owner occupation. *See* home ownership
Oxfordshire, community care, 231, 232

Packard, V., 144
Page, E., 124, 128
Pahl, R.E., 242, 243, 246, 266, 267, 280
Palmer, D., 271
Palo Alto school of 'communications theory', 22
Papandreou, V., 387-88
Parkin, F., 361
Parsons, D., 265
'participative democracy', 40
partnership approach, inner city planning, 3, 106, 109, 110-11, 113
  UDCs, 162-63, 168
part-time work, 351, 359, 416
party political emphasis, local government, 134-35
Patton, M.Q., 374
Payne, J. and Payne, G., 280
payroll giving, 69, 71
Peace, S., 236
Pearce, B., 312, 315
Pearson, R., 403
Peck, J., 365, 369
Pelgrum, W.J., 404
performance indicators, 46-47
  TEcs, 370-71, 378
peripheral housing estates, 275
Perlmutter, F., 66
'permanent innovation economy' (PIE), 22
Perry, R., 417
personal computer access, 89
Petchey, R., 23

Peters, T., 22-23, 28, 94-95, 87, 133, 134, 138, 142
Peterson, G.E., 139
Peterson, J., 72
PETRA programme, (EC), 408, *409*
Pfeffer, G., 83
Phillipson, C., 236
Pickup, L., 264
pilot schemes, information technology, 89
Pimlott, B., 157
place marketing, 161-62
'places', labour market, 349-52
   allocation to, 352-53
planning. *See* land use planning
planning equation, 'lagged response' model, 295-96
planning permissions model, 305-07, *306*
planning variables, housing models, 297, 299, 323-24
   planning permissions, 303, *314*, 315
   planning policy, 303, *304*, *306*, 307
'planning' theory, 105
Plomp, T., 404
pluralism, 61, 64-74
   finance, 69-74, *71*
   delivery, 64-68
   democratic, 62, 75, 165
   inner city policy, 119
   market, *136*, 137-38
   political, 59, 135, 147
   public sector provision, *136*, 137-38
   welfare, 58-59, *59*
pluralist collectivism, *136*, 137-38
Plymouth, labour markets, 350
Poland, institutional change, 2, 93-101
polarisation, tenurial, 266, 267, 268, 280
Policy for the inner city (White Paper), 110, 113, 156
policy-making, devolution of, 31-33
'policy orientation', 'policy sector' concept, 117
'policy sector' concept, 107-08, 112-14
   attributes, 113
   emergence, 112-13
   implications, 114
   interest structure, 108, 117-18
   organisation structure, 108, 115-17
   rules of structure formation, 108, 118-20
policy styles, UDCs, 160-01
political activities, charities, 73-74
political devolution, 32
political education, 147
political movements, local, 3, 133, 134
political pluralism, 59, 135, 147
political pressures, quasi-markets, 184-85
political struggle, inner cities, 156

political tensions, urban government, 133, 134-35
'politics of policy', 107
poll tax, 139-40
Pollert, A., 354
Pollitt, C., 39, 42, 44, 46, 143
Porter, D.O., 115
'positional goods', 358
Positively Discriminatory Vouchers (PDV), 186
Posnett, J., 72
post-bureaucratic management, 1, 2, *18*, 25-34, *30*
   delegated powers, 30-34
   freedom within boundaries, 28-30, *30*
post-Fordism, 3-4, 15, 345-47, 358-59
   and labour market, 9, 347-58, *348*, *349*, *355*
   UDCs, 166-67
   urban government, 137
post-modern ideas, Poland, 97
poverty, 'rediscovery of', 155-56
practical help, and housing improvements, 338-39
pragmatic partnership model, 59
'preference-guided society', 58-59
prescription costs, 225, *225*
Preteceille, E., 246-47, 266
price variables, housing models, 297, 305, 299, 323-24
prices, house
   and mobility, 264, 265, 269
   See also supply elasticity
'primacy of ownership', 258-59
Priority Estate Programme, 23-24
private health insurance, 220-21
private investment in housing, 334-39
privatisation, 3, 4-5, 131, *136*, 137, 138-42
   See also council houses: sale of; quasi-markets
'professional' control strategies, 17-19, *18*, 34-35
programme areas, inner cities, 109, 110, 111, 113
Propper, C., 205, 206, 207, 211, 212, 219, 221, 230
'provider' units, NHS, 191
public accountability, 45, 139-40, 146
'public dividend capital' (PDC), 192-93
public inquiries, UDCs, 161
public labour market agencies, 354
public/private sector partnerships, UDCs, 162-63
public sector investment, housing renewal, 335, 340-41
public service orientation, 51, 61, 143
public service reform, *136*, 137

collectivist solutions, 144, 145-50, *147, 148*
consumerism, 142-44
Puffer, F., 205, 206
Purcell, K., 356
purchaser-provider role separation, 199, 201-02
purchase-of-service contracts, voluntary sector, 64-66
'purchaser' units, NHS, 191

quality of outcome, quasi-markets, 184
quality of service delivery, xiv, xv, 39-56
  decentralisation, 39-40, 48-49
  model 41-46
  relationship with decentralisation, 50-51
  standards and monitoring, 46-48
quasi-markets, xiv-xv, 4, 175-88, 189-204, 230
  community care, 199-200
  education, 195-99
  health, 190-94
  housing, 200-01
  and welfare, 181-86

race
  employment, 358, 359, 400
  empowerment, 236
  Social Charter, 385
  training, 414-15
radical left strategies, 134
radical right strategies, 134, 138-42
Radice, H., 347
Ramon, S., 229
Ramsay, E., 276
Randolph, W., 267, 275
Rankin, M., 72
rationalistic management approaches, 19, 22
RAWP (Resource Allocation Working Party), 206
Raybould, S., 289
Reade, E.J., 119
Reagan administration, expenditure cuts, 138-39
Recommendation on Vocational Training for Women (EC), 407
recorded medical need, true need compared, 209
recruitment channels, labour market, 361
  institutional restructuring, 354-56, *355*
  places, 352-53
redundancy, and German NITs training, 413
Rees, G., 353, 400, 421
Rees, J., 128
Rees, T., 403, 404, 408, 412
regeneration, and UDCs, 163-64

regional differences, German NITs training, 412
regional dimension, housing, 264, 265, 267, 269, 273, 289, 291
  elasticity of supply, 310, 311
  tax subsidy effects, 315-16, *315*
regulation, and European labour markets, 391-92, 395
regulation view of UDCs, 167
Reid, M., 346, 347
Rein, M., 66
relocation of firms, 127-28, 272
remortgaging, 253
renewal, housing, 8, 325-42
  crisis, 326, *327*, 331
  grant provision, 327-30
  policies, 326-27, *327*, 331-34, 341-42
  public sector investment, 340-41
  stimulating private investment, 334-40
renovation grants, 326-27
rental housing, private, 263, 264, 271, 276-77
renting variables, housing models, *299*, 300
repairs, private housing. *See* renewal, housing
repossessions, housing, 263, 278
representative democracy, *148*, 148-49
research, and policy determination, 125
residential care for elderly people, 177, 185, 199-200
Resource Allocation Working Party (RAWP), 206
resource dependencies, 'policy sector' concept, 115-16
restructuring
  labour market, 347-58, *348*, *349*, *355*
  public sector, 15-17
  See also economic restructuring
results orientation, and decentralisation, 26, 30
retirement migration, 273
Reward Regional Surveys, 269
Rex, J., 244, 245
Rhodes, M., 388, 391
Rhodes, R.A.W., 141, 145, 146
RICS (Royal Institution of Chartered Surveyors), 295, 302
Ridley, N., 139, 140
Right to Buy loans, 278
risk-shifting, purchaser-provider contracts, 202
Robins, K., 166
Robinson, C.J., 133
Robinson, J., 184
Robinson, R., xiv
Robson, B.T., 244, 266
Rogers, A., 156

rolled up interest loans, and housing improvements, 335
Romano-Germanic labour market regulation, 392
Rose, D., 266
Rose, R., 124, 128
Ross, B.H., 145
Ross, S.A., 202
Rowntree Studies, 290, 312, 320
Royal Commission on the Distribution of Income and Wealth 1977, 250, 251
Rubery, J., 403
rules of structure formation, 'policy sector' concept, 108, 118-20

Sabel, C., 345
Salamon, L.M., 59, 63, 70, 73, 74
Salt, J., 270, 272
sampling differences, health expenditure studies, 206
Sanderson, K., 403
'satisfaction cards', 47
Saunders, P., 120, 165, 242, 246, 247-48, 250, 266, 268
Savage, M., 350, 352, 357
savings schemes, and housing improvements, 336
Scheffler, R., 184
Schein, E., 29
Schiersmann, C., 413
Schmehr, H.J., 402
Schneider, A.L., 374
Schon, D., 24, 134
Schonberger, R.J., 95-96
School for Advanced Urban Studies, xiii-xvii
schools
 open enrolment, 177-78, 196, 197
 opting out, 177, 178, 196, 197
Schweikert, K., 415
Scott, D., 65
Scottish Homes, *327*
second-hand houses, prices, 300, 301, 302
'secondary' external labour markets, 349, 351-52, 357
SEG. *See* socio-economic group
segmentalism, and bureaucratic control, 20, *20*, 21
segmentation, labour market, 9, 347-49, *348, 349*, 402-05
 access to NITs training opportunities, 405-420, *406, 408, 409*
 institutional restructuring, 354-56, *355*
 labour market 'places', 349-52
 recruitment channels and selection criteria, 352-54
segregation. *See* segmentation

selection criteria, labour market 'places', 352-53
self-employment, 8, 348, *248, 249*, 352
self-help groups, 60, 235
self-justified action, economic development programmes, 125
'self-reliant development', 96-97
self-training, information technology, 89-90
Sellens, R., 271
Seneviratne, M., 47
senile dementia, 236
Senker, P., 356
service delivery
 improving local government, 143-44
 and information technology, 82
 pluralism, 64-68
 quasi-market costs, 183, 189-204
 See also quality of service delivery; service pluralism, 61
'service providers', 43-44
'service users', 44-45
Sessar-Karp, E., 414
Sharpe, L.J., 151
Shefer, D., 374
Sheppard, S., 289, 290
Shostack, G.L., 44
Siemens, NITs training, 412, 414
Sills, A., 157
'simple' control strategies, 17, 18
simulations of housing policy impact, 307-20, *309, 314, 315, 317*
Single European Market (SEM), 383
skills training, information technology, 90
Sloan, F., 184
Smircich, L., 80
Smith, C., 352
Smith, M., 132, 143
Smolka, G., 70
Social Action Programme. *See* Action Programme
Social Charter, 10, 382-98
 history, 387-89
 impact, 394-97
 legal basis, 386-87
 scope, 383-86
 subsidiarity, controversy and diversity, 389-94
social criteria, recruitment, 353, 357, 400
social differences, and housing. *See* occupational class
'social dimension' SEM, 383
 See also Social Charter
Social Fund, 62
social movements, urban, 133, 135
'social partnership', Social Charter, 396
social policy, 4-6
 Poland, 96

See also community care; quasi-markets; voluntary sector
social protection systems, European diversity, 392, 393
social services. *See* community care
Social Services Inspectorate, 47, 229
Social Trends, 346, 347, 348, *348*, *349*, 361
socio-economic group (SEG), as ability-to-pay measure, 211, 214, 215, 218, 218, 220, 221, 222
Solesbury, W., 112, 158, 168, 169
Soskice, D., 416
South Glamorgan Women's Workshop, 418-19
spatial mobility, and housing, 262, 264-77, 283-84
and housing histories and assistance, 280-83, *283*
and tenure, 269-77
Speaker's Commission on Citizenship, 69
Specified Capital Grant (SCG), 332, *332*
Spector, M., 125
Spencer, K., 67
St Helens, community care, 231, 232
Staedelin, F., 390
standard of living, British, 347
standard-setting, service quality, 46-48
standardisation of need and expenditure, health care, 212, 215, 223-24, *224*, 225
Stanley, L., 355
state role, inner cities policy, 119-20
Stedman, M.S., 145
Stepney neighbourhood, 32-33
Stewart, J., 34, 41, 43, 51, 61, 143, 147
Stewart, M., xiv, 110, 111, 113, 115, 117
Stirling, J., 396
stock market deregulation, 346
Stoker, G., 40, 43, 49, 135, 139, 141, 160, 166, 167
Strasbourg summit, 388
strategic control, 25, 29, *30*, 31-32
strategic objectives, TECs, 377
strategy concept, NITs and change, 86-87
stratification, owner-occupation, 266
Strauss, A., 116
street-level bureaucrats, 43-44, 80
structure formation rules, 'policy sector' concept, 108, 118-20
subsidiarity, 389-94, 395
subsidies, housing
employer, 271-72
tax. *See* tax subsidies
subsidised loans, housing improvements, 335
Sullivan, O., 275, 279
summary measures, health expenditure, 207-10

Sunderland, council housing, 244
supply elasticity, housing, 288-324
area sample and data sources, 296-98, 320, 323-24
background, 289-91
model, 291-96, *293*, 294-95
private housebuilding modelling, 298-307, *299*, *304*, *306*
simulations of policy impact, 307-18, *309*, *311*, *314*, *315*, *317*
supply variables, housing models, 297, *299*, 323-24
Surrey County Council Planning Department, 274
Swales, J.K., 128
symbolic aspects, economic development programmes, 124-26
Syrett, M., 356
'systematic noise', labour market, 354-56, *355*

Tansik, D.A., 44
Targetti, F., 4
Task Force programmes, 405, 408-10, *409*
Tate, J., 253
tax liability, and housing improvements, 335
tax subsidies, housing, 7, 288, 290-01, 312-16, *314*, *315*
Taylor, D., 354
Taylor, G., 157
Taylor, M., 61, 72, 229
Taylor, M.J., 128
Teague, P., 387, 393
technical control, 17, *18*, 84
technical dimension of quality, 41-42, 51
'technical expert' approach, policy change, 84
TECs. *See* Training and Enterprise Councils
Temple, B., 355
TEMPUS programme, EC, *409*, 410
tenure
differentiation within, 249-50
and spatial mobility, 269-77
tenure mobility, 277-80
tenurial polarisation, 266, 267, 268, 280
Thatcher era
expenditure cuts and privatisation, 138-42
welfare provision, 60-63, 175-76, 189
Third Action Programme on Equality between Men and Women, 407
'third generation' evaluation, 374
third-party government model of welfare, 59
Thomas, A., 254
Thomas, H., 165

Thomas, R., 148, 157
Thorns, D., 266
Thriving on chaos, 94-95
time series approach, housing models, 289
Timms, D.W., 244
Tirole, J., 203
Titmuss, R., 268
Tolan, F., 135
Tomlinson, J., 347
'top-down' approach, policy change, 83-84
Tower Hamlets, London Borough, 32-33, 40, 148
trades union leaders, and European integration, 396
'trading down', home ownership, 252, 253
'traditional' internal labour markets, 8-9, 349
Trafford Park UDC, Manchester, 159, 160
training
    front-line staff, 44
    NITs, 90, 399-420
        EC 402-10, *406, 408, 409*
        Germany, 410-16
        UK, 416-20
    See also Training and Education Councils
Training and Enterprise Councils (TECs), 9, 169, 365-81, *366*, 417
    evaluation, 369-79
    structure and function, 366-69, *367*
training schemes, government, 354
transport vouchers, 180, 185-86
'truncated' internal labour markets, 9, 11, 349, 350, 351, 357
trust and devolution, 49, 50
Tsoukis, C., 289, 294, 305
Turnbull, P., 253
Tyne and Wear Development Corporation (TWDC), 161, 163

UDCs. *See* urban development corporations
UK
    NITs training, 401, 416-20
    See also urban government
Underwood, J., 110, 111, 113, 115, 117
Unell, J., 70
unemployment
    and German NITs training, 415
    and housing, 275-76, 279
    as local concern, 122, 124
    and self-reported morbidity, 215
    and Social Charter, 385
unfit dwellings, 326, *327*, 329, 330, 333
UNICE (Union of Industrial and Employers Confederation of Europe), 389, 395, 405
University Enterprise-Training Partnerships (UETPs), 410
university funding, 176, 178

Upward, R., 221
URA. *See* Urban Regeneration Agency
urban development corporations (UDCs), 3-4, 155-72
    as flagships of urban policy, 157-58
    future policy, 168-70
    results, 159-64
    views of, 164-67
urban economic development programmes, 3, 122-30
    symbol or substance, 124-26
    ultimate purpose, 127-29
    welfare versus market, 123-24
urban government, UK and US, 131-54
    changing pressures, 131-33
    developments in Britain, 135-38, *136*,
    emerging tensions, 133-35
    empowerment, 145-50, *147, 148*
    expenditure cuts and privatisation, 138-42
    public service reform, 142-44
urban policy, 2-4, 155-57, 168-70
    See also inner cities; urban development corporations; urban economic development programmes; urban government
Urban Programme, 110, 113, 156
Urban Regeneration Agency, 155, 167, 168, 169-70
urban social movements, 133, 135
Urry, J., 345, 347, 358, 360
USA
    economic restructuring, 360
    health service quality, 41-42
    UK urban government compared, 131-35, 138, 141, 142, 145, 150-51
use-need ratio (Le Grand), 207-10, 217, *218*
user empowerment. *See* empowerment
User empowerment in community care, 229
user groups, 60, 149
    and community care planning, 231-33, 235
    NITs, 89
user-led approach to informisation, 89
utilisation of health care, 205, 206, 207-11, 212, 216, 222

Ven, W. van de, 225
Venturini, P., 387
Vliet, R. van, 225
Vocational Training for Women Recommendation, 407
voice-driven approaches to empowerment, 230, 231
voluntary sector, 1-2, 57-78, 149
    changing welfare strategies, 58-60, *59*
    delivery pluralism, 64-68

financial pluralism, 69-74, *71*, 118
  Thatcher era, 60-63
volunteering, 69, 71-72
voucher systems, 179, 190
  childcare, 180
  education, 178, 180, 187, 195, 196
  health service, 178, 179-80
  social care, 177, 178
  transport, 180, 185-86

wage policies, European diversity, 392
Wagstaff, A., 207, 209
Wajcman, J., 404, 405, 417
Walby, S., 353, 402
Walker, A., 25
Walsh, K., 41, 43, 50
Ware, A., 58
Warnes, A.M., 127
Waste, R.J., 135
Waterman, R., 22-23, 87, 134, 138, 142
Watson, W., 265
Watzlawick, P., 22
wealth accumulation, and housing, 246, 248, 250-56, 282, 283, *283*
Webb, S., 215
Weber, M., 244-45
Wedgwood Oppenheim, F., 40
Weeks, G.C., 271
'welfare pluralism', 58-59, *59*
welfare provision, xiv, 1, 4-6
  and market goals, 123-24
  See also community care; expenditure distribution; GPs; health policy; National Health Service; quasi-markets; voluntary sector
welfare state, 58, *59*, 60, 175-76
Wellington, J.J., 417
Welsh Office, 225, *327*
Wener, R.E., 44
Wennlund, I.L., 43
Westaway, P., 289, 294, 305
Whitehead, C., 289, 291, 294, 310
Whittaker, A., 234-35

Widdicombe Report, 146
Wilcox, S., 312, 315
Wilkinson, S., 161
Williams, A., 270
Williamson, E.O., 187, 194
Williamson, H., 353
Willmott, P., 169
Wilson, G., 180
Winckler, V., 15, 27
Winkler, W., 353
Winter, D., 175
Wokutch, R.E., 374
Wolfe, B., 214
Wolfenden Committee, 58
women, and employment, 8-9, 10-11, 348, *348*, 351, 357, 358, 359, 399-405
  managers, xv
  NITs training, 11
    EC, 405-10, *406*, *408*, *409*
    Germany, 413-14
    UK, 416-20
  recruitment channels, 355, *355*
women-only training workshops, 418-20
Women in Technology (WITEC), 410
Women's Technology Scheme, 420
Wood, P.J., 128
Wood, S., 22, 27
work organisation patterns, and NITs, 400
workforce structures, European diversity, 393
working-class mobility, 264, 269-70
Wright, A., 33
Wright, S.J., 214

x-efficiency, 182-85

Yates, D., 145
Young, K., 3, 122, 125, 133, 147
Young, M., 179-80
Youth Training Scheme, 354, 368

Zeitlin, J., 345
Zweig, F., 243